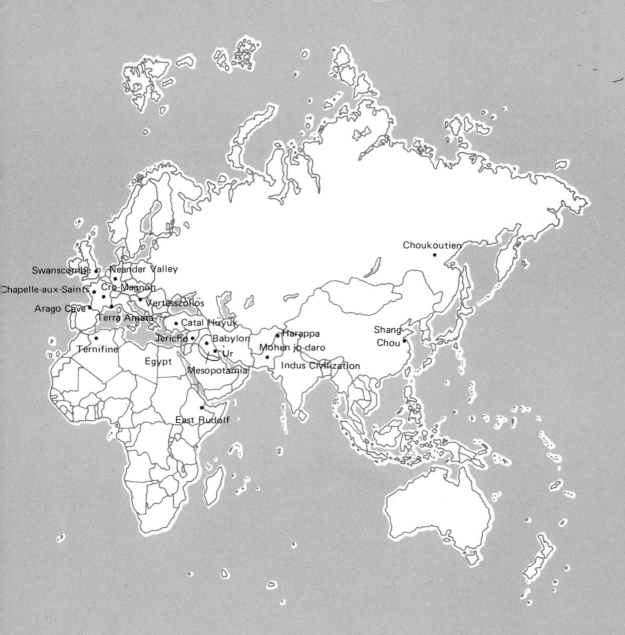

Choukoutien

Swanscombe •   • Neander Valley
Chapelle-aux-Saints •   • Cro-Magnon
Arago Cave •   • Vertesszöllös
   • Terra Amata   • Catal Huyuk
   Jericho •   • Harappa
Ternifine •   • Babylon   Shang
   Egypt   • Ur   Mohen jo-daro   Chou
   Mesopotamia   Indus Civilization

East Rudolf •

PREHISTORIC SITES MENTIONED IN THE TEXT

The
Human
Myth

To my mother and the memory of my father;
and Beatrice and Max.

The Human Myth

An Introduction to Anthropology

Michael D. Olien

The University of Georgia

Harper & Row, Publishers

New York   Hagerstown   San Francisco   London

Chapter-opening photo credits: 1. Mead, EPA; 2. Australian Information Service; 3. Wide World; 4. Milwaukee Public Museum; 5. Culver; 6. Harry Burton, The Metropolitan Museum of Art; 7. Courtesy of the American Museum of Natural History; 8. Michael D. Olien; 9. The Granger Collection; 10. Cartier-Bresson, Magnum; 11. Fujihira, Monkmeyer; 12. Felker, Monkmeyer; 13. Shostak, Anthro-Photo; 14. Wide World; 15. NASA.

Sponsoring Editor: Dale Tharp
Project Editor: Holly Detgen
Designer: Frances Torbert Tilley
Production Supervisor: Stefania J. Taflinska
Photo Researcher: Myra Schachne
Compositor: Progressive Typographers, Inc.
Printer: The Murray Printing Company
Binder: Halliday Lithograph Corporation
Art Studio: Danmark & Michaels, Inc.
Cover Photo: Emily Harste

THE HUMAN MYTH: AN INTRODUCTION TO ANTHROPOLOGY
Copyright © 1978 by Michael D. Olien

Library of Congress Cataloging in Publication Data
Olien, Michael D
  The human myth.

  Bibliography: p.
  Includes index.
  1. Anthropology. I. Title.
GN25.044   301.2   77-12802
ISBN 0-06-044918-7

Contents

How Do Humans Compare with Other Primates?   133

Why Shouldn't I Collect Artifacts?   181

What Are Non-Western Peoples Like?   297

Humankind and the Natural World   337

Contents

Religion, Witchcraft, and the Supernatural World 375

Family Ties and Sex Categories 415

Who's in Charge Here?   A Look at Political Organization   453

What Will Humans Be Like in the Future?   491

Glossary   524

References Cited   539

Index   559

Preface

XiV

During the last half of the nineteenth century, anthropology crystallized as a unique discipline that was devoted to the study of a wide range of esoteric topics. This science singled out a domain of knowledge that had not been treated by other sciences. As the renowned anthropologist Franz Boas (1974:272) put it, anthropology encompasses "the biological history of mankind in all its varieties; linguistics applied to people without written languages; the ethnology of people without historic records, and prehistoric archaeology." Anthropology appealed to the romantic and to those especially fascinated by the seemingly strange customs of primitive peoples. As anthropology became an established part of the university curriculum in the post–World War II era, its body of knowledge was primarily of interest to those who intended to make anthropology their career. Nonmajors were often few and far between in the classrooms. Introductory textbooks were written primarily for those who planned to continue in anthropology, and anthropological concepts and vocabulary became increasingly specialized.

In recent years there has been a shift in the types of students who enroll in introductory anthropology classes. Most do not intend to continue in the field. Instead they are interested in learning what anthropology can tell them about a number of topics of current interest: Did visitors from outer space make the monuments of the ancient civilizations? Is there such a creature as Bigfoot? Unfortunately, these and similar topics have been of interest to the general public but not to anthropologists, even though their body of knowledge about humanity can be especially useful in clarifying the issues surrounding these questions. Anthropologists have generally avoided these issues in their textbooks and have assumed that those reading introductory texts wish to become anthropologists and will therefore want to know the totality of anthropological knowledge. Introductory texts have thus been written primarily as encyclopedias of anthropological knowledge.

This book has been written as an alternative approach to the study of humans. It assumes that the student is interested in anthropology but probably will not choose anthropology as his or her major. Therefore an attempt has been made to present only some of the major themes and viewpoints of anthropology, in order to give some indication of how the anthropologists' ideas came to be accepted and to discuss some of the particular topics that are of interest to the student.

Any undertaking of this sort would be impossible without the aid of many individuals. I am happy to have this opportunity to express my thanks to the ones who helped me. Certainly the beginnings of this book must go back to my college years at Beloit College, where my interests in anthropology were nurtured, stimulated, and encouraged under the tutelage of Andrew H. Whiteford and William S. Godfrey, Jr. To both of them I owe a debt of gratitude that can never be repaid. I would like to thank Michael Brown for encouraging me to undertake this project and Dale Tharp for seeing the project to its completion. My sincere thanks to Holly Detgen, Project Editor. A number of reviewers have read various parts of the manuscript and have offered extremely helpful suggestions. Any errors in fact or judgment are of course my responsibility and must not be blamed on the reviewers. For their most constructive criticisms, I would like to express my thanks to Robert McC. Adams, John E. Blank, C. Loring Brace, Robbins Burling, Napoleon A. Chagnon, Brian M. du Toit, Arthur M. Haskins, Mary W. Helms, Dell H. Hymes, Grover S. Krantz, Harriet J. Kupferer, June Macklin, Magoroh Maruyama, Daniel E. Moerman, Robert A. Schiffman, Karl W. Schwerin, Alexander Sonek, Jr., George W. Stocking, Jr., O. Michael Watson, and Michael B. Whiteford. I would like to offer a special thank-you to Mary W. Helms for her continued support and encouragement during many bleak hours while the text was being written. Additional thanks are extended to Donald A. Graybill for allowing me to cite unpublished material from his archaeological research in New Mexico and Marshall G. Hurlich for calling my attention to several important sources on human evolution. This book has also benefited from the questions and comments of the students who have taken my introductory anthropology course over the past eleven years. To Louise Brice and Adrienne Seccia many thanks for their help with typing during the last hectic days of deadline pressures. Last but not least, I must single out for special thanks my wife Joan, who typed most of the manuscript and also edited the text and put it into readable form, and my daughter Karen, who assembled the material for the bibliography and glossary, and proofread the entire manuscript. For all of their time and effort, they deserve to be considered coauthors.

MICHAEL D. OLIEN

The
Human
Myth

I
Studying the human myth

Anthropologists contribute to the human myth.

Anthropology is the study of human beings.

Anthropology is divided into four subfields: physical anthropology, archaeology, anthropological linguistics, and cultural anthropology.

Anthropologists have a unique perception of humankind.

Of all the creatures on earth only humans question their existence. What are we? What were we? What will we become? Perhaps these questions are unanswerable; nevertheless humans strive to find answers.

While all people may reflect on the nature of their existence, the anthropologist is a specialist who devotes full time to attempting to understand the nature of humankind. *Anthropology* is the study of human beings. The term is derived from two Greek words, *anthropos* (human being) and *logos* (study or science). As a specialist the anthropologist has become uniquely trained to delineate the epic of human beings. Like the mythmaker or epic poet of ages past, the anthropologist has the task of explaining what it is to be human, of glorifying humanity by composing the human myth. Stone Age hand axes had no meaning to humans until anthropologists in the nineteenth-century incorporated them into the human story by showing the part they had played in conquering the environment. The sounds made by Australian aborigines were thought to be imitations of the sounds of nature until anthropologists incorporated them into the human myth by showing that the sounds of aborigines constitute a language just as do the sounds of English.

Anthropology studies human beings.

The anthropologist Miles Richardson (1975:530) has eloquently summarized the work of the anthropologist in the following statement:

> Like the poet recording the exploits of the epic hero, the anthropologist mythicizes the human record. He takes the discrete bits of human data, the pelvic girdle, Acheulean handaxes, Eskimo kinship, and phonemic contrasts, and narrates the human story, how we came to be, how we fought in the past, how we live today. As teller of the human story, the anthropologist cannot falsify what we are. He seeks to find the full range of human variation, the cruelty, the magnificence, the love that is in us all and in all of our cultures. But the anthropologist is recorder of human data; he searches for the human secret.
>
> In telling the human myth, of how men wrestle with the problem of being human, of how people envision a society of love but live in a society of hate, of how they conceive of a collective soul but live in individual cells, the anthropologist may find his own salvation.

Every *society*, or large group of people who share a common culture, creates myths to help explain the unexplainable. A myth is a sacred narrative explaining how the world and people came to be in their present form. Although the term *myth* is often used interchangeably with *error* or *fallacy*, *myth* in the narrow technical sense refers to a narrative or story believed to be true by the people who relate it. Myths are dynamic and eloquent articulations of our perceived place vis-à-vis our fellow humans, the gods, and the universe (Dundes 1976:279–281). Anthropology is the myth of humankind, an explanation of our nature. It is an attempt to explain human beings in all places and in all times by studying human cultural and biological diversity.

Anthropology is the myth of humankind.

The human myth, like other myths, deals in part with reality, but in a sense it is more than reality. Like any myth, it is subject to the biases of the storyteller. Our sensory perceptions and our cultural training condition the way we interpret things. They create the conceptual frameworks within which we see the world around us. On the one hand these frameworks are blinders, because they limit *what* we see and the *way* we perceive the world around us. On the other hand, without some sort of framework we would see nothing at all. Arrowheads would remain mere pieces of rock. As the biologist Lawrence S. Dillon (1973:v) has observed:

Culture and sensory perception condition the way we interpret things.

> Theories can have two opposing effects. By means of them, the mind is enabled to make meaningful that which otherwise would be unintelligible. Furthermore, they make possible projections into the unknown and thereby open new channels to exploration. Yet, when adhered to overtenaciously, concepts may act as blindfolds and prevent the perception of new truths or even obvious facts.

As human beings, we see what we want to see; in other words we have selective perception and memory. Likewise as members of a particular society we are taught to view the world around us through a set of biases which act as filters between ourselves and reality. We strive for understandings but the biases, the conceptual frameworks, are always there. As we try to understand humankind we arrive at many realities, but never Reality. Anthropologists can never be more than mythmakers, for they, too, are human. They hope that their myth will provide insights into Reality. If people are able to reach new insights about themselves through the human myth recorded by anthropologists and if this in turn saves a Brazilian Indian tribe from extermination or a crucial prehistoric site from destruction, the anthropologists' attempt to understand humankind will have been worthwhile.

As conceptual frameworks change, so too does our understanding. Yesterday's fact becomes today's fiction, and sometimes yesterday's fiction becomes today's fact—perhaps to become fiction again tomorrow. The human condition is an elusive

tale we will never fully tell, but our attempt to understand ourselves may be our greatest undertaking.

Anthropologists are professional mythmakers. Folk anthropologists are nonprofessionals who also have an interest in the
human myth. Ever since the era of recorded time began, and
probably before, humans have struggled with the phenomenon
of humankind. There is actually a variety of human myths, with
many different ways of understanding humanity. Often folk
anthropologists attempt to answer questions for which the professional anthropologist has no answer. Or they may question
that which the professional anthropologist has no interest in, as
a result of his or her particular framework, such as the existence
of Bigfoot or ancient "astronauts." In other cases the human
myth created by the folk anthropologist is based on theories or
findings that were once accepted by professional anthropologists but have since been rejected or replaced by newer concepts.

*There are both profes-
sional and folk anthropo-
logists.*

In this attempt to present the human myth, it will be assumed
that there is no absolute truth other than that in which people
believe. All of our views of humankind are colored by our biases.
At the same time, however, it is impossible to proceed with the
study of human diversity without some sort of theoretical
framework. This book will deal with the assumptions and concepts which affect our view of the human myth. At a number of
points the theoretical framework of professional anthropology
will be contrasted with that of folk anthropology, in an attempt
to understand better the nature of the human myth.

The Divisions of Anthropology

Professional anthropology approaches the human myth from
four different but interrelated areas of research: physical
anthropology, archaeology, linguistics, and cultural anthropology. The professional anthropologist is first and foremost a general anthropologist, but he is also a specialist within one of these
four subfields.

Physical Anthropology. Physical, or biological, anthropology
deals with human biological diversity. The physical anthropologist is concerned with the changes that have occurred in the
human physical form over time. Were creatures living 2 million
years ago ancestral to modern humans? Which pieces of fossilized bone that have been discovered are from creatures related
to humans and which are not? The physical anthropologist

*Physical anthropology
studies human biological
diversity.*

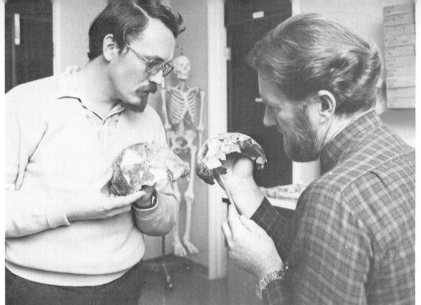

Physical anthropologists
comparing fossil skull caps.
(Australian Information
Service)

Performing an autopsy on a ▶
3,000 year old Egyptian to
learn the cause of his death.
(Wide World)

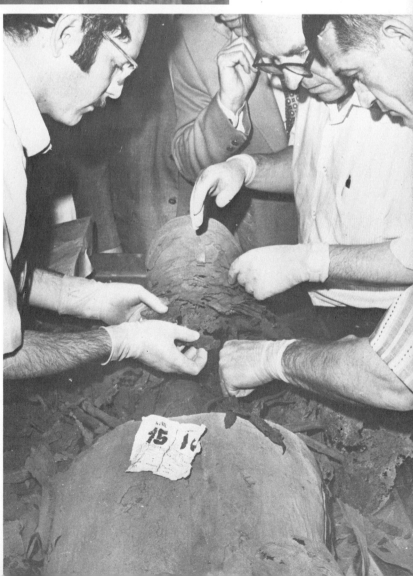

studies ancient human forms and seeks to discover their place in the human myth. He is also interested in contemporary biological diversity. What do differences in body shape, skin color, and genes mean? Is there any correlation between race and intelligence? What mechanisms bring about physical changes in human populations? What are the effects of the physical environment on humans? What aspects of human behavior are genetically programmed and what is learned?

In recent years a number of physical anthropologists have turned their attention to the study of the Primates, that order of animals that includes humans, apes, monkeys, and a lesser known group called prosimians. Primates are the creatures considered to be closest to humans. We are able to learn what is uniquely human and what we share with other primates by contrasting human anatomy with that of other primates.

Primates are humans closest relatives.

[The physical anthropologist is interested in the behavior of primates as well as their anatomy] Physical anthropologists spend months and sometimes years living in the wilds alongside various types of primates, observing their behavior; for example, Jane van Lawick-Goodall studies the chimpanzee and Diane Fossey studies the gorilla. Their work has been described in the *National Geographic* magazine and has been the focus of

Physical anthropologists study primate behavior. (Hidy, Anthro-Photo)

Archaeologist studying early Mesoamerican stone monument with date carved on it in bars and dots. (Wide World)

several television specials. The anthropologist is able to obtain insights about human beings by contrasting the behavior of humans with that of other primates. The study of primate behavior has also provided clues about the nature of fossil humans.

The remaining three subfields of anthropology are concerned with cultural diversity, spatially and temporally. Each subfield focuses on a particular aspect of this diversity.

Archaeology. The archaeologist reconstructs ways of life in the past by studying remains that have been left behind. These remains, such as arrowheads and pieces of pottery, are called *artifacts* and are reflections of what life was like at some period in the past. A great deal of American archaeological research is concerned with *prehistory*, the period prior to writing, a period that stretches back in time millions of years. Most of our history occurred before writing was invented, since humans learned to write only a few thousand years ago.

The popular stereotype depicting the archaeologist as an elderly, bearded, eccentric adventurer who, with pith helmet, magnifying glass, and beautiful daughter, wanders through the jungles of Africa in search of lost cities, is incorrect. Instead, the

Archaeologists study life in the past.

Skeleton and grave goods. (Wide World)

modern archaeologist is a scientist who often spends many more hours in his laboratory than in the field, analyzing artifacts, bone, soil, pollen, and remains of plants, often with the aid of expensive, sophisticated equipment such as a high-speed electronic computer and scanning electron microscope. The interpretation of archaeological data has become so highly complex that the archaeologist must have some knowledge of a number of the natural sciences, especially astronomy, geology, physics, chemistry, botany, and zoology. The archaeologist is an interpreter of humanity's past who uses artifacts and other data to reconstruct what life was like in the past.

While a great deal of archaeological research involves the study of life prior to the invention of writing, some archaeologists are committed to the study of early civilizations as well as prehistory. The majority of civilizations studied by archaeologists have produced written records that can be translated. The written records left behind by the people of a past society are filled with detailed insights into their lives. In contrast, the information of the prehistorian has to be gleaned from such nonwritten sources as artifacts, remains of food from garbage dumps, and the pollen of plants.

In recent years some archaeologists have become interested in an attempt to solve the problems that face contemporary humans by utilizing traditional archaeological methods and theories. For example the methods of archaeological research have been applied to the analysis of household refuse from a stratified sample of households in Tucson, Arizona. The nutrient composition of food waste is being studied in order to estimate the nutrients that are being wasted by sample households with different socioeconomic and demographic characteristics. The

Hundreds of workmen are employed to remove debris from Egyptian site. (Wide World)

archaeologists believe that this kind of information will be useful in resource-management, recycling, and nutrition-education programs.

Anthropological Linguistics. Linguistics studies another manifestation of human cultural diversity: language. The linguist is concerned with various aspects of language. While linguists are fascinated with the history of language, most of the research on how languages change has been limited to the study of Indo-European languages, where writing has a long tradition. Only where writing occurs can language change be documented. A great deal of the research undertaken by the linguist involves

Linguistics studies various aspects of language.

the study of languages as they are spoken today. Because many of the languages of non-Western peoples are unwritten, it is impossible to study change in these languages. In many cases, as the linguist records a language, he is the first to put this language into a written form. Sometimes the linguist aids in educational programs and creates textbooks to enable speakers of the language the linguist has studied to read and write in their own language. Not all linguists are anthropologists. Linguistics also exists as a separate discipline. Only the anthropological linguist has internalized the anthropological perspective. The anthropological linguist is an anthropologist who has specialized in the subfield of anthropology that studies language. As an anthropologist he is especially interested in the relationship between language and human behavior. The nonanthropological linguist, on the other hand, is primarily a linguist and tends to view language apart from the social and cultural context in which it exists.

The goal of many linguists is to record native languages before they disappear. Some languages that were once widely used are spoken by only a few individuals today. If the language remains unwritten and unrecorded, it will become extinct once the last speaker dies. When societies become extinct, they leave behind cultural remains that can be analyzed by the archaeologist to partially reconstruct the way of life of a people. However, when

Cultural anthropologists studying coffee processing in Costa Rica. (Michael D. Olien)
▼

▲
Cultural anthropologist photographing Mexican children. (Michael D. Olien)

an unwritten language becomes extinct, there is little that can be learned about it other than what can be inferred from languages of the same language family. In order to understand human cultural diversity, linguists are collecting information on many unwritten languages before they become extinct. The linguist's primary concern has been the structure of the language—the sounds, and the rules that govern the arrangement of sounds in larger units of discourse.

Linguists also contribute to our understanding of human history by classifying languages into various language families. By discovering which languages are historically linked, the linguist is able to derive theories about contact between peoples. Such information is of considerable importance to the archaeologist.

In looking at linguistic diversity, the anthropologist is also concerned with the universal features of language. What aspects of language structure are shared by all languages? How does the verbal communication of humans compare with forms of communication used by other animals?

Anthropological linguists study the cultural content of languages, that is, the categories that speakers use to divide the world around them into meaningful units. What do these categories tell us about the culture? How are these categories related to the way that people think? Anthropological linguists and cultural anthropologists are both interested in the answers to these questions. Related to the study of the cultural aspects of language is a relatively new subfield of linguistics known as *sociolinguistics*, which deals with linguistic variation. It is concerned with language use, in particular with how language serves as a social identity of various groups and with how linguistic variations are used in different kinds of social settings.

Cultural Anthropology. Cultural anthropology, sometimes called social anthropology, studies the cultural diversity of contemporary societies, with particular emphasis on a people's belief system. A *culture* is a system of knowledge by which people design their own actions and interpret the behavior of others. For example, an American believes that eating with one's mouth closed is proper, while East Indians know that to be polite one must chew with one's mouth open. Anthropologists have learned that there is nothing preordained about cultural categories—they are arbitrary. The same act can have quite different meanings in various societies. For example, when adolescent boys walk holding hands, it signifies friendship in Hindu culture, while to Americans the same act may suggest homosex-

Cultural anthropologists study the cultural diversity of living peoples.

uality. Cultural anthropologists recognize that human experience and behavior are largely products of symbolic meaning systems. Thus in order to understand the behavior of people in any society, the cultural anthropologist must first learn their system of knowledge—in other words, their culture (Spradley and McCurdy 1977:3; Spradley and McCurdy 1975:5).

Cultural anthropology has two aspects: ethnography and ethnology. *Ethnography* is the fieldwork aspect, in which a specific society or subculture is studied over an extended period of time by an anthropologist who lives with the people and participates in their daily lives. *Ethnology* is the theoretical aspect and relies on the cross-cultural comparison of a number of societies in order to test hypotheses. Each cultural anthropologist is both an ethnographer and an ethnologist.

> Cultural anthropology is comprised of ethnography and ethnology.

Most people think of the cultural anthropologist as someone who studies nonliterate societies exclusively, yet cultural anthropologists have within the past 30 years extended their interests to include virtually every kind of society or subculture. Today the cultural anthropologist studies longshoremen in Portland, Oregon, retirement communities in California, or hippie ghettoes in Florida, as well as peasant villages in Mexico or bands of aborigine hunters and gatherers in Australia.

As an ethnologist, the cultural anthropologist is interested in theoretical issues that transcend the study of a particular society or subculture. Whereas ethnographic research provides the raw data of cultural anthropology, ethnology is the attempt to utilize these facts as the building blocks of theory. These two aspects of cultural anthropology, ethnography and ethnology, are interrelated. As facts are collected through fieldwork, they yield new theories. These theories in turn raise new questions that require further fieldwork.

A special subfield of cultural anthropology is known as *applied anthropology*. Applied anthropology is the use of anthropological knowledge gained from the study of many different societies of the world toward the solution of contemporary social, economic, and technological problems. Most of the work of the applied anthropologist has been conducted in the underdeveloped countries. Applied anthropology also involves the testing of theory in clinical settings, an effort which contributes to the general body of anthropological knowledge and helps to refine both theories and research methods (Foster 1969:152). A great deal of applied anthropology involves programs of planned improvement in agriculture, health, medical services, education, and social welfare services.

> Applied anthropology is a problem-solving subfield.

The Culture Area

Besides concentrating on a particular subdivision of anthropology, the professional anthropologist is generally interested in a specific region of the world known as a *culture area*. A culture area is a geographical region within which there is a similarity of culture between societies. Anthropologists associated with universities and colleges are usually required to teach a course on a major culture area of the world in which they have field experience. The culture areas covered by these courses are quite broad. Traditionally they have included such areas as Europe, the Near East, South Asia, Oceania, Africa, Latin America, and North America.[1] Anthropologists who teach these courses usually have more specialized interests. For example, an individual who teaches a course on Latin America may be interested mainly in the peoples of South America, and his or her field experience may be limited to a particular region of South America such as the Andes, or the Africanist may be especially interested in the urban areas of the Union of South Africa. Nevertheless the professional anthropologist maintains a familiarity with the research being conducted throughout the entire culture area.

The Professional and the Folk Anthropologists

Although some professional anthropologists major in other disciplines while undergraduate students, all received graduate training in anthropology at universities. As part of this training the professional anthropologist internalizes a distinct anthropological perspective. It is this particular perception that distinguishes the professional anthropologist from the folk anthropologist, not the fact that anthropology is the professional anthropologist's occupation. Anthropologists David Hunter and Phillip Whitten (1975) have suggested that there are five themes in particular that form this unique anthropological perspective or point of view: the comparative perspective, the holistic perspective, the systems and process perspective, the emic/etic perspective, and the case study perspective.

Professional anthropologists develops a unique perspective because of their training.

Five themes make anthropology a unique discipline.

The Comparative Perspective. Although many anthropologists conduct research in a single society (ethnography), it is gener-

---

[1] The North American culture area is the only one in which modern peoples are excluded from coverage, being specifically limited to Indians.

ally assumed that the data collected will serve as part of the factual base for developing meaningful theories that interpret the
behavior of all peoples. Such general theory rests on the systematic comparison and analysis of data from a large number of
different societies (ethnology). *Synchronic studies* compare a
number of societies at one point in time. *Diachronic studies* compare cultural remains as they change through time in a specific
geographical area. The synchronic studies provide understanding of the regularities of human behavior around the world
at a given point in time. From diachronic studies, conclusions
can be reached regarding the evolution of human beings and
their cultures.

The Holistic Perspective. Anthropology, more than any other social or behavioral science, has resisted simplistic, reductionistic
explanations of social phenomena. The holistic perspective
encourages anthropologists to consider a wide range of causal
factors when attempting to understand human behavior—
biological, social, cultural, psychological, economic, political,
ecological, and many others. Anthropologists are sensitive to the
complexity of human behavior. According to Hunter and
Whitten (1975:3),

> This [holistic] perspective sets anthropology apart from sociology,
> which rarely considers more than the social and sometimes the
> cultural system; and psychology which is often criticized by
> anthropologists on two counts: (a) ignoring cross-cultural, compar-
> ative data, and (b) focusing almost entirely on psychological data,
> with a very deterministic dependence on biological data when
> these are available.

The Systems-and-Process Perspective. The major current trend
in professional anthropology is to move away from static
descriptions of societies to a consideration of processes. Because
of its holistic orientation, anthropology approaches human
behavior in terms of various systems which contribute to it,
such as the social system, the biological system, and so on.
Anthropologists study the internal dynamics of each of these
systems and also the interaction among systems as a dynamic
set of processes.

The Emic/Etic Perspective. Because of anthropology's emphasis
on cross-cultural fieldwork, the professional anthropologist has
been forced to acquire a working knowledge of linguistics in
order to learn the language of the people that he or she studies.
Anthropologists working in another society must continually

deal with the difficulty of translating the culture they are studying into categories meaningful to Westerners. Much of cultural anthropology involves maintaining a delicate balance between the world view of the people being studied and our own assumptions regarding the nature of the universe. Anthropologists find it necessary to keep these two domains separate in their descriptions and analyses. Anthropologists have adopted the terminology of the linguist and distinguish between *emics*, a set of categories through which the people of a given culture view the world, and *etics*, a set of categories used by the Western social scientist to explain social phenomena. Keeping the two domains separate is often a very difficult task for the anthropologist, both in research and in analysis. The anthropologist is generally more sensitive to the problems posed by emic/etic differences than most other social scientists, and consequently the anthropologist has learned to appreciate on its own terms the way of life of the society she or he is studying. Anthropology has devoted many years to challenging *ethnocentrism*, the belief that one's own way of life is the best, or the correct way. Anthropologists instead emphasize *cultural relativism*, the notion that judgments should not be made concerning the merits of one way of life over another. Anthropologists believe that each way of life is a valid one.

The Case Study Perspective. The growth of cultural anthropology involved the study of small, isolated non-Western societies. The research technique that came to be relied upon most is known as *participant observation*. This approach involves participating in the day-to-day life of the people being studied by living with them over an extended period of time. The use of this research method is necessary because more formal research tools, such as questionnaires, are often not applicable: Where very little is known about a society, the construction of a questionnaire is impossible; likewise, the obvious difficulties of learning the native language make it impossible to construct a questionnaire that does not distort the native point of view. While anthropologists appreciate the importance of statistical analysis, their orientation is to look at the rich description of setting and behavior found in case studies rather than focusing on great volumes of standardized data. The distinction between the intensive study and the extensive survey approach represents a major difference between anthropology and sociology. The sociologist tends to be quantative, while the anthropologist tends to be qualitative. Sociologists generalize from broad

Anthropologists emphasize a qualitative approach.

Margaret Mead living
among the Manus of
New Guinea in 1929.
(Reo Fortune)

surveys of large numbers of people, usually from their own society. Anthropologists rely upon close and intimate knowledge of
a small group of people to form their impressions. The anthropologist will spend weeks tracing a lead to the answer of a particular question, because of his or her intense personal involvement in the study; sociologists cannot afford to become deeply
involved with their informants if they intend to survey large
samples of the society. The cultural anthropologist John Friedl
(1976:31–32) sums up the difference in approach between sociologists and anthropologists with the following tongue-in-cheek
definition: A sociologist is someone who spends $50,000 to find a
house of ill repute, only to find an anthropologist playing the
piano in the parlor.

The professional anthropologist also differs from the folk
anthropologist, in that he or she devotes full-time attention to

the study of human diversity whereas the folk anthropologist's involvement with the human myth may be limited to interest in a current topic of conversation, such as the recently discovered "Stone Age" Tasaday of the Philippines; a hobby of collecting arrowheads that prompts some thought about what the maker of an arrowhead was like; or watching a television special about race and IQ. While the folk anthropologist is often truly interested in these exposures to the human myth, these topics are not primary concerns. But the human myth is the professional anthropologist's life work. Anthropologists spend most of their waking hours teaching anthropology, carrying out anthropological research, or reading what others have contributed to the human myth. They attend meetings and exchange ideas about anthropology with colleagues. During the course of a career the professional anthropologist reads a sizeable number of books and articles on human diversity, and writes articles and sometimes books about anthropology. In order to undertake these endeavors, the professional anthropologist must receive specialized training in areas outside of anthropology, becoming fluent in at least one foreign language, gaining a grasp of statistics and computer programming, and in particular cases, undergoing special training in psychological testing, bone identification, pollen analysis, film making, and so on. Exposure to a vast amount and variety of scientific information gives the professional anthropologist a different perspective than the folk anthropologist, who has to rely on the mass media or folk beliefs for an understanding of the human myth.

Besides internalizing a special framework or bias for viewing humanity, the professional anthropologist also learns the scientific approach which becomes the standard for accepting or rejecting data. The truth value of information is generally measured by criteria of usefulness—its ability to predict and explain our experiences in the natural world. The professional anthropologist must learn how to judge another researcher's work and decide whether to believe the other anthropologist (Pelto 1970:2). (While folk anthropologist's generally do not initiate research, they, too, wonder whether to believe a writer on an anthropological topic or not; for example, is Erich von Däniken, who is not an anthropologist, correct when he theorizes that civilization was brought from outer space?)

The professional anthropologist has internalized a conceptual framework by which he or she evaluates data. The scientific researcher must have sets of procedural rules, including concepts and definitions, by which to transform raw data into generalizations about phenomena. One of the goals of all scientific disciplines is to link low-order generalizations into larger networks of propositions that will make possible the prediction and explanation of specific phenomena within a given domain. These networks of propositions are called theories (Pelto 1970:3) and can be accepted, rejected, or modified, depending on how well they seem to predict or explain. Thus professional anthropologists are continually revising their understanding of human diversity as new data is discovered or better theories are developed.

Because anthropology is not a full-time interest of the folk anthropologists, they perhaps have a less coherent view of humankind. They are able to retain contradictory beliefs without being aware of the contradictions. They can simultaneously accept the concepts of God's creation of humans and human evolution, or have mixed feelings about whether extraterrestrial beings have visited the earth. In professional anthropology the conceptual framework focuses on humans; this is not the case with folk anthropology, where beliefs and theories of humankind are aspects of various conceptual frameworks but are seldom the focus. Thus it is possible for the folk anthropologist to hold contradictory beliefs about humans without realizing it. Arrowheads are not connected to human evolution in the mind of the folk anthropologist. The behavior of the major-league baseball player who eats fried chicken every day at 4:00 PM, keeps his eyes closed during the national anthem, and changes his sweat shirt at the end of the fourth inning each night during a batting streak, is not thought to be related to the practice of vodoo on the island of Haiti. To the professional anthropologist these phenomena are interrelated, and it is only through the professional anthropologist's conceptual framework that one is able to see a connection. It is this conceptual framework that has helped to create the human myth.

Anthropology Vocabulary

Note: All vocabulary words are defined in the Glossary at the end of the book.

anthropological linguistics	comparative perspective	emic/etic perspective
anthropology	cultural anthropology	ethnocentrism
applied anthropology	cultural relativism	ethnography
archaeology	culture	ethnology
artifacts	culture area	holistic perspective
case study perspective	diachronic studies	myth

participant observation
physical anthropology
prehistory

primate
society
sociolinguistics

synchronic studies
systems-and-process perspective

Review Questions

1. What is the human myth? Why are anthropologists involved in its creation?
2. How are the four subfields of anthropology interrelated? What special
   areas of interest in the human myth are found in each of the subfields?
3. How does the perspective of the professional anthropologist differ
   from that of the folk anthropologist?
4. In what ways is anthropology relevant to the problems of the modern
   world?

Recommended Reading

Downs, James F., 1975, *Cultures in Crisis,* 2nd ed. Beverly Hills, Calif.: Glencoe
  Press. This book demonstrates how anthropological theory relates to many of
  our contemporary society's problems.

Frantz, Charles, 1972, *The Student Anthropologist's Handbook: A Guide to Research, Training, and Career.* Cambridge, Mass.: Schenkman. Basic information about becoming a professional anthropologist.

Fried, Morton H., 1972, *The Study of Anthropology.* New York: Crowell. Additional information on becoming a professional anthropologist. It deals with
  undergraduate study in anthropology, as well as graduate work.

Hunter, David E., and Phillip Whitten, eds., 1975, *Anthropology: Contemporary
  Perspectives.* Boston: Educational Associates. An excellent collection of very
  readable articles on topics relating to the four subfields of anthropology.

Kluckhohn, Clyde, 1949, *Mirror for Man: Anthropology and Modern Life.* New
  York: McGraw-Hill. Still an interesting introduction to anthropology written
  for the layperson.

Oliver, Douglas, 1964, *Invitation to Anthropology.* Garden City, N.Y.: The Natural History Press. A brief and easy-to-read description of the theories and
  methods of modern anthropology.

Pelto, Pertti, J., 1965, *The Nature of Anthropology.* Columbus, Ohio: Merrill. An
  introduction to the character of anthropology as a discipline, including information on its history and scope.

Spradley, James P., and David W. McCurdy, eds., 1977, *Conformity and Conflict:
  Readings in Cultural Anthropology.* Boston: Little, Brown. Interesting articles
  on various aspects of culture, including a number of studies of the United
  States' culture.

Whitten, Phillip, and David E. Hunter, eds., 1976, *Encyclopedia of Anthropology.*
  New York: Harper & Row. An important source of background information on
  all aspects of anthropology, including a number of biographies of famous
  anthropologists.

Wolf, Eric R., 1974, *Anthropology.* New York: Norton. (Originally published in
  1964.) An examination of the ways American anthropologists have approached and interpreted their subject matter in recent years.

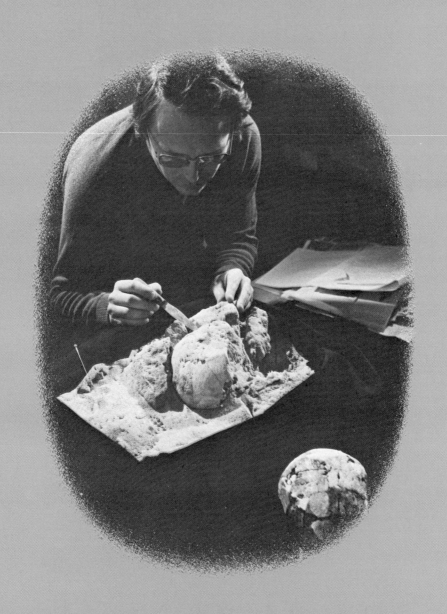

2

Where did humans come from?

Creationism and evolution represent two opposing views of human origins.

Darwin emphasized natural selection in his evolutionary theory.

Genetics contributes to an understanding of the mechanisms of evolution.

Humans evolved from earlier, prosimianlike forms.

Human remains appear in the fossil record at least 5 million years ago.

Neanderthal was our ancestor.

On the stifling-hot morning of July 13, 1925, a trial began in the small town of Dayton, Tennessee, which was destined to attract worldwide attention, *Tennessee* v. *John Thomas Scopes*, No. 5232. The defendant was a local high-school science teacher and football coach who had reluctantly agreed to be arrested so that a test case could be brought against a recently passed state law—the Butler Act—which made it a criminal offense to teach evolution in Tennessee public schools.

While technically it was Scopes who was charged with a misdemeanor, in reality it was evolutionary theory that was on trial. Since 1859, when Charles Darwin published *On the Origin of Species,* the battle lines had been forming between those who closely followed the teachings of the Bible and those who favored Darwin's theory of evolution. In the post–World War I South there had been a rapid growth of Fundamentalism, and the Butler Act was an outgrowth of that movement. In many peoples minds the Scopes trial was to be the ultimate showdown between religion and science. Each side was defended by an eloquent spokesman. On the side of the state, and against Scopes and evolution, was the three-time Democratic presidential nominee and former secretary of state, William Jennings Bryan, a leader in the Fundamentalist movement; for the defense was the world-renowned lawyer Clarence Darrow.

While the Scopes trial did not live up to the public's expectations of a battle to the death between science and religion,[1] the publicity devoted to the trial by the mass media did bring the controversy clearly before the public. The trial centered around the legal issue of whether or not Scopes had the right to teach concepts of evolution in his science classes. The larger issue involved, however, was the origin of humankind. Had humans been created by God as the Bible describes, or had they evolved from a lower form of life, as Darwin suggested? Were humans special creatures distinct from animals or were humans themselves animals, sharing a common ancestry with the great apes?

The legal issue was settled in 11 days. Scopes was found guilty and fined $100.[2] The Butler Act remained in effect in Tennessee until 1967 but was never again enforced following the Scopes

The Scopes trial made public the evolution-Creation controversy.

[1] Judge John T. Raulston ruled that the trial involved only one question: Whether or not Scopes had taught evolution in the high school. As a result seven of the eight noted scientists that Darrow had assembled as expert witnesses on evolution were not allowed to testify, nor was Bryan able to deliver a speech he had prepared attacking Darwin.
[2] The case was dismissed by the Tennessee Supreme Court in 1927, on a technicality involving Scopes' fine.

trial. The more basic issues of the origins of humankind have not yet been resolved in the minds of many people. Both points of view exist today, as well as various intermediate views that attempt to integrate both a religious and scientific explanation of human origins. In this chapter both of these two points of view, Creationism and Darwinism, will be examined, and the evolution of primates in general and humans in particular will be discussed.

Creationism

In 1863 the famous British naturalist Thomas Henry Huxley wrote, "The question of questions for mankind—the problem which underlies all others, and is more deeply interesting than any other—is the ascertainment of the place which Man occupies in nature and of his relations to the universe of things." The conflict between the Bible and evolutionism centers around this problem of discovering humankind's place in nature.

If there were such a thing as a time machine that could take us back to the time when humans first appeared on earth, we would have a definite answer about our origin. Since no such machine exists, different methods of viewing the origin of humans must be used. One approach is through faith. Many people believe that the Bible's account of Creation in Genesis is absolute truth and must be accepted as written. On the other hand the scientific point of view rejects the Bible as a book of science. The scientific point of view holds that the most reasonable theory to explain the known facts surrounding human origins should be accepted. Because new theories emerge and new facts are discovered, the scientific interpretation changes more readily than the religious point of view.

Throughout most of the Middle Ages the Bible represented the primary source of explanation for all questions about human origins and about the relationship of humans to their surrounding world. Yet as a book of science the Bible suffers from several flaws. First, it was written primarily as a book of religious teaching and not as a scientific text. Second, it was written several thousand years ago, when learned people understood less about the world around them than they do today. For example, the Biblical writers believed that the earth was flat and a sea lay under it (see Ps. 136:6; Ps. 24:1–2; and Gen. 7:11) or that the earth was stationary and the sun, moon, and stars circled the earth (Ps. 93.1; Ps. 104:5; and Gen. 1:14–18). A more serious objection to the use of the Bible as an explanation of human origins stems from the fact that the Bible contains two contradictory stories of Creation, one in Gen. 1 and 2:1–4a, the other in Gen. 2:4b–23.

There are two contradicting accounts of Creation in the Bible.

These two accounts of Creation arise from the fact that the books of the Bible were written by different people at different times. When the kingdoms of Judah and Israel were united, their sacred books were combined. The religious book of the Judahites has come to be known as the J narrative; that of the Israelites as the E narrative. Only the J narrative had an account of Creation. When the sacred books were combined, the story of Creation in the J narrative was left intact as Gen. 2:4b–23 and in front of it was placed a new and different account of Creation, Gen. 1 and 2:1–4a (Moody 1953:428).

The newer account of Creation is generally the more familiar one, with its division of Creation into six days. The creation of lower animals occurs on the fourth and fifth days and the creation of humans on the sixth day. There is no mention of Adam and his rib in this account, which reads instead, "male and female created He them." In the older J narrative there is no mention of six days; lower animals are created after Adam, and Eve is created from one of Adam's ribs after the lower animals have been created. If one accepts the Bible's account of Creation as absolute truth, which account is to be accepted? The supporters of an interpretation of human origin based on the Bible have generally accepted the more recent account, Gen. 1 and 2:1–4a.

If the judge had allowed Clarence Darrow to introduce his expert witnesses at the Scopes trial, Rabbi Herman Rosenwasser, a Bible expert, would have testified that there were many different Bibles in addition to the King James version that the Fundamentalists had accepted. The Bibles published in English were translations of Greek and Latin texts that were themselves translations from earlier Hebrew and Aramaic texts. The King James version differs from its own revision in some 30,000 respects (Ginger 1969:122). Since the Scopes trial the discovery and translation of the Dead Sea Scrolls have shown how the text of the Bible has changed considerably since the original texts were composed, during the period from about 250 BC to AD 68 (Gaster 1964:v).

The Bible and the Growth of Science. People look to the Bible for an understanding of human origins because the Bible has long been a major source of explanation in Western history. Throughout the Middle Ages scholars accepted the Bible as their final authority. The use of the Bible to answer all questions continues today in fundamentalist sects. By the Renaissance a few scholars began to publicly question the authority of the Bible in matters pertaining to what is now called "science." Eventually certain areas of science—those least related to the study of humankind, such as astronomy and physics—were accepted regardless of the fact that their findings challenged statements in the Bible; however, statements about *humans* that deviated from the Bible were not tolerated. In most people's minds, God had created each type of organism separately in its present form.

Throughout the seventeenth and eighteenth centuries certain information about living organisms contained in the Bible was accepted as basic "scientific fact." These "facts" formed the framework upon which all scientific theory was built during this time period. First it was assumed that the age of the earth was very brief. In the middle of the seventeenth century, James Ussher, archbishop of Armagh, Northern Ireland, came to the conclusion that the earth had been created in the year 4004 BC, based on his calculations regarding the generations since Adam recorded in the Bible. This calculation had a profound effect on the thinking of the time. In fact the belief that the earth was created about 6000 years ago continues to be accepted by some people even today. Working independently of Ussher, Dr. John Lightfoot, vice-chancellor of Cambridge, came up with an even more precise calculation of when Creation had occurred: October 23, 4004 BC at nine o'clock in the morning. In a sense, humans were thought to have hardly any history.

If the history of earth and humans was of such a short time span, there was no reason to assume that humans or any organism might have changed over time. Therefore it was accepted that all living organisms, humans included, had been separately created in their present forms by God. This belief was known as the belief in "special creation" (McKern 1974:6). Any attempt to suggest that one form could change into another form over time was discouraged and viewed as a form of heresy.

Given the short span of earth history and special creation, the notion that forms had become extinct was not generally accepted. As late as 1785 the great scholar and statesman Thomas Jefferson declared, "Such is the economy of nature, that no instance can be produced, of her having permitted any one of her animals to become extinct; or her having formed any link in her great work so weak as to be broken" (McCown and Kennedy 1972:8). In the Middle Ages scholars such as Saint Augustine

Archbishop James Ussher.
(The Granger Collection)

Archbishop Ussher believed the earth had been created in 4004 BC.

and Saint Thomas Aquinas applied a concept that had its origin, in a somewhat different form, in the writings of the classical Greek philosophers. This concept came to be known as the *Great Chain of Being* (Figure 1). Scholars believed that there was a hierarchy in nature, a chain composed of an indefinite number of categories or links, ranging from the lowest forms of life on up to God (Lovejoy 1936:59). Each link differed from the link above and below it in the least possible degree. The organisms representing each link were considered immutable. Since it was assumed that the ordering of the links was static from the time of Creation, there was no thought that any of the links might share evolutionary affinities. Not only was each form created independently, each was thought to have a different purpose.

> The Great Chain of Being was composed of living organisms, linked hierarchically in nature.

By the end of the seventeenth century, science had established a new view of the universe that included a number of radical departures from Biblical writing. First, it was assumed that there were other planets in our solar system inhabited by rational creatures. Second, it was asserted that the size of the universe was infinite. Third, it was conceived that stars were suns, each with possible planetary systems (Lovejoy 1936:108). Science was beginning to discover new ways of viewing life on earth and was beginning to challenge the literal interpretation of the Bible.

Due to the pressures of the new scientific discoveries, the Church began taking a new stand about the nature of humans. Church leaders hoped that science and religion could still be re-

Figure 1 Illustration of the Great Chain of Being from Raymond Lull's *Liber de ascensu et descensu intellectus,* published in 1512, showing humans (*Homo*) in the middle of the chain. (From Margaret Hodgen, *Early Anthropology in the Sixteenth and Seventeenth Centuries,* 1964, University of Pennsylvania Press.)

conciled. The development of astronomy, physics, and mathematics suggested there were natural laws, which could be discovered. Natural laws, the Church suggested, were those that God wished humans to understand; in fact people *should* try to understand the divine plan of nature. As scientific investigation continued, the credibility of accepted traditions was further strained. Most damaging was the increasing discovery of new fossil types and the inadequacy of the older scientific theory to explain their existence.

Fossils: A Puzzle

Fossils were discovered by the ancient Greeks. They were puzzled by fossils and realized that an explanation was needed to account for the fossilized remains of sea creatures on mountaintops many miles from the ocean. The Greeks viewed the history of the earth in terms of cycles. Fossils were thought to be the remains of former earth cycles. A similar explanation of fossils appeared in the Middle Ages, but now fossils of marine life were thought to have been deposited on mountaintops by the Great Flood described in the Bible. Perhaps in the Middle Ages fossils were of greater importance as "ceraunia," a category that included fossils of sea urchins and belemnites, prehistoric artifacts, and meteorites. These objects were valued for the medical and magical qualities they were believed to possess (McCown and Kennedy 1972:7–8).

Beginning in the fifteenth century, the Renaissance ushered in an era of the collecting of exotic curiosities. In 1700 the earliest human fossil remains were discovered in West Germany (Brace 1967:7). However, the significance of fossils was not appreciated until the process of evolution was understood. After all, if the earth was only 6000 years old, there was still little reason to suspect that humans or any organism had changed over time. Yet the collecting continued. It was assumed that survivors of forms represented by the fossilized organisms would be discovered in unexplored regions of the earth, since it was still thought that forms did not become extinct. This did not prove to be the case. Instead, each newly discovered region yielded its own living forms and unrelated new fossils.

About 1800 the fossil footprints of dinosaurs were discovered in New England, in the Connecticut River valley, but they were given a Biblical interpretation. It was assumed by some that Biblical animals were of a very large size. Therefore the fossil tracks were presumed to be those made by the raven that Noah had sent from the ark in search of dry land (Wood et al. 1972:73).

As the eighteenth century drew to a close, it was becoming apparent to some researchers that creatures must have become extinct, because their fossil remains were unlike any existing forms. With this view came the even more important implication that some links in the Great Chain of Being had been lost. The remains of mastodons and mammoths were being discovered in the United States and Siberia, once again with no living counterparts. The famous French paleontologist Baron Georges Cuvier described and classified the remains of 23 kinds of extinct animals (Greene 1961:119). If the world was not static but had changed since Creation, a new scientific framework was needed to reconcile the recent fossil discoveries and the religious beliefs of the time. Early research in geology showed that each of the various stratigraphic layers of the earth showed the remains of different animal forms. Cuvier proposed an explanation to reconcile the extinct forms with the religious beliefs of the time, an explanation known as *catastrophism*. He hypothe- | Cuvier explained fossils by catastrophism.
sized that the world had been subjected not only to the Great Flood but to a whole series of worldwide catastrophic events, each one involving crustal upheaval, such as an earthquake that was then followed by a great flood. Each catastrophe had destroyed all existing life forms. Cuvier also suggested that the fossils of each geologic stratum thus represented the organisms that had suddenly been destroyed by that particular catastrophe. Cuvier suggested that there had been a succession of special creations, one following each catastrophe. He believed that the account of Creation in the Bible represented the latest special creation, in which all living organisms were created. Humans did not exist prior to the last Creation; thus for Cuvier there could be no fossil humans (McKern 1974:7; Brace 1967:8). Cuvier's catastrophism became popular because it took into account the fact that the earth had changed—to a certain extent—without giving up the belief that life forms were static and immutable. Thus Creationism continued as an explanation of human origins although the new Creationism of the early nineteenth century was very different from the Creationism of the Middle Ages. It had changed to accommodate people's changing view of the world. However, in the last half of the nineteenth century this view of catastrophism lost out to Darwinism.

A New Theory of the Earth's Age. Two Scottish geologists, James Hall and James Hutton, spearheaded the first revolution in geologic thought, at the same time that Cuvier was advocating his theory of catastrophism. Hall and Hutton studied rocks exposed on the rugged coast of Scotland. They began to realize that enormous spans of time were required to produce the rocks of the earth's crust. Their doctrine, which came to be known as *uniformitarianism*, maintained that the process of nature seen in action today—such as flooding, wind erosion, earthquakes—can account for all past formations of rock and all present features of the landscape. This principle of uniformity ruled out any supernatural events that would contradict physical laws acting today, such as Cuvier's worldwide catastrophes (Strahler 1977:4). Hutton published the doctrine of uniformitarianism in 1795 under the title *Theory of the Earth*. Hutton saw the actions that changed the face of the earth as the work of God (Greene, 1961:84–87; McKern 1974:8). Yet Hutton's work was considered heretical by the Church and many of his fellow scientists. To many, his views differed too much from the accepted views of Creationism. Hutton's belief that geologic phenomena should be explained in terms of everyday processes of nature rather than catastrophes suggested that the earth must be much older than the 6000 years that Ussher had hypothesized. In fact it might require millions of years for natural phenomena to have brought about the changes of the geologic strata suggested. To Hutton this was no problem. "Time, which measures everything in our idea, and is often deficient to our schemes, is to nature endless and as nothing" (Hutton 1795:221–222). To many scholars Hutton's theory was extremely radical. It suggested the continual change of the earth's surface, while other theorists considered the immutability of the earth a basic assumption.

Uniformitarianism suggested a long earth history.

Hutton died only two years after the publication of his book. In 1797, the year of Hutton's death, another man, Charles Lyell, was born who would later build upon Hutton's germinal theory. In 1830 Lyell published the first volume of his *Principles of Geology, Being an Attempt to Explain the Former Changes of the Earth's Surface, by Reference to Causes Now in Operation*. This book, which formed the basis of modern geology, reintroduced Hill and Hutton's idea that changes in the earth's surface in the past were due to natural causes that are still operating. This idea of gradual change eventually replaced the older notion of worldwide catastrophes. If one accepted the theory of gradual change, then one also had to accept the great antiquity of the earth. Lyell's work was important to Charles Darwin, because it introduced the theory that the earth was very old, without which Darwin's concept of evolution would have been untenable.

Charles Darwin. (Courtesy of
the American Museum of
Natural History)

Charles Darwin and Natural Selection

Charles Darwin took the ideas of many earlier writers and combined them with observations of his own to form a new framework for viewing humans origins, and the world never again was the same.

Darwin's early childhood suggested he might not be a success. Unsure of his future he eventually entered Edinburgh University to study medicine. After a short time he decided he would study for the clergy, which he did at Cambridge University for three years. He then learned of an opening for a naturalist on board the HMS *Beagle*, which was about to make a world cruise. As Darwin had been an avid collector of natural phenomena since childhood, he applied to Captain Robert Fitz-Roy for the position but was almost not accepted. As Darwin later recounted (F. Darwin 1961:43), "On becoming very intimate with Fitz-Roy, I heard that I had run a very narrow risk of being rejected on account of the shape of my nose! He was an ardent disciple of Lavater, and was convinced that he could judge of a man's character by the outline of his features; and he doubted whether anyone with my nose could possess sufficient energy and determination for the voyage. But I think he was afterwards well satisfied that my nose had spoken falsely."

One of the books that Darwin took with him on the cruise was the first volume of Lyell's *Principles of Geology*, which he had not read previously. The voyage lasted from December 27, 1831 to

October 2, 1836. The HMS *Beagle*, a ten-gun brig, was supposed to survey the South American coastline and undertake chronometrical measurements around the world (Eiseley 1967:27). During the voyage Darwin made extensive observations of nature, many of which supported the theory of uniformitarianism. Darwin also noticed variation within species, especially in the Galápagos Islands, 600 miles off the coast of Ecuador. He discovered that plants and animals showed considerable variation from island to island; for example, he noted there was great diversity in the beaks of finches. By the end of the voyage Darwin seems to have been convinced that forms could change over time. Still, he did not yet understand how evolution operated. He felt that somehow the variation that existed among the members of any species was important. From his knowledge of domestic plants and animals he recognized that selective breeding resulted in improvements. However, this was *artificial selection*. This type of change was brought about by human interference and did not account for change in wild forms.

It was not until 1838 that Darwin realized that selection—natural selection—also occurs among wild plants and animals, when he read Thomas Malthus' *Essay on the Principle of Population*, written in 1798.[3] Writing about the human population, Malthus suggested that the reproductive potential for humans far exceeds the natural resources necessary to support an ever-increasing population. This imbalance results in a struggle for existence. Darwin applied Malthus' theory to all organisms. He saw all life, not just the human population, as being in a struggle for existence. He argued that this struggle under changing environmental conditions ultimately resulted in changes in the physical structure of organisms. The variation within species that he had observed on board the HMS *Beagle* and elsewhere was fortuitous and random. The struggle for existence perpetuated "advantageous" variations by means of heredity. The "unfit" were eliminated, while the "fit" (those with the best heredity for any given environment) were selected to be the parents of the next generation. This was the process Darwin called *natural selection*. Just as the breeder artificially selects the best forms for procreation, nature also selects. Since life and the environment are ever-changing, evolution is perpetual. No life form is ever in complete equilibrium with its surroundings (Ei-

Darwin explained the origin of species by natural selection.

---

[3] There is disagreement among the biographers of Darwin as to the actual influences that stimulated the development of Darwin's theory of natural selection. Darwin (F. Darwin 1961:58) and Himmelfarb (1959) gave credit to Malthus, but Eiseley (1959) and Poirier (1974:22), among others, suggest that the writings of Edward Blyth and perhaps others were more influential, though Darwin never credited them.

seley 1967:30). Changes, often imperceptible from one generation to another, over many generations can result in new species. Thus Darwin had his explanation for the origin of species.

Charles Darwin realized that to envision the world as he did was considered heresy in the 1830s. He decided that it was absolutely necessary to fully document his argument. He investigated every exception to his theory fully until it could be explained. He explored every other possible explanation of the evidence. Yet as if fearful of ridicule, he delayed publishing his theory. His friends encouraged him to publish the massive collection of data that he already had assembled. He procrastinated. Lyell warned that others might eventually arrive at the same conclusion and receive credit for it. His warning was to no avail. Darwin continued to collect data.

Darwin conceived of a massive volume with an enormous amount of data written to convince other scientists of his theory of natural selection. He had no thoughts of a book for the general public. On June 18, 1858, after Darwin had worked on his theory more than 20 years, his world exploded. He received a manuscript from a young naturalist, Alfred Russell Wallace, who was working in the Malay Archipelago and who had been corresponding with Darwin for about one year. Wallace's manuscript outlined Darwin's theory of natural selection. Darwin (F. Darwin 1961:196) wrote to Lyell:

Wallace independently also discovered natural selection.

Down, 18th (June 1858)
My Dear Lyell,
    Some year or so ago you recommended me to read a paper by Wallace in the Annals, which had interested you, and, as I am writing to him, I knew this would please him much, so I told him. He has to-day sent me the enclosed, and asked me to forward it to you. It seems to me well worth reading. Your words have come true with a vengeance—that I should be forestalled. You said this, when I explained to you here very briefly my views of Natural Selection depending on the struggle for existence. I never saw a more striking coincidence; if Wallace had my MS. sketch written out in 1842, he could not have made a better short abstract! Even his terms now stand as heads of my chapters. Please return me the MS., which he does not say he wishes me to publish, but I shall of course, at once write and offer to send to any journal. So all my originality, whatever it may amount to, will be smashed, though my book, if it will ever have any value, will not be deteriorated; as all the labour consists in the application of the theory.
    I hope you will approve of Wallace's sketch, that I may tell him what you say.

                              My dear Lyell,
                              yours most truly,
                                      C. Darwin

Stunned, Darwin suggested to close friends that perhaps he should destroy his own manuscript lest anyone think that he had stolen the idea from Wallace. However, Lyell and the biologist Joseph Hooker arranged for a short summary by Darwin of his work to be read along with Wallace's manuscript when the latter was delivered as a paper before the Linnaean Society on July 1, 1858. The two papers drew little attention. Wallace's paper forced Darwin to publish what he considered an abstract of his definitive volume. *On the Origin of Species by Means of Natural Selection, or the Preservation of Favoured Races in the Struggle for Life* was published in November 1859. The first edition of 1250 copies (which was more than twice the amount that Darwin thought the book would ever sell) sold out on the day of publication. A second edition of 3000 copies also sold rapidly and was quickly translated into a number of foreign languages.

While Darwin was interested in describing a system operating by natural selection, he did not completely eliminate God from his theory. Darwin believed that the first living thing or things were created by God and that from then on natural selection took over. In the last sentence of his book, Darwin (C. Darwin 1958:450) observed, "There is grandeur in this view of life, with its several powers, having been originally breathed by the Creator into a few forms or into one; and that, whilst this planet has gone cycling on according to the fixed law of gravity, from so simple a beginning endless forms most beautiful and wonderful have been, and are being evolved."

Thus far, no mention has been made about human evolution. Darwin purposely avoided discussion of humans in *On the Origin of Species* for fear that it would create controversy and detract from his argument for natural selection, which he considered of primary importance. All that he ventured to say about humans was, "Much light will be thrown on the origin of man and his history" (C. Darwin 1958:449). Darwin's fears were proven correct. Even though Darwin had not discussed humans, much of the controversy over the book centered on human beings, and particularly on the implication that if all of life gradually changes over time, some forms becoming extinct and other forms evolving into new species, then humans too must have begun as some other form.

Darwin's friend Thomas Huxley was the first to apply the principle of natural selection to humans, in his book *Man's Place in Nature*, which was published in 1863. After writing *On the Origin of Species* Darwin took another 12 years before completing his own work on the evolution of humans, which was entitled *The Descent of Man* and was published in 1871. In this book Darwin suggested that in the distant past there had existed an ancestor common to all primate forms, including humans. In 1871, there was little fossil data to support his point of view.

While Darwin was suggesting that humans and apes had descended from a common ancestor, critics of his theory accused him of saying that humans had evolved from modern apes and monkeys. To this day Darwin's theory is still referred to by some as "monkeyism." This mistaken notion about his theory upset the general public. Today the close relationships between humans and apes is easily accepted yet in Darwin's era there was a tremendous reaction against viewing these organisms as even distantly related. The public was not yet ready to accept humans (themselves) as animals, much less as cousins of apes.

Darwin believed that humans had descended from some earlier primate form.

Darwin's theory challenged a number of assumptions of the nineteenth century:

1. The earth was unchanging, except as a result of catastrophes sent by God.
2. The earth was recently created.
3. Living forms were unchanging.
4. Living forms had each been specially created.
5. Humans were different from animals.
6. Humans were not related to monkeys or apes.

Darwin's theory contradicted many of the theories of his time.

The theory that Darwin presented provided a new way of looking at the world and at humankind. His theory was based partly on assumptions that could not be proven in the nineteenth century, for the following reasons: Geological information was lacking, there was little fossil evidence of human antiquity, dating techniques did not exist, comparative anatomy was in its infancy, and the science of genetics had yet to develop. As a result it was possible for Darwin's nineteenth-century critics to suggest that Darwin's account of natural selection was "merely a theory." Many people still hold this view.

Most of the research on evolution since Darwin has attempted to document the process of evolution that he described. The most important advance since Darwin has been the acquisition of knowledge about how heredity operates from generation to generation. Darwin speculated on this point but was unable to find a satisfactory answer. Like others of his time, Darwin assumed that each trait of an offspring was a blend of traits from both parents. However if this were true, it raised a serious problem for Darwin's theory of natural selection: If a particular variation within a population was advantageous in terms of natural selection, would it not become "diluted" through mating with individuals who did not have the characteristic, or perhaps even disappear after a few generations? Darwin was unable to provide the answer. Instead it was an Austrian monk, Gregor Johann Mendel, who discovered the answer, as a result of experiments that he undertook on the common pea plant, in a small garden of the monastery where he lived and taught mathematics.

Gregor Mendel and Genetics

Gregor Mendel obtained purebred varieties of peas that differed in a number of characteristics, such as color of seed and vine height. Cautiously he grew each of these purebred varieties for two years, in order to verify that each bred true to type.

Gregor Mendel.
(The Granger Collection)

While these pea plants are normally self-fertilizing, Mendel was able to artificially cross-fertilize the plants. Thus he was able to cross various purebreds and observe the characteristics of the offspring that these cross-fertilized purebreds produced. He prevented the pollen of other plants from affecting the experiments by covering the buds of these plants with small bags. Mendel found somewhat surprisingly that the offspring traits were not blends of both parents, as Darwin had believed, but rather showed the characteristic of *one* of the parents.

Mendel observed seven different traits: seed shape, the interior color of the seed, the color of the seed coat, the shape of the pod, the color of the pod, the position of the pod, and the length of the stem. Two forms of each were represented by the various purebreds that he used. For example, the stem length of a particular plant could be either long or short, or the color of the pod could be either green or yellow. For each trait in the first filial generation (the first generation of offspring) there was no blending, but rather the appearance of one of the two characteristics for each trait. For example, the stem length of *all* of the plants in the first filial generation was tall and the pod color of *all* plants was green. Mendel continued his experiments and next crossbred the hybrids of the first filial generation with one another. The result of these experiments was that in the second filial generation *both* of the original traits appeared. For example, both tall and short stem lengths occurred, as did pods of solid green and solid yellow. But each set of characteristics did not appear in equal numbers. Instead, 75 percent showed the characteristic of the first filial generation—in other words, tall

stems or green pods—while 25 percent showed the characteristic that had not appeared in the first filial generation, namely
short stems or yellow pods.

Characteristics such as the tall stems and green pods that appear as the only characteristics of the first filial generation and
as the most frequent characteristics of the second filial generation are called *dominant*. Those that are absent in the first filial
generation and that appear infrequently in the second filial generation are called *recessive*. Mendel's discovery was of the utmost importance in answering the question that had plagued
Darwin. Hereditary material from both parents does not blend
to produce a trait, although material from both parents (called
genes) is present for each trait. Some of these genes transmit
dominant characteristics. Whenever this occurs, the plant has
the appearance of the dominant characteristic. Only in the absence of the dominant characteristic does the recessive character appear. Mendel made another important distinction. He realized that the outward appearance of the plant, today called the
phenotype, was misleading as an indicator of what hereditary
traits it carried. For example, some tall-stemmed plants contain
only genes for tallness. Other tall-stemmed plants, such as those
of Mendel's first filial generation, contain a combination of dominant and recessive genes. Thus the internal or genetic makeup
was different from the outward appearance of the plant. This internal makeup is called the *genotype*.

Mendel concluded that each of the seven traits he was studying was determined by a pair of genes. The genes comprising a
given pair can be alike or different. For example, a purebred tall
plant is said to be *homozygous* for tallness. It has two genes that
are the same. It also contains the dominant genes and therefore
is referred to as a *dominant homozygote*. A plant that has two
genes for shortness is also homozygous, but is a *recessive homozygote*. Plants that are crossbred, such as those of the first filial
generation, have a *heterozygous* condition. Genetically they
carry one dominant and one recessive gene. In this condition,
the dominant gene typically masks the expression of its partner,
the recessive gene (Volpe 1967:18).

By his experiments Mendel was able to demonstrate that
heredity does not involve a blending of genes, as Darwin
thought, but rather that genes act as independent units. This important finding has come to be known as the *law of segregation*.
Mendel also learned that each of the seven traits of the pea
plants that he studied operated independently of one another.
For example tall stems could occur with green pods or yellow

Mendel's experiments showed that hereditary material from both parents does not blend to produce a trait.

pods as could short stems. This discovery has come to be known as the *law of independent assortment*.

Mendel published his findings in *The Proceedings of the Natural History Society of Brünn* in 1866, only seven years after Darwin's *On the Origin of Species*. Unlike Darwin's work, Mendel's discoveries were ignored. The significance of his research was not understood by the scholars of his time. It was not until 1900 that his work was rediscovered. In that year three botanists[4] independently came to the same conclusion that Mendel had arrived at in 1866, and each independently rediscovered Mendel's publication. With the rediscovery of Mendel's contributions, the era of modern evolutionary theory was underway. By the 1930s the discoveries of the new field of genetics could be interrelated with Darwin's theory of natural selection to form a more comprehensive theory of evolution. In 1942 Julian Huxley, the grandson of Thomas Huxley, published a major book entitled *Evolution: The Modern Synthesis*. This book outlined the *synthetic theory of evolution* which combines the theories of genetics and Darwinian natural selection to form the foundation of modern biology, paleontology, physical anthropology, and other life sciences (Weiss and Mann 1975:22–23).

Since Darwin's discovery of natural selection it has been learned that there are three other ways in which evolutionary change takes place. Darwin was able to base his theory only on observations of differences in physical features, or phenotypes. Today biologists analyze evolutionary change in terms of changing genetic frequencies in populations that form breeding groups. Any process that affects the frequencies of various genes within such a population brings about evolutionary change. Besides natural selection, biologists now recognize that *mutations*, *genetic drift*, and *migration* also bring about changes in the frequencies of genes in breeding populations.

A mutation is a sudden change in genetic material. In many cases a mutation is lethal and therefore is not passed on to the next generation. In other cases mutations are neutral and introduce new genetic material into the population. The neutral mutations remain in the breeding population, increasing the range of variation within the population. Mutations interact with natural selection, which increases the frequency of the few adaptive mutations and decreases the frequency of those that are maladapted.

Genetic drift also affects the frequencies of genes in a breeding

Darwin's natural selection and Mendel's genetics are the basis of synthetic theory of evolution.

Evolutionary change is a result of natural selection, mutations, genetic drift, and migration.

[4] Hugo de Vries, Karl Correns, and Erich Tschermak.

population. Genetic drift is an abrupt change in a frequency due to the smallness of the group size. It is assumed that genetic drift was especially important in the evolution of early forms of humans, who lived in small groups. In such a small group the loss of one or two individuals could mean that a particular gene was completely lost from the population. Genetic drift has nothing to do with natural selection, because drift works entirely by chance. For example, two hunters of a small population might be killed by lightning and might be the only carriers of a particular gene in that population.

Migration represents another cause of change in the frequencies of genes in a breeding population. Like genetic drift, migration is especially important in small populations. As individuals leave one breeding population and join another, the frequency of genes in both populations may be significantly altered. Migration is also important because it ensures that adaptive mutations will be introduced into other populations.

The changes in genetic frequencies brought about by mutation, genetic drift, and migration may or may not be adaptive. However, evolutionary change is adaptive, a fact that natural selection is primarily responsible for. It selects among variants according to their adaptive value. Natural selection works because individuals with different genetic makeups have different chances for reproducing (Weiss and Mann 1975:28).

The Fossil Evidence for Evolution

Charles Lyell, Charles Darwin, Gregor Mendel, and others provided the theoretical framework for a comprehensive theory of evolution. Yet the question remains: Does the fossil evidence *prove* the theory?

Since the first discovery of a fossil human in 1700 in West Germany, sufficient evidence has been accumulated to prove Darwin's theory that humans, like other organisms, change over time. The data show a gradual change from an early form at least 5.5 million years ago until modern humans emerged about 40,000 years ago. The primary problem of contemporary scientists is no longer to prove the existence of earlier forms of humanity but rather to understand the interrelationships between the various forms. While the broad outlines of human evolution can be reconstructed, the task is fraught with problems. At best the scientist is able to provide what appears to be the most reasonable interpretation based on the present data.

Interpreting the fossil record is difficult.

Excavation of a fossil skull. (Courtesy of the American Museum of Natural History)

But often, just one new discovery or one new technique for more accuracy dating fossils can radically change our picture of human evolution.

The following reasons explain why the data from fossils are inadequate for providing a definitive description of human evolution:

1. Fossils result from chance discoveries. Frequently one cannot predict where fossil discoveries will be made with any great precision.
2. Fossil skeletal material represents a rare combination of circumstances that have brought about its preservation. Usually a skeleton decays after death, leaving behind no traces of its existence. However, once in a great while a complex combination of events will result in the fossilization of the skeleton before it decays. Apparently most of human evolution occurred in the tropical zone, where the chances of preservation are especially poor.
3. Even where skeletal material has fossilized, there is usually little chance of finding a complete skeleton. Early forms of humans did not bury their dead. Parts of the carcass were dragged off in different directions by scavengers. Often only a single bone of a skeleton is discovered. Therefore the scientist is often put in the uncomfortable position of having to compare a leg bone from Africa with a piece of jaw from Asia.
4. The farther back in time one goes, the smaller the human population and, by extension, the fewer the skeletons to be left behind.
5. It is often very difficult to date skeletal remains. The bones of early forms of humans cannot be dated directly. Instead they must be dated in association with certain types of rock, which can be dated. Often the associations are questionable, and scientists will disagree among themselves over the date.
6. Any view of human origins and development is colored by the accepted theoretical viewpoints of the time.

In light of these and other problems it is easy to understand how scientists are able to arrive at different interpretations of human evolution and why these views change. If anything, it is remarkable how much has been learned within the last 50 years about humankind's past. In the section that follows, the basic outlines of human development will be presented, along with the problem areas remaining today in the interpretation of human evolution.

Primate Evolution

Humans are classified as members of the taxonomic order Primates, which is a subdivision of the class Mammalia (mammals). The living primates include prosimians, monkeys, apes, and humans.[5] Human evolution leads from ancient prosimians through early forms of monkeys and apes to early forms of humans. For the most part, these ancient ancestors did not look like contemporary prosimians, monkeys, apes, or humans. Modern primates have evolved from ancient forms unlike any living form. Of course, that is exactly what Darwin suggested the case would be: Organisms change over time. This applies as much to nonhuman primates as it does to human beings.

> Primates is the subdivision of Mammalia that includes humans.

The earliest fossil evidence for any creature that might be considered an ancestor of the primates is a single tooth from the late Cretaceous period (Figure 2), about 90 to 100 million years ago, found in a fossil site in Montana. A great number of primate teeth from the Paleocene epoch, dated at 75 million years ago, have been found at the same site. All of these teeth have been classified in the same genus, *Purgatorius*.

> The oldest ancestor of primates date back to the Cretaceous period.

Early prosimian ancestors suggested little of the potential of the primates. Primates share more biological characteristics with insectivores—such as the shrews, moles, and hedgehogs—than with any other mammalian order. It is believed that the early ancestors of the primates exhibited many features of the insectivores, such as a long snout, small size, eyes on the sides of the head, and an insect diet. Well-developed hearing and a keen sense of smell were of major importance to these first primates because they were ground-dwelling.

These earliest primates appeared toward the end of the era of the dinosaurs, in a period of rapidly changing ecological conditions. At present it is believed that these early forms moved into trees, where there were fewer predators than on the ground.

---

[5] The basic characteristics of the primates will be described in Chapter 5.

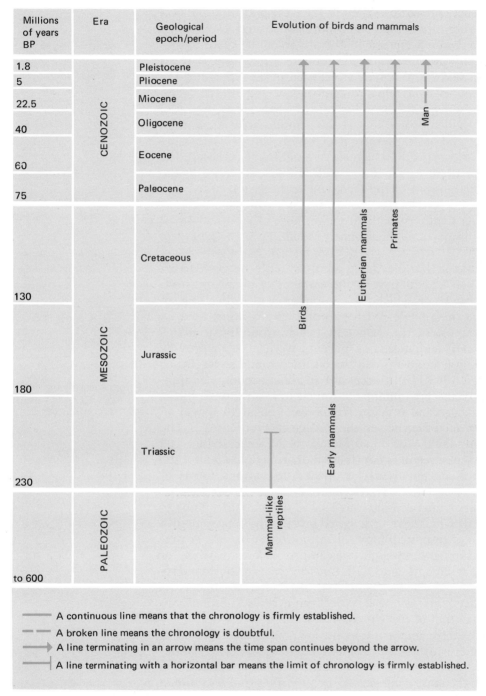

Millions of years BP	Era	Geological epoch/period	Evolution of birds and mammals
1.8	CENOZOIC	Pleistocene	
5		Pliocene	
22.5		Miocene	
40		Oligocene	Man
60		Eocene	
75		Paleocene	
130	MESOZOIC	Cretaceous	Eutherian mammals / Primates
180		Jurassic	Birds
230		Triassic	Early mammals
to 600	PALEOZOIC		Mammal-like reptiles

A continuous line means that the chronology is firmly established.

‑ ‑ ‑ A broken line means the chronology is doubtful.

→ A line terminating in an arrow means the time span continues beyond the arrow.

A line terminating with a horizontal bar means the limit of chronology is firmly established.

Figure 2 Geological time scale of the Mesozoic and subsequent epochs. (From W. G. Osman Hill, *Evolutionary Biology of the Primates,* 1974, Academic Press, Inc., London, Ltd.)

Once these early primates moved to the trees, natural selection operated to adapt them better to arboreal life. First, the pattern of evolution shows a change in the shape of the teeth, cheek bones, and jaw muscles, to accommodate a new diet that included fruit, buds, and leaves as well as insects. Second, the skeleton changed over time to facilitate living in the trees. Jumping and grasping became a part of arboreal locomotion. Eventually, the hands and feet of the primate became adapted for grasping, and claws were replaced with nails. Eyesight became more important than hearing or smelling. As a result, the placement of the eyes gradually shifted from the sides of the head toward the front of the face, where the vision of the two eyes overlapped, creating *stereoscopic vision*, which is necessary for perceiving depth. As sight became more crucial and smell became less important, there was a reduction in the length of the snout.

Another change that may have occurred with the move to arboreal life was a reduction in the number of offspring, from eight or ten in a litter, which is common for ground-dwelling rodents, to just one or two. With parental care concentrated on just a few youngsters, the chance that each would live to maturity was greatly enhanced, as parents were able to provide better protection against predators, accidents, and so on (Brace and Montagu 1965:110). Successful in their arboreal adaptations, some of the prosimians continued to evolve, until forms that can be recognized as primitive monkeys began to appear 45 million years ago or earlier, in the Eocene epoch (Figure 2). The New World and Old World had already been separated for 100 million years, as a result of continental drift. In both areas of the world prosimians apparently evolved into various forms of monkeys, although Richard Hoffstetter (1972) believes some contact between the two land masses was still possible. Many of the advances of monkeys over early prosimians represented a continuation of trends already set in motion in the era of prosimian development. Eyesight was improved even further for the perception of depth, and with this there was a continued reduction in the reliance on smell. As a result, the snout was further reduced, giving the monkey face a more "human" appearance than that of early prosimians.

Primitive forms of monkeys appear in the fossil record during the Eocene epoch.

Perhaps the most important evolutionary change reflected in the fossil data regarding the development of monkeys was an increase in the size of the brain. Brace and Montagu (1965:111) suggest that the increasing size of the primate brain was due to the monkeys' arboreal existence:

Locomotion through the tree tops requires the continual making of choices—certainly to a much greater degree than would be the case for a terrestrial quadruped when there is virtual certainty that there will always be ground wherever one's feet are moved. In a tree, however, there is more space than support, and, in addition, locomotor decisions have to be made in three dimensions rather than in only two. Obviously an expanded choice-making mechanism, i.e., brain, is of relatively greater importance to an arboreal animal than it would be to an average terrestrial quadruped.

A new form of primate, the ape, evolved from some of the early forms of monkeys about 30 million years ago, in the Oligocene epoch (Figure 2). With some of the apes came a new form of movement, *brachiation.* For more than 40 million years, early primates, prosimians, and monkeys had moved by scampering along the tops of tree branches or by jumping from one branch to another. However, some of the apes developed brachiation, whereby they moved hand-over-hand from branch to branch, with their bodies hanging under the branch.

Fossil apes appear during the Oligocene epoch.

The important questions still unresolved concerning this new development are (*a*) When did brachiation begin? and (*b*) How does human evolution relate to brachiation? There seem to be at least three possible answers. First, there is the possibility that the line leading to human beings diverged from the line leading to modern apes after the specialization to brachiation had already occurred. If this was the case, our ancestors would have had to lost the specialized upper trunk of the brachiator skeleton. A second possibility is that not all fossil apes evolved into brachiators. Perhaps those that became brachiators led to the modern apes, while those that did not led to humans. Recently, a third and somewhat more controversial interpretation has been offered by the Finnish paleontologist Björn Kurtén. An Oligocene fossil form called *Propliopithecus* (*pro*, before + *plio*, more + *pithecus*, ape) known only by a jawbone and teeth, has been dated at about 30 million years of age, earlier than any clearly recognizable ape. To some it may represent a very early unspecialized ape, but to Kurtén it may represent an early hominid (a humanlike form). If *Propliopithecus* is a hominid rather than an ape, it would suggest that human evolution branched off *before* the development of the apes, and perhaps even that the apes evolved from this early form of human! Kurtén's theory has not found wide acceptance, but it does point out the need to keep an open mind when interpreting the fossil data to allow for alternative theories. The question of humankind's relationship to the apes can only be resolved through further fossil discoveries.

Most of the fossil ape data comes from the early Miocene epoch (Figure 2), some 10 million years after *Propliopithecus*. The Miocene material comes from Africa, Europe, China, and India and includes several hundred specimens, indicating a wide distribution of apelike animals in the Old World. Most of the Miocene fossil apes have been classified in the genus *Dryopithecus* (*dryo*, forest + *pithecus*, ape), whose descendants may include the chimpanzee, gorilla, and orangutan. The dryopithecine fossils are generally quite similar to one another, although they are divided into about seven species, differing primarily in body size.

The dryopithecines exhibit lower molar teeth with the same cusp pattern as both humans and modern apes. This pattern is known as the Y-5 pattern. Each lower molar has five cusps. Between cusps are grooves that form a **Y** shape. This pattern represents a more complex arrangement than that found in the earlier fossil monkey forms, perhaps suggesting changes in diet.

Relating the dryopithecines to more recent forms presents some difficulties. While they seem to lead to the modern apes, only the very recent *Dryopithecus* forms show some evidence of anatomical adaptations to brachiation. It is possible that brachiation developed as a response to Old World monkeys living during the same time period. While the unspecialized dryopithecines apparently died out, those with a specialized locomotor adaptation—brachiation—survived. Brachiation may have allowed these apes to avoid competition with the monkeys by utilizing different econiches. Researchers do not agree on the relationship of *Dryopithecus* to human evolution. One species, *Dryopithecus nyanzae* is thought by some physical anthropologists to represent the early Miocene ape form likely to have given rise to the line leading to humans. Other physical anthropologists are less convinced that any *Dryopithecus* form can be clearly identified as leading to human origins. Thus, in spite of a number of fossil finds from the early Miocene epoch, the relationship of the fossil apes to modern apes and human remains unclear.

Difficulties of Interpretation. Part of the difficulty of interpreting the fossil data of the Miocene epoch centers around the taxonomic classification of the finds. Each discovery exhibits both differences from and similarities to other finds. The problem is one of deciding whether or not the differences are great enough to establish a new type. Sometimes two fossil finds have been classified as separate types when the differences

The lower molars of the Miocene apes have the same cusp pattern as humans and modern apes.

between them may be no more than the differences between individuals of modern human populations. Elwyn L. Simons (1963), a leading authority on Miocene-Pliocene fossils, suggests that there are at least four reasons that new discoveries are so frequently classified as new separate types. First, many uncertainties of classification result from the incompleteness of the discovered fossils. Often the researcher has to compare the back of a skull from one fossil with the jaw of another. Second, there are doubts about the ages of fossils being compared. In other words, if the forms are contemporary, the differences might reflect separate species or genuses. If the skeletal data are from different time periods, the differences between the forms may represent the evolution of the same form over time. Third, there are problems of interpretation if the populations are widely separated geographically. Ecological barriers could have brought about the separate development of contemporary forms, ultimately leading to the growth of separate species. Fourth, there has been a tendency for some researchers to classify a fossil discovery as a new species or genus to establish themselves as the discoverers of a new form. Unfortunately personal motives such as these have sometimes confused the taxonomic issues.

As a result of these four factors there is disagreement over classifications and continual attempts to reclassify various forms. With each reclassification there is often the introduction of new terminology to describe the fossil data. Thus, certain fossil forms are referred to by three or four different terms. If this confusion is not enough in itself, there are also popular terms which are sometimes used for the forms.

Ramapithecus

In the late Miocene epoch, perhaps 10 to 15 million years ago, a form known as *Ramapithecus* (*Rama*, the god Rama of India + *pithecus*, ape) lived in India, Pakistan, East Africa, and possibly Europe and China. *Ramapithecus* is considered by many anthropologists as the most likely of all of the Miocene forms to have been in the line leading to humans (Tattersall 1975:28–29). The interpretations of *Ramapithecus* has been based on the analysis of only several pieces of bone from the mouth region. Thus our knowledge is extremely limited, and further discoveries will be needed to clarify the speculation about *Ramapithecus*' behavior and form (other than the shape of its teeth) and its relationship

Ramapithecus is considered the Miocene form most likely to have been in the line leading to humans.

to human origins.[6] Most of the recent discussions of *Rama-pithecus* center on whether it was a fossil hominid (a human) or a fossil ape.

The dentition of *Ramapithecus* is the most human of all the Miocene forms. Several features of the dentition have been especially important in the attempts to discern the evolutionary significance of *Ramapithecus*. In general the teeth are more like those of humans than apes. The canine teeth are small as in humans, whereas ape canines are large. It is generally accepted that the arrangement of *Ramapithecus'* teeth is similar to that of humans. The teeth of humans form a parabolic arch; in the ape the arch is more **U** shaped. Although no complete arch of *Rama-pithecus* has been discovered, it is believed by many that the teeth form more of a parabolic arch than a **U** shape. However, Alan Walker and Peter Andrews (1973) suggest that the jaws are so fragmentary they could also be reconstructed closer to an apelike **U** shaped pattern.

On the basis of what can be reconstructed of the face, it is assumed that this creature had a short face, which would make its shape more like humans than like the snout of the ape. An upper jaw with a canine fossa has been found. The canine fossa is a depression that occurs just below the eye socket and is found in humans but not in living apes or monkeys. In humans it serves as an anchor for a muscle controlling the movement of the upper lip, particularly in speech. The discovery of a canine fossa in the *Ramapithecus* fossil material does not indicate that this creature had the ability to speak, but more likely that the potential for speech was developing (Washburn and Moore 1974:57).

Because *Ramapithecus* is unusual in its small canines, several interesting hypotheses about *Ramapithecus* has been derived. In nonhuman primates, large canines are used for offensive and defensive actions, and especially for threats. It has been argued by some physical anthropologists that these functions of the large canines were taken over by the hand, with its ability to fashion and use tools and weapons, and consequently the size of canines was reduced (Washburn 1960). One of the foremost authorities on *Ramapithecus*, Elwyn Simons (1964:528), has suggested that in *Ramapithecus* forms, the hands were already playing a major role in food getting and defense. Is there evidence to support this point of view? Only of a very questionable nature. If *Rama-pithecus* used tools and weapons and perhaps even shaped them,

---

[6] In April, 1977, the discovery of fossils of 80 individuals classified as *Ramapithecus* was reported from Pakistan. Most of the specimens are fragments from the mouth region. New techniques of dating place these finds in the 8 to 13 million BP time period. These finds will help to clarify the nature of *Ramapithecus*.

the "artifacts" would be only slightly modified and not clearly distinguishable from forms that occur in nature.

Other physical anthropologists believe that canine reduction has no necessary connection to tool use. The British physical anthropologist Clifford Jolly (1970) has suggested that changes in dentition were related to changes in diet rather than tool use. He theorizes that the first hominids originated as small-object feeders who began extensive use of seeds as they moved from forests into open grasslands. Until then, grass seeds represented an untapped source of food, because the collecting of seeds required hands with great manipulative ability. Natural selection for manual dexterity in these early hominids, or protohominids, then opened the way for later development of tool use and toolmaking. In Jolly's theory, toolmaking would *follow* the reduction of canines rather than precede it.

Another inference that has been made from the small canine teeth is that *Ramapithecus* may have been the first creature in the line leading to man to exhibit upright posture. The reasoning goes something like this: The reduced canines suggest the possibility that *Ramapithecus* individuals must have used their hands, rather than their teeth, for food getting and defense. This suspected extensive use of the hands further implies that they walked upright. This is not to say that *Ramapithecus* walked upright continually as do modern humans. *Ramapithecus* may also have spent time in the trees, still having some ability for brachiation. But coming to the ground in search of food, at the edges of the forests, *Ramapithecus* may have walked upright. Some physical anthropologists have suggested the possibility that *Ramapithecus* walked on his knuckles like the modern gorilla does. However, R. H. Tuttle (1969) has shown that this theory is implausible on comparative anatomical grounds.

In summary, *Ramapithecus* is at present the only fossil form of the Miocene epoch that seems to be directly in the line leading to humans. On the basis of its dentition there is a strong possibility that this form can be considered a hominid rather than an ape. However, a clearer picture of *Ramapithecus'* role in human evolution awaits discovery of skeletal evidence.

Between the dates assigned to the known *Ramapithecus* data and the appearance of the first clearly human forms, there is a gap in the fossil data. The dates assigned to the *Ramapithecus* fossil material range from 10 million to 14.5 million BP (before present). The next fossil hominid material does not appear until about 5.5 million BP, when creatures referred to as *Australopithecus* appear in the fossil record, thus skipping the late Mio-

Australopithecus 5 million years ago was the first definite known hominid.

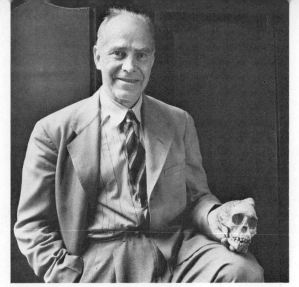

Physical anthropologist Raymond Dart and the Taung skull. (Jerry Cooke)

Artist's reconstruction of the head of the Taung Taung child, a gracile form of *Australopithecus*. (Courtesy of the American Museum of Natural History)

cene epoch. Supporters of some of the newer versions of creationism have taken this gap in the fossil evidence as proof that humans were created separately and therefore have no ties with *Ramapithecus* or any other earlier form. Anthropologists, on the other hand, interpret the gap in the fossil data to mean that fossil beds of the late Miocene epoch have not yet been discovered; they believe that given continued exploration, the fossil data will eventually be discovered in the 10 million BP to 5 million BP era.[7] Those who accept a special-creation explanation are still faced with the problem that *Australopithecus* was a protohuman with many apelike traits.

Plio-Pleistocene Hominids

The first discovery of Plio-Pleistocene hominids was made in 1924 in the Republic of South Africa, the skull of a six-year-old male now known as the Taung child. This fossil, and others like it, ultimately became known as *Australopithecus* (*australo*, southern + *pithecus*, ape). In recent years most of the Plio-Pleistocene research has centered in East Africa, where not only the largest number of *Australopithecus* fossils have been found, but also forms which have been classified as *Homo*, the same genus as modern humans. Although a large group of fossils has

---

[7] In 1973 a tooth believed to be that of a hominid was found in Kenya and was dated as 6.5 million years old (J. D. Clark 1976:9).

been collected, the data are confusing and lend themselves to multiple interpretations. Unlike *Ramapithecus*, for whom the data are skimpy and restricted to fossil material from the lower face, the Plio-Pleistocene hominids are represented by the remains of hundreds of individuals. Bones of most parts of the body have been discovered. In 1974, 40 percent of a complete skeleton of a female in her late teens was discovered in Ethiopia and dated at about 3 million years ago. She has been named Lucy by her discoverers and represents the most nearly complete early fossil hominid yet found. In the past ten years more than 20 Plio-Pleistocene sites have been discovered in the East Rudolf region of East Africa, and excavation or testing has been carried out at some ten localities (Isaac, Harris, and Crader 1976:533).

Primarily on the basis of material discovered in South Africa,

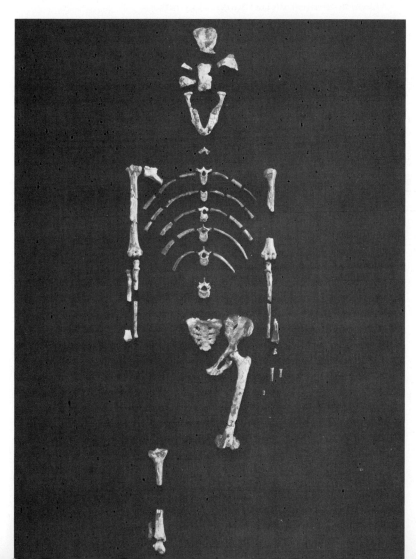

"Lucy," the most complete early fossil hominid discovered thus far. (The Cleveland Museum of Natural History)

anthropologists distinguished two types of *Australopithecus:* gracile (also called *Australopithecus africanus*) and robust (also called *Australopithecus robustus*). The discoveries in East Africa during the past few years suggest that the picture of early hominids may be more complex than originally assumed. It appears now that there may have been a *Homo* form contemporary with *Australopithecus.*

The gracile variety seems to have been the earlier form of *Australopithecus.* The Plio-Pleistocene population of about 5 million years ago is represented by a single mandible from Lothagam, in East Africa, which most closely resembles that of the gracile form. Several other fossils, dated at between 3 and 4 million years ago, also resemble the gracile *Australopithecus.*

From 3 million to 1 million years ago, the fossil record becomes both more extensive and more complex. By that time, perhaps three different forms of hominids were living together in Africa (Figure 3). Earlier than 3 million years ago, some East African australopithecine populations had diverged from the gracile line, emphasizing brain enlargement and an increasing cultural dependence. These were the *Homo* forms that eventually led to modern humans, several million years later. Other populations of the ancestral australopithecines began to differentiate in another direction from the *Homo* line, emphasizing cheek-tooth expansion and bodily enlargement, with a moderate degree of brain enlargement but with perhaps no major use of culture or development of toolmaking. Thus was produced the robust line of *Australopithecus.* Those of East Africa, sometimes called *Australopithecus boisei,* are characterized by extreme de-

Some early *Australopithecus* forms evolved into *Homo* by 3 million years ago.

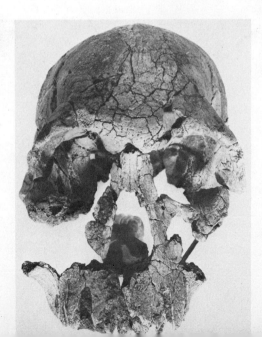

East African *Homo* form.
(National Museum of Kenya)

grees of specialization compared to the robust forms of South
Africa. The robust line was apparently sufficiently distinct in
behavior and ecological preferences from the *Homo* line that the
two lines were able to coexist for perhaps 2 million years
(Tobias 1976:406–408).

In South Africa (and perhaps East Africa) populations of the
gracile line persisted for some time, even after the emergence of
Homo in other parts of Africa. Just how long the gracile line continued is unclear. It may have continued another 2 million
years, or the gracile australopithecines may have died out soon
after they spawned the *Homo* line (Figure 3).

One of the reasons that the *Australopithecus* forms and the
early *Homo* are considered hominids is because they walked
upright. Whereas the question of the bipedalism of *Rama-*

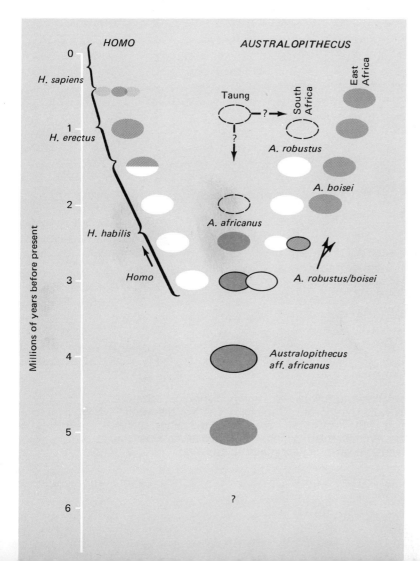

Figure 3 Hominid populations in Africa at various
time levels in the Plio-
Pleistocene. The oval figures at each time level
represent the systemat-
ically identified,
synchronic hominid popu-
lations known from the
fossil record of Africa at
that time. The question
marks indicate the ano-
malous position of the
Taung skull, for which the
dating is uncertain. (From
Glynn Ll. Isaac and Elizabeth R. McCown, eds.,
*Human Origins: L. G. B.
Leakey and the East Afri-
can Evidence,* copyright ©
1976 by W. A. Benjamin,
Inc., Menlo Park, Cali-
fornia.)

pithecus cannot be resolved, due to lack of skeletal data, the bipedalism of Plio-Pleistocene hominids is clearly demonstrated by the skeletal remains. While most of the skeletal structure of the *Australopithecus* form is adapted to upright posture, there are slight differences from modern humans in the placement of several muscles of the pelvis, the size of the anklebone, and the size of the head and neck of the thighbone (Figure 4). These differences suggest that *Australopithecus* was perhaps as efficiently bipedal as modern humans but that their pattern of bipedalism may have been different in some ways. In 1972 a complete thighbone and part of a shinbone were discovered in Kenya, East Africa, and dated at more than 2.6 million years ago. Although the date is the same as or even earlier than those of other *Homo* and *Australopithecus* finds, the bones are next to indistinguishable from those of modern humans. This may mean that

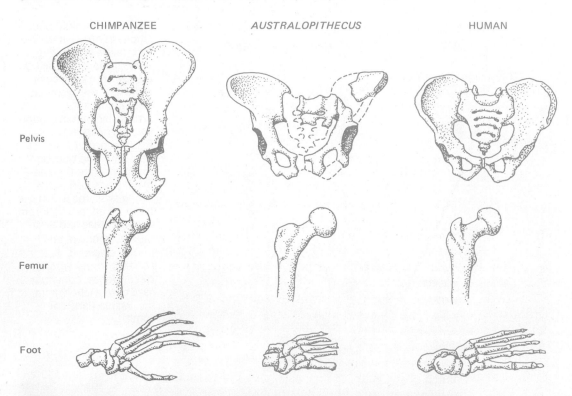

CHIMPANZEE   *AUSTRALOPITHECUS*   HUMAN

Pelvis

Femur

Foot

Figure 4   Comparisons of chimpanzee, *Australopithecus* and humans emphasize the humanness of *Australopithecus*. Note the shortening and broadening of the whole pelvic structure, the lengthening of the neck of the upper end of the femur, and the large and nonopposable big toe. (From Bernard Campbell, ed., *Humankind Emerging*, copyright © 1976 Little, Brown and Company, Inc. Reprinted by permission.)

some of the Plio-Pleistocene hominids, probably the *Homo* forms, moved about just as modern humans do, while the australopithecines maintained a slightly different locomotor pattern (Weiss and Mann 1975:179–181).

The primitiveness of the *Australopithecus* skulls has led to these creatures being classified as a different genus than the *Homo* forms. Generally the shape of the teeth is similar to modern humans and the arch of the jaw is parabolic, like that of modern people. Other features of the skull, especially in the robust type, are more apelike than the *Homo* forms. Both the gracile and robust types exhibit *prognathism* in the lower face. Prognathism is a protrusion of the jaw that causes the facial plane to slope outward. Both forms of *Australopithecus* have smaller brain cases than the *Homo* forms. The volume of the *Australopithecus* brain case ranges between 450 cc (cubic centimeters) and 550 cc, about the same as the modern gorilla, whereas modern humans average between 1350 cc and 1450 cc. The recently discovered *Homo* forms range between 650 cc and 775 cc.

The robust types also exhibit large back teeth (premolars and molars), massive jaws, heavy brow ridges above the eye sockets, and a bony crest along the top of the skull. Most of these features are directly related to massive muscles which operated the jaws. One of the muscles is so large that the bony crest developed to provide more space for the attachment of muscle fibers. Male gorillas also have such a crest on the top of their skulls, which serves for attachment of the muscle that operates the jaws. In the robust type of *Australopithecus*, the development of massive muscles controlling the movement of the jaws seems directly related to the large back teeth. Perhaps the large teeth and powerful jaws were part of a complex which developed for chewing tough fibrous foods. These features separate the robust types from the other australopithecines.

Before the discovery of the *Homo* forms, it was assumed that *Australopithecus* had been a toolmaker. Many physical anthropologists now believe that most, if not all, of the tools found from the early Pleistocene epoch were made by the *Homo* forms. The earliest stone tools thus far discovered come from East Africa and are dated at 2.6 million years ago. Most of the tools discovered from the era of *Australopithecus* and the early *Homo* forms suggest that the earliest stone manufacturing developed to help obtain and prepare food rather than to produce weapons. On the basis of what is known of modern hunting and gathering peoples, it seems likely that these early hominids relied

The early *Homo* forms were the first toolmakers.

primarily on gathering. In modern bands the vegetation gathered by women constitutes as much as 80 percent of a band's diet. Therefore it is possible that most of the first tools were used by females. Perhaps females were the first toolmakers as well. Many of the tools seem to have been used for chopping or mashing vegetable material; others were used for skinning and cutting. Certainly the artifacts do not support the popular notion that our earliest ancestors were aggressive armed killers. Besides choppers, flakes (chips from a core) of different shapes were also used. The complex of tools from the early Pleistocene epoch is referred to as the *Oldowan* industry (Figure 5). Because some of the first tools discovered were made from pebbles, these tools became known as pebble tools. However, this is a misnomer, as lava and quartz were also used for stone tools (Clark 1976:21–24).

The fossil record shows that the early *Homo* forms of East Africa evolved into the slightly advanced form of hominid known as *Homo habilis* and later into *Homo erectus*. The *Homo erectus* forms are spread more widely throughout the Old World than the East African *Homo* forms (Fig. 3). However it is possible that additional *Homo* forms will be found once physical anthropologists discover more Pliocene and early Pleistocene locations. Ecological conditions similar to those of East Africa may have existed in parts of the Near East and elsewhere.

Homo erectus represents the next stage in human evolution.

Middle Pleistocene *Homo erectus*

At the end of the Lower Pleistocene epoch and beginning of the Middle Pleistocene epoch, between 1.5 and 1.2 million years ago, *Homo* forms that have been classified as a single genus and species, *Homo erectus,* are found not only in Africa but also Java, China, and Europe. Of all of the stages of human evolution, it is the *Homo erectus* era that has resulted in the greatest agreement of interpretation among modern scholars. Unfortunately this concensus seems to be due primarily to sparseness of data. Whereas *Australopithecus* and the early *Homo* forms are represented by several hundred individuals, the *Homo erectus* finds represent a mere handful of individuals.

The first *Homo erectus* finds date from the 1880s, when the idea of fossil humans was not yet fully accepted. In 1883 a Dutch surgeon, Eugene Dubois, influenced by the controversy over human origins raised by Darwin's writings, set sail for the island of Java to find the "missing link" between humans and the

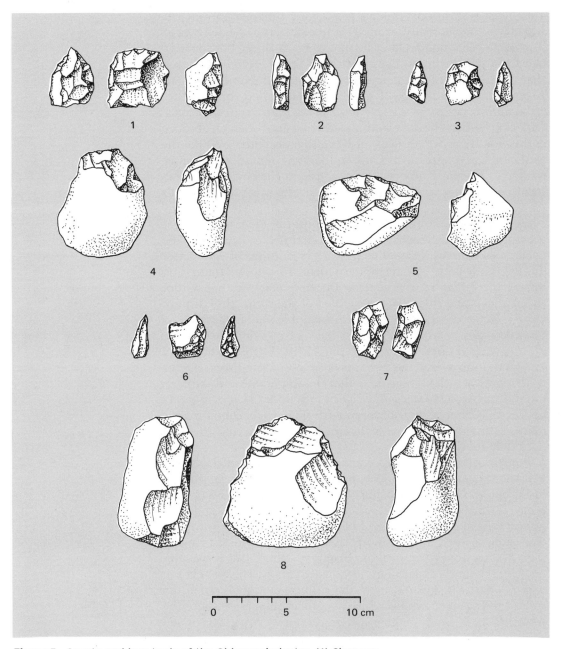

Figure 5 Quartz and lava tools of the Oldowan industry. (1) Chopper, (2) flake scraper, (3) flake, (4) chopper, (5) chopper, (6) flake, (7) modified chunk with notch, and (8) protohand ax. (From Glynn Ll. Isaac and Elizabeth R. McCown, eds., *Human Origins: L. S. B. Leakey and the East African Evidence,* copyright © 1976 by W. A. Benjamin, Inc., Menlo Park, California.)

apes. His excavations yielded important discoveries, but the world was not yet ready for fossil humans. In 1891 he discovered a skullcap. Ten months later he uncovered a thighbone, only 50 feet from where the skullcap had been found. Dubois believed that the two pieces of bone belonged to the same individual, or at least to the same type of individual. He called this creature *Pithecanthropus* (*pithec*, ape + *anthropus*, man); it also became widely known as the Java man. In 1894 he published an account of his findings, which was not readily accepted: While the skullcap was very primitive and unlike that of modern humans, the femur was very modern looking, and at the end of the nineteenth century, it was assumed by those who accepted Darwin's view of human evolution and antiquity that all parts of the body evolved at the same rate. Today this point of view is no longer acceptable. Fossil evidence has shown that the skeleton from the neck down became humanlike first. Only millions of years later did the skull evolve into its modern form. Thus today there is no longer any difficulty in accepting Dubois's original theory that the skullcap and thighbone were part of the same kind of individual. Since the 1960s *Pithecanthropus* has been classified as *Homo erectus*.

Later excavations in Java in the 1930s, 1950s, 1960s, and 1970s have uncovered the remains of several more *Homo erectus* individuals, which demonstrate that the thighbone and skullcap did indeed belong to the same type of individual.[8] Unfortunately no tools have yet been discovered with these early *Homo erectus* fossils of Java, yet there is little reason to believe that they did not make tools.

Other discoveries of *Homo erectus* fossils were made in China. For years peasants have been making a living by digging up fossil bones, which they bring to the cities and sell as dragon bones to "drugstores," where the bones are ground up and used in medicine and for potions of various kinds. In 1899 a European doctor discovered a fossil tooth that looked humanlike among the "dragon bones" in a Peking druggist's shop. But it was not until 1921 that an expedition began excavation. The site chosen was a small hill located near the village of Choukoutien, 25 miles southwest of Peking. This was one of the areas where the peasants had been digging dragon bones. Work continued through 1937, and during that time a number of *Homo erectus* fossils were uncovered. The skeletal evidence suggested simi-

---

[8] Recently, Day (1971) has suggested that the thighbone discovered by Dubois is not from the same creature as the skullcap. He suggests that the fossil discoveries from China represent the only known Asian *Homo erectus* limb bones.

larities to the Java forms. But the 1920s and 1930s constituted an era in which new discoveries were assigned to new genuses and species. As a result, the Chinese *Homo erectus* was given the name *Sinanthropus pekinensis* (*Sin,* Chinese + *anthropus,* man; *pekinensis,* of Peking) in scientific circles and Peking man in more popular accounts. By 1940, skulls, teeth, and other bones of about 45 hominids had been discovered. Along with the skeletal material, more than 100,000 stone tools and fragments were discovered in the caves inhabited by Chinese *Homo erectus,* as well as tools made from bone and antler. There was also evidence of extensive use of fire—a large number of hearths, some with charcoal 22 feet deep. This depth of ash suggests that fires burned continually.

The excavations in China were stopped prematurely with the Japanese invasion of northern China. Drawings and photographs were made of the fossils, and casts were made of the fossil skulls. The drawings and casts were taken to the United States, while the original fossils were left behind because they belonged to the Geological Survey of China. However, as the Japanese reached Peking, the Chinese scholars decided that the fossils should be sent to the United States for safekeeping. Boxes of fossils were given to nine United States Marines evacuating Peking. The marines were captured by the Japanese, and the fate of the *Homo erectus* fossil data remains a mystery. From time to time there have been rumors of someone having knowledge of their whereabouts, but the fossils have not materialized to date. Therefore, a great deal of our information about the Chinese *Homo erectus* is based on the casts of the skulls and the detailed descriptions that were brought to the United States.

Following the war, Chinese anthropologists continued work at Choukoutien and discovered another skull and a jaw. Other excavations, in 1963 and 1964 in Lantian District, produced a jaw, a skullcap, facial fragments, and a tooth. This material is older and more robust than the Peking material. It is contemporary with, and similar to, the fossils from Java.

At first it seemed that *Homo erectus* was strictly an Asiatic population, because the only known Middle Pleistocene hominids were those of Java and China.[9] In recent years evidence of *Homo erectus* has been found over much of the Old World. *Homo erectus* forms have been discovered in Asia, North Africa, South Africa, East Africa, and Europe (Figure 6). The South Afri-

Homo erectus has been discovered in Africa, Asia, and Europe.

[9] The Mauer jaw was discovered in 1907 in Germany and is classified by many anthropologists as a *Homo erectus.* In pre–World War II years its taxonomic status was uncertain. It is a massive jaw without a chin and with relatively small, modern-looking teeth.

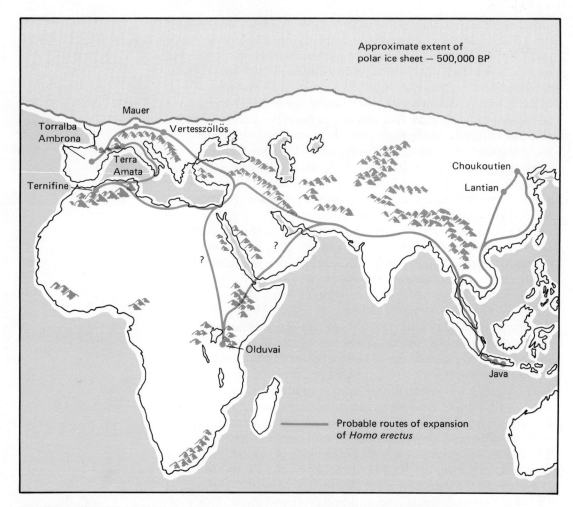

Approximate extent of
polar ice sheet — 500,000 BP

Mauer

Vertesszöllös

Torralba
Ambrona

Terra
Amata

Ternifine

Choukoutien

Lantian

?

?

Olduvai

Java

Probable routes of expansion
of *Homo erectus*

Figure 6   *Homo erectus* was much more widely dispersed than *Australopithecus* and
was the first primate to survive the winters of the north temperate region. This map
shows the sites of some major finds and gives an idea of the routes of expansion and
gene interchange. *Homo erectus* may have occupied many other areas as well. (From
Bernard Campbell, ed., *Humankind Emerging,* copyright © 1976 Little, Brown and
Company, Inc. Reprinted by permission.)

can *Homo erectus* material has been found among the remains of
the robust form of *Australopithecus,* suggesting that they may
have been contemporary. The East African finds appear to resemble the Asian *Homo erectus.* Recent discoveries of pieces of
the lower skeleton confirm Dubois's belief that *Homo erectus*
was an erect, bipedal hominid. In North Africa lower jaws and a
skullcap discovered at Ternifine, Algeria, suggest *Homo erectus*

forms that closely resemble the *Sinanthropus* variety of *Homo erectus* from China. In Europe, besides the Mauer jaw (see footnote), there is a skull from Vértesszöllös, Hungary, that was discovered in 1965 and has been assigned to *Homo erectus,* although some scholars believe it is more advanced.

The earliest *Homo erectus* forms appear in East Africa and date back to about 1.5 million years ago. By a million years ago *Homo erectus* was living in Java and China, and reached Europe by 750,000 years ago. These differences in time suggest that *Homo erectus* evolved from the early *Homo* forms of East Africa. *Homo erectus* then became the first hominid to move out of the tropics and face the problems of surviving in the severe and wintry world of Europe and China during the Ice Age. In both China and Europe there is evidence that *Homo erectus* adapted to the northern environments by making use of caves and fire. Fire was important not only for heat and for cooking but also as a form of protection from the animals that humans had to fight for possession of caves. Evidence from the earliest period of occupation at Choukoutien Cave suggests that *Homo erectus* was driven out of his home time after time over many generations by the large predators that lived in the caves. Eventually *Homo erectus* learned the use of fire, and from that time on he was able to inhabit the cave continually (Campbell 1976:237–238).

There have been sites discovered known to have been occupied by *Homo erectus,* even though no fossil material has been found at them. These sites tell us about the type of life that *Homo erectus* led. Several recent excavations in Europe have been especially important. In Spain several "kill sites" have been excavated. At Torralba as many as 40 or 50 elephants were killed and butchered; apparently the site was not a habitation site. Because the site was a bog, the hunters carried the meat to higher ground somewhere else.

In 1965 an open-air site was discovered in Nice, France, close to the shoreline of the Miditerranean. This site, known as Terra Amata, was probably a seasonal camp used by *Homo erectus* to exploit the local plant, animal, and seashore resources. The remains of Terra Amata suggest that the *Homo erectus* group that camped there between 300,000 and 200,000 years ago erected shelters. As shown in Figure 7, these structures were oval-shaped dwellings supported by poles and probably covered with interlacing branches (Weiss and Mann 1975:202–205).

The biological evidence suggests that throughout the era of *Homo erectus* there was a gradual growth of brain size. The earliest *Homo erectus* forms of Africa and Java had cranial capacities of about 775 cc. By the end of the era the *Sinanthropus*

Figure 7 Oval huts, ranging from 26 to 49 feet in length and from 13 to 20 feet in width, were built at Terra Amata by visiting hunters. (From Henry de Lumley, "A Paleolithic Camp at Nice," *Scientific American,* May, 1969. Copyright © 1969 by Scientific American, Inc. All rights reserved.)

varieties were exhibiting cranial capacities of 1225 cc, which is within the range of modern adult humans (1000 to 2000 cc).

The increasing brain size is also reflected in the improved manufacturing seen in artifacts. The crude Oldowan tools of the Middle Pleistocene epoch evolved into more specialized tool kits, perhaps reflecting the different kinds of environment to which the various *Homo erectus* populations were adapting. The early Oldowan and the later *Homo erectus* tool industries belong to the cultural period that archaeologists call the *Lower Paleolithic* (Lower Old Stone Age). During the era of *Homo erectus* two different stone industries evolved. One industry is known as the *evolved Oldowan* industry. While similar to the earlier Oldowan tools, the evolved Oldowan tools were better made and more varied (Figure 8). These tools have been found with *Homo erectus* fossils in South Africa at Vértesszöllös, Hungary, and in China. The most typical artifacts of evolved Oldowan are chopping tools. A second tool industry is known as *Acheulian* in which the typical artifact is a *hand ax,* measuring $3\frac{1}{2}$ inches wide, from 5 to 6 inches long, and teardrop in form. These hand axes have been found in Europe, the Near East, Africa, and India. There is no simple, clear association between tool types and varieties of fossil hominids. The Acheulian industry may have lasted for more than a million years and near its end seems to have been associated with hominids more like *Homo sapiens* than *Home erectus.*

With the advance of the second glacial period, about 300,000 BP, the fossil evidence becomes scanty for almost a 200,000-year period. Thus the line leading to modern humans once again becomes difficult to discern, and several interpretations have been given to the fossil data.

Homo erectus is represented by two stone tool industries: evolved Oldowan and Acheulian.

Figure 8 Evolved Oldowan and Lower Acheulian implements. *Evolved Oldowan:* (1) Multifaceted polyhedral, (2) double-notched scraper, (3) flake, (4) protohand ax, and (5) denticulate core scraper. *Lower Acheulian:* (6) Hand ax, (7) picklike hand ax, (8) picklike hand ax, and (9) cleaver. (From Glynn Ll. Isaac and Elizabeth R. McCown, eds., *Human Origins: L. S. B. Leakey and the East African Evidence,* copyright © 1976 by W. A. Benjamin, Inc., Menlo Park, California.)

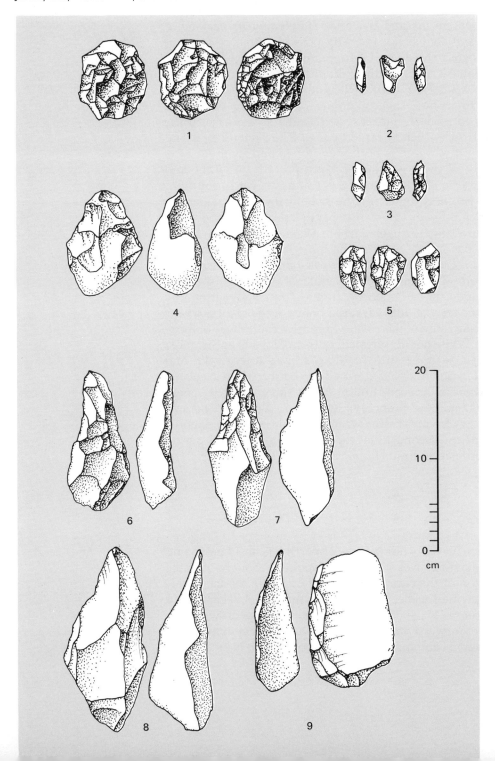

Several fossil remains dating from the second interglacial period and the third glacial period have been discovered in England, Germany, France, and perhaps East Africa. In many ways these forms are seen to exhibit features that are intermediate between *Homo erectus* and the later *Homo sapiens neandertalensis*. However, that is not the only possible interpretation. A few scholars view these fossil data as representative of a separate evolutionary line leading directly to modern humans (*Homo sapiens sapiens*), with little connection to the Neanderthal forms. Others have suggested that some of these forms gave rise directly to modern humans, while others gave rise to the Neanderthals, who then became extinct. The skeletal material that has been discovered is both incomplete and scanty.

The earliest of these remains is known as Swanscombe and was discovered in deposits along the Thames River in southern England. It has been dated to the second interglacial period. However, it is difficult to use this partial skull to support any theory, because only the back part of the skull was found. Bones of the facial region that contain the most important diagnostic features have never been found. The estimated cranial capacity of Swanscombe is about 1100 cc, not as large as either the average Neanderthal or modern human but well within the range of *Homo erectus*. Likewise, the bones of the skull are very thick, more like those of the earlier hominids than those of modern humans. While not all physical anthropologists agree, most now view Swanscombe and the other second-interglacial and third-glacial period finds as intermediate between *Homo erectus* and *Homo sapiens*. A recent find at Arago Cave in the Pyrenees Mountains of southern France which included a skull and several lower jaws from the third glacial period tends to support the view that the second interglacial and third glacial period was one of transition from *Homo erectus* to *Homo sapiens*.

Several fossil finds represent a transition from *Homo erectus* to *Homo sapiens.*

The First *Homo sapiens:* Neanderthals and Neanderthaloids

Of all the forms of early humans, Neanderthal is best known and most misunderstood. Neanderthal is popularly thought of as the personification of the cave dweller, a short, hairy, stocky creature of limited intelligence; the male is often depicted carrying a wooden club over his shoulder and walking stooped over, with his knees bent forward. In the mass media he is often juxtaposed with a presumed contemporary, Cro-Magnon, who is usually depicted as the exact opposite of Neanderthal. Cro-Magnon is portrayed as tall, slender but muscular, intelligent, carrying a spear, walking upright, and lacking the body hair that makes Neanderthal look like an ape. These popular misconceptions of what Neanderthal was like have come from the work of respected scientists who made many errors in analyzing and reconstructing some of the early Neanderthal finds.

Important Neanderthal fossil material was uncovered near Dusseldorf, Germany, in 1857 in the Neander Valley, shortly before Darwin's theory of natural selection was published.[10] Those who did not accept an evolutionary perspective dismissed the finds as the remains of a pathological being. Although as more Neanderthal finds were uncovered, this point of view became harder to defend, at first even colleagues of Darwin who accepted an evolutionary perspective did not see the skeletal material as proof that there had been ancient humans.[11] To Darwin's friend Huxley, the Neanderthal material was merely a degenerate form of modern human. In referring to Neanderthal, Huxley used the term *degraded*. Likewise, in 1858 Hermann Schaaffhausen (1971:162), who was the first to bring the Neanderthal discovery to scientific attention, suggested that the bones belonged to a "barbarous and savage race." Thus only a few years after the discovery, the Neanderthal find was being characterized in very negative terms. William King, of Queens College, Ireland, was the first scientist to recognize that the skeletal material belonged to a representative of a hitherto unrecognized type of human. In 1864 he classified the skullcap as *Homo neandertalensis*. But King also added to the brutish stereotype by writing, "The Neanderthal skull is so eminently simian . . . I am constrained to believe that the thoughts and desires which once dwelt within it never soared beyond those of the brute" (Constable et al. 1973:15). In 1868 the discovery of Cro-Magnon (today considered a more recent form than Neanderthal) in southwestern France was taken as proof that modern humans had always looked as they do today.

In southwestern France, in 1908, in additional Neanderthal skeletal material was discovered. One of these skeletons was selected for a detailed reconstruction of the typical Neanderthal. Unfortunately a poor choice of skeletons was made. Chosen for

When first discovered, Neanderthal was thought to be a degenerate form.

---

[10] Many accounts state that the discovery was made in 1856. Schaaffhausen (1971) writes in his account of the discovery that it was 1857.

[11] There had been two previous discoveries that are now classified as Neanderthal—the Engis skull, discovered in Belgium in 1828, and the Gibraltar skull, discovered at the Rock of Gibraltar in 1848. They were not accepted as fossil forms when first discovered, because of the prevailing antievolutionary views.

reconstruction were the almost complete, but poorly preserved, remains of an old male from a cave near the French village of La Chapelle-aux-Saints. Marcellin Boule, a paleontologist of the French National Museum of Natural History, undertook the reconstruction. Boule's reconstruction turned out to be a "misconstruction," which dominated anthropological thinking about the nature of Neanderthal for almost half a century.

In looking back at Boule's reconstruction, one must conclude that he did little that was correct. He reconstructed the big toe so that it was set off to the side, much like that of an ape. Boule then concluded on the basis of his erroneous reconstruction that Neanderthal had to walk on the outer part of the foot, like an ape. Incredible as it may seem today, Boule did not take into account the fact that the skeleton he was reconstructing had suffered from severe arthritis, which had deformed some of the bones. His incorrect reconstruction of the spine suggested that it lacked the curves of the modern spine and that Neanderthal was unable to stand fully upright. He incorrectly placed the skull on top of this spine in an unbalanced position. Boule also felt that Neanderthal could not fully extend his leg and walked with a bent-knee gait. Without any anatomical evidence, Boule concluded that the pelvic area was not human but apelike. By the time Boule was through, he had created a brutish, shuffling hunchback that lived up to his own belief of what Neanderthal had looked like. In spite of the skull's large cranial capacity (over 1600 cc), Boule concluded that the intelligence of the creature was much closer to the apes than to humans. Boule was a widely respected scholar, and his incredible reconstruction was widely accepted in scholarly circles.

It was not until 1955, when several scholars independently presented evidence of the inaccuracy of Boule's reconstruction, that scientists began to change their view of Neanderthal (Arambourg 1955; Patte 1955; Straus and Cave 1957). Unfortunately, the brutish image of Neanderthal was by then well entrenched in the public mind.

With evidence of what seemed to be such a grotesque, brutish form of human, here was an ancestor no one wanted. So the search was on for a more human type of fossil that might have been a contemporary of Neanderthal. Boule had suggested that there were two fossils that would qualify: Grimaldi man, which has now been dated as a more recent fossil, and Piltdown man, which was proven to be a hoax.

What Is a Neanderthal? Another source of confusion and debate over the Neanderthal finds has been an inconsistent use of the

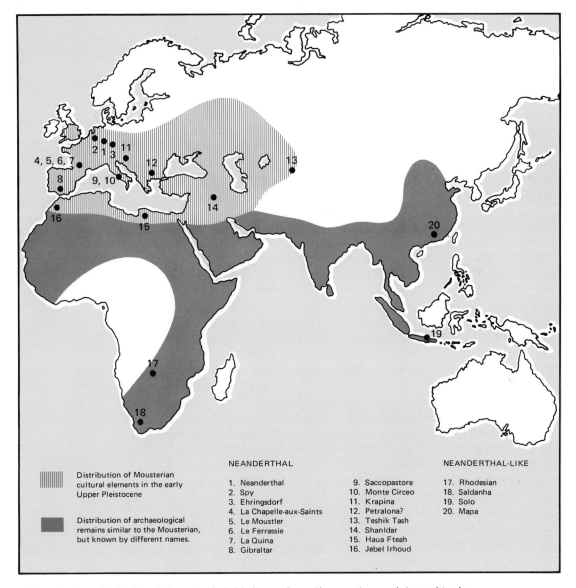

	NEANDERTHAL		NEANDERTHAL-LIKE

Distribution of Mousterian cultural elements in the early Upper Pleistocene	1. Neanderthal	9. Saccopastore	17. Rhodesian
	2. Spy	10. Monte Circeo	18. Saldanha
	3. Ehringsdorf	11. Krapina	19. Solo
	4. La Chapelle-aux-Saints	12. Petralona?	20. Mapa
Distribution of archaeological remains similar to the Mousterian, but known by different names.	5. Le Moustier	13. Teshik Tash	
	6. Le Ferrassie	14. Shanidar	
	7. La Quina	15. Haua Fteah	
	8. Gibraltar	16. Jebel Irhoud	

Figure 9 Neanderthal and Neanderthaloid sites, where the most complete and/or important specimens have been discovered. (From Brace, Nelson, and Korn, *Atlas of Fossil Man,* copyright © 1971 by Holt, Rinehart and Winston. Reprinted by permission.)

term *Neanderthal.* Since the first Neanderthal find, many similar fossils have been found in France, Germany, Belgium, Spain, Yugoslavia, Italy, Gibraltar, Russia, Czechoslovakia, Hungary, Israel, Lebanon, Iraq, and Morocco (Figure 9). The term *Neanderthal* has generally been applied to all of these finds. These

Neanderthals are considered a subspecies of *Homo sapiens* that inhabited Europe, North Africa, and the Middle East from early in the Upper Pleistocene epoch, about 100,000 years ago, until the middle of the fourth glaciation, about 40,000 years ago, when they disappeared. Less similar fossils of the same time period have also been found in sub-Saharan Africa, Java, and China and are referred to as *Neanderthaloids.* There is a minority opinion that several skeletons discovered in the New World are also Neanderthal or Neanderthaloid. However, the dating of these forms is still debated. Generally it is believed that the New World was not populated until after the appearance of modern humans. The taxonomic scheme that has been suggested by some physical anthropologists is that the Neanderthals of Europe and the circum-Mediterranean region should be classified as *Homo sapiens neandertalensis,* while those found in sub-Saharan Africa should be classified as *Homo sapiens rhodesiensis* and those of Java and China should be classified as *Homo sapiens soloensis.*

There is a considerable variation among the forms of Neanderthal classified as *Homo sapiens neandertalensis.* Those of western Europe have the most unique features and are sometimes called classic, or typical, Neanderthals. Their unique features are now interpreted to be adaptations to the extreme cold conditions in western Europe during the fourth glaciation. Neanderthal populations in eastern Europe and the Middle East were more generalized and perhaps closer to modern humans in appearance. The eastern European and Middle Eastern forms have sometimes been called progressive Neanderthals.

The archaeologist classifies the era of the Neanderthals and Neanderthaloids as the *Middle Paleolithic,* or Middle Old Stone Age. The major stone industry of this time period is called *Mousterian.* At first the term was used for artifacts associated with the western European Neanderthals. Today the term is applied by many not only to artifacts found with the western Neanderthals but also to those found with other Neanderthal and Neanderthaloid populations. Some archaeologists believe that the Mousterian industry gradually evolved out of the Acheulian. The typical Mousterian artifacts are points that are made from flakes removed from stone cores. These points were probably hafted to the end of a pole to form a spear. The Mousterian points were manufactured by a fairly complicated set of procedures. Other flakes were apparently made into tools used for scraping hides and tree bark. An increase in the variety of tool types suggests that Neanderthal was manufacturing spec-

Neanderthals have been found in Europe, North Africa, and the Middle East.

Neanderthaloids have been found in sub-Saharan Africa and Asia.

The Mousterian stone tool industry is generally associated with Neanderthal.

ialized tool kits for specialized jobs, some of which occurred seasonally.

The Neanderthal artifacts indicate a more complex cultural tradition than is evidenced by any of the earlier fossil types. The discoveries, many of them made fairly recently, suggest that this creature was becoming emotionally more like modern humans: With Neanderthal comes the first evidence of any fossil form having buried its dead, thus suggesting some feelings toward the deceased and perhaps even some notion of an afterlife. At the cave of La Chapelle-aux-Saints in France, the skeleton of a male was discovered laid out carefully in a shallow trench. A bison leg was placed on his chest, and the trench was filled with broken animal bones and flint tools. These items may have been placed there to serve as provisions for the world beyond the grave. In a cave not far from La Chapelle-aux-Saints, a "family cemetery" of six skeletons has been discovered which included a man, a woman, two children about 5 years old, and two infants. Flint flakes and bone splinters had been placed in the grave of the male, and a flat stone had been placed over his head and shoulders. The woman was buried in an exaggerated fetal position, with her legs tightly bent at the knees and pulled up against her chest. One of the children was buried with its head and body separated by a distance of about 3 feet. The skull was covered with a triangular limestone slab whose underside displayed a number of cup-shaped impressions that probably had some symbolic meaning (Campbell 1976:350–351).

> Cultural remains suggest Neanderthal had some notion of an afterlife.

It seems likely that Neanderthal practiced rituals that were related to problems of nature, perhaps hunting. In Lebanon, evidence has been discovered of a deer ceremony. Here, about 50,000 years ago, Neanderthals dismembered a deer, placed the meat on a bed of stones and sprinkled it with ocher. Ocher is a natural red pigment and perhaps symbolized blood.

In the Swiss Alps another cave has been discovered with evidence of what has been termed a bear cult. In this cave, archaeologists discovered a cubical chest made of stones. On top of the chest was a single massive slab of stone. Inside the chest were seven bear skulls, arranged so that their muzzles faced the cave entrance. Deeper in the cave were six bear skulls set in niches in the walls. In France, a pit has been discovered covered by a flat stone slab weighing nearly a ton. This pit held the bones of more than 20 bears. It is impossible to know what the significance of bear skulls was to the Neanderthals. However it is interesting to note that some of the tribal peoples of Siberia even today worship the bear as the mythical first human; or they consider the bear to be an intermediary between humans and the spirits (Campbell 1976:346–347).

By 40,000 BP, there were no more Neanderthals. From then until the present, the world has been populated only by modern humans (*Homo sapiens sapiens*). The seemingly abrupt disappearance of Neanderthal has long puzzled scientists. What happened? A number of explanations have been offered, but most are unsatisfactory, because they have been influenced by the older stereotype of Neanderthal as a brutish creature.

Modern humans appear in the fossil record about 40,000 years ago.

The most popular interpretation held by the general public, and perpetuated in the mass media, is that Neanderthal was conquered by tall, light-skinned modern humans of greater intelligence. In battle after battle the modern types defeated the poor brutish Neanderthals (who have sometimes been depicted as evil). Here is an explanation based on a catastrophist vision of a Europe overrun by modern invaders. This explanation raises the questions, Where did the modern humans come from? and Why do they seem to appear suddenly in the archaeological record? Those who accept some form of creationism see these modern humans specially created and then driving out the earlier specially created Neanderthals. In recent years another type of explanation, comparable to creationism, has become popular in folk explanations of human diversity: The abrupt change is explained by the appearance of creatures from outer space.

While scientists still have many unanswered questions about Neanderthal, recent improvements in techniques of dating and the discovery of non-European contemporaries of the European Neanderthals have added new insights. The most plausible explanation is that the *Homo sapiens* population of the era 100,000 to 40,000 BP most affected by glaciation was that of western Europe. The biological characteristics of the western European, or classic, Neanderthal suggest adaptations to life in a basically tundra environment. Not *all* of the western European populations lived in caves in tundra conditions, but perhaps most did. Some authorities have suggested that the jutting-out of the lower jaw of the western European Neanderthals was a result of their using of the teeth for chewing skins—much as Eskimos did until recently. Other western European Neanderthal adaptations to extreme cold included stocky build, increased blood flow to face and enlarged nasal and sinus passages. These western European Neanderthals were restricted in their contact with other contemporary populations farther to the east by glaciation. However, there was no time at which contact would have been impossible.

In eastern Europe, the Middle East, Asia, and Africa, Neanderthal and Neanderthaloid populations of the 100,000 to 40,000 BP time period were less affected by the conditions brought about by glaciation than those living in western Europe. The adaptations that these non–western European populations were making to their various environments produced somewhat more modern-looking physical types.

The retreat of the glaciers about 40,000 years ago allowed greater movement of populations. Apparently some of the more modern-looking forms of eastern Europe and the Near East began moving into western Europe; there they mated with the western European Neanderthals, who then gradually disappeared as a specialized form of Neanderthal, as a result of interbreeding. Eventually, after thousands of years, no clearly identifiable western European Neanderthal type remained, and only modern humans—*Homo sapiens sapiens*—inhabited the earth.

The earliest modern humans identified thus far are the forms called Cro-Magnon, after the site in France at which they were first discovered in 1868. But identifying Cro-Magnon as the first modern human, as some people do, may represent an unconscious form of Western ethnocentrism. It is certainly possible that discoveries in eastern Europe and the Middle East may confirm that the transition from *Homo sapiens neandertalensis* to *Homo sapiens sapiens* took place in that part of the world rather than in western Europe. Fossil research in both Asia and Africa has concentrated on early hominids, and therefore our knowl-

The Western form of Neanderthal apparently disappeared as a result of interbreeding with more modern-looking forms from eastern Europe and the Near East.

Cro-Magnon. (Courtesy of the American Museum of Natural History)

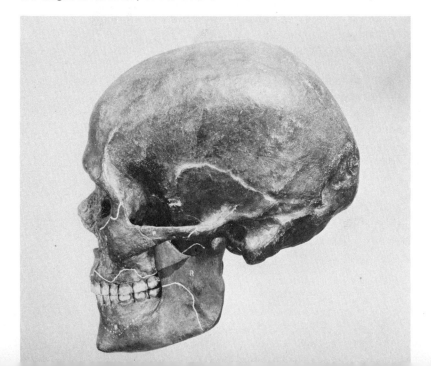

edge of the relationship of the Neanderthaloids to modern humans is very sketchy. What is clear is that shortly after the appearance of Cro-Magnon in western Europe, modern humans whose skeletal remains look very similar to Cro-Magnon appear in Hungary, Rusia, the Middle East, North Africa, South Africa, China, Southeast Asia, Australia, and North America.

Modern humans began to exploit a far larger number of different environmental niches, and the great diversity of their artifacts reflects these specialized adaptations. Archaeologists refer to the early period of modern humans as the *Upper Paleolithic* (Upper Old Stone Age). This time period is marked by the appearance of a new toolmaking technique called *pressure flaking,* in which a piece of bone is used to remove tiny flakes from the cutting edge of the artifact. With this technique it is possible to make arrowheads and spear points that are exceedingly sharp and effective.

With the appearance of modern humans, cultural development accelerated as never before. Cave painting and other art forms and religious symbolism are expressed to an extent never reached by Neanderthal. The human accomplishments of the past 40,000 years seem incredible in comparison to the first 5 million years during which humanlike forms existed.

Conclusion

The evidence for evolution is overwhelming, but there are still many gaps in the fossil record. Likewise there are still problems with dating fossil remains and deciding which fossil remains are from similar or different hominids, due to the great variability within fossil populations. Scholars disagree, both for the reasons above and because their preceptions of the data are influenced by their theoretical biases. In a sense each is creating his or her own version of the human myth. While scientists disagree over details, however, almost all accept an evolutionary perspective. There is a general pattern to the data in spite of many gaps. The closer in time fossil material is to modern humans, the more it resembles modern humans. Conversely, the older the fossil, the less it looks like modern humans.

The human myth that anthropologists have developed tells us that the origins of humankind began with a line of protohominids, called *Ramapithecus,* that eventually evolved into an early form of *Australopithecus* about 5 million years ago. This early form of *Australopithecus* gave rise to three different populations: the gracile *Australopithecus*, the robust *Australopithecus*, and the *Homo* forms. The robust and *Homo* forms began to differentiate about 3 million years ago. The *Homo* forms of East Africa began to evolve into *Homo erectus* about 1.5 million years ago. *Homo erectus* settled an extensive area of the Old World tropics and even moved north into the colder climates of Europe and China by 750,000 years ago. *Homo erectus* evolved into the early *Homo sapiens* by about 100,000 BP. These populations showed greater biological diversity than any previous hominid and spread over larger areas of the Old World. Western European *Homo sapiens* showed extreme biological specialization to the cold glacial environment. Some of the early *Homo sapiens* eventually evolved into *Homo sapiens sapiens*, or truly modern humans, by about 40,000 BP. These modern forms then settled the remainder of the world.

While fossil bones are the primary data of the physical anthropologist, biological and cultural evolution are closely related. Increases in the size of the brain; improvements in dexterity; upright posture; the manufacturing of artifacts; changes in diet; increasing complexity of language as a system of communication; and the growth of culture have all affected one another and have ultimately led to the development of the type of creature that we are today.

The evidence for evolution has been so overwhelming that many of those who previously accepted a special creation for humans have had to change their point of view. No longer is the Great Chain of Being concept promoted. Forms are no longer thought to be unchanging. The evidence against this notion is just too great. One version of creationism sees human beings as specially created, but from then on evolution is acknowledged to occur. Unfortunately, the origin of humans has now become a political issue in some states, just as it was in Tennessee 50 years ago. There have been attempts in various states to force boards of education to adopt biology textbooks that include a Biblical version of Creation as well as the theory of evolution. The advocates demand that the account of human origins in Genesis be presented as simple historical fact. However they apparently wish that only the first account of Creation in Genesis be accepted as fact. The contradictions between the two accounts of Creation are ignored by these advocates.

Unfortunately, those promoting any type of creationism do not understand the methods or rationale of science. The essential characteristic of scientific theory is that it is capable of contradiction by empirical data. Scientific theory is perfectible and

The evidence for evolution is overwhelming.

stands only as long as it has not been contradicted. Thus Darwinian evolutionary theory has been significantly transformed and enriched by the research of Mendel and others. Creationism, on the other hand, is a theory of primordial history, and as such, it follows different rules than does scientific theory. It is not subject to empirical testing, nor does it allow for improvement (Bevan 1972).

Anthropology Vocabulary

Acheulian industry
artificial selection
Australopithecus
Australopithecus boisei
brachiation
catastrophism
Choukoutien
classic Neanderthal
creationism
Cretaceous epoch
Cro-Magnon
dominant characteristic
Dryopithecus
Eocene epoch
evolved Oldowan industry
genetic drift
genotype
gracile *Australopithecus*
Great Chain of Being
hand ax
heterozygous
hominid

Homo
Homo erectus
Homo sapiens
Homo sapiens neandertalensis
Homo sapiens rhodesiensis
Homo sapiens sapiens
Homo sapiens soloensis
homozygous
law of independent assortment
law of segregation
Lower Paleolithic
Middle Paleolithic
migration
Miocene epoch
Mousterian industry
mutation
natural selection
Neanderthal
Neanderthaloid
Oldowan industry
Oligocene epoch

phenotype
Pithecanthropus
Pleistocene epoch
Pliocene epoch
pressure flaking
Primates
prognathism
progressive Neanderthal
Propliopithecus
prosimian
Purgatorius
Ramapithecus
recessive characteristic
robust *Australopithecus*
Sinanthropus pekinensis
stereoscopic vision
Swanscombe
synthetic theory of evolution
Terra Amata
uniformitarianism
Upper Paleolithic
Vertesszöllös

Review Questions

1. How does the evolutionary theory of human origins compare with Creationism?
2. Darwin's concept of evolution stressed natural selection. What other factors resulting in biological change have been added to evolutionary theory since Darwin?
3. What have been the general trends of primate evolution?
4. What is the significance of *Australopithecus* in human evolution?
5. What evidence is there to suggest that the biological evolution and cultural evolution of humans have been interrelated?
6. What are the problems in interpreting the transition from Neanderthal to modern humans?

Recommended Reading

Campbell, Bernard G., ed., 1976, *Humankind Emerging.* Boston: Little, Brown. Perhaps the best available introduction to fossil hominids. Extremely well illustrated.

Darwin, Charles, 1958, *The Origin of Species by Means of Natural Selection or the Preservation of Favoured Races in the Struggle for Life.* (Originally published in 1859.) New York: New American Library (Mentor Books). Perhaps the most important book of the past century. It should be read by anyone interested in evolution, because what Darwin says is sometimes different from what other writers say he said.

Darwin, Sir Francis, ed., 1961 *Charles Darwin's Autobiography.* New York: Collier Books. An interesting little book that provides background about how *On the Origin of Species* came to be written.

Dobzhansky, Theodosius, 1962, *Mankind Evolving: The Evolution of the Human Species.* New Haven: Yale University Press. A well-written explanation of human evolution, stressing the interplay between biology and culture in human evolution.

Ginger, Ray, 1969, *Six Days or Forever? Tennessee v. John Thomas Scopes.* (Originally published in 1958.) New York: Quadrangle. Provides a useful background to the famous Scopes trial.

Howell, F. Clark, and the editors of Time-Life Books, 1973, *Early Man,* 2nd ed. New York: Time-Life Books. Well illustrated overview of human evolution.

Poirier, Frank E., 1973, *Fossil Man: An Evolutionary Journey.* St. Louis: Mosby. An overview of human evolution. The author emphasizes behavior as well as skeletal data. A conscientious attempt to include alternative interpretations.

Washburn, S. L. and Ruth Moore, 1974, *Ape into Man: A Study of Human Evolution.* Boston: Little, Brown. A view of human evolution based heavily on recent findings in biochemistry and primate behavior studies.

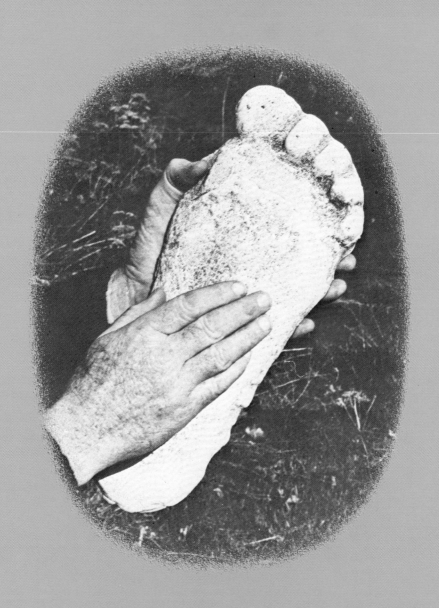

3

How many kinds of humans are there?

There are many beliefs about monstrous races.

There is only one kind of human being in existence today.

On October 20, 1967, near Bluff Creek, California, Roger Patterson was able to record the movements of a large, hairy creature on 24 feet of 16-mm color movie film.[1] The creature was estimated to be close to 7 feet high and weigh about 500 pounds. Because of its apparent pendulous breasts, it was assumed to be female. It was covered with short, shiny black hair. The creature walked upright, swinging its long arms as it moved. Footprints in the area were measured later and found to be 14½ inches in length, with a stride of 41 inches. Patterson, who has since died, believed that this was conclusive proof of the existence of a creature popularly known as Bigfoot. Does Bigfoot exist? Is Bigfoot possibly a remnant from the era of *Homo erectus* or Neanderthal? In this chapter we will attempt to answer these questions and to determine how many kinds of humanlike creatures exist.

Strange forms of humans have been reported by various societies for as long as there have been written records. However, the fossil record has provided no support for their existence; instead these creatures have been a part of the mythology and folklore of different societies.

Homo monstrosus

Monsters. The ancient Greeks recorded descriptions of a number of peculiar races that they believed existed or may have existed. Herodotus of Halicarnassus was one of the first writers to compile accounts of different societies, in his *Histories.* In the fifth century BC, he collected accounts of strange people like the Troglodytes of Ethiopia, who lived underground, ate snakes and lizards, and whose language resembled the screeching sounds made by bats; and the Arimaspi, who had only one eye, situated in the middle of their forehead. In some cases Herodotus included accounts of strange people that he didn't believe existed. Some of the monstrous people he described had been mentioned by earlier writers. Frequently these monstrous forms were thought to be similar to humans, but with at least one different primary feature (Figure 10); for example, some creatures had only one foot, such as the Sciapodes of India; some had the body of a human and the head of a different animal, such as the dog-headed Cynocephali of India; some had ears that extended almost to the ground, such as the Phanesians, also of India. The ancient Greek writer Empedocles suggested that various parts

The Greek writers described a number of monstrous races.

---

[1] The movie was eventually expanded to 320 feet by repeating parts of it and by using stop-frames to give extended exposure to certain areas (Hunter and Dahinden 1973:123).

Figure 10 Representatives of monstrous tribes from *Liber Chronicarium,* by Hartmann Schedel, published in 1493. (From the Rare Book Division, The New York Public Library, Astor, Lenox and Tilden Foundations.)

of bodies originally existed separately from one another and were scattered about in space. These parts combined at random, sometimes producing "normal" humans and at other times producing monstrous forms. Thus Empedocles provided one of the earliest explanations of how monstrous races could come into being (Malefijt 1968).

In the first century AD the Roman naturalist Pliny the Elder assembled for his encyclopedic *Historia Naturalis* all the known accounts of monstrous beings, including such peoples as the headless Blemmyae, with eyes and mouths on their chests; the Thibii, who had a double pupil in one eye and the image of a horse in the other; or the Strap-foots, with feet like leather thongs, whose nature it was to crawl rather than walk (Hodgen 1964:35–39).

By the thirteenth century, accounts of monstrous races were still being perpetuated by travelers such as Marco Polo, who wrote of the inhabitants of Andaman Islands in the Indian

Ocean, "You may take it for a fact that all the men on this island have heads like dogs, and teeth and eyes like dogs; for I assure you that the whole aspect of their faces is that of big mastiffs" (Polo 1958:230). One has only to watch the Saturday morning children's cartoons on television to realize that the fascination with monstrous races continues even today. The belief in monstrous creatures is important because it has colored the way in which Western people have viewed members of other societies.

Wild Individuals. In a similar vein there have also been beliefs about "wild people." In some cases these beliefs are interchangeable with those about monstrous races, but in many cases they have a different significance: Whereas the monstrous races were regarded as curiosities, wild individuals more frequently appear in literature as examples of "wildness" and "heresy." The wild person and his or her culture were used by Westerners to confirm the value of their antitheses: "civilization," "sanity," and "orthodoxy."

By the Middle Ages a distinction also emerged between the barbarian and the wild individual. Both were viewed as animal-like, unable to control their passions; as mobile, shifting, confused, chaotic; as incapable of sedentary existence of self-discipline, or sustained labor; and as hostile to normal humanity. However, there was one important difference between them: The barbarians lived in groups, while the wild person always lived alone, or at most with a mate (White 1972:4).

While monstrous races were thought of as entire groups of people, the wild individual always lived alone.

According to historian Hayden White (1972:20) the wild individual and the barbarian represented different kinds of threats to normal humans. The barbarian represented a threat to society, to civilization, to racial purity, to moral excellence, or whatever the ingroup took pride in; while the wild person was a threat to the individual, both as enemy and as representative of a condition into which an individual, having fallen out of grace or having been driven from his or her city, might degenerate.

In stories about barbarians, their home, like that of the monstrous races, is conventionally conceived to lie far away in space, and the time of their coming into the confines of civilization is conceived to be fraught with apocalyptical possibilities for all of civilized humanity. The wild man, on the other hand, is conventionally represented as being always present, inhabiting the immediate confines of the community—just out of sight, over the horizon, in the nearby forest, desert, mountains, or hills.

He sleeps in crevices, under great trees, or in caves of wild animals, to which he carries off helpless children, or women, there to do unspeakable things to them. And he is also sly: he steals the sheep from the fold, the chicken from the coop, tricks the shepherds, and befuddles the gamekeeper. In medieval myth especially, the Wild Man is conceived to be covered with hair and to be black and deformed. He may be a giant or a dwarf, or he may be merely horribly disfigured. . . . But in whatever way he is envisaged, the Wild Man almost always represents the image of the man released from social control, the man in whom the libidinal impulses have gained full ascendacy.

In the Christian Middle Ages, then, the Wild Man is the distillation of the specific anxieties underlying the three securities supposedly provided by the specifically Christian institutions of civilized life: the securities of *sex* (as organized by the institution of the family), *sustenance* (as provided by the political, social, and economic institutions), and *salvation* (as provided by the Church). [White 1972:21]

As will be shown later in this chapter, the Abominable Snowman, the Almas, and Bigfoot exhibit many of the characteristics of the wild person.

Feral Individuals. A special type of wild individual has been a part of the beliefs of a number of societies for many centuries. These are the feral people, human beings who have remained isolated from other human beings for a number of years during their early childhood. Lucien Malson (1972:62–71) distinguishes three types of feral individual: (*a*) Children who were purposely kept isolated from others but who had some type of contact with other human beings from time to time, such as Kasper Hauser, who at the age of 17 wandered into Nuremberg, Germany, one day in 1828. He had been held captive from an early age and had never seen his captor. (*b*) Children who were isolated from humans and had no contact with them, such as Victor, who was captured at the age of 12 running naked in the woods of Aveyron, France. He was studied by the great French doctor Jean-Marc-Gaspard Itard. Very frequently, such children had been abandoned by their parents, sometimes as a result of the ravages of war. (*c*) Children who had been isolated from humans at an early age but who had supposedly been raised by other animals.

These latter children are usually referred to as "wolf-children," although there are stories of children being raised by bears, sheep, cattle, pigs, snowhens, baboons, panthers, leopards, gazelles, kangaroos, and apes, as well as wolves. Actual discoveries of these types of feral individuals appear at least as early as 1344, with the Hesse wolf-child, and continue up to the present with Sidi Mohammed, the ostrich-child discovered in

Kaspar Hauser, feral individual. (The Granger Collection)

Feral individuals are humans who have remained isolated from other humans.

Victor, the so-called Wild Boy of Aveyron. (The Granger Collection)

France in 1962. Wolf-children are found in mythology at least as far back as the story of the founder of Rome, Romulus, and his twin brother Remus. Sons of Mars, they were left to die when they were babies and were reared by a she-wolf. In most accounts of wolf-child types, the child is supposedly suckled by the animal and then takes on many characteristics of the animal, such as walking on all four limbs.

Claims that children have been raised by animals are usually believed to be either hoaxes, lies, or a misunderstanding of the facts. While there have been many accounts of such children, none has ever been authenticated. In most cases, a child has actually been found, but proof of its having been reared with some animal is lacking or questionable. Perhaps the only case ever to be accepted by any scientists as authentic was that of the wolf-children of Midnapore, India, discovered in 1920 by Reverend J. A. L. Singh.

> The younger one was given the name of Amala and the older one Kamala. With both of them, the skin on their hands, knees and elbows was heavily calloused. Their tongues hung out through thick red lips, they panted and frequently bared their teeth. They suffered from photophobia and day-blindness, and spent their days crouched in the shade or standing motionless with their faces to the wall. They livened up at night, howling and groaning and hoping to escape. Amala—aged one and a half—and Kamala— aged eight and a half—slept only about four hours in twenty-four. They had two means of getting about: on their knees and elbows for short distances and on their hands and feet for longer distances or for running. They lapped up liquids and took their food in a crouching position. Their exclusive taste for meat led them to indulge in the only activity of which they were capable: chasing chickens or rooting around for carcasses and entrails. Though they took a slight interest in dogs and cats, they were completely unsociable and used to snarl at humans, showing particular hostility to Singh's wife. [Malson 1972:68–69]

The children were supposedly living in a wolf lair with three adult wolves and two cubs when they were discovered by Reverend Singh. The children were taken to his orphanage, where Amala died within a year and Kamala died eight years later. Reverend Singh kept a journal of Kamala's development, which was published by the anthropologist Robert Zingg (Singh and Zingg 1942), who strongly believed in its authenticity, although he had never seen the children himself. Other prominent scientists wrote forewords to the publication stating their belief in its authenticity. The physical anthropologist W. M. Krogman, however, having read the original manuscript, raised serious questions about Singh's journal (to which Zingg replied in the footnotes of the final publication).

The most devastating criticism of the Midnapore case came from the physical anthropologist Ashley Montagu (1943), who reviewed the book. He pointed out a number of problems with Reverend Singh's account of the children. They were supposedly found in a wolf den, but only Reverend Singh could testify to this fact. There is no confirmation of the story by any other eye-witness. Even if the children were found in a wolf den, Singh had no reason to assume as he did that a wolf had suckled the children. Reverend Singh stated that the children used to howl regularly every night at about ten o'clock and at one and three o'clock in the morning. Folk tradition has perpetuated the belief that wolves howl at regular hours every night, but observations of wolves do not support this belief. It is another folk tale that dogs do not sweat except through the tongue. This is an incorrect belief as dogs possess sweat glands all over the body. Thus Reverend Singh's contention that the children did not sweat is questionable. These and many other inaccuracies suggest that Reverend Singh was making up at least part of his narrative.

Following Montagu's review, W. F. Ogburn and N. K. Bose (1959) made extensive investigations in India. They discovered that two children named Amala and Kamala had lived for a while at Singh's orphanage, but there was no evidence to support the story of their being wolf-children. Also, the village of Midnapore, where the children had reportedly been discovered, did not exist.

In spite of the fact that some scholars accepted Amala and Kamala as the first legitimate case of human having been raised by an animal, this case as well as others, is not a very convincing one. There are too many questions raised by Reverend Singh's narrative that cannot be answered.

What, then, are feral types? In most cases they appear to be severely retarded individuals. It is not always clear in particular cases whether the child was retarded to begin with, this being the reason for its abandonment, or whether the retardation was due to the fact that during a critical period in its development the child was isolated from other human beings. Individuals do not become functioning human beings simply by being born; indeed they cannot become a functioning human beings until they are exposed to the humanizing influences of other human beings. The attributes that we associate with being human are a function of human society, of socializing factors acting upon a person's potentialities to be humanized (Montagu 1943).

From time to time there have been hoaxes by individuals claiming to have discovered some type of wolf-child who has taken on attributed of the creature who raised him or her. There is no evidence in any of these cases to support such a belief. Some circus "freaks" are promoted as if they had been born with the attributes of an animal. Just as Pliny the Elder wrote about dog-headed people in ancient times, the carnival has had its Dog-Faced Boy, Mule-Faced Woman, and Frog Boy. There seems to be no evidence whatsoever to suggest that any of the feral individuals, wolf-children, or carnival freaks are anything other than human beings. They do not constitute monstrous races.

The Ape as a Human Being. Throughout human history apes and monkeys have been mistaken for various monstrous forms of humans. The three largest apes were unknown to the Western world until quite late. The chimpanzee was not described until 1640, the orangutan not until 1658, and the gorilla not until 1847 (O'Malley and Magoun 1973). The description of a monkey or ape by a traveler was sometimes taken to be an account of a strange race of humans. Primitive humans, monkeys, and apes were frequently confused. By the eighteenth century there was a fairly common belief that both monkeys and apes interbred with humans in certain primitive societies, the results of such unions being fertile offspring, part human and part beast. One scholar of the time, Lord Monboddo, concluded that the orangutan represented a stage of human social evolution advanced over that demonstrated by feral children. He suggested that all that inhibited the orangutan from being able to speak was a sound Scottish education (McCown and Kennedy 1972:29).

Westerners were aware of monkeys and apelike creatures at least as early as classical times. Although these creatures were called apes in the writings of the time, they were not the great apes but were instead the tailless Barbary ape (not a true ape), the sacred baboon of the ancient Egyptians, and a variety of tailed monkeys. From the collapse of the Roman Empire to the thirteenth century, the official Christian view of the ape was that it was associated with the Devil or was the Devil himself. By the thirteenth century, the image of the ape was changing from that of the Devil to that of a deformed human in a state of degeneracy. The ape began to be cast in the role of sinner and was seen as the *victim* of the Devil rather than as the Devil himself. The apes were seen to have "devolved" from humans, usually as a result of some conflict with God. It was within this context that the great apes were viewed when they were discovered. There was a folk belief that apes were the offspring of human beings who had become lazy and weary of the discipline

Feral individuals are human beings.

Apes and primitive humans were often confused with one another.

of living in society and had taken to the forest, where they reverted to the animal state (Janson 1952). Thus one may understand the violent popular opposition that greeted Darwin and his supporters and their claim that humans descended from apes.

At various times, beliefs about monstrous races, wild individuals, and apes played a similar role in Western thought. They were all used as examples of what could happen to a civilized person who was not virtuous. More than anything, the stories of these creatures were moral lessons. The discovery of "primitive" people was viewed in the same sort of conceptual framework.

Primitive People. During the Renaissance, in the sixteenth and seventeenth centuries, when new peoples were being encountered by Westerners, "racial" differences between peoples were not stressed. At this time in Western society there were still no strong political or economic interests that prompted the debasement of a people on the basis of their skin color. There was an awareness of differences in skin color, but they were explained by the theory that all skins were originally white and that variations were due to differences in exposure to the sun. Assuming that all men were biologically the same, Renaissance scholars focused mainly on differences in language and religion. To the Renaissance European these were the basis of human diversity (Hodgen 1964:213–214). Scholars accounted for this diversity by some version of creationist theory.

> Renaissance scholars explained diversity by some form of creationist theory.

The early explorers were instrumental in changing the European attitude toward primitive peoples. They associated characteristics of primitive people with those of the monstrous races of ancient legends. People discovered living in caves were not reported as humans but described as the Troglodytes, recorded by Herodotus, living underground and eating snakes and lizards and screeching like bats. The Europeans explorers relied on hearsay and indirect evidence to support their view that the newly discovered peoples of the world were something other than humans. If the Europeans discovered tracks in the sand in an area they were exploring, they assumed giants lived there. Relying on hearsay in Haiti, Columbus reported a people who had one eye in their forehead. In his *Sphaera Mundi* of 1498, John of Holywood described the people of the New World as blue in color, with square heads.

Partly as a result of such reports, there was a gradual acceptance that primitive people were something less than human. Primitive peoples began to be viewed in the hierarchical terms

> Primitives were thought to be intermediates between modern humans and apes.

of the Chain of Being and were now seen as a lower link in the Chain than Europeans. The primitive, especially the African and the American Indian, was conceived of as a bridge between the apes and completely developed European humans. Related to this notion was the idea that primitives were unimprovable, because each link in the Chain was static. This belief became justification for the European to expropriate the lands of the primitives and to enslave them (Hodgen 1964:380–415).

By the middle of the eighteenth century differentiations between the inhabitants of the earth came to be based primarily on differences of skin color rather than on the cultural differences emphasized earlier. From that point on, the study of "race" began to emerge as a valid one for scientific research.

Ideas of semihuman creatures have been maintained tenaciously in folk anthropology. In some cases the ideas seem to have originated in hearsay accounts from ancient times, while other notions have come from legends of primitive societies. These legends became incorporated in European beliefs which were then often transmitted to other primitive societies, many of which already had their own beliefs in semihuman forms. For example, the oral tradition of Renaissance Spain contained the story of John, the bear's son, whose human mother had been captured by a bear. John was half-bear and half human, hair covered his entire body. This tale was carried by the Spanish to Latin America, where it is still told (Robe 1972:40–41). Anthropologists continue to discover beliefs in monstrous races among the people they study.

Are There Monstrous Races?

People believe in monstrous races; that is an established fact which can be verified. The actual existence of such beings is a much more difficult problem to deal with. There is no fossil evidence to support beliefs in monstrous races, yet the fossil record is an incomplete one. There have been many surprising discoveries in geology. Who would have believed 200 years ago that at one time the earth was populated by the likes of the dinosaur? Human understanding of its own past has often changed dramatically with a new fossil discovery. Thus, to say that there is no fossil evidence for the existence of monstrous races does not completely disprove the possibility. Nor have any of these creatures been captured long enough for scientific analysis, with one interesting exception.

The "Minnesota Iceman" was supposed to have been a Nean-

> There is no fossil data to support a belief in monstrous races.

derthal male found by fishermen floating in a 6000-pound block of natural ice in the Sea of Okhotsk, an oceanic enclave between the Kamchatka peninsula and eastern Siberia. It was exhibited in the United States in a sealed, ice-filled coffin in the late 1960s as the Siberskoye Creature. However, in 1969 a young woman, Helen Westring, claimed to have shot the creature in the woods near Bemidji, Minnesota, while it was assaulting her. Her story was carried in the June 30 issue of the *National Bulletin* under the sensational headline, "I Was Raped by the Abominable Snowman." In the magazine *Saga* the following year, the exhibitor of the creature claimed that he had shot the creature in the woods of Minnesota in 1960. The exhibitor allowed two zoologists, Ivan T. Sanderson and Bernard Heuvelmans, to study the creature, albeit in cramped quarters and through the plate-glass lid of the coffin. Both accepted the creature at face value. Both published articles on its existence in learned journals (Heuvelmans 1969; Sanderson 1969). However, before any serious study could be undertaken the creature disappeared and was replaced by an artificial copy. The entire series of incidents surrounding the Iceman are so suspicious that the physical anthropologist John Napier is convinced that the Iceman was a fake from the very beginning, a Hollywood-created monster (Napier 1972:98–114). In any case, the body, whether fake or real, is no longer available for scientific study.

The question still remains, then, as to what evidence there is to support the belief in monstrous races. Generally the "evidence" is of four types: Stories, sightings, footprints, and several motion pictures. Before reviewing the evidence, however, it is necessary first to consider the types of monstrous races that are thought to exist today. Leaving aside various types of transformers, such as werewolves and vampires, who are believed by some to change periodically from human form to something else, the most persistent beliefs about strange humanlike creatures center around two forms, the Abominable Snowman and Bigfoot. Considerable sums of money and a tremendous number of hours have been spent trying to capture or kill one of these creatures. Both the Abominable Snowman and Bigfoot are considered by many to be in the same class as the Loch Ness Monster and flying saucers. Many people do not know if these things really exist but are willing to keep an open mind to the possibility. Others accept the existence, or possible existence, of some of these phenomena, but not all. Those who believe they have observed one of these phenomena are convinced of their existence. Scientists have generally maintained a low profile concerning the issue.

Since it is extremely difficult to prove that something could not exist, scientists cannot completely dismiss the phenomena. At the same time the evidence of the existence of flying saucers, the Loch Ness Monster, the Abominable Snowman, and Bigfoot has not been hard data. As a result, most scientists feel that their time will be better spent engaging in other research until there is more evidence to work with, such as skeletal data. Therefore, almost all of the research has been carried out by folk anthropologists rather than professional anthropologists.

The major problem with the evidence for humanlike creatures is that it is generally circumstantial: footprints, sightings at night, stories heard secondhand. Authentication of the creatures is made more difficult by promoters, con men, and publicity seekers, who will often go to any lengths, including faking evidence. However, as the physical anthropologist John Napier (1972:203–4) points out in regards to Bigfoot,

> No one doubts that some of the footprints are hoaxes and that some eyewitnesses are lying, but if *one* track and *one* report is true-bill, then myth must be chucked out of the window and reality admitted through the front door.
>
>   The dilemma is simple enough. Either some of the footprints are real, or all are fakes. If they are all fakes, then an explanation involving legend and folk memory is adequate to explain the mystery. But if any one of them is real then as scientists we have a lot to explain. Among other things we shall have to re-write the story of human evolution. We shall have to accept that *Homo sapiens* is not the one and only living product of the hominid line, and we shall have to admit that there are still major mysteries to be solved in a world we thought we knew so well.

Napier has been one of the few professional anthropologists to consider the evidence for the Abominable Snowman and Bigfoot. He feels there is no clear evidence in support of the Abominable Snowman, or Yeti, as it is also called, but that an actual creature has made some of the Bigfoot prints.

The Abominable Snowman

Stories of sightings of the Abominable Snowman have survived for centuries among the peoples of the Himalaya Mountains. However it is difficult to separate fact from fiction in these stories, as any unexplained phenomenon tends to be classified as the Yeti by the natives of the region. Perhaps the first Westerner to record a belief in the existence of a strange humanlike creature to account for footprints in the Himalayan snows was a traveler named J. B. Fraser, who published a book in 1820 about his journey through the Himalayas. At one point he and his crew discovered tracks in the snow. His crew claimed the prints were not made by a tiger but rather by a creature they called the Bang, who was believed to be large and red and who was greatly feared.

It was not until 1921 that the Abominable Snowman caught the public's eye. That year marked the beginning of high-altitude mountaineering expeditions, which were newsworthy events in themselves. Therefore, whatever the expeditions encountered was carried in newspapers around the world. Lieutenant-Colonel C. K. Howard-Bury was the leader of the 1921 Everest Reconnaissance Expedition. At between 20,000 and 21,000 feet he came upon humanlike footprints. While Howard-Bury dismissed these tracks as having been made by a gray wolf, his porters believed it was the Metoh-Kangmi, or Abominable Snowman, that had made them. Howard-Bury did not take the Snowman story seriously, but the newspapers played up the story. For Howard-Bury the Snowman was just the Tibetan counterpart of our bogeyman, used to scare children into following proper behavior (Napier 1972:38–39). According to the porters the creature had his feet turned backwards so as to climb more easily, and he had long matted hair, which covered his face (Tchernine 1961:28).

An account by a British photographer-climber created even greater furor. In 1925 N. A. Tombazi reported seeing the creature at an altitude of 15,000 feet, at a distance of 300 yards. It looked human, walked upright, was dark in color, and wore no clothing. Although a photographer, Tombazi did not photograph the creature. He later returned to the area where he had sighted the creature and found 15 footprints that looked human, but each of which was only 6 to 7 inches long by 4 inches wide. Napier (1972:40) suggests these were probably the footprints of a bear; Tchernine (1961:164) accepts the account as an actual sighting of a Yeti.

In the 1930s there were continued sightings of footprints in the snow. In 1959 a Captain d'Auvergne, the curator of the Victoria Memorial in Calcutta, India, published a story of his alleged capture by a Yeti in 1938. He had been injured, and was saved by an 8- to 9-foot Yeti that carried him to a cave and nursed him back to life. His story has not been taken seriously.

The 1950s might be described as the Golden Age of Snowman hunting. The Nepal government required a special license for Yeti hunters costing £400 per Yeti. The Yeti was becoming a commercial success for the people of the Himalayas. Nepal was publicized in official tourist brochures as "the land of Mount Everest and the Yeti" (Napier 1972:47–48).

In 1951, members of the Everest Reconnaissance Expedition, Eric Shipton, Michael Ward, and Sen Jensing, discovered fresh tracks in deep snow that stretched for approximately one mile at an altitude of about 18,000 feet. Shipton took two photographs of the clearest footprint, one with Ward's booted foot as a scale and the other with an iceax as a scale. The footprint measured 13 inches by 8 inches. This is the only footprint photographed that Napier believes may provide some evidence in support of the Yeti, but even it is somewhat dubious. In fact, Napier suggests that the tracks may have been composite prints made by naked human feet (Himalayan pilgrims walk barefoot) following in the track of prints already made by feet wearing leather moccasins (Napier 1972:48–49, 141). However, according to Shipton, "There could be no doubt whatever that a large creature had passed that way a very short time before, and that whatever it was it was not a human-being, nor a bear, nor any species of monkey known to exist in Asia." He also adds, "Personally, I believe that there exists in one or more of the high mountain ranges of Central Asia a large creature of anthropoid form unknown to science" (Shipton 1961:9).

In the 1950s several unsuccessful Abominable Snowman expeditions were organized, three of which were sponsored by the Texas oil millionaire Tom Slick. These expeditions turned up no new evidence.

The Hillary expedition of 1960–1961 had as a secondary goal, that of Yeti-hunting. Giant footprints that were discovered during the expedition were shown to be small fox prints that

CENTIMETRES

Scalp attributed to the Abominable Snowman. (British Museum, Natural History)

had become larger by natural melting. A so-called Yeti skin in a villager's house at Beding was in fact that of a blue bear. The expedition discovered a so-called Yeti scalp in the village monastery of Khumjung, which was borrowed for scientific analysis and found to have been fabricated from the skin of a rare goat-antelope known as the serow (Napier 1972:56–58). This expedition tended to put a damper on interest in the Yeti. However, in 1970 the mountain climber Don Whillans photographed a trail of footprints at 13,000 feet in Nepal and that night saw a creature moving on all fours in the moonlight.

All told there is considerable variation in the accounts of the Yeti. Estimates of its height vary from $4\frac{1}{2}$ feet to 16 feet. Some observers emphasize that it walks on two legs; others that it walks on all fours. A number of the reported characteristics are classic monster-myth motifs found in the beliefs of people in many parts of the world, such as that they live in caves high in mountains; they are nocturnal; they raid villages to carry off humans; they have a strong, offensive body odor; they have tremendous physical strength, being able to uproot trees and hurl boulders great distances; the breasts of the females are so large they have to throw them over their shoulders when running or bending down; their long hair falls in their eyes and blinds them when they run down hill; and they are fond of alcohol, which can be used to trap them (Napier 1972:64–66). Napier, the only physical anthropologist to have devoted study to the Yeti, concludes that there is little evidence to prove their existence and that they are best understood as myth.

There are many differing descriptions of the Yeti.

The Almas

A second kind of humanlike creature has been reported from Central Asia. Although there are various names for these creatures, and perhaps several types, both Tchernine and Napier lump them together under one name, Almas.[2]

The Almas is a humanlike creature thought to live in Central Asia.

In the fifteenth century Johann Schildberger traveled in Mongolia and Siberia while a captive of various primitive peoples. He returned to Germany with an account of wild people that he had supposedly observed first hand. This account was later discovered by a Russian, Professor Boris Porshnev (sometimes spelled Porschnieff), who served on a commission established to study the Abominable Snowman. According to

[2] Other local names include Kaptar, Ksi-kiik, Golub-Yavan, Tok-Dzu-teh and Gin-sung.

Porshnev, the fifteenth-century German offered the following account:

> Crossing the Altai Ranges of Mongolia takes approximately thirty-two days to travel their whole length. The inhabitants of the region believed that behind the mountains there existed a desert (the Gobi Desert) which led to the end of the world! Wild people lived in the mountain fastnesses. They had no permanent homes. Their bodies, except for hands and feet, were covered with hair. Like animals they fed on leaves, grass, and anything they could find. The chief of that region presented Edigai (the chief who held Schildberger), when he visited him, with two wild people, a man and a woman who had been caught on the mountain. [Porshnev 1958, cited in Tchernine 1961:49–50]

This questionable account of monstrous races has been taken as factual by Porshnev and a few of his Russian colleagues. It is one of many accounts over the years describing various types of semihumans in Central Asia. Perhaps the most detailed description of the Almas comes from a Mongolian linguist, J. R. Rinchen:

> The inhabitants of the Gobi Desert gave eyewitness accounts of the Almas. They are very similar to humans, they say, but their bodies are covered with reddish-black hair which is not thick. The skin is visible through the hair, a non-existent factor in the case of the true wild animals of the desert. The Almas' height of body is Mongol. The posture is upright, with a forward bending slant. They walk with knees half-bent. The jaws are powerful, forehead low and receding. The brow ridges are prominent in comparison with the Mongolian brow. The females of the species possess long mammary glands. These creatures cannot light a fire. [Porshnev 1958, cited in Tchernine 1961:52]

In general the descriptions of the Almas are closer to those of wild people than they are those of monstrous races. However, in some accounts they are described as being much larger than a modern human. The Almas are regarded by some of the Russians as remnants of the Neanderthals. This explanation has also been suggested for the North American creature, Bigfoot.

Bigfoot

The North American counterpart to the Himalayan Abominable Snowman and the Central Asian Almas is the creature called Bigfoot in the United States and Sasquatch in Canada. Creatures identified as Bigfoot but not always having the same characteristics have been sighted in most states of the United States and most provinces of Canada. By far the largest number of

Bigfoot is known primarily by a number of footprints and sightings.

sightings and footprint reports come from northern California, Oregon, Washington, and British Columbia. Some of these accounts have proven to be sightings of escaped circus apes or other animals such as bears. In other cases, mountain men have been mistaken for the beast. In 1964 for example, George Warren, a prospector, was mistaken for Bigfoot in California. He weighed over 200 pounds, stood over 6 feet tall, wore a knee-length bearskin coat, which he seldom took off because his dog would fight it if he did, and he left large tracks with his size $11\frac{1}{2}$ foots. Warren came out of the hills and identified himself as a mountain man once he learned that the towns people of the area were hunting with guns for a monster in the hills (Anonymous 1964). Some accounts of Bigfoot have been outright hoaxes. In 1970 Joe Metlow, a prospector, claimed to have captured a Bigfoot in an abandoned mine shaft. Later he claimed he had a Bigfoot foot in his sister's freezer. He was unable to produce either (Hunter and Dahinden 1973:153–158). Other accounts can be dismissed less easily.

The zoologist Ivan T. Sanderson (1961) believed that unknown hominids like Bigfoot did exist, for two reasons: (*a*) there is a large number of eyewitness reports and (*b*) the serious reports of these creatures come only from montane areas to which the creatures could have migrated or where they could have evolved from earlier mammalian types.

Certainly for Bigfoot there have been numerous sightings and reports of tracks.[3] John Green, a newspaperman and Bigfoot

---

[3] For some curious reason the sightings of the animal have occurred primarily in Canada, while most of the tracks are reported from the United States.

Plaster cast of alleged Bigfoot print. (Wide World)

hunter, has published almost 500 reports in a recent book; and several Bigfoot newsletters have served as clearinghouses for sightings and reports of tracks, among them "Bigfoot Bulletin" (of which 26 issues were published) and "Manimals Newsletter," begun in 1972 when publication of "Bigfoot Bulletin" ended. As publicity about Bigfoot grew, the number of reports of tracks or sightings showed a tremendous increase. John Green's publication (1973) of what he considers the most reliable of the reports shows an increase from 14 sightings prior to 1900 to 18 between 1900 and 1925, to 38 between 1926 and 1950, to 57 between 1951 and 1960, to 266 between 1961 and 1969. He had collected 94 reports for the period from 1970 to 1972 before his book was published. Sanderson and Green, as well as other Bigfoot enthusiasts, believe that there is "something" out there because there have been too many sightings for there not to be. Green and others also raise an important question: What motive would all of these people have in lying about what they saw? Certainly some opportunists have invented stories for profit and publicity but the majority are accounts by honest people who have usually faced ridicule and in some cases even the loss of their jobs for revealing their experiences concerning Bigfoot sightings.

Perhaps a clue is provided by the folklorist Bacil Kirtley, who emphasizes one function of our human myth. He writes (1964:87–88):

> Have the multitude of witnesses who have described their meetings with man-beasts deliberately lied? Not necessarily. It would seem rather that their memories, translating experiences which perhaps were baffling and disturbing, short-circuited from the empirically defined mental world of normative reality into the realm of myth, an ideational sphere in which delusion and not deception rule.

Our perception is influenced by our conceptual framework. The folk anthropologist believes in Bigfoot, or is at least willing to accept the possibility of the creature's existence, and therefore any unexplainable phenomenon is explained as Bigfoot. The professional anthropologist generally does not accept the existence of such a creature. Bigfoot cannot easily exist within his or her currently held view of human diversity. As a result the professional interprets the unexplainable phenomenon as something other than Bigfoot.

Sanderson's belief that sightings have occurred only in montane areas is a less convincing reason for accepting the existence of unknown hominids than his first reason. While many reports of these creatures do actually come from montane areas, there are similar kinds of reports from other parts of the world as well, including the tropical islands of the Pacific. What the stories do seem to have in common is that the creatures are thought to exist in remote places. Humans have believed in monsters from at least the beginnings of recorded time, and since the monsters are never found, they are thought to live in remote areas. The mass media have perpetuated this belief by creating movies and television programs that depict the monster being discovered on some lost island or in the interior of the Amazon jungle or on some remote mountaintop. Certainly much of what has been written and told of Bigfoot falls into either the realm of folklore or that of hoax (for which the term *fakelore* has been coined). What then is the evidence in support of the existence of this creature?

There have been sightings, photographs, and casts made of the footprints, and they are difficult to dismiss completely. First, there are many of them. Second, they occur in remote, hard-to-reach areas where it would be difficult to bring in some type of machine to make the tracks if a hoax was involved. Third, the tracks show such a wide step that a normal human would find it impossible to duplicate. Fourth, the tracks seem to show that the makers of the prints have stepped over large logs and boulders without losing their stride, which a human could not do. John Napier, the physical anthropologist, has been especially impressed with the authenticity of one set of prints from Bossburg, Washington, that show a crippled foot (Napier 1972:123).

The American anthropologist Grover S. Krantz has analyzed plaster casts of two handprints and a number of casts of footprints attributed to Bigfoot (Krantz 1971, 1972a, 1972b). Krantz more strongly than Napier accepts the probability of some of the tracks being made by some type of gigantic hominids. On the basis of his measurements of Bigfoot casts, Krantz (1972a:101) observes:

> In general, the sasquatch foot differs from man's in having greatly enlarged ankle bones, especially the heel, very short metatarsals, and a more nearly equal set of toes. These characteristics are all logical requirements for an otherwise human foot adapted to a body weight of 500 pounds or more. These characteristics are also evident in preserved footprints.

After weighing the evidence for the tracks being made by gigantic subhuman primates or being faked, Krantz (1972a:103) concludes:

> There are a number of reasons to believe that at least certain sasquatch tracks could not have been made by hoaxers. Their obscure

locations would mean that perhaps a hundred times as many tracks were laid as have been discovered. Lengths of stride and obstacles stepped over often surpass anything a man can do. Depths of imprints would require a hoaxer to carry many hundreds of pounds of extra weight, thus making the walking accomplishments even more impossible. Independent toe movements as noticed in some tracks would require a special device to accomplish.

To all these must now be added the fact that our supposed hoaxer is an expert on human anatomy with a very inventive mind. He was able to create from nothing all the details of how a foot might be redesigned to support a body weight several times that of a man. And he has continued to plant these tracks over more than a lifetime, always showing only vague hints of these anatomical pecularities. These include great width of heel, a double ball, and a straighter row of similarly sized toes.

No matter how incredible it may seem that the sasquatch exists and has remained uncaught, it is even more incredible to believe in all the attributes of the hypothetical human track-maker. As Sherlock Holmes put it, ". . . when you have eliminated the impossible, whatever remains, however improbable, must be the truth." Even if none of the hundreds of sightings had ever occurred, we would still be forced to conclude that a giant bipedal primate does indeed inhabit the forests of the Pacific Northwest.

Besides numerous sightings and tracks, there are two other controversial pieces of evidence. One is the story told by a retired logger, Albert Ostman, from Fort Langley, British Columbia, who claims to have been held captive in a cave by four creatures for several weeks in 1924. He waited until 1957 however to make his story public, on the grounds that no one would have believed him at the time of his experience.

While on vacation searching for a lost gold mine, Ostman was carried off from his camp in a sleeping bag by a large male Bigfoot and taken to a cave. Living there were four Bigfoot: the adult male who had captured him, an adult female, a boy, and a girl. Ostman finally escaped by tricking the adult male into swallowing a tin of tobacco (Hunter and Dahinden 1973:52–62). Some writers have accepted this story as factual. Napier (1972:77) suggests that there appears to be nothing in Ostman's description of the creatures and their behavior patterns that seems false. However, one point makes Napier somewhat leery of the story. According to Ostman's description, the group must have weighed collectively over 2000 pounds. Yet Ostman mentions hardly any food collected. He supposedly witnessed the "mother" and "son" return to the cave with grass, spruce and hemlock tips, and tubers. The adult male brought in no food, unless it was Ostman himself. As Napier (1972:78) observes:

> Grasses and spruce tips, rich though they may be in protein, hardly seem an adequate diet for a bio-mass of close on 18 cwt. It

might be expected that massive creatures of vegetarian habits would receive vast quantities of low-energy foods, the collection of which would occupy each individual's entire waking hours; yet from Ostman's story this type of food-gathering does not seem to have been taking place.

The second controversial evidence of Bigfoot is the somewhat blurred film made in October 1967 by Roger Patterson near Bluff Creek, California, mentioned at the beginning of the chapter. In a clearing, Patterson and his partner saw a 7-foot, humanlike creature covered with short black hair. They estimated its weight at approximately 500 pounds. It was apparently a female with pendulous breasts. Patterson had a movie camera with him and filmed the creature for a short time until it disappeared in the woods (Hunter and Dahinden 1973:114). It was shown at movie theaters around the country and on television (Kirkpatrick 1968:43). The Bigfoot enthusiasts have accepted the film as convincing proof of the existence of Bigfoot. A few scholars have accepted the possibility of its authenticity but remain skeptical. D. W. Grieve, a British biomechanic who has analyzed the film has concluded that its authenticity may rest on one important fact—the camera speed at which the footage was shot. If it was taken at 16 or 18 frames per second Grieve believes it is probably authentic, because the gait of the creature would be different from humans. However, if it was taken at 24 frames per second, the gait of the creature would be almost identical to that of a man in an ape costume (Napier 1972:220). Unfortunately the question of the camera speed will never be resolved, as Patterson claimed not to know what speed the camera was set at and died before any further light could be shed on the problem. Other scientists doubt its authenticity. On the basis of his own numerous viewings of the film and on the basis of Grieve's analysis, Napier (1972:89–95) finds that the film presents at least one important contradiction. The size of the creature in the film does not accord with the measurements of the footprints later taken by Patterson. According to Napier either the film or the footprints has to be fake, or perhaps both were fake. Napier maintains that there is no way that both could be authentic. Krantz (in a personal communication) disagrees with Napier's conclusion. Krantz believes the size of the footprints and that of the creature in the film match perfectly. Napier's conclusion is based on the assumption that the Bigfoot creature had a foot-to-stature ratio of 1:6.6 (Napier's own ratio), which according to Krantz's interpretations it did not (Krantz (1972*b*).

In summary, the evidence for Bigfoot is inconclusive. In spite

Patterson's film proportedly of Bigfoot, is still considered inclusive evidence.

Rock and canvas bunker constructed for viewing Bigfoot in an area where Bigfoot has been reported, near Dalles, Oregon. (Wide World)

of numerous sightings and tracks, none has been captured. There have been several expeditions to search for Bigfoot, some well financed with helicopters, snowmobiles, and other modern technology but no Bigfoot has turned up. Some of these expeditions have proven to be fiascos, such as one sponsored by Tom Slick, the Texas oilman who also sponsored the Abominable Snowman expeditions to the Himalayas. Convinced that the Bigfoot expedition needed a sexual lure, Slick first thought of chaining a female human to a tree as bait. Abandoning this idea he proceeded with a new plan that involved sneaking into women's rest rooms at service stations and retreiving any used sanitary napkins deposited there, which he then nailed to trees. There were also attempts to lure the creature with food. Everything from sandwiches to fried eggs were placed all over the countryside, attached to trip-wires connected to Brownie box cameras (Hunter and Dahinden 1973:89). But all of this effort has thus far been to no avail.

Scientists are leery of becoming involved in the Bigfoot controversy for several reasons. The professional anthropologist who takes Bigfoot seriously does so only by rejecting the anthropological framework within which he or she has been trained. This is a difficult course of action and would involve much the

same kind of soul-searching that a person might undergo in rejecting the religion that he or she was brought up in. The names
of only three anthropologists appear frequently in the controversy. One of them, John Napier, was attracted to the Bigfoot
problem by a fascination with Eric Shipton's 1951 photograph
of a Yeti footprint. Another physical anthropologist, Grover
Krantz of Washington State University, has seen tracks on two
occasions in the state of Washington and has published three articles on his analysis of them. Finally, Donald Abbott, an archaeologist of the British Columbia Provincial Museum, has examined a number of Bigfoot tracks and has attempted to develop a
model of Bigfoot feeding habits based on the life-style of the wolverine.

A second reason that most professional anthropologists have
not become involved in the controversy is that the evidence in
favor of Bigfoot remains circumstantial. Even Napier, who accepts Bigfoot's existence, admits that the evidence is all "soft,"
but he feels it *is* evidence and cannot be ignored (Napier
1972:205). However, if we assume there is something to the soft
evidence, then we are faced with two further problems: an ecological one and an anatomical one.

From what is understood of living primates and their relationship to their environments, a creature the size of Bigfoot could
not survive in the environment in which it is found. It would require much more food than the environment could supply. The
largest of the known primates, the male mountain gorilla, which
weighs 450 pounds in the wild, spends 8 to 12 hours each day
eating. The environment in which the mountain gorilla lives
provides food all year round. Bigfoot has been reported mainly
in the rugged coniferous forest of the Northwest. While there are
obviously enough food sources for a creature of an estimated 800
pounds to exist through the summer months, because bears of
that size inhabit the area, the winter resources of the environment are so lacking that a creature could not survive if our ecological theories are correct. It would have to migrate, which it
apparently does not do, or hibernate like a bear. Although some
Russian scholars accept the fact that it hibernates, there have
been enough winter reports, especially of footprints in the snow,
to rule out hibernation. Although John Green accepts hibernation, his own records actually show 86 winter reports (Green
1973:63). Besides hibernation, the only other explanation of how
Bigfoot could survive through the winter months has been offered by the anthropologist Donald Abbott. He suggests that like
the wolverine, Bigfoot may store food during the summer
months in caches above the snow line, where the food would

freeze. Bigfoot could then consume the food during the winter months as food became scarce (Napier 1972:172).

Most anthropologists are reluctant to accept either the bearlike-hibernation or the wolverinelike-cache theory to explain the food habits of a creature that is supposed to be a primate. Before taking Bigfoot seriously, anthropologists want to have a model of food gathering that would fit better with what is known of the behavior of all other primates.

The anatomical problem concerns the taxonomic position of Bigfoot in the overall classification of living forms. If Bigfoot exists, where did it come from? Is it related to human beings? Lacking any "hard" evidence such as skeletal data, it is difficult to attempt an answer. Most explanations of Bigfoot's origin start with a basic assumption about Bigfoot—that it is the remnant population of some earlier humanlike form or fossil ape that has managed to survive in remote corners of the world. Three early forms in particular are suggested as the possible ancestor of Bigfoot: *Gigantopithecus*, *Homo erectus*, or Neanderthal.

John Green (1973:65) considers Bigfoot to be a direct descendant of the Asiatic fossil ape *Gigantopithecus* (Figure 11). Unfortunately it is difficult to compare the creatures, because there is no Bigfoot skeletal data and *Gigantopithecus* is known only by a number of large teeth and several lower jaws. When the first large teeth were discovered in 1935 it was assumed that the creature must have been of giant size. Recent discoveries in India of four additional jawbones dated at over 5 million years ago confirm that *Gigantopithecus* was a massive ape, perhaps 9 feet in height and weighing 600 pounds. While Napier (1972:176–179) does not consider *Gigantopithecus* a likely ancestor to Bigfoot, Krantz believes that the two creatures could be quite similar.

Homo erectus has been offered as another possible candidate for the ancestor of Bigfoot, and the Yeti as well. Those who consider *Homo erectus* the predecessor assume that this fossil type originated in Asia and later migrated to the New World. There is nothing in the reconstructed fossil evidence to suggest that *Homo erectus* was ever any larger than the average modern human—much less a giant. Its posture and style of walking did not differ from modern humans to any great degree. There is no fossil evidence to suggest large feet. Therefore, if Bigfoot were the contemporary descendant of *Homo erectus*, biological change would have been considerable. Also, the cultural advances of *Homo erectus* over *Australopithecus* would have been

Was the ancestor of Bigfoot *Gigantopithicus*, *Homo erectus*, or Neandethal?

Figure 11 An artist's conception of what *Giganto-pithecus* may have looked like. (By permission of R. F. Zallinger.)

lost somewhere along the line. It is difficult to explain how a human form such as *Homo erectus* would have lost such important knowledge as fire making, tool manufacturing, and big game hunting, which the archaeological evidence shows were a part of *Homo erectus'* life (Napier 1972:183).

Neanderthal (*Homo sapiens neandertalensis*) is perhaps the most frequently cited ancestor for Bigfoot. Yet Neanderthal is the least likely candidate. Only if we believe that Neanderthal was like the incorrect Boule reconstruction that caused so much confusion even in professional anthropology, can we even consider Neanderthal as a possibility. The folk anthropologist generally has not been aware that professional anthropology has changed its view of what Neanderthal was like. Folk anthropology still operates with the erroneous view that Neanderthal was a burly, brutish, hairy creature that walked with bent knees, being incapable of true upright posture. However, as was shown in the previous chapter, this impression was based on an inaccurate reconstruction. Today many professional anthropologists find Neanderthal so similar to modern humans that Neanderthals are put in the same genus and species. Because Neanderthal was more culturally advanced than *Homo erectus,* it is difficult to imagine how such an advance could have been lost over time. Given the remote possibility that a small population of Neanderthals could have survived, there is no reason to expect they would look different than modern humans.

Perhaps the most conclusive evidence against Neanderthal as ancestor of Bigfoot comes from Neanderthal footprints left in clay that have been found in Europe. These impressions of Neanderthal feet show a foot not much different from that of a modern human. The big toe is slightly larger and the foot is wider than that of modern humans, but the footprint is nowhere near the size of the Bigfoot prints that have been discovered (Napier 1972:189–190).

The most important reason that Bigfoot accounts have not received serious attention from professional anthropologists is that they conflict too greatly with the human myth. Over many years the discipline of anthropology has developed a theoretical framework within which human diversity is understood and explained. This framework is not a static one: Changes in our perception of humankind have been made. But to accept Bigfoot as part of our reality, professional anthropologists would have to reject all they have learned about humans during the past hundred years of anthropological research. Considering the circumstantial nature of the evidence for Bigfoot, this would be asking a great deal of anthropological science. Until there is hard evidence to support the existence of Bigfoot, professional anthropologists really have little choice but to accept our current understanding of human diversity and take a wait-and-see attitude about Bigfoot. We would gain little by rejecting our perception of humankind without a more adequate one to replace it. Let us examine the current anthropological perception of human diversity.

Human Diversity

In the previous chapter it was shown how fossil humans evolved into *Homo sapiens sapiens.* While the relationship between modern humans and Neanderthal is anything but clear, it was suggested that Neanderthal generally represented an earlier population than ancient modern humans. If small groups of the western European Neanderthal had remained isolated from the mainstream of human evolution, it is likely that they would have been absorbed into the more advanced population through miscegenation (interbreeding). As a result, anthropologists believe that all living forms of humans are part of the species *sapiens*, although there is a great range of variation within human populations. As the anthropologist Marvin Harris (1975:95) has observed, "When our ancestors finally crossed the threshold to fully human status they made the unity of *Homo sapiens* inevitable and unbreakable. There is only one human species, and no longer are there any parts of the world inhabited by hominids whose nature is less human than the rest." We will see in the next chapter how certain kinds of selective pressures and adaptations have brought about the physical diversity of humanity that does exist.

Anthropologists believe that all living forms of humans are of the same species.

Perhaps the fact that all of humans share basic physical similarities is less important for our conclusion that there is only one form of human than are the tremendous cultural changes that begin with ancient modern humans of the Upper Paleolithic, about 40,000 years ago. With the advent of *Homo sapiens sapiens* the archaeological record shows rapid technological growth. Perhaps it was a chain of intertwined cultural and biological factors that set off this advance. If recent research on the development of language is correct, modern humans were the first to use language in the sense that we know it today. Yet this use of language was possible only after certain anatomical changes occurred in the throat. Following the development of language, cultural change happened swiftly. Ideas were exchanged more rapidly from group to group. Cultural traditions were born that were then transmitted from generation to generation. In many ways cultural adaptations began to replace the biological ones. Cultural means of adaptation are, of course, unique to humans. For example, the Indians of the Amazon Basin did not evolve new digestive tracts in order to eat poisonous bitter manioc, but rather they developed complex cultural techniques for removing the deadly prussic acid from the root of the plant to make it edible. This kind of cultural development has allowed *Homo sapiens sapiens* to survive in environments in which they otherwise would have been biologically unfit. The reports of Bigfoot show evidence of neither language nor culture. Therefore, if Bigfoot exists there is little likelihood that it is closely related to humans.

There is no evidence that Bigfoot has culture.

Anthropology Vocabulary

Abominable Snowman	feral individuals	wild individuals
Almas	*Homo monstrosus*	Yeti
Bigfoot	Sasquatch	

Review Questions

1. How would the discovery of a Bigfoot change our notions of human evolution?
2. What do beliefs about the Abominable Snowman and Bigfoot share with the earlier beliefs in monstrous forms?

Recommended Reading

Burridge, Kenelm, 1973, *Encountering Aborigines—A Case Study: Anthropology and the Australian Aboriginal.* New York: Permagon Press. An interesting study showing how early anthropologists' concept of aborigines as the world's most primitive human colored their perception of these people.

Dudley, Edward, and Maximillian E. Novak, eds., 1972, *The Wild Man Within: An Image in Western Thought from the Renaissance to Romanticism.* Pittsburgh: University of Pittsburgh Press. A collection of aricles on the Western view of the American Indian and other forms of "wild people."

Green, John, 1973, *The Sasquatch File.* Agassiz, British Columbia: Cheam Publishing Ltd. Primarily a collection of eyewitness accounts of sightings and reports of footprints. It is of interest because of the number of conflicting reports it contains as to what Bigfoot looks like.

Hunter, Don, and René Dahinden, 1973, *Sasquatch.* Toronto: McClelland and Stewart Ltd. This book is an account of Dahinden's search for Bigfoot. It includes a great deal of information on the personality conflicts that have existed between the Bigfoot hunters.

Kirtley, Bacil F., 1964, "Unknown Hominids and New World Legends," *Western Folklore* 23:77–90. A folklorist who refutes Sanderson's book by regarding all accounts of monstrous races as legend.

Malson, Lucien, 1972, *Wolf Children and the Problem of Human Nature.* New York: Monthly Review Press. A discussion of the significance of wolf-children, including an account of Victor, the wild child of Aveyron.

Napier, John R., 1972, *Bigfoot: The Yeti and Sasquatch in Myth and Reality.* London: Jonathan Cape. A professional's attempt to synthesize the data on the Abominable Snowman and Bigfoot from a scientific point of view. Highly recommended.

Sanderson, Ivan T., 1961, *Abominable Snowmen: Legend Come to Life.* Philadelphia: Chilton. A zoologist's attempt to classify monstrous forms into four types.

4

What has anthropology learned about race?

Notions of racial differences are based on cultural and biological differences, which are often confused with each other.

Anthropologists now use a nonracial approach to human biological diversity.

"Race" and "intelligence" are two concepts that anthropologists are cautious about.

ince 40,000 BC, only modern humans (*Homo sapiens sapiens*) have populated the face of the earth; other human forms such as *Homo erectus* or Neanderthal no longer exist. Yet one can observe that living peoples do not look alike. Modern humans exhibit tremendous biological diversity. In this chapter the nature of human biological diversity as it applies to *Homo sapiens sapiens* will be examined, with special emphasis on the concept of "race."

Classifying Humans

As taxonomic classifications of living organisms became popular, some scholars of the eighteenth century made an important distinction between "species" and "varieties." Species were thought to be immutable prototypes created separately by God. They were the links in the Great Chain of Being. Varieties were different members of a single series, who differed in appearance because of the effects of conditioning factors such as climate and geography. The races of humans were considered varieties, not different species by many scholars (Gossett 1963:35). For example, in 1735 the great Swedish botanist Carolus Linnaeus divided humans into four varieties: American, European, Asiatic, and African.

Many eighteenth-century scholars considered races to be varieties rather than immutable species.

Linnaeus was concerned almost exclusively with assigning names to living organisms. He was not particularly interested in the theoretical bases of his taxonomic decisions. A contemporary of Linnaeus, Georges Louis Leclerc, conte de Buffon, attempted to explain the reason for the differences between varieties of humans proposed by Linnaeus. Buffon believed that species were changeable. In fact, Buffon had some inkling of evolution, but it was not explicitly stated in his writing. In distinguishing varieties of humans, Buffon introduced the term *race*. The distinguishing traits he used were skin color, stature, and bodily figure. He believed that humankind was of one species, which was originally homogeneous. As humans spread throughout the world, different populations were influenced by different climates, foods, living habits, diseases, and other factors, which over time led to the development of different races.

Johann Friedrich Blumenbach attempted a classification of humans into five varieties or races, in 1775. His terminology has been more popular than any other and has sometimes been codified into law. He divided humankind into Caucasians, Mongolians, Ethiopians, Americans, and Malays; or white, yellow,

Blumenbach's racial classification has been the most popular.

black, red, and brown. Blumenbach was the first to coin the word *Caucasian* to describe the "white" race.

While earlier classifications were extremely impressionistic, Blumenbach must be credited with introducing greater methodological rigor into the study of race. He compared numerous skulls, fetuses, hair samples, anatomical dissections, and illustrations. Unfortunately the scientific rigor of Blumenbach helped to establish a belief in the validily of race in the minds of both scholars and the general public.

Concepts of Race in the United States

Carolus Linnaeus. (Culver)

The physical anthropologist Ashley Montagu makes an important distinction between the social idea of race and the biological idea of race. As he points out (Montagu 1965:4), "These two separate concepts of 'race' need to be carefully distinguished from one another, for the one is general, popular, and widespread, and the other passes as scientific. Unfortunately, these two conceptions are usually confused with each other."

There has been confusion of social and biological concepts of race.

The biological idea of race is recent. Prior to the nineteenth century, Europeans envisioned the world as inhabited by people who differed socially or culturally: There were Christians and heathens; or slaves and slaveholders. But with Western expansion and the exploitation of small-scale societies, biological differences between groups of people became the primary rationale for imperialism. New myths were created which explained these differences.

The United States of the late eighteenth and early nineteenth centuries became a meeting ground of the world's major forms of humanity: the original Amerind[1] New World settlers, the European settlers and conquerors, the African slaves, and in later years the Chinese, who began to arrive on the West Coast. Like the Europeans, the Americans were curious about human diversity, but in the post-Revolution years, most assumed that humans were all of one kind, created by God. This point had been emphasized by Thomas Jefferson in the framing of the Declaration of Independence, with the passage "We hold these truths to be self-evident, that all men are created equal . . ." In Jefferson's day, these words meant that the signers of the Declaration of Independence agreed that all men had been *created*

---

[1] *Amerind* is a contraction of *American Indian* and is used in anthropology as a short term to distinguish the American Indian from West Indians of the Caribbean and East Indians from India.

equal. It was not merely a question of equal rights or equal opportunities. It was an acceptance of equality derived from the Biblical account of Creation.

Toward the end of the eighteenth century, two possible explanations of human diversity appeared. One point of view, taken by Samuel Stanhope Smith, professor of moral philosophy at the College of New Jersey, was that humans were of a single origin, a single species, and that the variations that appeared were merely varieties resulting from different climatic conditions. This point of view became known as *monogenism.* In 1787 Smith published his *Essay on the Causes of the Variety of Complexion and Figure in the Human Species.* Smith and other monogenists based their concept of species on John Hunter's (1775) criterion for differentiating species, the inability of different species to interbreed. They noted that various forms of humans were able to interbreed. Therefore, they reasoned, all humans must form a single species.

Monogenism attributed variations in the human species to the influence of climate.

Smith felt that biological differences could be explained by what he considered the ordinary laws of nature. Skin color, for example, was due to the effect of climate. He reasoned that since the sun causes freckles, the dark skin of the black was a kind of giant freckle. As proof that the sun was responsible for dark skin, Smith presented the case of Henry Moss, a black slave who at the age of 38 began to turn white-skinned and grow straight hair. The Moss case was taken as conclusive proof of the influence of the sun on the skin[2] (Stanton 1960:4–6).

While Smith deemphasized anatomical differences, he admitted different mental or cultural characteristics. It was Smith's belief that humans had been created with civilization. The state of the black's "savagery" was a result of degeneration. Blacks had forgotten the arts of civilized life (Stanton 1960:8).

Monogenism seems to have been popular because it did not conflict with the teachings of the Bible as traditionally interpreted. Yet there were other scholars who did not accept the orthodox account of Creation. They believed that there were several species of humans, each specially created. This point of view became known as *polygenism.* One of its earliest advocates was the English surgeon Charles White. In 1799 he published *Account of the Regular Gradation in Man.* White attempted to correlate human variation with the Great Chain of Being and saw the black as an intermediate form between the white and the ape. Relying on questionable evidence from travelers, White presented a number of anatomical differences he believed to exist between blacks and whites as proof that they were sepa-

Polygenists believed in the special creation of different species.

---

[2] Actually, Moss seems to have suffered from a disorder known as vitiligo.

rate species. In each case, the characteristic of the black was seen by White as closer to that of the ape than to that of the white person.

Like the monogenists, White attempted to reconcile his interpretation with the Bible. He pointed out that Adam and Eve had no daughters, so there must have been other people in existence whom the Bible did not mention; Cain had married *someone*.

Perhaps neither argument was really convincing to readers of the time. What was still lacking were concrete scientific data on racial differences. Both Smith's case and White's rested heavily on a single example or on second-hand stories. At the time, the issue of human diversity was still seen as only slightly related to the issue of slavery.

A number of individuals began to develop new techniques for comparing individuals, based on measurements. The most important work to result from these new approaches was a book entitled *Crania Americana*, published in 1839 by a Philadelphia physician and professor of anatomy, Dr. Samuel George Morton. Morton's careful measurements of skulls gave the false appearance of valid information. At the time, no one questioned whether the measurement from one point on the skull to another point really had any significance. Although it did not, Morton's work is important because it was an attempt to get beyond the simple aesthetic judgments of earlier writers by substituting mathematical measurements. With *Crania Americana*, Morton established himself as the father of American physical anthropology and a leading figure in the so-called "American school" of anthropology, a major center of polygenist theory.

> Morton introduced measurements into the study of race.

The concept of race had changed a great deal in little over a century. Since Linnaeus' completely arbitrary classification of humans, the notion of separate races had become an established "fact." The belief that measurements of skulls could prove the existence of separate races was now taken for granted. While debate continued over the ultimate origin of races and their actual number, the underlying assumption that races actually existed was no longer questioned, and humanity was no longer viewed as biologically one. Somewhat surprisingly, the polygenism of Morton and his followers never appealed to the southern slaveholders. Stanton (1960) suggests it was rejected by many southerners because it was considered heresy.

While followers of monogenism and polygenism may have disagreed about the ultimate origin of humanity, they could both conceive of the other races, especially the black, as inferior to the white. As John Haller, Jr. (1970:1323) has observed:

Samuel George Morton. (The Granger Collection)

Inferiority was a permanent stain on the race and marked the Negro for slave status [according to the polygenists]. But the monogenists, despite their insistence on environmental change through time, were no more favorable to the Negro, except in their remote theoretical stance. For all practical purposes, the monogenists accepted the known race stocks as "fixed" as a result of centuries of in-breeding. Change in the Negro's status, if it was to take place, would require undetermined generations and influences. Hence, almost the whole of scientific thought in both America and Europe in the decades before Darwin accepted race inferiority, irrespective of whether the races sprang from a single original pair or were created separately. Whether for or against slavery, anthropologists could not escape the inference of race subordination, either in the monogenistic degeneracy theory of Blumenbach or the polygenistic stance.

It was primarily in the writings of some of the abolitionists, such as Frederick Douglass, that attempts were made to demonstrate the equality or even superiority of the black, by claiming that the ancient Egyptians had been black and by publicizing examples of the creativity and accomplishments of black people. For example, Moncure D. Conway (1863) claimed that the most original scientific intellect that the South had produced was the black Benjamin Banneker, a self-taught astronomer who had corrected some of the errors of the greatest astronomers of his age. However, the views of these abolitionists were in the minority. The notion of black inferiority had become so prevalent by the Civil War that the Lincoln administration attempted a number of programs to relocate freed blacks in other countries after the war, on the assumption that whites and blacks could never live together (Olien 1977).

With the new theoretical framework advanced in Darwin's *On the Origin of Species*, the polygenism-monogenism debate no longer interested scientists: An evolutionary perspective was introduced into the study of societies. If organisms could evolve so too could societies. In the wake of Darwin's theory of natural selection came "social Darwinism," which used the theory of natural selection as proof of the prevalent belief that some races were superior to others.

Social Darwinism used the theory of natural selection to support the idea of superior races.

Social Darwinism was a collection of assumptions about society and human behavior that were in part analogous to Charles Darwin's biological theories. They were assumptions which Darwin himself never expressed, but rather are found in the writings of other nineteenth-century scholars who were impressed with Darwin's work. Darwin's notion of natural selection was translated into a struggle between individual members of a society, between members of classes of a society, between different nations, and between different races. The conflict that these writers described was seen as anything but evil. Instead it was thought to be nature's indispensable method for producing superior individuals, superior notions, and superior races (Gossett 1963:145). One of the leading proponents of social Darwinism was the English sociologist Herbert Spencer.

Spencer believed in the necessity of "progress" in the evolutionary process. In a book entitled *Social Statics* that was published in 1855, several years prior to *On the Origin of Species,* Spencer argued that individuals should be allowed to make fatal mistakes, because then stupid and inefficient persons would be gradually eliminated and the human species would be that much improved. For example, Spencer felt that if an individual is so ignorant as to consult a "quack" instead of a qualified physician and dies as a result, the species has been improved by his or her removal. Therefore, Spencer concluded, the government has a moral obligation not to interfere with a natural process by passing laws to protect the individual from misrepresentation and malpractice medicine (Kardiner and Preble 1965: 52). Likewise Spencer saw warfare between societies as necessary and useful in that inferior races would be killed off. Thus Spencer's beliefs served as a rationale for white Western imperialism. It was Spencer, and not Darwin, who first introduced the phrase commonly associated with the idea of evolution, "the survival of the fittest" (C. Darwin 1958:74).

Spencer's ideas of race differed from Darwin's concept of evolution on one very important point. Darwin believed that organisms change through accidental variations which turn out to have some sort of survival value and thus are perpetuated. Spencer, on the other hand, adopted a concept of change that had been advanced years earlier, the idea that *acquired* characteristics are inherited. Spencer thought that he himself had inherited small hands because his ancestors had been schoolmasters and had not engaged in manual labor, which would have enlarged their hands (Gossett 1963:151–152).

Besides the theories of Spencer there were many other concepts that appeared in the nineteenth century that were taken as proof of the existence of different races and of the superiority of some of these races. Many intellectuals were influenced by the popular "science" of physiognomy. Physiognomy used animal analogies in an attempt to determine the character of people on the basis of their physical characteristics. For example, blacks were classified as "stupid" by one of Morton's followers because he believed that blacks had longer "snouts" than other races of people; he compared them with the longest-snouted animals, which he believed to be the most stupid.

Other "proofs" of racial superiority and inferiority were introduced in the nineteenth century.

Physiognomy led to the development of another pseudo-science, phrenology, which stressed a relationship between the shape of the head and human character. Various areas of the skull were examined for their size and shape. Each area of the skull was thought to determine some aspect of character. The phrenologist believed that the most developed regions of a skull determined the dominant features of an individual's character. The phrenologist believed that he could detect areas of the skull that determined evil, secretiveness, firmness, and so on. Phrenology was then applied to races. The American Indian, for example, was characterized as not only inferior in intelligence but also hopelessly "savage." More and more attention was given to skull differences in the explanation of racial differences. In 1856 a French scholar, Gratiolet, proposed that the coronal suture of the skull of blacks closes at about the age of 13, thus preventing any further growth of the brain. He believed that the black child could be as intelligent as the white child until the approximate age of 13, and then his intellectual development would lag far behind. There was of course no scientific evidence to support Gratiolet's claim, yet in the United States his belief was used in the North as an argument against black education. It was assumed that any serious mental work attempted by a black would lead to a breakdown. The same argument was used later in anti-Chinese propaganda in California (Gossett 1963:72–75, 290).

Another version of racism is found in the writings of Sir Francis Galton, Charles Darwin's cousin, in his book *Hereditary Genius,* published in 1869. Galton developed the science of *eugenics,* which attempted to prove that geniuses came from "superior" human stock and that such things as feeble-mindedness and criminality were strongly influenced by heredity. In *Hereditary Genius* Galton used quantitative data to demonstrate that the great intellectuals of England came from a relatively small number of families that were closely related to one another. Galton hypothesized that heredity was of prime importance, whereas social and economic influence had a minimal affect on the individual's success or lack of success. For Galton, there were absolute hereditary differences between races. He believed that the blacks had very little ability. From American books he had read about black house servants, Galton (1891:338–9) concluded that great numbers of blacks were "half-witted." Galton was unaware that the blacks were actually engaging in a form of passive resistence to slavery called "quashee," in which black slaves consciously feigned being stupid and childlike in order to manipulate the slave owners and avoid extra work (Patterson 1967:170–181). The eugenics movement advocated greater production of children by the upper classes and fewer by the lower classes.

During the last half of the nineteenth century many countries were solidifying their national boundaries. It was an era of colonial expansion by Western countries; in the United States it was an era of immigration. While most of the pre–Civil War racism had been directed by whites against blacks and Indians, the new immigrants became subjected to a similar type of prejudice, as the concept of racial traits was extended from the "major races" to nationals of various countries. Cultural and linguistic differences were confused with biological differences.

Prejudices against immigrants resembled racism.

The new immigrants, primarily the Europeans in the East and the Chinese in the West, were willing to work for lower wages than the American laborers, and they were culturally and sometimes linguistically distinct. The Irish were described as "inherently deceitful and violent"; the Chinese, as "the most morally debased people on earth."

With the arrival of the European immigrant the rationale for the prejudices of the whites towards blacks and Indians was no longer adequate. The belief began to develop that not all whites were of equal superiority. Some whites were more advanced than others. In particular, different national origins were thought to produce biological differences between the whites. Since advocates of the superiority of specific national origin believed their own nation to be best, there was some disagreement as to which people were the most superior. Generally, those claiming to be superior stressed the superiority of one or another of the northern European peoples.

Works by American and English writers stressed the superiority of the Anglo-Saxons. To these writers the Anglo-Saxons were God's favored race. As the great colonizing race, it was the Anglo-Saxons' duty to expand their territorial possessions around the world. This notion in fact provided a rationale for United States participation in the Spanish-American War at the turn of the century. By 1915 the Ku Klux Klan was revived, on the belief that Anglo-Saxon civilization was being threatened by blacks and immigrants.

Two books were especially influential in the post–World War I era: *Essay on the Inequality of Races* and *Foundations of the Nineteenth Century*. A Frenchman, Count Arthur de Gobineau, published *Essay on the Inequality of Races* between 1853 and 1855. It was written as a defense of the French nobility. Gobineau was interested in why civilizations rose and fell. He found his answer in race mixture. He believed in three basic races: white (with the qualities of manhood, leadership, energy, and superiority); yellow (with the qualities of stability and fertility); and black (with the qualities of sensuality and artistic impulse). Civilization occurred when two races initially mixed. As civilization led to more and more mixing of "inferior blood" (yellow and black) with that of the ruling race (white nobility), Gobineau believed that the white nobility was inevitably "bastardized" and decadence set in (Barzun 1965:54). Gobineau used his concept of race mixture to interpret history. For Gobineau all modern nations represented advanced stages of "mongrelization." He saw no hope for any nation where democracy had replaced aristocracy.

In Germany, Gobineau's theories were reinterpreted as a basis for German nationalism. The operatic composer Richard Wagner was strongly impressed by Gobineau and modified Gobineau's ideas to fit his own notion of German history. Wagner believed it was not only the German aristocrats who exhibited Teutonic superiority, but *all* Germans. He agreed with Gobineau that German blood was not pure, but he disagreed with Gobineau that such a condition could bring about decline. All that was needed, Wagner believed, was to teach the German people to revere their Teutonic blood. It was not too late to avoid deterioration. As Thomas Gossett (1963:347) has noted, "Wagner exalted race to the status of a religion. He maintained that the Germans are a race superior to all others, that the German language is superior to other languages and is the direct reflection of German racial qualities, that music peculiarly expresses the German soul."

Yet it was Wagner's son-in-law, Houston Stewart Chamberlain, who carried German racism even further. Chamberlain's German fanaticism is all the more peculiar because he was born in England. He renounced his citizenship and became a citizen of Germany. In 1899 he published the two-volume *Foundations of the Nineteenth Century,* in which he rewrote history and created a new myth of racism. He believed that Christ was a Teuton and not a Jew because the ideas of Christianity were wholly consistent with those of the Teutonic peoples and inconsistent with those of the Jews. Likewise Chamberlain discovered Teutonic characteristics in the great men of other nations. Men like Marco Polo, Copernicus, and Galileo were in reality Germans, he claimed. He also attributed a person's better tendencies to Teutonic blood and thought that negative tendencies indicated Latin blood. For example, Chamberlain claimed that Louis XIV was Teutonic when he defended the liberties of French Catholics against Rome but non-Teutonic when he persecuted the Protestants. Chamberlain believed that race was internal and could not be studied by measurements of the skull, by skin color, and so on; instead one had to rely on intuition to determine a person's race (Gossett 1963:347–351). The works of Gobineau and Chamberlain are regarded as the spiritual progenitors of Adolph Hitler's *Mein Kampf* and the notion of *Herrenwolk*, or a master race. As John Oaksmith (1919:50) observed following World War I:

The essence of the racial theory, especially as exhibited by the writers of the school of Houston Stewart Chamberlain, is profoundly immoral, as well as unnatural and irrational. It asserts that by virtue of belonging to a certain 'race,' every individual member of it possesses qualities which inevitably destine him to the realization of certain ends; in the case of the German the chief end being universal domination, all other 'races' being endowed with qualities which as inevitably destine them to submission and slavery to German ideals and German masters. This essentially foolish and immoral conception has been the root-cause of that disease national egotism whose exhibition during the war has been at once the scorn and horror of the civilized world.

The writings of Gobineau and Chamberlain became important for American racists during and after World War I, when both books appeared in the United States in translated forms. Gobineau's work was accepted by the anti-immigrationists as important proof that the eastern and southern Europeans were diluting the superior Nordic race of the earlier American settlers. The writings of Chamberlain gave American racists the argument that a person's true race could be learned only from intuition, which needed no specific verification. Madison Grant's *The Passing of the Great Race*, published in 1916, was based on just those notions. He argued that the superior races of the United States were being overwhelmed by inferior immigrants.

Chamberlain provided a rationale for racists.

While individuals like Chamberlain and Grant were arguing that racial differences were best understood by intuition, there were others who felt that these differences could be accurately measured.

The Measurement of "Racial" Differences

As mentioned earlier, Samuel G. Morton's *Crania Americana* (1839) gave birth to the assumption that "racial" differences could be precisely measured and compared. Morton's comparisons focused on the size of the interior of the skull, or *cranial capacity*. Differences in brain size were inferred from differences in cranial capacity.

At the time that Morton was publishing his findings, a Swedish scientist, Anders Retzius, was developing a technique for comparing external dimensions of skulls. Retzius was interested in the relationship between Finns and Swedes. In 1842 Retzius published his findings, showing differences based on the measurement of the skull exterior. By dividing the length of the skull into the breadth and multiplying the quotient by 100 (to eliminate decimals), Retzius arrived at a figure he called the *cephalic index*. Long, narrow skulls with an index of 80 or less were called *dolichocephalic*, and short, broad skulls with an index of over 80 were termed *brachycephalic*. On the basis of this completely arbitrary measurement Retzius concluded that Finns and Swedes were racially different. The Finns were brachycephalic and the Swedes were dolichocephalic (Barzun 1965:39). The followers of Retzius continued to expand on his approach. By 1900 there were 5000 different ways that a single skull could be measured. The difficulty that all of the researchers encountered was the fact that the human skull is very irregular in shape and does not lend itself well to two-dimensional measurements. Two anthropologists seldom obtained the same figure in measuring the diameter of the same skull. Even worse, one anthropologist would frequently arrive at a *different* figure in a second measurement of the same skull (Gossett 1963:76). Other attempts at measuring "racial" differences included comparisons of human brains, the structure of hair, and types of body lice associated with particular races, among others.

The IQ test provides a new rationale for racism.

Perhaps the strongest arguments of the racists following World War I were based on a new kind of measurement, the mental test. There were various attempts to develop mental tests toward the end of the nineteenth century. The most influential test was that created in 1905 by Frenchmen Alfred Binet and Théodore Simon for the purpose of recognizing various degrees of feeble-mindedness. Ultimately the purpose of this test was changed, and it became the basis of the IQ (intelligence quotient) test.

Originally the Binet-Simon test established standards for different age groups; the concept "mental age" was used to indicate how a child might compare with other children of his or her own age. When the test was revised in 1908, "mental age" was measured in terms of the ability of a child to answer a group of questions which 75 percent of the children that age could answer. Binet and Simon recognized that environment and education would inevitably affect the achievement scores and therefore concluded that the tests would indicate the approximate intelligence only of those children who had closely similar environments (Gossett 1963:365).

Despite the warnings of Binet and Simon against interpreting tests as measuring hereditary intelligence without regard to environment, other scientists began doing just that. In 1912 the German psychologist William Stern introduced the notion of the "mental quotient," the comparison of one's mental age with one's chronological age. In 1916, in the United States, Lewis Terman and his associates published a revision of the Binet-Simon test known as the Stanford-Binet; they also coined the term *intelligence quotient* (abbreviated IQ). Psychologists and the general public became intrigued with the possibility of expressing a person's intelligence in absolute numbers, and the early Binet-Simon warnings about the effects of environment were forgotten (Montagu 1975:4–5). Furthermore, it was felt that the tests could determine innate differences which might exist in the intelligence of different races.

The tests began to show that the children of bank presidents, lawyers, and college professors did much better than the children of blue-collar workers. These results were interpreted as Galton might have interpreted them. It was inferred that good heredity was the key factor and that differences in social environments of children were insignificant. Without taking into account the effects of cultural and linguistic differences, Terman concluded that low test scores among blacks and among Spanish-Indians and Mexicans in the Southwest was due to racial dullness. He believed that the IQ test would discover significant racial differences. Terman suggested that such tests would demonstrate that many children were uneducable beyond the most rudimentary level of training and that no amount of school instruction would ever make them intelligent voters or capable citizens (Terman 1916:90–91).

In 1917 tests were employed on a massive scale in the military services. Because the military thought the tests could identify potential officers quickly, tests were given to more than 1,700,000 men coming into the armed services. Two tests were used, the "army alpha," which was the test generally used, and the "army beta," which was a nonlanguage test given to immigrants and illiterates. While the tests were given to measure intelligence, they did not really do so. There was considerable misinterpretation of the data. For many, the fact that blacks generally scored lower than whites "proved" the intellectual inferiority of the blacks. Since it was assumed that environ-

The IQ test has been misused in the United States.

Alfred Binet.
(The Granger Collection)

ment played no role in the test scores, it was concluded that the situation for blacks was a hopeless one. They were not capable of benefiting from improved education. Yet in spite of the racists' use of these scores for their own propaganda, there was one result that could not be explained simply through racial heredity. While blacks scored lower than whites in general, northern blacks scored higher than southern blacks, and even more importantly, blacks in 4 northern states scored higher than whites from 11 southern states (Gossett 1963:367–368; Montagu 1964:230). Obviously, the test scores were strongly influenced by cultural factors and socioeconomic conditions. These findings were of course played down by those who felt the tests demonstrated racial differences in intelligence.

The IQ tests are extremely biased in favor of the life experiences of the white urban population. While the tests have been thought by some to be culture-free, a number of studies have demonstrated that the tests are culture-bound. Sociologist Jan Mercer (Mercer and Brown 1973) has developed a list of cultural and social factors that allow her to account for IQ score differences between ethnic groups. She discovered that by giving weight to cultural barriers such as the absence of English in the home, to the person's test-taking behavior, and so on, she was able to account for differences between white, black, and Spanish-speaking groups of schoolchildren in average IQ scores. In fact, by adjusting scores in a standard way for each factor, she found that 99 percent of the differences among the three groups disappeared.

The IQ test is biased in favor of white, urban people.

Physical anthropologists Mark Weiss and Alan Mann (1975:389) recount the following story about a poor black child who was not performing well on an IQ test. It illustrates how differences in culture can affect IQ-test performance:

> His teacher, knowing the boy could do better, asked him: "If you had 50 cents and gave half to your friend, how much would you have left?" No answer. "I know you can figure this out. Why won't you answer?" The boy replied, "If I had 50 cents, I wouldn't give half to anyone." In white, middle-class American society, the question makes perfect sense, but in a culture built on poverty it is irrational. No wonder the poor don't perform well on an examination designed for middle-class society; they are from another society.

When IQ tests are devised on the basis of the life experience of ghetto children or those of various minorities, the ghetto and minority children do a great deal better than on the standard IQ test; at the same time, white, middle-class children exhibit very low IQ scores on these tests. In some cases, IQ test scores merely show differences in English language ability. For example, in San Francisco almost half of the Mexican-American schoolchildren who had been placed in classes for the "mentally retarded" were found to be of average or above-average intelligence when retested in Spanish (Herndon 1972: 96).

Despite the well-established racial, ethnic, and class biases of most intelligence tests, many teachers and school systems continue to use such tests as though they were valid instruments for the assessments of innate differences in mental endowment. The consequences of this continued acceptance of IQ tests by educators are often tragic. The tests create a self-fulfilling prophesy. When teachers learn the IQ scores of their students, this knowledge affects how many react to the children. Children with higher scores are considered to be brighter and are encouraged to do well in school, while those with low scores are often considered of limited intelligence and are discouraged from taking an active part in the learning process (Hodges 1974:404). According to Richard A. Graham (1968), head of the Teachers Corps, the typical school grading system plays a major role in institutionalizing the self-fulfilling prophesy created by the IQ tests. The grading system convinces students, their peers, and their parents that some children are unfit for education.

In the mid-1960s, standard IQ tests were administered to children in a predominantly lower-class elementary school in San Francisco. The children's teachers were informed—falsely—that certain children were "brighter" than others and that these children would learn more quickly than their less-gifted peers. The children were actually not the brightest, but rather were chosen randomly. On the average their IQs were equal to those of their classmates; but these children did much better than their peers—not because they were more intelligent, but because they were expected to perform better. They received the constant encouragement of the teacher that was denied the other students. Not only did the grades of these "brighter" students improve; so did their IQs—by an average of 24.4 IQ points in the span of a single school year (Hodges 1974:404). The teacher's attitude toward the schoolchild is often based on the child's IQ; the teacher's behavior affects the child's self-esteem, and self-esteem affects the child's performance in the school. IQ tests thus create a vicious cycle of failure for children with low scores.

IQ tests may measure certain genetic differences between individuals, but genetic factors cannot be distinguished from cultural factors. Likewise, there is no proof that IQ tests measure "intelligence." All that can be claimed for IQs is that they are the scores that individuals make on IQ tests. It cannot be assumed that the tests measure intelligence, that the ethnic groups to whom tests are administered are sufficiently comparable in life experiences to permit valid inferences to be drawn as to the quality of their intelligence, or that what IQ tests measure is to a large extent determined by genes (Montagu 1975:7).

Many of the popular beliefs about race that are held today have had their origins in the nineteenth century or earlier: that races exist, that some races are superior to others, that racial differences are primarily genetic and thus can be modified only slightly, and that racial differences can be scientifically measured. Scholarly interests in race have shifted from late-eighteenth-century questions concerning the significance of cultural and linguistic differences, with biological differences considered trivial; to an early-nineteenth-century interest in whether or not each race was specially created; to a late-nineteenth-century and twentieth-century interest in the superiority and inferiority of races.

Popular notions about race go back at least to the nineteenth century.

The concept that anthropologists took completely for granted was the one thing that required proof, namely that the concept of "race" corresponded to a reality that could actually be measured and verified. In other words, anthropologists accepted as true the belief that "in nature there exist groups of human beings comprised of individuals each of whom possesses a certain aggregate of characters which individually and collectively serve to distinguish them from the individuals in all other groups" (Montagu 1964:67).

How Many "Races" Are There?

During the first half of the twentieth century many anthropologists argued against the notions that some races were "superior" and that others were "inferior," and that race was the determinant of culture, but few anthropologists rejected the basic concept of race. As a result, much attention was given to attempts at classifying the various races. It is not surprising that there was little agreement in the classifications, since the basic assumption that there were races was fallacious to begin with.

There is little agreement over the number of races, because the concept of race is fallacious to begin with.

The early classifications of the eighteenth century grouped humans into a small number of varieties. Johann Blumenbach, for example, had proposed five categories: Caucasian, Mongolian, Ethiopian, American, and Malay. By the twentieth century, the classifications had become exceedingly complex. A number of races or subraces were identified, often on the basis of statistical differences in body measurements from one population to another. In 1900, for example, Joseph Deniker (1900) proposed a classification of 17 groups made up of 29 races and subraces.[3]

Some of the later classifications of the first half of the twentieth century had an even greater number of races and subraces. The lack of agreement among classifications was of course due to the nonexistence of races, in the biological sense. This does not mean that the concept of race as applied to humans has no social significance. In order to elaborate on this point it is necessary to distinguish the nature of these two concepts of "race," the biological and the social.

The Biological Concept of Race

The concept of biological race in organisms other than humans has had some taxonomic utility, but even some biologists[4] have been critical of the concept of race as applied to nonhuman animals. Both human and nonhuman species have been defined on the basis of the inability of two species to breed and produce fertile offspring. As mentioned earlier, humankind by this definition is considered a single species. This concept of "species" is at least 200 years old, appearing in the work of John Hunter in 1775, if not earlier. "Races" are thought to be some type of subgroupings within species. Races are capable of interbreeding, or they would constitute separate species. Biological concepts of race used in anthropology are of two kinds, the *typological* and the *genetic*.

> Biological races are conceived as either typological or genetic.

The Typological Definition of Race. The typological concept of race is the older of the two and is a direct outgrowth of classifications discussed earlier in this chapter. This concept of race is exemplified by the following definition (Coon, Garn, and Birdsell 1950): "A race is a population which differs phenotypically from all others with which it has been compared." This concept of race is generally nonevolutionary and lends itself to the belief that there are, or have been, certain "pure" races. Persons classified as Caucasian, Mongoloid, or Negro are more "pure" than persons classified as mulattoes (Caucasian-Negro admixture) or mestizos (Caucasian-Indian admixture) (Spuhler and Lindzey 1973:189).

> The typological notion of race reinforces the belief that there are "pure" races.

This typological concept of race has also led to the belief, both

---

[3] Deniker actually had a better understanding of the arbitrariness of racial classification than did many of his contemporaries or those who followed later.
[4] Cf. Calman (1949), Carter (1951), Wilson and Brown (1953).

in professional anthropology and in folk anthropology, that there are ideal types for each race; in other words, there is a Negro type, a Caucasian type, and so on, which can be readily identified. However, if one categorizes in terms of these stereotypes, one finds that real people do not conform very neatly to "types" (Bleibtreu and Meaney (1973:185). An interesting illustration of this point occurred when William Ripley was preparing his book entitled *The Races of Europe* (Ripley 1899). He wrote to the European physical anthropologist Otto Ammon, requesting a photograph of a "pure" Alpine type from the Black Forest. Ammon was unable to provide one, although 25 million Europeans had been subjected to anthropometric measurements, not one individual showed all of the characteristics of the type (Stocking 1968:58). Yet the popular notion persists that there are "typical" characteristics that members of races should exhibit. These notions have been perpetuated in the mass media. For many years, black actors were hired for movies only if they looked like the "typical" Negro; American Indians were seldom hired, because they did not look enough like the "typical" Indian.

The typological concept of race is a static one that does not allow for the normal process of evolution. While this concept of race remains the most popular in folk anthropology, it is no longer widely accepted in professional anthropology's human myth.

The Genetic Definition of Race. The other concept of race attempts to define race from an evolutionary point of view. Races are considered *Mendelian populations* (breeding populations) that change over time (Dobzhansky 1962:265). This concept of race emphasizes breeding populations that differ from one another in the frequencies of various genes. This concept of race makes it possible to understand why specific individuals do not seem to conform exactly to their racial "type."

> The genetic concept of race is based on closed breeding populations.

Individuals are members of populations: that is, they originate from a gene pool that has been established by a group which over the generations habitually exchanged mates. Such pools are "leaky" in that people immigrate and emmigrate [sic], yet at any one time an individual consists of a more or less random amalgamation of genes from that pool. Since there are thousands of loci in man and the possibility of multiple alleles [the different versions of a gene] at every locus, it is to be expected that, within a population, variation can be great. While the pool can be characterized in terms of gene frequencies and the population members can be described in terms of biological similarities, any one person will only represent a very small amount of the variation which could be expressed by the pool. [Bleibtreu and Meany 1973:185]

If one considers gene pools as races, one is faced with the problem that humans do not behave in the same way that other animals do when it comes to breeding patterns.

Humans are the only animals on the face of the earth that inhabit the entire globe yet remain a single species. In a family of insects, for example, there may be as many as 50,000 known species (Dillon 1973:288). The great number of species in families other than humans represent the process of *speciation*. In nonhuman forms, breeding populations may form truly closed gene pools. Races of the same species may become isolated from one another. Over time the frequencies of the genes in each gene pool may become so different—due to migration, mutation, natural selection, and genetic drift—that the races can no longer breed and produce fertile offspring. At this point what were previously the two races of a single species are considered to be two separate species.

The breeding populations of nonhumans are generally much easier to identify than those of humans. In humans, the populations have probably never formed completely closed gene pools. Any human is potentially capable of mating with any other human of the opposite sex and producing fertile offspring. Humans have always been highly geographically mobile. It is likely that mating has always taken place between human populations. Therefore any notions of originally "pure" races that have recently degenerated due to race mixing is incorrect. The populations that are identified as races have never been closed breeding populations. So-called "race mixture," then, is not a recent phenomenon but rather extends throughout the entire range of human history.

Nevertheless one can arbitrarily identify areas of the world where more genetic traits are shared within the populations than are shared with other populations. As the anthropologist Marvin Harris (1975:102) has noted, "Despite the internal variability of the major geographic races, it is usually easy to identify individuals drawn from European, African and Asian populations. Given a random sample of individuals from Europe, East Asia and Central Africa, one would make few mistakes in assigning them to the region of their birth. But if a random sample included individuals drawn from the remaining regions of the world, many mistakes would be made." Prior to Western expansion, as much as half of the world's population was settled in areas other than Europe, Central Africa, and East Asia, and individuals from these areas are not easily assigned to the so-called Caucasoid, Negroid, or Mongoloid races. These populations exhibit some traits of one of the major geographic races and

Subgroupings of humans do not form closed breeding populations.

some traits of others. Both professional and folk anthropologists have great difficulty assigning these individuals and populations to "races." They do not fit nicely into our stereotypes of races. Most of these races are classified on the basis of obvious phenotypic differences such as skin color, rather than less stereotyped genotypic differences.

Part of the problem of identifying races relates to the fact that human mating is not random. The choosing of one's mate involves sexual selection. While humans are not the only animals that have some sort of sexual selectivity, it is the most elaborate in humans. Most, if not all, societies have some form of incest taboo, which eliminates certain individuals, usually closely related ones, from serving as potential mates and marriage partners and thus prohibits close inbreeding. Incest taboos create the need to acquire mates from other groups.[5] Geographic proximity, social class, caste, religion, language, and phenotype, among other factors, have played a significant role in reducing the randomness of mating in humans.

The Nonracial Approach to Human Diversity

Because both the taxonomic and genetic approaches to race are based on at least partially arbitrary classifications, some physical anthropologists have suggested in recent years that the concept of race should be abandoned in the study of humans,[6] although not all physical anthropologists agree.[7] If the concept of race is rejected, are there alternative ways of looking at human biological diversity?

Perhaps the most interesting approach that has been suggested is one proposed by the physical anthropologist C. Loring Brace (1964a). Brace has pointed out that neither the use of "breeding population" nor "race," however defined, is sufficient for understanding the diversity exhibited in humans. Brace believes that an assumption that there is something significant in the fact that certain traits are shared by a single group of people obscures our understanding of the factors influencing the occurrence and distribution of any single trait. To understand human variation, one must study the selective pres-

[5] For a detailed discussion of the incest taboo in human matin   the reader is referred to Aberle, Bronfenbrenner, Hess, Miller, Schneider, and Spuiier (1963).
[6] See especially Livingstone (1962) and Brace (1964a and 1964b).
[7] See Lieberman (1968) for a discussion of the various points of view currently held.

sures which have operated to influence each trait separately. The selective pressures that operate on a particular trait often have no relationship to particular "races" or "breeding populations." According to Brace (1964a:108), "Human physical variation can be understood by relating the distributions of specific morphological features [biological characteristics] to the distribution and history (also the prehistory) of the relevant selective and adaptive forces."

It is possible to illustrate this nonracial approach to human diversity by actually analyzing the distribution of several morphological traits and the type of selective pressures that have affected them. Skin color, for example, is caused by melanin in the skin. Prior to the era of Western exploration, dark pigmentation was found only in the tropics of the Old World. Not everyone living in the tropics had dark skin: The inhabitants of Indonesia and northern South America did not have dark skin; but they were fairly recent migrants into the tropics, evolutionarily speaking.

Dark pigmentation seems to be a form of protection from the sun's rays for people who wear little if any clothing. Extensive melanin in the dead outer layer of the skin absorbs harmful ultra-violet radiation, stopping its penetration into the living skin. Solar radiation is especially strong in the tropics and could damage the living cells of the skin, resulting in skin cancer. Therefore, dark skin had survival value in open environments such as savannas, where persons born with lighter skin color would have been selected against. The jungle dwellers of Africa were a late adaption. Only after iron tools and specialized jungle crops were available were Africans able to settle in the jungle. These settlers of the jungle would have had dark skin before they moved into that ecological niche.

In other areas of the Old World tropics besides Africa, the earlier populations all seem to have had dark skin. Remnant populations in southern India, Ceylon, Malay, Andaman Islands, and the Phillippines are all darker in pigmentation than more recent populations that migrated into the tropics. Since humankind appears to have originated in the tropics of Africa, this distribution of pigmentation suggests that humankind's ancestors were dark in skin color. This view is of course a deduction made from the data. It will probably never be proved that this was the case, as it is highly unlikely, given the problems of preservation, that any *Australopithecus*, *Homo erectus*, or Neanderthal skin will ever be found. However, given the currently available information on fossil humans and the historic distribution of different

The nonracial approach emphasizes different selective forces operating on different characteristics.

Brace's theory assumes that early humans had dark skin.

pigmentation, this assumption seems the most valid.[8]

If we assume that early forms of humans had dark skin, then how do we explain the large number of individuals with light skin today? The answer is more difficult to discern from the data than the presence of dark skin in early humans. The archaeological and fossil data suggest that humans originated in the Old World tropics and were biologically and culturally ill equipped to survive in the colder northern environment. It was not until the third interglacial period that humans, *Homo sapiens neandertalensis*, moved northward as permanent settlers. Biologically, humans were still not much different from their ancestors, but culturally they had advanced to the point of being able to manufacture clothing from animal skins as protection from the cold. However, in doing so the survival value of dark skin was lost. With protective clothing it mattered little what color the skin pigmentation was. The genetic material controlling melanin production was free to vary, and the result was that mutations detrimental to melanin production occurred, creating depigmentation.

The degree of depigmentation in populations seems to indicate the length of time and the extent to which skin pigment has been reduced as an adaptive feature. The lightest pigmentation is found in people who can trace their ancestry back to northern Europe. The archaeological record suggests that the earliest use of clothing occurred in northern Europe.

The inhabitants of northern China and Mongolia are lighter than those of the tropics but not as light as those of northern Europe. Brace suggests that the ancestors of those living in northern China and Mongolia started relying on clothing later than the northern Europeans did. After depigmentation had occurred, populations of lighter-skinned peoples moved into tropical regions of the world such as India, Indonesia, the eastern Pacific, and the New World, thus accounting for the lighter-pigmented peoples also found in the tropics today.

If one considers only the distribution of skin color, it is difficult to see how Brace's approach differs from the racial approaches discussed earlier. The differences begin to appear as additional characteristics are analyzed. If one considers differences in shape of nose, body build, size of teeth, and so on, *each* of these characteristics is affected by different kinds of selective pressures than those which affect skin color. In other words, solar radiation has no affect on size of teeth, shape of

---

[8] This theory assumes that fossil hominids were more or less as hairless as modern people. If fossil hominids were covered with hair, then dark pigmentation would have had less or perhaps no survival value.

nose, and so on. The size of teeth is directly related to diet. Those people who have practiced farming for the longest period of time have the smallest teeth. Nonagricultural people or those who have acquired farming only recently have the largest teeth. Apparently, in hunting and gathering societies, people with small teeth were selected against. Agricultural life put less demand on dentition, and people with smaller teeth were no longer selected against. The shape of the nose, on the other hand, seems to be related to climate. A lengthened nasal passage has survival value in very cold and very dry climates. In cold weather it warms the air, and in dry climates it moistens the air.

While sufficient data is lacking to prove each and every one of Brace's interpretations conclusively, it is still possible to see the difference between his suggested approach and those that emphasize racial classifications. What Brace is able to demonstrate is that variations in traits are distributed according to the particular selective factors responsible for the expression of each trait and not because of race. As Brace (1964a:145) observes:

> Where the selective factors are related or happen to vary together, then the traits they influence will likewise vary together, but, as has been shown, it is commoner to see the selective forces and their corresponding traits varying more or less independently of each other and crossing geographical and population boundaries without regard to the supposed limits of human gene pools or areas of mating preference.

Brace's nonracial approach to human diversity allows one to understand why there is so much divergence within "races." It explains for example why there are blacks with a variety of body builds, different nose shapes, and so on. In a sense, Brace is reminding us of the discovery that Gregor Mendel made over a hundred years ago in his experiments with pea plants, the law of independent assortment, which states that each trait operates independently of other traits.

Social Race

In light of Brace's approach is it fruitful for anthropologists to continue racial studies? The answer is a definite yes, especially if we focus on the social significance of beliefs about race. People in many, if not all, societies recognize so-called "racial" differences. The types of differences recognized and the rationale for their existence vary from society to society. Thus concepts of race are of great importance to the cultural anthropologist. It is on the basis of how members of societies perceive one another

The rationale for race differs from society to society.

that they react to each other. Therefore the notion of race has great importance in understanding behavior. People are taught to perceive racial differences from the point of view of their own society. For example, in the United States we tend to dichotomize, grouping all persons of African heritage as "black" and all persons of European ancestry as "white." We recognize no intermediate categories, although mating between Europeans and Africans began as soon as the first slaves arrived. Yet seldom do we classify individuals as mulatto or some other form of intermediate. Individuals classified as mulattoes are considered to be in a subcategory of "black," in spite of the fact that the mulatto by definition has one white parent and one black parent. The extensive mating between blacks and whites in the United States is conveniently overlooked. Yet the studies that have been undertaken on miscegenation between blacks and whites in the United States between 1790 and 1950 have shown that 21 percent of all "whites" living in the United States in 1950 had African ancestry. This amounted to 28,366,000 persons. On the other hand, these same studies showed that 73 percent of all blacks in the United States in 1950 had non-African ancestry. This amounted to 10,980,000 persons being classified as black when in fact they were part white (Stuckert 1959). While the people of the United States acknowledge only the categories black and white and ignore any intermediate categories, other societies recognize various intermediate types. For example, the Brazilians recognize several hundred racial types (Harris 1970).

Not even the classification of who is white and who is black is as clear-cut as it may seem. In the United States, a person with the remotest black ancestry is classified as "black" once that ancestry has become known. The logic is reversed in much of Latin America, where an individual with the remotest white ancestry publicizes the fact in hopes of being classified "white."

Another aspect of social race that is of interest to the cultural anthropologist is its unfortunate relationship to patterns of discrimination and prejudice. In these patterns of discrimination and prejudice, one finds the "reality" of race. Because people act as if races exist, the notion of race cannot be ignored by the professional anthropologist. The anthropologist must attempt to understand the criteria by which members of the society he or she is studying perceive "racial" differences. In many societies it is skin color that is most important. For example, anthropologists have found that in many societies of dark-skinned individuals, light-skinned people are considered to be disgusting, and in some cases are even thought of as ghosts.

It is in the Western nations especially that racial differences have been interpreted from a hierarchical point of view, which served as an effective rationale for the exploitation of underdeveloped peoples during imperial expansion. In a sense, the notions of the Great Chain of Being and polygenism have remained with us, in the belief that some "races" are more advanced, are more evolved, or have been created superior to others. Perhaps the most ridiculous of these notions is that the "black race" is closer to the apes than is the "white race." The underlying assumption seems to be that blacks look more like apes than do the whites. But is this the case?

Both blacks and whites have black hair, therefore the fact that the chimpanzee and gorilla have black hair is not at all conclusive proof that blacks are more "apelike." The skin color of the apes varies from dark to lacking almost any pigmentation (Harrison and Montagna 1973:182–183). The black person has slightly longer lower extremities than do whites. In apes the lower extremities are shorter than in humans. In this characteristic, whites would be closer to apes. On the other hand, the upper extremities of the black are also longer than in whites. In this case the black more closely resembles the ape, because the upper extremities of the ape are longer than those of humans. In hairiness, hair form, thin lips, and other traits, whites resemble the apes more closely than do blacks. The point is that *both* blacks and whites share an apish ancestry (Montagu 1965:73–74, 78); and the units used for comparison ("blacks" and "whites") are themselves arbitrary constructs.

> Both blacks and whites share an apish ancestry.

Humans are unique in the animal world for inhabiting such widespread and diverse habitats while remaining a single species. While other forms have adapted to environmental pressures through biological changes, humankind's greatest adaptations since the appearance of *Homo sapiens sapiens* have been cultural. Thus humans everywhere are actually biologically quite similar but culturally quite different. Each society has its own cultural means of adapting to its environment and of surviving.

> Humans' greatest adaptations have been cultural.

Anthropology Vocabulary

eugenics	monogenism	social race
gene pool	polygenism	speciation
intelligence quotient (IQ)	race	species
Mendelian populations	social Darwinism	varieties

Review Questions

1. How were racial differences viewed by those who believed in monogenism? Why was polygenism generally a less popular interpretation of race?
2. What have anthropologists learned about the relationship of race and intelligence?
3. Why did physical anthropologists have difficulty determining how many races there were?
4. Why are the breeding populations of nonhuman animals easier to identify than those of humans?
5. What insights does a nonracial approach to human diversity provide?

Recommended Reading

Gossett, Thomas F., 1963, *Race: The History of an Idea in America.* Dallas: Southern Methodist University Press. An outstanding discussion of the role of race in American life from the colonial period to the present. Highly recommended.

Montagu, Ashley, ed., 1964, *The Concept of Race.* New York: The Free Press. A collection of articles by leading anthropologists that provide new interpretations of human diversity.

Montagu, Ashley, 1964, *Man's Most Dangerous Myth: The Fallacy of Race,* 4th ed. Cleveland: The World Publishing Company. An informative discussion of the popular notions about race, and the prejudices they create.

Stanton, William, 1960, *The Leopard's Spots: Scientific Attitudes Toward Race in America 1815–1859.* Chicago: University of Chicago Press. An excellent account of the development of the American school of anthropology in the pre–Civil War era. Highly recommended.

5

How do humans compare with other primates?

Humans belong to the order Primates.

Primates include prosimians, monkeys, apes, and humans.

Primates have elaborate systems of communication.

Early forms of humans were probably not as strongly aggressive as they are popularly described.

Kerchak was dead.

Withdrawing the knife that had so often rendered him master of far mightier muscles than his own, Tarzan of the Apes placed his foot upon the neck of his vanquished enemy, and once again, loud through the forest rang the fierce, wild cry of conqueror.

And thus came the young Lord Greystoke into the kingship of the apes (Burroughs 1963:82).

In 1912, Edgar Rice Burroughs introduced one of the most popular fictional wild men of the twentieth century, Tarzan, to the Western world. The popular story relates the rearing of the baby of Lord John Greystoke by Kala the ape, "a huge, fierce terrible beast of a species closely allied to the gorilla, yet more intelligent" (Burroughs 1963:30). The story of Tarzan and his relationship to the apes that raised him has served as an introduction to the great apes for many people. The story of Tarzan was elaborated upon by Burroughs in 22 novels, and in comic books, movies, and a television series. Burroughs had many remarkable insights into the differences and similarities between humans and apes. At the same time, his novels contained other information that was factually incorrect and which has misled the general public ever since. Perhaps part of the problem is due to the fact that the discovery and study of the African great apes is recent in Western culture. The lowland gorilla was first discovered by Europeans in 1847, and the mountain gorilla was not discovered by Westerners until 1903. A species of small chimpanzee found along the Congo River was unknown until 1929. In this chapter, the currently known similarities and differences between nonhuman primates and humans will be explored, in terms of primate taxonomy, anatomy, locomotion, and social behavior.

The Classification of Primates

Several previous chapters have already referred to the great classification of nature devised by the Swedish botanist Linnaeus and published under the title *Systema Naturae*. With the publication of the first edition in 1735, Linnaeus was the first scientist to classify humans with the rest of the animal world. Humans were considered quadrupeds and placed in the class Quadrupedia and the order Anthropomorpha, along with the ape and the sloth. In the much-revised tenth edition of this classification, published in 1758, Linnaeus proposed a new order of animals, which included humans. In Linnaeus' scheme, these animals were ranked the highest; thus he assigned the name *Pri-*

Linnaeus' *Systema Naturae* was the first taxonomic scheme to classify humans in the animal world.

Humans were first classified in the order Primates by Linnaeus.

mates, or primary animals, to this order. Included in his new order were different forms of humans, apes, lemurs, and bats. The sloth was no longer included in the grouping with humans (Bendysche 1863). Today the order name Primates remains, but a number of animals have been added to the order, while the bat has been deleted. Considering the date when this classification was published, it is not surprising that many individuals were shocked that humans were included in the same group as apes and monkeys. Therefore a number of alternative classifications that emphasized the uniqueness of humans were quickly introduced by other scholars. Nevertheless, Linnaeus' scheme survived the critics, and today it still forms the basis of our taxonomy of the animal world, even though the classification of the primates has become increasingly more complex and confusing. Today approximately 200 species and 55 genera (plural of *genus*) of primates are recognized by one or another authority. Linnaeus' original idea was to introduce taxonomic principles in order to simplify the identification of animals. Unfortunately, in the case of the living primates there has been a tendency to divide animals into separate species or genera when the differences are slight. As a result, there is a bewildering array of names and synonyms. (This same point was noted in the discussion of fossil primates.)

Linnaeus' scheme and those that followed represent only a European scientific approach to classification. These schemes emphasize the importance of certain characteristics while ignoring others. People in other societies classify their flora and fauna differently than we do. Anthropologists have begun to study systems of classification in other societies in order to discover new insights into the general process of categorizing and to learn what kinds of criteria besides those used by the Western scientist would provide a better understanding of humankind's relationship to the rest of the animal world.

Taxonomic schemes rely heavily on morphological differences. The anthropologist's classification system should consider total morphological patterns. However, in primate taxonomy one or a few traits are frequently used to separate one group from another. In some cases, species and genera are based only on differences in fur color. Many differences of opinion exist regarding primate classification, reflecting our incomplete knowledge of many forms of the primates. With the exception of a few pioneering studies, intensive research on primates in the wild is less than 15 years old. Prior to this period a great deal of our knowledge of primates was based on inaccurate reports of travelers and observations of captive primates in zoos, who were atypical. Therefore it should be kept in mind that our understanding of primates is in a state of flux, and many of our current ideas are subject to considerable revision as new information is obtained. In spite of the scholarly disagreements, however, it is possible to outline the major taxonomic divisions of the recent primates, although not everyone will agree with each grouping. The following chart includes the suborders, infraorders, families, and genera of the order Primates, as well as the common names of the genera and their geographical location.

The Living Primates

SUBORDER PROSIMII

Infraorder Lemuriformes		Madagascar
Family Lemuridae		
Genus *Lemur*	lemur (true lemur)	
Genus *Hapalemur*	gentle lemur	
Genus *Lepilemur*	sportive (weasel) lemur	
Genus *Cheirogaleus*	dwarf lemur	
Genus *Microcebus*	mouse lemur	
Family Indriidae		Madagascar
Genus *Indri*	indris	
Genus *Propithecus*	sifaka	
Genus *Avahi*	avahi	
Family Daubentoniidae		Madagascar
Genus *Daubentonia*	aye-aye	
Infraorder Lorisiformes		
Family Lorisidae		
Genus *Loris*	slender loris	southern India, Ceylon
Genus *Nycticebus*	slow loris	Southeast Asia
Genus *Perodicticus*	potto	Africa
Genus *Arctocebus*	angwantibo (golden potto)	West Africa
Family Galagidae		
Genus *Galago*	galago, or bush baby (includes dwarf species)	Africa
Infraorder Tarsiiformes		

Family Tarsiidae
Genus *Tarsius* tarsier Southeast Asia

**SUBORDER
ANTHROPOIDEA** *higher primates*

Infraorder Platyrrhina

Superfamily Ceboidea

Family Callithricidae
Genus *Callithrix* marmoset South America
Genus *Cebuella* pygmy marmoset South America
Genus *Saguinus* tamarin Central and South America
Genus *Leontideus* golden lion, tamarin South America

Family Callimiconidae
Genus *Callimico* Goeldi's marmoset South America

Family Cebidae
Subfamily Aotinae
Genus *Aotes* owl (night) monkey,
Douroucouli Central and South America

Subfamily Pitcheciinae
Genus *Pithecia* saki South America
Genus *Chiropotes* bearded saki South America
Genus *Cacajao* uakari South America

Subfamily Cebinae
Genus *Cebus* capuchin monkey Central and South America
Genus *Saimiri* squirrel monkey Central and South America

Subfamily Alouattinae
Genus *Alouatta* howler monkey Central and South America

Subfamily Atelinae
Genus *Ateles* spider monkey Mexico, Central and South
America

Genus *Brachyteles* woolly spider monkey South America
Genus *Lagothrix* woolly monkey South America

Infraorder Catarrhina

Superfamily Cercopithecoidea

Family Cercopithecidae

Subfamily Colobinae

Genus *Colobus*	guereza (colobus monkey)	Africa
Genus *Presbytis*	langur	India, Pakistan, Ceylon, Southeast Asia
Genus *Pygathrix*	douc langur	Laos, Vietnam
Genus *Rhinopithecus*	snob-nosed langur	West China, North Vietnam
Genus *Simias*	Pagai Island langur	islands off Sumatra
Genus *Nasalis*	proboscis monkey	Borneo

Subfamily Cercopithecinae

Genus *Macaca*	macaque monkeys (includes Barbary ape and Celebes black ape)	North Africa, Asia, Southeast Asia
Genus *Papio*	common baboons, hamadryas baboon, mandrill, and drill	from sub-Saharan Africa to part of Middle East
Genus *Theropithecus*	gelada	Ethipia
Genus *Cercopithecus*	guenon	Africa
Genus *Erthrocebus*	patas monkey	Africa
Genus *Cercocebus*	mangabey	Africa

Superfamily Hominoidea

Family Hylobatidae

Genus *Hylobates*	gibbon	Southeast Asia
Genus *Symphalangus*	siamang gibbon	Sumatra, Malay Peninsula

Family Pongidae

Genus *Pongo*	orangutan	Borneo, Sumatra
Genus *Pan*	chimpanzee	Africa
Genus *Gorilla*	gorilla	Africa

Family Hominidae

Genus *Homo*	human	worldwide

[Rosen 1974:26–28]

As an order, the primates are characterized by the following traits that set them apart from other mammals (Brace and Montagu 1965:65):

1. Generalized or primitive mammalian organization, including a well-developed collarbone, allowing great mobility of the arms, and five digits on each hand and foot.
2. Grasping ability, enhanced by the mobility of all the digits, especially the thumb and big toe.
3. Presence of nails rather than claws, indicating the development of a pad of well-endowed tactile sensory tissue at the end of each digit.
4. Development of the powers of vision, with stereoscopic vision in the higher forms.
5. Expansion of the brain, especially of the area known as the cerebral cortex.
6. Reduction of the muzzle, indicating both a decline in the importance of the sense of smell and its related organs and a reduction of the dentition.

The primates are also included in several levels of classification higher than the order level: They are considered a part of the kingdom Animalia, the phylum Chordata, and the class Mammalia. By these classifications we understand that the primates are animals rather than plants; they are animals with backbones; and more specifically they are warm-blooded animals with hair. Because the mammals constitute an extremely diverse range of animals, it has been useful to the taxonomists to further subdivide the mammals into various orders, of which Primates is one. The major divisions within the order Primates are between the suborders Prosimii and Anthropoidea. Of these suborders, only the suborder Anthropoidea has a great deal in common with Tarzan and other humans. The tree shrew is also included by some physical anthropologists as a suborder of Primates, although the current trend is to exclude it.

In many ways the tree shrew found in Southeast Asia and the Philippines is an intermediate form. It is not quite a true primate, and in fact many authorities prefer to include the tree shrew in the order Insectivores. Yet the tree shrew is probably closer in form than any other living creature to what the original primates looked like some 70 million years ago. Some genera of the tree shrew resemble rats, while others resemble squirrels. The muzzle of this tiny animal is very long and has an extensive rhinarium, much like a dog's wet nose. Unlike those of primates, all of the digits are clawed. The tree shrew does not

The tree shrew is perhaps the living animal closest in form to the earliest primates.

have the ability to grasp as do primates. It has relatively large eyes, positioned to the sides of the head rather than to the front of the face, making it unlikely that they have stereoscopic vision. Unlike primates, it has multiple pairs of breasts. On the other hand, the tree shrew has a relatively large brain compared to other mammals of a similar size.

The tree shrew is not at all like most primates in its behavior. For example, soon after birth the mother deserts her young, coming back only for brief feedings every few days. Nor do the tree shrews exhibit the more tender mother-infant relations of primates, which involve such things as grooming and fondling. But nonetheless, tree shrews could be representative of mammals from which primates evolved.

The Prosimians

The prosimians exhibit most of the basic primate characteristics, although some of the genera have unique adaptations to their particular ecological niches. The prosimians are found in the Malagasy Republic, Africa, India, Ceylon, and Southeast Asia. They show more basic variety than any other primate group. They represent a curious blend of primitive mammalian patterns and highly specialized traits. In fact most prosimians look more like raccoons, dogs, and cats than like other primates. Prosimians also share a few traits with the tree shrew: a projecting muzzle, a moist rhinarium, nonmobile upper lips that limit facial expression, a dental comb in some species, formed by a few lower teeth and used to groom their fur, an accessory tongue used to clean the dental comb, and multiple pairs of breasts.

The prosimians differ from the tree shrew in a number of important features: The hands show dexterity in holding and manipulating objects; all digits have nails except the second toe, which has a claw for grooming; the eyes are larger and positioned more forward, may distinguish color, and may have stereoscopic vision; dentition is reduced from the tree shrew's 38 teeth; and the brain is slightly larger in relation to body size.

Prosimians show advances over the tree shrew.

The Lemuriformes. The infraorder of the prosimians that includes the lemur, indris, sifaka, avahi, and aye-aye is called Lemuriformes. The modern lemuriforms are found only in the Malagasy Republic and on the Comoro Islands, between the Malagasy Republic and Africa. When the lemuriforms migrated there from Africa, these environments were free from competi-

Lemuriformes fill several eco-niches usual to primates.

Lemur. (Roos, copyright © *Animals, Animals,* 1972)

tion, and the lemuriforms were able to fill successfully several eco-niches that primates do not normally fill.

The lemurs vary considerably in size. The true lemurs are generally large and *diurnal* (active in the daytime); the small lemurs are *nocturnal* (active at night) and may weigh only a few ounces, with a body length of only 6 inches. The small lemurs are unique among the primates in their extreme susceptibility to temperature changes. During cool weather these tiny creatures go into a state of suspended animation. While most of the lemurs are tree dwellers, the ring-tailed lemurs spend some time on the ground (Rosen 1974:45).

The late physical anthropologist Ernest A. Hooton (1947:15) once commemorated some of the peculiarities of the lemur in a poem:

> The lemur is a lowly brute;
>   His primate status, some dispute.
> He has a damp and longish snout
>   With lower front teeth leaning out.
> He parts his fur with this comb-jaw
>   And scratches with a single claw
> That still adorns a hinded digit
>   Wherever itching makes him fidget.
> He is arboreal and omnivorous;
>   From more about him, Lord deliver us!

The indrises are the largest of the lemuriforms. Their bodies often reach over 3 feet in length, exclusive of tails. All forms of the indrises have hands well adapted for grasping tree trunks and branches, and all are tree dwellers. The hands and feet of some of the forms have digits that are partially webbed. Most are diurnal, but the avahi is nocturnal.

The lemuriform known as the aye-aye shows the greatest specialization from a basic primate pattern. At one time this unusual animal was classified as a rodent. Aye-ayes are strictly nocturnal, exclusively arboreal (tree dwelling), no larger than a domestic cat, not the least gregarious, and few in number (they are an endangered species). For these reasons the aye-aye has not been well studied. It has a dental pattern which is considerably different from any other primate. The adult has only 18 teeth, including 2 extremely large incisors. With these teeth the aye-aye is able to gnaw wood and open hard-shelled fruit, including coconuts. Unlike the teeth of other primates, these incisors grow continually as they wear. The aye-aye has also developed extremely long and slender middle fingers, which are specialized for spearing the larvae of beetles from holes in bark (Schultz 1969:18–19). It has been suggested that the aye-aye occupies the woodpecker's eco-niche in Malagasy Republic, since woodpeckers are not found there (Cartmill 1972, cited in Watts 1975:14). The aye-aye is fearless; it strikes at intruders, biting viciously if caught, while all the time making a harsh noise (Bourne 1974:34).

A second infraorder of the prosimians is known as Lorisiformes and includes various lorises, pottos, and the galago. The lorisiforms inhabit Africa, southern India, Ceylon, and Southeast Asia, which are also habitats of the higher primates. Lorisiformes is divided into two families, Lorisidae and Galagidae. All of the Lorisidae family live in dense forest and are nocturnal, probably as a result of competition from higher primates who are diurnal. In response to their nocturnal arboreal life, the lorisiforms evolved large, forward-placed eyes and powerful, grasping hands. The loris is a slow climber, while the galago is a fast hopper. Both forms of locomotion are successful though different adaptations to their eco-niche. The fast hopper is difficult to catch, and the slow creeper is difficult to spot in the dark.

The Tarsier. The tarsier is a small, rat-sized prosimian of the Philippines and Indonesia. This animal is enigmatic, because it retains some very primitive primate characteristics, yet in other ways it is more monkeylike than the other prosimians. As a result, some authorities, such as Napier and Napier (1967:5), place the tarsier as intermediate between the tree shrew and the prosimians; while others (Clark 1963:47) consider the tarsier as intermediate between the prosimians and the monkeys.[1]

Although a prosimian, the tarsier has some monkey-like features.

Like the galago, the tarsier is a leaper, capable of jumping as far as 7 feet, because its feet and lower limbs have become elongated to almost twice the length of its trunk. The tarsier probably relies on vision rather than smell. Its snout is reduced in comparison with the lemur. The tarsier has a true primate nose rather than a rhinarium. The tail of the tarsier is unique among the primates. It is long and slender and is used like the third limb of a tripod to aid the tarsier in sitting erect, much like the tail of a kangaroo. The tarsier stands up on its legs, clenches its fists, and spars like a boxer. In fact, F. Wood Jones had a tarsier in his home who would attack an intruder by springing at his face and biting whatever part of the face presented itself to the animal. All this from an 8-ounce primate! The tarsier is also able to swivel its head 180 degrees right or left (Bourne 1974:60–62; Hill 1972:156–160; Rosen 1974:59–61).

The Anthropoids

The New World Monkeys. The suborder Anthropoidea consists of the New World monkeys, the Old World monkeys, the apes, and humans. The fossil evidence for the New World monkeys is very poor. It is believed by some authorities that the early New World forms were prosimians that migrated across a land

[1] The English anatomist F. Wood Jones (1923) claimed that humans descended directly from the tarsier. This view has found little acceptance.

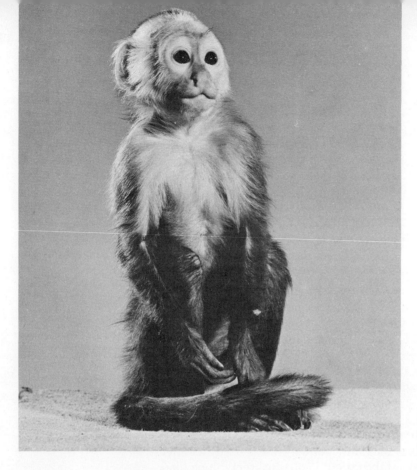

New World monkey. (Gili, copyright © *Animals, Animals,* 1972)

bridge that connected Europe and North America 30 million years ago or more; and that they eventually moved into the New World tropics of Central America and South America. A minority view is that monkeys originated in the New World and then spread westward into the Old World. For 30 million years the New World primates have evolved along their own lines of evolution, apparently with no further Old World contact. All of the living New World nonhuman primates are called "monkeys," but some seem to be closer to the prosimians than to the Old World monkeys. The New World primates are classified as Ceboidea, or platyrrhines. The name platyrrhine comes from the unique shape of the New World primate nose. The platyrrhine nose has round nostrils that are widely separated by a broad fleshy nasal septum, giving the nose a very flat appearance.

The New World primates are characterized by a great deal of variety, although all forms have tails. The New World forms are generally divided into two groups, the marmosets and the cebid monkeys. Of these two groups, the marmosets most closely resemble the prosimians of the Old World.

The New World primates have been separated from the Old World primates for about 30 million years.

The marmosets resemble prosimians in some respects.

Although the marmosets are referred to as monkeys, most have digits with prosimianlike claws. The marmosets, like the cebids, have an extra premolar not found in the Old World monkeys or apes. While most primates usually bear only one off-spring at a time, the marmosets have twins. The father begins to take care of the twins as soon as they are born and carries one on the upper part of each of his legs. The mother nurses them, but it is the father who weans them and teaches them how to behave. The marmosets are one of the few primates that live in monoga-mous units (Bourne 1974:66–80; Rosen 1974:67–69).

The cebid monkeys exhibit a tremendous variety of size, shape, and locomotion. Some of these monkeys, such as the owl, are primarily springers in their locomotion, much like most marmosets. The owl monkey is the only nocturnal New World primate.

Cebid monkeys are highly varied.

Other cebid monkeys are climbers. Included in the climbers are the saki monkeys, who are unique among the New World forms in that they exhibit marked male-female differences (sexual dimorphism). The squirrel monkey is also a climber. Its skull is the most humanlike of all the New World primates. Somewhat surprisingly, relative to body size its brain is larger than ours. A squirrel monkey named Miss Baker was one of the two monkeys that participated in the first United States space flight involving primates[2] (Bourne 1974:84).

Another climber is the capuchin, the organ-grinder monkey, which seems to be extremely intelligent and has great manual dexterity. Its brain is large and well convoluted. There is also increasing evidence that the capuchin is a tool-user and even a toolmaker. In the laboratory situation it has used sticks as weapons; in the wild it threatens predators by dropping tree branches to the ground. More importantly, it modifies branches and leaves to probe for larvae. This is a simple form of tool-making (Rosen 1974:75–76; Hill 1972:168–169). Some scientists rate the capuchin as not too different in intelligence from the chimpanzee. In fact, the capuchin is one of the few monkeys that will scribble or paint like a great ape. The animal shows great powers of concentration, working for more than an hour on a problem without losing interest. In 1933 Heinrich Klüver car-ried out a number of experiments with capuchin monkeys and discovered that both macaques and capuchins will tear apart any object that can be dismantled. While the macaque seems purely destructive, the capuchin takes the object apart with

---

[2] The other was a rhesus monkey named Able.

more care and examines it: It demonstrates an interest in the object and its component parts (Bourne 1974:88–89).

A third group of cebid monkeys are considered brachiators[3] by some anthropologists, or semibrachiators by others. The New World brachiators make use of a prehensile, or grasping, tail as a kind of third hand. The prehensile tail has a patch of skin at its end and strong muscles that give it a powerful grasp. None of the Old World monkeys have prehensile tails.

The brachiators are subdivided into two kinds: the howler monkeys and the Atelinae. The howler monkey does not make use of its ability to brachiate, preferring a quadrupedal gait. The howler is named for the loud calls it is capable of making, due to its highly specialized vocal apparatus.

The Atelinae subfamily is made up of the woolly monkey, the spider monkey, and the woolly spider monkey. Of these, the spider monkey is the most adapted to brachiation. For efficient brachiation the hand must be able to form an effective hook grip or the thumb will be in the way while brachiating. The spider monkey's thumb is reduced to almost nothing, and quite often it is absent. In many ways, the spider monkey is the New World counterpart to the Old World gibbon.

[3] Brachiation is a hand-over-hand, arm-swinging form of locomotion in which the body is suspended by the upper extremities.

Old World monkey. (Hidy, Anthro-Photo)

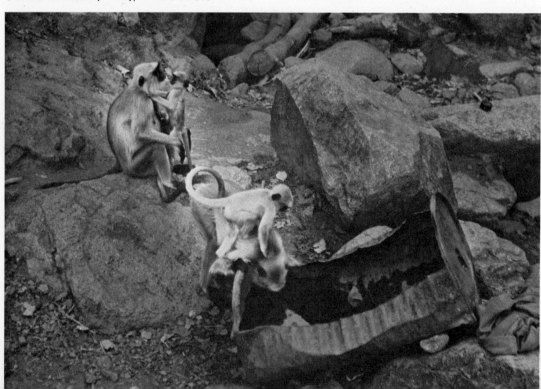

The Old World Monkeys. The Old World monkeys are widely distributed in Asia and Africa, in a variety of habitats that range from tropical rain forest to open grasslands, and even semi-desert, to the Himalayas. When compared with the New World monkeys, the Old World monkeys show a relative uniformity of anatomy, considering they are distributed over the largest area of the world of all the nonhuman primates.

The Old World monkeys differ from the New World primates in that they have catarrhine, or down-pointed, noses; they lack prehensile tails; all are daytime creatures; they are more robust; they possess sitting pads, called ischial callosities; the Old World monkeys share the dental pattern of the apes and humans, which includes fewer premolars than the New World monkeys; sexual dimorphism is common; some female Old World monkeys exhibit various sexual swelling when sexually receptive; and almost all Old World monkeys have opposable thumbs. The Old World monkeys are biologically closer to humans than to the New World primates (Rosen 1974:84–87).

The Old World monkeys have been divided into two groups, the Colobinae and the Cercopithecinae. The colobines are leaf eaters and have complex stomachs that aid in the digestion of cellulose, as well as enlarged salivary glands in the mouth to aid in the predigestion of food. The colobines exhibit less sexual swelling and sexual dimorphism than the cercopithecines. The colobines also lack cheek pouches, which are found in other Old World monkeys. While the colobines normally move on all four limbs (quadruped locomotion), they are considered brachiating leapers. However, they move primarily by leaping rather than by swinging, and as a result their hindlimbs have become lengthened, rather than the forelimbs as in most brachiators. The colobines are primarily tree dwelling. Finally, the colobines exhibit unusual nose shapes, particularly the male proboscis monkey of Borneo, which has a huge bulbous, pendulous nose (Hill 1972:173; Rosen 1974:88–89). The colobines include the colobus monkeys of Africa and a variety of Asiatic langurs.

The cercopithecines occupy a number of habitats throughout the Old World. Their stomachs are simple, and they are omnivorous. They are able to store large amounts of food in their mouths, due to the presence of cheek pouches. Cheek pouches are especially advantageous for ground-dwelling animals who may have to flee a grazing site quickly or give up food to a more dominant member of the group. Perhaps the two best-studied forms of the cercopithecines are the African baboons and Asian macaques, but the subfamily also includes other African forms; guenons, mangabeys, mandrills, drills, and geladas.

The Old World monkeys are widely spread over Asia and Africa.

Old World monkeys are divided into the colobines and the cercopithecines.

Baboon yawning; note large canines. (DeVore, Anthro-Photo)

The baboon was important in the belief system of ancient Egypt. It was depicted in their art, and mummified. The baboon was associated with Thoth, the god of scribes, and with the moon (Frankfort 1948:79). Baboons have figured in the mythologies of various societies ever since. In some cases baboons are believed to have special powers, often magical, and in other cases they are portrayed as licentious, especially toward human females.

Baboons are almost exclusively terrestrial. They utilize trees only for resting, sleeping, and fleeing danger. There is considerable sexual dimorphism among the baboons with the males having considerably larger bodies, much larger canine teeth, and larger jaws than the female. The baboons exhibit unusually large ischial callosities. While baboons are basically vegetarians, they occasionally eat small animals.

The savanna baboons have been the baboons most extensively studied in the field, especially through the pioneering efforts of physical anthropologists Irven De Vore and S. L. Washburn. The gelada and hamadryas baboons apparently manifest behavior that is different from the savanna forms.

The savanna baboons form troops of approximately 40 to 80 individuals, organized around a male *dominance hierarchy*. This hierarchy protects the rest of the troop and directs troop move-

The baboons are ground dwelling.

ments. The hierarchy is headed by a dominant male, who is usually the largest and who has exclusive priority over a female in estrus. Female hierarchies are also found in some groups (Napier and Napier 1967:247–257).

Among the hamadryas and the gelada baboons the main social unit is the "harem." A dominant male has a whole group of females (the "harem") under his control, while other less dominant males may have access to no females. Approximately 20 percent of the adult male population is without females (Rosen 1974:102–105).

The macaques have the widest geographic distribution of any primates other than humans and are divided into 12 different species. The macaques are also distributed over a tremendous range of elevations, from sea level to 13,000 feet. Species of macaques vary also in the amount of time they spend in trees and on the ground. The rhesus macaques of India inhabit temples and roam the street, occupying an unusual "urban" niche. Like the baboons, the macaques have well-developed male dominance hierarchies (Napier and Napier 1967:205–214).

The Japanese macaques have been studied since 1948 and represent one of the best-studied primate groups, in terms of behavior. The Japanese scientists were able to identify individuals of a troop living in a national park and thus were able to record their specific behavior. A dossier has been kept on each individual of the troop, and the group has now been observed over several generations. The scientists have also kept track of who was the mother of whom. Many of the first insights into the behavior of primates came from these pioneering Japanese studies.

The macaques, especially the rhesus, have proven invaluable for laboratory research. In fact, the Rh factor, which is of great importance to humans, was discovered as a result of research on the blood of rhesus monkeys. The abbreviation *Rh* comes from rhesus. Other experiments on the rhesus monkey led to the discovery of the vaccine for polio.

The Apes. The apes are the closest to humans of all of the primates. They are classified in the superfamily Hominoidea, along with humans. The apes are divided into two families, Hylobatidae and Pongidae. Hylobatidae includes the gibbon and the siamang gibbon, and these forms are less like humans than are the pongids. The hylobatids must have branched off from the line leading to humans very early, becoming greatly specialized for brachiation. The common gibbon is found in Southeast Asia. It is an arboreal animal living in fairly dense forest environments, including tropical rain forest, semideciduous forest, and

The apes include the hylobatids and the pongids.

Gibbon. (Roos, copyright
© *Animals, Animals,* 1972)

montane forest. Like all apes, the gibbon is tailless. It is the smallest of the apes, having an adult stature of about 3 feet and a body weight of 10 to 20 pounds. The siamang gibbon is larger, and some authorities believe it is closer to the pongids than the common gibbon.

All gibbons are fully adapted to brachiation and use this form of locomotion about 90 percent of the time. The forelimbs are extremely elongated to allow for the gibbon's graceful brachiation. Somewhat surprisingly, the gibbon's thumb is quite long. It is placed far back on the wrist and is turned across the palm to enable the gibbon to effect a hook grip while brachiating.

The gibbon is well adapted for brachiation.

The gibbons exhibit very little sexual dimorphism. Both sexes are similar in size, and both have very long projecting canines, which are well adapted to piercing the outer shells of fruit. The gibbon is also one of the few primates to live in monogamous units made up of a male, a female, and young offspring. The adult male eventually drives out the maturing male offspring.

The pongids form the great apes, which include the orangutan of Southeast Asia and the chimpanzee and gorilla of Africa. They are the largest and heaviest of the nonhuman primates and the most humanlike. All of the pongids are primarily vegetarians and have large projecting canine teeth used to open fruit and to strip vegetation. More than any other nonhuman primates, they can maintain prolonged semierect posture and bipedal locomotion. Fully erect posture is not possible, however, because the pongids cannot fully extend their knee and hip joints. Their brains are large, and more complex than any other nonhuman primates. While the great apes do not brachiate as much as the gibbon does, they are capable of brachiation, because of their long forelimbs and reduced thumbs. There is considerable sexual dimorphism in the adult forms.

The pongids include the so-called great apes—the orangutan, the chimpanzee, and the gorilla.

The orangutan is the only Asiatic pongid. Today it is restricted to Borneo and Sumatra, due to human activities, but originally it had a much wider distribution, which included the Asian mainland. Perhaps less than 5000 of the genus remain outside of captivity. Like the gibbon, the orangutan is almost exclusively arboreal.

Orangutan.
(Roos, copyright © *Animals, Animals*, 1972)

The orangutan is large, about 5 feet in height, and exhibits a great deal of sexual dimorphism. In captivity, females weigh about 180 pounds and males weigh about 350 pounds. In captivity, they often become obese due to inactivity and overfeeding. They weigh somewhat less in the wild, but the male still weighs approximately twice as much as the female.

The orangutan is well adapted for brachiation, as the bones of both the hands and the feet are curved into permanent hooks. The arms are exceedingly long, spanning over 8 feet in a large male. There is disagreement among physical anthropologists as to whether or not the orangutan brachiates in the same sense as the gibbon. The orangutan uses its limbs primarily to "hang." The coat of the orangutan is long and reddish-brown. Some of the males have enormous cheek pads that contain fat and connective tissue, which gives the face and neck a very broad appearance. The male also has a huge, pendulous laryngeal air sac, which hangs like an apron from the neck and is apparently used as a vocalization chamber. The female has a much smaller air sac.

> The orangutan is well adapted for brachiation, considering it is larger than the gibbon.

Very little is known of the orangutan's social behavior in the wild, as in-depth studies have only recently begun, but group size seems to be very small, usually two to four individuals. Lone males are common, as are females with their young offspring. However, families have also been observed.

The African pongids include the chimpanzee and the gorilla. Both of these forms are considered the closest to humans of all of the apes. Both spend more time on the ground than do the Asian apes.

The chimpanzee is the best known of the pongids, to both the folk and the professional anthropologist. For many of us, familiarity has come from the Tarzan movies and television series, which included Tarzan's constant companion, Cheeta the chimp, who exposed us to chimpanzee locomotion and behavior. In the early years of the "Today" television show, a chimpanzee, J. Fred Muggs, was co-star, and numerous other chimpanzees have appeared in movies and on television. Of all presentations about chimpanzees in the mass media Jane van Lawick-Goodall has presented the most thorough and accurate portrayal of the chimp in the wild.

The habitats of the chimpanzee include the tropical rain forest, forest-savanna mosaic, deciduous woodland in hilly country, and even montane forest up to approximately 10,000 feet. During the daylight hours the chimpanzee, in certain locales, spends 50 to 75 percent of its time in the trees. Each night it builds a nest in the trees, at least 15 feet above the ground (Napier and Napier 1967:238).

Chimpanzee sexual dimorphism is not as extreme as that of the orangutan. The chimpanzee is the smallest of the great apes. While roughly the same height as the orangutan, the male chimpanzee weighs only about 110 pounds and the female about 90 pounds, although the pygmy chimpanzee is somewhat smaller.

The chimpanzee has many of the characteristic specializations found in other brachiators. The forelimbs are elongated and the hindlimbs are relatively short. The thumb is short and the hands form hooks for brachiating. Because of the specialization that their hands have undergone for brachiating, it is impossible for any of the great apes to walk on the palms of their hands as Old World monkeys do. Instead, the orangutan walks on hands in a fist position and the chimpanzee and gorilla walk on their knuckles.

Chimpanzee extracting termites. (Giza Telecki)

One of the main reasons that most of us are more familiar with the chimpanzee than with the other great apes is that the chimpanzee is easier to work with and train, because of its personality, imitative behavior, and attention seeking. Consequently it is chosen for parts in movies over other apes. The chimpanzee is also easier to test. Whether or not this indicates greater intelligence is difficult to discern.

The chimpanzee's personality makes it easier to train than other apes.

Chimpanzees live in very loose-knit groups in the wild. Old members leave continually; new members are added. The size of the group fluctuates considerably, from just a few to as many as 80. Solitary chimpanzees are also fairly common. The only stable relationship in chimpanzee society is that of mother and offspring.

The chimpanzee society is quite a friendly one. When food is abundant, large numbers of chimpanzees will gather together. Announcements of the available food are sent throughout the forest by drumming on tree trunks. Greetings are almost humanlike, especially among those chimps who are friends. They hug, kiss, and pat one another.

Unlike most nonhuman primates the chimpanzee will occasionally cooperate with one another in hunting for fresh meat. Most of their diet consists of fruit, leaves, bark, seeds, palmnuts, and stems; it infrequently includes termites, bush pigs, monkeys, ants, fish, and native-cultivated fruit.

Chimpanzees are unusual in that they hunt in groups and make simple tools.

Jane van Lawick-Goodall has made field studies of the chimpanzees at the Gombe Stream Reserve in Kenya. Perhaps her most interesting and important discovery occurred in 1960, when she found that the chimpanzees were able to *make* tools as well as use them. One morning as she headed toward the area where she was observing a troop, she came upon one of the chimps, whom she named David Graybeard, in the process of trimming the edges from a wide blade of sword grass:

> He then poked his cleaned rod down a hole he had scratched in a large, domed termite nest. He waited a few minutes. Then he skillfully pulled out his rod and delicately licked it with his lips. He was termite fishing! When his first fishing rod weakened, he picked a piece of vine, stripped off its leaves, and continued his successful pursuit. Every now and then he would put his ear to the nest, listen carefully, and then scratch a new fishing hole. [Washburn and Moore 1974:45]

With this unexpected discovery Jane van Lawick-Goodall was able to question the old notion that humans were set apart from all other animals because of their ability to make tools. Clearly the line between humans and the chimpanzee was not as sharp as most authorities had thought. Later studies of the chimpanzees have added further examples of toolmaking and tool using: van Lawick-Goodall observed chimpanzees mashing leaves in their mouths and later using the leaves as sponges to obtain water; other observers have reported chimps using sticks as clubs (Rosen 1974:131–132).

The gorilla is the largest of the primates, exceeding even humans in average size. The males range from slightly over 4 feet to about 6 feet in height, while the females are usually less than 5 feet. The average weight of wild males is between 300 and 450 pounds, while some captive males obtain weights of over 600 pounds. The wild female probably weighs between 150 and 250 pounds (Schaller 1963:76).

While the mass media have generally depicted the chimpanzee as a lovable, intelligent rascal, the gorilla has been depicted as a terrifying, ferocious brute. Yet the stereotype of the gorilla is inaccurate. As is the case with so many animals, our knowledge of the gorilla was based on observations made of animals imprisoned in zoo cages. Studying these animals for clues to their behavior in the wild is much the same as observing the behavior of human prisoners and generalizing from these observations about the nature of nonprison society. In-depth knowledge of the gorilla in the wild did not begin until 1959, when an intensive study was begun on mountain gorillas living in the Albert National Park, Congo, by George B. Schaller, a zoologist.[4] Schaller found that the gorilla in the wild is aloof,

The stereotype of the gorilla is inaccurate.

---

[4] This expedition was described by Schaller in the entertaining book *The Year of the Gorilla* (Schaller 1964) and in the more technical account, *The Mountain Gorilla: Ecology and Behavior* (Schaller 1963).

shy, gentle, stoic, and even introverted. In the mass media and especially in travelers' accounts of Africa, the male gorilla was thought to be a highly lascivious beast who frequently attacked and raped native women. Such behavior does not seem to be a part of the gorilla's true life-style. The gorilla is shy of humans and probably would not attack a human without provocation. More importantly, Schaller discovered that the male gorilla has almost no interest in sexual behavior. In 466 hours of observations, representing over a year of fieldwork, Schaller observed only two copulations, and no sex play, homosexual behavior, or any other noncopulatory form of sexual expression (Schaller 1963:275–286).

Gorilla.
(Michael D. Olien)

Because of their large size and their vegetarian diet, which is low in nutrition, the gorilla spends most of its waking hours eating or looking for food—up to eight hours a day. The gorilla's huge canine teeth are used for stripping rough vegetation.

While the gorilla has the body structure of a brachiator, the adult is too heavy for very extensive brachiation. A quarter-ton gorilla has to be much more cautious of dead or weak tree limbs than does a 15-pound gibbon. As a result, it is mostly the young gorillas that brachiate. The adult gorilla spends about 90 percent of its time on the ground, where it is a knuckle-walker like the chimpanzee.

The gorilla has a well-developed laryngeal air-sac like the orangutan but one which is internal rather than external. Since the gorilla beats its chest, the air sac may serve as a resonating chamber.

The gorilla has no natural enemies except perhaps the leopard. Its greatest threat comes from humans. It is killed for sport, out of fear, and because it raids native gardens. While it is not yet at the point of extinction, its number is being greatly reduced by humans.

The gorilla's social organization is quite different from that of either the chimpanzee or the gibbon. Groups number from 5 to 30 members and are fairly stable. Most groups have twice as many females as males. Each group has one or more silverback gorilla males, only one of whom is dominant, one or more younger blackback gorilla males, and females and infants. It is the dominant silverback male and females who form the core of the group. While there is little overt dominance, one silverback male is considered the leader and the protector (Napier and Napier 1967:164).

In some ways gorillas might be considered nomads. Each day they travel approximately one mile, moving along and feeding, and finally bedding down wherever darkness overtakes them.

Their wandering occurs within about a 10- to 15-mile area, which they consider their home.

Special Features of Primate Anatomy

In contrast to the skeletons of many other mammals, those of the primates have remained generally unchanged from the primitive mammalian forms. While much of the primate skeleton remains generalized, there are several parts of the skeleton that have become highly specialized, in particular the hands.

The Hands. The hands play a very prominent role in the life of primates, serving many purposes. For this reason, the hands have undergone numerous adaptive modifications, while retaining the essentials of the original anatomical ground plan.

Primates hands have undergone many kinds of adaptations.

The fingers of the tree shrew, some of the prosimians, and the marmosets have claws rather than nails. In some of these forms the thumb is not truly opposable, and the sharp, curved claws become important for holding the light bodies of these small animals onto the rough surface of trees or bushes. The most extreme specialization is found in the aye-aye, where the middle fingers have become exceedingly slender, with a thin, sharp, claw at the tip, which is used to probe into bark holes and pierce and withdraw the larvae of insects (Schultz 1969:86).

The New World monkey's thumb is greatly reduced and not well adapted for grasping. The spider monkey's thumb is almost completely absent. This reduction of the thumb is apparently related to the fact that these monkeys tend to hold objects between the second and third fingers rather than between the first and second fingers, as is the case in the Old World monkeys. The hands of the prosimians and New World monkeys are capable of prehension, which is the ability to grasp an object by wrapping the fingers around it or by pressing it between the fingers and palm. (*Prehension* is also used to refer to the grasping of the prehensile tail.) With the capability of prehension the lower primates are able to hold objects in one hand. The tree shrew is the only primate without the capability of prehension. In order to hold an object, the tree shrew must use both of his hands, much as a squirrel does.

The Old World monkeys, the apes, and humans have true opposability of the thumb. With this ability these forms are able to grip objects more effectively. These forms use both a "power" grip and a "precision" grip. The power grip is one in which all four fingers are wrapped around an object and the thumb is firmly placed against the object to brace it—for example, the grip employed by humans while using a screwdriver to remove a firmly imbedded screw. The power grip is used for grasping a limb in locomotion or any time that strength is needed to grasp. It involves holding an object firmly between the fingers and palm. Precision grips are used when accuracy rather than power is needed. In the precision grip, the object is grasped between the fingers alone, usually between the thumb and the first one or two fingers on the thumb side of the hand (Napier 1962).

The Feet. The specializations of the primate foot are in many details remarkably similar to those of the hand in humans. For most primates the feet act as another set of hands, but in humans the foot has changed to accommodate upright posture. In humans the foot is basically nonprehensile, because the big toe has lost its opposability.

The foot represents a specialized aspect of human anatomy.

The human foot has a big toe that is in line with the other toes, rather than to the side like a thumb as in other primate feet. All of the toes but the big toe have become shorter and smaller in humans. The heel has increased in size and has extended backward. Likewise, two arches have developed at the instep, one running transversely and the other from front to rear.

The Pelvis. Besides the brain, skull, and foot, the pelvis represents the other highly specialized aspect of human anatomy. Like the foot, the pelvis of the human has changed for upright posture. The human pelvis is made up of six bones; pairs of ilia, ischia, and pubes bones, which are fused together in adults. The iliac portion, or blade, of the pelvis has been greatly broadened and shortened in humans to accommodate the body's changing center of gravity. In the monkeys the pelvis has something of a cylindrical shape, with the top and bottom having roughly the same diameter. In humans the pelvis is more funnel-shaped, the top opening being slightly larger than the bottom opening. This specialized shape of the pelvis for upright posture sometimes results in difficulties for females giving birth, especially when the fetus has a swollen brain case. The fetus may be able to pass into the top of the pelvis but be unable to pass the rest of the way through without the aid of surgery.

The human pelvis has undergone many changes for upright posture.

The Skull and Brain. Perhaps the greatest and most important specializations in human anatomy are found in the skull and the brain. The brain of recent humans is both large and complex, es-

The skull and brain are perhaps the most specialized human characteristics.

pecially the front part of the brain, which is called the cerebral cortex and is extremely convoluted. The size of the human brain ranges from approximately 1000 cc to 2000 cc, being on average about 1400 cc. In contrast, the largest nonhuman primate brain, the gorilla's, averages about 525 cc. The expansion of the frontal region of the human brain has brought about an important change in the shape of the skull: A true forehead is found only in humans.

The human skull lacks the heavy muscle attachment for the jaws that is found in apes. The massive bony ridges above the eye sockets in apes are absent in the modern human skull. The human face also lacks the prognathism of the mouth region found in all other primates: The modern human is the only primate to exhibit a true chin. The jaws and dentition of humans are much smaller than those of the apes. None of the human teeth are exaggerated in size. The aye-aye, on the other hand, has enormous incisors, and many other primates have large canines. Human dentition is balanced, allowing for great diversity of diet: As a result, humans are completely omnivorous. Human dentition is also arranged differently than that of other primates: While the dental arcade in the pongids is **U** shaped, that of humans is parabolic.

While facial musculature is minimal in the prosimians, it is more developed in monkeys, and has progressed most in the hominoids, attaining its extreme development in humans. This general trend toward gradual refinement is particularly marked in the muscles surrounding the mouth and has culminated in humans' ability to make a wide range of sounds modulated by the lips. Clear and marked facial expression, too, is directly related to the refinement of the facial musculature, since it depands on specialization for independent action in separate parts (Schultz 1969:223–225).

The skull of the ape is not well balanced on its neck; as a result, it has a tremendous amount of neck musculature and a large bony area at the back of its skull for attachment of this muscle. The human skull, on the other hand, is well balanced on the spine for erect posture and requires no heavy musculature to hold the head up.

Primate Locomotion

Many of the specializations of human anatomy are directly related to our upright, or bipedal, form of movement. Our full-time bipedal locomotion is unique among primates, although some nonhuman primates are capable of bipedalism for short distances. Actually, it is important to distinguish between posture and locomotion. There is a definite trend in the primates toward upright posture, in other words, holding the trunk upright. The prosimians are essentially upright in their posture, the arm-swinging monkeys and apes carry themselves in an upright position, and even those monkeys that walk on all fours sit with their trunks upright much of the time (Watts 1975:37–38). Three major forms of primate locomotion have been distinguished: quadrupedalism, brachiation, and bipedalism. Each is characteristic of a group of primates, but the categories are not mutually exclusive: Most primates exhibit more than one form of locomotion, although one form tends to predominate.

The full-time bipedalism of humans is unique among primates.

Primates use three major forms of locomotion: quadrupedalism, brachiation, and bipedalism.

Quadrupedalism. This form of locomotion is found among the tree shrew, some of the prosimians, all monkeys, the chimpanzee, and the gorilla. Quadrupedalism is four-legged walking or running and occurs both on the ground and in the trees. This form of locomotion is so diverse that several varieties of quadrupedal locomotion have been recognized. Slow climbing is most characteristic of the loris and potto. In this type of locomotion, three or four extremities are applied to the branch at any given moment. The movement is always slow and cautious. The limbs may act to suspend the body or to support it. The slow climbers have a well-developed power grip. Their index fingers are reduced, and the thumb and big toe splay out at a wide angle, allowing the animals to use their hands and feet like forceps to enclose a branch with a firm grip (Watts 1975:41).

Tree shrews, some prosimians, and some monkeys practice a second form of quadrupedalism, known as branch running and walking. This generalized form of quadrupedalism is simply running or walking in trees. It usually involves a prehensile grasp by arms or legs or both, although a few types hold on to branches with their claws. In most of these animals the arms and legs are of about equal length (Napier and Napier 1967:388).

A third type of quadrupedal locomotion is called ground running and walking. It is found among the ground-dwelling monkeys, such as the baboon. This is another generalized form of quadrupedal locomotion, which does not usually involve a prehensile grasp. Animals exhibiting this type of locomotion, run and walk on the ground, moving on the soles of their feet and the underside of the fingers of their hands. Their arms and legs are about equal in length. Because the ground runners and walkers do not have to grasp the surface on which they walk as the arboreal type does, the ground-type hand is shaped for a more effective precision grip (Watts 1975:41).

A fourth quadrupedal locomotion is called New World semi-brachiation. It is practiced by the howler monkey and the various spider monkeys. Semibrachiation is a type of arboreal locomotion in which the arms are used extended above the head to suspend the body or to propel it through space. In some cases the arms are used alone, and in other cases they are used in association with the legs and the unique prehensile tail of these animals. Quadrupedal walking and running are also used by the semibrachiating New World monkeys. Leaping is uncommon. Generally the trunk is short and broad, the arms and fingers elongated (Napier and Napier 1967:388; Watts 1975:41).

Old World semibrachiation represents a fifth type of quadrupedal locomotion. It is practiced by the Colobinae subfamily of Old World monkeys, such as the colobus and the langur. This form of semibrachiation differs from New World semibrachiation mainly in that leaping is employed more extensively. During leaping, the arms extend out ahead of the body to reach a handhold or to check momentum (Napier and Napier 1967:388).

The locomotion of the African apes, the gorilla, and the chimpanzee represents a sixth form of quadrupedalism, called knuckle-walking. This adaptation to ground living is a secondary one, as these apes are structurally still brachiators. As a result they have retained the long arms, long fingers, and short thumbs of their brachiating ancestors. It seems likely that these animals became quadrupeds because of their large size. When they walk and run, they do so on their soles and on their knuckles. Although they walk on all fours, their torso is actually slanted, with their head end higher, because of their disproportionately long arms, originally evolved for brachiation (Watts 1975:41).

Brachiation. Brachiation is the locomotion characteristic of the Asian apes. It is a form of arboreal locomotion in which the body weight is suspended from the arms and hands beneath the branches and movement is accomplished by swinging the body from one handhold to another. The legs are used to support the body in trees or on the ground in either the erect or the quadrupedal position. The gibbon and siamang exhibit true brachiation, whereas the orangutan's locomotion has been termed modified brachiation.

In modified brachiation, the feet as well as the arms play a role. The orangutan's feet are used for support, climbing, and hanging. In a sense orangutans resemble the quadruped slow climbers. They climb using any combination of their four grasping extremities. When they are on the ground they do not knuckle-walk like the African apes but walk on their hands in several positions; for example, they use fist-walking (Watts 1975:40–43).

Bipedalism. The form of locomotion used by humans is called bipedalism. It is a form of locomotion in which the body is *habitually* supported on the legs, which move alternately to propel it through space. One of the main advantages of bipedal locomotion is that it frees the hands, which can then be used to carry and manipulate objects such as tools.

While bipedalism in humans is considered specialized in comparison with the locomotion of other primates, it is not as specialized as the bipedalism found in some nonprimate animals. For example, the kangaroo is able to hop in 40-foot bounds with its powerful hind legs. Humans are capable not only of hopping; they can broad-jump up to 29 feet; can run at a speed of 15 miles an hour for several minutes and at a speed of more than 20 miles an hour over short distances; and can travel 50 miles or more on foot in a day, as well as swim rivers and climb mountains (Editors of Time-Life Books 1972:12–13).

Quadrupeds are capable of suspending themselves by the arms alone, in the manner of brachiating primates. The brachiators and knuckle-walkers adopt bipedalism for short distances when on the ground and in the trees. Thus the sequence quadrupedalism to brachiation to bipedalism represents a continuum of locomotor activity that can be divided into discrete categories only arbitrarily. There are in fact a number of primates that cannot be easily classified into one or another of the major categories (Napier and Napier 1967:389).

The origins of bipedalism are unclear. There seem to be two possibilities: Bipedalism evolved from quadrupedalism or it evolved out of an early stage of brachiation. It does not seem possible that it could have been derived from fully evolved brachiation, as was once believed, since quadrupedalism and brachiation are not wholly discrete categories. The quadrupedal subtype semibrachiation, for example, contains elements of both categories (Napier and Napier 1967:390–391).

Primate Communication

The primates are generally quite social animals. It is not surprising therefore that mutually understood communicatory signals play a very prominent part in their daily life and have evolved into intricate systems in all of the higher species. The study of nonhuman primate communication is extremely difficult: Some of the communication is carried out by scents, and humans are generally not as attuned to distinctions in smells as are the lower primates; nor are humans capable of hearing some of the high frequencies used by some primates in vocal communication. Perhaps the most difficult aspect of studying primate communication is that one can only infer its meaning. Not belonging to the species being studied, we are generally unable to know for sure what a signal means, because we are not programmed to do so. Most of the meaning that we can infer from the communication comes from observation of the stimulus and the response to the stimulus.

Primates use four basic systems of communication: chemical, tactile, optical, and acoustic.[5] While all primates utilize all of these systems to some extent, the lower forms generally rely more heavily on chemical systems, while the higher forms rely more heavily on optical and acoustic systems.

Chemical Systems. The chemical systems involve communication through organs of smell and taste. The initial response of individuals of all or most species to strange object or an animal of their own or another species is to sniff at it. The scents given off by primates seem to function as yes/no signals; in other words, a particular scent is either produced or it is not. At this stage in the study of primate scent it is unknown whether any of the primates are able to change the intensity of a scent, thus developing a more complex type of message. The one great advantage of chemical signals is their capacity to serve as vehicles of communication into the future, in the sense that once emitted, an odor is very likely to persist and thus convey a message after the departure of the animal who has left the scent. With odors an individual can send messages to another in its absence. In a very small way the use of scent is analogous to the human use of writing (Sebeok 1967:367). Most prosimians, especially the nocturnal ones and many of the New World monkeys,

Primates are social animals.

Primates use four basic systems of communication.

---

[5] Most likely there are other systems of communication used by primates that have not yet been identified, much less studied. The anthropologist Edward Hall (1966) recognizes another form of communication in humans which he calls thermal communication. He has found that the body gives off different amounts of heat in different behavioral settings, which in some cases can be interpreted as signals.

have specialized scent glands used for marking territories and routes, as well as for sexual attraction. These glands are located on either the throat, chest, arms, external genitalia, or anal region. The animals press and rub these glands against branches, and the odor left behind will be detected by others as a signal for receptivity to mating or as a warning of territorial possession. Scent seems to be used primarily by the nocturnal, arboreal primates, as a substitute for vision in the dark or in dense forest. The Old World monkeys and apes move over larger areas, which would be impossible to mark with scents. Likewise, in the Old World monkeys and apes, the signs of estrus are highly visual, thus reducing the need for olfactory signals (Marler 1965:549–550).

Perhaps the most peculiar behavior related to scent occurs in humans, and especially among the so-called "civilized" peoples. Millions of dollars are spent each year by these humans for underarm deodorants and vaginal douches in order to rid their bodies of the natural scents that the cosmetics manufacturers and advertising agencies claim are offensive. The same humans then spend additional millions of dollars on musk oils, perfumes, after-shave lotions, and fruit-flavored douches in order to give off olfactory signals that the advertiser claims have "sex appeal."

Tactile Systems. Almost as little is known about the tactile worlds of animals as about their chemical worlds. The hand is the most common part of the body used by primates to initiate physical contact, although the teeth, lips, tongue, nose, the tail when it is prehensile, the general body surface, the pelvic area, and penis may also be used in some circumstances or by certain species. All communications related to the sense of touch depend on the close proximity of individuals, in contrast to visual or auditory communication, which can occur over distances.

A prominent form of tactile communication among primates is grooming. The time spent grooming and the type of grooming vary widely with the species, age, and sex of the animals, as well as with social rank. In grooming, one animal manipulates and mouths the fur of another. While tree shrews use their teeth and tongue for grooming, the monkeys and apes generally use their hands. Almost any part of the recipient's body may be groomed, although much of the grooming seems to concentrate on the head, neck, and back, which are inaccessible to self-grooming, and on the anal and genital areas. These types of tactile communication play an important role in maintaining peace and cohesion in primate societies, especially in those species in which

Grooming is a major form of tactile communication.

dominance relations play an important role. In some cases, various grooming and sexual contacts are combined, producing an extraordinarily rich repertoire of tactile signals (Marler 1965:550–553).

Grooming behavior is important as a means of keeping the fur of a partner clean. It aids in keeping wounds from becoming infected and reduces the number of pests which could be transmitted within the group. Most of the grooming of the gorilla is limited almost exclusively to the cleaning function. On the other hand, grooming is important for more reasons than just cleaning, especially in baboons and rhesus monkeys, among whom it is a prominent part of social activity. In these species it is generally the females who initiate grooming, because they rank below the males in the dominance hierarchy most of the time. Grooming helps to relax tension between animals in potentially aggressive situations, as does mounting behavior in nonsexual situations (Marler 1965:553–554).

Visual Systems. Another form of communication involves optical systems. Visual signs (any information viewed with ones eyes) are both flexible and transient. They can be rapidly switched on or off. Visual signals are important (*a*) when fine discrimination of objects is needed, (b) when unfamiliar material is being comprehended, (*c*) when reference data have to be immediately available or where nearly simultaneous comparisons have to be made, (*d*) when the receiver must promptly select limited data from a large repertoire of information, and (*e*) when unfavorable environmental conditions hamper reception of other forms of communication (Sebeok 1967:367). As a result, visual systems allow for the exchange of sophisticated forms of information.

Visual signs differ somewhat for animals that move about during the day and those that are nocturnal because greater subtleties of information can be observed in light. The visual apparatus of the monkeys, apes, and humans is more highly developed than that of the prosimians. All visible parts of the body can contribute to optical signals. From an individual's size, coloration, and general appearance, its age and sex can be determined. Changes in posture or the mode of locomotion inform the observer about an individual's activity. By the position of its head, limbs, and tail, a primate can precisely express its temper or its intentions to others who are capable of interpreting the signals.

Among the higher forms of monkeys and apes, facial expressions are of primary importance in visual communication. The

In higher primates, facial expressions are important means of communication.

aspect of threat behavior most widely shared among species is the direct gaze. Often this gaze is sufficient in itself for a dominant monkey or ape to displace a subordinate. On the other hand, looking away is a widespread sign of submission. In some forms such as the macaques and baboons, stare threats are further embellished by eyelid fluttering, in which the raising of the brows and the lowering of the eyelids serves to set off the pale-colored lids against the darker background of the face. Imagine the plight of the poor monkey or ape who is put on display in one of our zoos. If staring is part of threat behavior in this species, the animal must be continually frustrated by the daily hundreds or even thousands of visitors who stop by its cage and stare at it.

The shape of the mouth is also an aspect of visual communication, and in some species its shape represents varying degrees of threat intensity, ranging from an "open-mouth" threat in which the teeth are not exposed to a "grimace" in which the corners of the mouth are drawn back exposing the teeth. "Lip smacking," in which the lips make kissing movements without the teeth coming together, is used in more neutral or pacificatory situations (Marler 1965:571–575). Due to the refinement in the muscles of their faces, the monkeys, apes, and humans are capable of the greatest amount of facial expression. The muscles are extremely complex in humans, providing by far the most varied facial expressions.

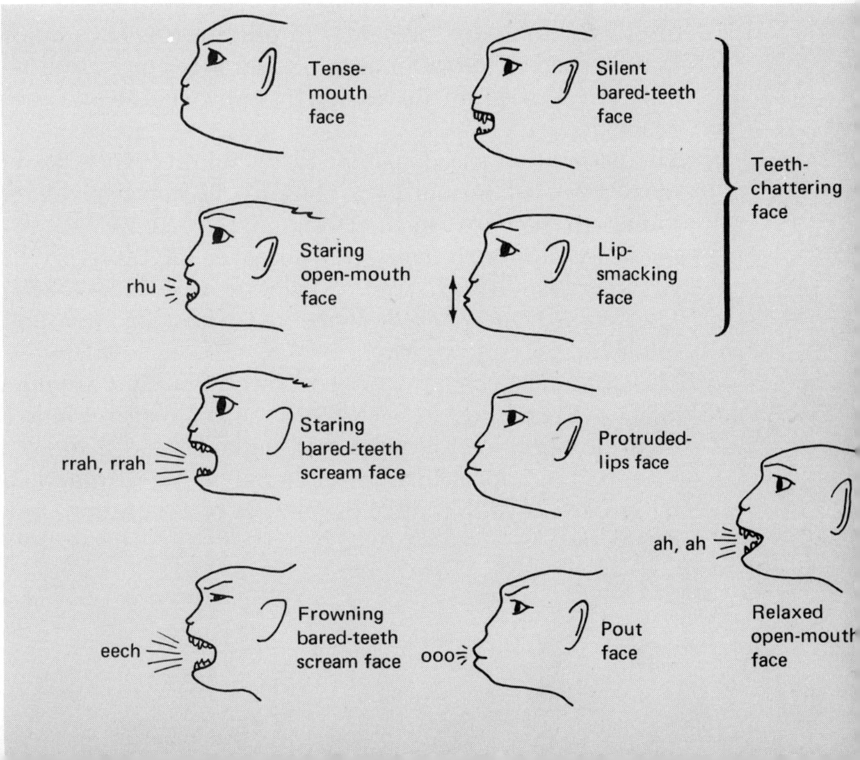

will evolve behavour adaptive.

Figure 12 Schematic representation of the main compound facial expressions in a *Macaca* type primate. (From Desmond Morris, *Primate Ethology*, 1967, Aldine Publishing Co.)

Van Hooff (1969:21–66) has identified the following 12 compound facial expressions observed regularly in most species of Old World monkeys and apes (also see Figure 12):

1. **The tense-mouth face**—used especially during a fast attack run.
2. **The staring open-mouth face**—used as a threat by the dominant animal. If the receiver of the threat does not back down at this point and indicate submission, the threat will lead directly to an attack.
3. **The staring bared-teeth scream face**—used most commonly as a response to an attack or a staring open-mouth display by a more dominant member of the group.
4. **The frowning bared-teeth scream face**—used by the subordinate animal as a reaction to an imminent or actual attack.
5. **Silent bared-teeth face**—does not give rise to attack. It may be used during fleeing, avoiding, or approaching and may alternate with other displays. It frequently leads to activities such as embracing, huddling, play, or visiting in each other's neighborhood.
6. **The lip-smacking face**—used quite infrequently when animals meet for the first time or after a period of separation. It acts both to lower the tendency to attack and to lower the tendency to flee. Thus it seems to have an important attracting function.
7. **The protruded-lips face**—used by some of the male macaques when a female is in heat. It is used by the male to induce the female to "present." In other forms of monkeys it may be used by two animals of the same sex or by animals of different sexes as an expression for approaching one another or for fleeing.
8. **The pout face**—used primarily by infants when they are away from their mothers. Usually the mother reacts by taking up the baby. In the chimpanzee the pout face is also made by adults. It has been observed of captive chimps when a person shows some attractive object like food.
9. **The relaxed open-mouth face**—used frequently when animals are playing together.
10. **The teeth-chattering face**—especially prevalent among macaques. Frequently it alternates with lip-smacking. It is often preceded or followed by avoidance and fleeing, or it may lead to approach. The teeth-chattering display is used by subordinates to reduce the chance of a dominant animal attacking.

11. **The relaxed face**—used when the animal is relaxed and not engaged in any activity.
12. **The alert face**—used in many social situations, including grooming and mounting.

The tails of primates are also of special significance in communication, although there is great variation in movements from one species to another. For example, among rhesus monkeys a subordinate monkey being attacked by a dominant one will place its tail between its legs. On the other hand, among baboons the *dominant* animal will have its tail between the legs. A dominant rhesus monkey will have a raised tail. In rhesus monkeys, tail movements upward or to the side are often associated with "presenting" of the anogenital region, which occurs both as a pacificatory gesture and as an invitation to mount for copulation. The langur's invitation to mount involves a lowered tail (Marler 1965:575–576).

Acoustic Systems. Acoustic systems add yet another dimension to primate communication. A sender can broadcast fairly directional sounds[6] when it is advantageous to the sender that its location be known. On the other hand, with the use of lower frequencies the sender's whereabouts may be kept concealed. Sound fills the entire space around the source and thus does not require a direct line of connection with the receiver. In other words, the signals can travel around corners and are not usually interrupted by obstacles (Sebeok 1967:368). In some primate species, observers have been able to identify over 30 different sounds produced by the vocal organs and used in communication (Struhsaker 1967:318). In addition a number of nonvocal sounds are made by primates. For example, adult gorillas regularly drum with their open palm on their chests as loud signals of challenge, and chimpanzees apparently enjoy producing as much noise as possible by stamping, hand clapping, kicking hollow trees, and so on. Yet vocalizations constitute the most frequent sound signals (Schultz 1969:226–227).

While there is tremendous species variation, it is possible to make some generalizations about certain types of sound signals and their apparent function. Barks, often shrill ones, are widely used to signal alarm. Screeching and screaming sounds are widespread signs of distress. Growling is widely used in association with agonistic (combative) behavior. Soft grunts are used by some groups of animals as they move along apparently as a

---

[6] Primarily those in the higher frequencies.

means of maintaining contact with each other. Also, many of the lower primates use clicking and chittering sounds (Marler 1965:566–568). If each of the sounds that has been identified by primatologists can convey different information by being repeated slowly or rapidly, or by being used in combination with other definite signals, the vocal communicative possibilities are quite elaborate for many species of primates.

Nonhuman Primate Societies

Charles Darwin's work established the importance of monkeys and apes to the study of humans. It stimulated the scientific study of the behavior of living animals. Most of the early research on primates in the late 1800s and early 1900s was carried out in zoos. The primary concern of much of this early work was to demonstrate that the behavior of humankind's closest relatives in the animal world was both complex and advanced. The early researchers believed that if Darwin's notion that humans are related to the apes was accepted, it was their duty to "elevate" these primates by finding in them as many similarities to humans as possible.

It was not until the 1920s and early 1930s that a number of independent pioneering studies were undertaken, initiating a new era of primate-behavior investigation. The German psychiatrist Wolfgand Köhler (1925) carried out classic tests of chimpanzee intelligence; in Moscow, Nadie Kohts (1935) undertook intensive comparisons of the behavior patterns of a young chimpanzee and a human infant; Robert Yerkes (1943) set up a major ape station at Orange Park, Florida; Solly Zuckerman (1932) made a detailed study of the social behavior of a colony of baboons in London; C. Ray Carpenter (1934) undertook the first detailed field study of a New World primate, the howler monkey; Henry W. Nissen (1931) studied the chimpanzee in the wild; and Harold Bingham (1932) observed the gorilla in its native habitat. However, World War II interrupted further research, and comparative primate studies were slow in beginning again. In recent years renewed interest in primate studies has expanded rapidly, and American, Swiss, British, and Japanese scientists have once again taken to the field. In the 1960s seven major regional primate research centers were established in the United States (Morris 1969:4–5). At present the study of primates is of interest not only to physical anthropologists, but also to psychologists, ethologists, and zoologists, as well as researchers the new discipline of primatology, which is devoted exclusively to primate research.

Currently, interest in primates studies is extensive.

The field research on primates has clearly established that most species of primates are social animals, living in groups of a few individuals to several hundred. This fact did not emerge from early studies of animals in zoos, because usually only one or two captive animals of a species were on display. Humans often view themselves as creatures of habit, bound by the traditions of their society, but they tend to view monkeys and apes as free to roam wherever they please, as their whims dictate. Such a picture could hardly be further from the truth. As the writer Sarels Eimerl and the anthropologist Irven De Vore (1965:129) have observed:

> Compared to the average suburbanite, the life of a monkey or an ape is monotonous, repetitious and humdrum. By every imaginable yardstick, the nonhuman primates are intensely conservative. They move back and forth, round and round, constantly retreading the same well-worn trails. Most pass their entire lives amid the same small group. Some join new groups, but even these do not venture beyond one tiny area of the forest or the savanna. All follow daily schedules almost as regular as those followed by many men.

Field studies have changed many of our stereotypes of primate behavior.

Primates seem to be organized into two radically different types of societies. Chance and Jolly (1970) have termed these "centripetal" and "acentric" societies. Each type of society copes with danger in a different way. In the centripetal society, the society is the focus of attention for the individual, whose behavior is organized around the group during all types of emotional arousal. Because the group remains together, members of the society are able to ward off predators. The societies of the savanna baboon, the macaques, the gorilla, and chimpanzee are examples of the centripetal society.

In an acentric primate society, the individual loses all social orientation when under predatory attack and escapes to the protection of the environment, so that the society falls apart. In other words, in time of danger it is everyone for him- or herself. The patas monkeys of Africa are typical of this type of society. Of primate societies studied, only the langur society appears to be intermediate, in that it can operate in either way when in danger (Chance and Jolly 1970:202).

Primate societies are primarily combinations of three components: female assemblies, juvenile clusters, and male cohorts. The female assemblies are comprised of several females and their young, together with attached females without young of their own. Female assemblies are a prominent feature in at least the following societies: the rhesus, the Japanese macaque, the langur, the savanna and gelada baboons, the patas monkey, the chimpanzee, and the gorilla. The female assembly tends to be

Most primate societies are combinations of female assemblies, juvenile clusters, and male cohorts.

less rigidly structured than the cohorts of males, but in some societies, the langur for example, there is a clear rank-order
among the females. Female assemblies are generally more evident at those periods of the day when the troop is not engaged in
major activities such as feeding, moving from one locality to another, or running from danger. The females of a society are
packed closer together in their assemblies than are the males in
their cohorts. Males show a tendency to maintain a greater optimum distance from one another than the females maintain
from each other. In female assemblies there is greater contact
between individuals than is found among the males. Aggression
in the female assemblies is expressed by hitting, snapping, and
biting rather than by the threats and chases so common among
the males (Chance and Jolly 1970:157–158, 202).

As the young become more or less independent of their
mothers, they join together with juveniles their own age and
older to constitute another major component of primate
societies—the juvenile clusters. Clusters of juveniles spend a
great deal of time at play. In some species these subgroups have
considerable mobility, moving freely between groups. The juveniles are generally tolerated by adult males, as long as their
antics do not become too boisterous or they do not get too close
to the females (Chance and Jolly 1970:158–159).

A third component of primate societies is the cohort of males.
Adult males that form a cohort remain together more or less
permanently and show some rank order. Very little is known of
the nature of the bachelor bands found among such forms as the
gelada and langur (Chance and Jolly 1970:159–160).

Most primate groups fall into one of three categories: multimale group, one-male group, and single pair of adults. The most
common of these is the multimale group, in which many males
and females live together without stable heterosexual bonds.
The second category, the one-male group, consists of a single
adult male and several females. In some species many one-male
groups periodically live together in a large troop. The third type
of group, the single pair of adults, is found only among a small
number of primates, including the gibbons, siamangs, and the
South American titi monkeys. All three types of groups also include juveniles and infants (Kummer 1971:33–34).

Spatial Relationships. All of the primate social groups, regardless of size or composition, live within circumscribed areas of
land, or "home ranges." Some social groups roam over miles,
whereas the ranges of others are concentrated into acres. Observers who study primates in the wild have been able to follow

group movements throughout the year, plotting routes taken and length of time spent in each area of their home ranges. Groups tend to spend the most time in certain locations, especially when there is a special food, a good water source, or favorite sleeping trees. Different parts of a home range may be used when seasonal changes in vegetation occur. Sections of the home range that are used most frequently are referred to as "core areas." Home ranges may overlap, with the same portions of land included in the home range of several troops of the same species. Normally the troops utilize the overlapping areas at different times, but occasionally there may be some feature in the overlapping area, such as a water hole, which is desired by more than one troop at the same time. When this is the case, the groups utilize the feature in such a way as to minimize the chances of the different groups coming into contact (Dolhinow 1972:358).

Species of several primate genera may live together in the same area. For example, in some African forests one might find chimpanzees, baboons, and several other species. Sometimes each species has a preference for a certain level of the forest; if the area is open, one species may move further from the nesting trees during the daytime. Likewise, one species will often have food preferences that differ from those of the other kinds of primates in the area, thus minimizing competition over available resources (Dolhinow 1972:358–359).

Under some circumstances, such as crowding or food shortage, a home range may be actively defended and other groups of the same species prevented from using the resources of the home range. Ranges that are defended are called "territories." Daily routines are organized in such a way as to maintain exclusive use of the territory. The boundaries of the territory may be marked with urine, feces, or other substances that smell. Loud calls are also used as boundary-marking mechanisms, signaling where the other groups should not trespass. When territory is violated, actual fighting may be engaged in. For the majority of species, fighting is rarely resorted to except under unusual conditions such as overcrowding, rapid changes in the habitat, and so on (Dolhinow 1972:359–360).

Hans Kummer (1971:74–76) has suggested that territorial behavior is caused partly by home ranges that are so small that the neighboring home ranges and groups become familiar and thus attractive to other groups. For example, in some langur studies in India and Ceylon it has been found that in two populations with relatively large home ranges (1.5 square miles and 3 square miles), relations between neighboring groups were gen-

> Primatologists distinguish between home range, core area, and territory.

erally peaceful and tolerant; while in two populations with very small home ranges (about 0.07 square miles to about 0.3 square miles), group encounters were frequent and aggressive. Likewise, the overcrowded city-dwelling rhesus monkeys of India will do anything they can to assure exclusive access to their territories (Southwick, Beg, and Siddiqi 1965).

Dominance. Another aspect of social life for some species is dominance. In some species, especially the baboons, the males are arranged in a dominance hierarchy. The male at the top of the hierarchy is considered the dominant male and is able to influence the lives of others. In human terms, he usually acts as the "leader" of the troop. There is a great range of dominance in the different primate societies but the dominant male often has priority over food and estrous females (females in heat). This male leads the group when moving, keeps order within the troop by stopping fights, and provides defense against predators and other threatening animals. Others in the troop show signs of submissiveness by lip-smacking, by grooming the dominant male, and so on. Other males of the troop are ranked individually in a hierarchy below the dominant male. Frequently several of the top-ranking males will cooperate with one another to maintain the status quo of the hierarchy. Less common females are also ranked in a hierarchy. Sometimes changes occur in the ranking. For example, a dominant male may lose his canine teeth and become an ineffective threatener and fighter, in other cases the change may be completely accidental. For example, Jane van Lawick-Goodall observed a chimpanzee who discovered accidentally that slapping empty tins caused such a tremendous racket that the other adult males were frightened. They credited the noise to the chimp, and he immediately enjoyed a rise in status, because the other males were now frightened of him.

In the long run, the dominance hierarchy actually promotes tranquility in the group, even though it may be based on force. As members of a troop grow up they learn which animals they can dominate and which they cannot. It would be dysfunctional for animals living together to have fights with one another every time an issue arose over food, space, estrous females, and so on. It is preferable for both the dominant and the subordinate to avoid fighting if the outcome of that fight is already predictable. Group-living primates have developed a substitute for frequent fighting—threat behavior. The dominance hierarchy allows members of the troop to make certain amount of prediction about the behavior of others in the troop. The ability to predict

Some primates have elaborate dominance hierarchies.

the behavior of others was basic to the evolution of the more complex social systems found in humans (Lancaster 1975:14–15).

Functions of Primate Social Organization. Before extensive fieldwork was undertaken, it was assumed that continuous sexual attraction between adults caused primates to live together. As a result of studies in the wild, it has been learned that mating systems differ widely and that many species have marked seasonal restrictions in their breeding, with little effect on their social organization. Lasting attachments between only two individuals of opposite sex or even one male and several females is found only in a few species. General promiscuity conditioned by the dominance hierarchy represents the most frequent mating pattern. Sexual behavior occupies only a small amount of time in the life of many mature female primates. For example, female monkeys are pregnant about half of the year and do not become sexually receptive again until their infants are weaned, a year or more after birth. Even after the infants are weaned, the female is actively interested in sex for only a few days, at the height of each estrus period (Schultz 1969:229).

While reproduction plays a role in the social group, other functions are of greater importance. Protection from predators is a basic function, especially in the centripetal form of societies. The young are especially vulnerable, and the social group, through cooperative watchfulness, is able to provide greater protection than could be provided solely by the mother. By laying claim to a home range, the social group is able to provide a certain amount of security for its members, in the sense that they are familiar with the resources. Also, the social group provides a context for learning. Because young monkeys and apes are generally left by the mother to learn many aspects of social behavior through observation, it becomes important for juveniles to learn to pay attention to the right things at the right time. Attention to others becomes a key element in primate learning. According to the physical anthropologist Jane Lancaster (1975:45) one of the important aspects of a dominance hierarchy is that it forms an "attention structure." Subordinate members are usually very much aware of what dominant animals are doing, even when the subordinates seem to be going about their business. Likewise, the individuals of mother-infant groups and peer play groups catch each other's attention. By noticing what is going on, the young of the social group are able to learn, and innovations can be passed from one member of the group to another.

Protection and learning appear to be of greater importance in primate-group cohesion than reproduction.

How Apelike Are Humans? If one is to believe the point of view presented in a number of popular books,[7] humans are little more than naked apes. Aggression, dominance, and territoriality are portrayed as primary factors in human behavior. The biological base of humankind is emphasized to the extent that culture is almost completely ignored. For example, in *The Territorial Imperative* Robert Ardrey (1966:4–5) states:

> Man, I shall attempt to demonstrate in this inquiry, is as much a territorial animal as is a mockingbird singing in the California night. We act as we do for reasons of our evolutionary past, not our cultural present, and our behavior is as much a mark of our species as is the shape of a human thigh bone or the configuration of nerves in a corner of the human brain. If we defend the title to our land or the sovereignty of our country, we do it for reasons no different, no less innate, no less ineradicable, than do lower animals. The dog barking at you from behind his master's fence acts for a motive indistinguishable from that of his master when the fence was built.

Popular writers such as Ardrey have discovered that humans are animals, and each author presents his discovery as if it is a startling new truth—although Linnaeus and others were aware of this fact several hundred years ago. The most extreme of these writers also argue that human behavior is out of tune with the needs of the modern world; that these behaviors are under genetic control and are largely determined by our animal heritage; and that there is little that humans can do but accept their fate. These same writers maintain that if humans insist on trying to change themselves, they will have virtually no success, because the natural human being—the naked ape—is far more like other animals than most humans admit. Humans are portrayed as so instinctively aggressive that they have no possibility of controlling this behavior.

The naked-ape argument suffers from two inadequacies: misinterpretation of primate studies and a general ignorance of the rich ethnographic data documenting the great cultural diversity of humans. Many field studies of primates have shown that aggressiveness is not the dominant instinct that Ardrey and others make it out to be. Only some types of primates exhibit strong aggressiveness. Aggressiveness occurs most strongly in groups whose habitat has been disturbed by predators, especially human ones, and also those whose habitat is primarily open country. The pioneering field studies of baboons were conducted on groups living under disturbed conditions. It is not surprising

The naked-ape argument misinterprets primate studies and ignores ethnographic data.

---

[7] The British zoologist Desmond Morris's *The Naked Ape* (1967) and *The Human Zoo* (1969); the American playwright Robert Ardrey's *African Genesis* (1961), *The Territorial Imperative* (1966), and *The Social Contract* (1970).

that these baboon troops exhibited considerable aggression. When forest groups of baboons living under more relaxed conditions were studied, it was found that aggression was very infrequent and male dominance hierarchies were difficult to discern (Pilbeam 1975:68–71). The naked-ape arguments overemphasis on the aggression, territoriality, and dominance of nonhuman primates is used as the basis for extrapolation from primate behavior to human behavior. It is overly simplistic to believe that human aggression is strongly genetically determined, when it is clear that many apes and monkeys are not particularly aggressive. Those who stress that humans are apelike, emphasize that aggression has been inherited from early forms of humans who were hardly more than "killer apes."

The notion of australopithecine aggression was first put forward by Raymond Dart (1959), who is convinced that humans originated when weapons for killing prey were invented. In *African Genesis*, Robert Ardrey elaborated on Dart's notion, proposing that hunting became an integral part of human behavior because the most skilled hunters would survive to maturity and pass their genes on to the next generation, through the process of natural selection. The behaviors of killing would become part of the neurological system. In time, every human male would be genetically endowed with a killer instinct. Recent chemical analyses suggest the *possibility* of a hormonal base to aggression in male baboons, chimpanzees, and humans, which would support the theory that aggression is genetically linked. Studies of ground-dwelling monkeys show that there is an increase of the male sex hormone testosterone in the blood of males who have been fighting. However, the research does not show whether the increase of testosterone in the blood initiates the aggression or whether the fighting itself stimulates the production of the hormone. If the hormone initiated the action it would provide strong support for the genetically based aggression; if the fighting caused an increase in testosterone, it would weaken, if not disprove, the aggression theory.

The relationship of killing and aggression in humans to the evolution of hunting is still being debated. The fossil remains at Olduai, East Africa, associated with *Australopithecus* include many animal skeletons, among them those of several large mammals. The problem is that no one can demonstrate whether the australopithecines hunted and killed these animals or found them dead and butchered them. Likewise, nothing is known about how much hunted animal meat these early creatures included in their diet (Weiss and Mann 1975:453). The rich ethno-

There is no proof that early humans were aggressive killers.

graphic data on many modern hunting bands shows a dependence on vegetable food and small game that far exceeds that of large game hunting. Primate studies and ethnographic studies of contemporary hunting-and-gathering societies indicate to many anthropologists that preurban humans would have used their evolving cultural capacities to channel and control their aggression. As the physical anthropologist David Pilbeam (1975:75) has remarked of the naked-ape argument:

> To be sure, we are not born empty slates upon which anything can be written; but to believe in the "inevitability of beastliness" is to deny our humanity as well as our primate heritage—and, incidentally, does a grave injustice to the "beasts."

The ethologist Irenäus Eibl-Eibesfeldt disagrees with Pilbeam's conclusion. Eibl-Eibesfeldt has worked with a team of researchers who have been studying the African Bushmen since 1970. On the basis of his own field observations, Eibl-Eibesfeldt (1975:177) believes that the anthropological data show that most hunters and gatherers have strong aggressive potential. Eibl-Eibesfeldt (1975:186) suggests that the Bushmen represent one of the groups in which these strong aggressive tendencies exist, but that these tendencies are in part tempered by a counter-tendency to share:

> I firmly believe that there is indisputable evidence of territoriality and aggression in Bushmen, thus indicating that men fought over the possession of land long before the advent of food production. At the same time, however, sharing, both of objects and game, does take place in Bushman society, despite the strong importance attached to ownership of personal items, and this would seem to suggest that the instinct of sharing may not have been completely dormant in early man.

We have seen that the debate over human aggression centers on the intensity of human aggression as well as on the reason for its occurrence. Physical anthropologists in general play down the aggressiveness of humans, while popular writers such as Ardrey and many ethologists emphasize a strong aggressive base in humans. In many cases these opposing points of view are based on the same factual data. Each group has its own perception of humankind, which it believes is supported by the facts. The physical anthropologists emphasize the importance of culture in distinguishing humans from the other primates; the popular writers and ethologists emphasize that humans are little more than naked apes. Each group is attempting to create its own myth of humankind's relationship to the nonhuman primates.

In general, anthropologists and other behavioral scientists question to what extent aggressive behavior is genetic. Many psychologists believe that frustration may be the most important cause of aggression. Some sociologists, cultural anthropologists, and psychologists believe that human aggression is produced by social deprivation, childhood maladjustment, mental illness, and other *social* factors (Weiss and Mann 1975:454).

Many anthropologists see aggression resulting from social rather than genetic factors.

It may be that all of the explanations of aggression are valid in one way or another. Certainly it is clear that the question of human aggression is exceedingly complex, but also exceedingly important in terms of humankind's future survival.

The Coming Extinction of Nonhuman Primates?

In this chapter, attention has been devoted to human's closest relatives in the animal kingdom, the nonhuman primates. The primate order of mammals is made up of almost 200 different species. Yet how many of these creatures have most of us ever seen? Unfortunately, many of these species are already considered endangered species and may be extinct before we ever have a chance to study them.

Various species have been able to maintain a balance with nature in the wild. In this century, humans have radically altered this balance, with disastrous results for the nonhuman primates. In some areas the animals are hunted for food and for their skins. In other cases the habitat has been destroyed by humans clearing the jungles and forests for farms. The monkeys and apes in particular have been captured and sent to zoos and laboratories around the world. Tens of thousands of animals are lost each year in this way. Hunters capture the young, often killing the mother first in order to make the capture less dangerous. The death of an adult female ape is especially unfortunate, because of the slow rate of growth and long interval between succeeding generations. Animals that are captured are usually sent to a central shipping point where they are often kept with other animals from many different regions. Under natural conditions these animals would never come into contact with one another. As a result the animals are not immune to one another's diseases, and many die even before they are shipped. Those that finally reach their destination are further affected by humans. Humans create a new and artificial environment in zoos. By introducing new diets and behavior patterns, humans

Many of the nonhuman primates are on the verge of extinction due to human activity.

produce new kinds of selective pressures quite different from those of the natural habitat. Humans may be creating new breeds of primates.

Fortunately many zoos around the world are no longer purchasing individuals who have been captured in the wild, thus lessening the demand for these primates; instead they have begun to purchase only animals bred in captivity. For some of the primate species, the help of the zoos may be too little or too late. It is somewhat ironic that just as the modern world is experiencing an almost uncontrollable cat and dog population explosion, many of humankind's closest relatives are on the verge of extinction.

Anthropology Vocabulary

acentric society
anthropoids
ape
arboreal
bipedalism
brachiation
centripetal society
chimpanzee
core area
diurnal

dominance hierarchy
gibbon
gorilla
home range
Lemuriformes
New World monkeys
nocturnal
Old World monkeys
orangutan
power grip

precision grip
prehensile
primates
prosimians
quadrupedalism
semibrachiation
sexual dimorphism
tarsier
territories

Review Questions

1. What are the major divisions of the primates? What are characteristics of the different forms?
2. What are the basic forms of locomotion used by the primates?
3. How do primates communicate with one another?
4. What kinds of societies do nonhuman primates have?
5. Are aggression, dominance, and territoriality basic factors in human behavior? How do ethologists and physical anthropologists differ in their views on these behaviors? Can anthropology's holistic approach account for the physical anthropologist's point of view?

Recommended Reading

Bourne, Geoffrey H., 1974, *Primate Odyssey.* New York: Putnam. A popular account of the primates, including a great deal of information on experiments being carried out at primate laboratories.

Chance, Michael R. A., and Clifford J. Jolly, 1970, *Social Groups of Monkeys, Apes and Men*. London: Jonathan Cape Ltd. An interesting evaluation of the nature and functions of different primate social groups.

Eimerl, Sarel, and Irven De Vore, 1965, *The Primates*. New York: Time-Life Books. A readable account of various primates, with emphasis on the baboon. Excellent illustrations.

Jolly, Alison, 1972, *The Evolution of Primate Behavior*. New York: Macmillan. An evolutionary perspective on primate ecology, society, and intelligence.

Kummer, Hans, 1971, *Primate Societies: Group Techniques of Ecological Adaptation*. Chicago: Aldine-Atherton. An interpretation of primate ecological adaptations, with excellent descriptions of the various types of primate societies.

Lancaster, Jane B., 1975, *Primate Behavior and the Emergence of Human Culture*. New York: Holt, Rinehart, and Winston. A brief introduction to primate communication, social organization, and adaptation.

Rosen, S. I., 1974, *Introduction to the Primates: Living and Fossil*. Englewood Cliffs, N.J.: Prentice-Hall. An excellent overview of living and fossil primates. Well illustrated.

Schultz, Adolph H., 1969, *The Life of Primates*. New York: University Books. A comparison of primate anatomical differences.

Watts, Elizabeth S., 1975, *Biology of the Living Primates*. Dubuque, Iowa: Brown. A brief anatomical and biochemical comparison of primates.

6

Why shouldn't I collect artifacts?

Archaeologists do not search for buried treasure.

Archaeologists are interested in artifacts because of the information they provide about the past.

Archaeologists use two strategies: the inductive and the deductive method.

Relative and absolute dating are both used to interpret the age of archaeological material.

Prehistoric artifacts have been discovered throughout the world. Artifacts come to light as a result of archaeological excavations, road construction, farming, and by other means. The significance of an artifact varies according to who discovers it. Some individuals value an artifact as a curio; to others an artifact is important for its monetary value. For the professional archaeologist, the importance of an artifact is in the information it yields about the people who manufactured the object. The archaeologist studies the context in which artifacts are found, as well as the artifacts themselves. In many cases the context yields more information than the artifact itself, providing data on climate, environment, the age of the material, and the relationships between artifacts. In this chapter each of the values of artifacts will be examined in terms of its effect on understanding the past.

Artifacts are valued as curios, for monetary value, and as information.

Artifacts as Curios

Artifacts are frequently found accidentally by an individual engaged in some other activity than hunting for artifacts. Chances are that many of us would recognize some artifacts as human products, especially if the artifact were an arrowhead or a piece of pottery. Yet other kinds of artifacts, such as stone scrapers or bison-scapula shovels, would be less easily identified by the nonprofessional as resulting from human technology. To many individuals these artifacts would look like just another rock or piece of old bone. As a result nonprofessionals may keep those things that strike their fancy as unique or unusual and leave behind artifacts they do not recognize as such.

In other cases, nonartifacts may be collected by the nonprofessional because they are thought to be artifacts. For example, avid collectors in southern Oregon value rocks that resemble the shape of a human foot. The collectors call these artifacts "moccasin lasts." They believe these rocks were used by prehistoric Oregon Indians as forms around which they shaped skins for their moccasins. Some proud collectors of the region have acquired hundreds of these rocks for their collections, the most envied being a 6-foot "moccasin last." These collectors have made a logical but inaccurate interpretation. They assume that the Indians of Oregon must have worn moccasins. Their knowledge of the American Indian has come from the mass media, which present *all* Indians as resembling those of the Plains, with feather headdresses, bison-skin clothing, and moccasins. But the archaeologists have found that the Indians of southern Oregon did not wear moccasins; they wore sandals. Besides, if these rocks had ever served as lasts, they would show some evidence of having been shaped to resemble the contours of the user's foot. Yet there are no signs of knapping (chipping of stone) on the "moccasin lasts." It is highly improbable, even if these Indians had ever worn moccasins, that *each* Indian would have been able to find *two* rocks that were naturally shaped just like his or her two feet.

In Oregon as well as other parts of the country, "arrowheads" are highly prized. When an arrowhead is discovered, it is almost always saved by the finder. Arrowheads are perhaps the single most popular artifact throughout the United States. Yet many artifacts discovered and considered "arrowheads" were not arrowheads at all. Many are too large to have been attached to an arrow shaft and propelled from a bow. Often these larger points were attached to a larger shaft of wood, which was used either as a spear, and hurled, or as a lance, for jabbing. In other cases an artifact identified as an arrowhead may have served an entirely different purpose: as a blade, burin, awl, or scraper, for instance. While the discoverer of the "arrowhead" may be interested in what it was used for, the primary importance of the discovery is the resulting ownership. The discoverer enjoys having the artifact whether it is actually an arrowhead or not. It is a curio and is saved because of its intrinsic qualities: unusual shape, beautiful color, and so on. As a curio the "arrowhead" may be displayed with other "arrowheads" in a design depicting the outline of an Indian chief, it may be imbedded in cement with other curios to form an interesting mosiac patio, or it may be stored in a drawer until it is eventually thrown away.

Artifacts of earlier times have always served as curios for later generations. Occasionally an ancient Mayan ceremonial center will yield an artifact of an even earlier culture than that of the Maya. These artifacts must have been considered heirlooms by the Maya. Recently in Cuba a native curer was found using an artifact from Mexico dating from about the time of the birth of Christ. The curer believed that the artifact had special magical qualities because it was a curio.

Collecting curios is a common practice, with a long history. Yet it is a kind of behavior that can be harmful to our understanding of the past. Let us suppose that each person in the United States found and saved just *one* arrowhead during his or her lifetime. It would mean that over 200 million artifacts would be removed from scientific analysis. Often the artifact itself is of less importance to the archaeologist than its context, such as the soil layer or the material found with it. The addi-

Curio collecting can be harmful to our understanding of the past because it destroys information.

tional facts gleaned from the context may allow the archaeologist to locate a new site, to identify the use of the artifact, or
perhaps date the artifact. Taking an artifact from the ground re-
moves it from its context.

The individuals of southern Oregon who collect moccasin
lasts also collect other kinds of artifacts. Collecting provides
these people a great deal of pleasure, as well as a hobby. They
may spend weekends and vacations looking for artifacts to add
to their collections. In doing so, they destroy sites that contain
valuable information. A typical site in southern Oregon has
circular or oval depressions, which are the remains of house
pits. Many of these collectors will dig into the middle of any
house pit that they discover, because they believe that artifacts
are always buried in the center of the pits. Besides being illegal,
as Oregon has a state antiquites law, this activity destroys the
house pit for any future archaeological research. If there were
only a few of these individuals, the situation would not even
merit discussion. However it is estimated that there are over
5000 such collectors in Oregon alone, and the same type of
collecting and site destruction takes place in every state in
the union.

Digging for Profit

Collectors are a serious threat to the preservation of archaeological material. They are misinformed or uninformed. If collectors understood the significance and the frequent illegality of
their actions, many would stop collecting or perhaps change
their approach so that they would contribute to rather than detract from archaeological research.

A more serious threat to world archaeology than the collector
is the growing number of individuals who make their living by
looting the past. Those who rob sites for profit are sometimes
referred to as "commercial archaeologists" or "grave robbers"—even if their looting takes place at sites other than
graves. "Commerical archaeologist" is truly a misnomer, because such an individual is not concerned with collecting information about the past.

The looting of archaeological sites for profit is a practice that
has considerable antiquity, especially in the areas of early civilization. Some of the earliest grave robbers were the Spanish conquerors, who acquired vast sums of gold and silver through
looting. The artistic skills of the ancient American metalworkers
were ignored, and their beautiful gold and silver work was

melted down to make bullion. In this process of destruction, thousands of exquisite artifacts were lost forever.

During the sixteenth century limekilns were operated in the Forum Romanum, the center of the ancient Roman capital. Temples were razed to provide stone for building material. Pieces of marble from the site were used by the popes to decorate their fountains. The Serapeum was blown apart by gunpowder and its stone used for decorating stables. The Roman Colosseum was used as a stone quarry for four centuries (Ceram 1951:22).

Grave robbing was important in the growth of archaeology. It was through grave robbing that many of the art objects of the early civilizations were first brought to light. A great deal of the early grave robbing was sponsored and financed by the European aristocracy, which began to value artifacts from the circum-Mediterranean area. Charles of Bourbon and his queen were instrumental in the excavations of Herculaneum in 1738 and Pompeii in 1748 because they were interested in expanding their collection of antiquities.

In 1798 Napoleon entered Egypt with an army and a scientific expedition of 175 learned civilians, who collected a tremendous amount of information on ancient Egypt. As interest in Egyptian art and culture developed in Europe, and later in the United States, a demand was created for Egyptian artifacts. The desire for artifacts in turn created a proliferation of grave robbing. The nineteenth-century grave robbers discovered that they had been beaten in their looting by several thousand years. Grave robbing was already popular in the days of the Egyptian pharaohs. Shortly after the body of a pharaoh was sealed in its tomb, the burial chamber was usually broken into and plundered. By the late nineteenth century, few tombs in the Valley of the Kings remained untouched.

As the Western world became intrigued with the artifacts of the ancient circum-Mediterranean civilizations, museums and private collectors acquired art objects by any means, whether legal or illegal. Although some countries took action to stop the flow of archaeological treasures from their borders, attempts at regulation were generally ineffective. When museums were not directly violating the antiquities laws of other countries, they were accepting collections of artifacts donated by private collectors who had acquired the objects through questionable means.

In 1922 Howard Carter's discovery of the tomb of Tutankhamen made world headlines because of the "Pharaoh's Curse." It was believed that the opening of the tomb had caused the

The Western world has long exploited the archaeological treasures of developing countries.

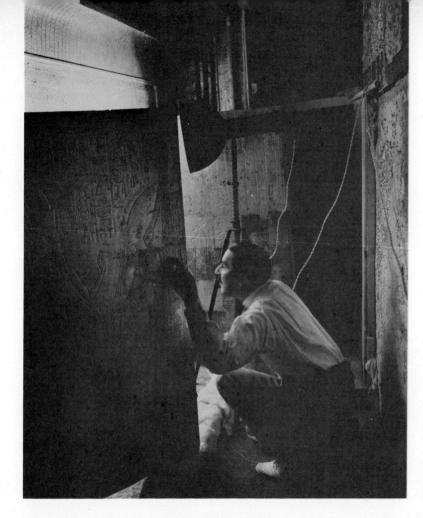

Howard Carter opening
the door to Tutankh-
amen's tomb. (The Met-
ropolitan Museum of Art,
photograph by Harry
Burton)

death of a number of the tomb's discoverers.[1] Interest in the ancient Egyptians was far-reaching, and tourists flocked to the
tomb in droves. Egyptian artifacts became more valuable and
looting more profitable than ever before.

The same story of plunder can be repeated with the discovery
of each ancient civilization. As a civilization is popularized its
artifacts are sought after. The artifacts command greater prices
and the looters are inspired. Looting in turn brings about the
destruction of the archaeological sites where the artifacts have
been discovered.

Until recently the art of pre-Columbian America did not command high prices on the art market. Pre-Columbian art was considered less sophisticated than that of the civilizations of the
circum-Mediterranean area. To be sure, there have been many
collectors. Looting of sites in Peru has occurred for hundreds of

[1] Actually the "Pharaoh's Curse" was a journalistic fabrication.

years. For example at Paracas, a site on the Peruvian coast, pre-Incan peoples wrapped bodies in cloth, together with objects of clay, gold, silver, and copper, forming *mummy bundles.* The mummy bundles were placed in large communal burial chambers. The extremely dry conditions of the Peruvian coast resulted in excellent preservation of the bundles. Because these bundles were concentrated in communal burial chambers, they fell easy prey to grave robbers of the past several centuries. One bundle after another was unwrapped for the treasures it contained.

Unfortunately for archaeologists, pre-Columbian art became popular in the late 1960s. The monetary value of these artifacts skyrocketed. In a matter of a few years an artifact that might have sold for an insignificant amount of money was commanding hundreds and in some cases even thousands of dollars. Acquiring pre-Columbian art became fashionable and a demand was created. The ancient art of Mexico, Guatemala, and Peru became especially valued. Even the less evolved art of the prehistoric Indians of the United States became sought after by the collector, once again inflating the price. A Mimbres pot from New Mexico that would have sold for $50 in 1960 was commanding thousands of dollars in 1970. Pre-Columbian art had set off another "gold rush," with many new looters joining in to make their fortune. Once again valuable sites were destroyed by the careless looters.

> Pre-Columbian art became valuable to collectors in the late 1960s, and many sites have been destroyed as a result.

The private collectors soon discovered that investments in pre-Columbian art could yield terrific tax write-offs. Objects could be purchased cheaply in Mexico or Guatemala, brought home illegally, and then appraised at the current United States market value. The objects were then donated to a museum or similar institution and the donation used as a tax deduction. The investment of several hundreds of dollars in Latin America resulted in a deduction of thousands of dollars. American taxpayers suffered, the archaeologists suffered, and the countries losing their national heritage suffered. The looting of pre-Columbian sites has become a lucrative business. In the richest archaeological regions, grave robbing was taken out of the hands of peasant families making a few extra dollars in their spare time with a machete and shovel; in their place came heavily financed, well-equipped looters.

The Mayan Area. In March of 1971 Ian Graham, a famous Scottish scholar who is photographing and drawing all known Mayan inscriptions, went to the remote Guatemalan site of La Naya with a party of workers. There they came upon a gang of looters cutting apart an ancient stone monument. The looters fled. As Graham was setting up camp, shots rang out, and one of his assistants fell dead.

Today's professional looter is well armed, sometimes with machine guns, and flies into sites by helicopter or carries out artifacts in expensive high-powered boats. Much of the recent looting activity is geared to procuring stone monuments. The monuments are so heavy they cannot be moved easily. Undeterred, the looters merely break up the monuments and take the pieces that will command the best prices. They use sledgehammers, chain saws, fire, and even dynamite to break up the monuments.

The ancient Maya were a literate people who used a writing system we have been unable to decipher. Every example of their writing that is discovered provides valuable clues toward translating their system of hieroglyphics. Almost all of the Mayan "books" of writing were systematically burned by the early Spanish missionaries. In fact only three, or possibly four, "books" have survived. Therefore almost everything that we can learn about the writing system comes from what has been carved in stone. Unfortunately, archaeologists are discovering that stone monuments are being destroyed, defaced, or removed faster than they are able to record information about them. At Naranjo, a Mayan site near the Guatemalan-Belize border, half of the 40 known monuments have been attacked by looters. Some of the finest examples of ancient American sculpture lie scattered in meaningless fragments over the ground. In their efforts to slice beautiful, thousand-year-old stone carvings into portable, marketable segments, thieves have totally destroyed many precious hieroglyphic inscriptions (Stuart 1975:769).

Looting is bringing about the destruction of the unexcavated Mayan site of Nakum, in the jungles of Guatemala. Thus far money has not been available for research at Nakum, even though it would probably provide important insights into the fall of the Classic Mayan civilization. Looters have penetrated 30 feet of solid masonary in order to get to tombs. The structures have become honeycombed with tunnels, trenches, and pits that many buildings are on the verge of collapse (Hellmuth 1975).

At another Mayan site, Tancah, the head of the Rain God, Chac, was removed from a beautiful and rare mural. The looter apparently just cut out a section of the limestone which he or she thought was marketable and left behind a hole—and a ruined mural—for future generations.

In 1972 two Americans and a national of British Honduras (Belize) were arrested and charged with conspiracy to transport in interstate and foreign commerce Mayan artifacts and art treasures stolen from Guatemala. These men had worked out a scheme for stealing artifacts from Mayan sites in the jungles of Guatemala and transporting them illegally to the United States, where they were offered for sale to museums, art dealers, and private art collectors. One of the artifacts found in the possession of these men was a sculptured stone monument known as the Machaquila Stela 2, dated at about AD 810. It was originally 82 inches in height and 48 inches in width. To facilitate its unlawful removal from Guatemala, the looters had cut the monument into 14 pieces and were offering the Machaquila Stela 2 for sale at a price of approximately $300,000 (Anonymous 1973:53).

In 1970, while the Mayanist Merle Greene Robertson was making rubbings of the stone monuments at the site of Itsimté, for Tulane University's Middle American Research Institute, she and her workers were held at gunpoint by six men with submachine guns posing as policemen. Fortunately the archaeologist and her workers were freed unharmed. However, after the crew left the site, the "policemen" returned and began sawing the monuments into smaller pieces. They were caught, but not before the monuments had been partially damaged (Robertson 1971:147).

Some of the Mayan stone monuments with hieroglyphic writing have been cut into hundreds of pieces, and the pieces have made their way to remote corners of the world. Even if all of the pieces of a monument could be assembled, the shattered fragments could not be put back together into their original form unless detailed photographs, drawings, or rubbings had been made before the monument had been broken into small pieces. In many cases no such records exist.

Once damaged or cut into pieces, monuments cannot be easily reassembled and valued information is lost forever.

Besides the stone monuments, the most promising collection of Mayan writing that might provide a clue to the decipherment of the hieroglyphics is found on the beautiful polychrome cylindic vases of the Classic Period. Like the monuments, these vases are sought after by collectors. Once in the hands of private collectors they are often no longer available to the scientific world for study.

> This is a tragedy for mankind, really, for each is, in effect, a new codex, replete with scenes of action—ball games, royal courts, ceremonies, and processions—most often with texts that explain them. One such vessel that was exhibited in New York City bore the pictures of 31 small figures, beings of the Maya pantheon, or mythology, hitherto unknown to archaeology. One can only wonder what else the looter found in the tomb that would have added to our knowledge of the Maya and the ways of the Maya mind. [Stuart 1975:791]

The incidents of looting which are occurring at the Mayan sites in Guatemala are also taking place on as extensive a scale in Mexico, Peru, the Middle East, South and Southeast Asia, and the United States. Each of these areas is rapidly losing a considerable part of its cultural heritage.

Attempts to bring an end to the looting in these areas of the world have thus far proven to be ineffective. There is still a market for the artifacts. Museums and collectors are willing to pay large sums of money for valuable pieces regardless of how the artifacts were obtained. Also, most countries are unable to control smuggling, because they have limited funds for customs officials and border guards.

In 1970 UNESCO adopted an international agreement to end the looting and smuggling of artifacts in an attempt to preserve the world's artistic and scientific heritage. In the same year, the United States and Mexico signed a bilateral treaty calling for cooperation in the restitution of stolen antiquities. However, measures such as these have not proven effective. In some cases United States collectors have been less willing to purchase looted material, but European and Japanese buyers continue to pay high prices, thus further stimulating the trade. Some additional help has come from a few museums which have taken a stand against acquiring any archaeological material that may have been obtained illegally: Not only will they refuse to purchase such material, they will not appraise it or even accept it as a donation. Unfortunately, most museums have not taken such a stand. Even if museums were to band together, there would still be private collectors eager to purchase valuable artifacts, no matter how they were obtained.

As some of the sources of artifacts have been reduced, the financial backers of the looters have begun to support artisans in faking artifacts. Millions of dollars have recently been made available by unknown sources for the creation of a highly sophisticated industry devoted to counterfeiting artifacts. In order to fake pre-Columbian jade pieces from Mexico, jade from Canada, which is the same type as that used in pre-Columbian times, is flown to western Mexico, where master crafters then duplicate the originals. Special techniques have been developed for faking pottery, including elaborate processes for giving pots the appearance of great antiquity. If museums eventually agree not to authenticate artifacts, it is possible that collectors will become fearful of purchasing fakes and less apt to purchase artifacts of questionable origin. This in turn might reduce the market for looted items and consequently bring about a reduction in the amount of looting.

The faking of pre-Columbian artifacts has become a major industry.

The only long-term solution to the problem seems to lie in creating pride in the cultural heritage of the areas where artifacts are being looted. Mexico has perhaps been most successful in this approach. The Mexicans have built a national museum of anthropology that has become a source of pride for the entire nation. However, there are over 11,000 archaeological sites in Mexico, most of which are unprotected. There are still some individuals in Mexico who put personal gain ahead of public heritage. In other countries, the situation is worse; people do not value artifacts as a vital part of their history.

The United States. In northeast Arkansas, the Arkansas Archaeological Survey has encountered a large number of grave robbers who have little appreciation of artifacts as information. Schoolteachers have been discovered who have traded high grades for artifacts or who have taken pupils out to help rob graves (Morse 1973:30–31). In this area, Mississippi Valley pottery, which is not particularly aesthetically pleasing, sells for from $5 to $1000 per piece. In northeast Arkansas it has been estimated that as many as 250 people are involved in grave robbing, and another thousand or more surface-collect for profit. Among these collectors the sole criterion of an artifact's worth is the amount for which it can be sold. The information it yields, or could yield if it were carefully excavated, is unimportant (Morse 1973:30–31).

Pottery found in New Mexico known as Mimbres pottery is sought after by museums and private collectors, because it represents some of the most aesthetically pleasing examples of pre-Columbian United States ceramics ever produced. For many years, curio collectors have sacked archaeological sites. In the past few years, as the value of Mimbres pots has increased, heavily financed looting has begun which will virtually destroy *all* known Mimbres sites.

Mimbres pottery has always commanded a good price but until recently was not considered as desirable or valuable as the art of many other regions of the world. Ten years ago the price of a Mimbres pot ranged from several hundred dollars to as much as $2000 for an exceptional piece. By 1973 the price of a single piece of Mimbres pottery had jumped to between $5000 and $15,000, with a few pieces being sold for even more (Donald A. Graybill, personal communication).

Along the northern Mimbres drainage, an area of Federally owned land, destruction of sites has been increasing at an alarming rate. Almost 87 percent of the larger sites of the area have been destroyed. Looters leave behind valuable artifacts

The development of pride in cultural heritage is the only long-term solution to the destruction of sites.

Extensive site destruction is also occurring in the United States.

and other data of importance to the archaeologist, as they search only for the Mimbres pottery. However, once these sites are destroyed, there is little that the archaeologist is able to learn about the people that once inhabited the region. Between 1900 and 1960, forty-seven square meters of site area were destroyed in the northern Mimbres drainage. Between 1961 and 1970, the additional area damaged included 273 square meters. In the year 1971 the rate of destruction per year increased to 1486 square meters and in 1972 reached 1670 square meters. If the destruction continues at the 1972 rate, all sites in this region will have been destroyed by 1977 (Graybill 1974).

Costa Rica. Costa Rica, the small Central American country northwest of Panama, has suffered a loss of its cultural heritage due to its citizens attitude toward artifacts. In Costa Rica many people make their living at grave robbing. They are called *huaqueros*. It has been estimated that about one percent of the total economically active population of the country is engaged in grave robbing—roughly 4400 persons. While this number may not seem especially large, it is more than all of the professional archaeologists in the world (Heath 1973:259—260).

There are more grave diggers in Costa Rica than professional archaeologists in all the world.

Many of the Costa Ricans, and especially the huaqueros themselves, view grave robbing as a kind of mining rather than a criminal act. Actually, grave robbing has been illegal in Costa Rica for only the last few years. There is little concern for or understanding of the irretrievable information that will be lost because of looting. The artifacts discovered and sold by the looters are considered an untapped natural resource. As long as the artifacts are not given importance as a vital part of the national heritage, many Costa Ricans will see no harm in digging up the artifacts and selling them, especially since 70 percent of the artifacts are sold abroad and constitute an appreciable source of foreign currency.

From the Costa Rican's point of view, everyone benefits from the grave robbing. It provides jobs for an extensive segment of the work force, many of whom might be unemployed without this income. Those unemployed would in turn depend on welfare and other governmental agencies, placing additional tax burdens on the average worker.

Looting is condoned because many people benefit financially from the activity.

But the benefits of grave robbing are much greater than this in the eyes of the Costa Rican. Store owners who supply equipment for digging and landowners upon whose land the huaquero excavates profit greatly. The landowner may be promised a royalty by the huaquero of 50 percent of the value of whatever is

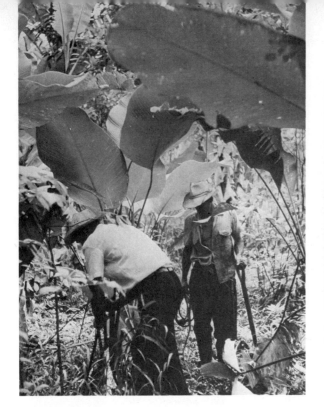

Costa Rican *huaqueros* testing for a grave.
(Michael D. Olien)

Costa Rican *huaqueros* displaying some
of their discoveries. (Michael D. Olien)

discovered at the site, although he seldom receives the percentage promised, because the huaquero makes low appraisals of
the artifacts. The landowner often has little knowledge of the
real market value involved. Nevertheless, in spite of the decep-
tion of the huaquero, the landowner may make more than the
market value of his or her land in just one month, for doing
nothing other than allowing a huaquero to dig on the land. Needless to say, the landowner is usually quite pleased about
the arrangement. Sometimes, in order to insure a fair share of
the profits, the landowner will employ a guard who will watch
over the dig. Since the digging is illegal, the local police occasionally accept bribes amounting to as much as double their
month salaries. In addition, they may confiscate a few choice
pieces and sell them for additional profit (Heath 1973).

Once the huaquero has uncovered artifacts, he may take them
himself to sell in San José, the capital, or he may sell them to an
intermediary. Much of the material brought to San José by the
huaquero or by the intermediary is sold to dealers who have
shops where the material is sold to the public. The dealers employ "runners." The runners are agents who know the special

interests of local collectors and take appropriate pieces to them in exchange for a commission of 10 percent. The dealer sets a minimum base price, and most runners will ask higher prices from collectors and pocket the difference (Heath 1973:263). Other artifacts are sold by huaqueros to agents in San José who deal on the international market and generally make a tremendous profit selling the items abroad, primarily in the United States, France, and Switzerland. In order to get the material out of Costa Rica, these agents must frequently pay bribes.

The availability of artifacts for sale in San José and the illegality of exporting them have led to several other occupations dependent on grave robbing: fakers and confidence artists. Fake gold work, jade, and pottery have become fairly common. A small number of fakes bring in thousands of dollars, especially from foreigners not too familiar with Costa Rican artifacts. Flimflams also occur. For example, a North American bought valuable jade work with the assurance that he could, with impunity, simply leave the country with the jade in his suitcase. Less than one hour after purchasing the jade, he was "shaken down" by a man posing as a plainclothes policeman, who visited his hotel room and threatened to arrest him if he did not pay $100 to fix things up (Heath 1973:264).

While the amount of money obtained from the sale of artifacts by the Costa Ricans is difficult to calculate, a cautious estimate of half-a-million dollars a year has been given (Heath 1973:260). In a country the size of New Hampshire and Vermont combined, with a total population in 1975 of approximately 1,970,000, this sum is considerable. Only 10 percent of the country's manufacturing establishments produced as much as grave robbing. With the grave robbing industry providing a livelihood for so many persons, it has been difficult to convince the Costa Ricans of the valuable archaeological information being lost.

Besides the professional grave robbers, there are thousands of Costa Ricans who, much like North Americans, enjoy digging for artifacts as a hobby and who destroy an additional large number of sites each year. At present the artifacts of Costa Rica, including beautiful polychrome pottery, stone work, jade, and gold, are little known on the international market. These artifacts do not yet command the prices of pre-Columbian objects from Mexico, Guatemala, or Peru, even when the quality of work and aesthetic value are comparable. If the Costa Rican artifacts increase in value over the next few years, the situation in Costa Rica will become even worse and a larger number of sites will be destroyed.

Artifacts as Information

The mass media have often incorrectly depicted the archae-ologist as either a collector of curios or an intellectual treasure-hunter searching for the gold of some lost city. Many people believe these depictions are exactly what archaeology is all about: the collecting of curios or the collecting of buried trea-sure.

In its infancy, archaeology was surely a little of both. The indi-vidual who perhaps did the most to popularize ancient Egyptian culture in the early nineteenth century, Giovanni Belzoni, would be considered a looter by our modern standards. On be-half of the British consul in Cairo, Belzoni roamed throughout the Nile Valley between 1815 and 1819 acquiring artifacts. He ransacked sites for their contents, paying little attention to the preservation of fragile objects. Plunder was his sole objective. His methods were uncompromisingly direct and his pace frantic. He opened secret doors with battering rams and moved hundreds of tons of rubble in his search for antiquities. In the Valley of Kings he discovered the tomb of Seti, father of Ram-eses the Great, which included an alabaster casket still intact. Belzoni also discovered the secret entrance to the Second Pyra-mid. Upon returning to London in 1819, he set up a spectacular exhibition in an Egyptian hall that had been built in Piccadilly. Thousands of people came to see the exhibit and became inter-ested in Egyptian culture for the first time. The artifacts that Belzoni plundered now form the basis of the Egyptian Room at the British Museum (Fagan 1973:49–51).

Giovanni Belzoni in Egypt.
(The Granger Collection)

It was not until the last half of the nineteenth century that artifacts began to take on a new meaning. From that point on, artifacts have interested the professional archaeologist primarily for the information they yield about the human past. Although the first archaeologists may have been primarily concerned with collecting, archaeology since the last half of the nineteenth century has been concerned with reconstructing the past. In this new framework, artifacts become just one source of information; other kinds of data such as pollen, bones, soil samples, and charcoal are as important to the archaeologist as artifacts. Perhaps the main concept that distinguishes the professional archaeologist from the curio collector and the grave robber, is the professional archaeologist's concern with context.

For the archaeologist, the context is often more important than the artifact itself.

The Importance of Context. The professional archaeologist has learned to control the initial instinct to remove an artifact as soon as a shovel or trowel exposes it. He or she has been taught that information about an artifact's position in the ground is often more valuable than the artifact itself.

Historians and the archaeologists are both concerned with reconstructing the past, but their subject matter is quite different. Historians rely on documents, as they deal with human history after writing was invented. Generally, the historian's "history" goes back no further than about 3000 BC. For the archaeologist, "history" begins with *Australopithecus,* 5 million years ago. Throughout most of the time-span that archaeologists study, there were no written records. The only information about human life prior to writing comes from the careful excavation of sites. Whenever an archaeological site is damaged or destroyed, invaluable information is lost *forever.* Archaeologists destroy sites while excavating, so they cannot afford to make mistakes. They will not be able to attempt the same excavation a second time, for they will have destroyed the context within which the artifacts have been found. To the looter and curio collector the context is unimportant, because their goal is to find artifacts. For the archaeologist, the context is a vital component in piecing together a picture of the human past.

The significance of the context of an artifact commonly results from the artifact's position in the ground and/or from the artifact's position vis-à-vis other remains. Both aspects of the context are valuable to the archaeologist. From the soil layer where the artifact is found, archaeologists are able to obtain clues about the age of the artifact. From its relation to other remains, they are able to learn about the function of the artifact, the exonomy of the group that made the artifact, the living habits of the people, or information on their kinship patterns and their beliefs. If the ground has been disturbed before the archaeologist begins a study, it becomes difficult—and often impossible—to date the artifact or to reconstruct the life patterns of the people who created it.

It is often assumed by the public that archaeologists dig only where there is valuable treasure. As a result, looters frequently sneak into sites during excavation in order to beat the archaeologist to the "goodies." What these looters do not understand is that the artifacts that the archaeologist considers of greatest value are those that yield important information, whether or not they have any monetary value. In other cases, looters are resentful of the archaeologist who is seen as interfering with their livelihoods. For example, in western Mexico so many villagers were making a living digging up artifacts that they deeply resented excavations in the area by professional archaeologists. Armed guards had to be posted to deter damage to the sites by the people of the villages. Given the chance, the villagers would have destroyed valuable contextual information by looting where the archaeologists were excavating. The looter or collector who digs into a site and disturbs the position of the material at the site is destroying irreplacable information.

How Does the Archaeologist Excavate?

Archaeologists come to excavate particular sites for one of three reasons: to collect data at an important site discovered by chance, to do salvage work, or to test hypotheses. While an archaeologist would perhaps wish to focus on the third of these, it is usually the first two reasons that result in excavation, at least in the United States.

A site may be a chance discovery, a salvage site, or a site chosen to test a hypothesis.

Chance Discovery. The chance discovery of important artifacts may find the archaeologist ill prepared for the excavation. For example, an archaeologist may be brought in to excavate when a road grader uncovers a skeleton or ancient projectile points. If the road crew can be convinced that they should hold up their work for a day or even longer, the archaeologist may have an opportunity to collect some data. However, under the pressures of road construction he or she may be unable to approach the material with normal thoroughness. Other chance discoveries of sites may not be as pressing, and in these circumstances the archaeologist visits the site, takes notes, and maps the area so that someone can return to the discovery at a later date. With thousands of sites being discovered each year, it is impossible—given the limited funds available for archaeological research—to excavate or even visit each site. Amateur archaeologists who are interested in making a contribution to our knowledge of the human past can do so by collecting detailed information about the sites they discover or visit.

Even with records made of their exact locations, many sites discovered but unexcavated cannot be relocated later because of human "progress." Barns are torn down, superhighways are constructed, and boulders are moved, so often that the major landmarks used to identify the site are no longer in the location that they were when the site was originally mapped. It has been estimated that as many as 50 percent of the sites visited and mapped by an archaeologist but not excavated cannot be relocated. Many of the sites that are not immediately excavated are probably of no great importance. Yet until they are studied, we cannot be sure what type of information they may yield. Unfortunately, when an archaeologist visits a site that has been discovered, collectors and looters consider this a validation of the importance of the site and often waste no time in attacking the site once the archaeologist leaves. Chance discoveries are very frustrating to the archaeologist, who has already committed most of his or her time and money to other sites and knows that very often the chance discovery will never be excavated before it is destroyed, either by looters or by "progress."

Salvage Archaeology. A great deal of current archaeology in the United States falls under the heading of "salvage archaeology." Before dams and other major constructions are undertaken in an area, archaeological survey and excavation are carried out, usually financed by the agency or company planning the construction. Unlike the chance discovery, where there is usually no financing available, salvage archaeology generates a great deal of research financing. The research is done under contract to the governmental agency or private company, with the extent of research, financing, and length of time clearly defined. Some state laws required archaeological studies where the environment is going to be changed; for example, in an area that will permanently under water with the completion of a dam. In the past few years the federal government has enacted legislation that requires environmental impact studies to be carried out prior to construction work that is federally funded, and some type of archaeological research is now frequently required.

Salvage archaeology attempts to extract as much information

A great deal of archaeological research in the United States is salvage work.

Missouri River basin salvage archaeology. (Michael D. Olien)

from an area as possible before the landscape changes, as valuable information is lost forever once construction work begins. The sites that are excavated in salvage archaeology may not be of immediate relevance to current archaeological questions. The archaeologist might prefer to study other sites, but is forced into the position of either doing the salvage work or losing potentially important data forever. The only information about the prehistory of the region that will be available to future generations will be the data that the archaeologist collects before the construction. Later, the site will be under water or concrete.

A great deal of salvage archaeology has been undertaken in river basins that have since been dammed and made into lakes. Concentration of archaeological research in the river basins biases our understanding of the prehistory of an area. As the archaeologists have to devote their limited time and funds to studying life along the rivers, they are unable to devote as much attention to other areas of the regions—flat plains, hilltops, and so on. What is typical of a people's adaptation at the river basin environment may be atypical of their adaptation to other eco-niches. Yet archaeologists may have to generalize about the prehistory of an area solely on the basis of the data obtained from the river basin. Likewise, it is possible that the adaptations identified along the river were seasonal. A group may have camped along the river during only one season of the year. If the archaeologists are unable to excavate other areas of the region, it is impossible for them to reconstruct the yearly cycle of the people.

Testing Hypotheses. A third reason that site excavation occurs is to test an archaeologist's hypothesis. On the basis of data already excavated and analyzed, the archaeologist is able to piece together a picture of life in the past. As the picture emerges, there may be insufficient data on certain subjects to provide a clear interpretation. At this point the archaeologist may conduct further excavation, carefully choosing the site according to a hypothesis about some aspect of life in the past. The site that he or she chooses may not yield valuable artifacts in the monetary sense; it may not be a site about to be destroyed due to construction; but it may yield precisely the information needed.

Sites chosen to prove or disprove a hypothesis are generally selected through careful and often complex sampling procedures. As a result, this third type of site is more representative of a region than the salvage archaeology site, which is chosen for its vulnerability to destruction rather than its representativeness in a sample. Sites selected to test hypotheses provide the most immediately useful data. This information can be used to answer a question that the archaeologist is puzzled about today, whereas the data collected from chance discoveries and salvage archaeology are usually stored for future inquires. Since most archaeologists prefer to collect data that are immediately relevant, they would rather select sites on the basis of their hypotheses. However, because of the imminent destruction of other sites, they are put into the position of spending much of their time doing salvage archaeology or investigating chance finds.

> Hypothesis testing generally yields the most immediately useful information.

The strategies utilized by the salvage archaeologist are generally different from those used by the hypothesis-oriented archaeologist. These differences in strategies represent one of the greatest conflicts of values in modern American archaeology. The salvage archaeologist uses an *inductive method*. The inductive method stresses data collection and assumes that synthesis and the generation of inferences can occur only after all the data have been collected. The archaeologist who follows the inductive approach believes that, potentially, every bit of information collected in an excavation can be used in the final synthesis. Presumably, all information at the site should be gathered, though this effort is usually thwarted by lack of sufficient funds, limited time, and so on; however, as much information is collected as is possible under the circumstances. Those who follow this ap-

> There is a conflict between archaeologists who value the inductive method and those who value the deductive method.

proach believe that data should be gathered without the use of a theoretical framework, in order to insure objectivity (King 1971:256–257). The strategy of the salvage archaeologist is analogous to the assembly of a jigsaw puzzle. When enough of the pieces of a puzzle have been collected, the overall picture will emerge. Thus salvage archaeology has centered on data collection, with much less effort exerted toward the synthesis of this data, because there are always more facts to be collected.

The archaeologist who operates on the basis of hypotheses follows a *deductive method*. Archaeologist who take the deductive approach assume that all data collection takes place in the context of some theoretical framework. For example, they believe that even the decision of the salvage archaeologist to excavate in one spot and not another is based on some theoretical assumption. Archaeologists following the deductive method believe that it is better to make the theoretical biases explicit and to use theory to guide the collection of data. The deductive research strategy requires the generation and testing of hypotheses and is much more problem-oriented than is the inductive approach of salvage archaeology. The deductive approach pursues answers to questions generated out of anthropological theory, or it attempts to explain the differences and similarities noted in the archaeological record through the utilization of general theory (King 1971:256). The collection of data and choice of site is both selective and intensive, focused on the hypothesis to be tested. The specific problem that the archaeologist is attempting to solve may require extensive and expensive interdisciplinary or technical studies and relatively little collection of artifacts. It may be necessary, in order to test the hypothesis, to sacrifice artifacts to concentrate, for example, on architecture or cemeteries, or vice versa. The deductive approach is fairly recent in archaeology and has been termed the "new archaeology."

Advocates of both the inductive approach and the deductive approach believe that their particular approach is scientific. Some archaeologists (Hawkes 1968) argue that the "new archaeology" is overly concerned with mathematical models and computer programming, while other archaeologists (Isaac 1971) see the emphasis on quantitative method in the "new archaeology" as part of the maturation of the discipline's methodology.

Excavation

Site Excavation. Site excavation follows a number of different plans, depending on the type of site. Archaeologists do not excavate the remains of a single Indian pit house, in which six people may have lived, in the same way that they excavate a large Mayan ceremonial center, that may have been inhabited by 2000 persons. At large sites a great deal of time and effort may be devoted to clearing and mapping before any digging takes place. In other cases, weather, fund limitations, and available labor affect the type of excavation techniques used. Many sites are located in areas of the world that have marked wet and dry seasons; often the only time that excavations can be conducted is during the dry season. With limited time, funds, and labor, the archaeologist may be able to sample only a small area of the site, to try to find answers to such basic questions as What is the settlement pattern, What is the age of the site, and What was the cultural tradition of the inhabitants? Where extensive funding is available, research may be conducted at the same site for ten years or more, and full-scale excavation can be undertaken, although some sampling is still likely to be done. While no single approach to excavation would be applicable to all sites, some of the most commonly employed techniques include test pits, grids, and trenches.

Before the major section of a site is excavated, a test pit is usually dug outside of the area of human occupation to determine the nature of the soil layers. The test pit will show the approximate thickness, color, and texture of each soil layer. It will also indicate which layers represent human occupations. At many sites, the same location was used over hundreds or thousands of years by different people. Very often the location is a strategic one—it has an ample supply of water, available natural resources, abundance of food, and so on—so that the same location has been appealing to different peoples over many periods of time. By digging a test pit, the archaeologist is able to prepare for the major excavation. While the test pit may not be completely typical of what the archaeologist will later discover, it gives valuable clues as to the number of soil layers and their characteristics.

After digging the test pit, the archaeologist will mark off the site into 2-meter squares, forming a grid over the section of the site that will be excavated. The squares provide convenient markers: The locations of all artifacts and other important features are mapped by squares as they are discovered. In some cases there is not enough time or money to excavate all of the squares of the grid. As a compromise the archaeologist will excavate a limited number of the squares, often adjacent squares stretching across the site, forming a trench. A trench can show the temporal arrangement of at least part of the site. The walls

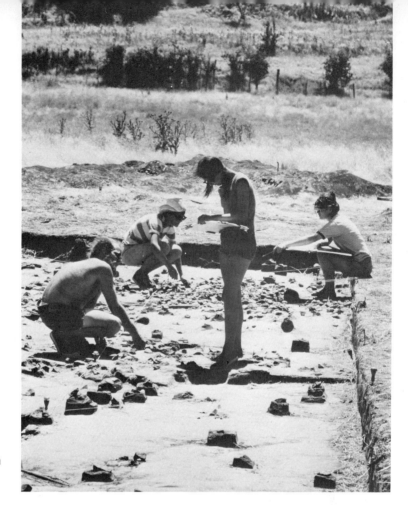

Archaeological excavation by squares. (Beckerman, EPA)

of the trench will show a *profile,* or cross section, of the soil layers. In other cases the archaeologist digs a series of alternate, rather than adjacent, trench sections.

The artifacts discovered are collected both by squares and by soil layers. By knowing the square, the archaeologist can later determine whether the artifact was near the center of the site or near the edges. Knowing the soil layer will aid in determining the age of the artifacts.

The archaeologist relies on the *law of superimposition* developed in geology to aid in dating the artifacts. The law of superimposition states that the soil layers closest to the surface are the most recent and those furthest from the surface are the oldest layers, if the layers have not been disturbed. The archaeologist assumes that the artifacts found in a particular soil layer are of the same time period as that soil layer. Therefore those artifacts found in the upper strata are the most recent; those in the lowest strata are the oldest. Stratigraphy (the arrangement of

The law of superimposition is valuable in dating artifacts in the field.

(a) Natural stratigraphy   (b) Cultural stratigraphy

Figure 13 Natural and cultural stratigraphy.

strata) provides a means of *relative dating* (Figure 13). The archaeologist can quickly learn which artifacts are older than others and which come from the same time period, but relative dating does not give the actual age of the artifacts. At one site, the artifacts of two different soil layers may have been manufactured thousands of years apart, while at another site artifacts of two soil layers may be only a few hundred years apart. The thickness of a soil layer is generally not an indicator of the age of the stratum. In some cases a thick layer may have been built up very slowly, over millenia. Other layers may have formed over a short period of years.

The stratigraphic sequence is further complicated by human activity. Sometimes holes are dug for semisubterranean houses, for burials, for garbage pits, for protective moats, or for caches. As a result of human digging, some artifacts of a time period may be buried farther down in the ground than other artifacts of the same time period, thus confusing the picture. Fortunately for the archaeologist, the human-made holes leave distinct changes in the pattern and color of the soil and are therefore recognizable, if workers proceed carefully with their excavation.

In most cases the excavation of a site does not involve total excavation. Many archaeologists prefer to leave at least a part of the site untouched, so that other archaeologists can later return to the site, after new methods, theories, and problems develop. Furthermore, many sites are too large for total excavation, given the resources available for the dig. Most archaeologists have to be selective in what is excavated. Some of the world's most important sites have been excavated selectively, for specific information, by the technique of *vertical excavation,* where limited areas are excavated to considerable depths. Selective excavation is especially informative in salvage work where large-scale operations are impossible. When larger scale excavation is undertaken, horizontal relationships as well as vertical ones can be discovered. Horizontal relationships are of primary interest when the archaeologist is concerned with settlement patterns. This larger-scale undertaking is referred to as *area excavation* and usually involves large areas excavated to a depth of at least several meters (Fagan 1972:84–85).

A growing number of archaeologists are beginning to rely on sampling techniques in their excavations. Sampling is an effort to control bias in excavation. Instead of choosing the site that *appears* to be the most important, the archaeologist uses sampling in selecting a site in order to ensure a statistically reliable basis of data from which generalizations can be made (Binford 1964).

Recording Information. As archaeological excavation is a form of site destruction, it is imperative that detailed records and accurate measurements be made. A major record book is kept by the director of the excavation; separate work diaries are kept by each worker. These notebooks are invaluable to the archaeologist, especially as questions develop after the excavation is completed. Drawings are made of everything of importance at the site: artifacts, bone, charcoal, timber, and so on. All of the information is plotted on maps. Once the material is removed from the ground, it is placed in a sack, and the sack is then labeled with a serial number, to indentify the level and square at which the material was found.

The stratigraphic layers appear on the walls of the excavated square as a profile. The layers of the profile show the various *occupation levels* (time periods in which the site was peopled) and the geological changes that have affected the area through time.

Professional surveying equipment is usually used for the measurements taken at a site, in order to ensure maximum accuracy. Since maps are generally two-dimensional, surface maps are drawn of the excavation at a number of levels, as digging uncovers new layers.

Photography represents another important means of data recording. General shots are taken of the site before any work is done. Photographs are taken at each phase of the research to document what is being done. In addition, each feature is photographed with an identification number and scale. Likewise the profiles are photographed. Frequently everything at the site is photographed in both black-and-white and in color. Infrared may be used to bring out certain profile distinctions. (While the cultural anthropologists normally work with 35-mm photographic equipment, because of its portability, archaeologists prefer larger formats, whose larger negatives allow sharper blowups of sections of a picture.) Finally, the most important artifacts are photographed separately once they are removed from their context.

Analysis

Following the excavation, the archaeologist begins the long process of classifying, preserving, and analyzing what has been excavated. The work following the field research is more time-consuming than the excavation. For every month spent in excavation, five months or more of processing and analyzing are required.

Before analysis can begin, the data from the excavation have to be processed. Artifacts are cleaned and then numbered. The number of each artifact is then listed in a record book, along with pertinent information about the artifact. Skeletal data have to be cleaned, numbered, and preserved with special coatings. Broken artifacts have to be restored, especially pottery. Metal, paper, and other kinds of artifacts often require unique techniques of cleaning or restoring that can be carried out only by a specialist.

Identification. Identification represents an important aspect of analysis. Often bones of many different animals are found during excavation. The archaeologist may need the help of a specialist to identify certain of these animals by species. The identification of the animals will be important later as the archaeologist attempts to reconstruct ecological patterns. Archaeologist Bruce D. Smith (1976:284–285) has outlined some of the kinds of questions now being asked about faunal material.

Data processing is more time-consuming than excavation.

Discovery of California
Indian burial. (Wide World)

a. What was the relative importance of various species of animals in the diet of prehistoric human populations?
b. Was exploitation of animal populations primarily a seasonal activity, and if so, during what season of the year was each species hunted?
c. What procurement strategies were employed to obtain exploited species?
d. To what degree was human predation of animal population selective?
e. What was the overall seasonal pattern and strategy of human exploitation of the faunal section of the biotic community?

The study of human skeletons may also require the help of specialists. While all archaeologists are able to distinguish human bones from those of other animals, they may find that deciphering important information from certain parts of the skeleton is beyond their expertise. For example, an archaeologist working with finds from the era of *Australopithecus* might need help from physical anthropologists, who could tell a great deal about the skeleton's posture and locomotion from the pelvis, leg bones, and bones of the feet. In other cases, detailed study of dentition might provide considerable information about diet.

The archaeologist must also attempt to identify the artifacts. In many cases identification is simple, but in other cases it is impossible to determine the use of an artifact. Artifacts that were made for social or ritualistic purposes may be especially difficult to identify. The interpretation is further complicated by the fact that few prehistoric artifacts are so specialized in form as to be useful for just one task. Since the archaeologist is usually dealing with the remains of people who were nonliterate, there are no written records to tell what the various artifacts were intended for. Frequently the archaeologist can only make an educated guess as to what the artifact was used for and hope that future excavations will shed more light on the problem. The identification may be extremely tenuous, especially where a unique artifact has been discovered. The most confident interpretation of a prehistoric artifact can be made when it is discovered that a similar or identical implement is used by a living people, especially if there is a historical link between the living and prehistoric people. Nevertheless, the archaeologist has to proceed cautiously with such an identification, because the meaning of an artifact can and does change over time. Often fewer than half of the artifacts from a site can be clearly identified (Anderson 1969).

The remains of wood, pollen, and other vegetable matter are also subject to analysis and identification. By identifying the species of wood, the archaeologist may be able to reconstruct the environment. Pollen and other plant remains tell the archaeologists about not only the previous climate of the region and the diet of the people but also which plants were domesticated and which were not. Since this material is highly perishable, the archaeologist will at best discover only a small amount of the flora used by a people. Yet the amount of information that the archaeologist is able to extract from the analysis of a small amount of vegetable material is amazing. A considerable understanding of the entire process of the domestication of maize and of the beginnings of settled farming life in Mexico has come from the careful analysis of a small number of corn cobs discovered during excavation in the Tehuacán Valley.

A new approach to the identification of artifacts and structures involves experimentation. For example, archaeologists have frequently discovered subterranean chambers called *chultuns* at Maya sites. Those first recognized were in the northern regions of Yucatan, where water scarcity is a problem. These chultuns were identified as chambers for water cisterns as

Experimentation is an important new approach to identification.

early as 1843, by the explorer John L. Stephens. These northern chultuns were generally found at sites lacking natural wells. They were lined with stucco or plaster to make them water-proof. The chultuns were bottle-shaped in form, with depths of 6 meters or more.

When smaller subterranean chambers were also discovered at archaeological sites in the wetter southern Maya lowlands, the term *chultun* was extended to these chambers as well. However, the southern chultuns differed considerably from those of the north. Instead of being deep and bottle-shaped, most of the southern chultuns are small lateral chambers that often can only be reached from the surface through a small and shallow antechamber. These chultuns are rarely more than 2 meters deep and show no evidence of stucco or plaster lining. Because these chambers were dug into very porous limestone, they could not have been used to store water without some type of lining. Therefore the chultuns must have been used for something other than storing water.

A variety of guesses as to the function of the chultuns have been made, including burial chambers, latrines, and food storage. Archaeological excavation has demonstrated that the first two purposes can be ruled out. A few have been found that were used for burials, but the chambers thus used did not seem to have been constructed with a burial in mind. The vast major-ity of chultuns were never used for burials. Latrines are ruled out because of the lack of any fecal remains, and also because burials would not have been placed in latrines, even infre-quently. Furthermore, it is believed that the disposal of human feces was left to vultures and dogs. Thus food storage seemed the most likely use. But archaeologists did not know what food might have been stored in the chultuns.

Experiments were undertaken at the large Mayan site of Tikal to see what type of food might best be preserved in a chultun. The known basic crops of the Maya included corn, beans, squash, cassave, and sweet potato. All of these foods were placed in a newly built chultun. In the high humidity of the southern jungle, none of the crops fared well. Within 11 weeks all of the food was seriously affected by fungi and rodents. How-ever, the following year it was learned that there is a close corre-lation between the present distribution of the ramon tree and the remains of Maya house platforms, suggesting that these ramon trees are the descendants of trees cultivated by the Classic Maya of Tikal in the vicinity of their homes. The ramon seed was found to have high nutritional value as a carbohy-drate and a staggering productivity as well. As a result of their newly discovered potential as a food crop, ramon seeds were placed in the chultun. It was found that they stored well, because of their low water content, which was not seriously affected by the very high humidity. After 13 months of underground storage, these seeds were still in excellent condition and completely edible. The southern type of chultun is not used today by the Maya; thus no ethnographic analogy could be drawn. However, the distribution of the ramon trees in relation to the houses of the ancient Maya, plus the experiments with the chultun, suggest that the ramon was an important food source that has since ceased to be a staple crop (Puleston 1971).

Another example of experimental archaeology comes from a study of notched deer ribs from Colorado. Large-mammal scapulae and ribs showing considerable wear along a jagged or notched edge have been discovered in a number of North American archaeological sites. The bones appear to have been deliberately broken in order to make a working edge. The notched bones were assumed to have been used as hide-scrapers. Two archaeologists (Morris and Burgh 1954) carried out experiments to discover if the notched bones were effective as hide-scrapers. They found they were not.

The production of cordage was one of the major industries of the Basket Maker communities where the notched bones were found. The principal source of fiber was leaves of the yucca plant. Thus it was hypothesized that the notched bone had been used to separate the fiber from the leaves. Morris and Burgh carried out experiments and discovered that the notched bones were quite effective in preparing the fiber for the making of cordage. Further support for this identification of the function of the artifact came both from the discovery of sap imbedded in a notched deer rib recovered at one site and from an ethnographic analogy found among the Pima Indians, where the deer scapula is used to separate pulp from the fiber of the maguey plant.

Not all problems of identification lend themselves to experimentation. Likewise some experiments that might produce valuable information are either too expensive, too time-consuming, or too impractical. For example, hundreds of years of experimentation might be needed to study the rate of decay of an artifact in the ground.

Although ethnographic analogy may be useful in identifying some things, the archaeologist must always be cautious in drawing inferences of this type (Binford 1967). The same artifacts can have different meanings or uses in different societies. Likewise, within the same society meanings and uses can change over time; yet if carefully handled, experimentation and ethnographic analogy can be valuable to the archaeologist.

Dating

Dating the material found at a site is another aspect of the analysis. The types of dating fall into two major categories, *relative dating* and *absolute dating.* With relative dating the archaeologist is only able to learn that something is older or more recent than something else. Absolute forms of datings provide specific dates.

Dating techniques are either relative or absolute.

Relative Dating. While relative dating may not provide an actual date, it can be very important. It is generally most important in determining temporal relationships at a specific site or a set of closely related sites. It is not useful for the comparison of material from one part of the world with another. Perhaps the most important source of information used in relative dating is *stratigraphy.* Stratigraphy doesn't tell the archaeologist how much older the artifacts of the lower layers may be, just that they are usually older than those closer to the surface.

Stratigraphy provides an important form of relative dating.

Not only are the naturally formed soil layers superimposed, so are human occupations at a site. Fires, floods, earthquakes, wars, and other disasters often level towns or partially destroy them. Yet the reason the site was chosen for settlement to begin with may still remain: It may be located on a trade route, it may be easily defended, it may be near water, and so on. As a result, the community may be rebuilt on top of the remains of the previous town. Thus, one period of human occupation is superimposed over another. In the Middle East, there are massive mounds called *tells,* which are the layered remains of a number of ruined cities, built one on top of another because of the desirability of the location.

Pleistocene *geochronology* represents a special form of stratigraphy, based on climatic changes reflected in the advances and retreats of the glaciers or the rising and falling of sea levels. Human remains associated with particular glacial or interglacial periods, or with changes in sea level, can be placed in a relative chronological sequence.

Another type of geochronology comes from the study of extinct fauna found in Pleistocene sites. Many animals hunted by humans and therefore associated with sites became extinct at different time periods. In many localities the paleontologists have been able to classify Pleistocene fauna and have built up a relative chronology of mammal types throughout the Pleistocene. A fairly reliable relative date can be assigned to a site on the basis of mammal bones. However, not all mammals are as good indicators of climatic changes as others are. Also it is sometimes difficult to distinguish between chronological change and variation between local populations.

Pollen analysis is another form of relative dating. It was first developed in northern Europe in 1916 and is now used in a number of countries. Under certain conditions, especially in bogs and marshes, the grains of pollen shed by trees and other plants will survive for thousands of years. Like the soil and artifacts, the pollen of each time period is superimposed over the pollen found in earlier soil layers. From the pollen in samples of different soil layers, the paleobotanist can reconstruct the proportions of different species of vegetation at different time periods. In some parts of the world, this information has been used to construct a sequence of time periods based on pollen analysis. An archaeological object found in a bog or in pollen-bearing mud can thus be assigned its place in the sequence. The pollen from an archaeological layer can tell a great deal about both the natural vegetation and the plants that were introduced by humans (Paor 1967:67–70).

A number of other forms of relative dating are also based on the law of superimposition, including interpretation of dune drifting and stream meanders. Once geologists are able to piece together the sequence of changes in dunes or streambeds, the sites associated with the different dunes or stream locations can be relatively dated. For example, stream meanders can provide a quick clue to the relative age of sites located on the banks of various old beds.

At a single site, several types of chemical tests can also provide relative dates. Perhaps the most famous of these tests is *fluorine dating*. It was used in unraveling the turn-of-the-century hoax known as Piltdown man. In 1911 a fossil skull was found in England which did not seem to fit into any existing theories of human evolution. Its cranium was not too different from that of modern humans, but its jaw was unlike any human fossil ever discovered. Controversy raged over this fossil find for many years, until 1953, when fluorine dating was being developed and the test was applied to the Piltdown material.

Fluorine dating helped expose the Piltdown hoax.

Fluorine dating is based on the fact that skeletal material in the ground absorbs water and, with it, fluorine. The longer a bone is in the ground, the more fluorine it will absorb. However, there is no constant rate of absorption: The rate will vary from site to site depending on the soil conditions. Yet the test is useful for dating bones from the same site, especially if the site has been disturbed and no soil layers are left for relative dating. At any given site, those bones that have been in the ground the longest will have the highest percentage of fluorine; and those bones that have been in the ground for the shortest period of time will have the least amount of fluorine. Bones that have been in the ground for the same length of time will have the same percentage of fluorine. Because the rate of absorption is not constant, the percentages of fluorine cannot be converted into number of years in the ground. Yet even with this limitation, the fluorine test proved of value in the case of Piltdown man. The test showed that the two parts of the skull were not from the same period of time. Once this was determined, other chemical analyses showed that the jaw was one from a non-human animal which someone had purposely reshaped to look human. Considerable effort had also been expended to make the jaw look old. The cranium was a legitimate fossil, a *Homo sapiens sapiens*, which someone had discovered and had reburied along with the bogus jaw.

A similar chemical test, *nitrogen dating*, can also be used on bones from the same site. With nitrogen the process is the opposite of that with fluorine: Once bones are in the ground, they begin to lose nitrogen. As with fluorine dating, there is no constant rate of change. However, at the same site one can compare percentages of nitrogen and learn which bones have been in the soil the longest.

Relative dating using changes in artifact styles is important in determining the temporal relationships between a group of related sites. This form of dating is known as *seriation* and is used primarily in the analysis of pottery types from a number of culturally similar sites. It is based on the assumption that a new artifact begins with a small distribution and ultimately reaches a maximum of popularity and then declines. In our modern life this process may take only a year or two. The popularity of hoola hoops spread rapidly in only a few years and the hoola hoops then were abandoned for new fads. Changes in prehistoric artifacts reflect more conservative changes. A pottery style may last a hundred years or more before it is abandoned. The archaeologist calculates the percentages of each type of artifact at each site being studied and then converts these percentages to bar graphs. Each stratigraphic layer at one of the sites is represented by a single strip of paper. These strips are arranged to provide the most viable seriated sequence showing the growth and decline of different artifacts, primarily pot sherds. Once the chronology at one site has been established, the seriated sequence can serve for dating the relative chronology of the same artifacts other sites of the area, even on the basis of samples collected on the surface. Because statistical methods are used to draw conclusions from seriation studies, procedures that ensure that the samples are selected randomly must be carefully followed.

Absolute Dating. While the various forms of relative dating are important, they are of limited value for cross-cultural comparisons. For example, it would be impossible to prove that the earliest pottery in the New World had diffused from Japan unless the archaeologist could demonstrate that Japanese pottery was earlier than any New World pottery. While it is of considerable value to know that something is older than something else, the archaeologist often needs to know exactly how much older one artifact is than some other artifact. Therefore, archaeologists and others have devoted considerable effort to inventing methods of absolute dating. Yet the archaeologist's dates are considerably less precise than the historian's. The historian's dates usually come from the documents left behind by people who had writing systems. Thus the historian can pinpoint events to the exact year and sometimes even the exact day. The archaeologist usually cannot. The dates for fossil populations may be off by 50,000 years or more, while dates of pre-Columbian Indian villages in New York may be inaccurate by several hundred years or more. Yet for the archaeologist, dates as inaccurate as these are of great value.

Absolute dating can be used for cross-cultural comparison.

The most commonly used dating for the early forms of fossil human is *potassium-argon dating*, which is a form of geological dating. It determines the age of certain types of rocks, especially volcanic ones, by measuring the rate of radioactive decay. This technique is capable of dating these rocks back to the beginning of the earth. Because of the limitations of the current measuring devices used in this testing, it cannot successfully date rock formed more recently than about 400,000 to 100,000 years ago. Fossil remains can only be dated by association with the rocks that are tested.

Potassium-argon dating is used to date rocks associated with fossil humans.

More recent archaeological material has generally been dated with carbon 14 dating. Whereas the potassium-argon method dates rock, the carbon 14 method dates organic material such as bone, wood, and charcoal. Radioactive carbon (C^{14}) is in the atmosphere and is absorbed by plants. Animals absorb this material from the plants they eat. When a plant or animal dies, the absorption of C^{14} ceases and disintegration begins, with the

Carbon 14 is used to date organic material as old as 40,000 years.

C^{14} converting to nonradioactive C^{12}. It has been assumed that this conversion occurs at a set rate. Measurement of the number of radioactive emissions per minute from the organic material indicates the amount of C^{14} still residual in a specimen. Carbon 14 dating is reliable up to about 40,000 years. As laboratory techniques are refined, it will be possible to date material perhaps as old as 70,000 years. The value of carbon 14 dating is that it can be used anywhere in the world, making cross-cultural comparisons possible.

Recently, a basic assumption about carbon 14 has been challenged, and therefore the reliability of this important technique is now being questioned. It was originally assumed that the amount of radiation has been constant everywhere around the world and at all times. It is now apparent that there have been fluctuations. Only further research will determine the impact of these fluctuations on the dates that are being obtained.

Until 1973 there was a significant gap in dating material from 100,000 to 40,000 BC. Neither potassium-argon nor carbon 14 is capable of accurately dating material in that time range. A newly discovered technique called *amino-acid dating* now gives promise of dating organic material, especially bone, in this time-span. Amino-acid dating is based on the rate at which amino-acid molecules realign themselves following the death of an organism. This realignment process apparently occurs at a set rate. Amino-acid dating is proving especially valuable in the recent study of the Neanderthals, in which samples of bone are analyzed.

Amino-acid dating may be the most important method of dating Neanderthal finds.

One of the most precise forms of absolute dating is tree-ring dating, or *dendrochronology*. Dendrochronology is the study of variations in tree rings (new growth), one of which is added to a tree each year, as a means of establishing dates. Annual rings vary from year to year, with dry years producing limited growth and thin rings, and wet years producing wider rings of growth. Trees in the same climatic area have similar ring patterns. This system of dating has been perfected for the Southwest of the United States. In California, the archaeologists have been able to piece together a master chart that shows the yearly pattern of tree-ring growth since 6000 BC. The master chart has been compiled through a process of matching the rings of successively older samples of wood. For example, the pattern of a 150-year-old tree recently cut can be partially matched with an older tree that may have been cut for a pioneer cabin if the ages of the two trees overlap. The log from the pioneer cabin can also be compared with still older logs from a Spanish mission to see if the patterns overlap and so on. Dating is then possible when-

Dendrochronology is one of the most accurate dating techniques.

Tree-ring dating. (Laboratory of Tree Ring Research)

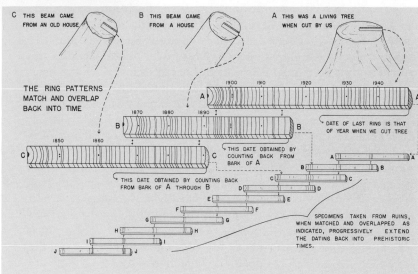

C THIS BEAM CAME FROM AN OLD HOUSE

B THIS BEAM CAME FROM A HOUSE

A THIS WAS A LIVING TREE WHEN CUT BY US

THE RING PATTERNS MATCH AND OVERLAP BACK INTO TIME

DATE OF LAST RING IS THAT OF YEAR WHEN WE CUT TREE

THIS DATE OBTAINED BY COUNTING BACK FROM BARK OF A

THIS DATE OBTAINED BY COUNTING BACK FROM BARK OF A THROUGH B

SPECIMENS TAKEN FROM RUINS, WHEN MATCHED AND OVERLAPPED AS INDICATED, PROGRESSIVELY EXTEND THE DATING BACK INTO PREHISTORIC TIMES.

ever pieces of wood are discovered at a site, especially if a piece shows a tree-ring pattern that extends over a period of 50 years or more. This pattern is matched against the master chart to give the exact age of the piece of wood. Although dendrochronology is a very precise form of dating, it has a somewhat limited application, because all parts of the area covered by the master chart have to be climatically similar. Tree-ring dating has been most useful in the Southwest, because of climatic homogeneity throughout the area, as well as the excellent preservation of wood due to the dryness. In parts of the world where there are tremendous differences within a region, a master chart must be constructed for each small area of similar rainfall before this form of dating is possible.

There are many other forms of dating. Unfortunately, few of them date the most common types of artifacts, stone tools and weapons. A new technique known as *obsidian hydration dating* has been increasing in importance for tools made from obsidian. This technique measures the absorption of water molecules in the obsidian. Rates have to be established for each area, because the rate varies by climate and quality of obsidian.

A second method of dating stone material is known as *thermoluminescent dating* and can be used for dating inorganic objects that have been heated, including tools made of flint and pottery. This method of dating depends on thermoluminescence, the production of light caused by shifts of atomic particles when certain minerals are heated. Such shifts occurred, for example, in clay fired by the heat of an ancient potter's fire or in flint chips that fell into a fire used by primitive people: Atomic particles in the clay or flint moved toward the centers of the atoms and released energy in the form of light. When the clay or stone cooled, the particles began to shift once again away from the atomic centers. Over time, more and more shifting of particles occurred. Thus the longer the time since the artifact was initially heated, the greater the shifting. The archaeologist reheats the stone or the pottery, and the amount of light released, which is measured by a sensor, reveals how long the particles have been shifting outward, and thus how long it has been since the object was first heated.

All stone artifacts that cannot be dated by these techniques have to be dated indirectly. For example, an arrowhead stuck in a bison bone can be dated indirectly by obtaining a carbon 14 date from the bone.

The dating of material is basic to archaeological research; therefore the search for new techniques of dating is unending. Archaeologists and scientists in a variety of fields experiment with many exotic approaches, never knowing when a new method of dating will be discovered. Some of the most important dating techniques have resulted from research on completely different problems: Carbon 14 dating was a by-product of the atomic bomb; dendrochronology was an offshoot of research on sunspots in astronomy; and amino-acid dating was discovered by an organic chemist at Scripps Institution of Oceanography.

Interpretation

For the archaeologist, the whole purpose of excavation, identification of artifacts, analysis, and dating of the material is to learn about human behavior in the past and to search for cultural processes.

An archaeologist's interpretation of data results in the description of a particular extinct society. Archaeologists use their information to reconstruct the settlement patterns, the types of land use, the demographic patterns, the crafts, religious behavior, social organization, trade, and as much as is possible of the belief systems of the society. Their goal is similar to that of the cultural anthropologist—a total picture of the society and its culture; but archaeologists are limited by their data in the questions they can ask. They are only able to utilize the evidence that has survived.

The second aspect of the archaeologist's interpretation involves cultural processes. Archaeologists are no longer content merely to observe, describe, and integrate; the modern archaeologist also wishes to explain the phenomena of the past. The excavation of a specific site yields unique data. Through the comparison of this date with information from other sites, the archaeologist is able to make greater generalizations about human diversity. A search to discover the laws that govern the adaptations of all people in similar habitats focuses the archaeologists's attention on recurrent patterns. The unique information of a single site becomes building blocks in the archaeologists's search for universals (Thomas 1974:4). Their attempts at theory-building distinguish the professional archaeologists from the collectors and looters. Only through explanatory theory can the human myth unfold.

In this chapter the professional archaeologist's quest for information has been contrasted with the destruction of information about our past by curio hunters, looters, and "progress." The destruction of sites has always occurred, but what is so shocking today is the rate at which this destruction has increased in just the past few years. If the destruction continues at the recent rate, there will be no prehistoric sites left in the United States by the turn of the century. In some parts of the country, the situation is so serious that few if any sites will be left by 1980. Archaeologists need public support to help preserve our past. As the archaeologist Charles McGimsey (1972:19) has so aptly observed:

> Archaeology presents the public with a problem which, unlike so many, will disappear completely if they continue to ignore it. But if this route is chosen, we and all succeeding generations will be infinitely poorer, and there will be no one to blame but ourselves.

The purpose of archaeological research is to reconstruct life in the past and to discover cultural processes.

Anthropology Vocabulary

absolute dating
amino-acid dating
area excavation
carbon 14 dating
chultun
circum-Mediterranean
deductive method
dendrochronology
fluorine dating
geochronology
huaquero

inductive method
law of superimposition
Maya
Mimbres
mummy bundles
new archaeology
nitrogen dating
obsidian hydration dating
occupation levels
pollen analysis
potassium-argon dating

pre-Columbian
profile
relative dating
salvage archaeology
site
stratigraphy
test pit
thermoluminescent dating
trench
vertical excavation

Review Questions

1. What effect have curio collecting and grave robbing had on the archaeological record?
2. How does the approach to artifacts of the professional archaeologist differ from that of the collector and the looter?
3. Why do archaeologists generally prefer to excavate sites in order to test hypotheses?
4. How do the inductive and deductive approaches differ?
5. What is the importance of the law of superimposition for excavation?
6. How do relative and absolute dating differ? Which is preferred? Why?

Recommended Reading

Deetz, James, 1967, *Invitation of Archaeology.* New York: Natural History Press. A short and readable overview of the archaeologist and his or her methods.

Hester, Thomas R., Robert F. Heizer, and John A. Graham, 1975, *Field Methods in Archaeology.* Palo Alto, Calif.: Mayfield Publishing Co. A comprehensive guide to the techniques of archaeological field work.

Hole, Frank, and Robert F. Heizer, 1969, *An Introduction to Prehistoric Archaeology,* 2nd ed. New York: Holt, Rinehart and Winston. A more detailed introduction to archaeology than that of Deetz.

Michels, Joseph W., 1973, *Dating Methods in Archaeology.* New York: Seminar Press. An up-to-date introduction to the major dating techniques of the prehistorian.

7

Did ancient astronauts bring civilization?

Many theories have attempted to explain the appearance of the early civilizations.

Anthropologists believe that the prehistoric and historic records show a gradual cultural development from early hunters and gatherers to modern civilizations.

The development of the world's first civilizations is one of the most intriguing topics that has been studied by archaeologists. Civilization emerges in both the Old World and New World and develops along similar lines. Did civilization develop independently in these two major areas of the world? Did civilization develop first in the Old World and then spread to the New World? Was civilization brought from outer space? In this chapter the nature of civilization will be explored and various explanations for its appearance will be examined.

The Discovery of a New World and Its Impact on European Thinking

During the Middle Ages of Europe, Westerners were little concerned about the glories of past eras. The Europeans recognized no significant difference between themselves and the people of the ancient world. There was little feeling of change. The world was basically static, and therefore it was assumed that the ancients behave in familiar ways.

The Arab world was a flourishing center of inquiry during the "Dark Ages" of Europe. Arab scholars made important advances in mathematics, medicine, astronomy, geography, poetry, and other forms of art. Equally important, the Arab world preserved many of the important contributions of the classical world, which were forgotten in Western Europe during the Middle Ages. When the Moslems occupied Spain they brought with them many writings of Aristotle and other valuable philosophical works, which were then translated into Latin and read by European scholars.

With the emergence of the Renaissance there appeared a new spirit of inquiry in Europe. The European began to be interested in the ruins of ancient monuments, often at his back door. What did these monuments represent? Who created them? How old were they? Stimulated by Arab contact during the fourteenth century, European scholars became increasingly interested in the writings of the ancient world and began to search for old manuscripts. By about AD 1430 almost all of the Greek and Latin literature which had survived had been discovered.

Ciriaco de' Pizzicolli is generally given credit for establishing the discipline of archaeology. In 1421, after studying the Latin inscription on the triumphal arch of Trajan at Ancona, Italy, he concluded that such monuments could provide important information about ancient times. He devoted the rest of his life to

In the fourteenth century, Europe became interested in the past.

studying ancient monuments in the field, making copies of inscriptions and recording ancient sculpture and architecture in Italy, Dalmatia, Greece, Turkey, and Egypt. In 1471, Biondo Flavio of Forlì produced the first archaeological monograph intended for publication, *Rome Restored*, a study of the monuments of the ancient city based on both literary evidence and observations of surviving remains. This work was followed by *Italy Illustrated* in 1474 and *Rome Triumphant* in 1473. This last work was important because it contained more than just a description of monuments. It included sections dealing with religion, government, military organization, life and customs, dwellings and transportation, and public honors (Rowe 1965:10–11).

In this era of intellectual curiosity, Columbus set sail for the New World, in 1492. Of course he went to his grave believing that he had discovered a new route to the East Indies. His discovery of "Indians" in the New World was not unexpected. Everyone knew that there were people in the East Indies. It took almost 75 years for the Europeans to realize that Columbus had sailed somewhere other than the East Indies. Thus, although the initial discovery spurred some interest in the nature of the place and people, Europeans' interest in America was considerably less than their interest in other areas of the world. For example, in a survey of sixteenth-century reading tastes in France, a list of geographical literature written between 1480 and 1609 showed four times as many books devoted to Turkey and Asia as to America (Elliott 1970:12).

The final realization that the New World was not the Indies did create speculation about just where Columbus had gone, and this speculation continued to grow with each generation. Here was a landmass populated by millions of people unknown to the Western world. How was it to be explained? The most common technique used to account for the New World inhabitants was to search for "lost" groups in the historical record. The European perspective was strongly influenced by the teachings of the Bible and by the writings of the recently discovered classical thinkers. These works were scrutinized for any unaccounted-for peoples. While many possibilities were offered, the two most influential theories were that the inhabitants were the lost tribes of Israel or the survivors of Atlantis.

The Lost Tribes. Abraham's grandson Jacob (also known as Israel) had 12 sons. The Twelve Tribes that later made up the Jewish people all descended from Israel's sons. Eventually, after the tribes had settled in the area around Jerusalem, the Twelve Tribes split into two groups. Ten of the tribes set up a northern kingdom, known as Israel and two established a southern kingdom known as Judah. The history of the lost tribes began when the Assyrian kings deported many thousands of Jews from the ten tribes of the Northern Kingdom of Israel to other parts of their empire in 721 BC. These Jews are referred as the ten lost tribes. Some were lost in various military conflicts, others may have been taken captive, and still others wandered off, or perhaps were assimilated into the society where they had settled. Hundreds of years later a great exodus of Jews from the southern kingdom occurred following the fall of the Jewish Commonwealth and the establishment of Roman rule 70 BC. Many settled in Egypt, Greece and all parts of the Roman Empire.

In the ninth century AD a man named Eldad ben Nahli Ha-Dani appeared among the Jews of northern Africa and told an incredible story. He claimed to be a member of the tribe of Dan and to have come from a distant land where Israelites of other tribes also lived. There is disagreement among scholars as to where Eldad had come from: Some believe he was from Ethiopia, others believe he was from Persia, and still others believe he was a fraud. Many of the Jews of Eldad's day believed his story and were convinced that mighty Jewish tribes lived in some far-off land. The story spread and developed for centuries, both among Jews and Christians, and was still remembered by the Europeans when another such Jew appeared about AD 1525, relating another tale of the lost tribes. David Reubeni arrived in Rome announcing that he was the emissary of his brother, who was king of a Jewish kingdom somewhere near Arabia, a kingdom whose population was descended from the lost ten tribes. Again, scholars are divided as to whether Reubeni was an imposter or whether he actually came from a forgotten settlement in Persia or Ethiopia (Grayzel 1968:255–256; 372–373). The importance of these individuals is not whether they were authentic members of a Jewish enclave or imposters, but rather that they helped to create a myth of the widely spread lost tribes.

About the middle of the seventeenth century, the Marrano Jew Antonio de Montezinus reported the fantastic story of Jews of the lost ten tribes whom he had met living among the Indians of South America (Ausubel 1953:217). In 1650, the Jewish scholar Menasseh ben Israel of Amsterdam, accepting Montezinus' account, published a book entitled *The Hope of Jews*, which promoted the idea that the American Indians were the lost tribes. The evidence given in support of the lost tribes theory for American Indian origin was slight—a few words that might be consid-

The American Indians were thought to be the lost tribes of Israel.

ered similar in an Indian language and Hebrew, or the fact that the Jews and the Maya both practiced circumcision. While the lost tribes theory was soon superceded by other more popular theories of American Indian origins, the notion of the lost tribes was never completely rejected and surfaced again in the nineteenth century.

Atlantis. In 1729 Gregorio Garcia's book *Origen de los indios* (*Origin of the Indians*) was republished. Originally written in 1607, it stressed a multiplicity of explanations for the origins of the American Indian, including the settlement of the New World from Atlantis. The second edition of the work stirred the imaginations of other writers. Yet Garcia's work was not the first to consider Atlantis as a possibility. The early writers who had described America were men who had had considerable faith in the works of the classical writers. For example, August de Zárate, who wrote *A History of the Discovery and Conquest of Peru* in 1555, considered Plato's account of life on the lost continent of Atlantis as an accurate description of customs that were still being preserved by the Indians of Peru. Zárate (1968:21) notes:

> Plato tells many most remarkable details about the customs and riches of this island, in particular about a temple standing in the principal city, the walls of which were covered with plates of gold, silver and brass. He says much else which it would be tedious to repeat, but which can be read at full length in his original works. Many of the customs and ceremonies which he there describes can be seen preserved to this day in the province of Peru.

What was this Atlantis of Plato's writings that Zárate and others referred to? L. Sprague de Camp (1970) and other writers have shown that Atlantis was a creation of Plato's imagination. There has never been any geological evidence to substantiate the notion of a lost continent in the Atlantic Ocean.

About the year 355 BC Plato wrote two dialogues narrated by Socrates, *Timaios* and *Kritias*, in which the basic story of Atlantis was told. In the story of Atlantis, Plato's relative Kritias relates how, a century and a half earlier, Solon, a half-legendary Athenian, heard a story from a priest while traveling in Egypt. According to this tale, Athena had founded a great empire about 9600 BC. There was at the same time a mighty empire, Atlantis, centering on an island west of the Strait of Gibraltar, which was larger than North Africa and Asia Minor combined. The Atlanteans had tried to conquer the entire Mediterranean area and had spread their rule as far as Egypt and Tuscany, where they were finally defeated by the Athenians. Then a tremendous earthquake and flood devastated Athens, swallowed the Athenian army, and caused Atlantis to sink into the Atlantic (de Camp 1970:3–8). Plato was creating a story with his account of Atlantis. There is no mention of any sunken island in the Atlantic by any writer before Plato. Nevertheless, the story that Plato wove evolved into a myth. Stories of the discovery of islands in the Atlantic thought to be the remnants of Atlantis continued throughout the Middle Ages. With the renewed interest in the writings of the classical scholars by the Renaissance writers, Plato's account of Atlantis was in the minds of the Europeans when the New World was discovered. Thus, like the lost tribes, Atlantis became a convenient explanation of Indian origins. Other writers of the sixteenth century besides Zárate, such as the Spanish historian Francisco López de Gómara and the Englishman John Dee, considered the New World inhabitants to be descendants of the Atlanteans.

> Atlantis was fabricated by Plato.

By the end of the sixteenth century Europe was no longer curious about the great indigenous civilizations of the New World, and these civilizations were forgotten. As the historian J. H. Elliott (1970:70) has observed:

> The reluctance of cosmographers or of social philosophers to incorporate into their work the new information made available to them by the discovery of America provides an example of the wider problem arising from the revelation of the New World to the Old. Whether it is a question of the geography of America, its flora and fauna, or the nature of its inhabitants, the same kind of pattern seems constantly to recur in the European response. It is as if, at a certain point, the mental shutters come down; as if, with so much to see and absorb and understand, the effort suddenly becomes too much for them, and Europeans retreat to the half-light of the traditional mental world.

The Demise of American Indian Civilization. When the Spanish arrived in the New World they discovered three highly civilized societies: the Aztec in central Mexico; the Maya in Southern Mexico, Guatemala, and Honduras; and the Inca in the Andes of South America. Many of the Spanish conquerors were amazed and impressed with the Indian societies they encountered. Several eyewitness accounts of the conquest of the Aztecs of Mexico have survived. One of these accounts, related by a soldier who accompanied Cortés, Bernal Díaz (1963:214), tells of the Spaniards' entry into the Aztec capital:

> Next morning, we came to a broad causeway and continued our march towards Iztapalapa. And when we saw all those cities and villages built in the water, and other great towns on dry land, and that straight and level causeway leading to Mexico, we were as-

tounded. These great towns and *cues* [temples] and buildings rising from the water, all made of stone, seemed like an enchanted vision from the tale of Amadis [the hero of several medieval romantic works]. Indeed, some of our soldiers asked whether it was not all a dream. It is not surprising therefore that I should write in this vein. It was all so wonderful that I do not know how to describe this first glimpse of things never heard of, seen or dreamed of before.

In other parts of the New World, the American Indian had less complex forms of organization than found among the Aztecs, Maya, and Inca. In some areas, especially Canada and the southern half of South America, the Indians lived in small nomadic bands. In many regions of the United States, the Caribbean, Central America, and northern South America, excluding the Andean area under the Inca, the Indians were farming people living in small villages.

The European conquerors had a tremendous impact on native American life, by introducing new technology and spreading new diseases. The areas of high civilization were hardest hit by European contact, as tens of millions of natives died during the first century as a result of warfare and, most of all, disease. The American Indian had no immunity to the European diseases. Smallpox, typhus, measles, influenza, and syphilis were as effective in eliminating the indigenous population as atomic bombs. For example, it is estimated that the population of central Mexico numbered over 25 million at the time of conquest. By 1605, a little over one million natives remained. In the Andes, an estimated population of 30 million declined to 1.5 million by 1650 (Dobyns 1966:415). With the loss of so many people and the pressures of the newly imposed European traditions, the older native systems of organization broke down. The native empires ceased to function in the Aztec and Inca areas. City-states collapsed and were abandoned in the Maya area. Natives who did not die were often relocated. Native life was reduced to the farming-village level. No great new ceremonial centers were constructed like those which the first conquerors had marveled at and then destroyed. Native religious leaders were killed; native written material was burned. The Indians' religions were systematically dismantled by the Spanish priests. Is it any wonder that by the end of the sixteenth century the native civilizations no longer existed? Only beliefs survived. The once-great ceremonial centers fell into ruin and were forgotten by Spaniard and native alike. In the Inca and Aztec areas, the Spanish built their cities on top of the rubble of the ancient centers. In the Maya area the jungle swallowed the once-magnificent ruins.

Contact with the West destroyed many native American societies.

A new world had been discovered by the Europeans, but they had never fully realized the significance of their discovery. The wonders of the New World were quickly forgotten, and instead, Europeans projected their stereotypes of what the New World was like into the accounts about it. Even where the descriptions of the New World Indians were fairly accurate, the illustrations that accompanied the works were often full of inaccuracies. In fact, sometimes a publisher might include scenes of Turkish life in a book on the Indians of Brazil, just because he happened to have them in stock. In the sixteenth century, pagan idolatry and cannibalism characterized the New World for many. By the seventeenth century, the accomplishments of the New World civilizations were almost totally eclipsed by the growing number of accounts about the Indians of the United States. All Indians of the New World came to be thought of as "primitives." For some writers the Indian was a "noble savage"; for others the Indian was a childlike creature; and for still others, a cruel savage.

Civilization Rediscovered

The First Views. In the mid-eighteenth century the relatives of a priest living near the village of Palenque in southern Mexico explored the surrounding jungle and reported finding curious "stone houses." The priest died before he could investigate, but the story was circulated among the relatives and eventually made its way to Joseph Estachería, president of the Royal Audiencia of Guatemala. Estachería ultimately sent Antonio del Río who was a military officer to investigate. He was accompanied by Ricardo Almendariz, an artist.

Today the site of Palenque is partially restored and is recognized as one of the most beautiful and important Classic Period Mayan sites. However when del Río arrived on May 3, 1787, the trees and undergrowth were so dense, one person could not see another from a distance of 5 feet. It took 79 Indian workers 16 days to partially clear the site so that it could be investigated. Del Río described the strange ceremonial center as best he could, often making comparisons of what he saw at Palenque to the idolatry of the Romans, Greeks, and Phoenicians. Almendariz made 25 drawings. Neither man seemed especially interested in what they had discovered. Del Río submitted a report in 1787, which was sent to Spain and filed away in the archives and forgotten (Brunhouse 1973:6–13).

Between 1805 and 1808, Guillermo Dupaix, a retired captain in the Spanish army, and an artist, José Luciano Castaneda,

In 1787, del Río rediscovered Palenque and Mayan civilization.

were commissioned to examine the pre-Columbian remains of Mexico. They visited a number of sites, including Palenque. Especially at Palenque they were amazed and impressed with the artistic abilities of the people who had built the ceremonial center. "Who were these people?" wondered Dupaix. He concluded that the inscriptions found at Palenque were different from the writing of the Egyptians. Also, the flattened heads of humans depicted on the walls convinced him that this was a race of humans unknown to historians. He believed the contemporary Indians of the area could not have been related to builders of Palenque. He felt that perhaps the inhabitants had come from Atlantis, but also that there must have been a long period of independent development in Mexico. Dupaix's report and drawings were filed in Mexico City and forgotten (Brunhouse 1973:17–28).

While these early reports were ignored by the Spanish, a copy of the del Río report eventually made its way to England, where it was translated and published in 1822 as *Description of the Ruins of an Ancient City*. It received little attention until the 1840s. Yet the book is important, because it did stimulate further research in the Maya area. An artist by the name of Jean Frédéric Waldeck had been employed to engrave the plates that accompanied the report. As a result Waldeck was attracted to Palenque, and in 1832 he spent a year sketching the ruins of Palenque and other sites. He made many errors in his drawings. Most notable was his mistake of portraying the long-nosed mask of the rain god as an elephant's head. He attributed the sites to the Arabs, Asiatics, Chinese, Egyptians, Greeks, and Phoenicians.

At about the same time that del Río's report appeared in England, an English nobleman, Lord Kingsborough, was relentlessly tracking down every fragment of information on pre-Columbian civilization known to exist in Europe. This material was compiled to support his belief that the native Americans were the survivors of the ten lost tribes. Between 1831 and 1837 he published a series of volumes entitled *The Antiquities of Mexico*.

During this era of initial rediscovery, the builders of Palenque and other ruins were always identified as having originated somewhere else: Atlantis, Asia, or the Middle East. The reason was that this research was conducted prior to the acceptance of evolutionary theory. People and their cultures, like all forms of life, were thought not to change. The stereotype of the native American was now that of a "primitive." It was assumed that primitive humans had always been primitive and would remain

It was assumed that primitive societies were static; therefore civilization had come from elsewhere.

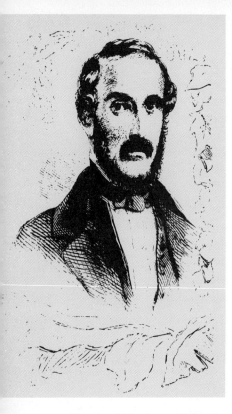

John Lloyd Stephens. (Culver)

Catherwood's drawing of the Gateway of the Great Teocallis at Uxmal, Mexico. (University of Georgia)

primitive. If the native Indians were primitive, then the question remained: Who could have built the centers of the great civilizations now being discovered in the jungles? Each speculator utilized some non-American source as an explanation. Besides the older explanations of the lost tribes and Atlantis, a new explanation for the origin of New World civilization was added at the beginning of the nineteenth century: Egypt.

With Napoleon's invasion of Egypt in 1798, the Western world began to learn of the wonders of what was then considered to be the world's earliest civilization. Egypt had been little known to the Western world until the arrival of the French. It was quickly assumed by many that Egypt must have been the "cradle of civilization" that had given rise to later civilizations elsewhere in the world. This view was held especially by those who believed that primitive societies were static.

In the 1840s, two explorers, John Lloyd Stephens and Frederick Catherwood, proposed a new interpretation of the Mayan ruins. Stephens was an American who had turned from the practice of law to writing travel books. Catherwood was an English architect. Both men had traveled extensively throughout the

Old World, and both had viewed the ruins of Egyptian civilization firsthand.

While visiting London in 1836, Stephens had stumbled upon a copy of the report on Palenque by del Río. His interest in the lost civilization in the tropics of America was heightened by the publication of Lord Kingsborough's *The Antiquities of Mexico*. Later, a friend showed Stephens a portfolio that contained the drawings of Waldeck. While in London, Stephens met Catherwood. The two became close friends and Stephens called Catherwood's attention to del Río report. They decided to see the ruins for themselves. In October 1839 the two explorers set out from New York for Central America, with Stephens as writer and Catherwood as artist.

The first major Mayan site that they visited was Copán, in Honduras. From Copán, on the southern fringe of the Mayan area, they traveled northward, across the entire region that had formed the ancient civilization. Along the way, they located and studied more Mayan sites than anyone previously. After almost three years in Central America and Mexico, they returned to New York in June 1842. Stephens had collected information for two books on their explorations[1] and Catherwood had made hundreds of drawings. Using a camera lucida,[2] Catherwood had set a new standard of accuracy in depicting Maya art and architecture.[3]

Returning with more accurate firsthand knowledge about the Maya than anyone previously, Stephens came to several important conclusions about the Mayan ruins that were contrary to what others believed. First, he suggested that Mayan civilization had flourished at a relatively recent date, not in extreme antiquity as was generally assumed; he decidedly did not believe it was as old as ancient Egyptian civilization.

Secondly, Stephens concluded that the civilization of the Maya had developed independently of that of the Old World civilizations. On the basis of his knowledge of Egypt, he was able to discern that the Mayan pyramids were unlike those of the Egyptians. Likewise, on the basis of his travels throughout Greece and Italy, he was convinced that the Mayan remains did not resemble those of the ancient Greeks and Romans. Stephens

Stephens believed that Mayan civilization was recent and had developed independently of the Old World.

[1] *Incidents of Travel in Central America, Chiapas and Yucatan*, published in 1841, and *Incidents of Travel in Yucatan*, published in 1843.
[2] An apparatus containing a prism or an arrangement of mirrors for reflecting the image of an object onto a surface so that its outline can be accurately traced. Earlier explorers had made freehand sketches of Mayan art and architecture.
[3] Many of his drawings were unfortunately destroyed in a fire shortly after his return to New York. However, 25 illustrations were published by Catherwood as *Views of Ancient Monuments in Central America, Chiapas, and Yucatan* in 1844. Two hundred and five of his drawings appeared in Stephens' books.

(1841, vol. 2:442) noted of the Mayan art and architecture, "It is the spectacle of a people skilled in architecture, sculpture, and drawing, and beyond doubt, other more perishable arts, and possessing the cultivation and refinement attendant upon these, not derived from the Old World, but originating and growing up here, without models or masters, having a distinct, separate, independent existence; like the plants and fruits of the soil, indigenous."

Finally he concluded that the ruins had been built by the ancestors of the Maya Indians who were then living in the area, a shocking statement for the time.

Considering the amount of information on the ancient Mayan civilization that had come to light, Stephens' observations were remarkably accurate for the time. His conclusions were soundly reasoned and based on more data than any of the previous theories about the Maya. Likewise, Stephens and Catherwood were the first Maya explorers to be knowledgeable about the known civilizations of the Old World. While Stephens' books were widely read, his conclusions fell mostly on deaf ears. The public and most scholars were unwilling to credit the American Indian with any great accomplishment. This attitude held not only for the Mayan area but for the United States as well.

The Mound Builders. As the settlers of the United States pushed westward across the Allegheny Mountains, they discovered tens of thousands of earthen mounds made by humans. The mounds were taken to be the work of a long-vanished race that had

> Stephens concluded that ancestors of the Indians still living in the area had built Palenque.

Grave Creek Mound, West Virginia, originally attributed to the "Mound Builders." (From E. G. Squier and E. H. Davis, *Ancient Monuments of the Mississippi Valley, Smithsonian Contributions to Knowledge,* vol. 1, 1848)

erected the mounds over hundreds of thousands of years and had then disappeared from North America. The local Indians were never seriously considered as the descendants of the mound builders "because the Indians of the mound area, as the settlers found them, were semi-nomadic savages, few in number and limited in ambition. They seemed obviously incapable of the sustained effort needed to quarry tons of earth and shape it into a symmetrical mound. Nor did these Indians have any traditions of their own about the construction of the mounds; when questioned, they shrugged, or spoke vaguely about ancient tribes" (Silverberg 1970:3).

In the Old World there had been many peoples who were mound builders. Almost all of these different peoples were at one time or another thought to have visited the New World. These hypothetical Old World builders of the New World mounds were believed to have been exterminated by the savage American Indians. Thus a myth was born that dominated the American imagination throughout the nineteenth century: The builders of the mounds were transformed into the Mound Builders, believed to have been a diligent and gifted lost race (Silverberg 1970:5).

The archaeological research of the twentieth century has shown that there was no vanished race of Mound Builders. Instead, the mounds were built by a number of different Indian societies at different periods of time. The Indians found at the time of exploration were the descendants of the peoples who had built the mounds. In some cases, the Indians were still using the mounds when the first Europeans arrived. Hernando de Soto witnessed many thriving centers with temple mounds being used in the Southeast in 1540. Like the eyewitness accounts of the early Spanish conquerors in Mexico and Peru, de Soto's description was forgotten and the builders of the mounds became a mystery.

> Archaeological research has shown there were no Mound Builders.

The Lost-Continent Theory Revived. In the second half of the nineteenth century, lost continents once again were used as an explanation for civilization in the New World. In the 1850s, the Frenchman Charles Étienne Brasseur de Bourbourg discovered in Mexico and Guatemala a number of important documents that had been written at the time of the Spanish conquest and one book, the Troano Codex, that dated from pre-Columbian times.[4] He became convinced that the origins of Mexican and Central American civilization were to be found in Plato's story

---

[4] Most important of his discoveries were the *Popul Vuh*, the Anales de Cuauhtitlan, the *Annals of the Cakchiquels*, Landa's *Relación de las cosas de Yucatán*, and the pre-Columbian Maya *Codex Troano*.

of Atlantis. While the Troano Codex remains untranslated even today, Brasseur believed that he could interpret it and that it told the story of how Atlantis submerged.[5] In "translating" the Troano Codex, Brasseur de Bourbourg used a Mayan alphabet that Bishop Landa had compiled shortly after the conquest of the Maya and included in his *Relación de las cosas de Yucatán*. Later efforts have shown that this alphabet was inadequate for translating Mayan writing. Nevertheless, on the basis of Landa's alphabet, Brasseur translated as "Mu" the symbols that he believed stood for the Mayan name for the submerged continent.

Perhaps the most influential book on Atlantis was published in 1882. It was entitled *Atlantis: The Antediluvian World* and was written by Congressman Ignatius Donnelly, who had twice run unsuccessfully for vice-president of the United States on the Populist ticket. His book has been reprinted more than 50 times and recently has been made available in paperback form. Donnelly went far beyond anything found in the writings of Plato. Plato never claimed that Atlantis was the source of all civilization; Donnelly did. Donnelly believed that a landmass had actually existed in the Atlantic and that it was on this landmass, Atlantis, that humans first rose from a state of barbarism to civilization. According to Donnelly, Atlantis eventually became a populous and mighty nation that colonized the shores of the Gulf of Mexico, the Mississippi River, and the Amazon; the Pacific coast of South America; the Mediterranean; the west coast of Europe and Africa; and shores of the Baltic, the Black Sea, and the Caspian. Donnelly believed that the oldest of these colonies was Egypt, whose civilization was a reproduction of that of Atlantis. Plato had never suggested this in his story; Donnelly was adding his own embellishments to the growing Atlantis myth. It was also Donnelly's contention that the knowledge of metallurgy and writing was derived from Atlantis. After Atlantis sank, civilization was maintained by some of her colonies. Following after Donnelly's promotion of the myth of Atlantis, another individual, James Churchward, began to explain the origin of civilization and Old World–New World similarities by hypothesizing a lost continent in the Pacific.

In 1926 James Churchward published *The Lost Continent of Mu*. Churchward suggested that Atlantis and Mu were not the same continent, but rather that there had been two sunken continents: Atlantis in the Atlantic and Mu in the central Pacific. Churchward was obsessed with the notion that there was once a universal esoteric language of symbols that the ancients used in

---

[5] Later it was demonstrated by scholars that not only had Brasseur failed to make sense of the text, he had even begun at the wrong end of the Codex.

recording their secret wisdom. He believed that by staring at ancient symbols, an intuitively gifted person could conjure their meanings out of his inner consciousness and thus recover forgotten historical facts (de Camp 1975:49). Such an approach is considered useless by the anthropologist, because without specific data, any person is able to claim that any enigmatic symbol represents whatever that person wishes it to represent. Churchward asserted that the rectangle stood for the letter *m* in the Muvian alphabet and that therefore the rectangle was a symbol for Mu itself. As a result since rectangles are found everywhere—even in an ordinary brick—Churchward was able to derive all persons and all things from Mu.

The interpretation of the symbolism of another culture cannot be accomplished by intuition.

The Egyptians. The theories of Atlantis and Mu put forth by Brasseur, Donnelly, and Churchward were not accepted by the scientific world, yet the theories became popular with the lay public. The theories provided a framework within which cultural evolution could be ignored. The notion of static "primitive" societies did not have to be rejected as long as some lost group could be credited with the accomplishments of civilization. At the same time, the scientific world became divided into several camps concerning the explanation of civilization in the New World. Those influenced by Darwin's notion of evolution saw the growth of civilization in the New World as a natural occurrence. Many anthropologists, however, were still influenced by the notion of static societies and were unwilling to credit the Indians with the development of civilization. Unlike the popular writers who credited the development of civilization to inhabitants of lost continents, these scientists sought to prove that civilization had been brought to the New World from one of the Old World civilizations. Egypt seemed to be especially favored as the source of New World civilization, because it was still the oldest known civilization, and both Egypt and the New World had pyramid-type structures. Perhaps the strongest proponent of New World civilization coming from Egypt was Grafton Elliot Smith.

Atlantis and Mu continue to be seen as the origin of New World civilization in folk anthropology because many people still hold the notion of static societies.

Smith received his training in anatomy rather than archaeology or cultural anthropology and therefore did not require the same evidence to substantiate his cultural theories that an anthropologist might. While investigating the skulls of mummies in Egypt, Smith became deeply impressed with the accomplishments of this civilization. He eventually developed a theory that a complex of traits was developed by the Egyptians and then directly carried to other parts of the world, including India, Malaysia, the Pacific, and the New World. The traits included sun worship, large stone monuments, mummification, the symbol of the swastika, serpent worship, head deformation, ear piercing, tattooing of women's chins, the Great Flood myth, and the couvade[6] (Hays 1964:286–287). This theory was based primarily on the assumption that the process of mummification was too complicated to have been invented more than once. Thus, wherever mummification was found, Smith hypothesized contact with the Egyptians. Unfortunately Smith's theory did not take into account problems of chronology. All the civilizations that were supposed to be linked to the Egyptians had originated at different time periods; some were considerably later than the Egyptians and a few were earlier. While few scholars ever put any faith in Smith's scheme, the belief that the Egyptians spread civilization to the rest of the world has never died. Thor Heyerdahl's Ra expeditions represent the latest revival of this notion.

Ancient Astronauts

In recent years there has been a flood of publications hypothesizing that civilization did not originate on earth but was brought to the earth by beings from another planet. Examples of this theory include Andrew Tomas' *We Are Not the First*; Jacques Bergier's *Extraterrestrial Visitations from Prehistoric Times to the Present*; Robert Charroux's *Masters of the World*; W. Raymond Drake's three books, *Gods and Spacemen in the Ancient West*, *Gods and Spacemen in the Ancient East*, and *Gods and Spacemen of the Ancient Past*; L. M. Lewis' *Footprints on the Sands of Time*; Eric and Craig Umland's *Mystery of the Ancients*; and the writings of Erich von Däniken. Perhaps the most popular of these writers is von Däniken whose books *Chariots of the Gods?*, *Gods from Outer Space* (originally called *Return to the Stars*), and *The Gold of the Gods* have been read by millions of persons around the world. While von Däniken has generally taken credit for originating the theory that extraterrestrial visitors brought civilization to the earth, other writers, such as Charroux, introduced the belief prior to von Däniken. What von Däniken has done is to present more data in support of the point of view and to successfully popularize the notion. To some, von Däniken's writings have taken on the aura of religious texts. Yet the scientific world has generally ignored his books and others of a similar genre. Why? Because von Däniken's approach to civilization is similar to most of the previous theories discussed in this

---

[6] The couvade is a practice found in some societies in which the father, rather than the mother, recuperates after the birth of a child.

chapter. Like those earlier proponents of the lost tribes, Atlantis, Mu, or the Egyptians, von Däniken bases his theory on the assumption that "primitive" societies are static and that New World civilization must have come from somewhere else. Given the assumption that "primitive" societies are static (which in itself is incorrect) the lost tribes, Egyptians, Atlantis, and Mu theories suffer because of a major inconsistency. These theories could explain the remains of civilization among historically known non-Western peoples, but they could not explain how those groups that were thought to have spread civilization, such as the Egyptains or Atlanteans, had obtained their civilized status in the first place. With von Däniken's theory, many folk anthropologists believe this problem has been resolved: Civilization did not originate on earth but rather was brought by aliens from another planet.

One of the difficulties in assessing the merits of von Däniken's theory is that his discussion of aliens is unclear and often inconsistent. In *Chariots of the Gods?* he suggests that the human race is the result of the deliberate "breeding" by unknown beings from outer space with some form of human beings already in existence on earth (von Däniken 1971:43). Is he referring to the appearance of *Homo sapiens* more than 100,000 years ago or to the appearance of *Homo sapiens sapiens* about 40,000 years ago? The appearance of civilization occurred much more recently than either of these two dates. Moreover, the emergence of civilization occurred at different times in different places on earth, sometimes hundreds and sometimes thousands of years apart. In order to attribute the appearance of modern humans and the emergence of a number of civilizations to ancient astronauts, von Däniken would have to prove that aliens visited earth not just once but a considerable number of times, or that the aliens civilized one group, which then civilized the other groups.

A second problem with von Däniken's writings is that he includes few specific references to the information that his theory is supposedly based on. Professional anthropological writing requires that the researcher include careful referencing to sources of information. This rule of writing is followed by scientists not because they are sticklers for detail but rather to aid their readers in locating the sources that have been used, so that if readers wish to, they can read quotations in their original context or evaluate the original sources for themselves. Von Däniken makes many startling statements about strange artifacts or secret caves, but without references. Thus the reader is able neither to check the authenticity of his statements nor learn more about the phenomenon cited.

Outer-space theories of civilization are also based on the notion of static societies.

Perhaps the most devastating criticism of von Däniken's theory is that it is based on inaccuracies, misinterpretations, misrepresentation of the data, and outright fabrication of data. As one of his most outspoken critics, Clifford Wilson (1975:168–169), stated when asked if he took von Däniken's conclusions seriously:

> Many of his hypotheses cannot be substantiated. He tends to distort facts according to his own preconceived notions. He belittles scholarship when that scholarship is opposed to his own hypotheses—this is especially so in the field of archaeology. He carries his readers along by flattering them with a "We know better" approach. Evidence opposing his viewpoint is brushed lightly aside. He confuses chronological and geographical data. He seems relatively unaware of the great technological achievements of men who lived thousands of years ago—by his hypothesis, the only really satisfactory explanation for those achievements is that astronauts intervened in the affairs of men.

Von Däniken started with the assumption held so often in the past that ancient humans were incapable of any spectacular accomplishments. The basis for von Däniken's assumption is that *he* could never have accomplished any of these feats of ancient humans—which is probably an accurate observation. Most likely, von Däniken and similar writers are truly incapable of building a Washington Monument, a Colossus of Rhodes, or an Egyptian pyramid. Von Däniken unfairly projects his own inabilities on all humanity. For example, in discussing the construction of the Great Pyramid in Egypt, von Däniken (1971:75) observes:

> I shall be told that the stone blocks used for building the temple were moved on rollers. In other words, wooden rollers! But the Egyptians could scarcely have felled and turned into rollers the few trees, mainly palms, that then (as now) grew in Egypt, because the dates from the palms were urgently needed for food and the trunks and fronds were the only things giving shade to the dried up ground. But they must have been wooden rollers, otherwise there would not be even the feeblest technical explanation of the building of the pyramids. Did the Egyptians import wood? In order to import wood there must have been a sizable fleet, and even after it had been landed in Alexandria the wood would have had to be transported up the Nile to Cairo. Since the Egyptians did not have horses and carts at the time of the building of the Great Pyramid, there was no other possibility. The horse-and-cart was not introduced until the seventeenth dynasty, about 1600 BC. My kingdom for a convincing explanation of the transport of the stone blocks! Of course, the scholars say that wooden rollers were needed.

Von Däniken is able to conjure up a dilemma only by ignoring well-established facts. Egyptian murals depict masons at work

Outer-space theories ignore well-established facts.

and show the tools that they used and their methods of dressing stone. They also depict teams of men pulling on ropes as they haul loads of many tons mounted on wooden sledges. Likewise, Egyptian texts from the Fourth Dynasty describe timber trade with Byblos (on the coast of Lebanon near Beirut), a consignment of 40 vessels with timber being recorded. Importing cedar logs was well within the technical capacity of the pyramid builders (Bracewell 1975:99–100). Anthropologists have assembled tremendous amounts of data testifying to the ingenuity and brilliance of human beings.

In other cases von Däniken uses data out of context, without any attempt to research archaeologists' interpretations and the factual data upon which their interpretations are based. For example, von Däniken has claimed that a stone carving found in the Maya area shows an astronaut in a spaceship. In the photographic section of *Chariots of the Gods?* von Däniken identifies this figure as a drawing from Copán, Honduras, while on page 100 of the same book he describes the same figure as a stone relief from Palenque, Mexico, representing the god Kukumatz which was discovered in 1935. The figure was actually found at Palenque but was first discovered in 1953 and is carved on the lid of a crypt. It is not a representation of the god Kukumatz but rather of a Palenque ruler named Pacal who was buried in the crypt. Von Däniken's interpretation reveals his biases and his lack of understanding of Maya iconography. He states (von Däniken 1971:100–101):

> There sits a human being, with the upper part of his body bent forward like a racing motorcyclist; today any child would identify his vehicle as a rocket. It is pointed at the front, then changes to strangely grooved indentations like inlet ports, widens out, and terminates at the tail in a darting flame. The crouching being himself is manipulating a number of indefinite controls and has the heel of his left foot on a kind of pedal. His clothing is appropriate: short trousers with a broad belt, a jacket with a modern Japanese opening at the neck, and closely fitting bands at arms and legs. With our knowledge and similar pictures, we should be surprised if the complicated headgear were missing. And there it is with the usual indentations and tubes, and something like antennae on top. Our space traveler—he is clearly depicted as one—is not only bent forward tensely; he is also looking intently at an apparatus hanging in front of his face. The astronaut's front seat is separated by struts from the rear portion of the vehicle, in which symmetrically arranged boxes, circles, points, and spirals can be seen.

The interpretation of Mayan symbolism by anthropologists has been a long and tedious process. Many symbols remain uninterpreted. Nevertheless, archaeologists have made some headway in interpreting the carving that von Däniken views as a space traveler. Those who are at all familiar with Mayan art will recognize that the headgear is typical of Mayan rulers. Similar feathered headdresses are depicted on all types of Mayan pottery and sculpture. The Mayan ruler may have been depicted barefoot in order to illustrate two of his physical deformities: his right foot was clubbed and his left foot shows a split big toe. The most recent interpretation of what the carving depicts is as follows (La Fay 1975:760):

> Pascal, the great ruler of Palenque, drops at the instant of death into the jaws of an underworld monster, just as the sun sinks each day in the west. This interpretation holds that, again like the sun, he will ascend into the heavens, thus fulfilling a cosmic cycle. This exquisite bas-relief is carved on a 12-foot sarcophagus lid of limestone. The cross behind the ruler represents the sacred *ceiba* tree with roots in hell, trunks in life, and branches in the heavens, where a celestial bird perches.

While much of von Däniken's data has been shown to be inaccurate or based on his misunderstanding of facts, an even more serious criticism has been made of his writing in recent years—von Däniken has fabricated information when there were no facts to back up his statements. His greatest hoax thus far occurs in his third book, *The Gold of the Gods*. He claims to have visited fantastic underground passages in Ecuador with his guide Juan Móricz. In the tunnel system, he supposedly observed a room full of animal figures made of solid metal, furniture made of a plastic as hard and heavy as steel, and most importantly, a metal library. Von Däniken (1974:9) describes the scene:

> The library of metal plaques was opposite the zoo, to the left of the conference table. It consisted partly of actual plaques and partly of metal leaves only millimeters thick. Most of them measured about 3 feet 2 inches by 1 foot 7 inches. After a long and critical examination, I still could not make out what material had been used in their manufacture. It must have been unusual, for the leaves stood upright without buckling, in spite of their size and thinness. They were placed next to each other like bound papers of giant folios. Each leaf had writing on it, stamped and printed regularly as if by a machine. So far Móricz has not managed to count the pages of his metal library, but I accept his estimate that there might be two or three thousand.

If von Däniken's findings were true they would necessitate a drastic revision of the archaeologists' perception of the pre-Columbian Incan and pre-Incan societies of the Andes. Is von Däniken's account true or is it fantasy?

Shortly after the publication of *The Gold of the Gods*, editors from the German magazine *Der Spiegel* went to Ecuador to check von Däniken's story. They interviewed Juan Móricz, and later they interviewed von Däniken. According to Móricz, a Hungarian now living in Ecuador, von Däniken never visited the cave and so could never have seen the room with strange furniture, metal animal zoo, and metal plaques he describes in his book. Rather, von Däniken's account was based entirely on information he had obtained in a conversation with Móricz at the Atahualpa Hotel in Guayaquil, Ecuador's seaport, on March 6, 1972. Later von Däniken admitted to the *Der Spiegel* editors that he had never been to the part of Ecuador that he described in his book. The photographs of the tunnel that are included in the book were not taken by von Däniken but rather by Móricz, during a 1969 expedition on which no artifacts were discovered. The "artifacts" photographed by von Däniken were supposed to have come from the tunnel. Actually they are in the collection of Father Crespi in Cuenca, Ecuador, and are fakes according to Móricz (Editors of *Der Spiegel* 1973:12).

Like earlier writers about Atlantis, Mu, the lost tribes, and so on, von Däniken begins with the erroneous assumption that non-Western humans of the past could never have accomplished great works without some type of outside help. If von Däniken's theory is inadequate, erroneous, and even partially fabricated, why has it received such popularity? The answer lies in the fact that many people want to believe that extraterrestrial beings visited the earth, in spite of the facts. Von Däniken and similar writers constitute a different kind of mythmaker than the anthropologist. They create myths that attempt to *dehumanize* the story of humankind, by attributing to extraterrestrial beings any accomplishments of the past.

> Outer-space theories dehumanize humanity's accomplishments.

Explaining the Rise of Civilization in the New World

The theories that have been discussed thus far have stressed the spread of civilization from one place on earth to other areas of the earth or from another planet to various parts of the earth. Such a process, which involves the spread of traits and ideas, is called *diffusion*. Diffusion is an important concept in archaeology. Since archaeologists find little evidence of the spread of ideas, they concentrate their efforts on the diffusion of artifacts. Artifacts that can be demonstrated to have diffused from one place to another can be used for dating and for inferring cultural history and contact.

> Diffusion is an important concept.

From their knowledge of contemporary societies, cultural

anthropologists are able to find sufficient examples to demonstrate that the process of diffusion occurs. Traits from one contemporary society can be followed as they spread to other societies.[7] In archaeological sequences, the process of diffusion is more difficult to interpret. Traits found in two different areas frequently are similar but not exactly alike. Does this mean that diffusion occurred? For example, in both India and Mexico ancient toys have been discovered that depict wheeled animals. Thus far archaeologists have found no other strong evidence for the use of the wheel in ancient America. Is this a case of diffusion? Since the toys are not indentical, it is impossible to give a simple answer. Time and time again the archaeologist is faced with this kind of dilemma in the material that he excavates. If it can be demonstrated that two complex artifacts found in two separate areas are the same, a case can then be made for some type of contact between the people of the two areas. But what type of contact? Certainly, one similar artifact is not proof of sustained or even significant contact. Perhaps the most conclusive proof of contact between two areas occurs when the archaeologist discovers in the two areas a *group* of artifacts that are the same, both in form and use. Dating is also an essential aspect of proof. The archaeologist must be able to show that the two groups of artifacts are from roughly the same time period.

In only one case have archaeologists been able to demonstrate to the satisfaction of most scholars that diffusion occurred between the Old World and the New World once the New World was populated. Beginning in the last years of the tenth century AD and continuing into the early years of the eleventh century, Norse ships in all probability made stops along the coasts of Labrador and Newfoundland. Excavations at the site of L'Anse aux Meadows in northern Newfoundland, dated at AD 1000, suggest that this site does represent a transient Norse settlement. Archaeologists have uncovered houses, a smithy, and a soapstone spindle whorl of a type commonly found in Norse ruins in Europe and Greenland (Taylor 1971:247). The Norse contacts do not seem to have been sustained and apparently had little impact on the general cultural development of the New World.

There is only one clear-cut case of Old World-New World contact.

Instead of clear-cut examples of transcontinental contact, in most cases there are a number of "maybes." A case in point is the pottery discovered on the coast of Ecuador, dated at about 3000 BC. This is the earliest date attributed to pottery in the New World. If someone had invented pottery in the New World, it

---

[7] The reader is referred to a classic article entitled "One Hundred Per Cent American" (Linton 1937), in which it is shown that many elements of our society that are considered genuinely "American" have diffused from other societies.

could be expected that the pottery would be extremely crude until the skills of shaping, tempering, firing, and so on were perfected. The Ecuadorian pottery is well made, however, suggesting that an earlier, cruder form of pottery preceded it somewhere; but no such earlier pottery has yet been found in the New World. The archaeologists who excavated this pottery believe that it diffused from Japan. Pottery discovered in Japan dated at roughly 3000 BC is similar to the Ecuadorian pottery. There are earlier, cruder forms of pottery in Japan, contrary to the situation in the New World. Therefore, if diffusion occurred, the pottery would have had to diffuse from Japan to Ecuador.

Would the Japanese have been capable of ocean travel to the New World in 3000 BC? Historical records show that Japanese fishermen of later time periods were sometimes lost at sea and managed to survive for months on end by catching fish and drinking rainwater. It is possible although not probable, that a fishing vessel or some other type of small craft used in Japan in 3000 BC could have survived a voyage across the Pacific, if it were lost during the time of year when winds and currents were favorable.

However, the journey of a single fishing raft is probably an insufficent explanation of pottery similarities in the two areas: As the Japanese pottery was not a crude type of pottery, the knowledge would have to have been carried by a potter. Thus the odds against diffusion via a single vessel are increased: The chances of a single fishing boat being lost at sea during the right season and surviving the transoceanic voyage *and* being operated by a crew that just happened to have a potter are very slim indeed. However, if diffusion occurred, it is possible that more than a single boatload of Japanese made the voyage. If this were the case, however, why are not other aspects of Japanese culture present in the New World?

Another problem that the archaeologist encounters in interpreting possible cases of diffusion is that artifacts from two different areas are usually not exactly alike. Determining the amount of similarity, then, becomes a matter of individual impression and perception. For example, how similar do certain designs have to be in order to be considered the same? Some archaeologists look at a set of designs and feel that the similarities are great enough that the artifacts are the same. Other archaeologists look at the same materials and feel that the similarities are not great enough to consider the artifacts the same. In the case of the Ecuadorian pottery and the Japanese pottery, the opinions of the archaeologists are split as to whether the pottery is the same, similar, or different. Other factors can also influence how the archaeologist interprets this pottery. For example, if earlier, cruder pottery is discovered in South America that can be linked stylistically to the Ecuadorian pottery, archaeologists will be less likely to interpret the Ecuadorian pottery as coming directly from Japan.

In other cases where Old World–New World contacts have been postulated, the evidence is even more confusing than in the case of the Ecuadorian pottery, especially where emerging civilizations are concerned. Comparisons of artifacts from emergent civilizations are complicated by the fact that art styles were more developed than the early pottery. Furthermore, civilizations all over the world probably arose as a result of similar responses to similar conditions. Thus, some similarities between civilizations are not due to diffusion but rather to the nature of civilization itself. On the other hand, long-distance travel increased in the era of civilization, making the diffusion of traits and ideas more possible than in any of the previous eras.

There is sufficient evidence to convince many archaeologists of at least the possibility of random transoceanic contact. The question that remains unresolved at present is whether or not wide-scale diffusion occurred between hemispheres. This question will continue to interest archaeologists for years to come, because its solution will provide an important component of the human myth. It is vital for our understanding of the human past that we ultimately learn whether or not the New World civilizations had indigenous origins. With our present knowledge of American archaeology, we are unable to attribute the origins of New World civilization to diffusion from the Old World with any assurance. At the same time, with our current knowledge of prehistory, we are unable to demonstrate conclusively the independent origin of New World high culture (Riley, Kelley, Pennington, and Rands 1971:457). While further evidence may tip the balance in favor of diffusion, at the present time most archaeologists believe that the New World developed with no significant influence from the Old World other than the original peopling of the hemisphere.

> Most archaeologists believed that civilization developed independently in the New World.

The Anthropologists' View of the Past

Von Däniken and other popular writers assume that earlier people were incapable of inventing a civilized way of life. If that assumption were true then it would be necessary to look for the origins of civilizations in places such as outer space. While diffu-

sion of a civilized way of life did occur in some cases, archaeologists have found that the first civilizations can be attributed
to ancient humans, not ancient astronauts. Archaeologists have
pieced together an evolutionary sequence that suggests the
growth of civilization out of earlier, less complex forms of organization.

Early Hunting and Gathering. With the emergence of completely modern humans (*Homo sapiens sapiens*) there began
rapid and important changes in human life ways. Perhaps these
changes were due primarily to greater abilities of communication than existed with the Neanderthal. At any rate, the
effects of change snowballed. Change in one aspect of life
brought about major changes in other aspects. For several million years, as initial human biological evolution was occurring,
the same basic cultural patterns had persisted. Here and there
someone figured out a new way to knap stone, but the basic pattern of life, as far as can be discerned from the archaeological
data, seems to have remained essentially the same throughout
the millions of years of biological change. Small nomadic
groups of hunters, fishers, and gatherers roamed the earth in
search of food. The food quest of these humans, like that of other
animals, may have consumed most of the group's time. Possessions were few, because they had to be carried by the individual.
Land had no value except for the food that the group was able to
find on it. There were probably few differences between the people of the group, other than those of sex and age. Women spent
more time gathering; men spent more time hunting and fishing. Older people were perhaps more respected because they
possessed more experience and more knowledge than younger
people.

The archaeological remains of hunting-and-gathering people
are sparse, being limited primarily to stone tools and camp
hearths. Because of the limited insights these kinds of data provide into the culture of the early hunting-and-gathering societies, archaeologists have had to rely heavily upon the research of ethnographers among historically known bands in
order to reconstruct this era of the human myth. The bands of
recent times may be quite different from those of the Paleolithic.
During the Paleolithic, hunting and gathering represented the
only pattern of subsistence on the face of the earth, and the natural resources were unlimited. By the time hunters and gatherers
were encountered by Western civilization, they had already survived for centuries, or in some cases millenia, in some of the
most marginal areas of the world, where their patterns of adap-

tation to the environment must have been considerably different from those of the earlier hunters and gatherers, who had access to all of the world's natural resources and could choose where they wanted to live. It must be added, however, that recent studies of some bands, in particular the !Kung Bushmen of Africa, suggest that the life of some present-day hunters and gatherers is less harsh than was once assumed. Not only do they make considerable use of vegetable resources, they have an enormous amount of leisure time and a life expectancy not much different from that of the average American.

Perhaps as early as 10,000 BC this pattern of life began to change, partly due to environmental changes. As the last glacial period ended, there were erratic fluctuations in temperature and climate. While there was a gradual warming trend, there were short periods of time, geologically speaking, in which the temperatures were much warmer or much colder than the general trend. The general warming trend brought about the extinction of the large Ice Age mammals that had provided a part of the food supply of the Ice Age hunters. Likewise, the climate shifts resulted in changes in the vegetation that provided the gatherers with food. Hunters and gatherers in both the Old and New Worlds were faced with a global food crisis, and they responded in similar ways in both parts of the world.

The Beginnings of Agriculture. The period from about 10,000 BC to 1000 BC was one of great experimentation around the world. New food sources were exploited that had not been utilized in earlier times because of the availability of other kinds of food. In some parts of the world, wild grasses began to play a greater role in food supply. The wild grasses that these people began to eat were not like the grasses that cover our parks today. Instead they were forms ancestral to our modern grain, which even in their wild state were partly edible. As greater dependence on the wild grasses occurred, new artifacts began to appear for harvesting and processing these grasses, including simple kinds of sickles—sometimes made from animal jawbones and in other cases from thin, small pieces of stone inlaid in bone or wood—and various kinds of grinding stones.

Groups slowly began to adjust their living patterns to the wild grains. A transition was made from nomadism to settled life. The continued reliance on the plants meant greater human interference in the natural growth cycle of the plants. At first, changes in plant structures apparently occurred by accident. Once it was recognized that weeding, watering, and seed selection could improve the plants, rapid changes began to occur,

Our notions of the hunting-and-gathering life are changing.

ultimately producing domestic plants that little resembled the original forms.

Why did humans begin to rely on these plants in the first place? It was assumed for many years that agriculture represented an important advance over the hunting-and-gathering subsistence system. Archaeologists viewed food production as a dramatic new source of energy and a labor-saving device that increased leisure time and left humans free to build culture. The ethnographic research of recent years seems to prove that this was not the case. If anything, the switch to food production meant that people had to work *longer* hours and endure *harder* work in order to produce *less* nutritious food than they had when they subsisted by hunting and gathering. In fact, the superiority of food collecting for the individual raises the question of why anyone would want to change to food producing. The answer seems to lie in the climatic shifts that lead people to eat wild grasses in the first place. In some areas, where traditional food resources were reduced while population remained the same or perhaps even increased, there were more people than could be supported by the food-collecting system. Overpopulation led to food production because this method had the primary advantage of producing a greater quantity of food in a smaller area. The change of food producing may thus have been a last resort for a society that could no longer maintain the hunting-and-gathering pattern and still feed its population

Famine and general food insecurity are recurrent problems only for societies that become dependent on producing their own food from domesticated plants and animals. Recent ethnographic research has shown that hunters and gatherers generally have a convenient cushion against food shortages, because their subsistence depends on natural or only partially modified ecosystems that are complex and stable. Hunters have the flexibility to change easily and can select from among a wide variety of wild foods in the event that specific food sources fail. Farmers, on the other hand, must rely on only a few species grown in artificial, highly simplified and relatively unstable ecosystems. Agricultural systems are quite vulnerable to many kinds of disruption; whenever crops fail, famine is almost certain to occur (Bodley 1976:95–96).

Another consequence of plant domestication, at least in the Middle East, was that cultivated grains quickly displaced wild legumes and grasses that had been highly valued as wild foods but which could not compete successfully with the domesticates. The wild plants that the gatherers had depended on were replaced by relatively useless weeds, wherever cultivated crops

Early farming may have been more difficult than hunting and gathering.

Plant domestication eliminated valuable wild-plant resources.

were no longer grown, and a major alteration of the native flora ensued. The early cultivators burned their bridges behind them, making a return to wild-plant gathering impossible because the edible wild plants were now extinct.

It was probably because the entire process took place so gradually—over hundreds or thousands of years—that no one realized the full implications of plant domestication. Given its many disadvantages, it seems remarkable that humans ever bothered with domestication (Bodley 1976:98). The only advantage of agriculture over hunting and gathering was that it supported a much denser population. If the pressure of overpopulation had not affected nomadic groups, it is possible that humans might never have changed to an agricultural base. Once groups changed to farming, however, the commitment was usually a permanent one. It was difficult to return to hunting and gathering, because the natural environment had been changed to accommodate agriculture.

Initially, while farming was conducted on a small scale, production was far below the maximum that might have been sustained, given the potential limitations of technology, labor force, and resources. The anthropologist Marshall Sahlins (1972:41) refers to this pattern as *underproduction*. Two reasons for this pattern were that the unit of production in early farming societies was the household; and that these societies generally lacked centralized authority. Thus production continued on a small scale. The advantage of underproduction is that it makes unlikely the possibility that a society will exceed the *carrying capacity* of its environment. The carrying capacity is the potential of an environment to support human life. As long as the carrying capacity is not exceeded, environmental deterioration and famine are held in check.

The new farming pattern eventually allowed spare time for at least a few members of the community, perhaps on a seasonal basis. With some leisure time and permanent settlement, new kinds of social and technological experiments were undertaken. Thus settled farming life not only transformed humans into food producers but craft producers as well. Pottery making, weaving, and metallurgy developed into complex processes, often requiring full-time specialization and specialized equipment. Once specialists no longer had time to farm, mechanisms of barter had to develop which allowed the specialists to exchange their skills for food.

As communities grew in size, the problems of organization resulted in the need for more specialized skills of administration than ever before, both in decision making and record keeping.

The only advantage of early farming was that it produced more, thus supporting denser populations.

Ultimately the knowledge of those who served as managers became increasingly esoteric, and the knowledge itself became a
base of power by which the managers began to separate themselves from the members of the society. In most cases, the religious leader emerged first as an effective manager; managers
concerned more specifically with secular matters appeared
later. The religious leader's power base was sacred. He was
thought to have the backing of supernatural beings—ancestors
or deities. Secular leaders began to appear whose power was
based on secular force—an army.

In part, managerial skills developed to regulate trade between
communities, often over sizeable distances. The earlier hunters
and gatherers were merely consumers of the environments
within which they roamed. They ate whatever food was available and made limited use of the natural resources, taking only
what rock or wood might be immediately needed. As crafts
developed, fostered by a settled life-style, people increased and
extended their use of natural resources. Surplus craft items
could be traded for items not locally available. Settled life also
placed certain natural resources within the territory of specific
groups. Control over raw materials such as salt, shell, certain
types of stone, and so on created trading advantages for some
groups, while groups without natural resources often played a
major role in transforming the raw material into usable items.

In some cases, farming villages grew into larger communities,
and their agricultural potential was pushed to its limits, leaving
little room for crop failure. It is not yet clear what conditions
changed the farming pattern from underproduction to overproduction (exceeding the carrying capacity of an environment).
Apparently a contributing factor was the growth of some type of
centralized power. If rapid growth of either population or food
production is to occur, a social system must develop that will
tap the resources not used with underproduction and transform
the individual-household mode of production into a system of
production based on larger units.

The Beginnings of Urban Life. In the Near East between 8000 BC
and 6000 BC, conditions such as strategic location along a major
trade route gave rise to larger communities. Excavations of sites
such as Jericho in Jordan and Çatal Hüyük in Turkey have
shown that the urban center appeared very early in the Near
East. At Jericho the remains of a site that was inhabited for over
65 centuries by at least ten different societies have been found.
Jericho is the oldest city thus far discovered. Although the walls
described in the Bible, which came tumbling down to the sound

Erbil, Iraq, a contemporary city, presents the same appearance that the site of Jericho might have had. (Aerofilms, Ltd.)

of Joshua's trumpets, have never been found, the most impressive features at Jericho are stone walls, the oldest of which is dated at about 8000 BC. The oldest wall was constructed of boulders that were dragged in from outside the town and set in place without the use of mortar. This wall was 6 feet 6 inches thick at the base and was perhaps 20 feet in height (Hamblin et al. 1973:29). Surrounding the wall was an enormous ditch 27 feet wide and 9 feet deep, carved out of solid rock. Inside the wall was a solid stone tower, standing 30 feet high, even in ruin. Another discovery suggests that the city had also constructed aqueducts. Perhaps the importance of this earliest of cities was as a strategic stop on an ancient trade route. Obsidian and greenstone were traded south from the Anatolian Plain and hematite and sea shells were traded north from the agricultural village of Beidha, south of Jericho. Jericho was a ready source of food, water, and salt for the travelers involved in long-distance trade.

The discovery in 1952 of the complexities of Jericho, dating to as early as 8000 BC, at first puzzled the archaeologists, who had assumed that the transition from farming village to city was a very slow process. The excavation of Çatal Hüyük, beginning in

1961, and the excavation of other sites in Turkey have shown that Jericho was no anomaly. Under certain circumstances, cities appeared earlier than had been assumed. The archaeologists are now attempting to discover exactly what set of factors could lead to the growth of urban life. Jericho's growth was due to its location along an important trade route. Was trade the reason that all the early cities appeared?

Çatal Hüyük, dating back to 6000 BC does not provide a clear-cut answer to the question. Its importance seems to have been only partially due to trade. Unusual findings at the site suggest that the city also served some important religious function. Perhaps it was a holy city. Archaeologists working at Çatal Hüyük have uncovered a number of ancient buildings that seem to have served as shrines (Figure 14), 40 out of the 139 buildings studied. Most of these shrines are larger than the structures used as houses but are similar in plan. Both the houses and the shrines were equipped with sleeping platforms, hearths, and ladders to the roofs. The major difference between the two kinds of structures is in their decoration. The shrines are elaborately decorated, and the art suggests a religious purpose (Hamblin et al. 1973:51).

Large communities appear early in the archaeological record of the Near East.

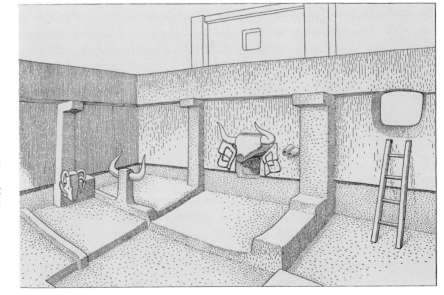

Figure 14 Reconstructed shrine, based on excavations of several shrines at Çatal Hüyük. (From James Mellaart, "A Neolithic City in Turkey," *Scientific American*, April, 1964. Copyright © 1964 by Scientific American, Inc. All rights reserved.)

The wall paintings that have been discovered at Çatal Hüyük are among the earliest paintings yet found on constructed walls. Fortunately the paintings have been fairly well preserved. The walls were frequently repainted while the original paintings underneath were still in good condition, thus protecting the original painting. The skill of the city's inhabitants in manufacturing textiles and objects of stone is also impressive.

Sites such as Çatal Hüyük and Jericho seem to show the evolution of important centers out of early farming villages. However, these centers in themselves cannot be considered civilizations. Additional events were needed for the emergence of civilization.

The Emergence of Civilization. While archaeologists are not in complete agreement as to the attributes of civilization, most accept the various characteristics suggested by V. Gordon Childe (1952), who was an authority on the Near East, as being important in most early civilizations:

A number of characteristics were shared by most of the early civilizations.

1. Increase in settlement size (urbanism)
2. Centralized accumulation of capital resulting from the imposition of tribute or taxation
3. Monumental public works
4. The invention of writing
5. Advances toward exact and predictive sciences
6. The appearance and growth of long-distance trade in luxuries
7. The emergence of a class-stratified society
8. The freeing of a part of the population from subsistence tasks for full-time craft specialization
9. The substitution of a politically organized society based on territorial principles, the state, for one based on kin ties
10. The appearance of naturalistic or representational art

Not all of the early civilizations had each of these attributes. Nevertheless, the early civilizations shared most of these attributes.

The archaeologist Robert Adams (1966:10–12) has pointed out several problems with Childe's list of traits. By giving all of the traits equal weight, he fails to separate the most important traits from the secondary ones, and the causes from the effects of civilization. Perhaps the most important of these traits are the appearance of cities and the emergence of a new form of organization, the state.

The state society is hierarchically organized along political and territorial lines rather than on the basis of kinship ties. Internally, even the earliest stages tended to monopolize the use of

The state form of organization brought with it many changes.

force for the preservation of order. Externally, they exercised a considerable degree of political independence (Adams 1966:14). Under the state form of society, food systems developed that contrasted strongly with patterns characteristic of the early farming villages. Through political coercion, states were able to extract food production from local villages and households in the form of taxes or tribute. The production levels needed to meet the tribute demands were far above the levels required for local needs.

Recent archaeological evidence from the Valley of Mexico suggests that during the period in which the state level of organization was emerging, there was a tendency for some settlements to grow to the maximum size permitted by their local productive systems. It is quite possible that the difficulties of maintaining these large regional centers generated pressures that brought tribute relationships into being: Unable to support all of its people, the large center solved its problem by using its population size to create a power relationship with smaller communities. The smaller, tribute-producing communities were then forced into overproduction to satisfy the tribute demands of the larger center. These demands then created severe population pressures in the smaller communities by limiting the local supplies of food (Brumfiel 1976:247–248).

The emergence of state-level organizations brought another change: Access to productive resources such as land and water was allocated according to the social class and status. Fairly large segments of the society were no longer involved in food production. Nutrients were no longer equally distributed in the society as they had been in hunting-and-gathering societies and the early farming villages. Some social classes suffered hunger, while other classes were overnourished (Bodley 1976:110).

The anthropologist Morton Fried (1960:728) has suggested several essential functions and institutions of the state. All states are stratified societies. Their populations are divided into two or more strata, which contrast in social status and economic prerogatives. The superior stratum enjoys privileged access to wealth, power, and other valued resources. The subordinate stratum is restricted in its access to strategic resources by members of the privileged group. The primary functions of any state, according to Fried, are to maintain general order and to support the existing socioeconomic stratification. States develop means of accomplishing these essential functions by the creation of special-purpose parts and subsystems, which also fulfill a variety of secondary functions, including (*a*) population control, which is accomplished by fixing definite boundaries, by establishing categories of membership, and by census taking; (*b*) the disposal of trouble cases, which is accomplished through the use of a system of laws and courts; (*c*) the protection of sovereignty, which is accomplished through the maintenance of military and police forces; and (*d*) taxation and conscription to support the state's various functions.

Civilization and Monumental Buildings

The Pyramids of Egypt. While urbanism and the emergence of the state are considered by anthropologists to be the most important characteristics of civilization, it is monumental architecture that has attracted the greatest attention from popular writers such as von Däniken. Although the archaeological record shows growing complexity in a number of areas of life through time, the popular writers have focused almost exclusively on large monuments, especially the pyramids of Egypt. How could ancient humans have constructed something as impressive as the Great Pyramid of Egypt without help from more technically sophisticated beings from outer space? some ask. Von Däniken suggests that the various mathematical equations represented by the Great Pyramid are so sophisticated that they would have required experts with modern computer technology. Unfortunately, von Däniken seems unaware that the calculations he refers to were proven to be incorrect a number of years ago. They are based on the calculations of Charles Piazzi Smyth, published in 1864. At the turn of the century the great Egyptologist Sir W. M. Flinders Petrie showed that Smyth's measurements were seriously inaccurate.

The Great Pyramid was not a sudden inspiration. Instead it represents the final success of a series of experiments, failures, and adjustments in earlier pyramids by the Egyptian builders. In fact the tools and techniques used in pyramid construction were in existence well before a pyramid was ever built. Prior to the era of pyramid building, the Egyptians had constructed fairly simple mud-brick tombs called *mastabas*, which were low and flat (Edwards 1947). The undertaking of pyramid building represented a change in scale. The pyramid could be constructed with the same kind of tools, but new technical difficulties arose due to the greater mass of the pyramids. Apparently, the first pyramid attempted was a mausoleum for King Zoser. This early pyramid differs from the later ones in that it is a step pyramid. It gives the impression that six stone

The pyramids of Egypt show a gradual growth of technological knowledge.

mastabas of diminishing size have been piled on top of each other.[8]

In the next stage of pyramid building, the Egyptians transformed the step structure into a true pyramid by first building a step pyramid and then adding an outer mantle that transformed the shape into that of a true pyramid. The pyramid built at Meidum and the pyramid at Dahshur show that the Egyptians were not always successful with their plans for pyramids. The Meidum pyramid was a transitional pyramid. Its underlying structure was a step pyramid. However, a collapse due to stress occurred when workers attempted to add a mantle to transform its shape. The Dahshur pyramid was being constructed when disaster occurred at Meidum. The builders at Dahshur then took steps to make sure that similar stress would not develop in the Dahshun pyramid, lowering the angle of elevation at the upper levels of the pyramid. The pyramid at Dahshur has come to be known as the "Bent" Pyramid.

By the era of the Great Pyramid, the Egyptians were experienced in pyramid building and were able to construct true pyramids, by using larger blocks and carefully squaring them off to insure less stress. Pyramid building in ancient Egyptian civilization clearly evolved out of the earlier, simpler mastaba-type tombs. Ancient astronauts are not needed to explain this technological achievement. The archaeological record clearly shows its development.

The Early Civilizations. While Egypt represents the most famous of the ancient civilizations, it is only one of six primary civilizations. The other civilizations include Mesopotamia, the Indus River valley, China, Mesoamerica, and the Andes. The earliest of these civilizations developed in Mesopotamia, the region in which the agricultural revolution first began.

The earliest known civilization emerged in Mesopotamia.

Mesopotamia refers to an area that is today called Iraq. It is a wide plain through which the Tigris and Euphrates rivers flow. In this region civilization arose about 3000 BC; the earliest civilization is known as the *Sumerian*. The Sumerian civilization is generally credited with the oldest writing system in the world. Sumerians initially were dominated by a priesthood. Subsequently there was an increase in warfare, with the successive rise and fall of military empires. The Sumerians were organized into a number of independent city-states. Perhaps the most famous of these cities was Ur, a community of an estimated

---

[8] Actually the construction is that of an interior tower whose masonry is held in place by outer buttress walls of diminishing height (Mendelssohn 1971).

360,000 inhabitants. Ur was divided into three parts: The first was a temple area that dominated the city. In this section was a stepped pyramid called a *ziggurat*, 68 feet high and constructed of mud bricks, and dedicated to the moon god. The second area of the city was the royal palace. The residential district formed the third area. Within this area were many unplanned streets, crowded with houses. The Sumerians were conquered by the Akkadians. Later, Mesopotamia was beset by disorders and wars.

About 1700 BC, the king of Babylon, Hammurabi, united much of Mesopotamia and elevated the local god of his city above all other gods and destroyed the temples of rival gods in all the cities he conquered. Thus monotheism was introduced in the Near East. Hammurabi also collected the old Sumerian laws and compiled a new legal code, which was then published and used throughout the empire. This set of laws, known as the Code of Hammurabi, later played an important role in shaping the Ten Commandments of the Old Testament. The peoples of Mesopotamia influenced both the Egyptians and the Indus Valley.

Civilization appeared rather suddenly in India, in the Indus Valley, about 2500 BC. It is not yet clear to what extent the development was indigenous and to what extent the people of the Indus Valley were influenced by the Sumerians. The civilization that developed in the Indus Valley had a writing system (as yet undeciphered), specialized skilled crafts, two planned cities as large as any in Sumer, irrigation and flood control, monumental architecture, and vast systems of transport, all of which were similar to those of Sumer. Likewise, there is clear evidence of trade with Sumer. Therefore it is difficult to assess the degree of independence of the Indus civilization.

The Indus civilization occupied a larger territory than either Egypt or Sumer and was dominated by two large cities, Harappa and Mohenjo-Daro. The two cities were built entirely of kiln-fired brick. Both cities were planned and laid out in a grid pattern with wide streets. Houses thought to have housed the elite were equipped with bathrooms, and there was an elaborate common sewer system. No large structures that might have served as religious temples such as those in Sumer and Egypt, have been found.

China appears to represent a case of independent growth of civilization. The Shang Dynasty (1766–1123 BC) and the Chou Dynasty (1000–256 BC) represent the beginnings of civilization in China. These dynasties are perhaps best known today for their bronze casting. During the era of the Shang and the Chou, China was basically a feudal society. The countryside was domi-

Teotihuacán, Mexico. (Wide World)

nated by many cities and walled towns. Centralization of government occurred under the Ch'in Dynasty. From that period on, the society was dominated by a complex bureaucracy. (Chapter 14 deals with the emergence of the Chinese state in more detail.)

The other two early civilizations developed in the New World, in Mesoamerica and in the Andes. The problem of transoceanic influence from the Old World has already been discussed. Archaeologists generally assume that in spite of the possibility of limited contact between the two areas, the major developments of the New World occurred independently of those in the Old World, although on both sides of the world the factors that led to civilization seem to have been similar.

Mesoamerica is the name given to one of the pre-Columbian areas of civilization. It includes most of Mexico and all of Central America except Panama and the southeastern half of Costa Rica. The first civilization recognized in this region occurred about 100 BC, in Central Mexico, at the site known as Teotihuacán. This site was the largest urban center of its time in the

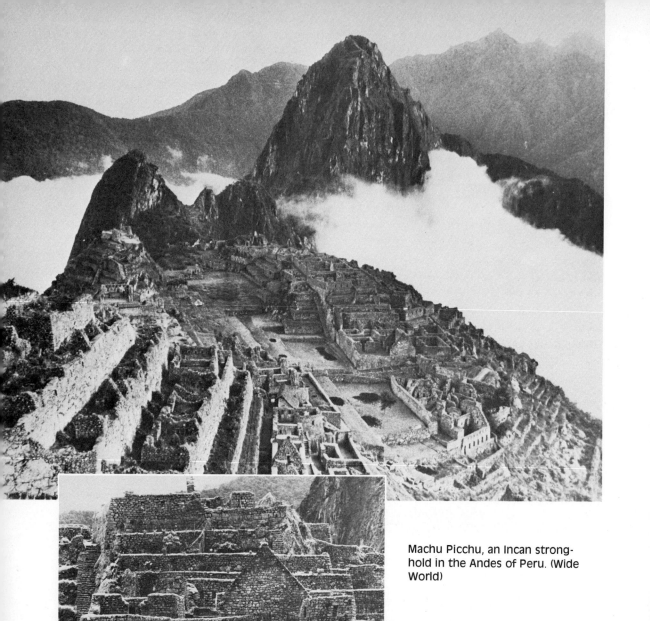

Machu Picchu, an Incan strong-hold in the Andes of Peru. (Wide World)

New World. Its important structures are oriented along a wide avenue known today as the Avenue of the Dead. The major structures along this avenue include the massive Pyramid of the Sun and Pyramid of the Moon. This city of perhaps 150,000 to 200,000 inhabitants dominated a large area of Mesoamerica, including the Maya area, either through military might or through trade—or perhaps both. Other major areas of civilization in Mesoamerica during the same period were located in the valley of Oaxaca in southern Mexico and in the Maya region (southern Mexico, Guatemala, Belize, and part of Honduras). With the fall of Teotihuacán in about AD 750, a series of civilizations influenced the development of Mesoamerica, of which the Aztecs were the last. Several systems of writing were developed in Mesoamerica.

In the Andes of South America, a second New World civilization developed, perhaps independently, although there is evidence to suggest some influence from Mesoamerica. The most important centers of civilization are located in Peru, although at different points in history, Bolivia, northern Chile, and Ecuador were also involved. Between AD 500 and 800, much of the area of Peru was united into an empire. The supposed capital of this empire was the city of Tiahuanaco, in the highlands of Bolivia. Tiahuanaco was an urban center with many thousands of inhabitants. The empire of Tiahuanaco was followed about AD 1000 by the Chimu Empire on the north coast of Peru, with its capital located at Chan Chan. Chan Chan was a large city of perhaps 60,000 inhabitants. The Chimu and other smaller groups were eventually conquered by the Inca, by AD 1450. Under the Inca, more than a third of a million square miles of territory were united into a single Andean empire. The Andes was the only area of the world in which civilization emerged without a writing system.

The professional archaeologists, through over 100 years of painstaking research, have been able to piece together a picture of human history that demonstrates considerable cultural evolution and some diffusion of artifacts from one society to another. The isolated cases that von Däniken refers to represent less than 1 percent of the archaeological record. Thus the human myth presented to us by the archaeologist can account for 99 percent of what is known of humankind. On the other hand, von Däniken's myth is capable only of explaining 1 percent of the archaeological material, while it is not applicable to the other 99 percent. Archaeologists are not impressed by von Däniken's myth, because they believe the past is human.

The archaeologists have pieced together a picture of human history that shows a gradual evolution.

Anthropology Vocabulary

Atlantis	Harappa	Mohenjo-Daro
Aztecs	Inca	Mound Builders
carrying capacity	Indus civilization	Mu
Çatal Hüyük	Jericho	Palenque
Chan Chan	L'Anse aux Meadows	Shang Dynasty
Chimu	lost tribes of Israel	Sumerian civilization
Ch'in Dynasty	mastabas	Teotihuacan
Chou Dynasty	Maya	underproduction
civilization	Mesoamerica	Ur
diffusion	Mesopotamia	ziggurat

Review Questions

1. What underlying assumptions about "primitive" peoples led to the acceptance of theories that civilization could be traced to the lost tribes or Atlantis. How do these assumptions compare with beliefs that civilization was brought from outer space?
2. Compare the implications of civilization's diffusing to the New World from the Old World with those of independent development.
3. Why do anthropologists now suspect that hunting and gathering may have been a less difficult life than early farming?
4. What is civilization? Where did the earliest civilization emerge?

Recommended Reading

Adams, Robert McC., 1966, *The Evolution of Urban Society: Early Mesopotamia and Prehistoric Mexico.* Chicago: Aldine. An interesting discussion of the rise of early civilization in two separate areas of the world that are not believed to be historically linked.

Adams, Robert McC., and H. J. Nissen, 1972, *The Uruk Countryside: The Natural Setting of Urban Societies.* Chicago: University of Chicago Press. A study of changing settlement patterns during the transition to a state society in the Near East.

Braidwood, Robert J., 1975, *Prehistoric Men,* 8th ed. Glenview, Ill.: Scott, Foresman. A clearly written introduction to the rise of agricultural society, with emphasis on the Near East, where the author has conducted fieldwork for many years.

Brunhouse, Robert L., 1974, *In Search of the Maya: The First Archaeologists.* New York: Ballantine Books. An entertaining account of eight of the first individuals to encounter the ruins of the ancient Maya first-hand.

Hamblin, Dora Jane, and the editors of Time-Life Books, 1973, *The First Cities.* New York: Time-Life Books. A well-illustrated account of the transition to farming life. Most of the material deals with the Near East.

Riley, Carroll L., J. Charles Kelley, Campbell W. Pennington, and Robert L. Rands, eds., 1971, *Man Across the Sea: Problems of Pre-Columbian Contacts.* Austin: University of Texas Press. A collection of articles that examines the evidence for transoceanic contacts, with an excellent introduction and conclusion by the editors that brings into focus the problems of investigating possible transoceanic contacts.

Sabloff, Jeremy A., and C. C. Lamberg-Karlovsky, eds., 1974, *The Rise and Fall of Civilizations: Modern Archaeological Approaches to Ancient Cultures.* Menlo Park, Calif.: Cummings Publishing Company. A collection of articles dealing with civilization in both the Old and New World. The articles include a number of the newer theoretical frameworks used by archaeologists in interpreting these data.

Sanders, William T., and Barbara J. Price, 1968, *Mesoamerica: The Evolution of a Civilization.* New York: Random House. A summary of the events and processes that led to the rise of civilization in Mesoamerica.

Stephens, John L., 1841, *Incidents of Travel in Central America, Chiapas, and Yucatan*, 2 vols. New York: Harper and Brothers; and 1843, *Incidents of Travel in Yucatan.* New York: Harper and Row. Stephens' exciting accounts of his expedition to the land of the Maya and the people and ruins that he found there.

Todd, Ian A., 1976, *Çatal Hüyük in Perspective.* Menlo Park, Calif.: Cummings Publishing Company. A summary of the archaeological research that has been carried out at Çatal Hüyük, an important Near Eastern site, and a consideration of the site's significance in the wider framework of Near Eastern prehistory.

8
Learning about language

The origins of language are human rather than divine.

Language is a system.

Language is distinct from speech.

Linguists study phonemic, morphemic, and syntactic structures.

Experiments with apes suggest they have greater language facility than previously believed.

Language is one of a variety of forms of communication. All social animals use communication. Some animals rely on acoustical communication (communicating by sounds) as do humans, while others rely primarily on visual, olfactory, or tactile communication. Thus, extensive communication through the use of sounds is not unique to humans in the animal world. However, the use of sounds organized into a language structure is generally thought to be uniquely human. Indeed, the human use of language is considered by many as a gift of God, which separates human beings from other animals.

Anthropologists have learned that the communicative forms of all animals are specific to their particular species. In other words, the sounds of a Persian cat will be the same regardless of whether the cat is raised in Mexico or the United States. The *capability* of using human vocal language is therefore specific to our own species. However, the details of this communication vary from one group to another. Languages are culture-specific. In other words, we can consider the ability to use human language a genetically programmed characteristic of our species. However, the particular language system that we use to communicate is culturally programmed by our having been raised in a particular society.

While there are many different definitions of language, a fairly typical and accepted definition is that offered by the linguists Bernard Bloch and George L. Trager (1942:5): "A language is a system of arbitrary vocal symbols by means of which a social group cooperates." By stressing that a language is a system, Bloch and Trager are emphasizing that there is an underlying structure to language that cannot be observed directly. It is this underlying system that the linguist attempts to describe. Most linguists have assumed that only humans internalize such a system as part of their socialization process.

> Language is an arbitrary, vocal, and shared system.

Certain biological adaptations occurred during human evolution, providing humans with the anatomical features necessary for speaking a language. The evolution of an enlarged brain and of a more complex oral passage produced an animal unique in the animal kingdom, a creature different from even the closest nonhuman primates. Improved language facility allowed humans to envisage new things about the world around them and to communicate this information to others of the same species through language. Because language is considered a vital part of being human, the human myth includes a number of beliefs about the nature of language. In this chapter some of these beliefs will be explored, including those that concern the origin of language, the structure of language, and the uniqueness of language.

The Origin of Language

Today the members of all known human societies communicate with one another through the use of spoken language. We know that there are several thousand languages spoken today and many others that have become extinct—some in recent times. What about earlier forms of humans? Did they all speak the same language? If so, when did language diversification occur? What kinds of information can anthropologists use to answer these questions? Perhaps it would be easiest to begin with the last question first.

Archaeologists explain the past on the basis of concrete data they have uncovered during excavations. The linguist interested in the history of language is less fortunate, because until the invention of mechanical recording devices, sounds were lost forever. Writing is a great help in historical analysis but does not extend back to the beginnings of human language, which must have originated sometime between *Australopithecus* and *Homo sapiens sapiens*. The earliest writing systems do not date much earlier than 3000 BC, besides which, some writing systems are only partially understood or translatable.

Actually, most languages of the world have no accompanying system of writing. When an unwritten language become extinct, we have only indirect information about the nature of the language. Nevertheless, linguists have developed effective methods of "reconstructing" languages, based on the comparative method, in which modern languages that are historically related are compared in order to infer what earlier forms of these languages must have been like. While the inferences made are matters of likelihood rather than absolute certainty, linguists have been able to achieve statements of very great likelihood in many cases. By the comparative method, linguists have been able to learn a great deal about the prehistory of the native languages of the New World, most of which were unwritten. The linguists are able to make reasonable estimates of the length of time many of the languages have been diverging from common ancestors, to reconstruct many features of the ancestral forms, and to trace the changes involved.

Linguists have been able to reconstruct unwritten languages.

Early Approaches. During the nineteenth century the primary technique of the historical study of language that developed was the reconstruction of "mother" languages, or protolanguages, from "daughter" languages still spoken or from earlier languages for which there were written records.

Throughout the eighteenth century it had been assumed by many scholars that Biblical Hebrew was *the* original language, that it had been a gift of God to humans, and that all languages were directly related to Hebrew. This assumption was based on the beliefs that God spoke Hebrew and that languages do not change. Linguistic research has since shown that all languages change over time. Therefore *no* contemporary language could possibly be the original language.

By the eighteenth century it was realized by some that languages change and that some languages become extinct. This was a startling conclusion, because Creation was thought to have occurred in 4004 BC. It was difficult for most people to accept the notion that languages had become extinct within a span of less than 6000 years, just as it was difficult to imagine extinct form of humans. Previously the great diversity of languages had been explained by the Bible, which told of differences in language having been caused by God at the construction of the Tower of Babel. Since the world's tremendous number of languages could be explained as a result of an instantaneous action, little thought was given to language change or extinction. New studies of language challenged the Biblical notion by proposing a genetic relationship between a number of languages such as Greek, Latin, Sanskrit (a language of India), and others, and at least the possibility that they were in turn related to some earlier language that was no longer spoken.

The proposal that languages in India, Europe, and elsewhere were historically linked allowed language scholars to theorize a *language family* that they called *Indo-European.* The technique used in studying the Indo-European languages was language comparison. By comparing a number of known languages (both spoken and "dead" languages known from writing) thought to be historically linked, the scholars were able to reconstruct the characteristics of a language that might have given rise to the languages still being used. This possible mother language became known as *proto-Indo-European.* Initially the attempts at Indo-European language classification and reconstruction were concerned at discovering the origin of the *speakers* of Indo-Europen rather than the origin of language per se.

Once the idea of language-family classification was recognized, attempts were made to classify other languages of the world into language families. These attempts have sometimes been less successful than the analysis of the Indo-European lan-

Language was originally thought to have been a gift of God.

Comparative study showed that some languages were related to one another and derived from extinct languages.

guages, because most of the other languages are unwritten and poorly described. Nevertheless, the languages of Africa, the Near East, Asia, the Americas, and the Pacific have been grouped into language families and in some cases attempts have been made to reconstruct the mother language of particular families.

By the end of the nineteenth century, due to the work of Darwin, paleontologists, and archaeologists, it was apparent that humans had been on the earth much longer than anyone had previously recognized. It became evident that even the protolanguages did not carry our knowledge of early language much beyond the era of writing. Put into an evolutionary perspective, it became clear that the earliest form or forms of language must have been considerably different and simpler than any known language or protolanguage; Biblical Hebrew or any other historically known language could not have been *the* original form of human language unless it had remained unchanged for tens of thousands of years. From the evolutionary point of view this seemed unlikely. Since the era of Darwin, the divine origin of language has no longer been seriously considered as an adequate explanation, and instead, human origins of language have been emphasized. In the past half-century our knowledge has been advanced concerning the communicative systems of primates and other animals, speech and brain mechanisms, language acquisition by children, language universals, human biological evolution, new techniques for linguistic reconstruction, and the interpretation of archaeological material (Stross 1976:20).

An Evolutionary Perspective. Perhaps the most important recent ideas about language origins are contained in the posthumously published book by Morris Swadesh entitled *The Origin and Diversification of Language.* Published in 1971, this controversial book contains many stimulating observations about the origin of language. Through language comparisons Swadesh attempts to unravel the basic characteristics of the first languages. While this approach is similar to that used by the nineteenth-century comparative linguists who studied the Indo-European languages, Swadesh's comparisons are of a wider scope. Whereas most comparative linguists have looked mainly at the similarities between languages within a particular language family, Swadesh begins his comparison with the assumption that there is an historical link between *all* languages—however remote the ties may be. Swadesh also differs from the earlier comparative linguists in that he compares different kinds of linguistic evidence. Most of the comparative studies have em-

Recent research in many fields has provided insights into the origin of language.

phasized the comparison of words. Swadesh also compares words, but goes beyond this to compare the various kinds of sounds used to express concepts such as near and far, motion toward and motion away, big and little.

The data that Swadesh present suggest that there is a distant common origin for all languages and that there are cross-cultural human tendencies toward certain common types of symbolism. Part of Swadesh's methodology involves not only a comparison of historically known language but a comparison of the various protolanguages that have been reconstructed. Swadesh compares these to discern what might be the common features of these older languages and to partially reconstruct a kind of "proto-protolanguage," thus extending linguistic analysis farther back in time than was done by previous comparative linguists. By this technique Swadesh has perhaps gotten closer to some of the features of the earliest forms of language than anyone previously. Swadesh's evidence does not *prove* that all languages have sprung from a common origin, since linguists must work with likelihoods in studying unwritten languages, but rather his work suggests new ways in which linguists can approach the problem of language origin.

Swadesh believes that in the era when prehuman communication was not yet really language, there could only have been one system common to the evolving species—with minor individual and subspecies differences. He believes that the cultural uniformity suggested by the material remains of *Australopithecus* allows the linguist to infer that there was no marked language diversity.[1]

As the brain case of *Homo erectus* shows marked increases in brain size over *Australopithecus,* as their cultural remains began to show greater diversity, and as they spread over a much larger area of the Old World, it seems likely that language diversity began in their era, perhaps a million years ago. Probably all three factors were important in language differentiation. The size of *Australopithecus'* brain case suggests limited ability of language communication. The increase in the size of *Homo erectus'* brain suggests greater language facility. The diversity of artifacts in the *Homo erectus* sites suggests that local populations were faced with different kinds of problems of survival and were coping by different means. Names may have been needed in one group for things that were not found in other local popu-

Swadesh has suggested that language diversity began as *Homo erectus* spread over the Old World.

---

[1] Swadesh died before the recent discoveries of early *Homo* forms in East Africa that were contemporary with *Australopithecus.* It is possible that he might have changed his point of view and allowed language diversification prior to *Homo erectus.*

lations. Futhermore, the era of *Homo erectus* was one of population spread. *Homo erectus* inhabited a greater area of the Old World than did *Australopithecus*. As Swadesh (1971:219) notes, "Linguistic differentiation tends to occur and language varieties to develop in every situation of reduced contact among the various parts of a language community. If all or part of the population moves, differences will appear more rapidly or more slowly in proportion to the degrees of isolation." However, since many of the communication devices were close to instinctive, differentiation of language must have occurred very slowly. Local differences began to occur more rapidly as *Homo sapiens sapiens* evolved. The time needed for the diversity found among the present languages of the world is calculated by Swadesh at about 20,000 years.

Local Languages served the needs of the hunter and gatherer and the early tribal peoples. As agriculture evolved as a way of life, many changes occurred in the life-style of the farming peoples. New equipment, new plants, new animals, and new forms of social organization all required new vocabulary. Over a period of perhaps 7000 years of agricultural subsistence, languages of a new kind evolved that were intimately tied with the first urban civilization and writings. These were the *classic languages* (a type of language shared by culturally diverse speakers) such as Latin, Greek, Egyptian, Hebrew, Persian, and Sanskrit in the Old World, and Nahuatl (the Aztec language), Maya, and Quechua (the Incan language) in the New World.

Both local and classic languages are still found today, but throughout much of the world they have been replaced by modern *world languages*. The world languages, such as English, Russian, and Japanese, are spoken by millions of people. These languages have such large and specialized vocabularies that no one possesses the language in its totality. It is characteristic of the speakers of the world languages to make use of dictionaries, encyclopedias, manuals, and tables of reference as the knowledge encompassed by world languages becomes more specialized. If anything, the dependence on extrahuman equipment will continue to increase, and the percentage of the total language known by any individual will decrease with each generation, as the societies and technologies of the world-language speakers become increasingly complex (Swadesh 1971:44).

While local and classic languages survive in isolated parts of the world, the contrast between them and the world languages is considerable. Whereas the local language is considerably restricted in distribution and number of speakers, like the lan-

Language shows an evolutionary development from local languages to classic languages to world languages.

guages spoken by the various Indian tribes of the Amazon Basin, the world languages are characteristic of complex societies that span oceans and continents. World languages have the large vocabularies; the local languages have relatively small ones. Nevertheless, all languages of the world are patterned forms of speaking and are considered equivalent or equally human.

Discovering Language Patterns and Sounds

The end of the eighteenth century ushered in the comparative and historical study of language. By the beginning of the nineteenth century, scholars were beginning to recognize that the comparison of languages required examining the total structure of each language. The comparison of a few isolated words was no longer adequate. This type of language comparison became known as *comparative philology*. A great deal of the important work in this field in the eighteenth century was undertaken by Germans, one of the most influential being Jakob Grimm.

Grimm made a fundamental contribution to the understanding of Indo-European language history, although he and his brother Wilhelm are better known to the public for the fairy tales they collected. Jakob Grimm was able to show that there were regular patterns of sound shifts in the Indo-European family; these patterns allowed the linguists to recognize that more words were actually related to one another than had previously been suspected. For example Grimm was able to show that words with the consonants *p*, *t*, and *k* in Latin, Sanskrit, and Greek shift to *f*, *th*, and *h* in the Germanic languages; Latin *pat*er becomes *fath*er in English, the Latin word *t*res becomes *th*ree in English, the Latin word *c*ornu (the *c* is pronounced like a *k*) becomes *h*orn in English. Likewise the *b*, *d*, and *g* sounds of Latin, Greek, and Sanskrit shift to *p*, *t*, and *k* in the same Germanic words; for example, Latin *d*entes becomes *t*eeth in English (also note the *t* shift to *th*). The description of these and several other patterns of regular sound shifts became known as Grimm's law. Although further modified by later linguists, this law was an important breakthrough in recognizing which words in the Indo-European languages were *cognates*. A cognate is a word in one language which closely resembles a word in another language—both in form and in meaning. The words resemble one another because each is derived from the same word in a third language that is parent of the other two. For example,

Grimm recognized that there are regular patterns to language change.

German *Fuss* and English *foot* are cognates, and both are cognate with the earlier Latin word *pes*.

While the comparative philologists continued to search for additional laws of language change, another group of linguists began to work on a different linguistic problem—how to record the sounds of an unwritten language. The problem of putting the sounds of language into writing was no real problem for people who had a writing system. Therefore as long as linguistic interest centered on the Indo-European languages, the transcription of sounds seemed no problem—the linguists merely used the conventional spelling of the language they were studying. However, as linguists attempted to record some of the local languages of the American Indians and other peoples, they realized that the alphabets of the Indo-European languages were inadequate for the task. Other language families contained sounds found in no Indo-European language. The first reaction to these new sounds was to record them using the Roman-alphabet symbols. There was often disagreement as to what sound in the recorder's language was the closest to a new sound. The Spanish conquerors of Mexico and Peru encountered a number of new sounds not found in Spanish. They frequently used the letter *x* to signify an unknown sound, even though this meant that several different sounds were recorded as *x*. The problem of transcription became even more acute as linguists began to study dialectical variations within various Indo-European languages.

Jacob Grimm.
(The Granger Collection)

In 1867, Alexander Melville Bell, the father of the inventor of the telephone, published a new way of translating the sounds of a language into written symbols. In his book *Visible Speech*, he presented a new set of symbols that were pictorial representations of the sounds. The symbols indicated the position of the throat, tongue, and lips in making sounds. It was Bell's aim to develop a system of transcribing sounds so complete that anyone could at first sight pronounce correctly any language written in these symbols. He succeeded in his aim of completeness, but his visible-speech alphabet was so revolutionary in form and contained so many symbols that few people could understand it. Bell's system fell into disuse because of its completeness which made it too cumbersome for the linguists. Nevertheless, it was widely used to teach the deaf to speak (Kantner and West 1960:309–310).

The most important advance in developing a system for writing languages was devised by the English phonetician Henry Sweet. Like Bell, Sweet wanted to devise a system that could record the nuances of sounds in different languages and dialects.

Apparently the character Professor Henry Higgins of George Bernard Shaw's *Pygmalion* and Lerner and Loewe's Broadway musical adaptation, *My Fair Lady*, was based on Henry Sweet. At first he attempted to devise a simplified form of Bell's visible speech, but even the revised form was too complicated. Therefore he developed a new set of symbols based mainly on characters of the Roman alphabet. These symbols were published in Sweet's *Handbook of Phonetics* in 1877.

The International Phonetic Association was founded in 1886, and in 1888 it adopted Sweet's set of symbols as the official *International Phonetic Alphabet*. The purpose of this association was to promote an official set of symbols that could be used by scholars all over the world in phonetic and other linguistic studies, as well as in the teaching of foreign languages. The International Phonetic Alphabet has been modified slightly from time to time since its inception and is widely used today by most of the world's linguists.

The International Phonetic Alphabet is widely used to transcribe languages.

Structural Linguistics

At the turn of the century, while the International Phonetic Association was struggling with the problem of how to record sounds precisely, another linguist was making a fundamental discovery about the nature of language. Between 1906 and 1911, the Swiss linguist Ferdinand de Saussure began teaching a new approach to the study of language at the University of Geneva that was to lay the foundation for modern studies in historical and structural linguistics. Earlier Saussure had made important contributions to the study of proto-Indo-European.

Language as a System. Language was studied piecemeal until Saussure introduced a new approach. Linguists usually focused on some minute aspect of language, without concern for how fragmentary facts fit into an overall pattern. As long as most of the linguists focused on historical studies, this atomistic approach was considered feasible. Furthermore, by emphasizing historical problems, the comparative philologists had tended to divorce language from humans. Since the speakers of the protolanguages they were reconstructing no longer existed, it was easy for the linguists to approach their subject matter in a mechanical, nonhumanistic way.

Saussure's new approach focused attention on the distinctly human side of speech. He conceived of language as a *system*, which is turn was related to the cultural tradition of the speakers. In taking this orientation Saussure was the first to present a coherent picture of the basic principles and methods of linguistics.

Saussure made a greater attempt than anyone previously to develop a rigorous series of distinctions and definitions. Saussure distinguished three ways of studying spoken language: First, it can be studied as a set of physical-physiological events, the approach used by phoneticians like Sweet, which involves a concern with sound waves and detailed transcription of them. Second, it can be approached from the point of view of the native speakers, with emphasis on what is heard rather than what is spoken (Linguists had not realized that there was a difference between what was spoken and what was heard. The phoneticians had concentrated only on the first approach and ignored the second.) And third, spoken language can be approached as a dynamic set of sounds, which undergoes change in the course of time. This third approach was the orientation of the comparative philologist (Wells 1958:1). The three approaches distinguished by Saussure have come to be known as *phonetics*, *phonemics*, and *historical linguistics*.

Ferdinand de Saussure. (The Granger Collection)

Saussure, a French speaker, distinguished between two aspects of language (*le langage*): *parole* and *langue*. Literally, *parole* can be translated from French as "speech" and *langue* as "language." As Saussure used these terms, what is actually spoken is *parole*, while *langue* is the system or code.

Saussure distinguished speech from language.

> No one really hears *langue* in reality; *langue* is in the long run really an abstraction from innumerable acts of *parole*. Yet each act of *parole* is performed in conformity to the norms and rules of the system called *langue*, for otherwise it would not be meaningful and therefore would not be *parole*. *Langue* is like the rules of a game; they do not in themselves constitute a game, yet no individual contest would be a game if the players were not conforming to a set of rules previously known to each. [Hughes 1962:23]

The acts of speaking (*parole*) are complex. As Saussure (1959:15) observed, "It would be impossible to provide detailed photographs of acts of speaking [*actes de parole*]; the pronunciation of even the smallest word represents an infinite number of muscular movements that could be identified and put into graphic form only with great difficulty." Attempts such as Bell's visible-speech system, mentioned earlier, were unusable because of the complicated system needed to record the nuances of speaking.

However, phoneticians were looking only at speech and devising more and more complex systems of notation, and complicated machinery for analyzing the sound waves made by speakers of a language.

Saussure's real contribution to linguistics was in recognizing another aspect of language—the underlying code—that had been ignored by linguists. Because *parole* and *langue* represent different aspects of language, an understanding of *langue*, the system or code, cannot be obtained merely by concentrating on speech (*parole*).

The modern anthropological linguist uses a structural approach in studying native languages. Linguists studying different languages of the world all collect similar kinds of data, representing three different levels of complexity in language. Each level is represented by its own form of language patterning. These three kinds of linguistic structure are referred to as the *phonemic structure*, the *morphemic structure*, and the *syntactic structure*.

The Phonemic Structure. Humans are capable of making an infinite variety of sounds, as phoneticians such as Sweet were able to demonstrate. However not all, or even most, of these sounds are used in any one human language. The sounds of most languages seem to number about 40 to 60 separate sounds. A few languages may include as few as 10 sounds, while other languages include as many as 150. The smallest sound units in a language that distinguish one word or syllable from another are called *phonemes*. The phonemes are the basic code elements that the rest of the language is based on. For example, in English the sounds "p" and "b" are separate phonemes. These two sounds interchanged in the same linguistic environment change the meaning of a word or syllable. If "b" is substituted for "p" in the word *pat* it changes the word to *bat*, which has a different meaning. Since the significance of sounds is culturally determined, the linguist cannot assume that all other, or even most other, languages will consider "p" and "b" as distinct phonemes. The main difference between the two sounds is that "b" is made accompanied by a vibration in the throat called *voicing*. The "b" sound in English is a voiced consonant, while the "p" is voiceless. In English, voicing is one feature that can distinguish sounds as separate phonemes: Thus voicing is considered a *contrastive* feature in English. There are other sound variations in English that do not make a difference between two words. These sound features are considered *noncontrastive*. For example, in English the sound "p" is sometimes released with a slight puff of air, called *aspiration*, at other times it is released without a puff of air. In both cases, the speaker of English hears

Phonemes are the smallest sound units that distinguish one word or syllable from another.

the same kind of sound, because aspiration is noncontrastive in English. Speakers of English have learned not to distinguish between aspirated and nonaspirated variations.

The linguist studying a language different from English will not know in advance which features such as aspiration and voicing will be contrastive and which will be noncontrastive. For example, an English-speaking linguist studying the language of the Menomini Indians would hear their word for "water" sometimes as "nipew" and sometimes as "nibew." To the English speaker this sounds like two separate words, because voicing (the difference between "p" and "b") is contrastive in English. But the Menomini do not make this distinction; in Menomini, voicing is noncontrastive. The speaker of Menomini has been taught to recognize no difference between "b" and "p," just as English speakers are taught to recognize no difference between aspirated and unaspirated consonants.

All that the linguist can confidently assume about the phonemic structure of a language to be studied is that it will be different from the phonemic structure of his or her own language. The linguist beginning an analysis has no idea which will prove to be contrastive sound features and which will not be significant. Therefore he or she begins the study by carefully transcribing the minutest differences in the sounds being spoken, using the International Phonetic Alphabet. Every sound feature has to be carefully transcribed so that no significant contrasts are ignored.

After transcribing utterances in careful phonetic transcription, the linguist sorts the variations he or she hears into the proper phonemes. In the initial stages of analysis there is considerable shifting of variants from one phoneme to another and discoveries that there are additional phonemes or that two phonemes are actually one, as more linguistic data is collected. Usually within a month a linguist has a pretty clear picture of the phonemic structure of a language, although slight modifications to the description are made throughout the entire analysis of the language. The linguist not only describes the phonemes of the language but also gives detailed information or rules describing the conditions under which each variant of a phoneme is used.

The Morphemic Structure. The phoneme is only a unit of sound. No meaning is attached to the phoneme. However the phonemes, or sounds, are combined in larger units to which meaning is attached. *Morphemes* are the smallest units of a language that have definite meaning. Morphemes may consist of a

Morphemes are the smallest units of a language that have meaning.

single phoneme, as in the English morpheme -s, meaning "two or more," or they can consist of strings of phonemes, as in *pit* (which is made up of the phonemes "p," "i," and "t"). Not all possible combinations of phonemes are given meaning in a language. In English, *pit* and *tip* have meanings, but *pti* and *tpi* do not.

Some morphemes, such as *tip*, have semantic meaning; other morphemes, such as *-ed* (past tense), convey grammatical meaning. A morpheme such as *tip*, which has semantic meaning by itself, is called a *free morpheme*. Other morphemes, such as suffixes and prefixes, which must be combined with other morphemes in order to have semantic sense, are called *bound morphemes*.

The Syntactic Structure. The linguist is also concerned with the basic rules of grammar. Each language has rules or restrictions on the formation of sentences and parts of sentences. These restrictions constitute the *syntax* of the language. The rules of syntax are based on strings of morphemes. The sentence *"John sold the horse"* has a different meaning than *"The horse sold John."* The order of the words produces the difference in meaning. As with the other levels of analysis, the linguist cannot assume the rules of arrangement in the language being studied will be the same as in his or her own language.

In many ways syntactic analysis is the most difficult. Whereas the total number of phonemes in the language can be determined in a relatively short amount of time, the linguist is never able to compile for analysis a listing of all possible acceptable utterances in the language. The number is infinite, because the speakers of any language are able to create combinations that have never been spoken previously but which are understood by the other speakers. Therefore, instead of concentrating on merely collecting a list of utterances, the linguist attempts to discover the underlying rules that the speakers of a language use to generate sentences.

Until the late 1950s, linguists analyzed syntax without concern for the semantic aspects (or meaning) of an utterance. Then in 1957, Noam Chomsky published *Syntactic Structures,* which revolutionized syntactic analysis. Chomsky's approach remains controversial even today, but its impact on modern linguistics cannot be denied. Chomsky's approach is to view all of the elements of a language, both structural and semantic, as a total system that has definite characteristic ways of operating. Chomsky does not think that traditional grammars account for all that governs the production of utterances. Chomsky's approach is called *transformational grammar*. Its basic principles were set forth in *Syntactic Structures*, while later works, especially Chomsky's *Aspects of the Theory of Syntax* (1965), elaborate on the approach.

Chomsky distinguishes between *competence* and *performance*. Competence is the speaker's grasp of the underlying principles of the language. Performance is his or her actual speaking. People are usually unaware of their language competence. They speak correctly without actually knowing why they do so. Chomsky feels it is possible to construct a grammer that can specify all of the rules concerning utterances in a particular language. Traditional approaches to syntax were unable to do this. Part of a human's ability to speak is the capability to say the same thing several ways. For example, a speaker of English can say "John loves Alice" or "Alice is loved by John" and convey exactly the same meaning. Chomsky suggests there are two levels of structure in every sentence: a *surface structure*, or verbal expression, and an underlying *deep structure*. The above examples have different surface structures but the same deep structure. On the other hand, a sentence such as "John loves Alice" can also have several meanings. It can mean that John has strong affection for Alice, or it can mean John makes love physically to Alice. In this case a single surface structure can correspond to several deep structures. According to Chomsky, it is only through context that we are able to understand what is actually meant. Traditional syntactic analysis has been concerned only with the surface structure; but transformational rules are used by speakers to translate the deep structure into the forms it takes as utterances (the surface structure). Chomsky's distinction of deep and surface structure strongly reinforces Saussure's distinction between language and speech.

All humans are capable of making transformations, whether the language they speak is Arunta or Swedish. Therefore Chomsky believes that all humans are born with a blueprint for language—the deep structure. If this is the case, then language is more genetically programmed than many linguists are willing to admit. In fact it suggests the possibility that all languages may share the same deep structure, which is expressed as a variety of different surface structures.

Semantics. Chomsky's work is symptomatic of a growing interest in meaning in anthropological linguistics. For many years linguists merely collected lists of words, which they compiled to form a dictionary. Today the study of meaning entails fruitful interaction between the linguist and the cultural anthropol-

> Transformational grammar represents a new approach to syntax.

> Chomsky distinguishes surface structure and deep structure.

ogist: The study of meaning obviously necessitates an understanding not only of a language but also of the speakers' culture—their system of knowledge. The shared interest of the two subfields of anthropology has led to the development of a specialty known as *ethnosemantics*. Ethnosemantics is the study of the categories that people of different societies use to classify the world around them. The approach of ethnosemantics is definitely an "emic" one—the linguist attempts to learn the native framework for classification. Some of the most interesting ethnosemantic research has considered how various societies classify their plant world or the color terminologies that are used.

> Ethnosemantics studies the categories that people use to classify their world.

Is Language Uniquely Human?

Primatologists have learned that African apes in the wild have a rather extensive system of communication based partly on sounds. While it is impossible to get inside the ape's brain to learn exactly what is meant by a particular sound, the observer is able to record stimuli and the responses to the stimuli. In this way certain patterns for the use of sounds were discovered among the apes. The chimpanzee makes certain sounds during certain situations; for example, when it is raining and the chimp seems to be angry about the weather condition, when it stops raining and the chimp is happy, when the chimp is nesting and so on.

For many years physical anthropologists have questioned whether or not apes could be taught to speak a language. All attempts thus far have failed. This suggested to scholars until recently that apes were incapable of learning a language. Baby apes have been raised with human infants for research purposes. In each case both ape and human learn at about the same rate until the human begins to speak; then human learning reaches such an accelerated pace that the young ape is left far behind. The world record for the number of words spoken by a chimp is held by Vicki, a chimpanzee who managed to learn four words in the 1950s. Of course, since the chimp's sound-producing mechanisms are significantly different biologically from those of humans, it is unlikely that the chimp, or any other ape, will ever learn to speak a human language. Yet Saussure has pointed out that speaking and language are two different phenomena. It is possible that apes could learn to use a complex system of symbols to convey information in some other form

> Attempts to teach apes to speak have been unsuccessful.

than speaking? Recently some very interesting experiments have been conducted to pursue this question.

Washoe Attempts to Learn a Language. Not all human beings are capable of speaking. Many individuals who are physically handicapped rely on a substitute for speaking—sign language. These humans very clearly illustrate Saussure's distinction between speech and language. Because of their human brain, these individuals have the capability of learning language systems, but they lack the ability to speak.

In observing films of Vicki, two American psychologists, R. Allen Gardner and Beatrice Gardner, were intrigued with Vicki's abilities to gesture with her hands in spite of her inability to speak. While most researchers thought that the experiments with Vicki were conclusive proof that the chimp lacked the mental capabilities necessary for language, the Gardners began to think that Vicki's deficiency was motor, not mental, and that perhaps an ape might be taught some language that did not rely on speech but rather exploited the ape's facility with its hands. Thus in 1966 the Gardners decided to teach a chimp a gestural language widely used by the deaf. They chose American Sign Language, or Ameslan.

The Gardners could have invented a new language to teach to their chimp, but they felt it would be too difficult to invent a new language. Among sign languages, two are used by the deaf in the United States: finger spelling and Ameslan. It was decided not to use finger spelling, because it is not really a language but rather a means of transposing any alphabetized language such as English into a gestural mode. Ameslan on the other hand is a bona fide language—although it is not spoken. It is comprised of basic signal units and a grammar that organizes gestures into sentences, although the grammer is significantly different from the grammer of spoken English (Linden 1976:18–19).

Studies had already been conducted on Ameslan's acquisition by the deaf. Therefore the Gardners would be able to compare the development of a chimpanzee's ability at language learning with that of deaf children, and the development of either with that of normal English-speaking children. Such comparisons would have been impossible had the Gardners attempted to invent a new language for their experiment (Linden 1976:19).

The chimpanzee selected for the experiment was a female born in Africa. She was about a year old when her language training began in 1966. Her new home was a 24-foot house trailer in the Gardners' backyard. As the experiments began, the

Gardners found that the chimp's development and needs were similar to those of a human baby of the same age. She slept a great deal, had just begun to crawl, and did not have either her first canines or molars. In fact, her daily routine during the first few months centered around diapers, bottles, and making friends with the Gardners. They chose a chimpanzee instead of a gorilla, orangutan, or gibbon because of the chimp's capacity for forming strong attachments to human beings. Since language acquisition is thought to be primarily social, it was felt that a high degree of sociability would facilitate the language learning. This first pupil of the Gardners was named Washoe (Fleming 1975:40–41).

The Gardners themselves first had to learn Ameslan in order to teach it to the infant chimp. They decided that in Washoe's presence they would not speak with one another but rather use only the sign language. The experiment was designed so that there would be continual interaction between Washoe and human beings throughout her waking hours, especially in the context of game playing

At first the Gardners were unsuccessful in their attempts at teaching Washoe the gestures of Ameslan. They tried to use various models of how language development occurs in human infants to teach Washoe, but either the models were incorrect or they did not apply to chimpanzees. Then the Gardners discovered success in the technique of "molding." This teaching method involved taking Washoe's hands and molding them into the proper configuration for a particular sign. For example, to teach her the sign and concept "hat," the Gardners would show Washoe a hat, then take her hand and put it in the correct position for the gesture "hat." In this case, one of the Gardners would take the chimp's hand and make Washoe pat the top of her head. This procedure would be repeated until Washoe began to make the sign without help, at which point the instructor would gradually loosen his or her hold on the chimp until she was making the sign by herself. In addition to learning through molding, Washoe learned a number of signs through other means. Some were learned by observing the Ameslan conversations of the Gardners when they weren't attempting to "mold" her. In these cases no attempts had been made to encourage her to use these signs, but rather she spontaneously started using signs that she had observed others using. The signs for "toothbrush" and "smoke" were learned this way. Another source of learning proved to be a number of gestures natural to wild chimps. The Gardners learned that Washoe quickly picked up signs of Ameslan that were similar to natural gestures. For example, the wild chimpanzee uses a begging gesture that is very similar to the Ameslan sign for "come" or "gimme." Likewise, agitated wild chimps often shake their hands to signal urgency, and this gesture is very similar to the Ameslan sign for "hurry" (Linden 1976:20–23).

Words into Grammar? By April 1967, less than a year after she had begun the language-learning experiment, Washoe began to produce her first combinations of signs. Some of these sentences were learned from the Gardners, but many were combinations created by Washoe, such as "gimme tickle" to request tickling. In some cases she invented new expressions that differed from what the Gardners had used. For example, she put together the signs "open food drink" to ask that the refrigerator be opened. The Gardners had been using the signs "cold box" to stand for refrigerator (Fleming 1975:41). This change in signs reflects an interesting difference in the perception of the refrigerator between Washoe and the Gardners. Washoe emphasized the contents (food and drink), while the Gardners emphasized the coldness.

The chimpanzee Washoe has learned certain aspects of language, using Ameslan.

Every language follows rules governing the order in which words occur in sentences, so that some combinations of words in sentences make sense and other combinations make no sense or are judged incorrect by the speakers of the language. In English, for example, the sentence "The dog barked because of a prowler" would make sense, while the sentence "The prowler barked because of a dog" would be unclear; and the sentence "Because barked the of prowler dog a" makes no sense whatsoever. The question that the Gardners hoped to answer about Washoe was whether or not she followed a consistent grammar, thus proving that she was trying to convey meaning. If the sentences made sense, then Washoe was operating with some type of patterning or language system (Saussure's *langue*). If the signs were combined at random, then Washoe has not really learned a language but merely the mechanics of making signs.

After four years the Gardners ended their experiment with Washoe. She was turned over to a student of theirs, Roger Fouts, for continued research. By then Washoe had acquired a 160-sign vocabulary. The question of whether or not Washoe had actually learned rules of grammar, however, was not clearly resolved. During the training program Washoe shifted from putting both the subject and object in front of the verb (such as "you me out") to putting the verb between the subject and object (such as "you tickle me"). This shift gave the impression to some of the scholars who evaluated Washoe's performance that she was stringing together words at random. On the other hand, in almost 90 percent of the combinations, Washoe put the subject before the verb, clearly nonrandom behavior (Linden 1976:46). Additional experiments with chimpanzees have supported the position that chimps can actually learn language systems.

The Gardners began raising a second chimpanzee, Mojo, who came to them on the second day of her life. Thus the Gardners will be able to provide even greater control over the experiments than with Washoe. Together with the Gardners, deaf children and adults are helping as signing partners for Mojo.

Washoe was moved to the Institute for Primate Studies just outside of Norman, Oklahoma. There Roger Fouts introduced her to the animals of the Institute farm. Washoe called the ducks "water birds," a combination of gestures that she invented. When she met the other chimps she labeled them "bugs." She had not seen another chimp for five years.

Washoe has now begun to teach Ameslan to the other chimps of the colony. At the same time, the Institute people are working with other young chimps, training them in the sign language. Thus there is a growing generation of chimpanzees, including Washoe's baby, who are now able to communicate with each other and with human beings by means of the sign language.

The Dutch psychologist Adriaan Kortlandt has observed that solitary chimps "talk" to themselves with gestures, and play with words in much the same way that solitary children name and talk to their toys. He feels that this type of play is very important in developing language skills.

> [Kortlandt] once watched Washoe "read" an illustrated magazine. As she did, she signed "cat" when she came upon a picture of a tiger, and "drink" upon seeing a vermouth advertisement. He refers to this as "thinking aloud," and he noted that when Washoe was not rewarded, she tended more to think aloud rather than talk to the Gardners. He feels this indicates that the "apes have a lot more to think about than to say," [Linden 1976:98–99]

Such thinking aloud with gestures is further evidence that the chimp has perhaps integrated a language system into its life and is not merely trying to please its instructors in order to receive rewards.

Other Experiments. The experiments with Ameslan sign language are only a few of those being carried out on language learning in chimpanzees. In California, David Premack, a psychologist, has been teaching language to a chimpanzee named Sarah using a graphic medium rather than a gestural one. Premack invented a synthetic language using tokens. Unlike the

Chimpanzee learning sign language. (Roger Fouts)

Chimpanzee practicing Ameslan. (Roger Fouts)

sign language used by Washoe, the synthetic language of Premack is a written language, and therefore lends itself more easily to the testing of snytax than does the gesture language. The language is based on arbitrarily shaped and colored plastic tokens. Each piece stands for a word. The research design used with Sarah has allowed the researcher to test other aspects of language learning not possible with the Ameslan experiments. Sarah has demonstrated ability in a number of language functions. At the end of two-and-a-half years she was able to use words, sentences, the interrogative, class concepts, negation, pluralization, conjunction, quantifiers, the conditional, and the copula.

Another important experiment in language training is being carried on at the Yerkes Primate Research Center in Atlanta, Georgia, by a team headed by Duane Rumbaugh. The chimpanzee used in this research is a chimp named Lana, who is being taught a special language called Yerkish. Lana has been taught to operate a kind of typewriter that has 50 colored keys, with a different white geometric configuration on each. Each white configuration represents a word in Yerkish. The keyboard in turn is attached to a set of projectors and a computer. The projectors flash the configurations that Lana selects on a screen, while the computer makes a permanent record of all selections,

Lana at the computer.
(Yerkes Regional Primate
Center)

analyzes the sequences she types, and rewards her when she performs correctly. Through the typewriter and the Yerkish language Lana asks for all of her food and drink, toys, music, movies, and human companionship. Lana's typewriter permits a spontaneity that is absent in Sarah's token language. Lana's abilities further demonstrate that chimps are able to generate and comprehend a level of sentence complexity never imagined previously.

It is as yet impossible to positively demonstrate that chimpanzees can use a language system in the same sense that humans can. Chimpanzees are physically incapable of human speech and could never be taught to speak more than a few words. The experiments with Washoe, Sarah, and Lana show that communication with chimps is possible through other means. The longer they are taught the greater the language capabilities they demonstrate. It is not clear what the maximum potential might be for these chimps. It is important to remember that the chimpanzees have only developed these capacities under laboratory conditions. In the wild they have the potential for aspects of symbolic thought and communication but have not actualized this potential to any great extent. Chimpanzees can learn human symbolic facilities to some degree, but only with human help.

Chimpanzees may never develop the facility to communicate by the complex systems that make up human language, but what interests the anthropologist is that chimps and humans are now able to communicate with one another at a level never before imagined. Perhaps our understanding of the kinds of categories and language functions that chimpanzees use will one

It is unclear what the ape's potential for language learning may be.

All of the chimpanzee language-learning has been under laboratory conditions.

day provide greater understanding of the origins and evolution of language and further enlighten us in our construction of the human myth.

Anthropology Vocabulary

Ameslan	historical linguistics	performance
aspiration	Indo-European	phoneme
bound morpheme	International Phonetic Alphabet	phonemic structure
classic language	language	phonetics
cognate	language family	Proto-Indo-European
comparative philology	*langue*	semantics
competence	local language	speech
contrastive feature	morpheme	surface structure
deep structure	morphemic structure	syntactic structure
ethnosemantics	noncontrastive feature	transformational grammar
free morpheme	*parole*	voicing
		world language

Review Questions

1. Why were the eighteenth- and nineteenth-century scholars interested in the origin of language? How does the approach to language origins suggested by Swadesh compare with the earlier approaches?
2. Why is Saussure's distinction between language and speech so important to linguistics?
3. What are the implications of Chomsky's deep structure and surface structure for the language-learning experiments being conducted on chimpanzees?

Recommended Reading

Bollinger, Dwight, 1968, *Aspects of Language.* New York: Harcourt Brace Jovanovich. One of the least technical introductions to general linguistics.

Burling, Robbins, 1970, *Man's Many Voices: Language in Its Cultural Context.* New York: Holt, Rinehart and Winston. An excellent introduction to many areas of language and culture.

Chomsky, Noam, 1968, *Language and Mind.* New York: Harcourt Brace Jovanovich. A good introduction to Chomsky's concepts of generative grammar.

Gumperz, John J., and Dell Hymes, eds., 1972, *Directions in Sociolinguistics: The Ethnography of Communication.* New York: Holt, Rinehart and Winston. A collection of articles dealing with a variety of topics relating to language and social life.

Hymes, Dell, 1974, *Foundations in Sociolinguistics: An Ethnographic Approach.* Philadelphia: University of Pennsylvania Press. An overview of the type of research and theoretical orientation currently found in sociolinguistics.

———, ed., 1974, *Studies in the History of Linguistics: Traditions and Paradigms.* Bloomington, Ind.: Indiana University Press. Currently the best coverage of the history of linguistics. Many of the articles are difficult for nonlinguists but are certainly rewarding.

Explaining cultural diversity

Initially, interest in non-Western peoples focused on the strangeness of their customs.

Anthropologists view culture as a system.

During the Renaissance and the age of exploration, the discovery of many new societies resulted in more extensive study of human differences. In previous chapters, the significance of biological and linguistic differences has been discussed. In this chapter, interpretations of cultural differences will be explored.

The Study of Custom and Diversity

Today there is no longer any question that all humankind belongs to the same species. While physical differences persist between human groups, cultural differences are often more striking. An interest in the differences in customs of various societies, as well as a concern with the origin of the customs, led to the development of the fourth subfield of anthropology, *cultural anthropology*.

The beginnings of interest in cultural diversity centered around description of the customs of exotic peoples. The emphasis was usually on the "strangeness" of a custom. In the Middle Ages non-Western people were described by travelers, traders, pilgrims, and later missionaries and colonial administrators. These outsiders made little attempt at understanding the meaning of a custom within its cultural context. Thus they had little perception of its meaning to the natives. Instead they unconsciously (and sometimes consciously) compared the other society's custom with a comparable custom in their own society. Because of their ethnocentricism, they assumed their own society was superior in every way. They saw no reason to allow the natives to retain their various practices. In the name of "improvement," the traditional customs were destroyed.

As early as the ancient Greeks information had been collected about various peoples of the world, including many second- and thirdhand accounts that were often incorrect. These accounts of strange customs were generally compiled in encyclopedias. Encyclopedists of one generation usually plagiarized the work of earlier writers without any concern for the accuracy of the information. This practice continued throughout the Middle Ages.

In the sixteenth and seventeenth centuries, a shift developed away from mere collections of curious customs of other societies to attempts at explaining why cultural diversity existed. The sixteenth-century writer assumed that there was a natural hierarchy of things and that everything on earth fit into the hierarchy somewhere. The existence of "savage" peoples raised the

Initial interest in cultural diversity focused on the strangeness of non-Western customs.

Sixteenth-century writers emphasized the Great Chain of Being.

question of just where they fit in the Great Chain of Being. The Chain of Being imposed on the European the need to reconsider the possibility that there was more than one form of humanity. Polygenists believed that several forms of humans had been created. If there were several forms of humans, then some must rank higher or lower than others in the hierarchy.

Scholars who accepted the notion of a hierarchy were further conditioned by another medieval and Renaissance belief that all forms were immutable. Each form had its place in the hierarchy and was destined to remain in that position. Therefore, if one accepted the point of view that "savages" represented different positions in the hierarchy than Europeans, one had to assume the savages could never change. This doctrine was a most effective guilt-soother for nations embarking on the colonial quest of primitive groups. If primitive groups could never become like the Europeans, then there was no point in trying to help them to change. This point of view provided some rationale for slavery, but since it represented a view contrary to the orthodox religious monogenetic view, it was not as widely accepted as it might have been.

By the end of the sixteenth century, a number of changes in the approach to the study of humanity were bringing about greater objectivity. These changes included a separation from theology, a waning reliance upon the ancient and medieval authorities, and a consideration of literate as well as nonliterate societies for comparative purposes (Malefijt 1974:58). In the seventeenth century this greater objectivity was furthered by the discovery and application of scientific principles.

Progress and Evolution

In the late seventeenth and eighteenth centuries, two important changes in the explanation of human diversity occurred. One was the temporalizing of the Chain of Being, so that it was no longer thought to represent an ahistorical, or static, classification. The links in the chain were now conceived of as mutable. The Chain of Being came to represent a historical sequence, in which the lower-ranked forms were earlier than the higher-ranked forms. This change in hierarchical thinking produced an assumption that has been perpetuated in both professional and folk anthropology—namely that contemporary "primitive" ways of life are representative of earlier societies. Today this kind of assumption occurs when the Australian aborigines or the recently discovered Tasaday of the Philippines are described in the mass media as Stone Age people. Obviously they are "Stone Age" only in the sense that they use, or recently used, stone tools. A limited toolmaking technology does not make a people and their way of life "Stone Age." Rather, they are our contemporaries, who practice a different style of life. Nevertheless the equation of living primitive societies with life in earlier times has become generally accepted in much of Western thinking.

Another change in thinking, also related to the Chain of Being, was the spread of the notion of mutability, a belief that things or forms could change. This notion was further supported by great nineteenth-century scholars such as Lyell, and especially Darwin. Degeneration, which had been the only type of change easily incorporated into orthodox Christian thinking, was now replaced by the more secular notion of "progress." When the notions of progress and hierarchy were combined they provided the framework for the ethnocentric belief that not only could the living peoples of the world be plotted on a scale that reflected temporal differences, but also that the highest-ranked societies were those that had "progressed" farther or more rapidly. Having made the unproved assumption that primitive peoples were remnants of older ways of life, people then assumed that the customs of contemporary primitive peoples could be used to reconstruct what prehistoric societies had been like.

As it became apparent that societies change, the concept of degeneration was replaced by notions of progress.

The last half of the nineteenth century is usually recognized as the period when professional cultural anthropology began. The earlier interest that Renaissance writers had showed in reporting customs, especially those that were exotic and abnormal, was gradually replaced by a new kind of inquiry. Inquirers were now more concerned with explaining why human cultural diversity had occurred than with merely reporting strange customs. The organizing principle around which much of the inquiry was centered was that of cultural evolution and the related notion of progress. While evolutionary principles guided the interpretation of customs, there were a variety of theories of evolution. Perhaps the two most influential students of culture in the last half of the nineteenth century were the American Lewis H. Morgan and the Englishman Edward B. Tylor.

In the last half of the nineteenth century, cultural evolution became the most important explanation of cultural diversity.

Morgan suggested three stages of *cultural evolution* (savagery, barbarism, and civilization) that seem to reflect the general pattern of development that has occurred in human history and which has been documented by archaeology since Morgan's time. While the terms *savagery* and *barbarism* are no longer used, because of their offensive nature, archaeologists have found evidence of a historical sequence from hunting-and-gathering subsistence to the domestication of plants and animals. Morgan considered writing a characteristic of civilization as it is still considered today. Morgan was also correct in his observation that kin-based societies preceded state organization, that stratification became increasingly more important, and that concepts of property were not developed in earlier times, with the consequence that there was little concern with inheritance (Malefijt 1974:151).

Tylor was especially concerned with the "degeneration versus progress" controversy and took issue with the degenerationists. In much of his early writings, Tylor was concerned with cultural history rather than evolution. He was interested in tracing the history of myths, riddles, customs, rituals, games, artifacts, and so on, rather than the general process of evolution (Carneiro 1973:61). Nevertheless, Tylor was convinced there had been a general pattern of progress. In dealing with progress or evolution, Tylor utilized the same basic stages that Morgan had had introduced, namely "savagery," "barbarism," and "civilization." However unlike some of the other nineteenth-century evolutionists, Tylor took more care to note that the stage model was an ideal scheme, that it represented one possible order of evolution, but that there were tendencies in other directions. For Tylor the course of progress was not always as uniform as Morgan's scheme had implied (Malefijt 1974:141).

Tylor was especially interested in reconstructing the evolution of particular traits or institutions, rather than in establishing specific overall stages of development. In order to study the development of particular traits or institutions, Tylor used a variety of techniques, some of which were already being used in the seventeenth century, to account for human diversity. The technique most closely associated with Tylor is the study of "survivals," traits that are remnants of earlier time periods.

Morgan and Tylor represented different approaches to cultural evolution, yet both seem to have been guided by what was known as the *comparative method*. The comparative method was similar to that used by the nineteenth-century linguists in the reconstruction of proto-Indo-European. The comparative method, as used in the study of culture, assumed that contemporary "primitive" peoples reflected early human conditions. Evolutionary sequences could thus be established by comparing various aspects and institutions of "primitive" societies and placing them in a sequence from simple to complex (Malefijt 1974:129).

With the nineteenth-century evolutionists, anthropology began to crystalize as a distinct discipline devoted to the study

The cultural evolutionists used the comparative method.

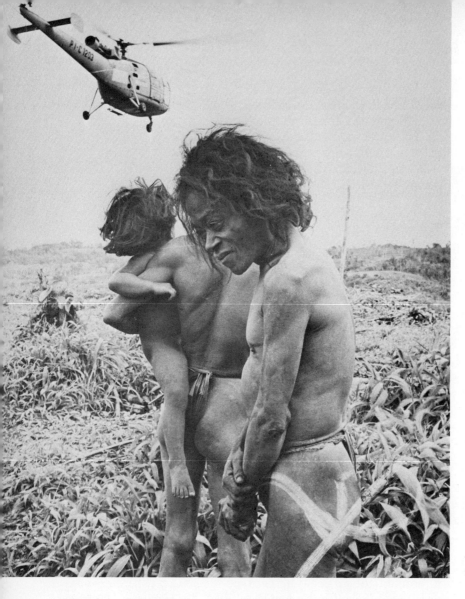

Tasaday's exposure to
Westerners. (Wide World)

of humankind. Evolution became the first important conceptual framework of cultural anthropology. With the concept of evolution, cultural diversity and similarity could be explained.

To nineteenth-century evolutionists, anthropology owes a debt for changing the study of humankind from the collection of peculiar customs to the search for laws that operate in human societies and human nature; and also for removing the study of human diversity from theological debate and making it subject to scientific investigation.

The views of culture presented by scholars such as Morgan and Tylor represented a major break from the study of exotic customs, however the modern concept of culture had yet to develop.

Culture as a System

The word *culture* was originally a biological term, derived from the Latin words *cultura* ("a tending") and *colere* ("till," "cherish") and related to breeding and improvement of animals and plants. This earlier usage is still found in words such as *cultivate.* Its application to human societies occurred initially in Germany in the eighteenth century, and during that era it still carried the connotation of improvement (Kroeber and Kluckhohn 1963:13). Yet the notion of culture precedes the use of the term by thousands of years. Herodotus, for example, realized that human behavior patterns differed from group to group.

From the era of Herodotus until the late nineteenth century, attempts were made to explain the cultural diversity that various writers had observed. Explanations included differences in climate or environment, differences in mental capabilities, differences in natural laws that had caused some people to progress more than others, racial differences, and degeneration (Malefijt 1974:138–139). However, it was not until culture was conceived of as a system that insights could develop about the significance of cultural differences. Just as Saussure's discovery of language as a system provided the key to understanding the nature of language, so too did the discovery of culture as a system provide the key to understanding the nature of culture.

Edward Tylor first offered a definition of culture that rejected both the notions of degeneration and of divine intervention. In *Primitive Culture*, written in 1871, Tylor (1958:1) wrote, "Culture or civilization, taken in its wide ethnographic sense is that complex whole which includes knowledge, belief, art, morals, law, custom, and any other capabilities and habits acquired by man as a member of society." Thus, by Tylor's definition it became possible to speak of the cultures and civilizations of peoples who had been commonly considered to lack either (Lienhardt 1969:88). With the inclusion of "primitive" peoples among those with culture, the notion of culture took on primary importance for the cultural anthropology that was to follow.

Two key terms in Tylor's definition are *acquired* and *complex whole.* That culture was acquired meant it was a product of social learning rather than biological heredity. Likewise the notion of a complex whole implied that culture included all socially learned behavior, whether it seemed trivial or not. Every

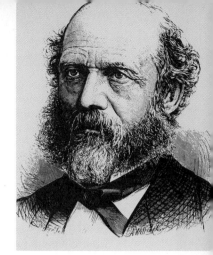

Lewis H. Morgan. (The Granger Collection)

Tylor is credited with the first modern definition of culture.

Edward B. Tylor. (National Portrait Gallery, London)

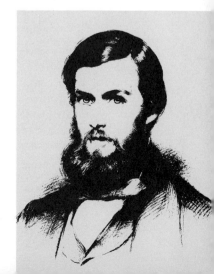

aspect of social life was worthy of study because it contributed to the understanding of humankind.

As anthropology was emerging as a distinctive discipline, the concept of culture as defined by Tylor offered a new orientation for explaining diversity. Although biological and environmental differences were still considered important, greater attention was now given to cultural differences. The Eskimo, the Samoans, the Sioux, and hundreds of other peoples were now seen as each having a distinct culture. Each of these cultures was now viewed as a unique complex of beliefs and behavior learned by members of each generation of a society. It has become a goal of modern cultural anthropology to describe the culture of as many of the world's societies as is possible and to understand the beliefs and behavior from their particular society's point of view. Thus cultural anthropology, which began as the collection of strange customs, has become the systematic study of culture.

Does Culture Make Humans Unique?

In the discussions of physical anthropology and linguistics, it has been shown that humans are not as distinct in the animal world as was once assumed. The widespread belief in the special creation of humans influenced how both the general public and scientists viewed the nature of humankind. This belief became so entrenched in European thought,[1] it was considered a basic assumption in theories about humankind.

Tylor's definition of culture stressed the human ability to learn behavior. It was thought by most anthropologists that other animals behaved according to instincts. The field studies of the ethnologists and primatologists suggest that a great deal more of the behavior of the primates and other animals is learned than was previously suspected, thus making learned behavior less of a diagnostic characteristic of humans. At least one anthropologist has raised the question of whether "culture," as defined in Tylor's terms with emphasis on learned behavior, is really a scientific concept at all. John H. Moore (1974) has taken the position that the preoccupation with finding some criterion for separating humans from other animals results from religious and philosophical ideology rather than rational science. He stresses that anthropologists who adopted Tylor's definition of culture were taking an ideological position that was congruent with prevalent notions about the place of human

A minority point of view in anthropology sees the concept of culture as learned behavior as merely an attempt to set humans apart from other animals.

[1] Some cultural traditions emphasize instead a very close relationship between humans and other animals; for example, see the discussion of the Australian aborigines in Chapter 10.

beings in the order of things, that humans were somehow distinct from other animals.

Within the past decade all of the criteria that have been used to demonstrate the uniqueness of humans have been challenged: tool using, toolmaking, biochemical differences, comparative anatomical differences, use of language, and culture defined as learned behavior. Most are no longer thought to be the exclusive property of humans, and the rest are being seriously questioned. The question of the uniqueness of humans is no longer a very productive one. As a result, cultural anthropologists have begun to approach culture differently. Instead of trying to prove human uniqueness, cultural anthropologists have become more concerned with explaining human cultural diversity. The definitions of culture in recent years have shifted from emphasizing that culture is learned to stressing that culture is an ideological system. The current direction of cultural anthropology seems to be toward the description of various systems of knowledge and belief. In this endeavor the concept of culture is basic.

> The most recent definitions of culture stress that it is an ideological system.

Anthropology Vocabulary

comparative method	cultural evolution	Tasaday
cultural anthropology	culture	

Review Questions

1. How did the early travelers and missionaries explain the cultural diversity they observed?
2. In what ways did the theory of cultural evolution conflict with and resemble the notion of the Chain of Being?
3. Why is the notion of culture as a system important? How does this notion compare with the notion of language as a system?

Recommended Reading

Darnell, Regna, ed., 1974, *Readings in the History of Anthropology.* New York: Harper & Row. An excellent collection of articles and excerpts that cover a wide range of topics related to the history of anthropology.

Hodgen, Margaret T., 1964, *Early Anthropology in the Sixteenth and Seventeenth Centuries.* Philadelphia: University of Pennsylvania Press. An outstanding summary of the early origins of anthropology. Highly recommended.

Malefijt, Annemarie de Waal, 1974, *Images of Man: A History of Anthropological Thought.* New York: Knopf. A good introduction to the development of anthropological theory.

10
What are non-western peoples like?

Non-Western societies are subject to change just like those of the West.

There is great diversity among non-Western societies.

Western culture cannot be assumed to be superior to other ways of life.

During the Middle Ages non-Western peoples were of interest to the Europeans only because their customs were considered strange and amusing. By the Renaissance, "savages" were being brought to Europe by explorers such as Columbus, and Westerners had an opportunity to view so-called "primitive" peoples in the flesh. The Europeans were disappointed, because contrary to what they believed, the "savages" were not very different from themselves. These first Indians to be brought from the New World actually had little effect on the strongly negative European stereotype of non-Western peoples. Notions such as monstrous races, static societies, "primitives" as prehistoric beings, degeneration, and the "progress" of Western culture all combined in the European mind to form a picture of non-Western peoples as filthy, lazy, naked, lascivious, stupid, pagan, childlike, animallike, cannibalistic, and lacking in the rudiments of culture and language. Unfortunately this stereotype is still with us. One has only to turn to the Sunday newspaper's comic strips to see cartoon after cartoon depicting non-Western peoples as almost naked, carrying spears, frequently having large (perhaps human) bones tied in their hair (possibly to symbolize more clearly that the non-Westerner is cannibalistic), and cooking missionaries or explorers in huge pots[1] over raging fires.

Western culture developed a negative stereotype of primitive peoples.

Our stereotype of "the American Indian" is equally inaccurate. The Indians portrayed in our mass media are usually shown in buckskin clothing and feathered headdresses, riding horses, hunting buffalo with bows and arrows, attacking whites in large groups, taking scalps from their enemies, abducting white women, whom they desire sexually, being less resistant to the effects of alcohol than whites, being humorless and taciturn, and speaking simple languages (often consisting merely of grunts).

While some of the characterizations, such as the feathered headdresses were correct for perhaps two dozen Plains tribes in the late 1800s, most of the characteristics were incorrect for the remaining Indian groups—over 500—in North America. Most North American Indians did not regularly ride horses, hunt buffalo, or wear buckskin clothing or feathers in their hair. Many lived in agricultural or fishing groups. They wore robes of woven bark or cotton cloth. The diversity of Indian culture is seldom portrayed in the mass media. The movies have been so effective

Our stereotype of the American Indian is incorrect.

---

[1] A pot of the size drawn in the cartoons would indicate previous trade with the Western world. The pot would have to be made of metal, as it would be too large to be made of clay. European drawings done shortly after contact with the non-Western world usually depicted cannibalistic societies roasting humans rather than boiling them.

in creating an unreal stereotype of the American Indian that for many years true Indians found it virtually impossible to find employment in the motion-picture industry, because directors did not think they looked or acted as Indians should (Price 1973:153–154, 164–165).

It is unfortunate that so many of the European stereotypes of non-Western people have survived, as these negative attitudes continue to affect development plans adversely in many emerging nations that include tribal peoples. For example, in 1966 a group of scholars and administrators met to discuss new policy directions for the hill tribes of northeastern India. One of the Indian professors suggested that the Garo people still maintained crude customs and traditions and were steeped in primitive ignorance; an educated tribal member characterized his people as backward, lacking in culture and living in darkness; and an official suggested that "they do not have a language, what they speak is an illiterate dialect, lacking grammar and orthography" (Chatterjee 1967:20). Of course these statements are incorrect, but they reflect the kinds of ethnocentricism that still exist in the Westernized world or among the elite classes of the emerging nations. Three notions about primitive peoples contribute to ethnocentricism and stereotyping: (*a*) the belief that primitive societies are unchanging; (*b*) the belief that all primitive peoples are the same; and (*c*) the belief that Western culture is necessarily superior to non-Western ways of life.

Static Non-Western Societies

By the nineteenth century, contemporary non-Western societies were equated with ancient societies. Contemporary tribal peoples were thought of as unchanged survivors of early societies; while Western societies, on the other hand, had progressed from the same beginnings. This notion was widely accepted after the introduction of evolutionary theory. The basic assumption was that non-Western societies were static. The fact of the matter is that *all* societies change. Archaeological and historical records are filled with examples of migrations, exchanges of artifacts and ideas, innovations and adaptations in each society.

All societies change.

The non-Western societies that became the subject matter of nineteenth- and twentieth-century anthropology were anything but static. The era of Western expansion affected most of not all non-Western societies. In many cases, the Western colonization of areas formerly held by non-Western peoples brought with it a holocaust from which many groups never recovered. The white

Maori chief signing treaty with the English. (New Zealand Consulate General)

world's diseases brought death to untold millions of tribal peoples. For those who survived, life with Westerners was often worse than death itself.

In Africa tens of millions of humans were lost to the slave trade: the weak and elderly were often killed by slave raiders; others died in stockades waiting to be loaded on board slave ships; still others perished in transit as a result of the abominable conditions in the ship's holds; and finally, many died or suffered once they arrived at their destinations. In the New World the enslaved person was humiliated, tortured, separated from his or her family, and often worked to death. The slave's life expectancy in the New World was only seven years. Europeans introduced disastrous change for those who remained Africa. Protestant and Catholic clergy struggled against each other for souls, and in so doing turned African groups against one another. Rifles and rum obtained by the African slave raiders for the slaves caused great suffering among the Africans due to the effects of alcoholism and more intense warfare between African groups. European nations divided up Africa among themselves and introduced colonial adminstrators and modern technology to extract whatever natural resources were available. Few non-Western groups remained the same through all of the changes that occurred during the eighteenth, nineteenth, and twentieth centuries. Some were able to retreat into unoccupied areas, but usually not before their societies had been affected by Westernization.

On the Pacific islands, the destructive impact of the European was great. In most cases, there was no place to which the native could escape: Many of the islands were too small to avoid contact with the Europeans for very long. Especially disastrous was the exploitation of the blacks of the western Pacific (Melanesia) under the system of labor recruiting known as "blackbirding," which was practiced between 1860 and 1910 as plantations were being developed in Australia and Fiji. In both places there were shortages of cheap labor, and the planters sent ships into Melanesia to obtain natives to work their plantations. While the system was technically one of contract labor, in reality it amounted to little more than slave trading and kidnapping. In most cases, the natives were tricked into signing three-year contracts they did not understand, and they received little for their labor other than misery and death. Village life was disrupted, new diseases were introduced, and a large proportion of the male population was removed from the native social system.

The missionaries made continual efforts to convert the natives on the islands of the Pacific to Christianity and brought about disastrous changes in native traditions. For example, missionaries were shocked by the nakedness of the Pacific islanders and equated it with sin. The natives were forced to wear European clothing that was ill suited to a tropical environment with heavy rainfall. Nakedness was well adapted to this type of environment, as wet skin dried quickly. European clothing, on the other hand, remained damp for hours, and sometimes days, causing pneumonia and other diseases.

In some parts of the New World the effects of the Western world were felt prior to the arrival of the European. The Alaskan Eskimo of the coastal area traded with natives of the Bering Strait Islands. The islanders in turn traded with people on the Siberian mainland who had access to metal goods. By this network of trade the Eskimo acquired copper kettles and metal knives without having face-to-face contact with the Europeans. Likewise, rifles were traded into the Eskimo area from Indians in Canada, who obtained them from the Hudson's Bay Company. By the time the first encounter between Eskimos and Europeans occurred, over 100 years later, these trade items had already affected Eskimo culture. The actual arrival of whites brought with it great changes in Eskimo life. Alcoholism and tuberculosis spread widely. The whaling industry brought with

In some cases the effects of Western civilization were felt before contact.

it tremendous demographic changes, as almost all inland Eskimos moved to the coast, where they settled in more permanent kinds of communities than had been traditional inland.

In other areas of the New World the effect of Westernization and the reaction of the natives were quite different. From as early as 800 BC, native civilizations expanded at the expense of other native peoples in the region from Mexico to Peru. Many hunters and gatherers and tribal peoples were pushed out of their homelands, because they could not compete with the armies of the expanding empires. Others were incorporated into the empires with drastically changed lives.

Some groups in the New World preferred to hide rather than fight native conquest states or, later, the Europeans. They moved into new environments, especially the jungles, where they were difficult to find. In the jungle environment small groups were able to elude raiding expeditions and postpone encounters with foreign intruders for generations, and sometimes centuries. Nevertheless, in relocating frequently and rapidly and adapting to new environments, they had to change various aspects of their culture and societal organization. A number of hunting and gathering bands encountered by the Europeans apparently had lived in larger, more complex groupings prior to Western contact. In fact, the forager groups of South America seem to represent cases of cultural *devolution,* in which simpler societies emerged out of formerly larger and more complexly organized populations, as an adaptation to Western expansion (Martin 1969).

The natives of some areas of the New World rapidly acquired the horse after its introduction by the Europeans. In each group that adopted the horse into its cultural pattern, changes in economy, settlement patterns, and relations with neighboring groups occurred. The impact of the horse on the way of life of the Plains Indians of North America in 1650 was comparable to the effect of automobiles on American culture in this century. Many of the inhabitants of the Great Plains were agriculturalists prior to the introduction of the horse. At first, they slaughtered horses and used them as a source of food, but they learned from the Indians of the Southwest that horses were more useful for riding than for eating. Once this was discovered, an entirely new way of life began on the plains that attracted other Indians from surrounding areas. Former villagers now combined hunting with farming. Men were absent from the villages for the entire summer. The introduction of the horse also placed great emphasis on the warrior in Plains culture. New symbols of military distinction were introduced, and bravery, individualism, and stoi-

The introduction of the horse had tremendous impact on many New World societies.

cism were glorified. The use of the horse also made a different type of housing possible. Tepees, which were originally no more than 5 or 6 feet in height, could now be carried on a *travois,* an **A**-shaped frame pulled by a horse, with the narrow end over the horse's shoulder and the broader end dragging behind. Tepees could thus be made larger, in heights of 12 to 15 feet, allowing larger groups of people to share the same shelter.

Because pottery was too easily broken to be useful to people on horseback, pottery users abandoned their pottery and switched entirely to leather containers. Likewise, a new piece of clothing was introduced: The tailed warbonnet, which was a symbol of prestige. The warbonnet was a feathered headdress with long, flowing streamers. It could not have been worn easily except on horseback, because it was so heavy and cumbersome. Even though the world has come to think of "the" American Indian as wearing a warbonnet, it was really only the mounted Indians of the Plains who wore them.

As Indians of the Plains were able to travel greater distances by horse, groups traveling about encountered other tribes, who spoke different languages. Moreover new Indians were moving to the Plains who spoke languages different from those of the established Plains Indians. In order to communicate between tribes the Plains Indians developed a sign language. The ideas expressed through this sign language were limited but proved useful for trading and treaty making.

The people of the Plains lived in basically egaliterian soci-

Miskito Indian at dry season fishing camp. (Mary W. Helms)

eties prior to the introduction of the horse. The horse and bison hides obtained through hunting on horseback created a socio-economic system based on valued material possessions, in which men were ranked by wealth, with the horse representing the most valued possession (Garbarino 1976:252–261).

Thousands of other examples could be presented of changes, many dramatic, that have occurred in non-Western societies in both prehistoric and historic times. Some of the so-called "primitive" societies did not really come into being until the historic era. These societies, sometimes referred to as "colonial tribes," were formed in frontier regions by refugees of diverse groups who retreated into refuge areas and banded together as new groups for mutual protection (Helms 1969). The post-conquest Seminole of Florida (Garbarino 1972) and the Miskito of Nicaragua and Honduras (Helms 1971) are examples of colonial tribes.

By the time cultural anthropology began as a professional endeavor at the turn of the century, there were no groups anywhere so remote that they had not felt the impact of Westernization either directly or indirectly. The anthropologists attempted to collect data on the way of life at the time of the first contact with Western civilization, a point in time referred to by anthropologists as the *ethnographic present*. Descriptions of cultural traditions were written in present tense but dealt with traditions of the past, some of which had long since been lost. By concentrating on the so-called "ethnographic present," these early fieldworkers were perhaps guilty of perpetuating the mistaken notion of static non-Western societies. In many instances, anthropologists recognized that the people they were studying had changed somewhat from precontact times. But while they recognized that such traits as the horse, rifle, and modern medicine had been adopted from Western culture, they ignored the context of colonialism and forced change within which these traits were frequently adopted. The early fieldworkers in cultural anthropology had little understanding of or interest in changes that were going on at the time of their studies; nor did they understand the nature of asymmetrical power relationships in the meetings of Western and non-Western societies.

Anthropologists have since learned through archaeology and archival research that non-Western societies have changed through time and that in many cases their simple contemporary form has been a devolution from a more complex form, brought about by contact with the West. Anthropologists now realize that the historical development of any nonliterate group can be an exceedingly complex problem. One cannot assume that

Tracing the historical development of nonliterate peoples is an exceedingly complex problem.

non-Western societies of recent history such as the Australian aborigines have been unchanging through time. While it is true that many tribal groups fought valiantly to maintain their traditional culture, it was often those who resisted Westernization the most fiercely whose culture changed the greatest amount. For example, some of the remnant groups of the Incan army attempted unsuccessfully to resist the Spanish following the Spanish conquest of the Inca in Peru. While they hoped to drive the Spaniards from the Andes and restore the traditional Incan way,[2] their only success occurred through adoption of Spanish warfare techniques. Manco Inca, the leader of these Incan troops, had been a protégé of Pizarro, from whom he learned Spanish military tactics. The Incan troops came to rely on Spanish horses and weapons obtained through raiding. Thus they became Hispanicized during the very act of attempting to maintain their cultural identity. This process has occurred frequently in the confrontation of the Western and non-Western worlds. To resist at all successfully, non-Western societies have had to acquire items of Western technology time and time again. Once these items—guns and axes, for example—are acquired they bring about changes in the native tradition.

The modern fieldworker now recognizes the organic nature of culture and no longer accepts the notion that non-Western societies are static. Since World War II cultural anthropology has had a great deal of interest in the analysis of cultural change itself. The anthropologist investigates how native societies have reacted to the encroachment of Western civilization and "progress." The anthropologist no longer ignores the role of the colonial administrator or missionary, as once was the case. For example, Bronislaw Malinowski, one of the most famous British social anthropologists, portrayed life in 1914 in the Trobriand Islands, off the eastern tip of New Guinea, as if he were describing a "pristine" culture not yet affected by the Western world. In fact, the Trobriand Islands had been under colonial administration for a number of years, and missionaries had been active for about the same length time and had built a mission station on the island of Kiriwina.[3] In modern fieldwork the roles of the administrator, missionary, and other agents of Westernization are studied along with native tradition. The emphasis in modern cultural anthropology is on studying a society as it exists

> Anthropologists no longer view "primitive" societies as static.

---

[2] The Inca way of life itself was less than 100 years old and had been imposed on many culturally diverse groups shortly before the arrival of the Spanish.

[3] Compare, for example, Malinowski's professional description of the Trobrianders (Malinowski 1922) with his personal diary (Malinowski 1967), which was published after his death, or with the account of the same Trobrianders written by one of the colonial administrators (Rentoul 1931).

today, as an ongoing system, regardless of how traditional the various aspects of that society might be. There is no longer an attempt to write about precontact culture on the basis of post-contact ethnographic fieldwork. Those interested in precontact culture turn to archaeology, oral tradition, and archival research to reconstruct past traditions, while the fieldworker tries to describe the society and culture as they now exist. Frequently examination of the power relationships between native peoples and the missionaries, colonial administrators, and other Westerners helps to clarify aspects of the present way of life. Non-Western societies are no longer viewed as static by the professional anthropologist in piecing together of the human myth, however the notion continues to persist in the beliefs of the folk anthropologist.

A Savage Is a Savage
Is a Savage?

Among the stereotypes of "primitive" people that became established in the Western belief system during the Renaissance was the notion that all non-Western people were the same, or at best could be grouped into one of two categories: the cannibal and the noble savage. Firsthand accounts by those encountering native societies were conveniently ignored.

Non-Western people depicted as cannibals. (The Granger Collection)

Two developments in cultural anthropology have helped to improve our understanding of the nature of non-Western societies: First, the nineteenth-century evolutionists helped to incorporate the so-called "primitive" societies into humankind at a time when many believed that "primitives" were a separate and lower form of animal. Thus, non-Western people could be studied as human beings who possessed the same mental and physical capabilities as Westerners. Second, through fieldwork the cultural anthropologist has provided the Western world with detailed descriptions of non-Western peoples as they really are, without the extreme ethnocentricism that clouded the accounts of tribal societies by earlier missionaries, travelers, and administrators. By giving up the many creature comforts of Western civilization and living for years in the midst of non-Western peoples, cultural anthropologists are able to acquire intimate firsthand knowledge of the culture they are studying. They accept the members of another society as equals rather than as inferiors. They assume that the culture of these people, however strange to the outsider, makes sense to the members of the society who share the culture. The role of the cultural anthropologist is that of student, while the natives are the teachers. Anthropologists go into the field neither to criticize nor to change another way of life. They are there to understand. In the process of fieldwork, cultural anthropologists have uncovered a rich diversity of culture among non-Western peoples. Each culture represents a valid attempt at being human; each is a part of the human myth.

Anthropologists have discovered that there is considerable diversity among "primitive" peoples.

The strange customs collected in the early Renaissance had little meaning when pulled from their cultural context other than as trivia. The Renaissance approach to the customs of "primitive" peoples still survives today in Ripley's "Believe It or Not." The cultural anthropologist has learned that these so-called strange customs become understandable once they are viewed as the insider vews them—within the cultural context.

Seemingly strange customs are not strange when viewed in their cultural context.

The great cultural diversity of non-Western societies has allowed native peoples to adapt to and survive in countless different environments with a minimum of technological development. If a sameness in humankind occurs, it is among civilized peoples, where millions drink soda pop, watch television, drive automobiles, and share many other characteristics. More people have been forced to share or adapt to Western culture as the civilized world has continued to encroach upon native societies. Yet among non-Western societies, diversity still rules.

Groups a short distance apart can maintain systems of belief that differ radically. Thus, while environmental differences can sometimes account for cultural differences, it does not explain diversity between groups in the same eco-niche. Anthropologists must look for cultural rather than ecological factors in those cases of diversity. In the sections that follow, something of the range of cultural diversity among native groups will be presented.

The Australian Aborigines

It has been estimated that by 1788 there were roughly 300,000 aborigines spread over Australia and Tasmania, divided into approximately 500 tribal groups, many of which spoke languages that were mutually unintelligible. By 1876 the aborigines of Tasmania had become extinct, as a result of systematic extermination by European settlers. The aborigines of Australia had large desert wastelands in which to avoid the white settlers more easily than the Tasmanians had been able to, yet the Australian aborigines suffered severe depopulation, 80 percent of the aborigines dying as a result of contact with Western civilization. Thus the way of life practiced by the simple hunting-and-gathering bands ultimately studied by anthropologists may not resemble that practiced prior to the arrival of the Europeans.

The life of the aborigine was possibly much different before Western contact.

An outstanding study of one of the Australian aborigine groups, the Arunta, was undertaken in the early 1890s by Baldwin Spencer, a zoologist, and by F. J. Gillen, the Sub-Protector of Aborigines at Alice Springs. Their study, *The Native Tribes of Central Australia*, which was published in 1899, remains today one of the most complete, detailed, and balanced accounts of an aborigine group. Many of the anthropologists' views of traditional aboriginal life are based on Spencer and Gillen's early research. Most of the modern studies of the aborigines did not begin until after 1926, when attempts were begun by the Australian National Research Council to collect information on traditional aboriginal life before it completely changed or disappeared (Elkin 1964:xii–xiii).

Material Possessions. While the aborigines' material possessions were minimal because of their nomadic existence, the range of possessions varied greatly from one local group to another. Material possessions included barbed wooden spears, spear-throwers, hitting sticks, stone axes, wooden dishes, grinding stones (left at campsites that were returned to periodically as part of the nomadic cycle), digging sticks, firesticks, boomerangs, shields, fishing nets, baskets, and a few sacred and magical objects. Somewhat suprisingly, the boomerang is absent from many groups. The boomerang is primarily a plaything, with one exceptional use—in hunting, as a projectile thrown into flocks of birds.

While the possessions of the aborigines are sparse, they have been sufficient for maintaining their desert life for thousands of years, even in desolate areas where Westerners still find survival difficult or impossible, even with modern technology. To many Westerners the simplicity of material possessions is taken as a sign of the simplicity of aboriginal culture. Ethnographers have found that this is not true. Instead, the aborigine kinship organization, rituals, and beliefs that anthropologists have analyzed are some of the most complex and interesting anywhere in the world. As the noted anthropologist Margaret Mead (1964:viii) has observed of the Australian aborigines:

> Poor and crude as their weapons and utensils were, in their social organization and their articulate relations with their environment, their cultures were complex and beautiful. They are perhaps the outstanding example in the world of how a people who remained at a very simple technological level could still develop a poetic and artistic approach to life, expressed in long liturgies that were closely bound up with the special country in which each tribe lived.

Perhaps the most complex aspect of Australian aboriginal culture is the kinship systems. Anthropologists have found them so complicated that they have had to invent a new technical vocabulary and mathematical models in order to analyze and discuss the various aboriginal systems. Differences in the theoretical orientation of cultural anthropologists and the considerable variations of the kinship systems themselves have made interpretation difficult.

Local Groups. Aborigine local groups do not correspond well to our Western concepts of the tribe, although these groups have been labeled as tribes. The Australian groups average 15 to 30 persons related by blood or marriage but might be as large as 50. This size group would habitually camp together, hunt, forage, and travel as a more or less coherent unit. However, depending upon the availability of food and water, some nights the entire group would gather together, while many other nights they would disperse in small family units. As the seasons changed, two or more local groups would camp together for ceremonial purposes, to settle disputes, to feast together, to initiate or to make part-payments on a variety of transactional arrangements. It is this kind of interaction between several local groups

Australian aborigine hunter with boomerang. (Courtesy of the American Museum of Natural History)

The aborigines have a rich and complex culture.

Aborigine hunter. (Courtesy of the American Museum of Natural History)

that has given rise to the groups being designated a "tribe." Membership in either a local group or tribe is quite fluid. Membership is not enforced; individuals or families that want to wander off and live by themselves or join another group are free to do so. Part of the difficulty of interpreting the nature of these groups and the conditions under which they fluctuate is the fact that no Westerner, anthropologist or otherwise, has actually lived and traveled with an aboriginal group through its entire annual cycle of nomadism. What is known about local groups and tribes is learned from Westerners who have encountered and interviewed such groups either by the wayside, in their camps, or when they have come to a government station. With the advent of the automobile it became possible to seek out aboriginal camps, stay with them for a while, and accompany them on short hunting and foraging trips. Nevertheless, detailed knowledge of the annual cycle is lacking, especially information on the many days when the small family groups roam in search of food and water, when no important ceremonies take place (Burridge 1973:128–130).

Aborigine Kinship. Although the aborigines live in small local groups, the ties of kinship that bind the group together and which tie a local group to other local groups seem to the anthropologist to be exceedingly complex and somewhat awe-inspiring. The family unit, which is also an autonomous unit during certain periods of the annual cycle, consists of a man, his wife or wives, and children. This family is a self-sufficient economic unit, in that the partners can between them obtain and prepare all that is required for daily life. However, to obtain brides and to fulfill the requirements of ceremonial life, the aborigine family must cooperate with other family units. Some of the variables of Australian kinship that lead to the complexity of the system for Western observers are as follows:

1. A classificatory system of kinship in which there is a greater grouping together of kin under the same kin term than in our own system. For example, an individual's mother's sister is classified with and called "mother," and the person's father's brother is classified with and called "father." Likewise, a grandfather's brother is called "grandfather," and so on, and as a result of this classification certain consequential relationships follow; for example, since father's brother is considered "father," his son will be "brother" rather than "cousin." However, not everyone is grouped this way by generation. The children of a brother and those of a sister are distin-

guished by separate kin terms, and an individual observes different behavior towards each set of relatives. Thus a male calls his own child and his brother's child "son" or "daughter," while he refers to his sister's child as "nephew" or "niece."

2. Sibling exchange is practiced in which a male in one group will exchange his own sister for a sister of a male in another group. By this system of exchange, both males are able to obtain a wife without either group having fewer females.

3. Many groups practice some form of preferred-cousin marriage, especially the form in which a male is supposed to marry his mother's brother's daughter. In other Australian aborigine groups an individual is prohibited from marrying any first cousin, but second-cousin-preferred marriage is practiced.

4. In many areas of Australia, aborigines belong to totemic clans. The clan is a grouping of kin to which an individual belongs on the basis of descent traced through either father or mother but not through both parents. A person is born into only one clan. All members of a clan are related to one another, because they share a common descent line. In a *totemic clan* a distinguishing feature is that all of its members profess a relationship not only with one another but also to a natural species that serves as their totem. The aborigines believe that the totem is their own flesh, or meat; conversely, if you ask a native "What is your meat?" he or she will give you the name of his or her clan totem—for example, the kangaroo, the emu, a particular bird, a species of plant or some other source of food. The totem is considered as a friend or guardian that must not be injured, killed, or eaten. To marry anyone who claims the same totem is considered incest.

5. The social organization of many aborigine groups is further complicated by the fact that members of the group are divided into marriage sections. Some groups have two marriage sections, but others have four, eight, or even sixteen different sections. A person is assigned membership to a particular section on the basis of the sections that his or her mother and father belong to. The marriage section that one belongs to determines from which section one may take a spouse. For example in the four-section system, if a male from section A marries a female of section B, their children will be classified in section D and will only be able to marry someone from section C. If a male of B marries a female of A, their children will be C and able to marry someone who is a

Marriage sections help to determine whom one marries.

D. When individuals from C and D marry, their children are A or B, by the same principles[4]

All of the variables mentioned above combine to form an exceedingly complex organization for the Westerner to understand. The system does not seem complicated to the aborigine, who has been born into the system and begins utilizing the classifications of kin at an early age.

The Aborigine Belief System. The Australian aborigine's belief system reflects a view of the world in which the individual is thought to be intimately related to other human beings, the environment (especially through the totems), and the past. The nineteenth-century evolutionists believed that the aborigines represented the earliest and simplest form of society, and proceeding from this notion they assumed that the religion of the Australian aborigine was representative of the earliest form of human religion. Emile Durkheim (1912), Sigmund Freud (1950), and others used the Australian aborigine religious beliefs as examples of the earliest forms of religious concepts and practices. Modern anthropology no longer accepts this assumption. Instead the aboriginal belief system is studied as a body of knowledge that helps aborigines understand their existence. It is a system of belief that has probably been conservative and has changed slowly, at least prior to the arrival of the Europeans; but certainly it is not the same as the beliefs held by humans tens of thousands of years ago. Therefore the Australian aborigine beliefs are no longer placed at the bottom of an evolutionary sequence of religious beliefs but are viewed in a relativistic manner, with emphasis on understanding how these beliefs function within the society.

The aborigines are no longer thought to represent the earliest form of human culture.

Besides the notion of totem, another important concept in the aboriginal belief system is the notion of *the Dreamtime* or *the Dreaming*. Aborigine children learn a mythology from the elders of their group that explains the origin of their culture. These myths deal with the creation of the various totemic groups by the ancestors, in the mythical past called the Dreamtime. During this time the ancestors laid out the contours of the land, created the flora and the fauna, provided the techniques whereby nature's bounty might be available, and made humans

The Dreamtime is a key concept in aborigine culture.

---

[4] A (male) marries B (female) offspring are D
B (male) marries A (female) offspring are C
C (male) marries D (female) offspring are B
D (male) marries C (female) offspring are A
If "=" stands for marriage: $\begin{array}{c} A = B \\ C = D \end{array}$

of themselves.[5] These divine powers also created the sacred storehouses, the souls, and *churinga*.[6]

For example, among the Arunta of central Australia it is believed that the great supernatural ancestor-creator *Numbakulla*[7] made the natural features of the country, the totems, the churinga, and so on. The original spirits associated with the churinga were thought to have come from the body of Numbakulla. Numbakulla also gave each churinga a secret name. Subsequently the churinga split in two; half of the churinga had a man's soul, the other half had a woman's soul. The souls arose from the churinga and gave rise to men and women, each with a secret name. Numbakulla explained the traditional knowledge to the first human ceremonial leader: How to carry out the various initiation ceremonies, including the rituals of circumcision and subincision, and how to fashion new churinga. Then Numbakulla disappeared (Service 1971a:24–25).

For the aborigine, creation is a continuing fact as well as a unique historical event. Created once and for all time, the world and everything in it die and are renewed or recreated. For example, the parched Australian desert, baked and cracked after years of drought, comes to life after rain with lush grasses and a variety of blooming forms. Animals gather, feed, mate, and die as the land reverts into desert again. Dearth succeeds plenty as night follows day. The aborigines believe that the world was created and that creation continues: Created and creating are one (Burridge 1973:74).

Just as humans are thought to originate from divine creators associated with a particular locality, the divine creators are explained in terms of another greater power, located in the sky. This power is generally associated with thunder, lightning, rain, flood, the rainbow, the serpent, phallus, streams, and semen. The power located in the sky is thought of as the life-source of all things. In the aborigine system of belief, this life-source was sometimes conceived of as concentrated in a single thing or phenomenon, while at other times it was manifested in the multiplicity of creators, each with its own sphere of influence. According to the anthropologist Kenelm Burridge (1973:74):

> The idea of Oneness, of a unity, was contained not in an idea or manifestation abstracted from or subsuming the millions of partic-

---

[5] Some of the myths relate that human beings were created from the plants, animals, and natural features that are the totems of the present groups.
[6] The *churinga* are usually flat, oval pieces of wood or stone carved with symbolic designs. Some, with a hole at one end to which a string is attached, are called bullroars and are whirled in the air.
[7] This name translates as "always existing" or "out of nothing."

ulars observable and experienced, but rather in the multiplicity it-self. All taken together made an integrated and organic whole. As the fact of birth was a corporeal proceeding and separation from the incorporeal divine powers of the dreamtime—which though it existed *then*, still exists today—so the life cycle was a series of ri-tualized exits and entries from one field of moral being to more ex-tensive fields of moral being and responsibility. Death signaled the passage from moral being into a reaggregation with the powers of the dreamtime.

At death a person's spirit makes the journey into the Dreamtime only if all moral obligations have been met. If not, the spirit will remain close at hand, manifesting itself to kinsfolk as a ghost or similar kind of being until it has been appeased by rituals, feasts, and offerings. The spirit is later reborn as a human of the same totemic group.

All of the various totems, whether plant or animal, are thought to have spiritual residing places called *totem centers*, which are located somewhere in the territory of the local group to which they belong. The totem center is also where the spirits of the human ancestral members of the group are thought to re-side. Thus the totem center provides a link to the Dreamtime. When a women who has married into a particular local group becomes pregnant, it is believed that the impregnation has been caused by a spirit from the local totem center which entered her body. Thus, a child born into a totemic group is tied to that locality forever, because it is the residing place of his or her progenitor, the ancestral spirit. The living father's most impor-tant role is as social father rather than progenitor.

The totem center pro-vides a link to the Dream-time.

Occasionally each totemic group performs ceremonies in order to increase the fertility and well-being of the plant or an-imal they believe they represent. Failure to perform these cere-monies periodically will cause the particular food species they represent to perish.

The totem group has a ceremonial leader, who is the caretaker of the local group's totemic center. The center serves as the storehouse for the churinga within which the spirits of the group reside. Each member of the local group possesses a churinga, but only the initiated men of the group are permitted to see them. Women play an insignificant role in the ceremonial life of the local group because (*a*) females born into the group will marry out of the group and live with their husband's local group, and (*b*) women married to men of the local group have come from outside. The men play the major role in ceremonial life, because they are believed tied to the spirits of the totemic group. In order to protect the secrecy of the ceremonies, some of the churinga are used as bullroarers. Their whirring noise serves as a sign that important rites are taking place and that the uninitiated should stay away.

Among the Arunta, the ceremonies to promote the increase of the group's totem are usually held at the time of year when that particular totem species produces fruit or seed or gives birth to its young. While ceremonies vary considerably from one local group to another, many share the following features: (a) the focus of the ceremony is a special and often very detailed ritual performance which it is believed will help to increase the numbers of the totem plant or animal; (b) the local group ceremonial leader eats a small amount of the species; (c) then the other members of the local group ritually eat a small amount of the totem species; and (d) finally, other people, often guests from a very wide area (but who have not been allowed to witness the secret aspects of the ceremony) feast freely on the totem pieces.

Other ceremonies of importance among the Arunta are tied to the individual's life cycle and again stress the tie with the spirits and the Dreamtime. At the birth of a child, the paternal grandfather and some of the elders of the local group take a piece of wood or stone from near the group's totem center and, in secret, fashing a personal churinga for the child, which is then stored with the other churinga. The child receives two names; one is personal and the other is secret. The secret name is associated with the churinga and is bestowed by the paternal grandfather. This secret name is considered sacred and is known only to fully initiated men. It is used only on important ceremonial occasions when women and children are absent.

Initiation Rites. While both boys and girls go through initiation rites, those of the male last longer, are more complex, and are considered more important. A boy must pass through four different ceremonies before he is considered a full-fledge initiate of the local totemic group. The first ceremony involves only members of the local group and occurs when a boy is between 10 and 12. The boys participating in the ceremony are thrown into the air several times by the men while the women dance in a circle around them. Their backs are then painted ritually by their prospective brothers-in-law, and their nasal septum is pierced so that it can hold a nose bone. After this ceremony the boys are no longer considered children and are able to join the men in their economic activities.

After boys have reached puberty, the second ceremony occurs. The adult men collect food and firewood and store it in a secret hideaway; then the boys are seized and taken to the hiding place. First there is ritual dancing and singing of myths related

Male initiation rites have great importance and involve four ceremonies.

Aborigine blood-letting ceremony. (Courtesy of the American Museum of Natural History)

to the ceremony. The boys' heads are bound with strands of fur string, and a girdle made of human hair is placed around the waist of each boy. They are then taken to another secret place, where they receive three days of instruction. Following the instruction there are recitals of tribal myths and ritual pantomimes. This is the first time the boys receive full knowledge of the sacred lore of the tribe. Several days later the boys are circumcised in a complicated ritual, and remain in seclusion until they recover. During this time the adult men visit the initiates and bite their scalps several times until blood flows freely.[8]

After several weeks of recovery from the second ceremony, the boys undergo a third initiation rite. This time the ceremony involves subincision. The adult men go to the secluded place where the boys recovered from the circumcision ceremony and relate the group's myths and engage in ritual pantomimes once again. The boys are then subincised. Subincision is a practice in which the ventral surface of the initiate's penis is slit to the urethra with a stone knife. This practice is a religious act done in emulation of ancestral creator-beings who are believed to have practiced the same ritual during their Dreamtime. Among some Australian groups subincision is practiced in emulation of the emu, a large flightless bird that has a distinct penile groove (Tonkinson 1974:31).

The fourth ceremony that a boy must pass through is considered the climax to his admission into adulthood. Whereas the early rites involved only members of the local group, the fourth ceremony attracts people from great distances and even from

_____

[8] It is believed that this practice promotes the growth of hair.

other language groups. If there is sufficient food, the various mass dances and celebrations may last for several months. During the fourth ceremony the boys undergo a complicated series of fire ordeals and bloodletting ceremonies. Various totem groups carry out special rituals, and the initiates receive the ultimate knowledge of the churinga, learn their secret names, and are finally accepted as full adult members of their local group (Service 1971*a*:20–21).

Perhaps the most important knowledge acquired during the initiation rites is the secret of the power of the churinga. The churinga are revealed as symbols of the ancestors of the eternal Dreamtime. They are the means by which life and power are mediated from those ancestors and from the eternal Dreamtime. Sick persons are made healthy by having the churinga rubbed on them. To take a churinga on a hunt ensures success, but the food thus acquired takes on a sacred quality, and only the fully initiated may partake of it, and then only after the observance of the proper rites. To lend a churinga renews or strengthens a friendship and gives the friendship the sacred qualities of the Dreamtime. When the newly initiated male is allowed to see and handle these objects for the first time, he is rubbed with them and brought into conscious touch with the eternal Dreamtime. Through the initiation rites the individual is made sacred and a sharer of the sacred life of both the local group's ancestral heroes and nature. In many Australian groups the term used for "churinga" is also the term used for the eternal Dreamtime, the myths and rites through which the initiated enter into their sacred condition, and even for the initiates themselves.

During initiation, boys learn the secret of the churinga.

The Dreamtime. While the notion of the Dreamtime represents only one concept among many in the Australian aborigine belief system, it demonstrates something of the rationale of the system. With their system of belief, the aborigines are able to comprehend their world. The beliefs and practices that have been discussed are not miscellaneous strange customs. Instead they fit together like the pieces of a jigsaw puzzle to provide the aborigines with a world view which to them is coherent.

For example, the concept of the Dreamtime also directs the nomadic pattern of the aborigine. The whole Western Desert, where many of the aborigines live, is crisscrossed by tracks followed by the aborigines between the main bodies of waters. These tracks extend in every direction from one site to the next and incorporate all topographical features that are economically or spiritually significant to the aborigine. It is believed that these are the tracks taken by mythic beings in the Dream-

Even the desert tracks are thought to be linked to the Dreamtime.

time. These mythic beings are eternal and continue to exist in spirit form. Although in the creative era they traveled across the country leaving tracks, they eventually turned into other forms. They were metamorphosed as rocks or trees or went into the ground at a particular place and perhaps reappeared at another location. Some of these tracks are very extensive, traversing the full width and breadth of the desert region and embracing a number of local groups, while others are quite localized. The tracks do not take the shortest distance between two points. The aborigines follow the tracks for their mythic importance rather than their directness.

Myths are guides to action without which the Australian aborigines could not easily have existed in the desert. To the aborigines, each site along the tracks crisscrossing the Western Desert is a visual and tangible expression of a segment of a myth, and each segment provides information that is vital to their survival. For example, myths specifically locate the sources of fresh water. The myths also indicate the characteristics of a site or local area by explaining the main features of the immediate environment, its resources, and whether or not increased rituals must be performed by the group to ensure their continuation. The myths of the Dreamtime thus represent a corpus of information on economic resources. Some of this information is transmitted during early childhood or in the course of the initiation rites. A great deal is transmitted as narratives or in song form during the performance of sacred rituals.

Since they extend in all directions across the desert, the mythic tracks also represent channels along which trade items are passed. Trading occurs within the context of ritual, primarily at the large initiation ceremonies. Thus, even trading is linked with the notion of Dreamtime. The aborigine's mythology represents *in toto* the experience and heritage of the people concerned, a basis for social as well as economic living. Viewed in this framework, the aborigine's mythology and notion of the Dreamtime is by no means nonrational or rooted in fantasy. On the contrary, it is highly practical, directly relevant to ordinary everyday living (Berndt 1972:182–188).

While the traditional system of belief formed an integrated whole, contact with the Christian missions has brought about the disruption of the native system that was based on such a delicate balance of humans and nature. The Christian missions have attempted to destroy the secret rituals practiced by the men, yet aborigine males have found it difficult to accept a religion in which women are admitted to all of its mysteries (Elkin 1964:195).

Aboriginal Culture and Westernization. Aborigine culture has survived in parts of Australia in spite of the missions. However, the survival of tradition has not occurred without change in aboriginal life. Many aborigines still see their well-being as dependent upon continued reciprocity with the spiritual realm and the faithful following of the total life-design laid down for them in the Dreamtime. Within this context, the aborigines in some cases have been able to accept Western material goods without threatening the belief system. In other cases, the introduction of a single new item of Western material culture has been disastrous to the traditional way of life. The anthropologist Lauriston Sharp (1952) has documented the impact of the introduction of steel axes into the Yir Yoront aborigine group on their traditional culture.

Prior to the establishment of a mission station in the territory of a neighboring tribe in 1915, the Yir Yoront had used stone axes. The stone axes played an important role within the traditional culture. The stone for the ax heads had to be obtained through trade from quarries 400 miles from Yir Yoront territory, as no locally available stone was suitable. The exchange of stone ax heads for fighting spears tipped with the barbed spines of the stingray formed the basis of a chain of male trading partnerships, relationships between males of different groups. Most of the exchanges took place during the dry season, at times when the great aboriginal totemic ceremones and initiation rites were held, and there was generally a great deal of exciting activity besides trading.

In Yir Yoront society, adult males were the only ones who obtained ax heads and who made the finished axes. The males considered these axes as their personal property. Women and children frequently used axes in cutting firewood. Because only adult men owned stone axes, every woman and child who needed to use an ax—and this might be frequently during the day—had to borrow an ax from a male, use it promptly, and return it in good condition. This necessary and constant borrowing of axes was done according to regular patterns of kinship behavior. Women generally borrowed from their husbands. If a woman was unmarried or her husband was absent, she would ask to borrow an ax from an older brother or her father. Children and young men likewise looked to their fathers and older brothers if they had to borrow an ax. The men allowed their axes to be borrowed only if they were on good terms with the borrower. This pattern of borrowing set up a number of social relationships with clear statuses of superordination and subordination. Women and children were dependent on, or subordinate to, older males in every action in which axes were involved. Among men, the younger person was dependent on the older person. Within families, older brothers were always superordinate to younger brothers. In the trade partnership, which was a brotherly type of relationship, one partner was always classified as older than the other and would have some advantage in case of dispute.

Stone axes were also important symbols of masculinity among the Yir Yoront. The masculine values represented by the stone axes were constantly being impressed on all members of society by the fact that females and nonadult males did not own axes and had to borrow them from adult males, whereas females and nonadult males never borrowed other masculine artifacts such as spears or fire-making sticks. The stone axes were also associated with the Dreamtime and were thus a part of mythology. The myths explained why the Yir Yoront used and should use stone axes. They also explained how the stone ax came to be used by the aborigines in the past.

The missionaries attempted to "help" the aborigines by giving them steel axes. However, the rewarding of aborigines with an ax did not follow the traditional patterns of superordination and subordination along age and sex lines. Instead the steel axes were distributed indiscriminately. If an aborigine attended one of the mission festivals where steel axes were given, he or she might receive one simply by chance. Or an aborigine might—again through chance—be given a brief job in order to earn a steel ax. Because the older aborigine men were the most suspicious of the missionaries, they tended to appear at the mission station less frequently then any other age group. On the other hand, young men, women, and children generally had a better chance of obtaining a steel ax, because they interacted with the missionaries to a greater extent. By winning the favor of the mission staff a woman might be given a steel ax that was clearly intended as her personal property. Furthermore, young men or even boys might also obtain steel axes directly from the missionaries. The new pattern of distribution introduced by the missionaries created a situation in which an old man might have only a stone ax, while his wives and sons had steel axes, which they considered their own and which he might even desire to borrow from them. This new pattern led to a confusion of sex, age, and kinship roles, with a major gain in independence and loss of subordination on the part of those now able to acquire steel axes who in the past had been unable to possess stone axes.

The trading partner relathionships were affected when missionaries distributed steel axes to the aborigines without con-

Steel axes upset the traditional system.

sideration of their social order. The "young brother" of the relationship, who had traditionally been in the subordinate position, often had greater access to the mission station and its steel axes. The access reduced his position of subordination. In many cases the younger partner began to prefer giving steel axes to his sweethearts in return for favors, rather than to his trading partner. Among other things, this change in trading patterns curtailed some of the excitement surrounding the ceremonial gatherings of the dry season. These gatherings had traditionally been the climactic point of the annual cycle for exchanges between trading partners, and at these gatherings a man might acquire an entire year's supply of stone ax heads. With the changing pattern the older men found that they often had to prostitute their wives to almost total strangers in order to obtain steel axes. With trading partnerships weakened, there was less reason to attend the ceremonial gatherings and less enjoyment for those who attended. Thus the well-meaning attempts of the missionaries to "help" the Yir Yoront resulted in major changes within the society. Older men no longer had the prestige they once possessed. Age and sex positions within the society were no longer as clear-cut as they once had been. The steel axes had no myths attached to them explaining how they fit into the Dreamtime, and the aborigines began to question the myths of the Dreamtime. In many instances the aborigine abandoned his totemic system of belief. The results of this abandonment have been observed by Sharp (1952:22), who notes:

> With the collapse of this system of ideas, which is so closely related to so many other aspects of the native culture, there follows an appallingly sudden and complete cultural disintegration, and a demoralization of the individual such as has seldom been recorded elsewhere. Without the support of a system of ideas well devised to provide cultural stability in a stable environment but admittedly too rigid for the new realities pressing in from outside, native behavior and native sentiments and values are simply dead. Apathy reigns.

Not all aboriginal groups have suffered the fate of the Yir Yoront. Other native groups have adopted some Western material goods but have been able to retain their traditional culture. In his study of the Christian mission at Jigalong in the Western Desert, the Australian anthropologist Robert Tonkinson (1974) found that the resistance of adult aborigines to alien nonmaterial cultural elements was demonstrated most clearly in their rejection of Christianity. Although many of the children of the aborigines living near the mission attend the mission school, they quickly discontinue most of the behaviors taught to them by the missionaries when they are through with school at age 14 or 15. As young adults they express a firm belief in the reality and truth of the Dreamtime and seek to emulate the rest of the community in following their traditional ways. In 24 years of attempting to change the aborigines, the Jigalong mission has won only one convert (Tonkinson 1974:109–110, 118).

The Semai of West Malaysia

Mainland Southeast Asia is a peninsula that lies east of India and south of China. Malaya represents the central tine of the peninsula, almost reaching the equator. Malaya now forms the western portion of Malaysia. The major people of the Malay Peninsula are the Malays, who form about 50 percent of the population. The Chinese represent a population almost as large. Twentieth-century immigrants from India represent slightly less than 10 percent of the population. Indigenous minorities comprise less than one percent of the total population of West Malaysia. The indigenous people number between 50,000 and 60,000. The most numerous of the native groups are the Senoi,[9] who account for approximately half of the total indigenous peoples of West Malaysia (Provencher 1975:1, 111–139). It is believed that the Senoi were among the earliest inhabitants of the Malay Peninsula. Where they originally migrated from is unknown. The Senoi languages are related to a language spoken by peoples scattered throughout Burma and Indochina. One of the Senoi groups is known as the Semai.

The original inhabitants of the peninsula such as the Semai were forced to give up their lands to the technologically superior Malays. Generally, the Semai and other native groups fled to the hill areas to avoid fighting. This policy may have encouraged the development of an emphasis on nonviolence that characterizes the contemporary Semai. In the fourteenth century AD the Malays were converted to Islam, further irritating relations between the Malays and the indigenous peoples. Malays apparently had attitudes about the Semai and other native peoples of the peninsula that were comparable to the beliefs Europeans held about non-Western peoples. The Malay viewed the native peoples as culturally inferior and pagan, good for nothing but slavery. The Malay raided Semai settlements for slaves until the beginning of the twentieth century.

Further interaction with the outside world was imposed upon

[9] The Senoi are also known as the Sakai, the Malay word for "slave" (Cole 1945:95).

the Semai during the early 1950s, when a Communist uprising occurred. The Communist guerrillas took refuge in the hills occupied by the Semai. The British, who ruled the area as a colony, tried to relocate the indigenous peoples in camps outside their rain-forest homes for their own protection. The Semai still view this relocation of their people as an attempt by the British to exterminate them, because the death rate in these camps was so high. When the camps failed, the British settled the Semai around strategically placed "jungle forts" where their activities could be supervised. During this time period, Semai from the more remote areas had their first opportunity to acquire Western goods such as wristwatches and woven cloth. Also during this era, a special Malayan agency was formed for the purpose of looking after the welfare of the indigenous peoples (Dentan 1968:2–3).

The Semai Environment. The Semai are slash-and-burn rain-forest horticulturists. They are able to use a plot of cleared land for as long as eight years by planting different crops on it each year. Families maintain more than one field and are able to harvest all year round in fields of different ages, each having its own kind of crop. A newly cleared field will usually be planted in millet or maize, along with fruit trees such as durian. Manioc is planted after the first crop has finished producing. A year or two later bananas replace manioc. In addition, greens, pumpkins, sweet potatoes, yams, taro, onions, and chili peppers are planted, along with other crops. The fruit trees that were planted when the field was first cleared will begin to bear when the forest is allowed to reclaim the plot. The Semai supplement their gardening by hunting and gathering (Provencher 1975:139–140).

> The Semai practice slash-and-burn agriculture.

To the average Westerner, the tropical jungle home of the Semai would represent an incredibly hostile environment. Diseases that afflict the population include tuberculosis, whipworm, typhoid, paratyphoid, malaria, hepatitis, yaws, and elephantiasis, among others. The mountainous terrain makes travel very difficult. The heat, slippery clay slopes, and biting insects make walking in the rain-forest an unpleasant experience. The Semai do not take strolls in the rain-forest. Many plants have poisonous spines or bristles. There is also danger of falling on split bamboo and being impaled on its razor sharp edges near cleared fields. This can be fatal. P. D. R. Williams-Hunt, an administrator and the only person to work extensively with the Semai prior to 1960, died as the result of such a fall (Dentan 1970:94).

> The Semai survive in an environment that seems incredibly hostile to the Westerner.

The eco-niche of the Semai is hot and wet. Daily temperatures range from 85° to 95°F and it rains about 200 days a year. Thundersqualls periodically hit the Semai villages with winds of 40 to 50 miles per hour, accompanied by torrential rain and flooding.

The fauna of the Malay Peninsula is varied—for example, there are 129 species of snakes—and includes many dangerous forms. Tigers, elephants, leopards, and bearcats attack both the people and their livestock. Reptiles include the reticulated python which grows to a length of 35 feet and a weight of an eighth of a ton; the king cobra, which grows up to 18 feet long and is both poisonous and aggressive; a smaller cobra that can "spit" a spray of venom a distance of 3 feet, causing temporary blindness; 3 kinds of kraits, which are deadly to humans; 12 other species of poisonous snakes; and crocodiles. Other forms of animal life include a spider large enough to eat birds and mice; black scorpions the size of New England crabs; deadly house scorpions; venomous centipedes over a foot long; black land leeches; and cockroaches so numerous that the Semai do not bother to brush them off their bodies (Dentan 1968:26).

The characteristic of the Semai that the outsider finds most interesting is their emphasis on nonviolence. The Semai conceive of themselves as nonviolent people. Those who have spent only a short time with the Semai inevitably use adjectives such as *timid* or *weak* to describe them. Those who have spent a few weeks with the Semai describe them as "carefree" or "jolly." One never finds in descriptions of the Semai terms such as *hostile* or *insolent,* which Renaissance Europeans used to describe all natives.

The Concept of Punan. The Semai believe that it is wrong to display the emotion of anger. A rationale for their nonviolence is found in their belief system, and especially in their concept of *punan. Punan* translates roughly into English as "taboo." Implicit in their thinking about punan is the idea that causing someone unhappiness, especially by frustrating his or her desires, will increase the probability of an accident that will injure him or her physically. The term *punan* refers to both the offending act and the resulting proneness to accidents. According to the Semai, punan accidents result somehow from the fact that the punan victim's heart is "unhappy." The concept of punan acts as a sanction that enforces what the Semai consider to be proper behavior. For example, if someone does not provide food on request, it is believed that harm will come to the person who requested the food. In other words, in the Semai system of

The concept of *punan* embodies the Semai emphasis on nonviolence.

sanctions and taboos, the punishment afflicts the victim rather than the offender (Dentan 1968:55–56).

While the Semai generally do not become angry, there are times when someone refuses the legitimate request of another Semai. The person making the request is put into punan. When this happens, the victim has two courses of action: enduring the punan or asking the offender for compensation. A man who has been refused a girl's sexual favors normally endures punan, and it is believed that he will very likely injure himself accidentally while in that state. In other instances, the victim seeks compensation from the person who has refused his request. To reverse the situation of punan the offender must apologize and pay a fine, so that the victim's "heart will be happy again." The amount of compensation demanded by the victim is proportionate to the amount of emotional distress the offense has caused. The Semai victim uses one of two means to attempt to collect compensation. In some cases, the victim sets a fine, often beyond the offender's ability to pay. Then the amount is discussed, and usually a minimal gift such as a cooking pot is agreed upon to repair the breech between offender and victim. The second means of collecting compensation for punan is used if the victim thinks it unlikely that the offender will pay compensation voluntarily. The victim will wait patiently until the unwary offender presents him or her with an opportunity to "confiscate" the compensation. For example, the victim may take the clothes the offender has left on the shore while bathing. Because offenders know they are guilty of punan, they usually offer no argument to such ploys, because they realizes that public opinion would be against them. In a society such as our own, in which courts are increasingly turned to for settlement of disputes, it is easy to underestimate the power of the opinion of one's neighbors in a small community (Dentan 1968:56–57).

While the belief in punan reduces hostility between individuals, there are other examples of the nonviolent orientation of the Semai. Alcoholic beverages have normally not been a part of the Semai's traditional culture; today some Semai will drink beer or palm wine. Although they seldom drink enough to become intoxicated, when it does occur that a Semai becomes drunk, he or she does not become violent like members of some other societies, but instead becomes extremely talkative. Likewise, the Semai seldom hit their children and never administer the kind of beating that has been traditionally considered a routine part of the socialization process in Western society. The Semai are uneasy about killing animals, especially those they have raised themselves. Most animals are raised for barter or for sale to the

Malay and Chinese traders. Murder is nonexistent among the Semai. The first census taken among the Semai was conducted in 1956. Since that date not one instance of murder, attempted murder, or maiming has come to the attention of the authorities. Prior to British administration, the Semai did reluctantly abandon very old or hopelessly sick people who were completely unproductive. They were left to die in a hut with a small supply of food and water. However, the Semai do not think of this abandonment as killing, but merely as allowing someone in great misery to die (Dentan 1968:57–58).

While the Semai are appalled by violence, removed from their traditional setting they are capable of killing. In the early 1950s some of the Semai were recruited by the British to help fight Communist insurgents. The Semai were good solders, in spite of the fact that they are traditionally nonviolent; however, some of the Semai soldiers overreacted to violence. Communists killed the kin of some of the Semai serving in counterinsurgency troops. The Semai soldiers appeared to have been swept up in a kind of "insanity" which they call blood drunkenness. They killed the enemy with vengence, and some drank the blood of their victims. When they returned to their homes the Semai troops seem to have had little difficulty reverting to the nonviolent behavior of their culture and were as gentle and as afraid of violence as anyone else. In compartmentalizing their violent behavior the Semai are able to maintain belief in the necessity for nonviolence as the model for village living as strongly as in precontact times.

The Yąnomamö of Venezuela

Halfway around the world, in roughly the same longitude, is another rain-forest-dwelling primitive group, the Yąnomamö. Unlike the nonviolent Semai of the Malay Peninsula, the Yąnomamö consider themselves fierce people and emphasize fierceness throughout their behavior with one another and with outsiders.

The Yąnomamö emphasize fierceness.

The Yąnomamö number about 15,000 people, living in some 150 villages on the Venezuela-Brazil borderlands. It is believed that until recently the Yąnomamö were one of the largest unacculturated tribes left in all of South America. In recent years new mission posts have been constructed, along with airstrips. The airfields attract the planes of government officials, many of whom are attempting to open up the sparsely populated interior of Venezuela for development. New diseases—measles and

The Yąnomamö are currently undergoing increasing culture contact.

influenza, introduced by outsiders—have taken a heavy toll on the Yąnomamö. Competition for metal tools and weapons, especially the shotgun, has had a dramatic impact on the scale and seriousness of wars between the inhabitants of villages that had previously not been enemies (Chagnon 1976:213).

Like the Semai, the Yąnomamö practice slash-and-burn agriculture and relocate their fields periodically due to the exhaustion of the soil. However the Yąnomamö gardening is further complicated by warfare. Raids and fear of them cause the rapid relocation of villages. The major crops of the Yąnomamö include plantains, bananas, sweet manioc, taro, sweet potatoes, maguey, and the peach-palm. Maize is cultivated as an emergency crop, because its seeds are light and easily transported. A village that must relocate its garden at a distance can carry large quantities of maize seed and produce a substantial crop in a relatively short period of time.

The aggression of the Yąnomamö affects their subsistence pattern, their demography, and their sociopolitical organization. Village size ranges from 40 to 250 inhabitants. The inhabitants of small villages must make alliances with inhabitants of larger villages in order to survive. A village must be able to assemble a raiding party of at least 10 men, plus a few additional men who will remain behind in the village to protect the women and children, in order to be successful. On the other hand, the inhabitants of villages usually fission into two or more groups once the population reaches about 150 persons, because internal feuds and fights are so frequent that peace becomes almost impossible to maintain. If a killing occurs within the village, the guilty

The Yąnomamö. (Chagnon, Anthro-Photo)

party and those aligned with him must flee far away and seek refuge in the village of an ally until they can establish their own garden. In other cases, where the basis for fission is less serious, the two resulting villages remain in the same general area, so that they can reunite when either is threatened by raids (Chagnon 1968:39–41).

A small group that has broken ties with its former village is the center of hostility from the inhabitants of other villages. Because the newly formed village is small and weak, it is continually attacked and its women are abducted by men from stronger villages. In order to survive, the inhabitants of the various Yąnomamö villages attempt to develop stable alliances with neighboring villages, so that if need be they can rely for long periods of time on the gardens of neighboring villages— often a year or more, until a crop can be harvested. However, the hospitality of an ally is not given without certain demands. The allies normally expect to receive some of the local groups' females as their wives. The longer the visitors remain with their hosts the greater the number of women demanded, so visitors usually make every effort to establish their new gardens as quickly as possible and to move as soon as they begin producing.

Host villages make demands on visitors for their women.

The Yąnomamö believe that strong villages should take advantage of weaker ones and coerce them to give up their women. In order to avoid such a fate, the Yąnomamö males of all villages act as if they are strong. The military threat that exists everywhere among the Yąnomamö creates a situation in which intervillage alliances are desirable; but at the same time, allies cannot really trust each other, because they are obligated by the Yąnomamö way of life to behave aggressively toward each other in order to display their strength. Napoleon Chagnon (1968:99), an anthropologist who has spent nearly four years among the Yąnomamö since 1964, has observed:

> Political maneuvering in this milieu is both a tricky and potentially hazardous undertaking. Each principal in the negotiation must establish the credibility of his own threats, while discovering the point at which his partner's bluff will dissolve abruptly into action; he must discover the point beyond which he must not goad his ally, lest he himself is prepared to suffer the possibly violent outcome. It is a politics of brinkmanship, a form of political behavior in which each negotiator is compelled to expose his opposite's threats as bluffs at the risk of inciting him to violence—a club fight immediately and honorably, or, later and treacherously, a feast in which the hosts descend on their guests to kill their men and abduct their women.

Because of their self-image of fierceness, the Yąnomamö

cannot present themselves at the village of a potential ally and request military assistance, revealing that they are being raided by superior forces. This type of action would be an admission of inferiority and vulnerability, and might even result in an attack by the potential ally. Therefore the Yąnomamö try to conceal their true motive for coming to a potential ally's village under the guise of trading and feasting. The trading creates frequent interaction between villages, a prerequisite to stable alliances. An alliance between two villages may stabilize at any one of three points: (*a*) sporadic reciprocal trading, (*b*) mutual feasting, or (*c*) reciprocal exchange of women. These are generally cumulative levels in a sequence. In other words, allies who exchange women also feast and trade, while allies who merely feast together also trade but do not exchange women (Chagnon 1968:100–101).

Feasting and trading between potential allies is carried out in a hostile atmosphere. Trading occurs when visitors make requests through their headmen for items they desire. The headmen of the host group then encourage their own men to give up the item. The item is usually thrown at the feet of the person who requested it. He first ignores it, then gives it a cursory examination and throws it back on the ground. Usually his mates examine the item in greater detail and try to convince him of its merits, while the giver may apologize for its defects. If the object is particularly poor the giver will extoll the item's not-so-obvious merits, while the recipient draws attention to the conspicuous shortcomings. In every trade the host villagers always feel they have been overly generous. On the other hand, after they depart, the visitors usually complain that they have not received enough gifts. The hosts try to conceal their choicest items from the visitors. If the visitors request any choice items, the hosts vigorously deny having them. The guests frequently do likewise; for example, they may sink their prize bows in a river before arriving to trade and carry inferior bows should such an item be requested by the host (Chagnon 1968:111–112).

Another aspect of aggressiveness and fierceness among the Yąnomamö is the chest-pounding duel. When heated arguments develop during feasts, one of the hosts and a guest may square off for a chest-pounding duel. The duel begins when one man from each side steps into the center of the crowd that has formed to observe the contest. One of the men spreads his legs apart, bares his chest, and holds his arms behind his back, daring the other to hit him, while permitting his opponent to adjust his chest or arms to allow him even further advantage when he strikes. The opponent then prepares to deliver a close-fisted

Village alliances develop through a sequence of trading, feasting, or exchanging women.

blow by painstakingly adjusting his own distance from his victim, by measuring his arm length to the man's chest, and by taking several dry runs before actually delivering his blow. He then winds up somewhat like a baseball pitcher and delivers a tremendous blow with his closed fist to the opponent's left pectoral (chest) muscle, putting all of his weight into the blow. Often the victim's knees buckle, and he may stagger around for a few minutes, but he remains silent, expressing no pain. After each blow the companions of the deliverer cheer. The victim's supporters urge him to take another blow. If the delivery is made forcefully enough to knock the recipient to the ground, the deliverer will throw his arms above his head, roll his eyes back, and prance victoriously in a circle around his victim. A good fighter receiving blows will usually be able to stand poised, taking as many as four blows before demanding the opportunity to hit his adversary. The recipient is entitled to strike his opponent as many times as he himself has been struck, provided that the opponent can take it. If a person has delivered three blows, he has to receive three, or else he is shown to be a poor fighter. He can retire with fewer than three only if he is injured. Then one of his comrades can replace him and demand to hit the victorious opponent. Any blows that the injured man still had coming are considered cancelled, and the man who delivered the victorious blow has to receive a greater number of blows than he delivered. As a result, the best fighters are at a disadvantage. They have to receive disproportionately more punishment then they can deliver. However, their reward is prestige. They earn the reputation of being fierce. Chest-pounding duels may last as long as three hours, with some men taking several turns (Chagnon 1968:113–117). These duels can escalate into the more severe side-slapping duel,[10] club fight, ax duel, or all-out warfare. Thus the feast is always potentially dangerous for both host and guest, even though its purpose is to cement alliances.

The Yąnomamö have evolved a very distinct way of dealing with their social universe. Whereas the Semai stress the importance of nonviolence to an extreme unusual among the people of Southeast Asia, the Yąnomamö emphasize aggressiveness in social action to an extreme uncommon in the jungles of South America. The tropical forest tribes of Brazil and Venezuela are varied in their behavior patterns. Some, such as the Shavante, are as violent as the Yąnomamö.[11] Other groups, such as the Ka-

---

[10] Almost identical to the chest-pounding duel, except for the blow that is delivered with an open hand to the side of the opponent, striking between his rib cage and pelvis bone.

[11] See David Maybury-Lewis' account of the Akwe-Shavante (Maybury-Lewis 1965 and 1967).

lapalo,[12] reject such behavior as entirely inappropriate and instead emphasize nonviolence to the extent that it is stressed in Semai society. Anthropologists have not yet found an answer to why these differences occur among the tropical forest peoples. Perhaps part of the problem stems from the fact that very little historical analysis has been carried out on any of the Brazilian-Venezuelan tribal groups. Until extensive archival research has been undertaken, it will be difficult to determine the extent and nature of the outside contact that these groups have experienced. It is possible that the Yąnomamö have had more contact with the outside world than is currently suspected. In fact the discovery of such contacts might provide some clue as to why the Yąnomamö are so fierce. Outside contact may have subjected them to land pressures and other problems that resulted in stresses to their social system.

Recently two events occurred that will have a major impact on the Yąnomamö way of life. In 1974 the major artery of the Trans-Amazonic road system was constructed through the tribes's land and in 1975 one of the world's largest uranium deposits was discovered in Yąnomamö territory (Davis 1977:470). Needless to say, the Yąnomamö will undergo rapid changes in the next few years.

The Nacirema

Among the least known peoples in anthropological literature are the Nacirema, a North American people living in the territory between the Canadian Cree of southern Canada and the Yaqui of northern Mexico. They are known primarily from an article by Horace Miner (1956), who has spent a number of years living among them.

Whereas Australian aborigine culture might be characterized by its emphasis on oneness with the past, the future, and the natural surroundings, and the Semai and Yąnomamö are characterized respectively by nonviolence and fierceness, the focus of Nacirema culture is on body ritual. According to Miner (1956:503), the fundamental belief underlying the whole culture system is that the human body is ugly and its natural tendency is to debility and disease, with the only hope of averting these characteristics being the use of ritual and ceremony.

In order to keep the body from being ugly or contacting disease, the Nacirema perform daily rituals at one of the shrines found in every household. These shrines are often a reflection of

The Nacirema emphasize body ritual.

---

[12] See Basso (1973) for a description of the Kalapalo.

the owner's wealth. The more opulent a family, the more likely they are to have more than one such shrine. While the shrines are family-owned, the rituals associated with them are not family ceremonies but rather are private and secret. These private rites are discussed only with the children of the family, and then only when they are being initiated into the mysteries of the shrine ritual (Miner 1956:503).

Miner was able to collect information on some aspects of the ritual in spite of the secrecy surrounding the ritual. Apparently the focal point of the shrine is a chest built into the wall. In this chest the Nacirema store the many charms and magical potions without which the natives believe they would die.[13] Most of the preparations are obtained from various specialized practitioners. The most powerful of these practitioners are the medicine men, who require substantial gifts from those they help. The medicine men, however, do not provide curative potions for their clients. This is considered the domain of another specialist. The medicine man decides what ingredients the client should take and writes these down in a secret language. This writing is understood only by the medicine man and by the herbalist, who provides the client with the required charm for an additional gift.

Beneath the chest where the charms are stored in a small font. Each day, every member of the family enters the shrine room alone, bows his or her head before the cham-box, mixes hot and cold holy water in the font, and proceeds with a brief rite of ablution. The holy water used is secured from the water temple of the local community. At the water temple, other specialists conduct elaborate ceremonies to make the liquid ritually pure. The daily body ritual performed by each Nacirema includes a mouth rite. The ritual consists of inserting a small bundle of hog hairs into the mouth, together with powders or pastes that the Nacirema believe have magical qualities, and then moving the bundle in a highly formalized series of gestures. The Nacirema have an almost pathological horror of and fascination with the mouth. They seem to believe that the condition of their mouth has a supernatural influence on all social relationships. Were it not for their rituals of the mouth, they claim that their teeth would fall out, their gums bleed, their jaws shrink, their friends desert them, and their lovers reject them (Miner 1956:504).

Besides their daily private mouth rites at their home shrines, the Nacirema seek out the aid of holy-mouth-men called *st-sitned*, once or twice a year. These practitioners use an impres-

Body ritual is secret.

---

[13] For a detailed description of the contents of one of these chests see Salinger (1961:75–76).

sive array of paraphernalia consisting of a variety of augers, awls, probes, and prods. The use of these objects in the exorcism of the evils of the mouth involves almost unbelievable ritual torture of the client, who gladly brings great gifts for the practitioners, in spite of the pain they inflict. Having observed a holy-mouth-man in ritual performance, Miner (1956:505) gives a vivid account of what is involved:

> The holy-mouth-man opens the client's mouth and, using the above mentioned tools, enlarges any holes which decay may have created in the teeth. Magical materials are put into these holes. If there are no naturally occurring holes in the teeth, large sections of one or more teeth are gouged out so that the supernatural substance can be applied. In the client's view, the purpose of these ministrations is to arrest decay and to draw friends. The extremely sacred and traditional character of the rite is evident in the fact that the natives return to the holy-mouth-men year after year, despite the fact that their teeth continue to decay.

While the data on the Nacirema is extremely skimpy, it is clear that their way of life adds yet another aspect to the diversity of human societies. It is hoped that anthropologists will have the opportunity to undertake further research among these curious people before either they or their culture becomes extinct.

The Superiority of Western Culture?

Another belief generally held about native peoples is that Western culture is necessarily superior to the non-Western way of life. Because people in all societies tend to think their own way of life is better than others, we assume that our culture is superior to the world's non-Western cultures and that we are helping to improve their situation by forcing them to change. Is this necessarily so?

Economic development and progress are generally taken by members of the Western world to be unquestionably beneficial goals for all societies to strive for. The "superiority" of societies is then measured by the Western world in terms of the amount of economic development and progress that have occurred. The social advantages of progress—usually defined in terms of increased incomes, higher standards of living, greater security, and better health—are thought to be positive, *universal* goods, to be obtained at any price. It is usually the decision of government planners throughout the world that native peoples must sacrifice their traditional cultures in order to "benefit" from progress, but this is thought to be a small price to pay for the "obvious" advantages. Yes the "advantages" of progress and change are not all that obvious to many non-Western peoples who have lost their lives by the millions, lost their land, lost their political sovereignty, and lost their right to follow the life-style of their own choosing (Bodley 1975:150–152).

The spread of Western culture brings with it an increased disease rate for native groups. It introduces diseases of Western civilization such as diabetes, obesity, hypertension, and a variety of circulatory problems to which native people become suddenly vulnerable. At the same time, traditional environmental balances are disturbed, often resulting in the dramatic increase of certain bacterial and parasitic diseases. The crowding of native peoples into urban slums brings with it an assortment of diseases associated with poverty (Bodley 1975:152).

For thousands of years non-Western societies have generally maintained a delicate balance with their ecosystem. Western culture and its "progress" are changing this. With the advent of the industrial revolution, industrial nations rapidly consumed their own local resources, as the population and demands for goods increased. For example, in England, after only a hundred years of industrial progress the island was no longer able to meet its basic needs for grain, wood, fibers, and hides. Between 1851 and 1900, 35 million people left Europe because it could no longer support them. By 1970, Americans were consuming per capita 15 times the world average of nonrenewable resources (Bodley 1975:4–5). Because the industrial nations can no longer support themselves with resources within their own boundaries, they have expanded into the areas of the world held by native people, under the guise of bringing economic development and progress. In every case, the Western world has benefited at the expense of the native.

Perhaps the observations of the explorer Lewis Cotlow (1971:225–226) are most pertinent here:

> Let me put the matter squarely. What we have done, as a civilization, is not only to assist in the destruction of life systems that are incalculably old; we have participated in the banishment from earth of peoples whose right to exist and whose style of existence are as sacred as ours. We have also obliterated systems of survival that for all their variety and strangeness to us have been successful for others.
>
> We have learned that victories over nature usually come at a high price. The primitive, too, is a conqueror of nature, although more often he seems to be its partner. He does it with all the seen and unseen resources of his wits, physical prowess and imagination. He has not, on the whole, had to pay dearly for the conquest.

Anthropologists have struggled to bring before the general public a view of humankind in which each society's way of life is

The "advantages" of Western civilization are not always so obvious to those they are imposed on.

seen as a legitimate adaptation to survival. It is only through comparing the cultures of many societies that we can eventually learn what is truly "human nature." Because anthropologists have demonstrated that there are many viable approaches to life, Westerners can no longer assume that their way of life is the only way or that their way of life is necessarily the best. Anthropologists have discovered that we must not judge other societies by our own standards. Each society has its strengths and weaknesses. From the anthropological perspective, all societies must be examined from a *cultural relativistic* point of view, in which societies are considered neither good nor bad but rather as successful alternatives in humankind's cultural diversity.

> All societies represent successful alternative ways of being human.

Anthropology Vocabulary

Arunta	Dreamtime	Semai
Australian aborigines	ethnographic present	totem center
churinga	marriage section	totemic clan
clan	Nacirema	Yąnomamö
devolution	*punan*	Yir Yoront

Review Questions

1. What effect did the arrival of Westerners have on the non-Western world during the era of exploration?
2. How has cultural anthropology changed our notions about "primitive" peoples?
3. What is the importance of the Dreamtime to the Australian aborigines?
4. The Semai and the Yąnomamö represent interesting cultural contrasts. What factors might have led to the different orientations of the two societies?
5. What is progress?

Recommended Reading

Bodley, John H. 1975, *Victims of Progress.* Menlo Park, Calif.: Cummings Publishing Co. An excellent account of the impact of Westernization on tribal peoples in different parts of the world. Challenges many of the stereotypes about "primitive" peoples.

Chagnon, Napoleon A., 1977, *Yąnomamö: The Fierce People,* 2nd ed. New York: Holt, Rinehart and Winston. A vivid account of a tribal people on the Venezuela-Brazilian border. This book offers the best overall view of the Yąnomamö of any of Chagnon's publications.

Denton, Robert Knox, 1968, *The Semai: A Nonviolent People of Malaya.* New York: Holt, Rinehart and Winston. An introduction to the culture of the Semai.

Elkin, A. P., 1964, *The Australian Aborigines,* 3rd ed. Garden City, N. Y.: Doubleday. This book remains one of the best introductions to the world of the Australian aborigines.

II

Humankind and the natural world

Environment has been incorrectly seen as a cause of cultural diversity.

Anthropology views humans as a component of the environment.

Economic and political power affect ecological decisions.

Many societies have maintained an antiecological approach to their environment.

Human interest in humankind's place in nature has led to an interest in nature itself. Scholars of the Middle Ages were searching for laws of nature long before they were concerned with any laws of human behavior. According to the geographer Clarence J. Glacken (1967:vii–viii), throughout Western thought people have repeatedly asked three questions about the habitable earth and their relationship to it: (a) Is the earth a special creation designed for humans to control? (b) Has the environment influenced the moral and social nature of individuals and has it had an influence in molding the character and nature of human cultures? and (c) In what manner have humans changed the earth from its hypothetical pristine condition? The first two questions have been expressed frequently, the third less so, although it has often been implicit in writings about humans and nature.

Was the Earth Made Especially for Humans?

Traditional Judeo-Christian beliefs about the creation of the earth and humans have emphasized the important place of humankind. Humans are thought to have been made in the image of God and given control over all living things. After creating the first man and woman, "God said unto them, Be fruitful, and multiply, and replenish the earth, and subdue it: and have dominion over the fish of the sea, and over the fowl of the air, and over every living thing that moveth upon the earth" (Gen. 1:28). Until very recently, orthodox Christianity has accepted the point of view that the earth was designed for human use and exploitation. This belief has led to an anti-ecological morality. Contrasting the Christian ethic toward nature with the views of other religious traditions of the Eastern world, Lynn White (1969:348–349) points out that the Eastern traditions tend to view humans as an integral part of nature. Humankind is a partner with but not the controller of nature. White (1969:351) feels very strongly that most of our ecological problems today relate to this Christian point of view toward nature.

While perhaps a strong case can be made for the impact of Christian teachings about Creation on the relationship of humans to their environment, these teachings should not be taken as the sole cause of ecological problems. Later in the chapter it will be shown that the non-Western, non-Christian Subanun of the Philippines have created their own ecological

The Judeo-Christian tradition views the earth as created for humans to control.

difficulties as a result of quite different factors. Religious conviction obviously represents only one of a number of potential variables affecting the environment. Nevertheless, in the Western world, the Christian philosophy of human dominance over nature has played a significant role.

How Does Environment Affect Culture?

While the belief that the earth was created for humans grew out of mythology, theology, and philosophy, the question of how the earth's environment has influenced human character and society originated in medical theory, pharmaceutical lore, and weather observations. One of the most influential works shaping opinions on this question was *Airs, Waters, Places*, written in the late fifth century BC and traditionally attributed to the Greek physician Hippocrates. The growth of formal medicine is thought to derive from Hippocrates. The Hippocratic system diffused from the ancient Greeks to the Arab world, where it was carried to Spain during the Moorish invasions. Hippocrates' basic concepts were utilized by doctors until the nineteenth century, when other systems of medicine replaced that of Hippocrates. However, many of the concepts survive today, especially in the Latin world, as folk medical beliefs.

At the heart of the Hippocratic system of medicine, described in *Airs, Water, Places*, was the *humor theory*.[1] The Greeks recognized four basic elements in nature—earth, air, water, and fire. Since the human body is composed of the same elements as all other natural phenomena, these elements were thought to exist also in the human body, in the form of humors rather than in their external forms. Air, consisting of hot and moist, was thought to be represented in the body by the humor blood; fire, a mixture of hot and dry, was thought to be represented by the humor yellow bile; water, thought to be cold and moist, was represented by the humor phlegm; and earth, a mixture of cold and dry, was represented by the humor black bile or melancholy. Good health consisted of a balance of the humors. Ill health was brought about when some aspect of the physical environment, usually temperature, resulted in the dominance of one humor over another. This notion formed the basis of medical theory. The curing process involved an attempt to restore a balance between the humors.

The humor theory was originally a medical belief.

[1] *Humor* refers to a variety of body fluids believed to determine a person's health and disposition rather than to the quality that makes something seem amusing.

The doctrine of humors was thought to be related to differences not only between individuals but between whole groups of people. The dominance of different humors was believed to be closely tied to differences in regional climates or to seasonal variations within a single climate. The humor theory was used to explain not only physical and mental health but the physical and cultural characteristics of a people as a whole. For example, it was believed that warm climates produced passionate natures; cold climates produced bodily strength and endurance; temperate climates produced intellectual superiority (Glacken 1967:81). By the eighteenth century, racial and cultural differences were interpreted as being caused by climate. Eventually, these points of view became known as *environmental determinism*.

> The humor theory was later applied to groups of people and thought to be caused by climate.

Between 1721 and 1748, there was a revival of interest in the writings attributed to Hippocrates, especially for his insights on communicable diseases, their relation to quick changes in temperature, and the influence of air on them. One of the writers who had access to an abbreviated version of *Airs, Waters, Places* was Baron de la Brède et de Montesquieu, a French lawyer turned writer and traveler. In his most famous book, *The Spirit of Laws*, published in 1748, he discussed the kinds of government that had appeared in history and used climatic theory to account for the differences. By Montesquieu's lifetime the influences of climate on the physical state of the human body were explained by a theory somewhat different from the doctrine of humors. Montesquieu embraced the theory of a celebrated English doctor, John Arbuthnot, who had published a theory of health and climate based on some of the general philosophy of Hippocrates but supplemented by the results of contemporary investigation. Arbuthnot's theory of the relationship of the atmosphere to disease, and especially to seasonally recurring diseases, was published in 1731 in a work entitled *An Essay Concerning the Effects of Air on Human Bodies*. It suggested that climate affected the human body by causing contractions or expansions of nerves and blood vessels and affecting the circulation of the blood. Following Arbuthnot's theory, Montesquieu concluded that people were more vigorous in cold climates because "here the action of the heart and the reaction of the extremities of the fibres are better performed, the temperatures of the humors is greater, the blood moves more freely towards the heart, and reciprocally the heart has more power" (Montesquieu 1899, cited in Glacken 1967:568–569). He saw the people of northern Europe as having few vices, many virtues, and a great deal of frankness and sincerity. In southern Europe,

> Environmental determinism viewed climate as the cause of cultural differences.

primarily Spain and Italy, he felt that people lacked morality and committed all types of crimes. Montesquieu believed that in France, which he classified as a temperate climate, the inhabitants were inconsistent in their manners as well as their vices and virtues and that this was because the climate was neither as cold as in the northern countries nor as hot as in the southern countries. He also tried to demonstrate further correlations between climate and religion (the religions of the East were unchanging because of the hot climate); climate and drinking alcohol (a law prohibiting the drinking of wine in hot climates was considered reasonable, while a law forbidding wine drinking in a northern climate would be improper); climate and laziness (slavery arose in countries whose climate induced such great laziness among the people that their masters could force them to work only by threat of punishment); and climate and sexual desires (in hot climates women mature sexually at an early age, before they attain maturity in their reasoning. As a result they become dependent upon male dominance, and therefore in hot countries one finds the widespread practice of plural wives. On the other hand, in temperate climates women's beauty, reason, and knowledge tend to keep pace with one another and mature together. Therefore they have more of an equal status with their men, and these conditions favor monogamy). For Montesquieu, different needs existed in different climates and brought about different ways of life; and these in turn required different kinds of laws (Glacken 1967:568–574).

While many writers before Montesquieu had emphasized the effects of climate on culture, it was his reformulation that made these ideas so powerful in the second half of the eighteenth century and the early part of the nineteenth century. However, not all of his contemporaries accepted Montesquieu's point of view. In particular, Johann G. Herder was a strong critic. Herder believed that even if environmental factors can be shown to influence the physical and mental characteristics of the individual, it does not follow that they have the same effects on whole groups of people. Hot weather may cause debility in an individual, but one cannot conclude that all peoples of hot countries lack the energies to create a civilization. In spite of Herder's warnings, the reasoning of Montesquieu and his followers has characterized much of the thinking on climatic influences in the nineteenth and twentieth centuries. Perhaps the strongest advocate of an environmental deterministic point of view in modern times was Ellsworth Huntington (1915:286), who stated, "In the South [of the United States] we find less energy, less vitality, less education and fewer men who rise to eminence than in the North, not

because southerners are in any way innately inferior to north-
erners, but apparently because of the adverse climate. In the Far
West people seem to be stimulated to such a degree that nervous
exhaustion threatens them."

One of the contributions of modern cultural anthropology has
been to show that simplistic theories such as those put forth by
Montesquieu and Huntington are inaccurate. Because anthropologists have collected extensive information about most of the
world's societies, they have been able to show that although
there may be certain influences of environment on culture, one
has to examine the interaction of environment and culture at
the local level. Knowing only climatic conditions does not allow
one to predict cultural patterns. For example, in the previous
chapter it was shown that although both the Semai and the Yan-
omamo live in tropical rain forests, their ways of life are almost
diametrically opposed.

One thing the environmental determinists did not take into
account was the great complexity of eco-niches in many parts of
the world. For example, wherever there are major differences
in elevation in the tropics, there is a great diversity of environments. Two entirely different environments may exist side by
side only a few miles apart. In the Central American republic of
Costa Rica, a country roughly one-half the size of the state of
Virginia, there are 13 different environmental zones, each as different from the others as the vast Corn Belt of the United States
is from the great Southwest. Writers from temperate countries
often fail to realize the rich ecological complexity of the tropics
and generalize as if all tropical eco-niches were the same. While
many tropical environments are hot and wet, there are many
others that are either cool or dry.

One can understand the interrelation between a society and
its environment only through extended field study, because beliefs affect the way in which a people perceive their environment
and the way that they react to it. This point will be illustrated
later in the chapter when the Subanun perception of their environment is discussed.

Anthropologists have
shown that one cannot
predict cultural patterns
from climate.

Humans' Impact
on the Environment

The third question that Glacken has found recurring through
Western thought concerning humankind and nature is the question of human impact on the environment. While the effects of
environment on humans were observed by the Greeks as they

developed theories of disease, there has been less concern with humans' effects on the environment. The concept of humans as causal agents apparently grew out of observations about everyday activities and skills such as cultivation, carpentry, and weaving. For example, agriculture frequently decreased the forests and increased the amount of grassland. This third notion was accommodated within Western thought because humans were considered partners of God who through their arts and inventions improved upon and cultivated an earth created for them (Glacken 1967:vii–viii).

Agriculture represented a major change in humans' relationship to nature from the earlier hunting-and-gathering way of life. During the seventh century AD the introduction of a new kind of plow changed the entire pattern of agriculture in Europe. Previously, plows were drawn by two oxen and did not normally turn the sod, but rather scattered it. Cross-plowing was used, and fields tended to be square-shaped. This system worked well in the fairly light soils of the Near East where agriculture had developed, as well as in the Mediterranean. However, this type of plowing was inappropriate to the wet climate and sticky soils of northern Europe. By the late seventh century, some of the northern European peasants began using a new type of plow, equipped with a vertical knife to cut the line of the furrow, a horizontal share to slice under the sod, and a moldboard to turn the sod over. The friction of this plow with the soil was so great, it required eight oxen to pull it. The plow cut into the soil so effectively that cross-plowing was not needed, and as a result, fields began to be shaped in long strips rather than in squares. While single families had been able to farm under the scratch-plow method, the new plow required a different kind of organization. Peasants had to pool their oxen to form the large oxen teams needed to use the new plow (White 1969:345–346). This plow did much to change the relationship of humans to the land; humans became more effective exploiters of nature than ever before. The belief that humans had been put on earth by God to rule over an earth created for them provided the rationale for a modification of the environment that has been increasing ever since.

The discovery of the New World offered Europe a new source of natural products to be exploited, and this provided her with so many new resources the Europeans did not think in terms of limited or finite supply. Hardwood forests were cleared and the land planted. Neither the mother countries nor the colonists reflected on the long-term effects of their actions on the environment. In particular, human settlement was highly mobile in

Agriculture represented a major change in human relationships to the environment.

Humankind's impact on the environment. (Brody, EPA)

North America, quickly expoiting the capital potential of the available resources and then moving on to untouched lands.

The first European of any note to discuss in detail what humans were doing to the environment was Comte Georges Louis Leclerc de Buffon, the eighteenth-century French scholar. He believed that modification of nature and the rise of civilization went hand in hand. In *Des Epoques de la Nature* he pointed out that humans have a tremendous impact on their environment:

> Finally the entire face of the Earth bears today the stamp of the power of man, which although subordinate to that of Nature, often has done more than she, or at least has so marvellously aided her, that it is with the help of our hands that she has developed to her full extent and that she has gradually arrived at the point of perfection and of magnificence in which we see her today. [Buffon 1749–1804; cited in Glacken 1967:668]

Buffon emphasized the contrasts between environments scarcely touched by humans and those which had long been the scene of human settlement. Uninhabited lands have rivers with many cataracts, and the land is often flooded with water or burned by drought. Trees grow on every spot capable of supporting them. There are few woods, lakes, or marshes in countries that have been inhabited for a long period of time. Humans give a totally different appearance to the face of the earth. Through human endeavor, untamed rivers acquire a fixed course as their waters are confined and directed. In general, Buffon found the changes introduced by humans to have positive effects on the landscape.

A different point of view concerning the impact of humans on nature was expressed in the nineteenth century, in the writings of George P. Marsh. In 1864, Marsh published *Man and Nature; or Physical Geography as Modified by Human Action*, introducing the pessimistic notion that certain kinds of environmental changes are irreversible. Marsh's theme was that humans disrupt the fundamental harmony or balance of nature. In other words, it was humankind that exerted a revolutionary effect on nature and not the reverse.

The warnings of Marsh were not taken seriously by his contemporaries. Westerners continued to utilize ever-larger quantities of energy in order to satisfy their demands for comfort and wealth, and the effects of the Industrial Revolution spread across the face of the earth. Having used up many of their own natural resources, the Western nations acquired the natural resources of the underdeveloped countries as well, spurred on by the Western values of growth and progress.

On August 6, 1945, 92,000 individuals died at Hiroshima, Japan as a result of the atomic bomb. Three days later 40,000 persons lost their lives at Nagasaki. The shocked world was faced with the reality that humankind now had at its command the power to destroy all of nature, including itself. Radiation poisoning became the first serious ecological issue to elicit global concern. Fallout shelters were constructed throughout the United States to protect citizens in case of a nuclear attack. Numerous science fiction movies depicted the potential havoc humans could unleash with atomic radiation. For the first time, many people began to question whether humans have the right to dominate the natural environment. Many feared that not all of those who would have access to nuclear power could be depended upon to act in a responsible manner.

By the 1960s a number of persons in the United States had become aware of the increasing environmental problems caused by our life-styles. Deforestation, air pollution, water pollution, and other problems were publicized by an articulate minority of concerned citizens. The general public seems to have viewed the conservationist movement as idealistic. Most people continued consuming vast quantities of products that were depleting the earth's supply of natural resources at an alarming rate.

It was not until the 1970s and the fuel crisis caused by the Arab oil embargo that the vast majority of people in industrial nations around the world finally realized that we live in a natural setting that does not have an endless supply of raw material. For too long, the earth has been considered a God-given gift for humans to extract from as they wish. We are only now beginning to recognize the fallacy of this thinking. As the lawyer Earl Murphy (1967:170) has noted:

The Arab oil embargo made many realize that natural resources are finite.

> Renewable resources have never been free. On a planet for which a population of from 30 to 50 billion is predicted within six generations, and for which an urban industrial revolution on the Euro-American model is also prophesized, there can be no change in this fact. Not even the most arcane technology can make the supply of air, soil, water, game, grass, and trees truly free.

What happens when supplies of natural resources are limited? The powerful nations acquire their needs at the expense of the poor nations. For example, anchovies caught off the coast of Peru are ground to meal and exported to the United States, where they are fed to chickens. Peru is already overfishing its anchovy stocks. This is leading to the death of the guano birds who feed on the anchovy school and will ultimately result in destruction of the fishing industry in Peru once there are no anchovy stocks left. At the same time, Peru's population, especially those living in the Andean highlands, is short of protein. Yet the Peruvians get no fish meal, because the United States can afford to pay for it (Anderson 1974:268–269). Thus, economic and political power also enter into the environmental problems.

We are becoming aware of the fact that nature and humans affect each other and that it is difficult to set humans apart from the environment. Humans and their culture must be seen as part of the ecosystem. The ecosystem approach focuses on feedback relationships between all parts of the environment considered. In other words, all things in the system are thought to have some effect on all other things (Abbott 1970:25). Most attempts at developing ecosystems include the human being as one of the many animal forms within the system. Many biologists play down the importance of culture. However, the anthropologist John Bennett has recently proposed that the most significant aspect of human relations with nature is that humans have increasingly considered nature a part of their culture. Recently Bennett (1976:3) introduced the concept of the *ecological transition*, which he defines as "the progressive incorporation of Nature into human frames of purpose and action." He elaborates on this important notion of ecological transition in the following observation (Bennett 1976:3–4):

Humans incorporate more and more of nature into their culture.

> My fundamental assumption is that the history of human-environment relationships, especially since the appearance of Homo sapiens, has featured a growing absorption of the physical environment into the cognitively defined world of human events and actions—indeed, to the point where the argument seriously can be advanced that the concept "human ecology" is a myth, and that there is (or shortly will be) only, and simply, Human Society: people and their wants, and the means of satisfying them. An example can be found in the old distinction between material and nonmaterial culture, which contained a proposal to the effect that water flowing over a dam becomes an item of material culture, since man is using the water as he uses any tool. Hence, humans are constantly engaged in seizing natural phenomena, converting them into cultural objects, and reinterpreting them with cultural ideas.

The archaeological record shows an increasing technology that has allowed humans greater control over the environment with each new era, but the process of ecological transition did not become overwhelming until the Industrial Revolution. Along with an increasing technology there developed hierarchies of status that differentiate humans into those who have power and those who do not. The ecological transition is also expressed in the breakdown of local self-sufficiency, as local groups become unable to satisfy their needs with existing resources in a particular geographical range. As the ecological transition has proceeded, local groups have cultivated wants that could be satisfied only by resources from great distances. Often people have subjected nature to intensive exploitation merely to acquire wealth and status, a purpose unrelated to biological survival.

In the sections that follow, two primitive societies and their relationship to their environment will be examined and contrasted with the relationship of a multinational corporation to the environment it exploited. Each of these cases is representative of some of the issues concerning humans and their environment discussed earlier. Each example is based on extensive fieldwork by anthropologists. The studies show another aspect of the human myth—the great complexity of ecological problems faced by different kinds of societies and the different ways in which the people cope with their environmental problems. The Bushmen of Africa illustrate that the life of the hunter and gatherer is not always as precarious as generally assumed. The Subanun of the Philippines represent agricultural peoples practicing slash-and-burn agriculture and the kinds of ecological alternatives they must choose between. Finally, the United Fruit Company's banana operations in Costa Rica raise the issue of powerful nations' exploitation of the environments of developing nations.

What Do Hunters Do for a Living?

The hunting-and-gathering economy was once representative of the way of life of all societies on the face of the earth. The population of the world in 10,000 BC is estimated to have been about 10 million persons. One hundred percent of them were hunters and gatherers. By the age of exploration, roughly AD 1500, the world's population had risen to about 350 million, and almost all lived in societies practicing some form of agriculture. It is estimated that only one percent of the population were still hunters and gatherers. In less than 500 years the world population has increased over 11 times, to a present total of almost 4 billion individuals. Less than one-thousandth of one percent (0.00l) of the population of the world still maintain a hunting-and-gathering existence. While the percentage of hunters and gatherers is very small today, it should be remembered that humans have been on this earth for millions of years; and for over 99 percent of this period they have lived as hunters and gatherers. It has been estimated that a total of some 150 billion

The environment has come to be used increasingly for acquiring wealth rather than for biological survival.

humans have lived on earth. Over 60 percent of this total have lived as hunters and gatherers, about 35 percent have lived as agriculturalists, and the remainder have lived in industrial societies (Lee and De Vore 1968:3). While the hunting-and-gathering economy represents the earliest form of human subsistence, it should be noted that not all of today's hunters and gatherers have always practiced this form of life nor are the subsistence techniques used today necessarily the same as those used in prehistoric times. Some contemporary hunters and gatherers were originally subsistence farmers who were pushed out of their homeland into more marginal areas, where they switched to the simpler form of subsistence because their agricultural practices were unsuccessful in the new environment.

While the hunters and gatherers generally inhabit the most marginal areas of the world today, the same was not the case in precontact times. Many lived in richer environments than they do today. A number of the classic studies of hunters and gatherers by anthropologists (for example, the !Kung Bushmen of Africa, who will be discussed in this chapter, and the Arunta of Australia, who were discussed in the previous chapter) have been made of the most isolated peoples, who have managed to avoid contact and survived only because they chose to live in extremely marginal areas. Therefore what we know of these hunters today should not be taken as typical of hunting-and-gathering life even several hundred years ago (Lee and De Vore 1968:4–5).

Hunters did not always inhabit marginal areas.

The Bushmen of southern and southwestern Africa today number about 45,000. While in the past these people have been hunters and gatherers, the majority of the Bushmen no longer follow the traditional pattern of subsistence. Most are attached to the Tswana tribes as serfs or to Europeans as servants or laborers and have undergone intensive culture change in the process. About 5000 Bushmen still pursue their aboriginal nomadic mode of life (Murdock 1968:15).

One of the most thoroughly described groups of Bushmen are the !Kung[2] Bushmen of Botswana. They inhabit the semiarid northwest region of Africa's vast Kalahari Desert. Because the region is faced with drought every second or third year, it is an environment marginal for human habitation. Precisely because of its marginality, the land has not appealed to the !Kung's agricultural and pastoral neighbors, and the !Kung have been left in relative isolation. The cultural anthropologist Richard B. Lee

[2] The ! symbol is used by the linguist to represent a consonant that does not occur in Western languages and for which none of the letters of the alphabet could serve. It is a click sound.

has studied the !Kung who live in the Dobe area, near the Southwest African border, some 125 miles south of the Okavango River. The !Kung of this area share part of the region with Bantu pastoralists of the Herero and Tswana tribes.

The Bushmen of the Dobe area number slightly fewer than 400 permanent residents, living in independent camps, lacking firearms, livestock, and agriculture. The !Kung rely occasionally on the Herero for milk and with this exception are entirely dependent upon a hunting-and-gathering economy for their survival. Technically they are under the political control of the Tswana, yet they pay no taxes and they receive only nominal government services. The Dobe !Kung are separated by an international border from the Nyae Nyae !Kung, who live in South Africa. Although the Dobe !Kung have had contact with outsiders since the 1880s, the majority maintain their hunting-and-gathering subsistence, because there is no alternative locally available to them. European contact amounts to an overnight stay by a government patrol every six to eight weeks (Lee 1968:31). The !Kung live in independent camps associated with the permanent water holes. During the dry season the entire population clusters around these water holes and exploits a hinterland of about a 6-mile radius around the water hole for vegetable and animal foods. At the end of the dry season most of the available food in the 6-mile radius has been consumed, and individuals must travel beyond the radius in search of food, carrying water with them.

The people of a camp form a self-sufficient unit. During the day the members of the camp hunt and gather, and in the evening they pool the collected food so that every person present receives an equitable share. While little food is traded between camps, people do move freely from camp to camp. On an average, individuals spend a third of their time living only with close kin, a third visiting other camps, and a third entertaining visitors from other camps. Because food is shared by the entire group, little surplus food is ever accumulated. Generally there is a two- or three-day supply of food on hand at any given time. As a result the !Kung must continue hunting and gathering every third or fourth day throughout the entire year. There is no off-season for the hunter and gatherer.

The vegetable food collected by women comprises from 60 to 80 percent of the total diet by weight. The collecting involves two or three days of work per woman per week. While the men collect some plants and small animals, their primary contribution to the group is the medium and large game that they hunt. While the men and women put in roughly the same amount of

Bushman.
(Shostak, Anthro-Photo)

Vegetable food collected by women comprises the bulk of the Bushmen's diet.

Bushmen women gathering food. (Shostak, Anthro-Photo)

hours in the food quest, the women provide two to three times as much food as the men. The most important food of the !Kung is the mongongo nut, which accounts for more than 50 percent of the vegetable diet by weight. The nut grows abundantly through much of the year and produces more food than the Bushmen utilize. Tens of thousands of pounds of the nuts are harvested each year, while thousands more rot on the ground because they have not been picked. In some ways the mongongo nut is comparable to a cultivated staple crop of an agricultural people. Nutritionally, the nut contains five times the calories and ten times the proteins per cooked unit of cereal crops. Daily, an individual consumes about 300 of these nuts, which would yield approximately 1260 calories and 56 grams of protein. The average daily per capita consumption of the nuts, roughly 7.5 ounces, contains the caloric equivalent of 2.5 pounds of cooked rice and the protein equivalent of 14 ounces of lean beef. At the same time, the mongongo nut is drought-resistant and is abundant in dry years, when the crops of the neighboring agriculturalists fail (Lee 1968:33).

Besides the mongongo nut, the !Kung Bushmen make use of 84 other species of plants, including 29 species of fruits, berries, and melons, and 30 species of roots and bulbs. Some of these species are considered less desirable than others and will only be consumed during the dry season, when the resources are more limited. Actually, 23 of the species account for about 90 percent of the vegetable diet by weight. The Bushmen are also selective in their meat-eating habits. They have names for 223 local species of animals but consider only 54 of these edible; and of these, only 17 are hunted regularly. The most important game is the warthog. Only a few of the birds, reptiles, and small mammals of the region are taken as food. Animals such as rodents, snakes, termites, grasshoppers, and lizards, apparently eaten by some Bushmen, are despised by the Bushmen of the Dobe area.

While some hunting-and-gathering populations move frequently over vast areas, the Bushmen move their camps only five or six times a year, and the camps are not moved very far. The Bushmen set up a rainy-season camp in the nut forests that is generally less than 12 miles from their home water hole. Often new campsites are moved only a few hundred yards away from the previous one. The only reasons the Bushmen travel long distances are for visiting, trading, and making marriage arrangements, not for subsistence reasons. Throughout most of the year, the food they utilize is nearby. A day's round trip of 12 miles by each individual serves to define a core 6 miles in radius. With individuals and small groups fanning out in all directions from the central water hole, the members of the camp can utilize the food resources of well over 100 square miles of territory by a two-hour hike from the well.

The life of the hunter and gatherer has often been characterized as nasty, brutish, and short. The assumption has been that this type of life is so difficult, the members of the society are rapidly worn out and meet with an early death. The statistics compiled on the !Kung Bushmen of the Dobe area refute this picture. In a total population of 466 at the time of Lee's study in 1964, there were 46 individuals (17 men and 29 women) over the age of 60, a proportion that compares favorably with the percentage of elderly in industrialized populations. In many ways, the aged in Bushmen society have a more respected place than in our modern industrial societies. The Bushmen elders are the effective leaders of the camp. They are fed and cared for by their children and grandchildren once their productive years have passed. The blind, the senile, and the crippled are respected for their special ritual and technical skills. For example, the blind may play an active role in both decision making and ritual curing. At the same time, young people are not expected to contribute to the work force nor are they expected to provide food regularly, at least not until they have married. The age of marriage for females is between 15 and 20 and for males between 20 and 25. Healthy, active teenagers spend a great deal of time visiting from camp to camp, while their elders provide them with food. The work force is comprised of people in the age group of about 20 to 60, who support not only themselves but a large number of nonproductive young and old people, roughly 40 percent of the population. The allocation of work to young and

The life of the Bushman is not as difficult as was once assumed.

middle-aged adults seems to allow for a relatively carefree and undemanding childhood and adolescence, and a relatively pleasant and secure old age (Lee 1968:35–36).

Hunters and gatherers are usually portrayed as spending all of their time every day searching for food in order to survive. Again, the !Kung Bushmen do not seem to conform well to the stereotype. The average adult spends only 2.3 days in subsistence activities per week. Since the average working day lasts approximately 6 hours, the !Kung of Dobe, despite their harsh environment, devote only about 12 to 19 hours a week to obtaining food. The pattern that is generally followed by a woman is to gather enough food on one day to enable her to feed her family for three days. She then spends the remainder of her time resting in camp, doing embroidery, visiting other camps, or entertaining visitors. Each day that she is at the camp, food preparation (such as cooking, nut cracking, collecting firewood and fetching water) occupies only one to three hours of her day.

Hunters tend to work more frequently than the women gatherers, but their schedule is more uneven. A man may hunt avidly for a week or more and then do no hunting for several weeks. If they experience a run of bad luck, the men may discontinue hunting for a month or more. During their leisure periods the men engage in visiting, entertaining, and dancing. A trance-dance is the focus of ritual life among the Bushmen. Over 40 percent of the men in the Dobe group have received training as trance-performers and regularly enter trance states during the course of their all-night dances. In some of the camps the trance-dances are held as frequently as two or three times a week, and those who engage in the dance rarely go hunting the next day.

The Bushmen have developed a diet that serves them well. While no detailed medical studies have been made, malnutrition does not seem prevalent among the Bushmen, while it is widespread in other parts of Africa. Analysis of the Bushmen diet shows that each person consumes 2140 calories and 93.1 grams of protein per person per day. The recommended daily allowance for persons of the small size and stature but vigorous activity of the Bushmen is estimated at 1975 calories and 60 grams of protein per person per day. Actually the situation may normally be even more favorable for the !Kung. The analysis of their calories and protein was made during the third year of one of the worst droughts in South Africa's history: The agriculturalist and pastoralists of the region were having to forage on Bushmen land for their survival. Thus at the time of the study, the natural resources of the Dobe area were carrying a higher

The Bushman diet exceeds requirements and is perhaps superior to that of surrounding farming and herding peoples.

Bushmen.
(Lee, Anthro-Photo)

population than usual. Nevertheless, this added pressure on the land did not seem to have much of an adverse affect on the Bushmen (Lee 1968:37–38).

The Dobe Bushmen live well in the least productive area of the territory they held before being pushed out by others. It is probable that in the past the hunting-and-gathering pattern provided an even greater subsistance base. While the hunting activity of a hunting-and-gathering economy is usually emphasized, it appears that groups such as the Bushmen that subsist primarily on vegetable food have an easier time surviving than those hunting-and-gathering groups that subsist almost exclusively on hunting. Hunting serves as the dominant mode of subsistence only in the world's highest latitudes—60 or more degrees from the equator. In the Arctic there is almost a complete absence of edible plants, which means that hunting has to provide almost the entire subsistence base. As a result, peoples like the Eskimo face a more serious problem of survival than the Bushmen. Without a vegetable base, the Eskimo today have extreme difficulty surviving, because of the great irregularity of hunting success.

In historic times, the Eskimo had a much greater abundance

of seals, caribou, and whales, all of which were decimated by Westerners. When the hunters owned the world, their life was secure: Hunters and gatherers make use of the natural resources of their environment while modifying it little. Today the type of environment in which they live does sometimes make their lives more precarious. The difficulties that some native groups now face are primarily a result of their having been pushed into very marginal areas. In other cases, as with the Eskimo, Westerners have upset the delicate balance with nature that the hunters and gatherers had achieved.

A Short-Range Strategy: The Subanun of the Philippines

The impact of hunters and gatherers on the environment is difficult to measure, because the greatest changes they caused to the ecological setting occurred in quite distant prehistoric times. The discovery and use of fire may have led to the destruction of considerable vegetational areas and may have produced the grasslands of the world. The impact of an agricultural way of life on the environment is more easily discernible. In many areas of the world, the agriculturalists have removed or are removing forests. Rivers have been dammed and their courses changed. Irrigation systems crisscross the land. Grasslands have been broken by the steel plow. In each instance, the agriculturalists have had to weigh alternatives in their relations with the land. Their success depends upon both the short-range and long-range effects of decisions that are made. Each decision has far-reaching consequences. The Subanun are a people who have based their subsistence patterns on maximizing the immediate returns of their agricultural production, at the possible expense of the loss of their land in the long run.

> The Subanun have stressed short-run gains at the possible cost of long-term disaster.

The Subanun are slash-and-burn agriculturalists who live in the tropical rain forests of Zamoanga Peninsula on the island of Mindanao in the Philippines. In its natural state the tropical rain forest is radically different from the ecological setting needed for farming. As result the Subanun modify their ecosystem to make it suitable for their type of agriculture. The Subanun are not as extreme in their changes of the environment as some agricultural peoples. The wet-rice farmers of the Far East, for example, permanently replace the natural environment with a completely different kind of biotic world.

The world's slash-and-burn agriculturalists follow one of two general patterns of settlement. Some form nucleated villages

Bushmen in camp. (Shostak, Anthro-Photo)

with more or less permanent dwellings. Individual fields are dispersed around the village. Because slash-and-burn agriculture requires frequent clearing of new fields, the nucleated settlement pattern has a disadvantage. After a few years the farmland near the village has been used up, and individuals must go farther and farther away from the village to find new lands. This sometimes result in hours being spent each day walking to and from the fields. The Subanun follow a different pattern of settlement. It is one of clusters of several fields, with an individual family house located in each cluster. Each cluster of fields and a house is separated from other Subanun fields and houses by an area of tropical rain forest, so there are no nucleated villages.

The Subanun seem to apply the following rules in determining their settlement pattern: (*a*) They attempt to minimize the amount of wild vegatation between the fields of a cluster. As a result, a new field is cleared as close as possible to older fields in the cluster. (*b*) They attempt to minimize the house-to-field distance by building their house within the field. This pattern results in their constructing new houses frequently as new land is cleared. Yet the Subanun prefer rebuilding periodically to walking great distances to their fields daily. (*c*) They attempt to maximize the distances between houses. The Subanun prefer that their house be far enough away from any neighbor so that family conversations and arguments cannot be overheard (Frake 1962:56–57).

The Subanun settlement pattern is based on ecological considerations as well as the sociological consideration that relations with neighbors require that houses be built at a distance from one another. The ecological consideration most important to the Subanun is controlling animal pests with a minimum expenditure of time and energy; by building their house within the field itself, a family is able to keep close watch over its fields. This practice also reduces the need for building fences or a second field-house (used by some who follow the village settlement pattern when their fields are at great distances from the village), and reduces the travel time from house to field.

The Subanun consider these benefits to be of the utmost importance to them. Yet they may suffer in the future because of their faming and settlement patterns. The practice of clearing large areas of the tropical rain forest adjacent to previously cleared areas increases the probability of an ecological succession to grassland instead of forest. When large areas are cleared, the land cannot revert back to forest but remains permanently as grassland. If the land does not revert back to forest, the Subanun can no longer farm the land with their slash-and-burn technology; they would have to adopt plow agriculture. Thus, by emphasizing the short-run gains of easy pest control and convenient walking distances, the Subanun are permanently destroying the land they count on for their survival.

This account of the Subanun is based on their patterns of subsistence over a period of several years. The cultural ecologist Robert Netting (1971:15) has noted that when anthropological data on a society are limited to only a few years, the success of a particular subsistence strategy cannot be properly evaluated. It is possible that over time the Subanun will be able to make adjustments in their subsistence patterns, turning from the disastrous path they now appear to be taking.

Power and Environment:
The United Fruit Company in Costa Rica

The greatest changes in humankind's relationship to the environment have taken place with the Industrial Revolution. With the growth of industry and big business, the Western world, and in particular the United States, has developed what the economist Kenneth Boulding (1966) calls a *cowboy economy*. The cowboy metaphor refers to a reckless, exploitive philosophy toward the environment based on two premises: more resources are waiting just over the horizon, and nature has a boundless capacity to absorb garbage. These premises made some sense during frontier days. There was some validity in seeking rapid improvements in human welfare strictly through economic development, with little regard for what kind of growth or waste accompanied it. However, the cowboy economy has led to an

We have had a reckless, exploitive philosophy toward the environment.

increasing demand for more resources, which are now imported from underdeveloped nations. The following data give some indication of the extent of our exploitation: Of the metals already mined, refined, and put into use, there are in the United States 10 tons of steel, 300 pounds of copper, 300 pounds of lead, 200 pounds of zinc, and 40 pounds of tin for every man, woman, and child (Ehrlich, Ehrlich, and Holdren 1973:66).

The success of the cowboy economy in the United States and in some of the European countries has been possible only because of the disparity of power between the developed and the underdeveloped nations, resulting from the Industrial Revolution. The industrial nations have been able to gain their wealth by passing the real costs of exploiting the environment on to others, usually the underdeveloped countries. In such maneuvers, political and economic power become vital ingredients of the ecosystem. The strategies used by the United Fruit Company to cope with the problems of soil depletion and banana disease in the Central American republic of Costa Rica during the first half of the twentieth century illustrate how differences in power affect how people are able to cope with environmental problems.

At the turn of the century, bananas were considered an extremely high-risk crop. Unlike a small-scale society such as the Subanun, which is taking a risk in terms of subsistence, banana producers were faced with a financial risk. The United Fruit Company (now a subsidiary of United Brands), which controlled the banana industry in Costa Rica, began its operations with company stockholders experiencing the greatest financial risk. In time, the company was able to transfer most of this financial risk to small banana planters. As a result, the United Fruit Company was able to abandon vast areas of banana land and not lose money—in the sense that stockholders were still paid substantial dividends. On the other hand, small planters were faced with economic ruin, forced to abandon their small plots of land due to the same ecological factors that led to the company's abandonment of land—banana disease and soil depletion. The success of the United Fruit Company and the failure of the private planter is not explained by differences in the level of technology, as the bananas were farmed in the same manner by both the company and the planter. Instead, the success of the United Fruit Company is explained by significant differences in power, both economic and political, as well as differences in economic organization, which allowed the company to pursue different strategies from those available to the private planter.

Multinational corporations are able to utilize different strategies than the small farmer.

The Plantation. Banana production in Costa Rica began as a by-product of a railroad system initiated in the early 1870s to link the highlands with the east coast. The Gros Michel banana was planted in the eastern lowlands beginning in 1874 by one of the builders of the railroad, a North American, Minor C. Keith, in order to provide revenue for the railroad as it was being constructed (Simmonds 1959:314). In 1899 Keith merged his interests in Costa Rica and other Latin American countries with the Boston Fruit Company to form the United Fruit Company. The United Fruit Company became one of the most successful of the early United States-based multinational corporations. As multinational corporations developed, they took one of two forms: a market-oriented form or supply-oriented form. The market-oriented corporations sold mainly to host countries; these corporations emerged primarily in industrial nations. The supply-oriented corporations predominated in the less developed nations as the primary exploiter of the raw resources of the natural environment (Wilkins 1974:92). The United Fruit Company was a supply-oriented corporation.

The eastern lowland area known as Limón had neither been heavily populated nor seriously exploited by the Costa Ricans. The majority of Costa Ricans preferred the temperate climate of the central highlands to the hot, humid jungles of the lowlands. Because the highlanders lacked interest in Limón, the United Fruit Company was able to acquire large tracts of land in the lowlands from the government at very low prices. By 1913 the company owned almost 250,000 acres— roughly 2 percent of Costa Rica's entire land area—of which approximately 50,000 acres were planted in bananas (F. Adams 1914:170).

By a number of means the United Fruit Company was able to establish a monopoly over banana production in Costa Rica, in contrast to the situation in other countries, such as Jamaica or Mexico, where it faced competition from other fruit companies and local cooperatives. In 1932 there were 4,313,000 bunches of bananas exported from Costa Rica, and of that amount 4,100,000 were exported by the United Fruit Company (Kepner 1936:67). As a result of its monopoly in Limón, the United Fruit Company was able to obtain *de facto* economic and political control over the Costa Rican lowlands (Olien 1970:21–38). To a certain extent the company became a self-contained system, operating its own railroads, shipping fleet, hospitals, radio stations, company commissaries, schools, housing, police force, and a work crew of some 6500 persons (roughly 2 percent of Costa Rica's entire population.

The United Fruit Company gained control over the lowlands by eliminating competition.

Headquarters of the United Fruit Company in Puerto Limón, Costa Rica. (From F. U. Adams, *Conquest of the Tropics,* Doubleday, 1914)

The Changing Environment. As the anthropologists Eric R. Wolf and Sidney W. Mintz (1957:398–99) have noted, the modern commercial plantation is specialized for the production of a single crop. When this crop fails the plantation is faced with economic disaster; the United Fruit Company was such a plantation. It was geared exclusively for banana production. Faced with the failure of the banana crop in the eastern lowlands, the United Fruit Company completely abandoned its banana operations in Limón in 1942 (Olien 1973:270). However, prior to final abandonment of the area, the company did attempt to find means by which it could cope with the changing environment and remain in Limón.

Banana production in the tropics has always been risky, as the plant is susceptible to diseases, pests, chills, wind damage, droughts, and floods. The 1920s were a decade of particularly heavy flooding in Limón that affected the banana crop. The depression of 1929 also had its effect on production. However, the major reasons for the abandonment of the lowlands by the United Fruit Company seem to have been two types of environmental change: soil depletion and banana diseases. Since there were no technological innovations at the time that allowed for improved production, the company adapted to the environmental change by improving its mechanisms for purchasing.

The first areas of the lowlands to be utilized for banana production were considered ideal for large-scale planting. The coastal, alluvial, and gently sloping piedmont plains of the Ca-

The company's production was seriously affected by soil depletion and banana diseases.

United Fruit Company town in the Costa Rican lowlands. (From F. U. Adams, *Conquest of the Tropics,* Doubleday, 1914)

ribbean lowlands were near the port towns, so bananas could be moved by cart or mule from the farms to railroads and then to the docks in 24 hours or less. Rapid movement of cut bananas was desirable to prevent ripening (Jones and Morrison 1952:3).

Because the physical features of the environment were at first favorable to banana production, plants matured to full size in one year. Eventually, the heavy rainfall of the lowlands, coupled with banana production, began to deplete the humus and nitrogen in the soil. The banana plants exhausted the soil of newly cleared land in from 5 to 20 years in the areas favorable to banana production.

At the same time that some regions of Limón were decreasing in productivity due to soil depletion, banana diseases began to destroy the crops. The bananas were affected first and hardest by the Panama disease, a root disease that began attacking plants as early as 1890 in some areas (McKenney 1910:750). Then sigatoka, a leaf-spot disease, began destroying plants in 1938. Some areas were also affected by a bacterial wilt disease, moko, as well as by the *taltuza*, a rodent that devours the roots of the banana plant (May and Plaza 1958:86; Kepner and Soothill 1935:31). The effects of the Panama disease were especially disastrous. In 1913, the peak banana-exporting year in Limón, the company had almost 50,000 acres in banana production; by 1934 the acreage had been reduced to less than 4000. The number of stems (bunches) exported declined from 11 million in 1913 to a little over 4 million by 1932 (Kepner and Soothill 1935:52, 113).

Strategies for Adjusting to the Changing Environment. The effects of soil exhaustion and banana disease required adjustments by the company in order to maintain a supply of bananas for its markets in the United States and England. Unlike the subsistence agriculturalist, who raises crops in order to provide enough food for the survival of his family, the United Fruit Company was concerned primarily about paying the highest dividends possible to its stockholders. The dividends paid between 1899 and 1933 represented an average annual income of almost 18 percent on the initial investment (Kepner 1936:23–24). This orientation toward profits rather than subsistence resulted in the company pursuing a different set of strategies than those used by the subsistence agriculturalist for coping with the environmental problems. In general the strategy followed was to limit the risk to the company by passing the risk on to others, primarily the private planters. The company used three means to cope with the changing environment: (*a*) experimentation with other commerical crops as substitutes for bananas, (*b*) changes in land tenure, and (*c*) reorganization of marketing procedures.

At first the company attempted to adjust to the changing environment by utilizing other crops to replace the banana. It experimented with cacao trees,[3] *abacá* (a banana plant used in manufacturing hemp), pineapples, rubber trees, coconuts, balsa, and other crops. None proved as commercially successful as bananas, due to problems of disease, marketing, insects, and shipping.

The company tried to find an alternative crop.

As the banana diseases spread, the company found it more profitable to abandon, lease, or sell its banana lands to small farmers (often former employees) and to purchase its export crop from the private planters. As the lowland territory began to experience soil exhaustion, plant diseases, and pests, it produced poorer-quality fruit for export. By switching from producer to purchaser, the company escaped financial losses due to the deteriorating quality of the fruit, passing them on to the planters. Although in the early years of the century the company had hoped eventually to grow 80 percent of its bananas itself, by 1929 it was purchasing 75 percent of its bananas from private planters (Kepner and Soothill 1935:271–273).

The company switched from producer to purchaser.

Fortunately for United Fruit, the period during which it shifted roles from planter to purchaser coincided with a period of strong anti-imperialist feeling in Costa Rica (Jones 1967:68–71). Many of the small planters in the eastern lowlands were Costa Rican nationals who had recently migrated to the area. Under the guise of "helping" the growing number of these small planters, the company used public sentiment to obtain even greater governmental export tax concessions than it already had. The company laid down new rail spurs and branches to more distant areas for the planters, areas that had not previously been developed by the company because of their inferior soil quality and their distance from the ports. The company also sold the planters the already deteriorated banana lands that were close to the rail lines. The company promoted the belief that an individual could become more acquainted than the company with the intricate problems a particular patch of land presented and therefore could still produce bananas on small plots (Shouse 1938:29). By its strategy of changing from major producer to major purchaser, the company was able to withdraw completely from banana production in the eastern lowlands by 1942, without having suffered from the economic plight that endangered the survival of the region's small plant-

---

[3] An evergreen that produces pods from which chocolate is manufactured.

Small planter taking bananas to market. (Michael D. Olien)

ers. Once the company became primarily a purchaser, it began to pursue new strategies, to ensure that it would purchase only the best fruit available and that it would pay the lowest possible prices.

The company faced considerable competition in some banana regions of the world, such as Jamaica, and was forced to purchase fruit by the bunch,[4] regardless of the number of hands (clusters) of bananas the bunch had. This system of purchase was advantageous to the farmer whose land was deteriorating and whose plants were producing smaller bunches of fruit. In Costa Rica, the United Fruit Company faced no competition and was able to purchase fruit exclusively by the number of hands on a bunch.

As the purchaser, it was difficult for United Fruit to regulate the supply of bananas to meet the varying demands of the foreign markets. Thus, whenever the company needed to limit the amount of bananas to be shipped, it employed tactics to avoid purchasing fruit from the planters. The company signed contracts with planters to ensure a steady supply of fruit. Under the terms of the contract, the company agreed to purchase certain amounts of fruit periodically. Yet the contract included a number of escape clauses allowing the company to refrain from purchasing bananas. One of the most common tactics used by the company for rejecting fruit was claiming that bunches were bruised, too ripe, and so on—all legal reasons, if true. Some days as many as 50 percent of the bunches brought to the docks were rejected. The rejected fruit was thrown into the ocean, since once it had been cut and transported to the docks it was

The company developed strategies to purchase only the best fruit at the lowest prices.

---

[4] Each plant that develops to maturity from the rhizome, bears a single "bunch" of bananas. This bunch is made up of "hands" (clusters), each containing from 10 to 20 individual bananas, or "fingers" (Reynolds 1927:63).

too late for the planter to find another means of selling the perishable fruit.

United Fruit pursued other means of reducing the amount of fruit that it had to purchase. By the terms of its contract with each planter, the company was obligated to give the planter a "cutting down" (an order to cut a certain number of bunches) at least once every week. Frequently when it did not wish to purchase fruit ready to be harvested, it issued limited orders (Kepner and Soothill 1935:267). The company also avoided paying for unwanted fruit by ordering its trains not to stop at signal stops to load fruit that planters had already cut. Also, the company sometimes rejected fruit under contract on the grounds that at some time in the past the planter had not lived up to the contract. Less fruit than normal was rejected, of course, when the demand for bananas increased.

One might wonder why the planter signed a contract with the United Fruit Company in the first place. The answer lies in the fact that the company maintained a monopoly over bananas in Costa Rica. At first it attempted to obtain a monopoly over banana production. As a result of the banana disease and soil deterioration, it turned its efforts to securing a monopoly over banana exporting. After the company obtained control over all the lowland railroads, docks, and shipping lines, the planters were left with no other sources for the sale of their fruit. The transportation of the bananas to the dock would have been impossible if company railroads could not be used, even if there had been other buyers.

While the planters were generally unhappy with their contracts, they found it difficult to organize and negotiate as a group, because the company's contracts were planned so that they expired on different dates. Thus, at any one time, only a

Bananas being inspected on way to Puerto Limón. (From F. U. Adams, *Conquest of the Tropics*, Doubleday, 1914)

Bananas being fed into loading machines at the dock, Puerto Limón, Costa Rica. (From F. U. Adams, *Conquest of the Tropics*, 1914)

small group of planters would be negotiating with the company for new contracts.

By 1932 the company's position as exclusive purchaser was secured through contracts and by apparent collusion with government officials, bribery, and acts of outright terrorism. The company then reduced the purchase price of bananas by 60 percent, giving as its excuse the effects of the Depression. This reduction in payments to planters resulted in dividends for the company's stockholders, which declined by only 15 percent. At the same time, the lowland railroads, all under the company's control, raised their rates for transporting bananas to the docks. This increase hurt only the independent planters and not the company.

As United Fruit gained greater control over the eastern lowlands, it was able to demand numerous concessions from the Costa Rican government. In particular, the company was exempted from heavy export taxes on bananas. Less than one percent of Costa Rica's total revenue in 1928 came from banana export taxes, although bananas accounted for about 25 percent of its total exports. While the value of coffee exports (a product not controlled by the United Fruit Company) was not quite double the value of banana exports, the taxes collected on coffee exports were nearly seven times greater than the taxes collected on banana exports (Kepner and Soothill 1935:213).

Even if the United Fruit Company had not been able to pass on the financial burden of soil depletion and banana disease in

Costa Rica to the private planters, it still would not have lost money in the long run. As a multinational corporation it would have been able to recoup its losses in other banana-producing countries under its domination. By the Depression, the United Fruit Company controlled over 80 percent of the world banana industry.

The Powerful and the Powerless. Large corporations around the world have generally been as successful as the United Fruit Company in extracting from the environment what they wish and passing any losses on to the powerless. Bennett suggests as a general pattern in the ecological transition that power groups gain control of resources, and their needs set the pace of exploitation. The powerless are promised they will benefit by a higher standard of living. He notes (Bennett 1976:12), "At the time of writing, there is no end in sight to this process, although spreading pollution and increasing materials shortages suggest the possibility of a slowdown."

> Multinational corporations have been able to take from the environment and pass any lose on to the powerless.

The cowboy-economy approach has led to our current ecological crisis. The world economic system is characterized by overuse of resources, whether by powerful nations consuming too much or by powerless nations forced to overdraw their resources or starve, rather than by efforts to protect the resources through sustained-yield (or balanced) management and recycling. Tremendous overdraft on the base is in turn matched by tremendous waste and inefficiency in resource use. Ours is an economy in which goods are used once and then thrown away (E. N. Anderson 1974:267). Thus far we have been told by the powerholders that recycling and sustained-yield management are too costly. And what happens when ecological reforms *are* instituted? The cost of these reforms is passed on to the powerless. This pattern has been clearly recognized by the anthropologist E. N. Anderson, Jr. (1974:268), who notes:

> The real costs of production (and consumption) are passed off on the general public; on the poor and the politically weak; or on those conveniently voiceless unfortunates, the future generations— including today's young people, not old enough to be politically visible. This is classic exploitation: X gets the profits by forcing Y to pay the real costs. In modern industrial economy, the whole system runs on profits that simply would not exist if this did not happen. The corporations, nations, and individuals who benefit from wrecking the ecosystem can benefit only insofar as they can make others pay the cost.

In looking specifically at the United States, Anderson (1974: 269–270) makes some pertinent observations.

We can observe the real costs being passed off by the corporations on the poor of their own polity. Freeways, reservoirs, and stream-channeling (despite this so-called "flood control," floods have worsened) projects displace the poor or expose them to maximal danger, because, on the cost-benefit accounting, the poor are more vulnerable. Also very noteworthy is the fact that the most polluted areas of cities are the slums, if only because everyone not poor has moved out because of the pollution. The pollution problems of the rich nations would no doubt end in a week if the rich had to live where the poor now do, instead of residing in remote, tree-shaded suburbs and exurbs. In agriculture, the rich agribusiness corporations use the pesticides, but the poor farm workers, being the ones who actually contact them in the field, are the ones who die from them.

The Industrial Revolution has brought with it an acceleration of the ecological transition as human societies have developed new economies, organizations, and technologies to remake nature into a cultural phenomenon. Human survival in the future will depend upon whether human beings realize the damage their present cultural adaptations have done to the environment. Many ecologists and others concerned with humankind's relationships to the environment have warned that the cowboy-economy attitude toward nature will lead to insurmountable problems in the near future that could bring about the collapse of modern civilization.

A Lesson from the Past?

There are rather intersting parallels between our own society and that of the Classic Period Maya, although we must be cautious in looking at situations of the past and comparing them to present-day situations. The Maya were a preindustrial people, a fact which means that they did not experience the impact of the industrial revolution that has so altered the face of the modern earth. Likewise some of the major ecological crises faced by modern society, such as air and water pollution, were not major problems for the Maya. Nevertheless, there are rather striking similarities between the problems faced by the Maya just before their collapse and those facing us today.

The Maya offer an interesting parallel to our own ecological problems.

The Maya Collapse. About AD 900 the major ceremonial centers of the Maya living in the rain forests of Mexico and Guatemala collapsed and were abandoned, although small groups of people inhabited a number of the sites for many years after the fall. Archaeologists have been puzzled for many years as to why the great Maya civilization, which reached its height between AD

There was a widespread collapse of Mayan ceremonial centers about AD 900.

300 and AD 900, seems to have declined so rapidly. In the past a number of explanations were presented, but none of them were satisfactory. Suggested as reasons for the collapse were: an invasion of people from outside the area, earthquakes, climatic change, epidemics, hurricanes, overpopulation, overfarming, peasant revolts, civil war, the breakdown of long-distance trade systems. Archaeologists have found that none of these explanations by themselves provide an answer. Earthquakes seem especially unlikely as a contributing reason for collapse. Other factors, such as overpopulation and peasant unrest, cannot be easily dismissed.

In 1970 a number of Maya specialists met to discuss what was known about the Maya collapse.[5] The most important conclusion of the meeting was that an explanation of the collapse of the Maya social system can be achieved only through a clear understanding of the way in which the system operated. As a result, the participants reexamined what was known about Classic Maya civilization and produced a model of the collapse that concentrated less on the causes mentioned above and more on the stresses that may have been inherent in the very fabric of Classic Maya society just before its collapse (Culbert 1974:111–113). At least seven interrelated stresses seem to have been operating at the time of the rapid decline of Maya civilization. None of these stresses by itself was the cause of the collapse, but the seven stresses (and perhaps others) operating together were disastrous for the Maya. The seven stresses are as follows (Culbert 1974:113–115):

Several interrelated stresses may have caused the collapse of the Maya.

1. A rapid rise in population occurred during the last half of the Classic Period, from roughly AD 600 to AD 900. While the increased population contributed to the size of the work force, it would also have created greater demands for all commodities. If the elite of the society enjoyed better health, due to greater nutritional levels and better sanitation, they would have increased at a more rapid rate than the masses.
2. In areas of high population density such as the large ceremonial centers, agricultural production would have constituted another point of stress in the society. In some cases the overexpansion of slash-and-burn agriculture due to the increased population would have brought about greater deterioration of farming lands than had been the case previously. Most disastrous would have been a shortening of the fallow cycle, so that land would have been reworked too quickly and the yield would have been poorer.

[5] The results of this seminar were published in 1973 as *The Classic Maya Collapse*, edited by T. Patrick Culbert.

3. A decline in agricultural production would have overtaxed the Maya ability to respond to subsistence emergencies. Most peoples are faced with occasional crop losses. However in the case of the Maya, a growth in population and soil depletion would have increased the frequency and magnitude of agricultural emergencies. These agricultural emergencies in turn would have consumed already critical wealth and labor supplies and perhaps would have increased the competition between political units.

4. The agricultural problems and overpopulation would have resulted in malnutrition and disease. Malnutrition would have resulted from either a reduction in the total food supply or a decrease in a key ingredient in the diet, such as protein. Malnutrition in turn could have raised the rates of bacterial and parasitic diseases from levels that had been acceptable for continued population survival to levels that would have contributed to the decline of the population. Both malnutrition and disease would have affected the labor output of the masses doing the farming and other manual labor. Thus labor shortages would have increased.

5. Competition between political units would have increased as a result of increased population densities and shortages of land and other resources. In some cases the competition may have taken the form of warfare, but most of the competition might have been more subtle. For example, ceremonial centers may have vied for wealth and status, competing with one another in lavish ceremonial displays, including the construction of increasingly larger ceremonial centers.

While these extravagant displays may seem quite wasteful to us in terms of labor and resources, they would not have been seen in that light by the Maya. Ceremonialism was part of a system that had operated successfully for many centuries for the Maya. Since human societies show a great deal of conservatism, it might have been impossible for the Maya to change, even if the ceremonialism brought about stresses in the system.

More important than conservatism in maintaining a system is another element that enters into the relationships between large-scale systems and their environment: power. The Maya seem to have been dominated by self-serving power groups whose primary concern was maintaining their status and prestige. The traditional way in which status was demonstrated was in lavish display and the building of new or larger ceremonial centers.

6. Another stress in the society might have come from an increased investment in the elite group. Since the elite class might have been growing more rapidly than the rest of the society because of superior health conditions and better sanitation, they would have required larger investments simply to maintain the level they already held. To the increased cost of just maintaining the elite would have been added the costs of the competition between centers and the agricultural difficulties. These factors would have led to a rapid escalation of demands upon the masses who supported the elite. Since most of the demands involved some sort of labor (farming, crafts, or military service), the burden would have fallen on those less healthy, who were becoming a smaller percentage of the society as the elite grew at a more rapid rate.

7. The management capabilities of the elite would have been severely stressed. As the population and the economic system expanded, greater management needs would have developed. Difficulties in record keeping, tax collection, and the transmission and enforcement of decrees would have become more pronounced. It does not seem that the Maya made any effort to alter the managerial system that had been well suited for them when they formed a much smaller society.

The seven stresses that it has been hypothesized operated on the Maya system were such that a difficulty of one type could easily have spread to other parts of the system, thereby increasing the problem. Pressure or a minor crisis at any of a number of sensitive points could have caused a whole set of interconnected stresses to affect the system. The present state of archaeological knowledge suggests that the causes of the collapse of the Maya system may have been inherent in the system itself.

Systems theory has provided a better clue as to the nature of the Maya collapse than any single-cause theory, because systems analysis stresses the interrelationship of parts rather than the analysis of parts in isolation. There are many kinds of complex systems. Some are extremely stable, with self-correcting mechanisms that maintain an equilibrium. Others are growth systems, in which parts are connected by growth loops, where an increase in one part causes an increase in a second part, which in turn feeds back to cause further increase in the first, and so on. The Maya with their continual expansion represented a growth system. A characteristic of any growth system is that it cannot grow forever. If it did it would eventually absorb all the energy and matter in the universe. Instead, at some point either the growth system reaches equilibrium and the growth slows and stabilizes, or the system outgrows its resources and overshoots. When the second possibility occurs, many of the same cycles that caused growth reverse themselves, and the system declines. The Maya seem to be a rather striking example of overshoot. They expanded too rapidly and used their resources recklessly in an environment that required very careful techniques of conservation. According to Maya specialist T. Patrick Culbert (1974:116):

> The Maya outran their resource base, not only in terms of farming capabilities, but also in terms of organization capabilities, the ability to distribute goods, and the ability to use manpower efficiently. Growth cycles reversed, and the resource base was so badly overstrained that the cycle of decline for the Maya could not be stopped, short of the final resting point of near depopulation. The ravaged land offered little potential for repopulation, and the rain forest home of the Maya still remains an unpopulated wilderness, with only the silent remains of the vast temple centers to remind the visitor of its once great past.

The Maya may have expanded too rapidly and used their resources recklessly.

Problems in Our Own Growth System. Our society is also a growth system. Projections made by computer simulation indicate that we and the rest of the world are headed for the same fate as the Maya. Many of the same stresses that have been suggested as destroying Maya civilization are occurring in our modern society. The world's population is growing at an unprecedented rate. In the 200 years between 1650 and 1850, the world's population doubled, from 500 million to 1 billion. By 1930, within 80 years, the population had increased to 2 billion. Another doubling of the world's population has occurred in just 45 years. The population in 1975 was about 4 billion individuals, more than *eight times* the world population during the era of colonization (Ehrlich, Ehrlich, and Holdren 1973:19–21).

Just recently we have seen the stress to the agricultural system of the United States that was brought about by the sale of large quantities of grain to Russia. Almost every aspect of farming was directly or indirectly affected in ways the government had not foreseen. The price of agricultural products skyrocketed, affecting the nonfarming sector of society.

Our society also suffers from health problems, albeit different from those of the Maya. Perhaps our biggest health problem today is the cost of medical service. Our technology is more sophisticated than that of the Maya, so that many diseases can be cured, yet many people are unable to obtain the medical care that our technology is capable of providing, due to the high costs of the treatment. As a result of the cost of medical care, only the wealthy are able to obtain the best treatment. While members of the lower class are often aided by government assistance, their care is usually minimal. Their chances of surviving then become less than those of the wealthy. In many instances, the elderly suffer great hardships. With no income other than social security, they must rely upon life savings for survival. The middle class suffers almost as badly as the lower class, because they can no longer afford much of the care they really need and at the same time are heavily taxed to help pay for the medical care of the poor.

Interrelated with the health problem is the tremendous growth of a managerial class, the bureaucrats. The growth of bureaucracy has been part of the reason for the high cost of medical care. Government-sponsored health care programs require large numbers of public officials to run them. Most of the health care money then has to be spent to pay the salaries of the bureaucrats, and little is actually passed on to those desperately in need of care. The poor management of health care, and most other government programs, results in increased taxes for those unable to invest in tax shelters. All levels of government have grown at rates exceeding the general growth of the economy. In 1953 an average family paid 11.8 percent of its $5000 income in direct federal, state, and local taxes. By 1974 the same average family had an income of $13,000 and paid 23.4 percent in taxes. The cowboy-economy rationale is that individuals must consume and be wasteful so that the economy can expand forever. Will we overshoot as the Maya did? There is of course no way of predicting with any certainty. Fortunately we still have time to modify our system, if the means can be found and followed.

Kenneth Boulding, the economist who introduced the term *cowboy economy*, has suggested a rational alternative to our present type of economy, which he terms the *spaceman economy*, in harmony with the emerging concept that earth is a "spaceship," dependent entirely upon the finite resources it carries onboard. Consistent with the fact that our planet's resources are finite and that the biological processes that support human life are fragile, such an economy would be a nongrowth one in terms of the size of the human population, the quantity of the natural resources used, and humankind's impact on the biological environment. Emphasis would be on the quality of goods rather than on our current use-and-throw-away philosophy. Automobiles do not have to be built with planned rapid obsolescence. Likewise, much of what is now being wasted can be recycled (Ehrlich, Ehrlich, and Holdren 1973:260–261).

The spaceman economy may provide a rational way to deal with our natural resources.

It is apparent that humankind cannot continue to live as it has been. We must realize that our notion of human domination over the earth is a false one. The ecosystem of any part of the earth is a delicately balanced system in which each form plays its part. Humans cannot remove links in the chain of life and expect to survive. As human beings we need our environment more than it needs us.

Anthropology Vocabulary

cowboy economy	humor theory	Maya
ecological transition	!Kung Bushmen	slash-and-burn agriculture
environmental determinism	Limón	spaceman economy
		Subanun

Review Questions

1. What is meant by an environmental deterministic point of view? How does this point of view compare with the modern anthropological view of the relationship between culture and environment?
2. What are the implications of the subsistence patterns of the !Kung Bushmen for archaeologists attempting to understand the way of life in the Paleolithic and Mesolithic (3 million to 10,000 BC)?
3. What is the cowboy economy? What have been its effects on our environment? How are political and economic power related to this concept?
4. Is our society similar enough to the Classic Maya for the lessons of their collapse to be applicable to ourselves? In what important ways are we the same? How do we differ?

Recommended Reading

Bennett, John W., 1969, *Northern Plainsman: Adaptive Strategy and Agrarian Life.* Chicago: Aldine. An important synthesis of how cultural values affect the ecological approaches of different groups. The study deals with the adaptive strategies of Indians, ranchers, farmers, and Hutterites in western Canada throughout the twentieth century.

———, 1976, *The Ecological Transition: Cultural Anthropology and Human Adaptation.* New York: Pergamon Press. An interesting theoretical statement on the relationship of culture and environment. More difficult than the other works listed here, but well worth reading, especially for its use of systems analysis.

Ehrlich, R., Anne H. Ehrlich, and John P. Holdren, 1973, *Human Ecology: Problems and Solutions.* San Francisco: Freeman. A readable introduction to the ecological problems facing modern humans.

Netting, Robert McC., 1968, *Hill Farmers of Nigeria: Cultural Ecology of the Kof-yar of the Jos Plateau.* Seattle: University of Washington Press. A detailed description of the relationship of an African society to its environment.

_____, 1971, *The Ecological Approach in Cultural Study.* McCaleb Module in Anthropology. Reading, Mass.: Addison-Wesley. A short but important state-ment of the difference between cultural anthropology's new ecological ap-proach and its older interests in environment.

Rappaport, Roy A., 1967, *Pigs for the Ancestors: Ritual in the Ecology of a New Guinea People.* New Haven: Yale University Press. A classic monograph on the cultural and ecological utility of the pig feast in New Guinea.

Vayda, Andrew P., ed., 1969, *Environment and Cultural Behavior: Ecological Studies in Cultural Anthropology.* Garden City, N.Y.: Natural History Press. A collection of some of the most important articles on cultural ecology.

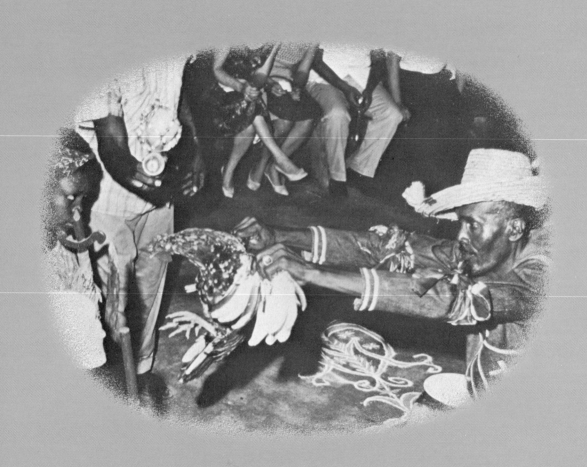

12

Religion, witchcraft, and the supernatural world

The origins of religion are to be found in shamanism.

Vodun represents a system of beliefs.

Anthropologists distinguish witchcraft from sorcery.

nthropological research has revealed that religion is a universal aspect of the human myth. All societies of the world have beliefs and behavior that can be classified as religious. However, the form of religious belief and ritual varies considerably from society to society, making a universal definition of religion for the anthropologist to devise. Most definitions of religion include a number of the following elements: Religion involves some belief in the supernatural; religion provides an explanation of life that people use to cope with the ultimate problems of life, such as death and evil; religion is an expression of what the members of a particular society consider to be sacred; and religion provides a moral code. The disagreements concerning a definition of religion result primarily over ideas and practices that might be included within the definition but which are not normally thought of as religious beliefs or behavior. Thus scholars have disagreed over distinctions between supernatural and natural, sacred and profane, and magic and religion. The first important controversy in anthropology concerning the nature of religion arose over its origin.

The Origin of Religion: Shamanism

The religions of other peoples were considered strange customs by Westerners of the Middle Ages. Because of the strong ethnocentrism of the Europeans, the Judeo-Christian tradition was considered the true religion, and other sets of belief were termed "superstitions." Evolutionary theory became the dominant theoretical framework for interpreting religion as anthropology developed as a discipline in the nineteenth century. It was generally assumed that the religions of non-Western peoples were representative of the earliest forms of belief.

Anthropologists believed that in the distant past humans had had no religious beliefs or practices. At some point in time humans discovered religion. How did it happen? There were many answers, all based on speculation. The theories all lacked the primary ingredient of modern cultural anthropology— ethnographic fact. None of the speculators on the origin of religion had ever conducted fieldwork among primitive peoples. As the British anthropologist E. E. Evans-Pritchard (1965:6) once noted:

> It is a remarkable fact that none of the anthropologists whose theories about primitive religion have been most influential had

In the nineteenth century, it was assumed that the religions of "primitive" peoples represented the earliest forms of religion.

ever been near a primitive people. It is as though a chemist had never thought it necessary to enter a laboratory. They had consequently to rely for their information on what European explorers, missionaries, administrators, and traders told them.

Many of the early descriptive accounts of non-Western societies that the nineteenth-century anthropologists relied upon were inaccurate. While some of the travelers and missionaries who wrote these accounts were able to speak a native language fluently, they usually did not understand the culture of the people they were writing about. Knowing the language of a people is merely one important prerequisite for understanding a people's religion. In addition there has to be an understanding of the entire belief system of which religious ideas are a part, or the native custom and ideas will be meaningless. Even though natives and missionaries may have used the same words, the connotations were often different. For example, on the Fiji Islands, in the Pacific, a missionary speaking of God would use the native term *ndina,* which to the missionary carried the connotation that all other gods were nonexistent. To the native Fijian, the term *ndina* meant that the god to which the missionary was referring was the only effective, reliable god; other gods might have been as effective at times but were not to be depended upon (Hocart 1914:46).

The travel accounts that the nineteenth-century anthropologist relied upon emphasized the sensational. Non-Western peoples were portrayed as strange, barbaric, mystical, monstrous, and superstitious. The nineteenth-century comparative method further distorted the facts by taking descriptions of specific religious beliefs and rituals out of context for comparative purposes. Each of these problems distorted the picture of "primitive" religions and confused attempts to discover the origin of religion.

At the turn of the century, three distinguished scholars, Emile Durkheim, Sigmund Freud, and James Frazer, offered views on the origin of religion based on available ethnographic data dealing with primitive societies. None of the three spent time living with non-Western peoples or observing first-hand their religious practices. These nineteenth-century scholars attempted to understand the origin of "primitive" religion through research in the libraries of Paris, Vienna, or London. They seemed to ask themselves, "If I were an Australian aborigine, how would I first discover religion?" Without any real first-hand knowledge of the aborigine, the scholars tried to construct a logical answer. Unfortunately the answers were just-so stories comparable to "How the Leopard Got His Spots" and were without validity as far as scientific replication was concerned. Reactions to the speculations about the origin of religion and the origin of language were similar: In both cases, the search for origins was abandoned. Since the turn of the century there have been few attempts to seriously consider the issue. However, recently an interesting, although controversial, theory for the origin of religion has been put forward by the anthropologist Weston La Barre.

La Barre's Theory of Shamanism. Today we know a great deal more about the past and about human beings than was known at the turn of the century, as a result of the extensive archaeological and ethnographic field research conducted during the past 50 years. Thus La Barre is able to base his argument concerning the origin of religion on facts that were unavailable when the earlier theories of religion were offered. At the same time, La Barre has had considerable field experience studying religious groups in a number of societies. Anthropologists have also recently learned considerably more about the wide use of various hallucinogens in prehistoric times and among a number of contemporary primitive peoples.

La Barre suggests that those speculating on the origin of religion have concentrated their attention on the wrong element, and states (1972:261) that "throughout history, extravagant attention has been paid to the nature of the gods, whose nature it is to be quite inaccessible to examination. The result of this preoccupation is that there is absolutely no consensus concerning the sacred." At the same time La Barre suggests that little attention has been paid to those who serve the gods, namely the prophets and shamans, who are quite available for study. La Barre hypothesizes that the alleged "supernatural" is only the human "subconscious." For La Barre the sacred world is merely psychological adaptations to inner anxieties. Some anxieties, such as those concerning death, are found in all societies. Other anxieties are created by variable and changing pressures in the particular cultures themselves, resulting in different sets of religious beliefs and practices.

According to La Barre, the archaeological record of the Upper Paleolithic and the Mesolithic suggests that the earliest religious functionaries were the *shamans* of hunting-and-gathering groups. The shaman is a part-time magicoreligious specialist who is adept at trance, divination, and curing. He derives his power directly from a supernatural source, usually through mystic experience, accompanied frequently by the use of hallucinogens.

La Barre believes that religion began with the shaman who frequently used hallucinogens.

The earliest known depiction of any religious functionary in the archaeological record was found at the southern French cave of Les Trois-Frères and dates from the Upper Paleolithic. It is a drawing that has been named the "Dancing Sorcerer" and is believed to have been a depiction of a shaman made by a Cro-Magnon artist. No gods are depicted in the hunter's art of the era preceding agriculture. Instead, the hunters and gatherers seem to have used the shaman as the group intermediary to the supernatural. The Dancing Sorcerer is not a supernatural being. He is clearly a human being dressed in animal skins and wearing an animal mask on his head.

Durkheim (1912) has suggested that certain kinds of religious notions are possible only after the growth of certain types of societies. The idea of a High God identified as "Emperor of the Universe" does not occur among the simple hunting-and-gathering societies, because their society is not a conquest state ruled by a strong leader. The Dancing Sorcerer, depicted only as a man dressed in animal skins, represents the focus of the Cro-Magnon hunter's small world. According to La Barre (1972:267), the shamanistic belief system accepts nature as it is, as opposed to large states which transform the environment. The shaman merely manages the changing elements in it, such as life and death, the weather, and so on.

> Durkheim has suggested that certain religious notions are possible only after certain kinds of societies appear.

Every religion derives from the beliefs and behaviors of identifiable humans. Each single item of religious information comes from the words of some inspired individual, whether shaman, prophet, or visionary; and the information is about that individual. In order to communicate with the supernatural, shamans use trance states and hallucinogens to reach the supernatural, but they are really only reaching their unconscious selves. As La Barre (1972:265) notes:

> Like the paranoid schizophrenic, the vatic [prophetic] personality pretends to be talking about the grandiose outside cosmic world, but he is really talking grandiosely in symbolic ways only about his narcissistic self and his inner world. The mystic pretends to discard his sensory self in order to meld with the cosmic Self; but in discarding his senses he abjures his only connection with the cosmos and re-encounters only himself. The realities he expounds are inside him, not outside in the world. He reveals only inner space, not outer space, in his revelation.

Anthropologists are discovering a wide use of hallucinogens among non-Western peoples for the purpose of obtaining the state in which they believe they are communicating with the supernatural world. The stimulants used include about half a dozen found in the Old World and 80 to 100 used in the New

World. Some of the most common include narcotic mushrooms, tobacco, peyote, coca, and native beers and wines. The archaeological evidence suggests that the shamanistic use of drugs diffused to the New World from the Old World either during the Upper Paleolithic or Mesolithic. Because hunting and gathering continued to be practiced by so many peoples of the New World, the shaman and the use of hallucinogens retained a central religious significance that persists even today among groups like the Yąnomamö, and hallucinogens continued to play a vital role even among peoples who developed more complex religions, such as the Aztec and the Maya. If anything, the emphasis on narcotics in the New World became greater than it ever had been in the Old World; thus the greater variety of hallucinogens.

Although new types of religions developed with the growth of new subsistence patterns such as agriculture and herding, La Barre (1972:269–70) believes that most religions are rooted in shamanistic beginnings. Among the Greek gods, for example, Poseidon carried the trident, which was symbolic of the shaman and was still being used as a symbol by shamans in Siberia as late as the eighteenth century. Joseph, who is believed to have lived during the sixteenth century BC, is an excellent example of the shaman of the Old Testament. At an early age he was already thought to have special powers as a dreamer. His brothers resented him because he dreamed that the entire family bowed down to him. In Genesis 37:20 the dreams are given as the primary reason Joseph's brothers attempted to do away with him and told their father that he had been slain by a wild beast. Many years later, Joseph gained great fame in Egypt as an interpreter of dreams and as a diviner. In the Old Testament, Moses and Aaron, who are believed to have lived during the thirteenth century BC, were represented as shamans at the court of the pharaoh. Moses turned his shaman's staff into a snake and back again; he afflicted Egypt with pestilence and plagues; he parted the Red Sea with his shaman-staff; and he struck water from a rock in the wilderness. According to La Barre, Moses is perhaps a compound of several traditional types of shamans. The God of Moses, Yahweh, seems to be the projection of Moses himself. The personalities are the same. The growth of Yahweh into Jehovah follows the hypothesis of Durkheim mentioned earlier. As Israel grew into a united kingdom under the Saul-David-Solomon line, the God of Moses was transformed into a Most High God, reflecting the new type of polity and the increased power of the secular ruler.

The history of religions other than the Judeo-Christian tradition also show evidence of shamanistic beginnings, with some form of hallucinogens playing an important role. Marijuana was already being used in China by the fifteenth century BC. The book *Rh-Ya* compiled at the time mentions the herb *Ma*, which is the marijuana plant. The book also describes the first shamanistic use of the plant recorded in writing. In India a variety of hallucinogens became a part of Hinduism, including marijuana, which was called the "heavenly guide," and a sacred hallucinogenic mushroom that was called *soma*. The *Rig-Veda* was an early Indian collection of hymns dating back to about the second millennium BC. One hundred and twenty hymns are devoted to the plant soma, which was deified (Wasson 1972a:201). Archaeological and linguistic evidence points to a much earlier origin of the soma in Siberia, where it continued to be used by shamans of hunting and reindeer-herding peoples up until recent historical times (Wasson 1972a:212–13). It is also believed that the "ambrosia" imbibed by the gods and heroes of ancient Greek mythology was also made from the same kind of hallucinogenic mushroom used in India and Siberia, known commonly as fly agaric (*Amanita muscaria*). It has also been suggested by John Allegro (1970) that Christianity began as a mushroom cult, but his evidence is not particularly convincing.

In the New World the use of hallucinogenic mushrooms was wide spread. The archaeological data suggest that from about AD 100 to 200 there was a shamanistic mushroom cult in western Mexico. The Aztecs and Maya both used the mushroom in their ceremonies. The Aztecs called the mushroom *teonanacatl*, "god's flesh." In central Mexico, frescoes with designs of mushrooms put the dating of its use at about AD 300. In highland Guatemala and southeastern Mexico, ancient evidence of the use of the sacred mushroom has been found, effigies (representations of various creatures) carved from stone dating as far back as 500 to 300 BC, with some dating back perhaps to 1000 BC. The effigies have a humanlike or animal face (often the jaguar) for a base, topped with a mushroom.

One of the earliest European accounts of the use of the mushroom is found in the Florentine Codex, written in the sixteenth century by Fray Bernardino de Sahagún, a Spanish missionary who was instrumental in recording a great deal of information about the Aztec culture shortly after conquest. According to Sahagún, the natives ate the mushrooms with honey and saw visions, felt a faintness of heart, and were provoked to lust.

> It is bitter and burns; it burns the throat. It makes one besotted; it deranges one, troubles one. It is a remedy for fever, for gout. Only

Hallucinogenic mushrooms were widely used throughout the New World.

two [or] three can be eaten. It saddens, depresses, troubles one; it makes one flee, frightens one, make one hide.

He who eats many of them sees many things which make him afraid, or make him laugh. He flees, hangs himself, hurls himself from a cliff, cries out, takes fright. [Sahagún 1963:130]

The Spanish friars found it very difficult to suppress the indigenous mushroom cults, although they were vehemently opposed to the use of the hallucinogenic mushroom.

The sacred mushrooms are still eaten by Indians in the isolated mountains and jungles of southern Mexico. In the remote mountain area of southern Mexico the mushrooms are used by the Mazatec Indians. Mushrooms are said to be gathered before sunrise by a female virgin and wrapped in leaves. In some villages the mushrooms are taken to the village church, where they are placed on the altar in a gourd bowl and left for some time. The Mazatec pick the mushrooms during the rainy season, June through August. This is considered the time for "consulting the mushroom." The native shaman prescribes the dose that each person takes. The mushroom is considered very dangerous, and there are a number of taboos surrounding its consumption. Those taking the mushroom assemble for an all-night session, in which the shaman watches carefully over those who have taken the hallucinogen. The participants are told not to leave the one-room hut in which they meet under any circumstances as long as the effect of the plant lasts. Afterwards the participants whisper among themselves about the events of the night (Wasson 1972b:195–196). Recently, Chol-speaking Maya Indians living near Palenque, an ancient Maya ceremonial center in the jungles of southern Mexico, were found still to practice the ritual use of hallucinogenic mushrooms (Furst 1972:x).

The theory presented by La Barre that religion originated in the Paleolithic with the shamans and their hallucinogens is recent. There are still a number of questions remaining that have not yet been answered by his theory, as well as some possible contradictory evidence. The well-known historian of religion, Mircea Eliade (1964:401) for one, has suggested that the use of narcotics and alcohol to trigger ecstatic trance states represents a fairly recent addition to the shamanist technique, a degeneration so to speak. On the other hand most of the linguistic, archaeological, historical, and ethnographic evidence tends to support the view that the widespread present-day use of botanical hallucinogens, fermented beverages, and tobacco in New World shamanism does in fact have remote origins in Old World Upper Paleolithic and Mesolithic shamanism and that the early Indian immigrants to the New World came culturally predisposed toward a conscious exploration of their new environment for hallucinogenic plants (Furst 1972:ix).

The Yąnomamö Shaman. One of the New World peoples who continue the practice of using hallucinogens are the Yąnomamö, described in Chapter 10. They view the relationship between humans and spirits as largely hostile. The shamans devote their time to casting spells on enemies and trying to get their own personal demons (called *hekura*) to help the people of their own village. These demons are believed to be tiny humanlike beings who dwell on rocks and mountains. The most successful shamans are those who can control the demons to such an extent that they live inside the shaman's chest. Magic and curing are the work of the shaman. Thus a great deal of his time is spent either causing or curing illness.

A man who wishes to become a shaman goes through a fairly simple rite involving fasting and abstinence from sexual relations. He sits in front of his house, eats very little, and spends most of his time in a contemplative stupor brought on by both hunger and hallucinogens. After several days he is considered to have entered into the world of the shaman and can begin causing or curing illness. After half of the men in a village will undergo this rite and become shamans. The obligatory chastity of the new shaman is very important, for it is believed that the hekura will not dwell in the chest of a novice shaman who con-

Yąnomamö shamans use hallucinogens today.

Yąnomamö shaman blowing *ebene*. (Chagnon, Anthro-Photo)

tinues to have sexual relationships. After a shaman has captured the hekura and they become acquainted with him, the shaman can resume sexual intercourse and they will not leave him (Chagnon 1968:52).

The shaman contacts the hekura by taking drugs. The hallucinogen is called *ebene* and is made from the moist inner bark of the ebene tree. The material collected is mixed with saliva and ashes and is placed on a hot piece of broken pottery so that the moisture will evaporate. The mixture is ground into powder as it dries. The men then blow the powder into one another's nostrils through a hollow cane tube about 3 feet long. An individual usually receives two doses of the drug, one in each nostril. Shortly after receiving the drug into his nostrils, the man vomits, gets watery eyes, and develops a runny nose. A great deal of the drug is actually lost in the nasal mucus that begins to run freely after the hallucinogen has been administered. Very quickly, the shaman has difficulty focusing his eyes and acts as if intoxicated. The Yąnomamö say that the ebene produces colored visions, especially, around the periphery of the visual field and it permits them to contact their hekura. The men chant to the hekura once the drug takes effect.

A few shamans are able to contact the spirit world merely by taking a pinch of the drug and inhaling from their fingers. Most, however, use the method of blowing the drug through a tube, While under the effect of the drug, the shaman prances back and forth in front of his house and chants to the hekura he attempts to control. The shaman tries to get the hekura to visit the villages of the enemies and cause sickness. If the shaman is curing he chants in front of the house of the patient, rubs the patient, and draws the evil spirit that is believed to be causing the illness to one of the extremities, such as an arm or leg. The shaman then sucks or pulls the evil spirit out and carries it away. Depending upon how the evil spirit was extracted, he will either vomit it or discard it. The traditional system of curing used by the Yąnomamö includes no medicines made from plants or animals. Instead, since all illness is thought to stem from supernatural ills, the curing relies exclusively on supernatural medicine (Chagnon 1968:23–24; 52).

The Growth of Priestly and Folk Religions

As many societies began to base their subsistence on agriculture during the Neolithic period in the Old World, the shamanistic practices of the hunting-and-gathering societies were replaced by new religious concepts that reflected the nature of the new forms of political, social, and economic organization within the societies. In many cases the shamans were replaced by priests.

Under certain conditions, farming economies made possible the rise of chiefdoms and states, and with these new forms of organization there emerged priests, who achieve their office differently than the shaman, and who play a different role in society. In particular, the priests serve to provide ideological support for the state, the rulers, and the elite. While it is possible that La Barre is correct in attributing the origin of religion to the shamans, most of religious ideology, the hierarchy of deities, and the ceremonial practices of the nations of antiquity must be attributed to the priests. In all likelihood, the great religions grew out of the early classic religions based on strong priesthoods.

Following the collapse of the Roman Empire, the rapid and extensive spread of monotheistic religions began. The Judeo-Christian tradition began in the eastern Mediterranean and spread into the western Mediterranean and then throughout Europe. Islam originated in western Arabia in the seventh century AD and spread across North Africa and eastward into Central Asia, India, Southeast Asia, and Indonesia. Hinduism, Buddhism, and Confucianism attracted large followers in the Far East. As these religions spread into areas controlled by "primitive" peoples, the monotheistic religions were often only partially or superficially adopted by the native people. Christianity and other major religions were introduced to native peoples during the era of colonialism, sometimes by force and sometimes peaceably.

While the orthodoxy of the major religions was perpetuated by the literati of each religion, many changes occurred in the beliefs and rituals of the religions at the local level—the tribe, the peasant village, and so on. A cultural anthropologist, Robert Redfield (1956), has made a useful distinction between the Great Tradition and the Little Tradition. *The Great Tradition* refers to the formal literary tradition of a civilization, which is maintained by the elite of the society and is generally found in the urban area. *The Little Tradition* refers to the culture of the rural villagers living within a civilization. Elements of the Great Tradition filter down to the village level, but in the process they are transformed or modified to fit the local peasant tradition. Thus, the village-level folk religion will not be the same as the orthodox religion of the city. The amount of difference varies ac-

In the evolution of society, the shamans were replaced by priests.

Redfield distinguished between the Great Tradition and the Little Tradition.

Catholic church fiesta celebrations, Mexico. (Michael D. Olien)

cording to a number of factors, such as the strength of native
tradition, the way in which the major religion was introduced,
and so on.

In some cases, folk religion represents a *reinterpretation*. The
famous anthropologist Melville Herskovits (1945:553) defined
reinterpretation as "the process by which old meanings are ascribed to new elements or by which new values change the cultural significance of old forms." For example, in the Catholic religion of the descendants of the Aztecs, Catholic saints were
equated with Aztec deities, and the Aztecs continued to worship
the saints in much the same manner as they had worshiped their
native gods. In other cases, folk religions result from a combination of native beliefs and those of a major religion. Herskovits
referred to this situation as *syncretism*. He defined syncretism as
a process whereby some of the old and new cultural elements

"are merged into a functioning unified entity of clear bi-cultural derivation" (Herskovits 1952:57). A new religion emerges out of the fusion of several existing religions in the case of syncretism. An excellent example of syncretism is the religion practiced by the peasants of Haiti known commonly as voodoo, a blend of Catholicism and native African religions.

Folk Religion as a System: Vodun in Haiti

The majority of the inhabitants of Haiti practice the Catholic religion. The elite of the society, many of whom live in the cities, practice the most orthodox form of Catholicism; or to use Redfield's term, they follow the Great Tradition. In the rural areas, the Haitian peasants also considers themselves to be Catholic and attend mass, but at the same time they follow a Little Tradition, voodoo, which in itself has incorporated many elements of Catholicism.

To those unfamiliar with voodoo, the term usually conjures up the notion of superstition concerned chiefly with charms or with putting spells on enemies. This is an incorrect assumption about voodoo. It is in fact a religion comprised of a system of beliefs and an organized set of rituals. The term *voodoo* itself is a part of our stereotype of the Haitian religion. It is the popularized version of the term used by the Haitian, which is *vodun*. The term *vodun* will be used here to emphasize the fact that we are discussing a folk religion and not superstition.

Roman Catholicism is the only approved religion in Haiti. No Protestant sect has ever gained great popularity. The Catholic Church dominates many aspects of Haitian life. Its churches are usually the most imposing buildings in the towns. The Catholic Church also directs much of the higher education of the country with state support and approval. The vodun religion is less visible. The state gives it no support, although from time to time a Haitian president has followed the practices of vodun, which are usually held in secret or at least without outsiders present, because of the continual pressures to stamp out vodun by the orthodox Church (Leyburn 1966:113–114).

Vodun had its origin in the colonial era of Haiti, during which time large numbers of slaves were imported from Africa. France enacted a strict code of laws for the planters to follow concerning the treatment of the slaves. This set of rules, issued by Louis XIV in 1685, was known as the *Code Noir* ("Black Code").

Example of a cultural reinterpretation. (Michael D. Olien)

Vodun is a folk religion.

Under these laws, all African slaves were supposed to be bap-
tized and receive instruction in the Catholic religion. However it
is doubtful that the instruction was ever extensive or meaningful to the transplanted African. The treatment of Africans at
the hands of the French planters was especially cruel. Because of
the high rate of death and the continually increasing demand for
more slaves, the number of Africans imported rose rapidly
throughout the colonial period. In a 12-year period (1779–1790)
shortly before the Haitian Revolution, almost a third of a million slaves were imported directly from Africa (Mintz 1972:8).
This steady arrival of new Africans throughout the colonial
period was important because it provided a continual reinforcement of African religious beliefs among the slaves.

The Code Noir also provided that assemblies of black slaves
were illegal unless it was for Catholic worship. Meetings of
slaves represented potential danger for the planters, because of
the possibility that a gathering might lead to a revolt of the
slaves against their masters. While meetings of slaves were illegal, they did occur, clandestinely. It is believed that in these
secret meetings the religious and magical rites of Africa were
kept alive. Between 1750 and 1790, vodunism began to take a
definite form, incorporating a number of elements from Islam as
well as African religions (Simpson 1945:35–36). In 1790 there
seem to have been few Catholic elements present in the
emerging folk religion.

The early leaders of the slave revolt against the planters were
practioners of vodun. The new cult became a rallying point for
the slaves, and their night meetings were now used not only to
practice vodun but to plot against the white planter. Many
blacks fought almost fanatically, because their leaders told
them that if they died they would come back to life in Africa.

In 1804 the blacks proclaimed their independence from
France, thus becoming the second independent republic of the
New World. Unlike the newly independent United States, Haiti
was made up almost exclusively of blacks. Considering the
world's prejudice against blacks at that time, it is not surprising
that Haiti found itself isolated. The United States did not recognize Haiti until 1862, when it was looking for a place to resettle
its own blacks. Without aid from the outside, Haiti's economy
stagnated. Its rich plantations had been destroyed during the
revolution; the ex-slaves became subsistence farmers. From
1805 until 1860 the Catholic Church withdrew from the rural
areas (Mintz 1972:9–10). Without the impact of the Catholic
Church, the African elements remained strong. The more or less

standardized vodun beliefs and rituals of 1790 became increasingly elaborate, and regional differentiations developed in the isolated rural areas. Today there is considerable variation in the beliefs and rituals practiced in the different parts of Haiti. Yet in many ways, vodun, in spite of the considerable variation, forms the national church of Haiti even today. Vodun was able to develop after the revolution because of the withdrawal of the Catholic Church. The blacks found themselves with no priesthood, with no written dogma, with no code, and with no missionaries. Thus vodun became the popular religion of the Haitians. Between 1915 and 1934, Haiti was occupied by the United States Marines. Considerable effort was exerted during that time to put an end to vodun. The past 50 years have seen some decline in the attraction of vodun, as well as the addition of greater Catholic elements; nevertheless, it has survived. Since there is considerable diversity in beliefs and rituals among vodun worshipers, beliefs found in one part of Haiti may not be shared by people in another part of the country. This situation makes it difficult to identify the primary beliefs and rituals. However, there are several elements that are widespread and form a core of vodun practice regardless of where it is practiced. They include the *loa*, the phenomenon of possession, the priests and priestesses, the twin cults, the role of the dead, and black magic. These elements will be examined in order to present at least a partial picture of the religion in terms of its beliefs and rituals.

The Loa. The most prominent figures in the realm of the sacred are the *loa*, or gods. Many loa are African deities who have been inherited through succeeding generations by the descendants of those who first brought them to Haiti. Other loa are indigenous to Haiti and have resulted from the deification of powerful ancestors. Some loa are widely known, others may be known to only a small number of individuals. The total number of loa in vodun runs in the hundreds. There are a number of contradictions in the beliefs of the followers of vodun as to the relationship of the loa and the Catholic saints. Many believe that at least some of the saints are loa and vice versa. Both saints and loa are thought to be intermediate between God and humans. God is considered to be too busy to listen to the pleas of humans, so the loa, most of whom are thought to live under the water, and the saints meet at the halfway point on the road between heaven and earth, and the loa relate the wishes of their human followers to the saints. The saints then return to God and report the

The loa are the most important sacred figures in vodun.

various appeals the humans have made to the loa, and God decides which requests to grant or refuse (Simpson 1945:38–39).

The worship of the loa is considered the essential purpose of vodun. The pantheon grows continually as new loa are added. Some are revealed and imposed upon members of a cult-group when one of the devotees is suddenly possessed by an unknown god who states his or her name, and demands to be worshiped. Others owe their existence to dreams. If an individual is visited by a loa during a dream, he or she hastens to make it the object of a cult. Sometimes an object found is kept as a talisman, and then, because it is unusual or because of the circumstances under which it was found, it may become a loa.

There are two main categories of loa: *rada* and *petro*. Most if not all Dahomean or Nigerian loa brought from Africa are placed in the rada loa group. The petro group also includes many African deities—but from other parts of Africa—as well as the majority of the loa native to Haiti. The two groups of loa are thought to have different characteristics. The petro loa are more violent and rough. They are specialists in magic, and all charms are thought to come under their control. A priest with too strong a preference for the petro loa will be thought to practice sorcery. The rada are considered more gentle.

The petro loa have the power to cure as well as cast spells. If a cure undertaken with the help of the rada loa is unsuccessful, a priest will advise that the patient use the petro and submit to rites, however frightening, which will bring about immediate cure. Whoever swears allegiance to the petro feels protected against any kind of witchcraft. He or she also expects to become prosperous, because the petro loa are givers of money. However, the price the petro claim for their favors is high. The Haitian considers that any transaction with the petro loa involves risk. A promise broken or a debt unpaid to a petro will get the client in serious trouble. Unlike the rada loa, the petro loa include in their numbers the "eaters of men" (devils). Those called "red-eyes" are without exception believed to be evil and cannibalistic. The most dreaded loa are automatically placed in the petro category.

As Durkheim's theory predicts, the supernatural society of the loa is almost the same as that of the Haitian peasant society which believes in it. The gods are all country people who share the tastes, habits, and passions of their followers. Like the peasants, they are fond of good living and are wily, lascivious, sensitive, jealous, and violent. They are capable of swearing, drinking too much, quarreling with other loa, and lying.

The worship of the loa is the main purpose of vodun.

There are two main categories of loa: rada and petro.

The peasants believe that the loa love them, protect them, and guard them. However, the good offices of the loa are never obtained without commitment. Whoever benefits from the loa must contract for definite obligations, the most important being sacrifices and offerings that have to be carried out at more or less regular intervals. To resist the will of a supernatural being is considered an act of rebellion. Such rebellion angers the loa. Supernatural punishments take many different forms, depending on the sex, character, and type of offended god. These considerations shape the justice meted out more than the nature or seriousness of the offense. Some loa are more severe than others. The loa who are worshiped by a particular family because they are ancestors of that family tend to be the most indulgent and show the greatest patience. Likewise, the more moderate loa punish gradually. They may start by sending a person a slight ailment, which will only become serious or fatal if the individual does not take the warning to heart. Madness and persistent bad luck are almost always attributed to supernatural punishment. It is also believed that the loa visit the sins of parents upon their children. The death of a child may be seen as the loa punishing the parent for some wrongdoing rather than as a result of any wrong behavior on the part of the child. Loa can also punish by showing indifference to their followers and withdrawing their protection. A person deserted by loa is considered to be at the mercy of his or her enemy's sorcery (Métraux 1972:86–99).

The loa make their desires known by possessing their devotees and speaking through them. This possession is one of the most widely publicized aspects of vodun, because it is primarily public, while other rites are carried out privately.

> Loa make their wishes known through possession.

Possession. Each follower of vodun has one or more important loa, but only one is considered his or her principal protector. Members of the vodun cult fall into four main categories: *hungans*, who are the vodun priests; *badjicans*, who are assistants to the priests; *serviteurs*, who are those who become possessed by the loa during ceremonies; and *fidèles*, who are the rank-and-file believers, who never become possessed at a ceremony. While northern Haiti may not be typical of the entire country, the percentage of peasants falling into each category gives at least a general idea of the number of individuals in each category. Less than 1 percent are priests, roughly 5 percent are assistants, 10 percent become possessed during ceremonies, and 85 percent are rank and file.

Most possession occurs following family ceremonies or at vodun dances. A person who is possessed is said to be "mounted" by a loa. The person becomes the "horse" of the god. A follower of vodun may come under the influence of a number of loa during a single ceremony or dance, one loa following another. It is believed that the first loa to enter a person constitutes that individual's chief loa and will be the leader of any deities subsequently possessing him or her (Herskovits 1971:146). It is also believed that each individual has two souls. The loa must drive out one of the souls in order to be able to enter the head of the individual. As the soul is driven out, people experience trembling and convulsions, which are considered the first stages of trance. People possessed experience a feeling of emptiness, as though they were fainting, once the soul has left. Their heads whirl and the calves of their legs tremble and they become instruments of the loa. From that point on in the trance, the peasant believes it is the god's personality that an individual expresses in both behavior and speech. Persons accustomed to possession are able to pass through these initial stages very rapidly and reach full trance. Those undergoing possession for the first time experience the wildest movements. The chaotic leaps and gestures of the newly possessed are said to be like the bucking of a wild horse who feels the weight of a rider on its back for the first time. The movements of an individual accustomed to trance are more passive. However, even among the possessed, behavior varies, because of the nature of the gods. The rada gods are more gentle to their mount, while the petro loa are said to rush into their mount with the violence of a hurricane. Possession may last a few seconds or many days (Métraux 1972:120–24). The Haitians make a very clear distinction between possession by loa, which is sought after and much desired, and possession by evil spirits, which is considered very frightening.

It is during possession that the loa communicate with their followers. Those assembled at the dances or ceremonies talk with the gods. At the same time the gods criticize the behavior of those who have acted improperly. In this way possession acts as a means of social control. The accused is ridiculed in public by an accuser who cannot be challenged, because the actions of the possessed who is doing the ridiculing are not thought to be his or her own but rather those of the possessing loa.

Possession serves as a form of social control.

The Hungans and Mambos. The priests of vodun are called *hungans* and the priestesses are called *mambos*. Each is the au-

Alter of a vodun sanctuary. (Alfred Métraux)

tonomous head of a sect or cult-group. There are no priests and priestesses who have authority over other priests and priestesses. However, some hungans and mambos enjoy great reputations and many clients, while others are little known and have only a small number of village followers. It is said that they vary in their "knowledge." *Knowledge* in this sense means supernatural insight and the power that is derived from this insight. The gift most prized in a priest is second sight, the ability to read people's thoughts and reply before being asked. Good priests and priestesses can perform the functions of priest, healer, soothsayer, exorcizer, organizer of public entertainments, and choirmaster. They are influential in politics and are often paid handsomely by public officials for their help. Besides possessing some supernatural power, the priest or priestess must also acquire a technical knowledge of vodun: he or she must know the names of the spirits, their various attributes, their emblems, their tastes, and the liturgies appropriate to the different kinds of ceremony (Métraux 1972:64).

The loa are not the only supernatural powers the hungans, mambos, and their followers must take into account. There are also the twins, who are considered extremely powerful, and the dead, who insist on sacrifices and offerings and are thought to exert a direct influence on the fate of the living.

The Twin Cult. Whether living or dead, twins are thought to be endowed with supernatural power that makes them exceptional beings. Any family that practices vodun and includes twins among its living members or in its ancestral line, must serve these twins with offerings and sacrifices. If a child is born with webbed feet, it is considered as a twin, because it is believed that the child has eaten its twin while in the womb. The child who follows twins immediately in order of birth is thought to have the power of both twins.

Twins are thought to have supernatural power.

It is normal for twins of this cult to hate each other. When twins are of different sexes it is believed the male prospers at the expense of the female. Twins have to be carefully supervised so that they do not harm one another. At meals they are distracted so that the parents can switch their plates, to enable each to eat the other's food. It is believed that this effort helps to restore a good relationship between the twins. They must also be treated exactly alike, so that jealousy can be avoided. Their clothes must be identical if they are of the same sex, their share of food must be equal, and praise must be divided evenly between them. Twin sisters must marry at the same time if at all possible. It is believed that even death does not break the bond between twins. The surviving twin puts aside a symbolic portion of whatever he or she eats or receives, as a present for the deceased.

Once a year, on the Day of Kings, on Christmas Day, or on the Saturday before Easter, whoever is related to twins must offer the twins a feast as a sacrifice, with the usual offering being a brown-skinned young goat and a speckled hen. The offering has to be equally divided between the twins. Taboos surrounding particular twins have to be scrupulously observed; for example, some will not eat a certain food, some require that their food be served only on a banana leaf, some cannot stand the sight of knives, forks, or spoons, and so on. Any mistake in the ritual may offend the twins and initiate the possibility of cruel vengeance. If the sacrifice is being performed for dead twins, food offerings are buried in three holes dug near the family house. If the meal is given for living twins, they eat first, until they have satisfied themselves; then the remainder of the sacrifice is served to the guests. Throughout the meal the twins are showered with attention (Métraux 1972:150–152). Some families with no known twins will celebrate because a vodun priest has divined that the family's unknown African ancestors included twins.

Twins are believed to have considerable ability to predict rain. Their ability to bring about an excellent harvest is considered greater than that of the loa or the dead, especially if the twins are promised offerings. Because they are capricious, the twins will do harm if they are not humored. Therefore it is believed that twins must be given whatever they ask for (Herskovits 1971:203–204).

The Cult of the Dead. In vodun belief, the dead rank second only to the loa. Some of the dead become loa, but even those who do not achieve this distinction must be shown respect. The dead are thought to be everywhere; they are the invisible living. They are thought to retain interest in this world and, like the loa, are capable of favoring or destroying its inhabitants (Simpson 1945:52).

The dead are almost as important as the loa.

The cult of the dead has greater Catholic influence than either the worship of the loa or the twin cult, although there are still a considerable number of African aspects in the belief and ritual of the cult of the dead. At the death of a peasant, the family must complete a series of ceremonies that are usually spread over several years. Most individuals plan carefully so that they will receive a proper funeral when they die. Some purchase a coffin while they are alive to ensure its suitability, others sell land to ensure that they will be enough money for a proper burial, and a few who are childless go so far as to adopt a child, just so there will be someone to pay for a funeral upon the death of the adoptive parents. Because the dead are so feared, even the most destitute peasant family will not hesitate to sacrifice its last bit of money or even go deeply into debt to ensure a proper funeral for one of its members.

If an individual who dies has undergone a vodun initiation, he or she will be under the protection of the loa. It is essential that this link between the individual and the loa be broken, or the loa will bring revenge on the living relatives. Therefore, a special ceremony requiring the hungan or mambo is supposed to take place immediately after death. With the priest's or priestess' help, the loa leaves the body of the corpse and frequently takes up residence immediately in some other person who has been appointed by the dead person as a spiritual heir. The newly possessed is expected to take over any obligations the dead person contracted with the loa.

The laying-out of the corpse involves a number of special procedures. The body is washed with special herbs, the nostrils and ears plugged with cotton, the mouth closed by means of a sling knotted on top of the head, the big toes tied together, the body and head shaved of all hair, the fingernails and toenails clipped, and the body dressed in new clothing with no buttons or pins. Placed in the coffin along with the corpse are a rosary, a scapulary, soap, a comb, a handkerchief, a pipe, face powder, and the hair and clippings that have been removed from the body.

The corpse is displayed in one of the rooms of the family's house. Someone is at its side at all times. Wailing continues throughout the night. In another room a group of individuals, mostly women, sing songs for the dead—both Church songs and songs created for the occasion. Outside the house, others gather to play games and tell stories. All of the games are entered into with enthusiasm, because the purpose of holding the wake is to amuse the dead person. The wake ends about five in the morning and the visitors return home, while the immediate family prepares for the funeral (Herskovits 1971:210–211).

The funeral follows the rites of the Catholic Church, varying primarily in the elaborateness of the ritual, according to the dead person's family's ability to pay. It is believed that the deceased must be taken from the house before dawn or another member of the family will die. Those carrying the coffin from the house take a devious route to the cemetery, trying to disorient the dead person by swift and subtle detours and changes in direction so that the deceased will be unable to find the way back home (Métraux 1972:250).

The family of the deceased lives in perpetual fear that the dead person will return following the burial. The fear is greatest during the first few days. The dead person is thought to be very lonely and obsessed by a desire to return and take with him or her those left behind. A novena, a nine-day period of prayers and devotion, is supposed to begin on the Saturday following the burial. At about eleven o'clock on the last night of the ritual, a special song follows the last prayer of the novena. This ritual is observed to drive the dead from the house. Refreshments are then served to those attending, many of whom stay through most of the night, playing games, telling stories, and singing (Herskovits 1971:213–214). On the following night, another ceremony is held and sacrifices are presented to other dead of the family.

The Haitians believe that a dead person will harass the living is they neglect him or her, if they do not wear mourning clothes, if they fail to remove the loa from his or her head, or if they do not provide a worthy burial place. If neglected, the deceased will appear in dreams and tell the family why he or she is unhappy. If they pay no attention to the dreams, the dead person will cause harm and even death to them. One who dies as a result of a dead person's vengeance comes back to warn his or her relatives that they must fulfill their obligations or they too will die (Métraux 1972:258).

Sorcery. Many of the elements found in the vodun religion, such as the loa and the dead, are also found in Haitian sorcery. The Haitians generally conceive of white magic, or "good" magic, as a part of their religion. Many of the ceremonies devoted to the loa include elements of "good," magic as does much of the curing practiced by the vodun priests and priestesses. Black magic—"bad" magic—or sorcery, is thought to be outside of religion, because it is practiced for evil purposes. Both the vodun priest and priestess and the sorcerer and sorceress are hungans and mambos. They have the same knowledge, but the sorcerer or sorceress is a hungan or mambo who puts this knowledge to evil purposes. The vodun priests and priestesses must know all of the techniques of sorcery, because much of their work involves counteracting these techniques. The sorcerer and sorceress obtain power from the evil loa. The gods of vodun priests are family gods whom the priests have inherited. They endow the priests with the knowledge that gives them control over the supernatural world. Sorcerers "buy" gods by making pacts with them, in order to gain power, although the power "purchased" is often at the price of eventual punishment (Herskovits 1971:224–225).

Priests and sorcerers both must make continual demonstrations of their powers, whether good or evil, in order to keep up their reputations. Those who are considered most effective attract large numbers clients and become both powerful and wealthy. Those whose cures or spells do not produce the desired effect soon lose clients. Many will not take a case if they think they will not be successful, for fear of damaging their reputation.

The evil powers that enter into the sorcery of Haiti are of both European and African derivation. From Europe has come the notion of the *démon* and the werewolf. The démon is a male and the werewolf is a female, usually an old woman. From Africa the sorcerer has taken the concept of the *baka,* an evil spirit actuated by a loa, which commonly takes the form of some animal when dealing misfortune. All the malignant powers of the belief system are thought to operate through the power of Lucifer and the Devil, who are conceived of as two separate beings. In addition, the cult of the dead, especially the concept of the *zombi,* contributes to the system of beliefs surrounding sorcery.

There are several types of baka. One type sends fatal illness or

Baka are evil spirits.

brings about accidental death. Another type stays at the house of its master or mistress, going forth only to procure riches for him or her by robbing others. Those of the second type are jealous spirits, who will ultimately destroy the members of their master's family, especially the children, if the master does not live up to the bargain made with them. Some Haitians believe that the baka are loa who change into these creatures from time to time or are animals who have been given power by the loa. They appear as small, bearded, humanlike figures with flaming eyes, or as cattle, horses, asses, goats, or dogs. Baka are often employed to guard buried money (Herskovits 1971:243–46). Démons are sometimes confused with baka, because it is believed that démons change into animals when they perform evil acts.

Werewolves are thought to make small children die by sucking their blood. The werewolf trait is thought to be frequently passed from mother to daughter. Certain loa are able to turn a woman into a werewolf as punishment for neglecting duties to the gods. In other cases, it is believed that the werewolf state derives from the penalty clause of a contract with a sorcerer or sorceress. It is the payoff for the advantages one enjoys as a result of having been given a powerful talisman by the sorcerer. The talisman brings luck, but because the sorcerer has "drugged" the object before giving it to the woman, it also has the power to turn her into a werewolf. At first the werewolf commits crimes without knowing it. Then gradually there is a realization of the transformation. When a werewolf has succeeded in killing a child, it is thought that she and her colleagues will go to the cemetery and dig up the corpse and eat it, after changing it into cod, herring, goat's meat, or pork. In some cases, cannibalism is not the werewolf's only motive for murder. It is believed the werewolf may kill a child because of an insult it suffered from the parents or that it may kill merely out of jealousy (Métraux 1972:300–304).

The *zombi* represents another category of spirits used in sorcery. The Haitian peasant believes that "unnatural" deaths are caused by sorcerers or sorceresses who may wish to use the dead person for evil purposes. If unnatural death is suspected, the family tries to take precautions in preparing the body for burial. Plants called *hoholi* are placed in the coffin with the body. It is believed that if the seeds placed in a dead person's coffin cannot all be counted before daylight, the sorcerer is unable to claim the body. The hoholi plants are said to contain so many seeds that when the sorcerer comes to take the dead person he or she is unable to count them all in time. A cross of pinewood made by

Zombis are thought to have died unnatural deaths and to be under the spell of a sorcerer.

the vodun priest or priestess to repel evil, is also put in the coffin. The body may be placed facing downward in the coffin, since it is believed that the discomfort of this position will cause the spirit of the dead person to avenge itself on the sorcerer who caused the death. Likewise, if the death is considered unnatural, the dead person is killed a second time by an injection of poison, stabbing with a dagger, strangulation, or a bullet fired in his or her temple. The person doing the second killing must stand behind the corpse in order not to become a substitute victim: It is believed that if the corpse sees this person, then the corpse, as slave of the sorcerer who killed him or her, will reveal the second killer's identity when ordered to do so by the sorcerer (Herskovits 1971:247–248; Métraux 1972:282).

If the victim of an unnatural death has not been protected by his or her family with the various rituals described above, the sorcerer or sorceress who killed that person will recover the body and use it as a zombi after the funeral. Deprived of the soul, which has already left its body, the zombi works for the sorcerer and will be able to return to its grave only when the time decreed by God for its natural death arrives, or if it is accidentally given salt. The sorcerer who controls the zombi can use it for many purposes. Sometimes a zombi will be transformed into a pig, sheep, or cow, and will then be killed and sold at market by the sorcerer. It is believed that zombi meat can be recognized by the fact that it boils rapidly and creates a great deal of white foam on the surface of a stew when it is cooked. Also, zombi meat sold as beef will turn as white as veal when cooked. One of the duties of a person's loa is to warn of the impending danger of eating such food unsuspectingly. One's arm becomes heavy and one shudders and continues to drop the piece of meat until one realizes it is a warning from the loa (Herskovits 1971:248–49).

Although the sorcerer brings the corpse back to life, the zombi is not completely like other humans. It moves, eats, hears what is said to it, even speaks, but has no memory or knowledge of its condition. The zombi is treated much like a beast of burden. The sorcerer or sorceress exploits it without mercy, making it work the fields, whipping it freely, and feeding it only a very meager, tasteless diet. The zombi is also used to steal the harvest of neighbors. It can be recognized by its absent-minded manner, its almost glassy eyes, and above all by the particular nasal twang of its voice. It remains docile as long as it is not given salt. A grain of salt can remove the spell and bring a zombi to consciousness, making it aware of its condition. Violent with rage and an uncontrollable desire for vengeance, the zombi will kill its master, destroy the master's property, and leave in search of its grave.

It is impossible to describe the richness of the beliefs and rituals of any religion in only a few pages, but this summary should at the very least dispel the image of vodun as nothing more than superstition and wild orgies. In doing fieldwork, the anthropologist learns that religious beliefs and practices, however strange in themselves, make sense to the people who practice them. They make sense because they are integrated into a system of knowledge by which the people view their entire universe, natural or supernatural. If some of the elements of vodun, such as the loa or possession, were removed, the religion probably would not make sense to the native either, unless adjustments could be made throughout the cultural system to compensate for the changes.

What is the Purpose of Vodun? Anthropologists believe that basic institutions such as religion must serve a purpose in the societies in which they are found, or they would not continue to be perpetuated in the cultural tradition. What purpose then, does vodun serve? First, simply because vodun is a religion it provides the peasants with an explanation of the universe and their place in it. Moreover, the anthropologist George Simpson (1945:55) believes that the vodun complex in its entirety, including sorcery, is an important institutional device for the release of aggressive impulses. The Haitian peasants' aggression, magical or otherwise, is seldom directed against those responsible for their impoverished plight, namely, the upper class of Haiti. Instead, aggression is directed at one's neighbors, and vodun functions as a means of coping with the problem they are thought to pose. Peasant children soon learn to be wary of neighbors, finding that their elders suspect the neighbors of causing many of the family's difficulties. Blaming misfortune on enemies near at hand and directing magic against them provides an opportunity for the release of aggressive impulses. The peasants feel they are at least doing something about their problems. This activity relieves tensions, even if there are no other results.

Vodun provides the Haitian peasant with an explanation of the universe and provides a channel for aggression.

Witchcraft and Sorcery

In the vodun belief system, emphasis is placed on the evil doings of the sorcerer. Other societies place the blame for evil doings or unnatural acts on witches. In Western culture the term *sorcerer*

Anthropologists interviewing Otomi Indian sorcerer, Mexico. (Michael D. Olien)

Zulu sorcerer curing patient. (Ewing Galloway)

and *witch* are frequently used interchangeably; however, anthropologists have found it useful to view each as a separate cultural category. The basic distinction between sorcerer and witch used by most anthropologists comes from the research conducted by E. E. Evans-Pritchard (1937) among the Zande people of Africa. The distinction they use has proven invaluable to anthropologists working in other societies. According to the Zande, a sorcerer achieves evil through the use of magic, while the witch achieves evil through some mystical power inherent in his or her personality, without the help of magic. From a scientist's point of view, there are no such things as witches, although there are accusations of witchcraft and there are people who are said to be witches. On the other hand, there are sorcerers, such as the vodun priests and priestesses, who can be observed using their magic. Sorcerers are thought to be ordinary humans; witches are not.

Sorcerers are thought to be ordinary humans; witches are not.

The anthropologist Philip Mayer (1970:47–48) has outlined some of the characteristics used to distinguish witches in a number of societies around the world:

1. Witches are almost always adults, very often women, and frequently belong to witch families. They often bear physical stigma such as a Devil's mark or a snake in the belly. They are often reserved, stingy, and quarellsome.
2. The misfortune that witches cause is often out of the ordinary.
3. Witches turn against their own neighbors and kin; they do not harm strangers or people living at a distance.
4. They usually work from envy, malice, or spite, against individuals, rather than in the pursuit of material gain. This is in contrast to the sorcerer, who frequently uses magic to become wealthy.
5. Witches always work in secret, especially at night.
6. Witches are not entirely human. The witch incorporates non-human power. In some cases, they are thought to change from human form into some other form while doing their evil.
7. Witches reverse all normal standards. They seem to delight in unnatural practices such as incest or bestiality. Witches eat their own children or dig up corpses. In Christian countries witches repeat prayers or even the whole Mass in reverse order.
8. Witchcraft is always immoral. At the very least, witches' behavior is socially disapproved; at worst, it inspires horror, like other practices that are thought to be unnatural.

Witches in a Mexican Village. The Valley of Mexico is one of the areas of the world where anthropologists discover individuals who are thought to be witches by members of the community. In the village of San Francisco Tecospa, not far from Mexico City, there are 800 Indians who still speak the language of and trace their ancestry from the ancient Aztecs. They also believe that witches live in their midst.

The ancient Aztecs believed in witches prior to the arrival of the Spanish conquerors. The *nahualli* were vampire witches who sucked the blood of children and frightened people at night. They had the power to transform themselves into animals, to fly, and to become invisible. It was believed that children born under certain calendar signs were fated to become nahualli. Aztec witches committed robbery and rape, first putting the occupants of a house into a trance. Witches traveled in groups in order to steal. Generally it was believed that one witch carried an image of the god Quetzalcoatl (the Feathered Serpent), while another witch carried the left forearm of a woman who had died in childbirth. When they arrived at the courtyard of a house, one witch would hit the soil and then hit the threshold of the house with the dead woman's forearm. With this act, the occupants of the house became drowsy or fainted. Some could hear and see what was happening but could neither move nor speak; others fell fast asleep (Madsen 1957:123).

The Spanish conquest of Mexico brought with it Catholicism and a sixteenth-century European notion of witches. It has been noted by Max Marwick (1970:14–15) that the European notion of witches at this time was rather unique. In most societies, witches personify evil in general, but in Renaissance European society, undergoing rapid change from feudalism, witchcraft became entangled in the new religious and political issues of the day. Witches were identified with heretics. In Europe, the moral indignation that already existed against witches was directed against those who failed to conform with official Christianity. It was in this context that European witchcraft acquired some of its distinctive features, the most important being the notion that witches had made pacts with the Devil.

Thus the motion of witches brought to the New World by the Spanish was somewhat different from that held by the Aztecs whom they conquered; yet on some points the similarities were striking. For example, a sixteenth-century European demonolatry document describes the witch's technique of putting people into a trance with the amputated hand of an executed criminal. The purpose of the trance was to enable the witch to rob a house. Other similarities between Spanish and Aztec beliefs in witches included the following: Witches possessed the power to transform themselves into animals; they could fly; they could harm by means of magical incantations; both sucked blood. The major differences concerned the source of a witch's power: The Aztecs believed people were born fated to develop supernatural power; the Spanish believed it was acquired as a result of a pact with the Devil. Another difference involved the material state of the witches: The Aztec witches were born destined to be poor, friendless, and unfortunate; Spanish witches, on the other hand, acquired riches, honor, and release from misery as a result of their pact with the Devil (Madsen 1957:130).

The Catholicism that was imposed on the Aztecs was only partially accepted. In some cases reinterpretation took place, in other cases a syncretism of the beliefs of the Aztecs and Catholi-

Both the Aztecs and the Spanish had notions of witches.

cism occurred. Today the descendants of the Aztecs living in San Francisco Tecospa consider themselves Catholic, but their form of Catholicism, like that of the rural Haitians, is not an orthodox one. The earlier Aztec belief in witches was reinforced by the belief in witches held by the Spanish. The modern Indians of Tecospa believe that there are two kinds of witches: *tlaciques* and *naguales*. A tlacique is a vampire witch who turns into a turkey or a buzzard in order to suck blood from humans; a nagual witch is one who can turn into an animal at will but does not suck blood. The nagual witch causes sickness through a variety of magical techniques.

The Indians believe that tlaciques suck human blood because they cannot eat meat. When they leave their houses at night to do evil, they light their way with a pot of fire. To avoid detection tlaciques either become invisible or put their victims into a deep sleep while sucking their blood. In spite of the fact that tlaciques transform themselves into other animals, they leave the marks of human teeth. The tlaciques are especially fond of the blood of newborn babies. When a child is born, the family places a cross formed with hatchets or knives in front of the door to keep out vampire witches. Many of the beliefs that the Indians hold about witches can be traced back to the Aztecs. They believe that witches are born destined to develop powers of witchcraft and that witches are fated to be poor, friendless, and unfortunate. They have accepted the Spanish belief that witches receive their supernatural powers from the Devil, but they reject the associated belief that witches make pacts with the Devil of their own free will in order to become wealthy (Madsen 1957:161).

The Tecospans tell a tale about a female vampire witch who lived in the village more than 50 years ago. As a young girl, she was fat, vivacious, and full of color. However, when she married, her husband did not allow her to go out alone at night, and she grew thin and pale and lacked energy. Everyone wondered why she had changed. Some blamed it on the husband's family, claiming they were not giving her enough food to eat. However, one day a friend told the husband that his wife was a tlacique and convinced him that he should observe her behavior for himself. The husband told the wife that he was leaving on a business trip. The wife appeared very excited. After pretending to leave, the husband hid in a nearby tree to observe:

> He heard her patting out tortillas and wondered what she was going to eat, because she had given all the food to him. After dark the door of his house opened and out flew a ball of fire. Later the ball of fire returned to the house. He saw his wife sit down at the table and pour a jar of hot blood into a bowl. Instead of using the

herb "epazote" to flavor her food she used human hair. Then she dipped the tortillas in the blood and ate until she drained every drop. After that meal her color came back and she was full of life again.

The next night her husband spied on her again and saw her take off her legs from the knees down and put them in the ashes under the comal [a clay griddle used for cooking] in the form of a cross. As soon as she finished doing this she left the house. Her husband came inside and burned up her legs. When she returned she couldn't find her legs and couldn't walk. Soon afterwards she died. [Madsen 1960:202–203]

While this witch supposedly lived in Tecospa over 50 years ago, the same kind of belief survives today. In the 1950s one of the most popular girls of Tecospa, who had jilted eight local suitors, announced her plans to marry a man from another village. Everyone was shocked, because they believed the man was a vampire witch. The girl did not know he was a tlacique (Madsen 1960:203). The people from Tecospa believe he occasionally comes to Tecospa to suck blood. His victims know he has sucked their blood because they can see his teeth marks on their bodies when they awaken the following morning (Madsen 1957:161).

Why Do People Believe in Witches? Why do accusations of witchcraft persist if there are no such things as witches? When routine responses alone do not give emotional satisfaction, the idea of witchcraft seems to be used as an explanation of events that are viewed as unnatural. Death and sickness create anxiety but can usually be dealt with through routine responses. For example, the routine response for death is a funeral; for illness, medical treatment. But when events run counter to the ordinary, witchcraft accusations may be invoked. Every culture defines what is unnatural differently, and as a result the circumstances under which a person is accused of being a witch will vary considerably. Among the Zande of Africa, death is considered unnatural unless the person is very old; all other deaths are explained as resulting from witchcraft (Mayer 1970:50).

Beliefs in witches also help to define more clearly the moral universe of a society. The witch is often the symbol of what is considered wrong in the society. Furthermore, the witch helps to preserve the belief system of the society. The anthropologist Philip Mayer (1970:53) has discussed how this operates:

> If you have cultivated your fields in the usual way, you may blame a witch for the failure of your crop, and so be saved from the thought that accepted farming techniques might be at fault. If your illness does not respond to treatment, you may blame a witch, and so be saved from doubting the worth of medical knowledge and

Witchcraft accusations occur when events run counter to the ordinary.

practice. The witch system can save other belief systems from being deluged with the blame which might otherwise often deservedly fall upon them. It gives a channel into which the blame can be turned more conveniently.

Witchcraft helps to account for sufferings that people cannot or will not explain otherwise, and it provides a pattern of action that sufferers can take when their misfortunes make them particularly uneasy. They can accuse someone of being a witch. The idea of witchcraft is also a force in relations. It can break up friendships, marriage, or even the community. It serves also as a banner under which people are able to hate, denounce, and even kill one another. The witch does not exist in his or her own right, rather it is society that creates the witch. Society decides on the characteristics of a witch and then pins this image on certain individuals (Mayer 1970:53–54).

Another important function of witchcraft is that it channels open hostility in small communities. Peasant communities or tribal villages are generally close-knit units of kin and neighbors where people live out their entire life. Witchcraft provides a means of channeling aggression to the supernatural, so that in most cases villagers do not have to engage in face-to-face confrontation. Several recent African studies suggest that as peasants and primitives move into cities and larger towns there is often an increase in tensions, accompanied by a decrease in the accusations of witchcraft. J. Clyde Mitchell (1965:201) has expressed the view that in the larger towns the preponderance of strangers, neither linked by kinship nor emotionally, makes it possible for hostility and opposition to be expressed quite openly rather than through use of supernatural rationales; and where tension between individuals arises, the typical urban solution is merely to move to another part of town or to another urban setting. In the rural village the peasant or primitive does not view moving away as an alternative and must rely on witchcraft accusations to reduce tensions.

Anthropologist Beatrice Whiting (1950:36–37) suggests that sorcery and witchcraft occur primarily in societies that lack formal procedures or judicial authorities to deal with crime and other kinds of offenses. Sorcery and witchcraft operate as forms of social control. Often in the absence of police and other full-time state officials, the only thing that prevents antisocial behavior is the fear of being called a witch or that others will seek vengeance through sorcery.

While Whiting's observation appears to be generally true cross-culturally, sorcery and witchcraft do exist in modern nations, including our own. If anything, there has recently been a marked increase in the number of individuals learning about

There has been increased interest in sorcery and satanism in our country.

sorcery and participating in satanism in our own country and in Europe. Edward J. Moody spent two years as a member of a satanic cult in San Francisco observing the rituals and behavior patterns of the group. He believes that although people from a variety of social classes and occupational backgrounds are attracted to satanism, many exhibit behavior identified in American culture as "pathological," such as homosexuality, sadomasochism, and transvestism. From psychological tests, extensive observations, and interviews, Moody found that nearly all of the members of the cult had a high level of general anxiety, related to low self-esteem and a feeling of inadequacy. The pattern appears to be related to intense interpersonal conflicts in the nuclear family during childhood. According to Moody (1977:429):

> Eighty-five percent of the group, the administrative and magical hierarchy of the church, reported that their childhood homes were split by alcoholism, divorce, or some other serious problem. Their adult lives were in turn marked by admitted failure in love, business, sexual, or social relationships. Before entering the group each member appeared to have been battered by failure in one or more of the areas mentioned, rejected or isolated by a society frightened by his increasingly bizarre and unpredictable behavior, and forced into a continuing struggle to comprehend or give meaning to his life situation.

Moody believes that individuals come to the satanic cults seeking help in solving problems that are beyond their abilities to cope with. For the most part the satanists can and do help these individuals, by providing them with a sense of power, a feeling of control, and an explanation for personal failure, inadequacy, and other difficulties. Thus it appears that sorcery and witchcraft fulfill not only certain social needs in societies but individual psychological needs as well.

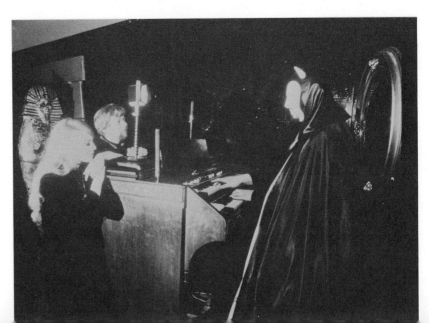

Satanic cult. (Low, Daily Telegraph, Woodfin Camp)

Nature and the Supernatural:
The Panare of Venezuela

In our society we separate that which we conceive of as "natural" and that which we believe is "supernatural," and generally do not view the two realm as interrelated. In other societies, such as the Panare of Venezuela, the two are more closely intertwined, to form a system of beliefs in which ideas about nature are reinforced by beliefs about the supernatural and vice versa. The discussion of the Panare which follows presents an example of another type of anthropological interests in beliefs, *cosmology*—the study of a people's view of the nature of the universe.

The Panare are a fairly isolated group of subsistence agriculturalists living not far from the Orinoco River. Recently they have studied by the anthropologist Jean-Paul Dumont. Most of the Panare settlements are located on the border of the conjunction between the tropical rain forest and the open savannas of the plains. Economic production is centered around gardening, a constant and regular source of food. However, the Panare are prouder of what is obtained through hunting, fishing, and collecting (Dumont 1976:41–43).

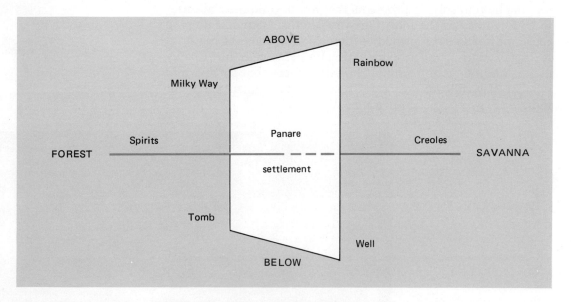

Figure 15 The conceptualization of Panare settlement position. (From Jean-Paul Dumont, *Under the Rainbow*, 1976, University of Texas Press.)

Among the supernatural beings of the Panare, the most important is Manataci, who appears in the form of a rainbow and is also a were-anaconda believed responsible for the present state of the world. It is believed that Manataci is responsible for the rains during the wet season and, by withholding the rain, also causes the drought that occurs during the dry season. When the water supply is exhausted in the dry season, it is necessary for the Panare to dig wells.

The Panare conceive of themselves as living between two waters.

The Panare envision a strong opposition between the forest and the savanna. The forest is believed to be inhabited by spirits, which are greatly feared by the Panare. No one dares venture into the forest after dark, for fear of meeting a spirit. The forest symbolizes the sacred world. The open savanna is not considered a fearful place. It represents the profane world. While the forest is dark, the savanna is a bright world of dazzling lights from the Creole towns. The Creole are the Hispanic, non-Indian people of the region. Figure 15 represents some of the basic oppositions in the Panare settlement pattern.

The Panare envision themselves as living between the forest and savanna.

According to Dumont's interpretation each Panare settlement is located conceptually at the intersection of one horizontal axis (where the savanna and the forest are opposed as nature and the supernatural) with a double vertical axis, depicting the opposition of life and death. The first vertical axis places the Panare settlement between two forms of death and opposes a rotting process (the natural decay of flesh and represented by human-made tombs) to a burning state (the souls of the Milky Way).

The Milky Way appears only during the dry seasons and is thought to consist of countless stars, each representing the burning soul of a dead Indian. The soul begins to glow in the sky only after all of the flesh of the corpse has decayed in the tomb in which it was buried (Dumont 1976:14). The second vertical axis places the Indians between two orders of life (supernatural and human) and opposes two types of water: One—the rainfall—is granted by the supernatural Manataci, a superior form of being, and is represented by the rainbow which appears only during the rainy season; the other, from the human-made well, merely insures physical survival during the dry season. Tombs are prepared for the rotting of the dead; wells are dug so that the living may not dry up (Dumont 1976:15).

The Panare see their culture as a mediator between the natural and the supernatural. Dumont (1976:15) notes:

Culture is the mediator between the natural and the supernatural.

> The locus of the settlement results conceptually from a confrontation between nature and supernature in which culture itself is the mediating agent. Supernatural causes, such as spirits for health

and Manataci for weather, bring about very natural consequences, such as death and drought. Through cultural manipulations (digging), religious in one case (the nonburied individuals would in turn become spirits), technological in the other one (the water shortage would lead to death), the settlement, a nexus of conceptual intersections asserts its own existence between these two orders: nature and supernature. At this cultural nexus, these two orders are rejected as alien; at the same time, they are mediated. This cultural mediation, strong dialectic of a frail balance, asserts itself as an order, that is, as the Panare order.

Where culture is unable to mediate nature and the supernatural, the results are disastrous. For example, the Panare believe that couples who have committed incest disrupt the order of the Panare universe. It is thought that the couple will escape into nature (the forest) and become incorporated into the supernatural (as spirits) if the culture does not serve as a mediator. On the other hand, if culture intervenes and the couple are clubbed to death and buried in tombs, they will rot naturally and their souls will glow supernaturally in the Milky Way. Harmony will have been restored. Mediation is considered a good thing, because everything happens according to the established order: The Corpses are manipulated according to cultural norms, and nature and the supernatural remain separated and under control. On the other hand, it is believed that the absence of mediation results in the collusion of nature with the supernatural, a situation that has serious consequences. For example, in the case of the incestuous couple, they would become spirits of the forest, and spirits are to be feared (Dumont 1976:99).

The Panare have integrated many oppositions and relationships into their belief systems. From the Panare point of view, the entire universe is divided into three planes: the natural, the supernatural, and the cultural. In their minds, they work diligently to keep the three planes separate, by using culture as mediator between the natural and the supernatural. The outsider's point of view would be, however, that the Panare's particular system of beliefs has integrated the entire universe into a single entity, Culture. In other words nature and the supernatural are all really part of the *same* cultural system.

The recent study of the Panare system of belief illustrates the direction that modern anthropology has taken in studying religion and the supernatural. Religious beliefs or beliefs about the supernatural are viewed within the context of the larger belief system. They help to explain beliefs about other aspects of the culture, such as the society's relationship to nature. At the same time, other kinds of beliefs in the system can aid the anthropologist in understanding the society's view of the supernatural.

The discussions of shamanism, vodun, witchcraft in Mexico, and the Panare have each emphasized a different aspect of the anthropological study of religion. Shamanism relates to the problem of the origin of religion, the relationships of hallucinogens to religious experience, and the anthropological interest in religious practitioners. The practice of vodun in Haiti illustrates how beliefs and practices in folk religion can be studied as integrated wholes. The description of sorcery and witchcraft shows the social importance of beliefs in witches and the functions of sorcery. The discussion of the Panare presents an example of cosmology. All of these areas taken together are relevant to the comparative study of religion. The features described for each society represent only one aspect of their total religious system and have been used only to illustrate a particular phenomenon studied by anthropologists. It should be kept in mind that all societies, not just the Panare, have cosmologies; most if not all societies have witches and sorcerers; and each religion has a definite framework of belief and practice. Besides being interested in beliefs, as discussed in this chapter, the anthropologist is also interested in the rituals that accompany the beliefs and the symbolic expression of beliefs.

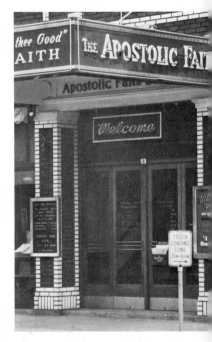

Modern religious sect. (Michael D. Olien)

What Is Religion?

At the beginning of the chapter it was noted that the considerable variation in religious beliefs and practice from society to society makes defining religion difficult. Having looked at some of the religious phenomena to which anthropologists devote their attention, it is possible to consider the definition of religion from a somewhat different perspective than that with which we began. Anthropologists, both professional and folk, have generally considered religion to be the belief in spiritual or supernatural beings or forces.

Recently, anthropologists have begun to shift the emphasis of their definition of religion from the supernatural to the recognition that religion is a cultural system. A definition of religion by the cultural anthropologist Clifford Geertz (1966:4) reflect this new emphasis in anthropology, "A religion is a system of symbols which acts to establish powerful, pervasive, and long-lasting moods and motivations in men by formulating conceptions of a general order of existence and clothing these con-

New definitions of religion emphasize that religion is a cultural system.

ceptions with such an aura of factuality that the moods and motivations seem uniquely realistic." This definition of religion not only emphasizes the importance of symbols, but it also helps to explain why people find their religion believable. A thorough anthropological study of a particular religious system must emphasize not only the beliefs that the people hold but also how these beliefs are symbolically expressed. Such a study requires an extensive understanding of the culture. The ethnographer cannot interpret the significance of a black candle placed on a vodun altar unless he knows what altars, candles, and the color black mean to the people engaged in the ritual.

In the nineteenth century, the human myth included only two kinds of religious beliefs and practices: the "true" religions of Westerners and the "superstitions" of non-Western peoples. During the twentieth century, anthropology has expanded the human myth, so that today we view all of the religions as "true," in the sense that all of the religions attempt to satisfy the same kinds of needs of their followers. Using the cultural relativistic approach, anthropologists have attempted to show that each religion is a valid approach to the kinds of questions that have haunted humans since at least the era of recorded history.

Anthropology Vocabulary

baka	Little Tradition	sorcery
cosmology	*loa*	syncretism
Creole	*mambo*	*teonanacatl*
cult of the dead	Manataci	*tlacique*
démon	Mazatec	twin cult
ebene	*nahualli*	vodun
Great Tradition	Panare	witchcraft
hallucinogens	reinterpretation	Yąnomamö
hekura	satanism	Zande
hungan	shaman	zombi

Review Questions

1. Do you accept La Barre's theory of the origin of religion? Does it explain the origin of the world religions?
2. Vodun is usually stereotyped in the movies. What are some of the misconceptions about this religion that movies usually promote? Do you believe that vodun in Haiti will increase or decrease in popularity? Why?

3. What distinction do anthropologists make between witches and sorcerers?
4. What is religion?

Recommended Reading

Castaneda, Carlos, 1968, *The Teachings of Don Juan: A Yaqui Way of Knowledge.* Berkeley: University of California Press.

———, 1971, *A Separate Reality: Further Conversations with Don Juan.* New York: Simon & Schuster.

———, 1972, *Journey to Ixtlan: The Lessons of Don Juan.* New York: Simon & Schuster.

———, 1974, *Tales of Power.* New York: Simon & Schuster. These four books by the anthropologist Castaneda describe his apprenticeship under a Yaqui shaman.

Evans-Pritchard, E. E., 1937, *Witchcraft, Oracles and Magic among the Azande.* Oxford: Oxford University Press. An important study that established a new approach to witchcraft and magic, in which their relationship to the belief system was stressed.

Lessa, William A., and Evon Z. Vogt, ed., 1971, *Reader in Comparative Religion: An Introduction to the Anthropology of Religion,* 3rd ed. New York: Macmillan. Generally considered the finest collection of articles on religion. A very wide range of topics is covered.

Malefijt, Annemarie de Waal, 1968, *Religion and Culture: An Introduction to Anthropology of Religion.* New York: Macmillan. A readable introduction to most of the topics that interest anthropologists about religion. Includes many of the theories about religion.

Marwick, Max, ed., 1970, *Witchcraft and Sorcery: Selected Readings.* Baltimore: Penguin Books. An excellent collection of articles and excerpts, covering a wide range of topics dealing with witchcraft and sorcery.

13

family ties and sex categories

Family organization takes many forms.

Other societies view kinship differently than we do.

Some societies recognize more than two sexes in humans.

families form the building blocks of larger societal units in almost all societies, yet anthropologists have had difficulty in learning how the family originated. Although the basis of the family is marriage, anthropologists have had difficulty defining *marriage* so that it has worldwide applicability. While kin ties beyond the immediate family are of little importance in most sectors of our society, anthropologists have found that such ties form the basis of organization in most of the world's societies. In each society there are different roles performed by each sex. Does this result from genetic differences between the sexes or cultural differences in the way the sexes are socialized? These and similar issues related to kinship have interested anthropologists since its inception. The anthropologist has learned that no single family or kinship form is "natural." Instead, there are many paths a society can take in forming units based on ties of kinship.

How Did the Family Originate?

Early travelers, missionaries, and colonial administrators were frequently shocked by the marriage arrangements they found in other societies. The forms of marriage and family found in the developed countries of Western civilization were taken to be the "correct" forms, and those of other societies were measured against these. Because these travelers understood so little of native customs, they were quick to report that some non-Western groups "lived like animals," that there were no real bonds of marriage, and that individuals merely paired off for random mating. When it was learned that in some societies where marriage was practiced, plural spouses were the rule, Westerners were often shocked, because of their ethnocentric point of view. Where males frequently had more than one wife, the members of the societies were characterized as sinful. Where females had several husbands, the society was viewed with abhorrence as abnormal, if not degenerate. In some cases, descriptions of primitive families were repetitions of hearsay going back to the classical writers. It was on this kind of inadequate observation of the "primitive" family and marriage that the nineteenth-century evolutionists built their theories of how the family originated and how it evolved.

The nineteenth-century evolutionists based their hypotheses about how the family originated on poor information.

One of the earliest publications on the origin of the family was *Das Mutterrecht* (*Mother-Right*), published by Johann Bachofen, a Swiss jurist, in 1861. Bachofen was one of the first to hypothesize a series of evolutionary stages in marriage and the family.

His controversial theory was that in the first human societies there were no rules of marriage, only random promiscuity. Males were sexually competitive and tyrannical, and females submissive. He further claimed that women invented marriage by stressing their *Mutterecht*, or mother-right, since they knew who their children were, even if the males did not. This was the beginning of *matriarchy*, a form of family organization in which females dominated. Descent was traced through a line of related females. Bachofen believed that once marriage was established, fathers came to know who their children were and began to exert their father-right. Thus *patriarchy* was established. Society was once again dominated by men, through whom descent was traced.

In the year that Bachofen published his theory, an English lawyer, Sir Henry Sumner Maine, published a different evolutionary scheme in his *Ancient Law*. Maine believed that marriage and the family began in the primitive horde when people limited sexual relations to recognized pairs and that in this earliest form of marriage and family, the male was dominant. Maine was convinced that patriarchy and not matriarchy was the most primitive family arrangement. Controversy raged throughout the last half of the nineteenth century over which form was the earliest, matriarchy or patriarchy. Most writers of the time seemed to accept some form of Bachofen's theory rather than Maine's.

In general, most evolutionary schemes of the era had as their first stage, sexual promiscuity. This stage was followed by family forms that traced descent through the females. Some theorists also believed the society was dominated not only socially by females but politically as well. The notion of society being dominated politically by women goes back to Greek mythology, which told of a race of warlike women known as Amazons, who made slaves out of captured men. Their queen was killed by Hercules. The Amazons were mentioned by Herodotus and later writers. During the era of exploration the Spanish reported a South American Indian myth about a tribe of female warriors very similar to those of the Greek legend. In the nineteenth century the Europeans still believed that such female-dominated societies existed.

The third stage in most of the evolutionary schemes of marriage and the family was the patriarchal family, ruled by males. The fourth and final stage in the evolutionary sequence was the monogamous family of Europe and the United States.

By the twentieth century, the speculation of the armchair anthropologists concerning the origin of the family was aban-

SIR HENRY MAINE, K.C.S.I.
Born 1822. Died February 3, 1888

Henry Maine.
(The Granger Collection)

doned for fieldwork. Once in the field, anthropologists realized the rich diversity of family forms and marriage that existed among the societies of the world. The archaeological record provides very little insight into the beginnings of the family or marriage. Therefore anthropological interest has switched from speculation on origins to studying the diversity of social forms found in living and historically known groups.

The Ties That Bind:
Marriage

The stereotype of marriage in our own society involves a wedding, in which one man and one woman are brought together to form the nucleus of a family. However millions of people around the world consider themselves married who have never wed. Because our popular view of marriage is too narrow to apply to societies different from our own, professional anthropologists have found it necessary to develop definitions of marriage that have greater cross-cultural utility. Regardless of the society, marriage seems to include the following elements: (*a*) It is a socially legitimate sexual union (*b*) it begins with some type of public announcement; (*c*) it is undertaken with some idea of permanence; and (*d*) it assumes some sort of reciprocal obligations between spouses and between the spouses and their future children (Stephens 1963).

Sexual unions occur in all societies, but only some are recognized as legitimate in the eyes of the members of the society. In our own society a civil or religious ceremony constitutes legitimate marriage. A man and a woman who have lived together for a number of years are considered, in at least some states, to have a common-law marriage. Any other sexual unions are considered illicit. The socially legitimate sexual unions in a modern society are carefully stated in codes of law. Anthropologists studying other societies cannot predict in advance what will be considered legitimate sexual unions. The anthropologist must learn what is considered legitimate and what is not, according to the rules of society. For example, in traditional China, a man's wife was clearly distinguished from his concubine; in Mexico and other modern societies, a man's wife is seen as socially legitimate, while his mistress is not.

In most Western societies, marriage begins with a public announcement that is called a wedding. For those attending, the wedding marks a clear-cut transition in status for the man and woman being married. The wedding has made their sexual

Weddings are not the only ritual of marriage.

union a socially approved one. All societies have some type of public announcement to mark the changed positions of the man and woman being married. Anthropologists must learn what is considered the public announcement of marriage in the societies they study. In our society, if one noticed an unmarried man and an unmarried woman in a restaurant together, no significance would be attached to the event. In some societies, however, the eating of food together in public is a public announcement of marriage, and the sexual union of a couple who have done so will be considered socially legitimate. In parts of India, the tying of a thread around the wrists of a male and female is considered a public announcement of their marriage. From that time on, the members of the society consider this couple married.

In some societies where weddings occur, the wedding is not the public announcement of marriage. On San Andros Island in the Bahamas, when a young man wishes to marry he must purchase a gold ring and obtain a document notarized by a government official of his intentions to marry a particular girl. The young man then presents the ring and the document to the girl's mother, and she then displays them to the villagers. The presentation of the ring and document mark the public announcement that creates a socially legitimate sexual union. Since the girl's mother has a signed document stating the man's intentions, it is believed that the man cannot change his mind from that point on, or he could be imprisoned for breech of promise. The couple begins living together, often in the mother's house, with the approval of the community. The actual wedding is anticlimactic and may not occur for a number of years as it may take the young man that long to build a house for himself and his wife. A wedding usually occurs once the couple have a place of their own. During the years between the presentation of the ring and document and the actual marriage, the couple may have produced several children. The children are considered legitimate, because the couple's sexual union prior to the wedding had social approval (Otterbein 1966).

A third aspect of marriage is that it is entered into with some idea of permanence. Fleeting sexual encounters, which occur in most societies, are not considered marriages. In our own society the wedding vows state that a man and a woman will remain married until "death do us part." In some Catholic countries this vow is taken literally, and husband and wife remain together their entire lives. In other countries the same vow may be taken, but eventually the marriage may end in divorce. Even though divorce occurs, however, the marriages are entered into with the idea that they will be permanent. The idea of permanence is relative. In some tribal societies, a marriage ceases when one or the other spouse sets the belongings of the mate outside their dwelling. Marriage is entered into with the idea that it is a permanent bond, unlike illicit sexual relations, which are never considered permanent.

Finally there has to be some understanding of the obligations inherent in marriage. In all societies there is a notion of obligations between spouses and between their children. In some societies a male also has obligations to his bride's parents: He is expected to work for them for a certain length of time in order to compensate them for her loss. In tribal societies marriage is an arrangement between two kin groups rather than between two individuals. Where the children of the marriage will belong to only one of the kin groups, the other kin group is often compensated for their loss. For example, the kin group of the male may be obligated to provide the female's kin group with six head of cattle. Part of this payment may be for the female, but often it is for the children she will produce, who will become members of her husband's kin group. If the woman is barren or dies before producing children, her kin group has not lived up to its side of the marriage contract and must either return the cattle, a thing which is often difficult or impossible to do, or send a substitute female to be the new wife.

Although there is great variation in the forms of marriage found throughout the world, anthropologists have created categories that allow them to classify most marriages into one of four major types. These categories reflect the anthropologist's view of humankind. The categories do not always coincide with the way the people of a particular society may think about their forms of marriage. The anthropologist uses etic forms of classification when making cross-cultural comparisons. In doing fieldwork in a specific society the anthropologist would attempt to learn how the people themselves think about marriage, the emic approach. Basically all marriages can be divided into *monogamy*, marriage between one man and one woman, and *polygamy*, marriage between plural spouses.

Monogamy. If all of the marriages in the world were listed and then tabulated, the vast majority would be classified as monogamous. In most societies, if not all, monogamy is the prevalent, but not the only, form of marriage. In some societies, such as our own, it is the only form of marriage allowed by law, but there are reports of polygamy, usually involving a male with more than one spouse. In some cases in our society, polygamy results

Marriages are either monogamous or polygamous.

from a legal technicality—persons have thought they were legally divorced from a former spouse when actually they were not; more commonly, the polygamous individual is maintaining two or more families at the same time, almost always without the plural spouses knowing of each other's existence. Only one of these marriages is legal; the others have no legal existence. Monogamy was not always the only form of marriage allowed in the United States. During the mid-1800s some members of the Church of Jesus Christ of Latter-Day Saints, commonly known as Mormons, practiced a form of plural marriage in which a male has two or more wives, termed *polygyny*. The church outlawed the practice of polygyny in 1890, after the Supreme Court of the United States ruled the practice illegal. A small group of Mormons wishing to maintain the custom of polygyny crossed the border and settled in northern Mexico.

In societies other than our own, monogamy may be the most common form of marriage; however, other forms are also considered acceptable. In many societies polygyny is not the most frequent form of marriage, but it may be the most preferred—it is generally the form of marriage which gives the male the greatest amount of prestige.

It is possible to distinguish several subtypes of monogamy. In societies such as our own where the incidence of divorce is very high, the term *serial monogamy* has been applied. Where serial monogamy is practiced, an individual has only one spouse at a time. However, an individual may be married to two or more different spouses during his or her life span.

In a few societies a rather unique form of monogamy has been reported. This form is called *brother-sister marriage*. The discovery of brother-sister marriage in a few non-Western societies shocked many Westerners, who considered it a violation of a basic incest taboo. However in the world view of the ancient Egyptians, Hawaiians, and the Inca, the custom was considered a necessity and was not viewed as repugnant. To understand the rationale of the custom, it should be noted that the practice was not followed by all members of the society. Not every male married his sister. In fact the practice was limited only to certain members of those societies in which the king or pharaoh was considered divine. In such societies it was believed that the divine ruler's marriage to a commoner would lessen his divinity. The ruler's sister was considered the least mortal of all of the females in the society. In Egypt, brother-sister marriage was practiced by the rulers of the Ptolemy Dynasty, which began in 306 BC, when one of Alexander the Great's generals (Ptolemy) assumed the position of king of Egypt. The dynasty ended in 30 BC

Brother-sister marriages occurred only where the ruler was thought to have supernatural powers.

with the death of Cleopatra, who had married her 12-year-old brother but had later had him murdered because of her interest in Julius Caesar. Following the demise of the Ptolemies, Egypt was ruled by the Romans. During that period of Egyptian history, brother-sister marriage became more widespread, as a means of keeping property within wealthy families.

On the island of Hawaii, the king, or paramount chief, was thought to be divine, and it was believed that he was born with sacred powers (*mana*). The mana was potentially of great danger to those of lower rank. As a result, a number of taboos surrounded the paramount chief: It was prohibited for a person's shadow to fall on the chief's house, back, robe, or any other of his possessions; it was prohibited to pass through his door, climb the stockade surrounding his house, put a racing canoe in the water before him, or wear his robe or other clothing; it was required that everyone kneel while he ate; it was prohibited to appear in his presence with wet clothing or with mud on one's head. In general the commoners could not touch anything that had been used by the chief. The ground on which the chief walked became charged with mana and was avoided by others. The chief was always preceded by heralds, who warned of his coming so that the commoners could prepare themselves. Given all the taboos surrounding the chief, the mana he possessed was a potential hazard to any woman he might marry. Only his sister was thought to possess enough mana of her own to make a marriage with the chief possible (Sahlins 1958:20–21).

Among the Inca of Peru the last few emperors considered themselves divine descendants of the sun. As a result, these rulers married their sisters, to perpetuate the divinity within the royal line. Nobles were allowed to marry half-sisters. Commoners could marry no one more closely related than a first cousin. Although the ruler's sister was his only socially sanctioned wife, the emperor did maintain a large number of concubines (Mason 1957:151–52).

Polygamy. Plural marriage can be divided into three major subtypes: polygyny, polyandry, and group marriage. Of these three, *polygyny*, the marriage of a man to two or more women at the same time, is by far the most frequent form. In a sample of 862 societies, 16 percent allowed only monogamy, 83 percent allowed polygyny, and less than 1 percent allowed polyandry or group marriage (Murdock 1967). Frequently where polygyny is practiced, a man will marry women who are sisters. This form of polygyny is called *sororal polygyny*. While women in our soci-

Polygyny is the most frequent form of plural marriage.

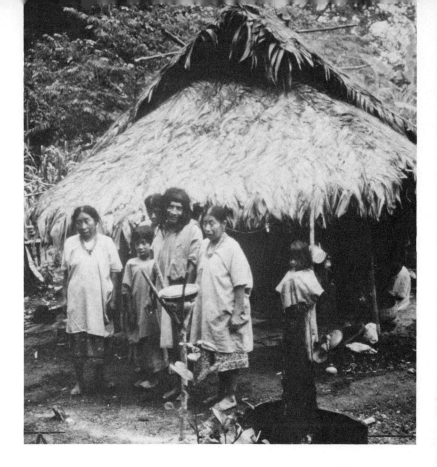

Polygynous Lacandon Maya
family, Mexico. (Jaroslaw T.
Petryshyn)

ety are usually appalled at the idea of sharing their husband
with their sister, the same is not true in many other societies.
Sisters sharing the same husband are able to cooperate with one
another more easily than can wives who are not related to one
another. The form of polygyny in which a man marries women
who are not sisters is called *nonsororal polygyny*. There is often a
great deal of hostility and competition between wives for the
attention of the husband in this form of polygyny. Typically in a
nonsororal situation, each wife will have her own dwelling, do
her own cooking and other chores, and raise her own children.
The husband can pursue a policy of divide and conquer in order
to have his demands met. He can play one wife against another.
This is more difficult to do in societies practicing sororal polygyny, because the wives are sisters and have grown up
together in the same kin group and so are better able to cooperate with each other in pressuring their husband to meet their demands.

A second form of polygamy, found in only a few societies of the
world, is known as *polyandry*. It is the marriage of a woman to
two or more men at the same time. The best known cases of

Polyandry occurs in only a
few societies.

polyandry occur among some of the people living in the Himalayas of South Asia and among some of the Eskimo. It must be
remembered that in societies where polyandry exists, most of
the marriages in the society are monogamous. A common
type of polyandry is the marriage of a woman to two or more
men who are brothers (to each other, not to the woman). This
variety of polyandry is known as *fraternal polyandry*. In some
cases the polyandrous marriage is a temporary arrangement,
in which an older brother is sharing his wife with a younger
brother until he is able to find a wife of his own, at which point
the two brothers will each be involved in a monogamous marriage. At other times the marriage arrangement is a permanent
one, and the brothers remain married to the same wife throughout their lifetimes. While it has been hypothesized that polyandry is caused by a sex ratio imbalance created by female *infanticide* (the killing of an infant), this does not seem to be the case,
and in fact some polyandrous societies have more females
than males.

A third form of polygamy is called *group marriage*. It is the
marriage of several women to several men at the same time. The
notion of group marriage seems derived from the stereotype of
the primitive horde held by the nineteenth-century evolutionists. Group marriage was seen by some evolutionists as an

Group marriage was once
thought to be wide-
spread; actually it is
found in only a few so-
cieties.

Members of a hippie commune. (Winston, EPA)

Commune family life.
(Conklin, Monkmeyer)

early stage in the evolution of the family, slightly more advanced than promiscuity. While it was once thought to be a common type of marriage arrangement among primitive peoples, ethnographic research has shown that it is actually quite rare. In a few cases its occurrence has been a result of relatively recent devolution, where the impact of the Western world has been so disastrous to a primitive group that their entire social system has been disrupted. This seems to have been the case with a few tribal peoples in the jungles of South America. A small group of individuals move about together, cooperating for their survival with apparently no formal pairing off of individuals within the group. Another example of group marriage is found in the Himalayas, among peoples who practice fraternal polyandry. In some cases where several brothers are married to the same wife, they will acquire additional wives who are shared by all of the brothers. This form of group marriage has been called *polygynandry* and can be defined as fraternal polyandry with multiple wives. Perhaps another example of group marriage is found in our own society. Some of the hippie communes are organized on the principle of group marriage. The entire group living together thinks of itself as a family. Some communes do not allow the permanent pairing off of mates. These come closest to true group marriage.

The cultural anthropologist Gerald D. Berreman (1975), who has done considerable research among polyandrous peoples in the western Himalyas of India, makes an important point that should be kept in mind in discussing any type of marriage. The types must never be thought of as rigid, since they are anthropological constructs. In each society there is usually more than one type of marriage practiced. Secondly the form of any given fam-

The form of a family can change over time.

ily can change over time. For example, in a polyandrous society several brothers may marry one wife. At this point in its developmental cycle, the family would be classified as fraternal polyandrous. After a few years the brothers may add another wife, thus creating a situation of a group marriage, specifically polygynandry. Later it is possible that the older brothers may die, leaving one brother and several wives, a polygynous situation. If some of the wives die, the family may eventually be made up of only the brother and one wife, in which case the family would now be classified as monogamous.

Some societies have customs of remarriage when a spouse dies. The two most common are the *sororate* and the *levirate*. The sororate is the marriage of a man to his deceased wife's sister. The sororate is a means of fulfilling the marriage contract between kin groups. If the male's group has given the female's kin group presents, her sister will be substituted for her if she dies before providing her husband's kin group with offspring. The levirate is the marriage of a woman to her deceased husband's brother. It represents one way of providing for widows in primitive societies and is usually practiced in societies where the woman lives with her husband after marriage and all of his brothers and their wives. When the husband dies, the woman is able to stay in what has become her home, looking after her children, who are considered part of her husband's descent line. One of the brothers merely assumes responsibility for the woman.

Not all societies have means of caring for widows. For example, in traditional India the devoted wife was supposed to throw herself on her dead husband's funeral pyre and be cremated along with him. Technically, then, there were not supposed to be any widows. But there were some wives who did not join their husbands as they were being cremated. For these women there was no place in the traditional society. They were hated by their husband's kin because they did not show the proper respect for him after he died, and they were shunned by their own kin because they brought shame to them as a result of their behavior. Often the only alternative for these women was to leave the traditional way of life and migrate to the cities where they ended up as maids or prostitutes.

Types of Families. Family forms can be divided into two major types: *nuclear* and *composite*. The nuclear family is the type of family most common in our own society and consists of a husband and wife and their children. The nuclear family is considered the building block of all family forms. During an individual's lifetime, he or she will normally belong to at least two

Families may be nuclear or composite.

White, middle-class American nuclear family. (Forsyth, Monkmeyer)

different nuclear families. An individual is born into a nuclear family, called the *family of orientation,* in which the person holds the position of child within the family. As the individual matures, he or she will normally marry and have children, forming a new nuclear family, known as the *family of procreation,* in which the individual now holds the position of parent in the family. In the United States the families of orientation and procreation are quite separate. They live under different roofs and even in different communities. If a married couple must live with one or the other set of parents, it is considered an undesirable arrangement and is usually viewed as temporary. In other societies there is great continuity between generations, so that parents will encourage children to stay with them even after the children have married. This results in a type of composite family known as the *extended family.* The extended family in its most common form involves three generations of kin living together: parents, their children, and the families of their children. If the parents die, their children may remain together, often with several brothers heading the household. This form of extended family, which involves the joining of two or more siblings' families, is known as the *joint family.*

Perhaps the most familiar example of the extended family is found in traditional China, beginning several thousand years ago and continuing until after the formation of the Republic of China in 1912. Some Chinese households contained as many as 200 persons. The oldest male of the family acted as the head of the household and directed family functions for everyone living with him. The elder male and his wife were shown great respect by members of the family, and his word was law. Not all

Chinese families were organized thus during the feudal era: The extended family was characteristic primarily of the wealthy gentry class. These families stayed together in order to preserve the wealth of the extended family. A joint family was usually formed upon the death of the elder male, with several brothers heading the family. Although it was highly advantageous to hold the family property intact, in time the joint families tended to divide into separate nuclear families, primarily because of the conflicts that developed between the wives of the brothers (Freedman 1958:21).

The extended family was much less common among the Chinese peasantry. Parents held little or no land. Therefore they had nothing to pass on to their children, and as a result were able to command little of the respect that the elder of a gentry extended family obtained from his children. In the peasant family, children moved out of the household and formed their own family of procreation at the time of marriage. If in later years the elderly peasant parents had to live with one of their children, they were considered a burden, since they were no longer productive members of the family.

Another form of extended family, found in modern societies, is known as the *matrifocal*, or mother-oriented, family. The matrifocal family generally consists of three successive generations of related females living together. This type of family is also characterized by the absence of permanent adult male members. A typical matrifocal family includes a woman, her daughter, and her daughter's children. However there is considerable variation, so that many matrifocal families also include some of the following female relatives: aunts, nieces, cousins, sisters, or grandmothers. The matrifocal family is widespread, being found primarily among blacks of the lower economic sector in a number of nonprimitive societies. While there is a high incidence of this type of family among blacks, it is found among other ethnic groups as well.

In the United States the lower-class black matrifocal family has been stigmatized by sociologists as "broken" or "disorganized." However this is an ethnocentric point of view on the part of those sociologists, who consider the white middle-class nuclear family as the only proper form of family organization. Some social scientists have hypothesized that African matrilineal descent (descent traced through a female line) accounts for the matrifocal family, because it was familiar to some of the blacks who were brought to the United States as slaves. This seems unlikely, as males play an important role in matrilineal descent. Others have tried to explain the matrifocal family as stemming from the days of slavery, when slave families were split apart and members of the family were sold to different planations. This reasoning may have some value in explaining contemporary matrifocal families, but other forces must be operating to perpetuate this form of family today.

In modern field studies, anthropologists have learned that the matrifocal family exists because it has survival value in situations of poverty, especially in those situations where the males of the lower sector are more economically marginal than the females. The females form the stable core of the family. They may either marry or have lovers, but the arrangements often do not last. The functions normally performed by a nuclear family can be performed by women of several generations living together. The mother may be too elderly to work, so the daughter is the member of the family most likely to be employed. However she would not be able to work if there were no one to watch her children. By living with her mother, she has close kin who will be responsible for her children when she is not at home. Husbands and boyfriends occasionally supplement the family income when they are able, as do unmarried males of the third generation still living at home. Women of matrifocal families often consider marriage a risk to themselves and their children because of the unstable position of the black male. Marriage is also seen as a threat to the durability of their kin group. Even if a man and woman sets up temporary housekeeping arrangements out of necessity, they continue to maintain very strong social ties with their own kin. Within the matrifocal family, the woman is able to maintain control over her children. The economic insecurity of the black male, and the availability of welfare in many modern societies for the female-child unit, make it difficult for an unemployed black husband-father to compete with a woman's kin for authority and for control over her children (Stack 1977:272).

Anthropologist Carol Stack (1974:115) has suggested that the matrifocal family is not a "family" in the traditional sense but rather a network of people who may sleep in different houses and take their meals in still other houses, yet which has continuity over time. The boundaries of this network expand and contract as members are added and leave.

Polygamy represents the other major type of composite family. It can be divided into two subtypes: polyandry, in which the family is composed of a female with multiple husbands; and polygyny, in which the family is composed of a male with multiple wives.

Generally there is a curvilinear relationship between family

The matrifocal family represents an adaptation to poverty where males are in a worse economic position than females.

and level of societal development. In simple hunting-and-gathering societies, the independent family is very important and the frequency of extended families is very low. There is a rise in the frequency of extended families in agricultural settings. In more complex urban-industrial societies, the frequency of extended families declines (Pasternak 1976:88).

Tracing Descent

The nuclear family forms the basis for more extensive kin ties that are determined by various patterns of descent. The particular kind, or kinds, of descent traced in a society form the basis for larger kinship networks or groupings. When anthropologists began to study other societies they quickly learned that kin ties, or descent, provided the organizing principle for a great deal of the behavior and beliefs of each society. In many primitive societies there is little distinction between political group, the religious group, the economic group, and the social group. They are all the same. It is the kin group that fulfills all these functions. The elder of the kin group deals with the matters of politics, organizes the religious rituals, directs subsistence production, and arbitrates in matters of kinship. Without a knowledge of a society's descent system the anthropologist would be lost in attempting to understand most behavior in the society. The kin group is the only effective group in many societies. Knowing how people are related to one another provides the key to why particular individuals hunt together or hold religious ceremonies in common.

In order to analyze kinship relationships in various societies the anthropologist has developed a set of symbols. These symbols are combined to form a *kinship chart*, which is used to show the way in which a particular society traces descent. A kinship chart is similar to a family tree or genealogical chart.

The kinship chart provides a simple means for describing kinship relationships.

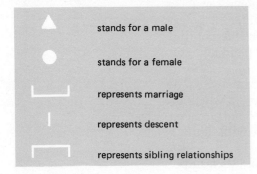

stands for a male

stands for a female

represents marriage

represents descent

represents sibling relationships

These five symbols form the building blocks of all kinship charts, whether large or small. For example, these symbols can be combined to represent a nuclear family, as illustrated.

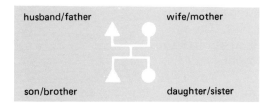

husband/father   wife/mother

son/brother   daughter/sister

It should be noted that there are several kinship terms for each position. Every individual fills a number of kinship positions: A man is someone's uncle, someone else's father, someone else's brother, someone else's grandfather, and so on. To avoid confusion over what kinship position one is emphasizing for a particular individual, the anthropologist selects one individual on the kinship chart as the person around whom the entire chart will be oriented. That individual is called the *ego* of the kinship chart and is clearly set off from the others on the chart by some means such as shading or the use of a different color. The nuclear family diagramed above would use only one term for each individual if an ego was added to the chart, as shown here.

While each society that the anthropologist studied yields new variations on the patterns of descent, it is possible to recognize two major types of descent: *unilineal descent* and *nonunilineal descent*. Each of these major types has several subtypes.

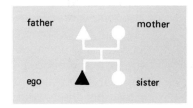

father   mother

ego   sister

There are two major form of descent: unilineal and nonunilineal.

Unilineal Descent. In our own society we view people as being equally related to their mother and her relatives *and* to their father and his relatives. In societies that practice unilineal descent, the kinship relationship is seen as existing between ego and father (and father's kin) *or* between ego and mother (and her kin). Unilineal descent can take one of three forms: *patrilineal descent, matrilineal descent,* or *double unilineal descent;* of the three, the patrilineal form is the most common. In a survey of 565 different societies it was found that 44 percent (248 societies) practiced patrilineal descent (Keesing 1975:26), making it the most widely practiced of any descent system.

In unilineal descent systems, descent is traced in order to establish which kinship group an individual belongs to. Kinship groups such as lineages or clans are the primary groupings of people in unilineal societies. *Lineages* are unilineal groups that have demonstrated descent. In other words, lineages are small kin groups in which all the members knows how they are related

Lineages and clans are the most important kinship groups in unilineal societies.

to everyone else in the group. *Clans* are unilineal groups that have stipulated descent, which means that clans are large kin groups in which the members do not know how they are related to everyone else; the members believe that they are related because they are all thought to be descended from the same clan ancestor—often a mythical being of the distant past. The unilineal descent form practiced allocates an individual at birth to a particular kin group, to which that individual belongs for his or her entire life.

In *patrilineal descent* an individual is assigned membership to a kin group on the basis of descent traced through males. Thus, at birth children automatically become members of their father's kin group. If the father belongs to a particular clan, all of his children will be considered of that clan as well. Generally the only people the child will consider kin are members of that kin group. In unilineal descent individuals are never allowed to marry within the same kin group. Women who marry males of the kin group do not become members of their husband's lineage or clan. As a result, ego's mother is not thought of as kin, because she does not belong to ego's kin group. The patrilineal kin group includes a line of blood-related males and their children. If members of the patrilineal descent line were plotted on a kin chart they would appear as shown in Figure 16. Patrilineal descent is reckoned in much the same way as surnames are passed from one generation to another in our own society, where children always take the last name of their father.

Patrilineal descent systems trace kin ties through a male line.

Figure 16 Patrilineal descent.

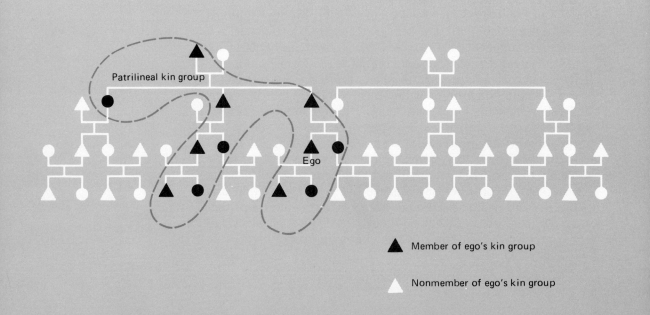

Patrilineal kin group

Ego

▲ Member of ego's kin group

△ Nonmember of ego's kin group

Patrilineal descent is often accompanied by the practice of *patrilocal residence.* This residence pattern locates a husband and wife with the husband's father. While women move out of their own kin group they never give up their membership in their own kin group, nor are they ever given membership in their husband's kin group. Patrilocal residence brings together the men of the male descent line and their wives.

Patrilineal descent is found in a number of different kinds of societies, with a variety of subsistence patterns. In this type of descent system, authority is vested in a male of the kin group, usually the eldest. The members of the kin group live together and frequently own land together. The land is considered the property of the kin group rather than of individuals. The headman is often in charge of allocating land to each family within the kin group. Patrilineal descent is common among hunting-and-gathering peoples, perhaps because it provides continuity among the male hunters. Since hunting is a group activity it is considered important that the men be related so that they can cooperate with one another. The female gatherers generally work alone or with their children, and it is therefore less important that they be related to members of the kin group.

A second type of unilineal descent is called *matrilineal descent.* In matrilineal descent, an individual is assigned membership to a kin group on the basis of descent traced through females. Thus in this type of descent, children at birth automatically become members of their mother's kin group. In its basic structure matrilineal descent can be thought of as the mirror opposite of patrilineal descent. Generally, a child's father is not considered kin, because the child's father belongs to a different kin group (his mother's group). The matrilineal kin group includes a line of blood-related females and their children. The men whom the women marry are not a part of the kin group. If members of a matrilineal descent line were plotted on a kin charter, they would appear as shown in Figure 17. In the sample 565 societies, matrilineal descent was practiced by 15 percent (84 societies).

Matrilineal descent systems trace kin ties through a female line.

Matrilineal descent is found primarily in simple agricultural societies where the women contribute most of the labor to gardening and the men have a somewhat peripheral role in the economy, supplementing the food supply by hunting and fishing. Matrilineal descent is not the exact opposite of patrilineal descent, because in matrilineal societies, women are not given power of authority. The matrilineal society is not a political matriarchy: It is not ruled by women. Instead an elder male of the descent group is considered headman or steward of the group. Frequently the individual in charge is ego's mother's

A male usually heads the matrilineal kin group.

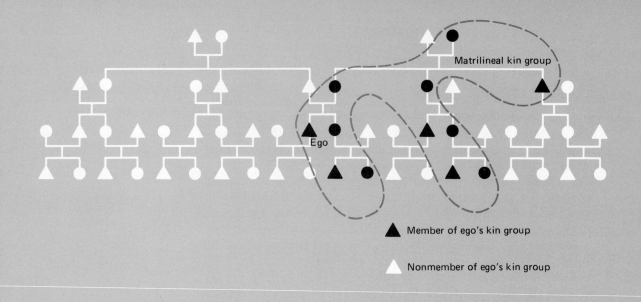

Figure 17 Matrilineal descent.

brother. Mother and mother's brother are in charge of disciplining the children. Father generally has little authority over his own children, because he is a member of a different kin group. The hostility that sometimes develops between father and son in our society develops between nephew (sister's son and uncle (mother's brother) in matrilineal societies.

In matrilineal societies the common residence pattern is called *matrilocal residence,* which means that the husband and wife live with the wife's mother in her village and sometimes even in the same house. In other words, upon marriage the husband leaves his kin group and goes to live with his wife and her kin group. Matrilocal residence brings together the women of the female descent line and their husbands.

The fact that a male of the female descent line must serve as headman complicates the matrilocal residence pattern. He would be unable to perform satisfactorily the affairs of his matrilineal kin group if he moved away when he married and lived with his wife if his wife's kin lived in a different village. As a result a few males must violate the practice of matrilocal residence in order to remain with their own kin group as headmen. Since the headmanship passes from mother's brother to sister's son, only those in line for the headmanship need practice a different form of residence. This second form of residence practiced in matrilineal societies is called *avunculocal residence,* which means husband and wife live with his mother's brother (his maternal uncle). The husband lives with his mother's brother and learns the duties of the headmanship from him. After the mother's brother dies, the husband will assume the office. Later he will train one of his sister's sons to follow in his footsteps. The sister's son will also have to disregard the normal matrilocal residence pattern and practice avunculocal residence instead. Avunculocal residence brings together males of the female descent line and their wives.

A third type of unilineal descent is less common than the first two. *Double unilineal descent* is found in only 5 percent (28 societies) of the 565 society sample mentioned earlier (Keesing 1975:26). In double unilineal descent, a person is assigned membership to *two* distinct kin groups, one on the basis of descent traced through males and one on the basis of descent traced through females. An individual is considered to be a member of both his father's patrilineal group and his mother's matrilineal group; see Figure 18. The two kin groups are mutually exclusive. It is usually only the patrilineal groups that are land-owning groups, whereas the matrilineal kin group may transfer movable property, be depended upon to administer certain legal responsibilities for its members, or be involved in ritual activities.

It is unclear why double unilineal descent occurs. In some cases it reflects an ongoing change in the descent system resulting from a native society with a matrilineal system being conquered by another group who practice patrilineal descent, or

> Double unilineal descent systems trace kin ties through both a male line and a female line.

Figure 18 Double unilineal descent.

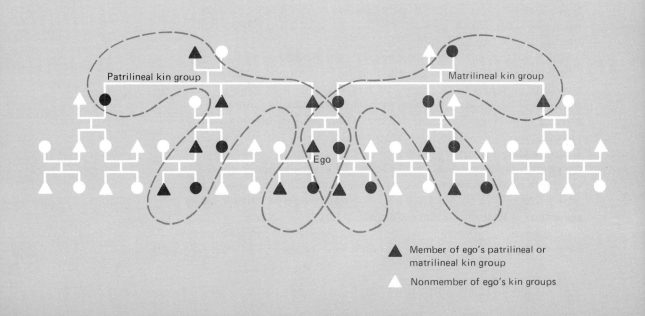

▲ Member of ego's patrilineal or matrilineal kin group

△ Nonmember of ego's kin groups

vice versa. However, some double unilineal descent systems seem to be very stable. Since only brothers and sisters normally belong to both the same patrilineal kin group and the same matrilineal kin group, people who are aligned against one another in one situation may well be allies in another. This type of descent helps to bind together the members of the society to a greater degree than is possible in patrilineal or matrilineal descent, where one belongs to one kin group and is aligned against all others.

In some patrilineal and matrilineal societies, several lineages or clans are allies because they belong to some higher order of kin grouping such as *moieties* or *phratries*. Moieties and phratries allow individuals to transcend somewhat the narrow loyalties imposed by matrilineal and patrilineal descent systems. A moiety is a large-scale division of society in which everyone is assigned to one or two kin groups on the basis of unilineal descent. The moiety is often composed of several lineages or clans that are thought to have some sort of mythical bond with one another. Moieties create a dualism in the societies in which they are found. For example, among the Eastern Timbira of Brazil each village is divided into "those of the east" and "those of the west" (Nimuendajú 1946:79). Moiety divisions often influence the settlement pattern of the village. In the case of the Eastern Timbira members of different moieties live on opposite sides of the village. Likewise moiety divisions create competition in sports and other activities between members of the moieties. The phratry is any large-scale grouping of clans or lineages other than the moiety. In other words, if the clans of a society are grouped into three or more higher-order groupings based on traditions of common descent or historical alliance, these groupings are considered phratries rather than moieties. Societies with phratries lack much of the dualistic symbolism found in societies with moieties.

In the various unilineal societies, certain kinds of kin relationships, frequently become strain points, for example, the relationship between a woman and her husband's brother in a patrilineal-patrilocal situation or between a man and his wife's mother in a matrilineal-matrilocal situation. Certain kinds of standardized behaviors have developed in these societies to relieve some of the potential pressure and tensions. In some cases, this behavior takes the form of joking between the people in the stressful relationship, with extreme license allowed; in other cases, it takes the form of avoidance, where extreme rules of decorum or even complete avoidance restrict interaction.

Moieties and phratries are larger groupings of kin than clans or lineages.

Nonunilineal Descent. For years anthropologists focused their attention on the unilineal descent systems and had little interest in other types of descent. Tribal societies without unilineal descent were relegated to the negative category of "nonunilineal." The technical vocabulary worked out by early kinship specialists were biased toward unilineal societies and left anthropologists ill-equipped to deal with the nonunilineal societies. Gradually anthropologists learned that more than one-third of all known tribal societies practice some form of nonunilineal descent (Keesing 1975:91). Because interest in nonunilineal descent is recent, there is still considerable disagreement over the nature of some of these systems, as well as disagreement over the proper terminology to describe the systems.

While there is still perhaps no consensus, there does seem to be a trend toward grouping the nonunilineal systems into one or the other of two types: *cognatic* and *bilateral.* Cognatic descent is most common among tribal peoples and chiefdoms, whereas bilateral descent is most common among hunting-and-gathering bands and modern industrial societies.

In cognatic descent a person is born with a potential claim on a number of kin groups. In a cognatic system, descent is traced back to an ancestor through any combination of male or female links. Cognatic descent groups include all those people who trace their ancestry back to a common ancestor. With the exception of siblings, each individual in a given group uses a different set of kinship links in order to validate his or her claim to the group.

Cognatic descent systems trace descent from an ancestor using both male and female links.

While our own society does not practice cognatic descent, it contains certain elements that help illustrate how cognatic descent operates. For example, individuals who trace their ancestry back to a famous ancestor, such as John Adams or George Washington, use whatever kin links they can find that will ultimately link them with the ancestor. One person may trace his ancestry back to John Adams through his mother, his mother's mother, his mother's mother's father, and mother's mother's father's father, and so on. Someone else might claim to be a descendant of John Adams through her father, father's mother, father's mother's father, and father's mother's father's mother. Whether the links used are male or female is unimportant. All that really matters to the descendant is to be able somehow to trace his or her ancestry back to that particular ancestor. In a cognatic descent system, an individual is able to trace ancestry back not to one but to a number of ancestors. For example, if an individual could trace a line of descent back to each of his or her eight great-grandparents, he or she could then make a legitimate claim for membership in eight different kin groups. Each of these kin groups would be composed of individuals who could trace their ancestry back to one of the eight great-grandparents. Theoretically, in a small society that practiced cognatic descent, a person could have a claim to all of the kin groups that existed. Since an individual could not possibly maintain membership in all of the cognatic kin groups to which he or she has a claim, at some point he or she must choose a group with which to live. A decision is usually made at the time of marriage, and the husband and wife will live with one of the groups to which one or the other has a claim. Having a number of kin groups to choose from adds flexibility to a descent system. The couple can choose that kin group having the most available land, knowledge of the most preferred craft, or some other advantage. Although the couple may choose a group in which parents of neither are living, the couple will still be living with some kin. The types of residence pattern that usually accompanies cognatic descent is called *ambilocal residence.* The ambilocal residence pattern is one in which the husband and wife live with kin of one or the other, the choice being based on relative need or some other advantage. In some cognatic societies, once a couple have made their choice of which group to live with, they

Figure 19 Cognatic descent.

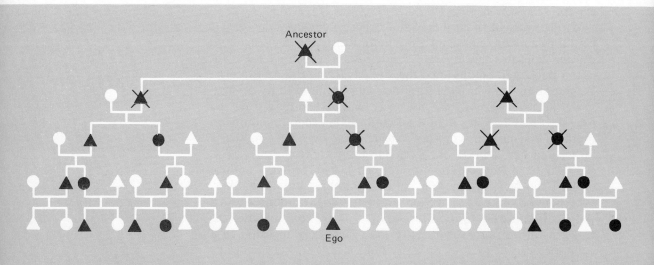

lose their claims on all other kin groups and must remain with the group of their choice from then on. In other societies the couple are allowed to maintain their claims on other groups and may relocate with another group at some time in the future if the group they have been living with is unable to provide them with land or there have been conflicts with members of the group. See Figure 19.

While our own society does not have a cognatic descent system, there are certain features that are very similar to cognatic descent in parts of the South, especially in the small towns and rural areas. Geographic mobility is still restricted in these areas, and many people remain in the same small town or rural area for their entire life. Some of the areas are settled by a few families who originally held large tracts of land. As the families grew, the land was divided among the offspring of the families. Members of one family married members of other families. In time almost everyone was related to everyone else in the town or area, although the link was often remote. For example, if one country in a southern state were originally settled by four families, Jones, Smith, Allen, and Clark, the original couple of each family would become the founder-ancestors of that family. Over time, members of the Jones family would marry Smiths, Allens, and Clarks, so that their children would be able to make claims of kin ties with more than one family. At the same time, members of the Smith family would marry Joneses, Allens, and Clarks; members of the Allen family would marry Joneses, Smiths, and Clarks; and members of the Clark family would marry Joneses, Smiths, and Allens. It would not be long before members of the most recent generation would have at least distant cousins, if not closer kin, in each family. Where geographical mobility was great, these kin ties would not develop. The southern kin ties do not result in kin groups comparable to those in true cognatic societies. However there is at least one social phenomenon that does bring a cognaticlike kin group together, the family reunion. The basis for an invitation to a family reunion is some claim of descent from some key ancestor. To use our example again, a family reunion might be called to bring together all of the descendants of Horace Jones, the original settler of the Jones family. Since the Joneses have intermarried with the other three families over a number of generations, the group celebrating the reunion would include many people with the last name of Smith, Allen, or Clark who could make a claim of descent from Horace Jones. Some would be able to make a claim through their father and some of his relatives; others would make the claim through their mother and some of her relatives; still others might be able to make a claim through both their mother and their father.

Besides cognatic descent, there is a type of nonunilineal descent called *bilaterial descent,* which represents the type of descent found in our own society. Bilateral descent is the reckoning of descent through both male and female lines, with an individual linked equally to relatives of both sexes on both sides of the family. Although our bilateral system of tracing descent seems logical and "natural" to us, in cross-cultural perspective it is perhaps the most unusual of all the descent systems. Our way of classifying kin would seem strange, if not incredible, to most of the world's peoples.

Some of the basic features of bilateral descent include the following: Kin are reckoned on both father's and mother's side of the family and are given equal status; relatives by marriage (called *affines*) are given equal status to blood relatives (called *consanguines*); bilateral descent does not result in kin groups; each individual has a unique network of relatives. Bilateral descent shares with double unilineal descent the feature of reckoning kin on both sides of the family—through mother and through father. See Figure 20. However bilateral descent differs from double unilineal descent in that it also includes as kin the spouses of blood kin and their children. In double unilineal descent, only blood kin are considered relatives and only those

Bilateral descent systems trace descent on both sides of the family, including affines as well as consanguines.

Figure 20 Comparison of descent systems.

	Types of Kin Reckoned	
Number of Descent Lines Recognized	Consanguines exclusively	Consanguines and affines
One	Patrilineal Matrilineal	
Two	Double unilineal	Bilateral
More than two	Cognatic	

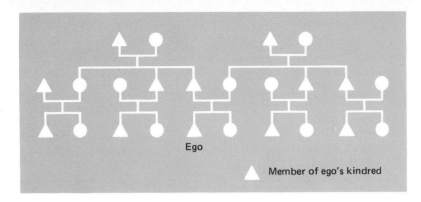

Ego

▲ Member of ego's kindred

Figure 21
Bilateral descent.

children who belong to the same kin group as ego are considered relatives. In our descent system we group together as kin, under the same kinship term, people who stand in several different kinship positions to us. For example, we call father's brother, father's sister's husband, mother's brother, and mother's sister's husband by the same kin term, *uncle*, and consider them all equally related to us. In partrilineal descent, only father's brother would be considered a kinsman. In matrilineal descent only mother's brother would be considered as kin, and in double unilineal and cognatic descent only father's brother and mother's brother would be considered kin. In all other systems of descent but the bilateral, the spouses of blood kin are not considered to be relatives. See Figure 21.

All of the descent systems described previously are organized around kin groups of one type or another. Bilateral descent is unique in that we have no kin groups. Instead, each individual recognizes a unique network of relatives. This network of relatives is called a *kindred*. One's kindred in bilateral descent is merely those people one considers his or her kin. Each individual's kindred is unique, except in the case of unmarried siblings. However these networks of kin overlap considerable. Ego will share one-half of his or her kindred with a cousin. For example, if the cousin is ego's father's sister's son, ego and the cousin will share the following kinds of kin: ego's father, mother, sister, father's brother, father's brother's wife, father's brother's children, father's sister, father's sister's husband, and father's sister's children. However, ego's kindred will also include all those kin related through is or her mother, none of whom will be part of the cousin's kindred. Likewise, ego's cousin will recognize a number of kin related through his or her father (ego's father's sister's husband) as part of his or her kindred. See Figure 22.

In the other descent systems, the kin groups play an important role within the society. The kin group is the group with whom ego lives, with whom ego owns land, and with whom ego

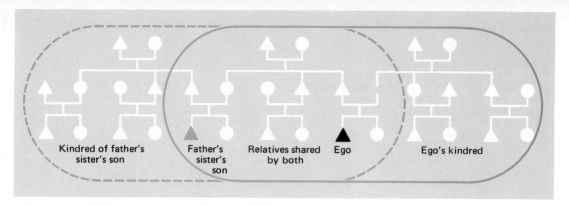

Figure 22 Two overlapping kindreds in bilateral descent.

carries out religious ceremonies. The kindred of the bilateral descent system does not have these functions. While ego may live with some relatives, he or she would not live with the entire kindred, nor would the entire kindred ever come together for purposes other than those that centered on ego. In our own society there is frequently conflict during family holidays. Should the family spend Thanksgiving with father's relatives or mother's relatives? Thanksgiving cannot be spent with both groups at the same time, because one side of the family usually does not know the other side of the family. Normally the only time individuals making up ego's kindred come together are for major occasions centering around ego: His or her confirmation, marriage, or funeral. Only in parts of the South do the kindred overlap to such an extent that something close to kin groups are formed, as ego begins to have relatives who are related through father and mother at the same time.

The kindred seems to have utility in a geographically mobile society such as our own. As people move from one part of the country to another, they may add or subtract individuals from their kindred. If you lived in Chicago you might have little or nothing to do with cousins living in New York and not even include them in your network of kin. However if you moved to New York you would probably begin to include those individuals in your kindred, while others in Chicago might now begin to be left out. One's kindred is highly personal. It includes only those relatives that one wishes to recognize as kin. Some people include as part of their kindred such distant relatives as fourth cousins three times removed. Others do not even include all of their first cousins in their kindred. The highly personal nature of the kindred has made it extremely difficult for the anthropologist to collect information relating to it. Since the concept of kindred is foreign to most people, the anthropologist cannot simply ask, "Who do you include in your kindred?" If the anthropologist asked, "Who are your kin?" he might receive an answer, but it would not necessarily include only the kindred. People may know of many more kin then they include in their kindred. Anthropologists have found no easy way to collect this information.

Fictive Kinship

While all societies recognize consanguineous kin, and societies with bilateral descent recognize affinal kin as well, many societies also recognize another kind of kinship, called *fictive kinship*. Fictive kin are make-believe kin. They are neither relatives by marriage nor blood relatives, yet they are often given the same status as true kin. Fictive kinship adds a certain amount of flexibility to the descent system. A number of forms of fictive kinship have been reported cross-culturally; several will be discussed here: blood brotherhood, adoption, *compadrazgo*, and *oyabun-kobun*.

Many societies recognize some type of fictive kin.

In tribal societies, trading with villages of the same tribe is considered safe, because one often has kin in the other villages. However, trade between villages of the same tribe does not occur frequently, because the villages produce the same goods. In order to obtain goods not produced within the tribe, it is necessary to conduct intertribal trade, which is considered highly dangerous. The members of another tribe are strangers—if not enemies. There is the constant threat of being killed when in the territory of other tribes. One solution to this problem is for the trading party to be accompanied by armed guards. Another solution is to establish trading partnerships with the other tribe. A *trade partner* is someone with whom one has a special relationship. Frequently, goods are given to the trade partner and whatever he gives in return has to be accepted. There is no bargaining with the trade partner. An individual gives up a certain amount of economic gain that might be possible if he traded his goods on an open market in the village. But on the other hand, the trader gains the security of knowing that he has someone in the potential enemy's village whom he can trust. In many cases the trading partnership is further solidified by the partners becoming blood brothers.

The ceremony of blood brotherhood is often similar to the ritual used among children in our own society. A cut is made in the skin of both individuals and several drops of blood are exchanged. In our own society and others the intent may be very similar—the individuals will become lifelong "brothers"—but the reality differs. Children move away from one another and forget both the ceremony and their blood brother; this is not the case in societies where the ritual is performed between grown men. In Africa and other parts of the world, once men become blood brothers their relationship will be the same as biological brothers. They are recognized as brothers by the members of their society. Trade partners who become bloodbrothers have a closer relationship than when they were merely trade partners. Each can now make certain claims on the entire kin group of his "brother." Thus the danger of trading in another tribe can be averted, because blood brothers would not harm one another. The reinforcement of trade partnerships is only one of a number of reasons that individuals enter into blood brotherhood relationships.

Perhaps the most common form of fictive kinship is adoption. Adoption is usually used to give an individual a position in the kinship structure. In our own society the most common form of adoption is that of young children, especially infants, by childless couples or by those wishing to have larger families. The ceremony that marks the child's and the couple's transition to a new status in our society is a legal one. The ruling of the court creates the fiction that the child is now the child of the couple and the fiction that the man and woman are the parents of the child. From that point on, the couple and the child act as if their relationship is a biological one. In some cases, even the birth certificate of the child is changed, showing the new fictive parents as the actual biological ones.

In other societies where adoption occurs, children may not be the primary candidates for adoption. Adoption may be used to fit a candidate for marriage into the proper position in the kinship structure. Some societies practice patterns of preferred marriage. In other words, an individual is encouraged to marry someone who stands in a particular kinship relationship to him or her. For example, in a matrilineal society, ego may be expected to marry his mother's brother's daughter. She would belong to a different kin group than ego. But what happens if mother's brother only has four sons? It might mean that ego would have to marry someone who was not in a preferred marriage category or not marry at all. A simple solution is for mother's brother to adopt an eligible young woman as his daughter. This enables ego to marry someone in the preferred status.

In other cases where adoption is practiced, it is used in the context of learning a craft. Kin groups not only own land and

In some societies, adoption of adults occur.

other tangible property, they also own certain kinds of knowledge, such as cures, religious rituals, and sometimes the specialized knowledge of a particular craft. On the island of Palau in the western Pacific, the kin groups are thought to own particular crafts. This is fine for the young man who wishes to learn the craft of his own kin group. However, what happens if he wishes to learn the craft that is not considered the property of his own kin group? Technically, another kin group cannot share that knowledge with him because he is not a member of the kin group. The Palauans solve this dilemma with adoption. A young man is adopted by an older man of the kin group whose craft he wishes to learn. He becomes that man's fictive son. He then has the right to learn the craft of the kin group. In some cases, a young man may be adopted several different times by men of different kin groups until he discovers a craft that he enjoys (Barnett 1960).

A third type of fictive kinship is called *compadrazgo* (or some variant thereof) and is widely practiced in southern Europe and Latin America. Compadrazgo is a set of complex relationships that develops out of the ritual of Catholic baptism and the naming of godparents. In the United States the naming of godparents at baptism is a fairly widespread Christian practice. But in our country the godparents do not play a major role in the child's life. Although the godparents agree to see that the child is raised in its faith and to serve as guardians of the child if the parents should die, in most cases the immediate family controls the child's religious training and if the parents died the child would most likely be raised by relatives rather than godparents (Olien 1973:200). In Latin America the institution of godparents operates differently.

In contrast to what happens in our own baptismal ceremonies, lifelong ties are established in compadrazgo, not only between godparents and child but also between godparents and parents. Once the ceremony has been performed, male godparents and male parents refer to one another as *compadres*, and the females refer to each other as *comadres*. Godparents are named for a number of other occasions besides baptism, such as confirmation, marriage, and even specialized ceremonies—for example, in highland Colombia, they are named for a child's first nail cutting, haircut, and ear piercing. The institution of compadrazgo allows the nuclear family to expand the network of people it can call upon in time of need. Individuals who become compadres are like blood brothers. It is unthinkable to turn down the request of a compadre.

Compadrazo establishes lifelong ties between parents and godparents.

Another example of fictive kinship is found in Japan and is known as the *oyabun-kobun* institution. Once widespread throughout Japan, today it is most important among hoodlums, neofascist political movements, and in remote rural areas. It is used especially by racketeers who are street-stall merchants. An individual wishing to enter the rackets must be adopted by a racketeer. The racketeer becomes the individual's fictive father (or *oyabun*) and the individual becomes the racketeer's fictive child (or *kobun*). The person who originally sponsored the rackateer becomes the new individual's fictive grandfather. Other men who were sponsored along with the fictive father become ego's fictive uncles. Later, as the individual becomes an established racketeer, he may wish to sponsor assistants of his own. They will become his fictive children. A retiring street-stall merchant is forbidden to transfer his economic interest and his sphere of influence to his biological son—it must be passed on to a fictive son.

Although fictive kinship customs are known to have been practiced from the beginning of Japanese history, the oyabun-kobun system seems to have developed in the late feudal period, about AD 1700. During the late feudal period, artisans, merchants, peddlers, and others of the commercial class organized guilds along the lines of the oyabun-kobun system. Lord-and-vassal relations were based on a similar pattern among the *samurai* (the military class) and upper classes. The oyabun-kobun system became especially important during the early industrial period, about AD 1900. Employment organizations for the recruiting peasants for factory work, various types of business associations, and labor organizations—especially among miners, stevedores, construction workers, and casual labor—were organized on oyabun-kobun patterns (Ishino 1953:698–99). In many ways it eased the transition from feudalism to industralism for the Japanese. Rural peasants who had normally oriented their world on the basis of kinship ties found it fairly easy to make the transition from farm to factory because of the oyabun-kobun system, whereas in our own country, the transition from farm to factory was a traumatic one. In Japan the factory often was operated as a large family in which everyone was a fictive relative of everyone else. The system created strong ties of loyalty to the company and resulted in little turnover of labor.

With the occupation of Japan by the United States following World War II, new institutions were introduced, such as national unemployment insurance and employment programs, and there was greater encouragement of labor unions. These

The *oyabun-kobun* system eased the transition to industrialization in Japan.

new institutions reduced the need for the oyabun-kobun system, and it declined in importance, although it survives today in a small sector of Japanese society.

Socialization and Gender Roles

The kinship ties discussed above bring individuals together into different kinds of groupings for many different purposes. Many of the functions served by the nuclear family in one society are taken over by lineages or clans in other societies. Where kinship ties are deemphasized, many of the family's functions are taken over by various governmental agencies or nonkin groups. For example, an interesting contrast between child-raising in the United States and among the Mundurucú, an Indian tribe of Amazon Brazil, is provided by the anthropologists Yolanda and Robert Murphy (1974:224):

> Mundurucú women, quite simply, do not spend as much time looking after children as American women do, nor are they as preoccupied with their welfare. The reasons for this have less to do with devotion than with the circumstances of life. Mundurucú mothers do not have to prepare their children for school and supervise their studies because there are no schools. Mothers do not watch while their children cross streets or caution them against traffic because there are neither streets nor cars. Women do not warn the young about "strange men" because there are no strangers. They are not obsessed by the life chances of their children because of the course of life is predetermined. Piano lessons, orthodonture, Little League, and all the other means by which the modern mother bedevils both herself and her children are absent. By the time the child is six or so, the burden of its protection and socialization shifts to the household, the peer group, and to the community-at-large. Mundurucú women are not "eaten up" by their young, as American women, and child rearing is less work. Moreover, those children they do tend are often not their own.

Although child-rearing techniques vary greatly from society to society, all children are taught that different behavior is appropriate for each sex. Although it is difficult to determine precisely how much of the differences in the behavior of males and females is genetically determined and how much is culturally determined, through cross-cultural comparison, anthropologists have learned that the range of culturally conditioned male-female differences is very great.

Only a few anthropologists have identified specific behavior differences between the sexes as hereditary. In recent years the most outspoken advocate of biologically determined sex role behavior has been the anthropologist Lionel Tiger. Anthropologists have found that in most societies the males organize themselves into the most important groups of their society. Tiger (1969) attempts to explain this pattern as a biological one. He suggests that males have an inherent drive toward banding together. This drive is hereditary, a legacy of hundreds of thousands of years of cooperative hunting that insured human survival. Intriguing as this theory may be, there is little or no genetic evidence to support Tiger's point of view. Furthermore, Tiger seems to ignore the number of societies in which there is no strong development of men's groups, where hunting is carried out by a single male, or where the women are more cohesive than the men.

While the evidence for male-group dominance as a genetically determined phenomenon is unconvincing, there is considerable cultural data to support the point of view that in a number of societies, men's groups are given higher status than women's groups. Moreover, much of the symbolism in different societies reflects the notion of male superiority: the notion of the "mighty hunter" (as opposed to the "lowly gatherer"), the elaborate male initiation rites, the elaborate male costumes, and so on. According to some anthropologists (Murphy and Murphy 1974:226), this symbolism functions to perpetuate an illusion. It conceals from the men the fragility of their own superiority. Men are born of women, nurtured and loved by women, protected and dominated by women, yet they must become men. The male bond with the mother is not easily broken, and a frequent fear of the male in many societies is that he will not become a man because of these strong bonds. Thus the male protects himself against these fears by a number of devices, including banding together with other males, wearing elaborate costumes, continually demonstrating his strength and independence. Margaret Mead (Murphy and Murphy 1974:226) has observed that "if the men really were all that powerful, they wouldn't need such rigmarole." Anthropologists are really only beginning to understand male and female behavior differences, and their incorporation of sex differences into the human myth is rapidly changing.

How Many Sexes Are There? It is usually assumed that biological sex differences are universally perceived as exclusively dichotomous—in other words, that people in every society determine a child's sex on an either-or basis, which derives from a judgment about the nature of the child's genitals. However, societies infuse even something as seemingly basic as physical male-female sex differences with cultural distinctiveness (Martin and Voorhies 1975:85–86). Human sex differences are *not* universally seen as either male or female. The folk classifications of some societies include certain intermediate categories.

There are individuals in any society who are born with genitals that are neither typically male nor female in appearance. The estimated frequency in human populations of this occurrence is between 2 and 3 percent. Thus the possibility is open for at least some societies to consider these individuals as a third sex. Among the Navajo, intersex individuals are called *nadle*. Their genital appearance sets them apart from both males and females. Their nadle status is considered distinct from masculine and feminine statuses. (Actually the nadle category is more complex than just described. Not only are there "real" nadle, there are others in Navajo society who pretend to be nadle. These pretenders can be individuals with either male or female genitals.) The nadle tend to wear women's clothing when doing women's work and men's clothing when engaged in male chores. The nadle are able to perform all Navajo tasks except hunting and warfare. In many ways the nadle follow female behavior. They assume the woman's role at dances, they are addressed by female kinship terms, and they have the social and legal status of a woman. The Navajo are a matrilineal people, and in many ways the status of women in Navajo society is greater than that of men. At the same time, the status of the nadle has certain unique aspects that clearly set them apart from either males or females. The nadle act as mediators in disputes between a man and a woman, have unusual sexual license, and may marry a spouse of either biological sex. They have special rights over the personal property of other members of their households and can even dispose of the private property of their relatives without their permission (W. W. Hill 1935).

In other societies more than two sex roles are recognized even though intersex individuals are not. Among the Mohave Indians, who lived in California and adjacent states at the time of contact, four different gender were recognized, even though the Mohave did not consider intersex individuals as a separate sex. A Mohave individual clearly male in gender could either accept the status of male or he could adopt a socially sanctioned femininelike role called *alyha*. A Mohave individual clearly female in gender could either accept the status of a woman or she could adopt a socially sanctioned masculinelike role called *hwame*.

Folk classifications of sexes in some societies recognize intermediate categories.

The Navajo recognize intersex as a separate sex category.

The Mohave recognized four different gender roles but did not recognize intersex individuals as a separate sex.

Boys who desired toys and the clothing of the opposite sex underwent a formal initiation ceremony that legitimated their change in status from male to alyha. They wore the clothing of women and adopted feminine names. The female apparently also underwent a ceremony if she wished to change her status to that of a hwame. She would then wear male paint, a breechclout, and adopt a new name. Her activities were then similar to the Mohave male. Some became shamans, others farmed and hunted. However the hwame was ineligible for tribal or war leadership positions (Devereux 1937:500–502).

The alyha and the hwame were able to marry individuals of their own sex. When the alyha married, "she" fictively created a first menstrual flow by drawing blood from "her" upper leg. Pregnancy was also acted out in an elaborate fashion. "Labor pains" were induced by the drinking of a severely constipating drug, culminating in the birth of a fictitious stillborn child. Because Mohave infants who were stillborn were customarily buried by the mother, the alyha's failure to produce a living baby was explained in a culturally acceptable manner.

The Navajo and Mohave are only two of a number of societies in which the members of the society view the biological differences between male and female differently than we do in our own society. Thus anthropologists studying another society cannot assume that it will be made up of men and women. Instead they must probe to learn what sex categories are recognized by the people and how they function in that society.

Anthropologists have found that family ties in the world's societies can be extremely diverse. However, in each society there are people who are thought to be related to one another. While the rules of decent that are followed are many and complex, it appears that the part of being human is recognizing a close bond with others.

Anthropology Vocabulary

affine	*comadre*	family of procreation
alyha	*compadrazgo*	fictive kin
ambilocal residence	*compadre*	fraternal polyandry
avunculocal residence	composite family	group marriage
bilateral descent	consanguine	*hwame*
blood brotherhood	double unilineal descent	infanticide
brother-sister marriage	ego	joint family
clan	extended family	kindred
cognatic descent	family of orientation	levirate

lineage	*nadle*	polygamy
mana	Navajo	polygynandry
matriarchy	nonsororal polygyny	polygyny
matrifocal family	nuclear family	serial monogamy
matrilineal descent	*oyabun-kobun*	sororal polygyny
matrilocal residence	patriarchy	sororate
Mohave	patrilineal descent	trade partner
moiety	patrilocal residence	unilineal descent
monogamy	phratry	
mother-right	polyandry	

Review Questions

1. Anthropologists have found a great range in the forms of marriage practiced among the world's societies. What common features do these marriages generally share?
2. The extended family is found most frequently in simple agricultural societies. What advantages might this type of family arrangement have in such a society?
3. What structural features distinguish unilineal descent systems from those that are nonunilineal? Why is our own type of descent system unusual?
4. Why is fictive kinship important?

Recommended Reading

Bohannan, Paul, and John Middleton, eds., 1968, *Kinship and Social Organization*. Garden City, N.Y.: Natural History Press. An interesting collection of articles of various aspects of kinship.

———, 1968, *Marriage, Family, and Residence*. Garden City, N.Y.: Natural History Press. A collection of articles dealing with the family and related topics.

Fox, Robin, 1967, *Kinship and Marriage: An Anthropological Perspective*. Baltimore: Penquin Books. A clearly written description of descent rules and the types of groupings that they form.

Keesing, Roger M., 1975, *Kin Groups and Social Structure*. New York: Holt, Rinehart and Winston. Informative work on kin groups. It is especially excellent in its discussion of nonunilineal descent.

Pasternak, Burton, 1976, *Introduction to Kinship and Social Organization*. Englewood Cliffs, N.J.: Prentice-Hall. A readable introduction to anthropological interests in the areas of kinship and social organization.

Schneider, David M., 1968, *American Kinship: A Cultural Account*. Englewood Cliffs, N.J.: Prentice-Hall. An anthropological study of our own descent system.

Schneider, David M., and E. Kathleen Gough, eds., 1961, *Matrilineal Kinship*. Berkeley: University of California Press. A detailed discussion of many areas of matrilineal descent.

14

Who's in charge here? A look at political organization

Not all societies have authority positions.

Sociopolitical organization has evolved from the band to the state.

The rise of great powers in Europe began during the late Middle Ages and was a movement that united the fragmented feudal domains of various lords. During the 1400s and 1500s, Spain and Portugal were among the first powers to develop strong centralized governments. England, France, and the Netherlands grew powerful in the 1600s, which saw the decline of Spain and Portugal. By the 1700s Prussia (later known as Germany) and Russia had become strong central powers.

As explorers, travelers, missionaries, and colonial administrators of these countries set out to explore newly discovered areas of the world, they assumed that they would find peoples with some type of centralized authority. This assumption reflected an ethnocentric point of view. Yet in some parts of the world their assumption was reinforced. Among the Aztec and Inca of the New World, among the kingdoms of West Africa, on the island of Hawaii, in parts of the Middle East, and in China and other areas of the Far East there were rulers surrounded with as much pomp and circumstance as any European monarch. In other parts of the world, where the Europeans encountered peoples without centralized authority, they found it difficult, if not impossible, to accept the fact that societies existed without anyone in charge. When a European asked to be taken to a native leader, his request was considered very strange, because there was no one who had the kind of authority the European assumed existed in all societies.

One of the best examples of the confusion in the European mind over the nature of the native sociopolitical organization is found in United States history, in the treaty making with Indian groups. The English colonists considered each Indian group an independent sovereign nation and treated each group as they would any nation—under the rules of international law. Of course "international law" was far from international and included only European notions of legality. The English settlers assumed that each tribe of Indians had a chief who had the right to enter into agreements for his tribe as its representative. In most cases there was no such person. Especially as the settlers moved inland from the East Coast, they encountered few groups with centralized authority. Nevertheless they were usually successful in finding someone who would sign a treaty, and on the basis of that individual's signature, the settlers assumed they had a valid agreement between themselves and an entire tribe—an incorrect assumption.

The American colonists had learned the official British policy of dealing with Indians: Indians were to be compensated for

Europeans assumed that all societies had centralized leadership.

their land. In many cases the compensation was incredibly small, yet for the Indian the sale of land represented the primary means of obtaining European metal implements, mirrors, glass beads, and firearms. In many cases, an Indian gave up rights to communally held land he did not own in order to obtain European trade goods. Not having a notion of private land ownership, the Indian did not realize that he was surrendering the land itself, rather than its use. On the other hand, the English settlers did not realize that the Indians did not share their idea of the exchange (Garbarino 1976:439–440). This lack of understanding on both parts led to white-Indian conflict in many areas, often with *both* sides believing they had been cheated.

The Study of Political Systems

Anthropological interest in political systems has developed more slowly than interest in other institutions. The reason there has been less study of political organization may lie in the nature of the societies that anthropologists have traditionally studied. In these societies it has been difficult, if not impossible, to separate matters of politics from matters of kinship, because the kin group was the political group. For one reason or another, anthropologists emphasized the study of kinship. At the same time, in many of these societies there were no group leaders or individuals who were considered strong leaders. It was not until the 1940s that anthropologists developed a theoretical interest in political organization.

One of the first detailed studies of tribal people in which detailed attention was given to political organization was E. E. Evans-Pritchard's study of the Nuer, an East African society, published in 1940 and titled *The Nuer*. It demonstrated that a people without government did have political institutions that helped maintain order within the society. Other anthropologists began conducting research on a variety of African societies at about the same time. In 1946 E. E. Evans-Pritchard and Meyer Fortes edited *African Political Systems*, a collection of case studies of different African societies, which provided some of the earliest modern theoretical statements on political organization. This important collection of articles was followed by even more extensive research on a number of African societies. In 1958 a second collection of articles was published, edited by John Middleton and David Tait and called *Tribes without Rulers*, in which stateless societies of Africa were reviewed. About the same time two important studies were published on Asian political systems. One, *Political Systems of Highland Burma,* published in 1954 by Edmund Leach, examined the political structures and organizations of the Kachin of Burma, while a second, *Oriental Despotism,* published in 1957 by Karl A. Wittfogel, a German economic historian, studied totalitarianism in the Far East. Both of these studies presented new approaches to the study of political systems. Leach's study showed that political structures are not always static. The Kachin political organization fluctuated between a hierarchically ranked system and an egalitarian one based on lineages of approximately equal status. Wittfogel influenced anthropology by creating an interest in large-scale state forms of political organization.

In recent years, two individuals, Elman R. Service and Morton H. Fried, have introduced schemes of sociopolitical evolution into anthropological theory. Service published an importan synthesis in 1962 entitled *Primitive Social Organization: An Evolutionary Perspective.*[1] In this book Service took a major step forward in defining the characteristics of four evolutionary levels of sociopolitical development: the *band,* the *tribe,* the *chiefdom,* and the *state.* Until Service's book, there was no standardization of the use of these terms, either by anthropologists or the general public. Thus, in one account, the Aztecs might be described as a band. In another work, they would be referred to as the Aztec tribe. More commonly, the Aztecs were described as a state. Service brought coherence to the terminology and a set of criteria for each level that could be tested by historical, archaeological, and ethnographic data.

In 1967 Morton H. Fried published *The Evolution of Political Society: An Essay in Political Anthropology.* Fried presented a somewhat different evolutionary scheme, one in which the evolutionary levels were based on different criteria from those of Service. The schemes agree primarily over the societies at the bottom and top of the evolutionary scale. They disagree over those placed in between. Those societies that are neither band nor state are less uniform and can be classified differently depending on which classification is used. Fried's scheme includes the following evolutionary levels: the *egalitarian society,* the *rank society,* the *stratified society,* and the *state.* With Service's and Fried's contributions, anthropologists have begun to reach a consensus as to the nature of political organization and thereby to clarify an aspect of the human myth about which there has been little agreement. In the sections that follow, Service's terminology will be used as an organizing framework; however, comparisons will be made with Fried's classification.

Service and Fried present two different views of sociopolitical evolution.

[1] A revised edition was published in 1971.

The Band

The egalitarian society proposed by Fried is one in which "there are as many positions of prestige in any given age-sex grade as there are persons capable of filling them" (Fried 1967:33). Of course, in any society, including an egalitarian one, some people are going to be more equal than others. However, in the egalitarian society their influence is slight compared to that of the ruler of a state. At best, some individuals in the egalitarian society can influence the decision making of those living with them, usually their kin. Those most likely to wield some authority are the elders and the shaman (the native priest), yet no matter what their own judgments may be, these individuals have little power to enforce their decisions; they must rely on supernatural sanctions and gossip to deal with those who deviate from the norms of the group.

The egalitarian society is based on hunting and gathering. From what can be inferred from the archaeological record, it seems clear that the hunting-and-gathering band was the first form of sociopolitical organization utilized by human beings. It also is the form which has the longest history—several million years.

> The band is an egalitarian society.

Almost all hunting-and-gathering bands are nomadic. Their personal belongings are extremely limited, because the hunters must carry all of their possessions with them whenever they move, which is frequently. The only major exception to this pattern are the Eskimo, who have sleds pulled by dog teams to aid in the transportation of their possessions.

The only permanent kin group in hunting-and-gathering societies is the family. Families in turn make up a larger, less close-knit unit called the band. The members of the band may live together as a group during certain seasons when food is plentiful. At other times of the year, as resources become scarce, the band splits into families, with each smaller group fending for itself.

> The domestic family is the only permanent kin group on the band level.

The band serves several important functions. First, members may share the same territory, although frequently the territory inhabited by one band overlaps that of another. The land itself is less important to hunters and gatherers than the natural resources it contains. Second, members of the band tend to form a ceremonial unit that maintains the various rituals of the society such as initiation rites. Third, the members of the band are forbidden to marry one another. It is this last feature of band organization that necessitates some type of interaction between bands. For the most part, the band is an autonomous political unit that is able to satisfy all the needs of its members, except that it is unable to provide its members with mates. The band frequently practices unilineal descent—usually patrilineal— and therefore everyone in the band is related by blood or is married to someone of the bloodline. Incest taboos dictate that mates must be obtained from outside the band.

Within the band there are no specialized institutions and, with the exception of the shaman, no specialists. The domestic family undertakes all roles. The only divisions within the society are those of age and sex. Individuals of particular age categories do certain tasks, as do members of each sex. In the egalitarian society, there is generally a clear-cut distinction between men's work and women's work. The men's work is usually social: It is more likely to be performed in groups, because of the tendency toward kin ties between males. The work of the women tends to be individualized and monotonous. The women of the group are not usually related by blood, and the largest female group may be that of a woman and her daughters. However, among many hunting-and-gathering bands the women's contributions are basic to the subsistence and very existence of the group. The vegetable material they collect may constitute as much as 70 to 80 percent of the total band diet.

The impact of a woman's contribution to the group is of special importance whenever a man seeks a mate. If the males of the band must find females from another group to marry, what inducement would make the other band give up any of its women? In agricultural and herding societies there are various kinds of inducements used. In some cases, gifts of cattle or other valuables, called *brideprice* or *bridewealth*, are given to compensate the female's kin group for her loss or for the loss of the children she might produce. In other cases, a young man may work for his bride's kin for a year or more, as a form of compensation called *bride service*. None of these compensations are possible at the hunting-and-gathering level. Since males of all bands need to find mates, bands have worked out a marriage arrangement whereby two males of different bands can each obtain mates, with neither group decreasing its number of women. This system, in which a male of one band exchanges his sister with a male of another band in return for that individual's sister, is called *sibling exchange*. In this way, each man obtains a wife and both bands retain the same number of women.

On the band level, economic relations are based on *reciprocity*. Reciprocity is the exchange of goods, favors, and labor among a group of people. Reciprocity is found at every level of sociopolitical evolution, but at the band level it is the only type of eco-

Band economic relations are based on reciprocity.

Brideprice on display at a wedding, Kaoka-speakers of Guadalcanal. (Ian Hogbin)

nomic relation practiced. Sharing is the most common form of reciprocity and is the basis of survival for the band. The members of the band share food with one another. Generosity is admired, while thrift is considered selfishness. The members of the band do not keep track of what they share with others. They assume that in the long run the giving and receiving will be roughly equivalent. Individuals are not supposed to keep track of what they give, and it would be considered an offense to suggest that a return was expected.

The sharing of food helps the group to survive. If one hunter is successful, he shares his game with others. In the future they will share with him. This is important, because the hunter may not have luck for several days or even weeks. In the meantime, he and his family can survive on what others share with him. This system of reciprocity works well on the band level, because there are few societies at this level that are able to store much of their food, because it is perishable. If game were not shared, much of the meat would be wasted since it could not all be consumed by a single family before it spoiled.

No one holds a great deal of power over others on the band level. Elders may make suggestions but are not surprised if their judgments are not followed. A great hunter may be admired and even assumed to have supernatural assistance, but the prestige that he enjoys as a hunter is not transferable to other areas of the society and does not constitute a firm basis for political power (Fried 1967:66). Without someone in charge of the group, social control operates primarily through social and supernatural sanctions. If someone is a perpetual wife stealer, there may be no effective way of dealing with that person. Gossip can be used, but only if the individual is sensitive to it. The supernatural can be called upon for retribution, but such punishment is often less effective than the forms of punishment utilized by the state form of organization, such as imprisonment or execution. Perhaps the only effective way of forcing the nonconformist to

Social control takes the form of social and supernatural sanctions.

follow the correct forms of behavior on the band level is for the group to stop sharing with that individual. Since the individual's survival may sometimes depend on help from others, the pressure is often enough to cause the individual to change his or her actions.

Blood feuds between individuals or families are also difficult to resolve at the band level, because there is no one who can act as an intermediary between parties. No one has the authority to arbitrarily decide that a death can be compensated by some form of payment. As a result, certain deaths are avenged by the family of the victim. In the revenge killing the murderer or someone of equal status in the murderer's kin group is killed. Thus, in times of conflict, the autonomy that the domestic families and the band enjoy for other purposes, is a hindrance, making resolution of conflict dificult—if not impossible.

The Copper Eskimo: An Arctic Band

The Copper Eskimo inhabit part of the central Canadian Artic area. They are descendants of people who spread from Alaska across Canada between AD 900 and AD 1200. Traditionally the Eskimo was a hunter of caribou and seal and a fisherman. There is little vegetable material to gather throughout most of the region. The Copper Eskimo remained isolated until the early years of the twentieth century, and from that time on the effects of Western culture have progressively influenced the aboriginal way of life. There has been an influx of trappers, traders, missionaries, prospectors, and others, culminating in the establishment of radar sites in Copper Eskimo territory.

The area that has traditionally been inhabited by the Copper Eskimo includes part of the northern Canadian mainland and the islands of the Arctic Archipelago. Most of the region is *tundra*[2] of various types. Vegetation is most abundant on the mainland. Much of Victoria Island is virtual wasteland, though some valleys support plant life such as mosses, grasses, and flowers. The region is characterized by long, cold winters and short, cool summers. Winter temperatures reach to −40 or −50 degrees Fahrenheit. Freezing temperatures can occur in any month except July. Precipitation is light and averages 6 to 10 inches a year, most of which falls in the form of snow. While the snow gathers in deep drifts wherever there are obstructions, much of the land is swept bare of snow even during the middle of winter. A solid sheet of ice forms over the straits and gulfs of

---

[2] Tundra is typically a vast, level, treeless plain so far north that the ground never completely thaws but south of the region of perpetual snow and ice.

the region beginning in autumn. Little ice remains from the preceding season at the end of summer, so that a new sheet covers the surface each year. Lakes freeze over by the end of September in most parts of the area. Many of the lakes continue to have ice cover until well into July. In some areas the ground is not free of snow until well into June and is again covered sometime in September. These extreme climatic conditions strongly influence the life of both the Eskimo and the game they depend upon for their survival (Damas 1972:7–11).

Famine was not uncommon in the precontact period, and female infanticide was practiced during difficult periods, especially when the group was moving. A census taken in 1923–1924 showed that males outnumbered females about three to two. The shortage of females seems to have been a contributing factor to the high rate of homicide among the Copper Eskimo. In many cases, rivalry over women set off a series of killings.

The economic cycle and the settlement pattern of the Eskimo were closely intertwined. During the winter months a large number of people lived together. Winter aggregations ranged from about 50 to perhaps 200 persons, with an average group of about 100. This range represented the optimum number of hunters that could adequately exploit an area around the camp 5 miles in radius. During the winter, hunters were engaged in breathing-hole sealing, a form of hunting requiring a large grouping of people, because each of the numerous breathing holes that a seal makes must be watched by a hunter in order to maximize the chances of success.

During the winter the Eskimo lived together in large groups.

In spring the large aggregation divided into smaller groups. At this time of the year the caribou were scattered in small herds, and the fish, the most important spring source of food, were not concentrated in any one place but were found in the numerous lakes and streams. Thus, exploitation of the fish could most effectively be accomplished by small groups.

In spring the Eskimo divided into smaller groups.

Beginning in July and extending through the autumn months, caribou hunting intensified, because the caribou were fat and had grown new coats at this time of year. Caribou drives were organized. Long rows of stones or scarecrows were set along ridges to resemble people. The caribou were then driven by shouting women and children between the rows of stones or scarecrows to a point where bowmen lay waiting in shallow pits. For a few days in late summer, in the middle of the caribou season, larger aggregations gathered again, this time at sites near the mouths of principal streams, to catch the large number of fish (mostly char) that were returning from the sea.

November usually marked the end of the caribou season. By

462

Who's in Charge Here? A Look at Political Organization

that time of the year it became dangerous to use a bow, because the low temperatures might cause frostbite. Also, the Eskimo had to stay close to the sea in order to catch seals. Seals were important both for the food they provided and for their fat, the primary and often sole source of fuel. Seal fat was burned in stone lamps, providing light, heat, and fire for cooking. During a period of two to four weeks in November or early December, the food supply was extremely sparse, and the Copper Eskimo existed on dried or frozen caribou meat and dried and frozen fish that had been stored in anticipation of the food shortages. Clothing was sewn for the winter months during this period of limited hunting and fishing. By December, camps of snow-houses were constructed on the ice of the frozen sea, within walking distance of seal breathing holes (Damas 1972:12–23).

Meat was distributed among the Copper Eskimo primarily on the basis of partnerships involving both kin and nonkin. This system of meat distribution was used mainly with the ringed seal. Fourteen major parts of the seal were assigned to individuals. Whenever a seal was captured, each individual received his section of the seal, no matter which hunter had actually killed the seal. The killer of the seal received only the skin, entrails, and fat of the seal. During the winter months, the distribution of seal meat was supplemented by the practice of communal eating. In some cases, the seal-share partnerships were extended during the summer months to include the sharing of fish and caribou among partners although the settlement was usually scattered into small groups. Likewise there was a certain amount of voluntary sharing, especially when those who were not partners were sharing the same snowhouse, although the amounts were considerably less than those given to partners. Sharing would take place during the period in which the families were coresidents of the snowhouse. As mentioned earlier, sharing on the band level insures a wide distribution of food and compensates for the vagaries of individual luck and for differences in skill.

Among the Copper Eskimo, as among other hunters and gatherers, there was no structurally defined institution of leadership. Some individuals received great respect because they organized hunts, practiced sorcery, or aggressively took what they wanted by force, including women. Yet none of these attributes led to a position of leadership. In fact, the aggressive individual was a constant threat to the harmony of the group and often met with a violent end, either by vindictive homicide or an execution-type killing, because the community had no effective way of controlling his aggression. There were few mechanisms

The Eskimo had no institution of leadership.

for settling disputes. As the anthropologist David Damas (1972:33) has observed of the Copper Eskimo:

> Without the existence of strong leaders or village councils, settlement of grievances became largely a private affair and often homicide was the only solution available. Some support from kindred can be seen in the existence of blood vengeance, which seems to have been rather highly developed in the area. The frequency of homicide, due to one cause or another, can be appreciated from Rasmussen's (1932) survey of an encampment of fifteen families where he found that "there was not a single grown man who had not been involved in a killing one way or another."

This pattern of ineffective social control on the band level due to a lack of leadership was not unique to the Copper Eskimo. For example, among the Eskimo of northern Alaska, the anthropologist Norman A. Chance found basically the same pattern. There were no formal positions of leadership. Outside of the ties of kinship, the north Alaskan Eskimo had few organizational ties. Like the Copper Eskimo his primary ties were with hunting partners and similar ties existed between members who hunted whales together. The north Alaskan Eskimo suffered the same problem as did the Copper Eskimo, that of not being able to deal effectively with the nonconformist. As Chance (1966:65) notes:

> Nonconforming individuals, such as an aggressive bully or persistent wife stealer, presented a continual problem in these settlements. If the nonconformist could not be curbed by the actions of kin or the force of public opinion, the one remaining alternative was to exclude him from participation in the community's economic and social life, a rather effective sanction given the unpredictable conditions of arctic life. If severe interpersonal conflicts arose between one or more members of different kin groups, the villagers were faced with a serious dilemma, for there was no available technique for resolving blood feuds once they had begun. It was not until the government assigned United States marshals to police this northern area that inter-family feuds disappeared entirely.

In some Eskimo groups, *song duels* were used to reduce aggression. When one Eskimo felt that he had been injured by another, he composed a satirical song which he sang at a public challenge performance. The person for whom the song was intended would respond in song. The audience served as a jury. When a decision was announced, the contestants had to be friends again, no matter what the results. The song duels were usually comic entertainment for the onlookers and revenge for one of the parties involved. The duel helped to channel aggression before it became physical, as it did among the Copper Eskimo, who did not observe the song duel ritual (Garbarino 1976:96).

The band then is a small, autonomous nomadic group whose subsistence is based on hunting and gathering. It is basically a leaderless society and one without effective mechanisms for resolving disputes. With the development of agriculture, human societies began to take on a new look.

The Tribe: Fact or Fiction?

When anthropologists began fieldwork at the turn of the century, many of the peoples they studied were organized into sociopolitical units classified as *tribes*. It had long been assumed by nineteenth-century evolutionists that the tribe represented an early form of organization that had been replaced in many areas of the world by more developed forms of organization such as the state. The tribe was thought to be a remnant or survival of an earlier way of life.

The term *tribe* has never satisfied anthropologists, because of its many uses and connotations. Societies that are classified as tribal seem to be very diverse in their organization, having little in common. Yet the belief that the tribe represents an early evolutionary stage of development continues today in the work of many anthropologists. Elman R. Service (1971b) and Marshall D. Sahlins (1968) have presented the most convincing arguments for a tribal level of development. The primary difference in their points of view is that Sahlins includes the chiefdom as a complex type of tribe, whereas Service views the chiefdom as a distinct evolutionary stage. In both cases they see the tribe developing primarily as a result of the origin of agriculture and the beginnings of settled village life. As new techniques of agriculture allowed the Neolithic tribal villages to transform their environment, their economy became more productive, and population density increased. The tribes were able to develop more power and resources than the bands. They spread at the expense of the bands, who were pushed into the more marginal areas of the world by these agriculturalists.

The anthropologist arguing most convincingly against this point of view is Morton H. Fried (1967, 1975a, 1975b). Fried contends that the term *tribe* is so ambiguous and confusing that it should be abandoned by social scientists. Fried also believes that the type of society to which the term has been applied does not represent an ancient form of organization. Instead, he argues, the tribal form of organization is something that came into being only *after* the emergence of the state. Concerning the nature of the tribe, Fried (1975b:12–13) observes:

Fried believes tribes originated as a result of states.

Social scientists, including most anthropologists, think of tribes as merely a stage in the evolution of political systems, occurring between family and the appearance of organized governmental bodies.

I disagree. I think there is ample evidence to indicate that states created tribes rather than having evolved from them. I believe that tribes first came into existence perhaps five or six thousand years ago. Considering that human culture may be as much as three million years old, the tribe must be regarded as a recent invention. Most tribes are much younger; some may even have been formed in the present century.

What Fried believes happened is that hunting-and-gathering bands and simple farming villages of prestate societies seemed so formless to encroaching colonial powers, including the expanding empires of the ancient world, that these powers had to transform the societies organizationally in order to deal with them. These societies then became tribes. The archaeological record shows that agriculture brought with it villages, but villages in themselves are not a sign of tribal organization. Where the archaeological data is examined for evidence of the tribe, the interpretation of the data is usually based on a projection of data from tribes of the twentieth century back into the past. This type of projection is risky, because there is no apparent reason that villages in the past had to have been organized in the manner that they are today. Fried (1975b:13) suggests that when archaeologists have discovered the remains of a number of unified bands or villages, which are characteristic of known tribes, it can usually be shown that this organization has been imposed by encroaching states.

Both Service's and Fried's points of view have their supporters in anthropology. Perhaps new approaches in archaeological systems analysis will ultimately solve the puzzle of whether or not any type of tribe existed in the past as an evolutionary stage. If it did, it may have represented a brief period in many areas of the world, being superceded by a chiefdom or state form of organization. In our discussion here, the problem of the tribe is not so critical, because the term *tribe* will be used only to refer to contemporary societies, regardless of whether they are the survivals of an early evolutionary stage or a secondary development of the state. Whatever the case, there are a number of contemporary primitive societies that are considered tribal and share certain characteristics.

According to service (1971b) the tribe is a fragile social body compared to the chiefdom or the state. It is composed of economically self-sufficient residential groups that recognize no higher authority than the village headman. In other words, the tribal village is much like a band of hunters and gatherers who have settled down and become farmers. The settled group is still basically autonomous and lacking in strong leadership, like the band, and the village is basically a kin group.

The tribe differs from the band in several features. It is primarily agricultural or pastoral rather than nomadic. The tribe is made up of a larger number of people than the band. Service believes that the most important difference between the band and the tribe is that the tribe is integrated by pantribal *sodalties*. A sodality, by Service's (1971b:13) definition, is "a nonresidential association that has some corporate functions or purposes." The pantribal sodality is some type of grouping that crosscuts the villages of the tribe. Some sodalities are based on kinship. In other words, in some tribes the members of a lineage or clan are found in more than one village. Other sodalities are nonkin. In these cases, age-grades, warrior societies, ceremonial societies, and so on include members from more than one village. The sodalities are important because they give the tribe a means of arbitration when disputes occur between villages. The kin of the same lineage or members of the same warrior society in the two villages can sometimes act as mediators, a mechanism lacking on the band level. However, the members of a sodality do not have authority, and the parties in conflict need not accept their mediation. Yet the sodality offers a potential for arbitration not present on the band level.

Although sodalities crosscut tribal villages, they do not give the tribe unity. For the most part, the members of a tribe do nothing as an entity. Instead, a large part of tribal life is carried out at the village level, where an elder of a village kin group serves as the headman of the village. Perhaps the only time that the members of different villages cooperate with one another as a tribal entity is during a period of conflict with other tribes. Tribal organization works on the principle known as the *massing effect*, in which progressively higher orders of groupings come into being in times of opposition (Sahlins 1961:332–333). For example, on a day-to-day basis, brothers of the same family may argue about their inheritance. If there are differences with kin of another family, the two brothers will cooperate with one another as members of the same family until the conflict with the other kin is resolved. If conflict arises with nonkin of the same village, all of the families of the kin group will cooperate against the other kin group. If two villages are in conflict over land, the various kin groups of the village will unite temporarily against the other village. The only time there is cooperation between the villages of the tribe is when the tribe is in conflict

Tribal peoples have pan-tribal sodalities.

The tribe cooperates as an entity only in times of opposition from another tribe.

with another tribe. For example, if one tribe invaded another's territory, the villagers of a tribe would cooperate with one another, temporarily, to defend themselves against the invaders. The village headmen might elect one headman to serve as war leader until the conflict had ended. Once there was no more opposition from another tribe, the war leader would have no authority over any village but his own. Likewise, if the problems with another tribe were resolved, the tribe would revert to a state of disunity in which village autonomy predominated.

Because of the fragile nature of the tribal organization, a particular type of lineage organization is found associated with the tribe, called the *segmentary lineage*. The segmentary lineage is one that fragments after only a few generations, so that members are continually splitting from the lineage and establishing their own new lineages. The Lugbara of East Africa are a tribal people who are organized into segmentary lineages.

The Lugbara: An African Tribe[3]

The Lugbara live along an international boundary in East Africa. They are found along the Nile-Congo divide where it forms the boundary between Uganda and Zaïre (formerly the Congo). The center of Lugbara country is between 4000 and 5000 feet above sea level and forms a clearly marked plateau. Almost all of Lugbara territory consists of open, treeless, rolling plains. The country is covered with a network of permanent streams and rivers. Across the open country one can see for vast distances. Two mountains rise in the center and are visible from virtually every part of the Lugbara territory in clear weather. These mountains have a conspicuous place in Lugbara mythology.

The Lugbara are sedentary cultivators whose main crops include millet, sorghum, legumes, and root crops such as sweet potatoes and cassava. Livestock, mainly cattle and goats, are also kept by the villagers. In general the residential groups—the villages—are economically self-sufficient as far as food is concerned. Water, firewood, ochre, clay, reeds, thatching grass, iron, calabashes, and other raw materials are found almost everywhere. Traditionally, there was little exchange of these materials, and individuals had little need to venture far from their own neighborhood to satisfy their wants.

There is no political centralization among the Lugbara, as one would expect for a tribal type of organization. The *family cluster* is the primary group of Lugbara society, being basically a small

---

[3] This description is based on the following sources: Middleton 1954, 1955, 1958, 1960, and 1965.

village. Relations between family clusters comprise the Lugbara political structure, which is made up of highly independent and autonomous territorial groups that are segmentary lineages. The only intertribal relations involve warfare.

The Family Cluster. The family cluster is a small group of about 25 people living in scattered groups of homesteads. The cluster has its own land, in which are located its compounds, fields, and grazing areas for its livestock. The family cluster is based upon a small patrilineage of three or four generations. The elder of the lineage is usually considered the headman of the family cluster. He holds this status by virtue of his genealogical seniority in the lineage. The family cluster allocates its own land. No higher kin grouping has any authority over the family cluster's land.

The headman has certain insignias of office, the most impor- tant of which is a special round stool made from a single piece of wood. Only headman may sit on these stools, which are in- herited. In some parts of the Lugbara territory, long sticks or wands are also considered marks of office. Only the headman may eat certain parts of the meat that are used for sacrifices—the spare meat of the chest, the liver, kidney, tes- ticles, penis, intestines, and usually the tongue. The headman is thought to have ritual authority over the members of the family cluster. It is he who consults *oracles* (mediums by which the an- cestors are consulted) and performs the most important rites of sacrifice. As secular authority within the family cluster, the headman has the responsibility of allocating land to the members of the cluster.

> The headman has ritual and secular authority over the Lugbara family clus- ter.

While each family cluster has its own landholding, there is a high density of population, and consequently sporadic and localized shortages of land. This results in the continual move- ment of certain individuals from one family cluster to another, as tenants. Also, there are almost constant tensions over land between family clusters and between each cluster's own mem- bers. When land becomes scarce, villagers attempt to take over unused land of neighboring villages. These factors, together with the lack of higher authority within the tribe, result in a high rate of segmentation at the family cluster level, as well as much fusion of family clusters that are alone and unable to maintain their rights over land vis-á-vis other groups that are increasing in size and strength.

Most of the members of the family cluster come under the do- mestic authority of the headman by virtue of kinship ties. An- other group of persons, the tenants, may also attach themselves to the group. Tenants are not under the ritual authority of the headman unless, in the case of men, they marry a daughter of his group; it is said among the Lugbara that a man can fight his tenants or even expel them and he will have the support of his own kin in doing so.

Most of the members of the group come under the ritual authority of the headman because they are kin. After a generation or two, the individuals of these attached families become so numerous, or there may be such a shortage of land, that some break away to become an accessory family cluster. Each new family cluster has its own headman and is independent in its internal affairs.

Relations beyond the family cluster are outside the control of the headman, who is primarily concerned with the ordering of relations within his group. The cluster's internal relations are seen in terms of personal kinship. The headman will sometimes initiate hostile or other actions against other groups, or he may decide to try to bring hostile relations to an end, although in either case, he has no control over the outcome because his authority is limited to the family cluster.

The headman is the highest authority in the tribal system. His family cluster is both kin group and political unit. Authority over the kin is passed through the patrilineal line. The most important recognition for the headman is internal recognition— that of his kin living in the village. External recognition for the headman—beyond the family cluster—occurs only after a person has gained internal recognition. An individual must first be accepted as headman by the kin of his village; he is then considered by headmen of equal status from other villages to be the legitimate representative of his village at ceremonies. However there is no higher-ranking external authority who must recognize his claim as headman.

The headman is the highest authority in Lugbara society.

The headman controls the allocation of land as part of his responsibility as head of the family cluster. Land plays a major role in the segmentation of the group. As land becomes scarcer, due to population increase and erosion, pressure is placed on the headman from within his kin group. He is expected to provide land for young people who wish to farm their own land. Eventually, such pressures will result in segmentation.

The Lugbara headman's authority in kinship matters extends over the entire village. Even those who are attached to the village as tenants must abide by his decision. His authority in political matters is not very significant. He assumes a political role only when the group has to interact with other groups, such as during periods of conflict.

The source of the greatest conflict for the Lugbara headman

comes from the competition of younger kin within his village who are constantly trying to take over his position. Conflict also occurs outside of the village, between headmen, over cultivable land, often leading to feuding between villages.

The effectiveness of the Lugbara headman is measured by his ability to summon the ancestors of the lineage. He is supposed to ask the ancestors for help whenever the lineage is in danger of being destroyed by the improper acts of an individual of the family cluster. The Lugbara believe that if a headman has the support of the ancestors, they will bring sickness to the evildoer or one of his relatives as punishment. If the headman proves ineffective in summoning the ancestors, it is assumed that the ancestors no longer support him. Those of the village wanting to challenge the headman will try to demonstrate that they have the ancestors behind themselves, thus threatening the position of the current headman.

The headman's power is based on his ability to summon the ancestors.

Individuals cannot move away from the village without upsetting the structure of the lineage, as most villagers are kin. The younger kin of the lineage will remain in the village as long as they feel there is a chance that they may be able to take over the position of headman. If the headman is absolutely secure in his position, the young kin tend to leave the village. At this point, the lineage may segment, with the young kin organizing their own autonomous groups.

The size of a village indicates something of the length of time which has passed since the kin group has last segmented. The larger the village, the more likely it is to be on the verge of segmentation. A large village will therefore be full of conflicts between the headman and the younger men of the village. Both the headman and the younger men will attempt to bring sickness to the kin of their village in order to demonstrate their effectiveness in summoning the help of the ancestors. On the other hand, a small village usually indicates that a group has recently segmented from another village. The shifting of nonkin tenants from one village to another is considered to neither increase nor decrease the power of either headman of the villages involved, since these nonkin are not really part of a village unless they marry into it. It is the kin of the village that the headman is mainly concerned with keeping in his village. When lineage segmentation occurs, another kin unit is established that is of equal status to the original village. While the original village and the new village are now considered autonomous, they will probably share ritual practices together, because they will continue to venerate the same recently dead ancestors of the lineage. These ties may cease after a generation or two, as each group will have its own recently dead ancestors to worship.

Accusations of Witchcraft. Sorcery, although it exists, plays an insignificant role in the conflicts of the Lugbara village. Of much greater significance are accusations of witchcraft within the lineage. Since only the headman is supposed to contact the ancestors, the use of lineage ritual is a socially sanctioned means of forcing deviants to conform to proper behavior for ensuring the perpetuation of the kin group. When someone acts in a way that endangers the group, the headman prays to the ancestors for their help. It is believed that if he is effective, the ancestors will cause misfortune to occur to the wrongdoer. As a village population grows, the younger kin of the group begin to question the headman's authority. They will claim that he is performing the ritual for his own selfish ends rather than for the good of the kin group. At first, this conflict is resolved by some of the young men moving away from the village. Frequently, however, the conflict between the headman and those who have remained in the village increases to the point where he is accused of using witchcraft against his own people. This is a serious charge, as witchcraft is an antisocial action, either because the witch's motives are selfish and malicious or because the witch ignores the socially approved means of dealing with offenders of kin beliefs. Witches are thought to deny and destroy the ties of kinship and community that are necessary for the perpetuation of any kind of orderly social life.

Social relations are structured by a network of ties of authority. The Lugbara realize that within this authority structure there will be some who will rebel against authority as they grow older. The authority against which they rebel is exercised by the headman. The young men usually do not try to escape from authority as such, only from the authority of a particular headman. They accept without question the ultimate authority of the ancestors. However there are always some people who either cannot accept authority as such or cannot accept any restriction on their personal ambitions and desires. These individuals especially try to destroy the authority of headmen by making accusations of witchcraft against them. If these same individuals themselves become headmen, they usually attempt to postpone either the legitimate aspirations of their own young men or those of their generational equals. They usually abuse their power of authority, using it for their own ends rather than the good of the kin. These individuals are then themselves frequently accused of being witches by their juniors.

In the Lugbara system of belief, witches are always men. Witchcraft is believed practiced only between people who are in some form of social relationship. Witchcraft accusations are made between headmen engaged in brideprice negotiations.

Among the Lugbara, only men are considered witches.

The Lugbara believe that a witch has the power to bewitch any person of his own neighborhood, kin or nonkin, but that he has no power to bewitch a member of another tribe. Elders are most often feared to practice witchcraft, because an individual can be bewitched only by a man older than himself, never by someone who is his junior.

Tenants are frequently accused of witchcraft. They are the first to be suspected, because their past is not as well known as that of the village kin. It is usually assumed that tenants leave their homes either because of famine or because they were banished as witches. The kinsman-tenant relationship is a strained one. The tenants are in a servile position and are usually poor. As a result they frequently dislike those who have taken them in and who have authority over them.

When a headman dies, it is often not very clear who should be his heir. At this point, those competing for the position will accuse the others of using witchcraft, and each will claim that the rituals he has performed have summoned the ancestors, thus demonstrating that he, and not his rivals, has the backing of the ancestors. John Middleton (1960:146), the British anthropologist who has studied the Lugbara, gives the following example of the type of competition that occurs over the position of headman:

Oguda and Ondua were half-brothers. Their father Dria had two wives. Dria had recently died, and it was not clear in the village which of his two sons should be the new headman. Then Oguda's grandson became sick with a prolonged series of low fevers. Oguda insisted on consulting the oracles. He went to the rubbing-stick oracle[4] for a séance. Oguda then maintained that he had made his grandson ill by invoking the ghost of his father, Dria, because Oguda's son, Jobi, had been insolent to him, the sickness sent by Dria had afflicted Jobi's son.

Oguda's half-brother Ondua refused to accept that verdict. He went to his own rubbing-stick oracle to confirm the verdict. Ondua then claimed that the rubbing-stick oracle did not confirm the verdict. He suggested that both he and Oguda should go to a neutral rubbing-stick oracle who would not be influenced by either half-brother. They consulted a famous oracle 7 miles from the village. Ondua gave the names of suspected agents to the oracle operator, including himself, Oguda, and several other individuals. The oracle gave the verdict that Ondua was the

---

[4] The rubbing-stick oracle is always the first type of oracle consulted. It consists merely of a stalk of sorghum, which is held in the operator's left hand and rubbed by a twist of grass or even by the fingers of the other hand. As it is rubbed, the names of suspected agents of a sickness are put to it by the operator. When the operator's fingers stick to the sorghum stalk, the oracle is thought to have given that particular name (Middleton 1965:77).

agent and that he had caused the boy to become ill. Ondua was pleased and agreed that he had made Oguda's grandson sick. He now claimed that it was he and not Oguda whose prayers were answered by the ancestors. In the eyes of the village, Ondua had been legitimated as successor to the headmanship because he demonstrated that he had the ability to summon the ancestors.

At this point, the loser in the competition, Oguda, and his followers segmented from the village and set up their own independent village, with Oguda as headman. Ondua and Oguda continue to have ritual ties in common because they both worship their father Dria. These ties will be broken by the next generation, as each village will focus its attention on the most recent ancestor. In Ondua's village they will venerate him, and in Oguda's village they will worship him. Thus, by the second generation, complete segmentation will have occurred.

The Chiefdom

The chiefdom represents a third type of political organization. Unlike the band or the tribe, the chiefdom is clearly a hierarchical society in which some individuals have leadership roles. A primary characteristic of the chiefdom is that an individual is given the position of chief in the society. Under the chief are a number of lesser chiefs and village headmen, all of whom are

The chiefdom has a clear hierarchy of authority positions.

Warriors of the Swazi chiefdom. (Wide World)

responsible to the chief. In Fried's terminology, the chiefdom is considered a rank society. According to Fried (1967:109), "a rank society is one in which positions of valued status are somehow limited so that not all those of sufficient talent to occupy such statuses actually achieve them." Thus in a chiefdom, people are less equal than they are in either the band or the tribe. According to Service (1971*b*:133), the chiefdom society transcends the tribal society in two important aspects. First, the chiefdom has a greater density of population, a gain made possible by greater productivity. Second, the chiefdom is more complex and more organized, with centers that coordinate economic, social, and religious activities.

In many cases the rise of chiefdoms in prehistoric times seems to have been related to a total environmental situation that favored specialization in production and redistribution of produce from a controlling center. Unlike the tribe, the chiefdom usually covers a large territory and includes several different kinds of environments, each with its own special crops or raw materials. With band and tribal organization, everyone in the society shares the same available resources and, in the case of the tribe, grows the same crops. There is really little need for an elaborate economic system. In both cases reciprocity serves as the basic economic system.

Reciprocity continues as an economic system within the chiefdom, but a new economic system called *redistribution* also operates. The redistributive system involves greater integration and centralization of the society. Because the territory of the chiefdom encompasses at least several different environmental zones, there is greater need for some sort of management of these resources. Surpluses from all of these zones are funneled into the chief's center and are redistributed by the chief and his assistants. More importantly, the chief does not usually redistribute all that comes to him. Instead, much of this surplus is channeled off to be used by the chief to support his political, social, and religious activities. It may also be used to help support artisans and other full-time specialists at the chief's center. Thus in the chiefdom, two categories of people, the producers and the distributors, emerge, corresponding precisely with the distinction between nonchief and chief (Sahlins 1958:4–5). The role of distributor confers prestige in the chiefdom society. In some cases the chief is expected to give away more than he receives and is forced to borrow from kin. Thus, it is possible for a chief to be impoverished and yet be accorded great prestige within the society. Such persons are considered rich for what they dispense and not for what they hoard (Fried 1967:118).

The power of the chief is derived from the redistributive system.

Whereas all members of the tribe, including the village headman, are involved in food production, in a chiefdom the chief is food distributor and is divorced from farming, as are a number of full-time specialists. The fact that the chief is given status as a distributor also raises the status of every member of his family above ordinary families, and ultimately the families of his local kin group as well.

The Luapula:
An African Chiefdom[5]

The Luapula live along the international boundary formed by the Luapula River between Zambia (formerly Northern Rhodesia) and Zaïre. The Luapula groups that have been studied by anthropologists live in Zambia. The total population of the Luapula is about 63,000.

The outstanding features of the topography are the rivers and the swamps. The British anthropologist most familiar with the Luapula, Ian Cunnison, describes the Luapula as "swamp-oriented." The Luapula differ from other groups of the same language family in that their economy is based primarily on fishing. The staple foods of the Luapula are fish and cassava. Fishing has replaced elephant hunting as the main source of wealth along the Luapula River.

The Luapula are ruled by a paramount chief, a number of territorial subchiefs, and village headmen. Each chief under the paramount chief controls the allocation of land to villages and has political control over the inhabitants of his territory. The boundaries of a chief's territory define the area within which a resident is allowed to cultivate without asking special permission from another Luapula chief. These boundaries are not significant, however, for carrying out other activities such as fishing, hunting, and cutting wood. Within the chief's territory, in contrast to the Lugbara village, there is little conflict over land matters. Villages, lineages, or any other kind of kin group, have no special rights over stretches of cultivable land. Unlike the Lugbara, individuals do not have to adhere to a kinship group before they can find land to cultivate; they need only be registered with a chief.

The Luapula lineage consists of those who trace their descent through the maternal line from an ancestor who was allocated land to settle a village. Elders of a matrilineage are in charge of

---

[5] This discussion of the Luapula is based on the following sources: Cunnison 1951, 1954, 1956*a*, 1956*b*, 1957, 1959; and Epstein 1954.

matters of succession within the lineage, and with this end in view, learn its genealogy. The lineage is the largest selection of clan whose comprehensive genealogy is known to any one person. The lineage leader and some of the elders live in the lineage center village. Meetings of members of a lineage to discuss lineage affairs take place at the center. The lineage is said to "own" the village. Although lineages have centers of this kind and select the village headmen from within their ranks, the lineages are in no way tied to the land, as village headmen have no control over the allocation of land. It is not uncommon for the members of a lineage to be scattered through a number of neighboring villages. Membership in a lineage does not determine residence as it does among the Lugbara. Although villages normally contain a nucleus of the headman's matrilineal descent group, kin of the headman do not account for more than a small proportion of the total village. The larger part of the village population is made up of individuals who, attracted by the prestige and personality of the headman, have migrated to join him. Although marriage is initially matrilocal, after the birth of two or three children, or before if the husband feels that witchcraft has been directed against him, he obtains the approval of his in-laws and takes his wife to his own village or wherever else he chooses to settle.

In the Luapula village, most members are not kin.

The Luapula village is a temporary association of people for the purpose of habitation. Membership in a village carries with it only a few political, ritual, and economic obligations. On the one hand, the name of the village and its continued association with a particular lineage and its comparative permanence on one site are long-lasting. On the other hand, the village's composition changes from year to year. At the same time, its structure is stable to the extent that a cleavage in kinship and interest always exists between the members of the owning lineage and the others—the strangers. Unlike the segmentary lineages of the tribe, the Luapula villages do not split apart because of this cleavage.

The Luapula village is part of a centralized political system headed by a paramount chief. The village headman is responsible, in political matters, to the chiefs above him in the political hierarchy. The members of the village owe most of their allegiances to the chief rather than to the headman of the village in which they live. Because of the political structure, people can move from one village to another and still remain under the same chief.

Among the Luapula there are two means by which an individual can become a village headman. The first is to succeed a former headman upon his death. A new headman is selected by the kin group from among the junior members of the lineage. This person can be any age when he becomes headman. The most important element in validating his position is being recognized as the new headman by the chief. Without the approval of the chief, no one can become headman, even though he has been chosen by his kin group. A headman chosen by his kin and approved by the chief is faced with the task of pleasing both his matrilineage and the other individuals living in the village. Once in office the headman is usually secure in his position until his death, unless he retires and names his successor.

A second means of becoming a headman is even more strongly dependent on external recognition (recognition from outside the kin group). If a man wishes to be recognized as a headman, even though his matrilineage has chosen someone else as headman of the village owned by the kin group, he applies to the chief to be "written" as a headman and to have his followers listed under his name. This requires that he have a minimum of ten taxpayers among his followers. If the headman establishes a new village, the land on which it is built is allocated by the chief and not by any kin group.

Whereas the Lugbara headman's authority in kinship matters extends to the entire village, the Luapula headman has such authority only over members of his matrilineage living in the village. Those not related to him do not have to follow the decisions he makes as representative of the matrilineage owning the village. The headman's political authority, however, affects everyone in the village, because he acts as the local representative of the chief. Thus in a chiefdom, kinship matters and political matters, while still intertwined, are often separate matters.

The Luapula headman's greatest competition is with other village headmen. Each headman tries to increase the population of his respective village by attracting people from other villages. There are no disputes over land between headmen—as is common among the Lugbara—because the chief controls the allocation of land. If there is any dispute over land boundaries, these are quickly settled by referring the matter to the chief.

The size of the village is very important among the Luapula because it is a measure of the headman's prestige. A large village indicates a successful headman. A large village is said to be a harmonious village, and it is believed to be relatively free from any illness and premature death. If some of headman A's people leave and move to headman B's village, this is taken as a decrease in prestige for headman A and an increase in prestige for

Headmen compete with one another for villagers in order to increase their prestige.

headman B. The movements indicate that headman B has better "medicine" (a substance believed to have magical power), allowing him to maintain a more pleasant village. A headman is usually assured that some of his kin of the matrilineage will always be living in his village. At any rate, their movements have little effect on the headman's prestige, as the number of kin in the village at any time is small. The headman is mainly concerned with keeping nonkin in his village; and they remain in the village only as long as the headman's medicine is considered powerful.

Among the Luapula, sorcery rather than witchcraft is prevalent. The people believe that the success of a headman cannot be achieved without the aid of "bad" medicine. Headmen are suspected of using sorcery, especially when they head large villages. Headmen use medicine against other headmen to attract people to their own village.

Sorcery is used by the headmen against one another.

Rituals are performed by a headman to benefit the entire population of his village. It is believed that rituals that are correctly performed will lead to protection from mystical dangers and will result in a harmonious village. The rituals are used to keep wild animals and sorcerers out of the village and at the same time attract and retain villagers. It is believed that if the rites are effective, they result in the absence of premature deaths in the village, because these are believed to arise either from sorcery by another village's headman or from some moral lapse due to lack of harmony in the village. Disharmony in the village is blamed on the headman's careless working of the ritual.

Headmen compete against one another with the same or similar medicines, and often with the medicines of the same magician. No headman admits that his own medicine is sorcery used to lower the prestige of another. Headmen insist that their medicines are "good" medicines, designed to secure the harmony of their own village, in other words, protective medicine. However, they view other headmen as enemies and potential sorcerers.

Chiefs are thought to have special medicines that are more powerful than those used by headmen. No magician would dare give the more powerful medicine to a headman, for fear of losing the favor of the chief. Thus the village headmen are not in a position to attack the villages of chiefs.

Unlike the Lugbara village, the Luapula village does not segment. Instead, the circulation of individuals is frequent, but with little change in political structure. Events that occur between the time a new headman takes office and the time he dies represent a recurrent village dynamic.

When a headman dies, a new headman is selected for the vacant position by the matrilineage that owns the village. He must then be recognized by the chief as the head of the village. The nonkin living in the village have no choice in the matter of who should be the new headman. If they do not like the person, they may move to another village under the same chief. Those who stay in the village accept the authority structure. The village is purified after the death of the former headman through a series of rituals performed by the new headman and a sorcerer that are thought to restore harmony in the village before the new man takes office. The new headman is therefore thought to begin his new role with a potentially harmonious village. The rituals that the new headman performs are supposed to keep mystical disaster away from the village.

To assure the success of the village, the headman obtains medicine from a sorcerer. He claims to have only good medicine that will protect the village, but he actually also obtains bad medicine to use against other headmen in hopes of attracting their villagers to his village. Change in the village takes one of two forms; either the village increases in size, or it decreases. If the size increases, the headman will continue to use his medicine in order to maintain his prestige or enhance it by attracting even more people to his village. If the village population decreases it is taken as a sign that the headman's medicine is weak and that other headmen are using sorcery against him. The headman will continue to use sorcery in an attempt to increase his prestige.

If a village is considered so unpleasant that it loses large numbers of people, it is moved to a new site, and a new ritual is performed establishing a new status quo and raising the prestige of the headman closer to what it was when he first became headman. Setting up the village at a new site allows the villagers to have a fresh start without their village being considered an unpleasant place to live. Then once again the size of the village can either increase or decrease. On the death of the headman, the village is again ritually purified and a new headman takes over a potentially harmonious village, and once again the population begins moving away from "bad" villages where there are premature deaths and the headman's medicine is weak to "good" villages where there are few premature deaths and the medicine of the headman is strong.

The State

Elman Service (1975) suggests that the level of evolution following the chiefdom is the state. On the other hand, Morton Fried

480

Who's in Charge Here? A Look at Political Organization

believes that there was an intermediate political form between the rank society and the state, which he calls the stratified society. Fried (1967:186) defines a stratified society as "one in which members of the same sex and equivalent age status do not have equal access to the basic resources that sustain life." Further, these societies are stratified but lack state institutions. At present there are no known examples of such a society. In all cases where stratification occurs, it is found with state institutions. Fried believes that such societies did exist in prehistoric times. Unfortunately, the invention of writing did not occur until the emergence of ancient states, so there is no written record of such societies. The stratified society was a fragile organization if it did exist, in that it was either quickly transformed into a state or built within itself great pressures for its own dissolution into a simpler kind of organization, either a rank society or an egalitarian one.

In order for a stratified society to exist, there would have to be sanctions of commanding power beyond the resources of egalitarian and even rank society. Kinship ties would no longer provide an adequate means of social control within the society. Fried (1967:196) considers the following conditions important in the evolution of the stratified society: population pressures, shifts in customary postmarital residence patterns, contraction or alteration of basic resources, shifts in subsistence patterns arising from technological change or the impingement of a market system, and the development of managerial roles.

If the stratified society grew out of chiefdoms or rank societies, it was often rapidly transformed into an even more complex form of organization, the state. Social scientists have presented a number of theories to account for the origin of the state, but the debate continues today. Two traditional kinds of explanation have been termed *voluntaristic* and *coercive*. Voluntaristic theories hold that at some point in the past certain peoples spontaneously, rationally, and voluntarily gave up their individual sovereignties and united with other groups to form a larger political unit. The coercive theories suggest that the state grew as a result of force and not enlightened self-interest. The coercive theories emphasize that war lies at the root of the state (Carneiro 1975:144–145). The archaeological and historical evidence strongly supports the coercive theory. In other words, warfare seems to be associated with the rise of every known state. However, warfare is not the only factor. Wars have been fought in many parts of the world where the state never emerged. In other words, war provides the mechanism of state

Fried believes there was a stage between the chiefdom and the state which he calls the stratified society.

formation, but it is also important to understand the conditions under which war gives rise to the state.

Robert Carneiro (1975:145–147) has developed the *circumscription theory* to account for the origin of the state. He believes that the most promising approach to determining the conditions under which the state came into being is to look for those factors common to areas of the world in which states first developed. What they seem to share is the fact that they are all areas of circumscribed agricultural land. Each of them is set off by mountains, seas, or deserts, and these features sharply delimited the area that early farming peoples could occupy and cultivate. Once the population began to outgrow its resources, competition arose over available land. This in turn led to ever-increasing warfare, in which the competing groups grew in size as villages either banded together or were subsumed by others. As these political units grew in size, they decreased in number, until eventually there was only one centralized political unit that had conquered all other political units of the area. This was the beginning of a state form of organization.

The circumscription theory emphasizes similarities between all the early states.

Top: The populations of states are highly stratified. *Bottom:* In the state form of organization, education is formalized. (Michael D. Olien)

States have formal military organizations. (Michael D. Olien)

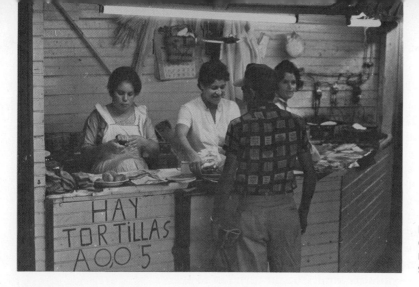

More complex systems of exchange based on money are found in the state. (Michael D. Olien)

Fried (1967:229–235) views the state as a complex of institutions by means of which the power of the society is organized on a basis superior to kinship. The specialized institutions and agencies of the state maintain an order of stratification. Several basic principles of organization are at the core of the state: It is a hierarchy; it has differential degrees of access to basic resources; its officials demand obedience; and it defends an area. All states face similar problems. They must learn to control the population and must have some means of identifying subjects, to distinguish them from nonmembers. Sometimes this is accomplished by establishing boundaries, but it can also be done through birth and parentage. In either case there must be some way of symbolizing the unit so that individuals can identify with it. States must also deal with trouble cases. Whereas kin-based political organizations rely on gossip, supernatural sanctions, and so on, the state relies on force. The state develops codes of law, giving itself the right to interfere legally in disputes between its members. The power of the state lies not only in its ability to muster troops against its enemies but also in such things as control of sources of information and the means of communication. The state also has a social sector that stands beneath the rulers but acts as the agency of control. In some states it is a large bureaucracy, while in others it is a military establishment or some type of priesthood.

In order to carry out all of its functions, the state must develop a means of transforming basic resources into more fluid kinds of wealth. There has to be some form of treasury, and in most states it becomes expedient to invent some form of all-purpose money. In order to survive, the state must have some means of obtaining surplus froms its producers. In other words, it needs a form of taxation (Fried 1967:240).

The Growth of the Chinese State

The early dynasties of China illustrate the problems confronting early states. The major problem, which took a number of dynasties to resolve, was the centralization of power. During the early dynasties, warlords, rather than the monarch, had considerable power. Over time, the monarchs were able to consolidate their power at the expense of the warlords, yet one dynasty after another collapsed, for more or less the same reasons. Karl Wittfogel has suggested that Chinese history was basically cyclical.

The first great powers of China were the Shang princes, who subdued 1800 city-states and established the first centralized authority. Their dynasty ruled from about 1766 to 1122 BC. They established capital cities with government buildings, palaces, temples, and mausoleums. They also made extensive use of an early form of writing. The Shang were most famous for their bronze work.

In the twelfth century BC, the Chou united with other groups to overthrow the Shang. The Chou Dynasty lasted until 256 BC. It is considered to have been a period of cultural flowering. When the Chou monarch came to power, he granted feudal domains to lords in return for their services. The lords agreed to send troops in time of rebellion or attack, and they organized communal labor service, using the peasants under their control. Although the monarch settled disputes between lords, the warlords had a great deal of autonomy within their territories, a situation that resulted in a great deal of political separatism. The warlords assigned less feudal domains, or fiefs, to lesser lords. These lesser lords owed their allegiances to the warlord rather than the monarch.

The Chou society was divided into two basic classes, the nobility and the peasantry. The Chou nobles followed a code of proper behavior known as *li*. This was a code similar to medieval European chivalry. Warfare was a pastime of the nobility, who engaged in chariot fighting. The peasants were the largest group in the society and were tied to the land in serflike fashion. The land of a lord was divided into nine squares. The middle plot was that of the lord. Each of the other plots was worked by a peasant family, who kept the produce of its own plot. In addition, all peasant families worked the plot of the lord, and all the produce from the lord's land was considered his.

In 771 BC, the Chou Dynasty was attacked and forced to move its capital. From then until the collapse of the dynasty, the authority of the Chou was greatly reduced, and different war-

The earliest Chinese dynasties lacked strong centralized authority.

lords continually attempted to increase their own power at the expense of the Chou. One of the groups that emerged victorious out of the struggles against the Chou were the Ch'in. The Ch'in Dynasty ruled only briefly, from 223 to 206 BC. Although brief, the period was an important one in centralizing China into the first true empire. The Ch'in introduced new military tactics. They rejected the Chou notion that the nobility should constitute the army. Instead, they utilized peasants and introduced the idea of archers on horseback. The Ch'in army, under the command of Chêng, was able to vanquish the last of the rival groups in 223 BC. Chêng then created the first empire and assumed the title of First Emperor—Shih-huang-ti—and established a system of government that lasted until the present century (Goodrich 1951:32). The Ch'in abolished the fief system and instead divided the country into 41 military areas, each with its military governor, its civil administrator, and its supervisory official. The ownership of land was turned over to the peasants, thus abolishing the feudal system that the Chou had introduced.

The Ch'in were able to increase agricultural production through the use of the plow, fertilizer, and irrigation. The increase in production led to a growth of population. The Ch'in also instituted reforms in taxation, creating a larger tax base than had existed previously. Shih-huang-ti increased the food reserves of the state and used them to support large-scale public works, using peasant labor. Some of the most important government undertakings of this dynasty included the construction of irrigation projects, the building of networks of tree-lined roads, the joining of sections of walls in the north to form the Great Wall, the deepening of waterways, and the digging of a 20-mile canal. With the death of Shih-huang-ti, the country was once again thrown into anarchy and was finally united by a new dynasty known as the Han.

The Han ruled from 202 BC to AD 220.[6] At the beginning of the Han period there was a brief return to feudalism. The first Han emperor parceled out feudal domains to his relatives and friends as spoils of war. However, this policy continued for a very short period of time, and then the Han court took measures to end the power of the feudal lords. Han Wu-ti, the greatest of the Han emperors, whose reign lasted from 140 through 87 BC, was able to force the lords to place themselves under the district representatives of the emperor. The Han changed the inheritance pattern by which the eldest son inherited all of his father's land. Instead, each son was to become an equal heir, thus frag-

The Ch'in introduced many changes in Chinese society that increased the powers of centralized government.

---

[6] Han rule was interrupted briefly between AD 9 and 23, when the Hsin Dynasty assumed power.

A section of the Great Wall of China. (Wide World)

menting any private concentrations of power and wealth. The Han introduced a system of civil service examinations for choosing public officials. These exams primarily tested a person's knowledge of the teachings of Confucius. By the middle of the Han Dynasty, there were some 130,000 civil officials.

Karl A. Wittfogel (1957) sees the growth of large-scale irrigation systems under the control of the state as the major reason for the development of what he terms Oriental despotism. Oriental despotism refers to Asiatic forms of government based on large-scale irrigation and connotes an extremely harsh form of absolutist power (Wittfogel 1957:101). The term applies to all of the dynasties based on large-scale irrigation. Wittfogel (1959) maintains that there are two kinds of agricultural systems: One requires the construction of an irrigation and drainage systems; the other operates with rainfall. According to Wittfogel, the

The Han introduced further reforms that increased the power of centralized government, including civil service examinations.

former system tends to generate great and repressive institutions of government; the rainfall system does not. With the Han Dynasty, there was established a pattern of almost absolute tyranny, in which the government exerted great control over the masses. The Han put into practice five institutional supports that helped to maintain a centralized government. One of these was the civil service examination system. It gave the government greater control over who would serve as a public official and to a certain extent kept the offices from being inherited. This reduced the likelihood that power that could challenge the centralized authority of the state would remain concentrated in any family. The civil service exams also allowed a small number of peasants to enter the bureaucracy. Wittfogel (1957:348) suggests that about 8 percent of the officials had a commoner background. A second technique used by the Han to consolidate their power was to shift officials so that they would not be serving in their home areas and thus be influenced by kin. Third,

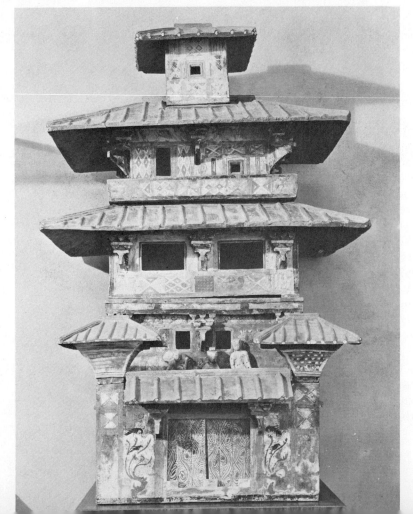

Model of a house from the Han Dynasty. (Collection, William Rockhill Nelson Gallery)

the government used *eunuchs* as officials wherever possible. These were individuals who had been castrated so that they could produce no heirs. Unlike the regular officials, the eunuchs did not usually come from prominent families. They were generally trusted and devoted attendants who own everything they had and everything they were to the ruler. A fourth institutional support of centralized government was the use of repressive measures against merchants. The government was fearful that the merchants might accumulate great wealth and thus challenge the power of the dynasty. The government therefore created a number of governmental monopolies on such commodities as iron and salt as well as on public construction. The fifth support used by the government was the Chinese writing system, beginning about AD 100. The system of writing was compiled by an unknown author and contained 9353 different characters, with meanings that could be read and understood by officials in any part of the country, even though the different spoken "dialects" were almost mutually unintelligible.

Beginning with the Han Dynasty, Chinese dynastic history reflects a series of cycles in which dynasties rise to power, establish stability, and ultimately collapse. While some scholars have explained this recurring cycle in terms of weak and strong emperors, Wittfogel (1957) suggests that the dynasties collapsed after their control over irrigation and nature weakened. The following is an abstract model of the cycle that occurred in Chinese history with each new dynasty, starting from the Han and continuing up until the establishment of the Republic in 1912.

Wittfogel suggests that each dynasty followed a similar cycle.

At the beginning of each dynasty, the new rulers found that much of the land lay idle because of the recent war that brought the new dynasty to power. There were many wanderers and bandits throughout the land. The irrigation systems were in disrepair, and both productivity and population had declined. The new dynasty repaired the irrigation systems, thus increasing the amount of usable land. The armies were enlarged and peace was established in the countryside. As a result, wanderers settled down on the new land. The dynasty reinstituted the bureaucracy. As stability was established, the dynasty came to the height of its power; then decline began. The redistribution of tax money was upset: Through collusion with government officials, powerful families did not pay their share of taxes. The government was faced with two alternatives. It could either reduce its budget or increase the taxes of those who were already paying. The dynasty always chose the second alternative. With the money that they were withholding, the powerful families either

488

Who's in Charge Here? A Look at Political Organization

purchased land from those who were forced to sell land to pay taxes or they lent money to the poor taxpayers at high rates of interest. In either case these wealthy families became wealthier. Hunger increased as the population increased. With hunger and high taxes, peasant discontent arose. Some of the peasants were forced to sell their land, and they became wanderers or bandits. This crises usually culminated in a rebellion just when the government was least able to stand one. Then either a rebel leader took over and started a new dynasty, or invaders attacked from outside the boundaries of the empire. As the new dynasty took over it found that much of the land lay idle. There were many wanderers and bandits throughout the land. The irrigation systems were in disrepair, and productivity and population were decreased due to the rebellion. The new dynasty repaired the irrigation systems, thus increasing the amount of usable land. The armies were enlarged and peace was established in the countryside. As a result, wanderers once again settled down on the new land. The dynasty reinstituted the bureaucracy and the whole cycle started over again.

Once states like those of China were established, they spread over the face of the earth, absorbing all other forms of political organization. Today, all peoples live within the boundaries of some state. Even the contemporary bands and tribal peoples are directly affected by the institutions of the state. It is no longer possible to view any contemporary political organization outside of the context of the state. There is now someone in charge of every society in the world. However, the individual in charge of egalitarian societies is not a member of the native group. He is a government administrator imposed by a state, who has the authority to make decisions that affect a group's most basic patterns of living.

Anthropology Vocabulary

band
brideprice
bride service
caribou
chiefdom
Ch'in Dynasty
Chou Dynasty
circumscription theory
Copper Eskimo

egalitarian society
Han Dynasty
li
Luapula
Lugbara
massing effect
oracle
rank society
reciprocity

redistribution
segmentary lineage
Shang Dynasty
sibling exchange
sodalities
song duel
state
stratified society
tribe
tundra

Review Questions

1. Why did Western societies encounter problems in their dealings with many non-Western societies?
2. What are the basic characteristics of the band? How do you think modern bands differ from those that existed 15,000 years ago?
3. How do Service and Fried differ in their views of the tribe?
4. What types of changes in chiefdom organization could have led to the rise of the first states?

Recommended Reading

Cunnison, Ian, 1959, *The Luapula Peoples of Northern Rhodesia: Custom and History in Tribal Politics*. Manchester, England: Manchester University Press. The most detailed ethnographic account of the Luapula.

Damas, David, 1972, "The Copper Eskimo." In: *Hunters and Gatherers Today*, M. G. Bicchieri, ed. New York: Holt, Rinehart and Winston, pp. 3–50. Most up-to-date summary of the Copper Eskimo. Includes recent ethnographic data collected by the author.

Fried, Morton H., 1967, *The Evolution of Political Society: An Essay in Political Anthropology*. New York: Random House. A thought-provoking work that challenges the traditional notion of the tribe.

Middleton, John, 1965, *The Lugbara of Uganda*. New York: Holt, Rinehart and Winston. A concise case study of the Lugbara by the British anthropologist most familiar with their way of life.

Sahlins, Marshall D., 1968, *Tribesmen*. Englewood Cliffs, N.J.: Prentice-Hall. An evolutionary perspective on the rise of both the tribe and the chiefdom.

Service, Elman R., 1966, *The Hunters*. Englewood Cliffs, N.J.: Prentice-Hall. An overview of the basic characteristics of band societies, with ethnographic descriptions of the remaining hunting-and-gathering peoples of the world.

_____, 1971, *Primitive Social Organization: An Evolutionary Perspective*, 2nd ed. New York: Random House. An important attempt to clarify the evolutionary trends of sociopolitical organization. It includes detailed discussions of the band, the tribe, and the chiefdom.

_____, 1975, *Origins of the State and Civilization: The Process of Cultural Evolution*. New York: Norton. A companion work to *Primitive Social Organization*, dealing primarily with the state level of organization.

Wittfogel, Karl A., 1957, *Oriental Despotism: A Comparative Study of Total Power*. New Haven, Conn.: Yale University Press. A classic study of the relationship between state organization and large-scale irrigation systems, especially in China.

15
What will humans be like in the future

The study of the future involves options and alternatives, not predictions.

Biological and cultural change can each affect the other.

Anthropology can play an important role in the future.

ill the human of the future consist of a large mass of brains and little else? Will humans live in colonies in outer space? With our rapidly increasing pollution, overpopulation, and the proliferation of nuclear technology, will there even be a world of humans in the future? Will humans live in families, and if so, will their composition be heterosexual? The folk anthropologist generally thinks about the future in terms of predictions. The social scientist has generally found attempts at predicting the future unfruitful. As a result, the social scientest approaches the study of the future in terms of possibilities, options, and alternatives.

Social scientists approach the future in terms of options and alternatives rather than predictions.

There are many writers of the modern era who attempt to describe life in the future. A great deal of this literature is classified as science fiction. Some of the classic works of science fiction were written in the last half of the nineteenth century, as modern science and technology came into its own. The French novelist Jules Verne envisioned the kinds of changes that would occur in the twentieth century as a result of technological growth. He accurately predicted the invention of airplanes, submarines, television, guided missiles, and space satellites. Some of his most popular works included *From the Earth to the Moon* (1865), *Twenty Thousand Leagues Under the Sea* (1870), and *Around the Moon* (1870). The English novelist and historian H. G. Wells wrote several popular science-fiction works that had a great impact on the thinking of Western society. These included *The Time Machine* (1895), which dealt with the transporting of individuals into the future, and *The War of the Worlds* (1898), which described an invasion of the Earth by creatures from Mars. The American writer Edgar Rice Burroughs, creator of Tarzan, was equally popular for his many science fiction novels about life on other planets, the first being *A Princess of Mars* in 1917.

The early science fiction works dealt primarily with technological advances of the future or with the life of imaginary beings on other planets. While these elements remain important even today in science fiction, a new note was added in 1932. In that year the English writer Aldous Huxley published *Brave New World*, in which he described a totalitarian society that disregarded individual dignity and worshiped science and machines. Huxley believed that science was destroying human and political values. This work was followed in 1949 by the publication of *1984*, written by the English novelist Eric Blair under the pen name of George Orwell. Following in the same direction as *Brave New World*, the novel *1984* presented a frightening portrait of a totalitarian society that punished love, destroyed privacy, and distorted truth. Perhaps the frightening aspect of both

Brave New World and *1984* is that they deal with *human* society in the future and not some make-believe culture of another planet. The works of Huxley and Orwell marked a turning point in science fiction writing. Since that time a number of authors have directed their attention to considering what human society will be like in the future.

By the 1960s there were a number of individuals in various disciplines attempting to consider various aspects of the future. *The future* is a very broad term and covers everything from the coming year to millions of years into the future. Many future studies concentrate on possibilities of changes that may occur to humankind during the remainder of this century. The year AD 2000 has become a rather convenient point for orienting future studies.[1] Several groups have been organized to focus special attention and a variety of expertise on the problems of life at the turn of the century, such as the American Academy of Arts and Science's Commission on the Year 2000, the *Futuribles* project in France, and the English Social Science Research Council's Committee on the Next Thirty Years.

According to anthropologist Magoroh Maruyama (1973:346), human *futuristics*, a study of future cultural alternatives, limitations, and choices, will not constitute another branch of science in the traditional sense. It will differ from sciences as we now know them in several important aspects. First, future societies are not existing phenomena that can be observed, analyzed, and explained. Second, future societies cannot be predicted by extrapolating the past pattern of change, the past rate of change, or even past rate of acceleration of change. There are too many unprecedented innovations taking place that make extrapolations invalid. Third, culture changes do not happen in and of themselves. People make these changes happen. Therefore culture changes must be viewed as continually subject to people's goals, imagination, will, and choice.

Generally there has not yet been much interest in anthropology concerning humankind's future. Anthropologists' broad understanding of the past and present of humankind through the entire world ought to give them a unique perspective from which to view the future of human beings. Yet anthropologists have been slow to bring their expertise to bear on the problems of the future. While it seems likely that considerable human creative energy in the future will be devoted to new types of technological discoveries, this chapter will be devoted primarily to

> Futuristics studies future cultural alternatives.

---

[1] For example, Fritz Baade's *Race to the Year 2000* (1962), Daniel Bell's *Toward the Year 2000* (1969), and Herman Kahn and Anthony Wiener's *The Year 2000* (1967). A few writers such as Nigel Calder followed Orwell and used 1984 as the projection date. These have been collected in *The World in 1984* (Calder 1965).

human biological and cultural changes. New technology will be discussed only as it is thought to affect humankind's biological and cultural development.

Biological Changes of the Future

It is impossible to make a sharp division between human biological evolution and human cultural evolution, because there is such a great interplay between the two. Cultural changes radically affect human biological evolution, just as biological changes affect culture. Biological and social factors are mutually causal aspects of evolution.

In popular magazines there are frequently drawings of artists' conceptions of what humans will look like in the future. Several physical characteristics of future humans seem to be emphasized more frequently then others: lack of feet, lack of a mouth, and the development of a large brain. The creature portrayed without feet is derived from the notion that humans of the future will do less walking and rely more on mechanical means of transportation. The artist apparently assumes that there will be no need for feet in the future and that therefore they will disappear. Certainly humans rely on automobiles, airplanes, and the like, in contrast to our earlier ancestors; however walking has remained a vital means of locomotion for several million years, and it is unlikely that any change as radical as the loss of feet will occur in human evolution. Such a change would necessitate an entire reordering of the human skeleton.

A second possible change in human anatomy depicted in popular science fiction literature is the loss of the mouth. The rationale behind this notion is that speech will not be used for human communication in the future, because at some point in time human capabilities will develop to such an extent the telepathic communication will make the use of sound unnecessary. While extrasensory perception (ESP) and other nonverbal forms of communication may become more important in the future, they will have little impact on the mouth, because speech seems to be a secondary development of the mouth region. Its primary purpose is to process food entering the body. Even if humans were to alter their diet to consist only of liquids taken intravenously, it is unlikely that humans would lose their mouths, because the mouth has been present throughout the entire history of primate evolution. If such a biological change were to occur, the process would take millions of years.

The growth in size of the human brain is perhaps more de-

batable than the first two features. Humans consider themselves the most intelligent creatures on earth, and much of human evolution in the past has involved the growth of the brain. However it appears from fossil records that an optimum in brain size was reached with the appearance of Cro-Magnon, about 40,000 years ago. If measurements of cranial capacity are an accurate reflection of brain size, it seems likely that the size of the brain of modern human is slightly *less* than that of these earliest *Homo sapiens sapiens*. While there are only a small number of fossil skulls in comparison to the millions of contemporary beings whose skulls can be measured, the fossil data is the only data available relating to the size of the brain of the first *Homo sapiens sapiens*. It is quite possible that the human brain developed greater complexity rather than size following Cro-Magnon. Whether this greater complexity reflects any change in intelligence is difficult to discern, because, as discussed in Chapter Four, measurement of intelligence is difficult if not impossible. If increasing brain complexity rather than increasing brain size is the evoluntionary trend of *Homo sapiens sapiens*, the human of the future may have a more complex brain, but not a larger one.

The evolutionary trend may be one of increasing brain complexity rather than size.

Because evolution is a continuing process, it is apparent that humans will not be the same in the future as they are now. It is clear that the anatomical changes of the past have developed over long periods of time, and changes in the future may occur as slowly. Artists' sketches of humans of the future propose that radical modifications of human anatomy will occur; the fossil evidence, however, suggests that there has been only limited structural change in humans over millions of years.

There is one factor, however, that cannot be accounted for in any discussion of future human biological evolution, and that is culture. Biologists have recognized the process of natural selection since the concept was introduced by Darwin and Wallace in the 1850s. The process of *cultural selection* may be equally important in humans. For example, in contemporary American society, females with legs that are more slender and longer than average are frequently considered aesthetically preferable; in Polynesia, extremely obese young girls are believed to possess great beauty. In each society, individuals with the biological characteristics considered desirable by members of that society will have a greater chance of mating and producing offspring than those who lack the features (Maruyama 1963:169). It also is possible that in the near future scientific technology (a part of culture) will alter human anatomy at a much greater rate and in more directed ways than have occurred in the past as a result of

Cultural selection may be important in biological change.

natural selection. As scientific technology is now capable of creating working genes, it is not impossible that someday science will be able to create living forms as complex as human beings, with shapes controlled and modified for different purposes.

Diet. At least three factors will have an important impact on human biology by the year 2000: diet, population size, and mutation. Since human anatomy has changed little in the past million years, it would not be an exaggeration to say that humans still retain the body of their hunting-and-gathering ancestors.

Part of our inheritance from early humans is the ability to produce adrenalin. Adrenalin provides an extra source of energy during times of stress. Carbohydrates stored in the liver are released into the bloodstream in the form of sugar, which is quickly converted to energy. Adrenalin also increases the flow of blood to the heart, lungs, central nervous system, and limbs, while decreasing the flow of blood to the abdominal organs. These kinds of changes aid in mobilizing the muscular and nervous reserves of the individual, allowing him or her to withstand fatigue, move more rapidly, and endure longer. The adrenalin is released into the body during periods of intense emotion. Such a reserve of energy has great survival value for hunting-and-gathering peoples such as the Bushmen, the Eskimo, and the Australian aborigine, who must face crises daily. It allows them to run after animals and track them for many miles, often with only brief pauses for food. Adrenalin provides the stimulus they need for a prolonged effort. Other materials, such as cholestrol and fatty acid, are also built up in the bloodstream as a result of the release of adrenalin. These other materials are worked off, converted to energy during sustained hunting (Campbell 1976:429–430).

Modern humans share the same kinds of reactions to stress that have been found in hunters and gatherers of the past and present. All living humans are *physically* hunters and gatherers. Our glands react as they have been reacting for hundreds of thousands of years. What differs is that modern humans are not able to burn off the cholestrol and fatty acids that aid the hunters and gatherers. Our lives are basically sedentary. Instead of our stresses being confined primarily to the hunt, we are faced with continual stress, producing cholestrol that is only partially used up.

The physical anthropologist Bernard G. Campbell (1976:430–431) recounts the types of stresses faced by the modern executive in our society:

We are still physically hunters and gatherers, but our diet and culture has changed.

Consider the plight of the businessman on his way from his home
to an important conference. Success or failure for him may ride on
how well he aggressively takes charge of the meeting, beats down
the arguments of others, rallies support to his own point of view.
Although no physical energy will be expanded, this promises to be
a real battle nonetheless, and in preparation for it his system has
been churning out hormones ever since breakfast. Thoroughly
aroused by a challenging situation, and repeatedly rearoused as
further crises in the meeting itself trigger off still higher levels of
cholestrol and fatty acids in his blood, he leaves the meeting at the
end of the morning and sits down to a heavy lunch preceded by a
couple of cocktails. Then the meetings continue in the afternoon. If
he does not succeed in his purpose, the high hormone level and resulting tension may remain through the evening and far into the
night.

The businessman's glandular system responds as if he is still a
hunter, but his style of life is such that he does not engage in the
kind of vigorous physical activity that would burn up the cholestrol in his bloodstream. The end result is frequently abnormal
heart condition. The businesswoman is faced with similar kinds
of stresses and her glandular system reacts the same as the businessman. Humans of the future will probably face even greater
cholestrol problems, unless the modern world can either significantly reduce stress, the cholestrol level, or both.

Lack of vigorous physical activity represents only one of a
complex series of problems, many of which have resulted from
changes in modern diets. The kinds of foods introduced by modern civilization have altered the diet that humans followed in
earlier societies. The use of so-called convenience food or "junk
food" seems likely to spread even further in the future. Junk
food is closely related to a changing work pattern. In the past,
working people in cities of many countries of the world took two
or three hours for their noon meal. Shops were closed during
those hours. The noon meal was the largest meal of the day, with
supper representing a smaller, lighter meal. Considerable preparation went into the noon meal. As new working and eating
patterns have spread to many countries, the traditional patterns
of other countries have been or are being replaced. Businesses
remain open during the noon hours, and employees eat a brief
lunch. The change to brief lunch hours has resulted in the
growth of quick-service food processing. Hamburgers, hot dogs,
pizza, french fries, fried chicken, and soft drinks have replaced
traditional dishes that were made "from scratch," using natural
foods that had been neither processed nor "enhanced" with
questionable additives. The main meal of the day also often consists of convenience foods; it now takes place in to the evening
hours, when the digestive system has less opportunity to digest

the food before the individual goes to sleep. Another factor in the reliance on junk food has been the increase of women in the work force. With both spouses employed, neither has a great deal of time to spend on food preparation.

One serious aspect of the spread of the reliance on convenience foods is the incredible increase in the intake of concentrated carbonhydrates, especially sugar and white flour, by civilized peoples. The surgeon-captain of the British Royal Navy, Dr. T. L. Cleave, has grouped together a number of seemingly diverse diseases, including dental decay, peptic ulcers, obesity, diabetes, constipation, and varicose veins, and refers to all of these illnesses under a single category, "the saccharine disease" (Bodley 1976:215). Sugar did not become an important part of the civilized world's diet until the seventeenth century. Although available to Europeans centuries earlier, it was too scarce and expensive to be widely used. In the United States today, the average person consumes about 100 pounds of sugar per year in various forms. Sugar accounts for nearly 500 calories per person per day in the United States. The extensive use of sugar seems destined to spread to developing countries in the future.

Population. A second factor likely to have an effect on human biology in the year AD 2000 is the size of the world's population, which today is approximately 4 billion individuals. Estimates for the world's population in the year AD 2000 are about 6.5 billion. It is also estimated that the greatest growth will occur in urban areas. Present urban centers will become even larger, smaller cities will grow into large urban centers, and perhaps even new planned cities will be created. If the estimates of growth are correct—and there are many problems with any estimate—the results of this rapid increase in world population are difficult to comprehend. For every large city now in existence, there will have to be another new city of equal size to accommodate this huge population. For every New York, London, Tokyo, Moscow, and Peking, there will be a comparably sized new city by AD 2000.

While the worldwide pattern is one of growth, the amount of growth will probably vary significantly from country to country. The rates of growth have slowed in most developed countries, while many developing countries are growing at a very fast rate. Under "primitive" conditions, birth rates are high because infant mortality rates are generally high. Once modern medical technology has been introduced into an area, the life expectancy generally increases, yet the high birth rates continue.

It is estimated there will be 6.5 billion people by AD 2000.

Overpopulation and crowding
in Calcutta, India. (NASA)

High life expectancy rates and high birth rates represent the
patterns found in many countries of the world today. The most
technologically developed countries have increased their life ex-
pectancies and have also begun to lower their birth rates, partially due to a growing interest in planned parenthood and concern over the rapid growth of the world's population. It seems
unlikely that by year AD 2000 there will be sufficient interest in
planned parenthood in developing countries to curb the growth
of population. In some developing countries the government
encourages high birth rates in order to increase its own population, often in hopes of gaining political advantages, such as expansion of its borders, because of the large number of nationals
it would have at its disposal as a fighting force. Thus the estimates about rapid population increases in the near future are
probably accurate. However the possibility of unforeseen circumstances could alter the situation.

War on a global scale could result in such a reduction of population that the estimates of 6.5 billion individuals by the year AD
2000 would be far from correct, especially if the war were a nuclear one. A second possibility that could affect the rate of
growth is based on Malthus' theory (1807) that there are certain
natural limitations to population growth. It is possible that 6.5
billion individuals would be too large a number to be supported
by the natural resources of our planet. The result could be death
on a large scale, possibly through malnutrition.

Malnutrition is already a serious problem in a number of
countries. As early as 1905 the Harvard geologist Nathaniel
Shaler warned that the world was very near the limits of its car-

rying capacity. By 1965 George Borgstrom, a food scientist, declared that the world had failed in its ability to feed itself and that hunger constituted the major issue of our time. In 1967 William and Paul Paddock, authorities on tropical agriculture and national food systems in developing countries, predicted that by 1975 the United States grain surpluses could no longer compensate for world food shortages and that a period of disastrous famines would begin after that date. Also in 1967 President Lyndon B. Johnson's Science Advisory Committee, making use of the knowledge of 115 experts on all aspects of the food crisis, published a 1200-page report confirming all of the pessimistic predictions of recent years. The committee's major conclusion was that "the scale, severity, and duration of the world food problem are so great that a massive, long-range, innovative effort unprecedented in human history will be required to master it" (United States, President's Science Advisory Committee, 1967, vol 1:11; cited in Bodley 1976:90). The United Nations World Conference in 1974 reported that 460 million people were already threatened with immediate famine.

It is difficult to estimate the extent of hunger throughout the world as health specialists use different standards of measuring malnutrition. In 1963 a U.S. Department of Agriculture report estimated that nearly 80 percent of the developing world's population, or roughly 56 percent of the world, were below acceptable caloric levels. Some writers consider these estimates as extreme and argue that individuals can live on a lower average per capita requirement than that used by the U.S. Department of Agriculture, while others believe that the estimates may be too conservative (Bodley 1976:92–93). As a result of food shortages, developing countries suffer a number of deficiency diseases and death. Where protein-calorie deficiencies are serious, infant mortality rates are high and include deaths from common childhood diseases that in developed countries are seldom fatal. There is also growing evidence to suggest that protein-calorie deficiency in infancy may be linked to mental retardation and growth impairment (Cravioto 1970; Eichenwald and Fry 1969).

The Ik of Uganda. Some anthropologists believe that the life patterns of an African group known as the Ik, situated in the mountainous northeast corner of Uganda, provide a glimpse into the future of all humankind if solutions are not immediately found to the problems of hunger, disease, and overpopulation. Up until World War II the Ik had lived a nomadic hunting-and-gathering life over a large territory that included not only a part of Uganda but the bordering countries of Kenya

Some believe that the Ik provide a glimpse into the future for all humankind.

and Sudan as well. Their major hunting area was the Kidepo Valley in Uganda. Just before World War II the Ik were encouraged to settle in the mountains of northeast Uganda, which represented only a small section of their previous territory. After the Ik settled in the mountains the Kidepo Valley was made a national park, and the Ik were forbidden to hunt or gather there from that time on. As a result of these changes imposed upon the Ik by the outside world, their traditional way of life has been disrupted, and each individual of the group is now engaged in a life-and-death struggle for survival.

The Ik have been studied by the British anthropologist Colin M. Turnbull, who had previously studied the BaMbuti pygmies of the Ituri rain forest in Zaïre. He assumed that the Ik would be somewhat similar to other hunting-and-gathering groups, displaying characteristics such as kindness, generosity, consideration, affection, honesty, hospitality, compassion, and charity, because these traits are necessities for survival in bandlike societies. Instead, he found that the Ik were no longer hunters and gatherers but had become subsistence farmers on drought-stricken land. They were "as unfriendly, uncharitable, inhospitable and generally mean as any people can be" (Turnbull 1972:32). Why? Because the Ik are faced with cultural disintegration that has been intensified by starvation. Too many have been crowded onto impoverished land.

The result of cultural disintegration among the Ik has been a breakdown of the family and an emphasis on individual survival—an "every person for themself" policy. The overriding concerns in Ik society are food and water. During the day each individual fends for himself, secretly eating whatever food he obtains. Most food is eaten raw, for fear that the smoke of a fire would attract others, who would make demands for the food. Likewise, food is consumed on the run so that the individual can have it all to himself (Turnbull 1972).

The elderly and the young have the least chance of survival. As the elderly get weak, food is taken from their mouths by those still stronger. The Ik believe this is proper behavior, because if the weak consume the scarce food, it only briefly prolongs the inevitable, death. The weak appear to understand this belief and seem passive when food is taken from them, even reacting with laughter. The strong Ik delights in giving food to a very weak person, watching him struggle, and taking the food from his mouth just as he weakly attempts to swallow it.

Parents consider children a burden. Therefore children are not allowed to sleep in the parents' house once they reach the age of about 3. A child of this age has no chance of surviving by itself, so the children form age bands. The junior band consists of children between the ages of 3 and 7; the senior band consists of children 8 to 12 years of age. Within the age band the child seeks the defense his parents do not provide. The friendships of the age band are temporary, and children eventually turn on one another. The weakest children soon die in this system. The strongest achieve leadership in the band but are eventually driven out. The leader then joins a senior band and begins as its most junior member. By the time children reach the age of 12 or 13 they leave the band and operate alone.

Young Ik girls become prostitutes because it is the only way in which they are able to earn money to buy food. They sell themselves to men of other tribes who pass through their area. By the time the Ik girl reaches her late teens she is no longer considered attractive and is generally no longer successful as a prostitute. From that point on her chances of survival are greatly reduced.

The Ik have become partially dependent on government aid. Famine relief has been initiated but not in the villages. The Ik have to travel to other areas to receive government food. Only the fit are able to make the journey. Although the Ik are given extra food for those who are too weak to travel, those making the trip eat the extra food themselves. In describing the return of those who had received help while Turnbull was doing field-work, he noted (Turnbull 1972:222-233):

> When they came back the contrast between them and the others was that between life and death. Villages were villages of the dead and dying, and there was little difference between the two. People crawled rather than walked. After a few feet some would lie down to rest, but they could not be sure of ever being able to sit up again, so they mostly stayed upright until they reached their desti-nation. They were going nowhere, these semi-animate bags of skin and bone, they just wanted to be with others, and they stopped whenever they met. Perhaps it was the most important demonstra-tion of sociality I ever saw among the Ik. Once together they neither spoke nor did anything together, they were together and that seemed enough.

The Ik pattern does not change even when their fields prosper. The crops are not harvested, and what is not eaten is left to rot. People steal food from each other's fields, and many intention-ally allow their crops to waste away, because they fear that if their fields are too successful the government will stop their famine relief.

Turnbull believes that modern society may be headed in the same direction as the Ik, because we are becoming increasingly individualized and desocialized in our own society and because the family has become less important. However he is optimistic

that we can bring about radical changes in our society before the situation becomes as hopeless as that of the Ik, where each human is concerned only with his own survival. It should also be noted that in other societies faced with starvation, the people have been able to maintain their cultural patterns without the extreme breakdown of society that has characterized the Ik.

Mutations and Eugenics. When early forms of human existed as hunters and gatherers, mutations were so disabling that the individual born with a defect did not stand much chance of surviving to maturity, mating, and passing the mutation on to the next generation. Thus many potenitally harmful genes were lost in only one generation. As humans switched to a settled farming way of life, some of the defects that could have been disastrous to a hunter had little effect on the life of the agriculturalist. Individuals born with these defects not only lived but were able to mate and pass their mutations on to succeeding generations in increasing numbers. Thus the stabilizing effect of natural selection was disrupted. Medical technology of the twentieth century has allowed an even greater number of individuals with mutations to survive than was the case during the era of early farming peoples. Individuals saved by modern medicine are carriers and transmitters of mutations that would formerly have been lost under the normal process of natural selection.

> Cultural changes have allowed increasing numbers of individuals with mutations to survive and produce offspring.

Some writers, of which the zoologist H. J. Muller is perhaps the most verbal, fear that due to a weakening of the stabilizing effect of natural selection, genetic decay of the human species is now occurring and will become even more serious in the future. While this theory remains a possibility, it should be kept in mind that genes are neither intrinsically beneficial nor harmful; they become so only when placed in a particular environment. A gene that is harmful in one environment may be neutral or useful in another kind of environment. The greater the variety of environments to which a population is exposed, the greater the chance that some mutants may be useful in some of the environments. Human environments have been endlessly diversified through culture. While a stabilizing type of selection is conservative and helps to maintain a status quo, a diversifying type of selection brings about genetic diversification and enables life to become adapted to a variety of environments. A population or species that has considerable genetic variety may be better adapted to the complexity of environments with which it is confronted than would be a genetically uniform population (Dobzhansky 1962:288).

> Mutations create greater diversity in the human population.

Those who see the future of *Homo sapiens sapiens* as one in which the genetic load of mutations and other kinds of defects will become so great as to be disastrous to humankind frequently advocate some form of *eugenics,* a method of improving the human race by careful selection of parents. Scientists such as Muller (1960) have proposed that certain individuals—those of high intelligence and lacking in genetic defects—should be encouraged to produce children, while those whose intelligence is below average or who have genetic defects should be discouraged from producing offspring. The most extreme advocates of eugenics demand governmental controls over reproduction as a means of improving the human species. Muller has proposed that programs of artificial insemination of human females could be improved, as a starting point. Artificial insemination is used primarily by women whose husbands are sterile. The sperm donors are not chosen on any genetic or eugenic basis. What Muller suggests is that individuals of the most outstanding native mental ability be used as donors.

There is a possibility that in the future a question may be raised by political leaders as to whether or not people have the right to have children at all. It would be possible for a government to place additives in food that would prevent all of its population from reproducing. Conceivably the government could then provide chemicals that would reverse the effect of the birth preventative for those selected to reproduce (Crick 1963:275).

The science of eugenics was begun by Sir Francis Galton in the 1880s, but it has not gained widespread acceptance. Most people believe such programs violate human rights, or they object on religious grounds. There is also fear that once a government assumed control over the reproduction of its members, this control might be misused. Memories of "experiments" in Nazi Germany are still vivid in the minds of many.

Science has progressed to the point where genetic counseling is being conducted on a limited scale. Couples contemplating having children are able to receive information about certain possible birth defects that might occur if they were to reproduce. This type of counseling is voluntary, and the decision about whether or not to have children remains with the couple.

Some states have laws that prohibit the mating of individuals such as the criminally insane. These laws act as another type of control over genetic defects.

Much of the controversy over eugenics surrounds the issue of who is the most fit. Which individuals should be encouraged to produce more children and which should produce less? If it were technologically possible to create a million Einsteins from frozen sperm and artificial insemination or other processes,

would this be desirable? Many geneticists believe that programs of eugenics would weaken the adaptive ability of the human species, which has resulted from the extreme diversity now found in humankind.

Many geneticists believe that eugenics would weaken the adaptive ability of humankind.

In looking toward the year AD 2000 and considering both the issue of overpopulation and eugenics, it is possible that as nations begin to compete more earnestly for the natural resources still available, strong prejudices will develop against those countries reproducing more rapidly than others. As noted earlier, the developing countries have been increasing in size faster than the developed countries. However, increase in population is only one part of the picture.

Our own country's population is growing at only about one-third of the rate of developing nations. Yet we are perhaps creating greater problems, because our demands for the world's resources are growing more rapidly than those of other nations. In terms of damaging the environment and utilizing the world's resources, the people of the United States are the world's most irresponsible and dangerous citizens. When ecological factors are taken into consideration, the birth rate of the United States is actually 25 times more important than the birth rate in India in determining whether our world has any ecological future at all. The following is a list of some of the things that the average American baby born in 1971 will consume, spend, or throw away during his or her lifetime (Meadows 1976:63):

One American will require:	One American will throw out:
26 million gallons of water	10,000 no-return bottles
28 tons of iron and steel	17,500 cans
1200 barrels of petroleum	27,000 bottle caps
13,000 pounds of paper	2.3 automobiles
50 tons of food	35 rubber tires
$10,000 in public expenses	126 tons of garbage
	9.8 tons of particulate air pollution

Remnants of America's cowboy economy. (Sachs, NASA)

Technology and Biology. Several other means of directing human biological evolution may develop as important technological breakthroughs before the year AD 2000. These techniques include chemically induced mutations, gene grafting, cloning, and bionics. All of these possibilities are quite familiar phenomena to science fiction enthusiasts.

In an article dealing with long-range biological possibilities, the geneticist J. B. S. Haldane (1963) has suggested that changes in genes can be chemically induced. Such changes could be used to alter the human genetic makeup, or perhaps scientists will synthesize new genes and introduce them into human chromosomes. Haldane believes that a more extreme possibility is the hybridization of humans with animals possessing specific characteristics that could be useful to a particular individual but not to humankind as a whole. Experiments in gene grafting have been carried out successfully on flies and bacteria. Haldane sees this type of experimentation as especially useful in space travel and in the possible colonization of other planets where the environment is very different from that of earth. A new World monkey with a prehensile tail is in many ways better suited to space travel then humans; human legs and much of the human pelvis are detriments to long periods of space travel in limited-size vehicles. As Haldane (1963:354) observes:

> Men who had lost their legs by accident or mutation would be specially qualified as astronauts. If a drug is discovered with an action like that of thalidomide, but on the leg rudiments only, not the arms, it may be useful to prepare the crew of the first spaceship to the *Alpha Centauri* system, thus reducing not only their weight, but their food and oxygen requirements. A regressive mutation to the condition of our ancestors in the mid-Pliocene, with prehensile feet, no appreciable heels, and an ape-like pelvis, would be still better.

The recent research in genetic engineering suggest that some of Haldane's possibilities are already a reality. A number of a scientists have been successful in combining genetic material (DNA) from the bacterium *E. colis* with genetic material of plants, animals and other bacteria, thus creating forms of life different from any that exist on earth. This new technique has come to be known as *recombinant DNA* and has raised considerable controversy over its morality and potential dangers.

Recent scientific experiments have produced yet another possibility for controlling human evolution. This procedure is called *cloning* and is the duplication of living forms. Scientists are learning to cause isolated living cells to multiply and differentiate by inducing chemicals. Each cell of a living organism contains the same genetic information as every other cell. Dif-

Some biological change of the future may be directed.

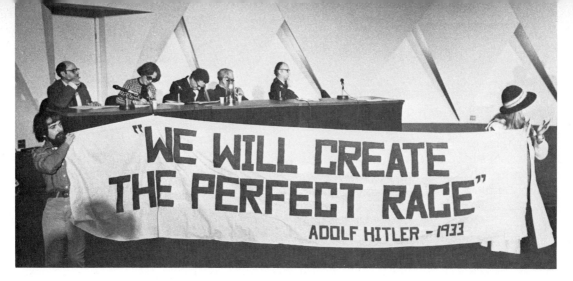

Protest against DNA research at Washington forum. (Paul Conklin)

ferent cells differentiate to express only a special portion of the total genetic information within them. Each cell has the potential of every other cell, thus cloning can make use of any cells of the organism in its duplication of the organism. Clones have already been produced from carrots and frogs. In the experiment with frogs conducted at Oxford University a clone was produced from an African clawed frog. The nucleus of an unfertilized egg cell from the frog was destroyed by radiation. The nucleus was then replaced with the nucleus of a cell from the intestines of the tadpole. The egg began to divide as if it had been normally fertilized, resulting in a frog that was the twin of the donor tadpole. Some scientists estimate that human cloning will be possible by the end of the 1970s (Rivers 1972:26).

The technique of cloning brings with it the possibilities of new kinds of social problems. For example, situations such as the following could become commonplace. A dictator could have skin tissue scraped from his arm. Nine months later 500 babies would emerge from a factory that contained 500 artificial wombs, and each baby would be the genetic carbon copy of the dictator (Rivers 1972:23). Over a reign of 20 years, if the dictator did not enlarge his "womb factory," he could have produced some 13,350 copies of himself. One wonders what a future world might be like with 13,350 Hitlers. Ira Levin's novel *The Boys from Brazil* describes just such a possibility.

The geneticist Haldane (1963:352) believes that cloning would offer many benefits if the process were controlled so that only exceptional people were cloned. Exceptional people frequently experience unhappy childhoods because they are not well understood by their parents, teachers, and peers, who force them to conform to ordinary standards. A great mathematician or painter could educate his own clonal offspring so that they could avoid most of the problems that normally plague a young genius. It is also possible that cloning could be used as a means of duplicating a person's vital organs, which could then be frozen and sorted until the person needed them at some time in the future. The clonal organs could be used to replace worn-out organs of the original donor, and the clonal organs might offset the rejection problems so common in organ transplanting thus far.

Television has created interest in the possibility of humans having machinery substituted for parts of their bodies. The term *bionic* has become popular in this context. The term *cyborg* has been used more traditionally to refer to a part-human, part-machine being. Michael Crichton's novel *The Terminal Man* deals with such a being, an individual suffering from violent epileptic seizures who undergoes surgery in which a miniature computer is implanted in his brain. At present, simple machines such as pacemakers are implanted in patients' hearts. The possibility of more complex machine parts being used in the future seems inevitable. A problem that will have to be faced by society is the question, When does a partially machine-made human actually become a machine? If a computer is used to control the individual's brain, is he or she still a human being? The fictional hero of *The Terminal Man* was faced with just such a dilemma, which drove him insane.

Technological changes of human beings may become commonplace in the future, but the potential power of these changes is frightening. What factors will be taken into consideration in deciding who will be chosen for cloning? Who will make these decisions? Will certain kinds of people—a minority group, the poor, those with low IQs, those opposing the government—be forced to undergo "cyborgization" in which their brains will be controlled by machines? Who would control these machines? Answers will have to be found to these questions, or the future may be as terrifying as that depicted in Huxley's *Brave New World*.

An implication of widespread cloning and cyborgization is that there may be an increasing homogeneity of humankind in the future. The possibilities of cloning suggest that large numbers of people may look alike; the possibilities of cyborgization suggest that large numbers of people may think alike. Yet our understanding of the evolutionary process suggests that heterogeneity, variety, changeability, and flexibility are the keys to survival.

As our technology advances rapidly it is important that

Cloning and cyborgization might result in greater homogeneity.

human beings generate cultural goals that anticipate technology and can serve as guidelines for its use. Maruyama (1973:351) has noted that we are entering an era in our discoveries and inventions are able to change a part of what has been considered "human nature" and gives humans the power to change it. Humans may transform themselves into monsters, or they may attain a new unkown civilization. The choice that we make requires some kind of philosophy. Yet the existing philosophies by which we operate are inadequate to serve as guidelines for our future decision making and action. It will be necessary to develop new types of philosophy. Since people are diverse, cultural goals generated by them will be diverse, according to the needs and tastes of individuals and groups. The future society must aim for diversity and heterogeneity if humankind is to survive and not merely make token allowances for "marginal" diversities, as the goals of non-Western peoples are often viewed. Instead, a heterogeneity based on symbiosis will give humankind the greatest survival advantage. The survival of the fittest does not mean the survival of the strongest. Instead it means the survival of the most symbiotic. The "strongest" individual or species who destroys others and its environment cannot survive at all (Maruyama 1976:274).

Survival of the fittest means the survival of the most symbiotic.

Cultural Changes of the Future

Many of the cultural changes that humans face in the immediate future are directly related to the problems of biological change. Any of the changes in human biological evolution will have to be accompanied by social and political reforms. Overpopulation, for example, is a social as well as a biological problem. It can lead to overcrowding accompanied by violence and breakdown in social services. These relationships are reciprocal, as political and social changes cause biological changes as well.

Future Shock. Culture shock is the disorientation that people often experience when they live in a society with a cultural system different from their own. The writer Alvin Toffler (1971) has introduced the notion of *future shock*, the disorientation brought on by drastic, rapid changes in one's own culture. According to Toffler (1971:11):

Our culture is experiencing future shock.

> Future shock is a time phenomenon, a product of the greatly accelerated rate of change in society. It arises from the superimposition of a new culture on an old one. It is culture shock in one's own society. But its impact is far worse. For most Peace Corps men, in fact most travelers, have the comforting knowledge that the culture they left behind will be there to return to. The victim of future shock does not.

Whereas human biological changes may not be great between now and the year AD 2000, cultural changes are accelerating at such a rate that many of us are no longer able to comprehend them.

In the traditional societies that have been examined by anthropologists, the elders are usually the bearers of knowledge of the society. They are esteemed for their long life and experience and for the knowledge they pass on to the young of the group. The anthropologist Margaret Mead (G. Harris 1970) has noted that in the modern world one is faced with a quite different phenomenon. Changes in technology and knowledge are occurring very rapidly. For the most part, it is the young of the society who are becoming the most knowledgeable about new discoveries and best able to adapt to rapid changes. They are taught the "new math," transformational grammar, and calculator skills. Older individuals are able to assimilate this new knowledge only if they are "reprogrammed." In academic disciplines with rapidly changing bodies of knowledge, such as mathematics, individuals in their late twenties are considered to be at their lifetime peak. In later years they will be outdated by younger mathematicians. The psychiatrist Erik H. Erikson (1968:237) predicts that in the future the younger generation will be divided more clearly into the "older young generation" and the "younger young generation." Erikson believes that the older young will grow in importance in future societies, and as they assume more responsibility for the conduct of the younger young, they may take over some of the traditional sanctioning powers of parents.

According to Toffler (1971:31) the future may include tremendous geographical mobility, involving extensive travel for both business and pleasure as well as resettlement. People in the future may be less place-related, with no long-term attachment to any place in which they are residing. This factor alone would have considerable impact on one's style of living. For example, while inhabitants or a rural town may live out their lives in the same place, developing strong ties with their neighbors, kin, and community, people in the future may own only weak allegiances to city or state, because they would see themselves as only temporary residents. In many cases people in the future may instead develop strong allegiances, to corporations, professions, or some other type of voluntary association, rather than to localities (Toffler 1971:92–93).

Toffler believes that the increased mobility he predicts illustrates one of the overriding patterns of the future, *transience*. Not only will home and community be temporary; so will most

Transience may be a general pattern of the future.

other aspects of life. The future, as Toffler sees it, will include a growth of the "throw-away" attitude and planned obsolescence. Transience will affect personal relationships and the nature of organizations. Because individuals will be on the move even more frequently than now, long-term friendships will be less useful than short-term ones. In primitive societies, friendships are few in number but holistic in nature, with the friendship extended to all aspects of life. It is believed by Toffler that in the future society, most friendships will be short-term and very specific in nature, based on perhaps one point of mutual interest.

According to Toffler (1971:187), a second aspect of the society of the future will be novelty:

> If transience is the first key to understanding the new society, therefore, novelty is the second. The future will unfold as an unending succession of bizarre incidents, sensational discoveries, implausible conflicts, and widely novel dilemmas. This means that many members of the super-industrial society will never "feel at home" in it. Like the voyager who takes up residence in an alien country, only to find, once adjusted, that he must move on to another, and yet another, we shall come to feel like "strangers in a strange land."

The Future Family. Perhaps some of the most interesting kinds of novelties Toffler foresees will occur in the forms of the family that may be found in addition to the nuclear family. Our modern, mobile life has brought about an emphasis on one type of family, the nuclear family. Toffler (1971:242) believes that increasing mobility in the future will result in even smaller families: a man and a woman. He states that people will either not have children or they may delay having a family until retirement. If some of the technological developments discussed earlier in this chapter actually occur, it might be possible for older couples to have children. Thus childlessness might spread among young and middle-aged couples, while the post-retirement family could become a recognized social institution.

Communes of different types might offer alternative forms of family life. In general they would be based on the practice of group marriage, but with modern trimmings. For example, three to six adults might adopt a single family name, live and raise children in common, and incorporate legally to obtain economic and tax advantages. Many of the individuals of the first communal families might be people who were dropping out of the frantic pace of the times, perhaps not wishing to relocate continually.

Conceivably the demands for mobility in the future could result in the rise of polygynous families. There are already some polygynous families in the United States, but all are illegal and underground. Some estimates indicate that there may be as many as 30,000 people living in polygynous family arrangements. In the future the polygynous family might become a fashionable form of marriage for the commuting male executive who spends part of the week in one city and part of the week in another, maintaining two separate households. A major difference between future polygyny and that practiced in non-Western societies today is that in the future the wives would probably demand extramarital rights before accepting such an arrangement.

The various marriage arrangements mentioned thus far will probably constitute the minority types. However, even the "normal family" of the future may live differently than it does today. The future family may be monogamous but will possibly practice serial monogamy more frequently than presently. Higher incidence of divorce and remarriage seems likely.

Another aspect of the family in the future is that gender roles will become less important. Anthropologists have found that gender roles have provided a means of social specialization within the various societies they have studied. The complementary roles of women and men have had the function of organizing societies in such a way that each group performs separate tasks, eliminating the need for everyone to do all tasks on an individual basis. Sexual anatomy has proven to be the simplest criterion for the social classification of people. The newborn infant is allocated at birth to the sex-identifed group to which he or she will belong for life. In the simplest societies, age and sex differences constitute the only major classifications. In large-scale societies sex difference represents only one of many ways of grouping people. Gender categories have considerably less adaptive significance in modern industrial societies than in non-Western societies (Martin and Voorhies 1975:406–408).

Settlement Patterns of the Future. If the world's population actually increases to 6.5 billion people by AD 2000, many writers believe that only urban settings will be able to accommodate such masses. A considerable part of the countryside would be transformed into urban centers. There may be underground cities as well as cities built on water. In the more distant future, human beings might live in colonies in outer space.

Human settlement patterns of the future may take on many new forms.

The biochemist and science fiction writer Isaac Asimov (1971:54–55) has proposed that by AD 2068 the number of cities on the earth's surface will begin declining; humans will have begun construction of new communities under the ground. He states further that the majority of the population will still be living aboveground in 2068, but that the future will see the rapid growth of underground settlements, and by 2068 each city will have a portion of its population living in subterranean suburbs. The primary advantage of the underground city would be that it would be free from climatic problems as well as day-night changes. There would be no heat waves or snow to shovel. Once the entire planet's population was underground there would no longer be a need for the day-night cycle or the different time zones based on it. Every society could operate on one universal "planet-time." As humans relocated underground, the earth's surface could be transformed into parks and other desirable phenomena. Instead of having to drive 20 or more miles to reach the countryside, like today's urban dweller, the underground dweller would merely rise a few hundred feet in an elevator and emerge in a surface park.

In addition to planned cities above and below the earth's landmass, there may also be cities in the future constructed on the earth's oceans. The oceans, which make up three-quarters of the earth's surface, must inevitably play a more important role in the future, not only as a source of food but as the permanent home of some of the world's increasing population. The British have been developing plans for Sea City, an offshore island of glass and concrete, to be constructed on a shoals area some 15 miles off the east coast of England where the water is about 30 feet deep. The main structure of this city would be a 16-story amphitheater supported by piles and protected on the seaward side by an encircling breakwater. The city would extend 4700 feet from north to south and would measure 3300 feet across at its widest point. The terraced city walls would hold 16 stories of centrally heated or air-conditioned apartments, which would accommodate some 21,000 residents. Other residents might have individually designed houses, on islands at the southern end of the city's lagoon, adding another 9000 inhabitants to the city's population. To reduce noise and pollution, all internal transportation would be provided be electrically powered boats and water buses. The city would include all of the services and activities found in most cities: libraries, tennis courts, hospitals, schools, and so on. Sea City's biggest contribution to the fight against the world food shortage would be a highly efficient fish-farming industry (Jellicoe, Mills, and Arup 1971).

R. Buckminster Fuller, the individual who introduced the notion of "spaceship Earth," has designed a floating community, made up of neighborhood modules designed to accommodate 3500 to 6500 people. Each neighborhood would average about

Earthling on the moon. (NASA)

5000 persons, the number required to support a school, super-market, convenience stores, and so on. Neighborhoods would be linked together to form Triton City, a community of 100,000. Like Sea City, Triton City would be built over water with a depth of about 30 feet. Over 80 percent of United States metropolitan areas with a population of one million or more are near bodies of water sufficiently deep to accommodate such floating communities. In water with a 30-foot depth, buildings with a maximum average height of 20 stories can be floated.

Triton City could be built up gradually. Three to six neighborhoods might be established to form a town of 15,000 to 30,000 people. At this point, a new town module could be added to the neighborhood modules, containing a high school, more commercial, recreational, and civic facilities, and possibly even light industry. When the community reached the level of three to seven towns, it would become a full-scale city, and a city-center module could then be added, containing governmental offices, medical facilities, a shopping center, a community college, and even specialized industry. Triton City would consist of a basic platform containing prefabricated units that could easily be replaced whenever a unit became outmoded (Sadao 1971).

If the specialists who consider the future are correct, humans will live not only on land, sea, and underground; they will also inhabit outer space. Speculations about space colonies are both numerous and varied. Plans for actual colonies may not materialize in the immediate future, but they do make interesting subjects for long-range speculation. Space colonies represent another form of planned community. One space-colony design will

Humans may have to inhabit outer space.

serve as an illustration of the type of communities being planned and some of the problems in the implementation of these planned colonies.

One of physicist Gerard K. O'Neill's proposed colonies would be contained in a cylindrical vessel 4 miles in diameter and 16 miles long. This vessel would rotate on its axis once every 1.9 minutes, producing a centrifugal force exactly equal to gravity on earth. People in the cylinder would feel that they were walking on level ground; however their visual impression would be that they were standing at the bottom of a rounded valley. Trees growing on the sides of the valley would look as if they were leaning downhill (because they would have grown up toward the axis in the direction opposite to the centrifugal force). Cylinders would be divided lengthwise into six long strips, each 2 miles wide. Every other strip would function as transparent windows, letting sunlight through onto the three solid strips of steel and soil that would form the inhabited valleys. To keep the sun fixed in the habitat's sky, three giant mirrors attached at one end of the cylinder and projecting outward would be used to deflect sunlight through the three windows into the cylinder (Bracewell 1975:120).

The valleys of the cylinder colony would be laid out as meadows, forests, lakes, villages, and mountains, just as on earth, and certain locations on earth known for their natural beauty could be duplicated for the space vessel. Such colonies could be used to manufacture space structures and to supply power to the earth (Bracewell 1975:121–124). Questions relating to such a self-contained colony include what types of animal or vegetable life would be acceptable. Could certain links in the ecological cycle be eliminated?

O'Neill and his associates have also designed other models, including wheel- and hat-box-shaped colonies. The wheel-shaped or torus community could be constructed over a mile in diameter and could accommodate 10,000 people.

As the limits to growth on earth become increasingly evident, more attention will probably be given to space as a frontier region for human settlement; however, the nature of space settlement is still unclear. There are at least three possibilities for outer space: inhabitation of other planets of this or other solar systems; the establishment of small space stations; or settlement on large space communities on space satellites. It is possible that the space station will be used initially, because it is the least expensive. Space stations could be used as centers for space industries, perhaps the most important of which would be the harnessing of cheaper sources of energy than those available

Space habitation may take three different forms.

on earth. As space stations began to pay for themselves, larger space communities could be constructed.

The construction of extraterrestrial communities provides humankind with a larger number of cultural options than have ever before been available in human settlements. Space communities can be designed to take into account, and utilize, humankind's cultural diversity. If heterogenity is the key to future survival, communities should not be designed in the same fashion. Instead, different communities should be planned to appeal to individuals with different outlooks and philosophies.

Language in the Future. Evolutionary trends suggest that language complexity will increase in the future. The evolutionary trend in language has been the development of smaller numbers of languages—called world languages—involving greater numbers of speakers with increasingly complex and specialized vocabularies. Between now and the year AD 2000 an even greater number of individuals may learn one of the world languages, as populations increase and as more non-Western people learn a world language as a second language. It is unlikely that any of the world languages will grow to such an extent that it will eliminate all others—at least not by AD 2000, although English is rapidly becoming the world's most widely used scientific and technical language. Nevertheless, there will undoubtedly be improved communication between speakers of different languages in the future, as a result of computer technology.

As computer technology has an increasing effect on our lives, a growing number of people will probably become familiar with computer languages. These computer languages will not replace world languages, because their uses are different, being primarily oriented toward the rapid storage and retrieval of quantities of data rather than for literary purposes. However, computer languages programs are universal and allow for computer communication between societies. In the future it is likely that communication between speakers of different languages will most often occur via computer. Thus computers may provide a means of universal communication that is lacking today. Just as households of the present have calculators and television sets, the households of the future will probably have computers.

Computer programming may provide more universal communication.

Education in the Future. Computer technology may also have an impact on the nature of education in the future. Schools will make use of time-shared computers. The psychologist George A. Miller (1968:260) envisions the following classroom in the future.

Imagine a classroom partitioned into semi-isolated booths. In each booth are a pair of headphones, a typewriter keyboard, a screen similar to a television set's, and a photosensitive "light gun." All of these stations (and others in other classrooms) are in communication with a central computer. A student communicates with the computer by typing on the keyboard or by touching his light gun to designated spots on the screen; the computer communicates with a student by playing recorded speech through the student's earphones, or by writing or drawing pictures on the cathrode ray tube. Each student can be working on a different lesson, or two on the same lesson can progress at different rates. A teacher walks from booth to booth, answers questions, sees that the stations are operating properly, and supervises requests for new materials.

Such innovations are being tested in pilot studies and seem likely to be adopted on a permanent basis in the future.

The possibility of computer-based education raises the question of whether or not teachers will be a necessary part of education in the future. In traditional societies, elders constituted human storehouses of knowledge. It was from the elders of the group that the children received their education. With the growth of sedentary societies and the invention of writing, education became the realm of specialists. With the increasing complexity of society and growth of knowledge, parents and kin were only partially able to educate their children. The learned individual had to receive specialized training in order to read and write and understand the discoveries being made of the world around him. By the 1800s the concept of public education was beginning to spread throughout the Western world. Today the teacher and classroom form the fundamental structure of the school system. With the advent of television and videotape, some changes in this structure were introduced, especially at the university level. It was found that a lecturer could teach one class of 1000 in which many of the students viewed the lecture over closed-circuit television, a far more efficient method than lecturing to ten classes of 100 students each. Computer technology of the future may switch the focus of education away from the classroom altogether and eliminate the need for teachers as they function today.

It is possible that education of the future will be home-based; however, unlike the home-based education of children of the traditional society, future education may come from a computer. Students of the future would not have to travel to school each day if computers were made available in the home. Those who serve as teachers today would probably function as consultants in the future. Videotapes would replace textbooks, and home computers would be linked with huge master computers, nationally and internationally. Videotape instruction would allow

Education of the future may be home-based rather than school-based.

children to proceed at their own pace. A student who did not understand a videotape lecture or program could press a replay button as often as needed. Questions could be answered through a hot line to a computer librarian.

Because the amount of knowledge will continue to grow rapidly, it is likely that all members of the family will receive continuing education via their computer. Individuals in any profession would be able to receive constant updating whenever they wished. The computer would also make available reeducation for persons who wanted to learn a new profession. Experts in every field could be called upon to produce videotapes. Video learning tapes could be updated on a periodic basis. Modern skills of television programming could be utilized to develop innovative means of presenting information that might be considerably more interesting and informative than typical classroom lectures.

The computer would also function as one's library. Every family that owned a computer would have access to all information available in the libraries of the world. One would merely give the computer instructions on what kind of information was required, and information from any book, manuscript or article ever written on the topic, as well as movies, videotapes, and information from other media, would appear on the computer screen. If the viewer wished to have a permanent record, he or she could make a duplicate by merely pushing a button as the information appeared on the screen.

Because the opportunities for improvement in our educational system are limitless, computer technology will be capable of revolutionizing every aspect of education. The invention of the transistor made the rapid expansion of computer technology possible, and the recent invention of fiber optics, or light-beam communication, could make low-cost computer centers available in every household.

Anthropology of the Future

All subfields of anthropology will probably be immensely affected by computer technology in the future. While the computer is used in all subfields of anthropology today, the sophistication of technology and new inventions will probably expand the anthropologist's reliance on this type of machine.

Anthropology will probably be affected by computer technology advances.

Physical Anthropology. Computers are currently used in the measurement and comparison of fossil data. Improvement in computer programming will result in more accurate analysis in the future. At the present time the physical anthropologist has difficulty measuring three-dimensional objects such as fossil skulls. The use of computer technology will resolve this problem, and an accuracy of three-dimensional measurement, analysis, and comparison never before obtained in fossil studies will be possible. Other technological advances will also greatly benefit physical anthropology. Certainly new dating techniques will be discovered that will provide more precise dates for the entire spectrum of human history. Finally, it is possible that new types of sensing devices will be invented that will aid in locating new fossil sites.

Archaeology. Of the four subfields, archaeology uses computer technology most extensively. Archaeology will also benefit from any discoveries of new dating techniques and new means of locating sites. It is possible that eventually site excavation will be a thing of the past. At some point in the future the archaeologist may use a type of sensing devise that will penetrate the earth, perhaps to a depth of several hundred feet, and project a picture on a television screen, much like a television camera taking a picture. This device would penetrate the soil and provide the archaeologist with videotape recordings of everything in the ground. Soil stratigraphy could be recorded through the use of different filters on the camera. Probably only very unusual or important artifacts would be excavated. For artifacts that were recovered, new laser technology would then be used to photograph them in the form of *holograms,* which create three-dimensional images. Holograms could be stored in computer banks so that any archaeologist in the world would have access to a three-dimensional image of an artifact.

Linguistics. Certain areas of the study of language lend themselves to the use of computers. The computer may provide some of the most important breakthroughs in linguistic research. Computers could eventually be developed that would have considerable skills of translation. Native languages, ancient languages, and modern occupational argots fed into the linguistic computer could be analyzed in a matter of seconds. A printout could provide a detailed description of the phonemics, morphemics, and syntax of a language. The linguist's time could then be spent in research on more detailed problems of the language.

It seems only a matter of time before computer technology ultimately breaks the linguistic codes of all untranslated writing of the past. This would greatly enhance our understanding of many ancient societies. The Maya, for example, left behind a large corpus of written material carved in stone and in other forms, which up until the present has been translated only on a quite limited scale; the same is true for the writing of the Indus civilization.

Computer programs will also become more accurate in their comparisons of languages and in their grouping of languages into appropriate language families. Once the groupings of language families become more accurate, the linguist will be able to utilize the computers to better reconstruct protolanguages.

Cultural Anthropology. Like the other subfields of anthropology, cultural anthropology will rely increasingly on computer technology. Computers are today being used in fieldwork in order to analyze large masses of data more rapidly and accurately than the individual can do. The computer can discover new patterns or inconsistencies in the data that can be further investigated by the ethnographer. In his study of the Yąnomamö, Napoleon Chagnon has made extensive use of the computer in manipulating the data he has collected on genealogies. The data he collects in the field are punched onto data-processing cards, which are then manipulated by a computer in a matter of minutes. The printouts then clearly show conflicts, gaps, and inconsistencies in the data, which Chagnon checks when he returns to the field. Chagnon (1974:117) makes the following observation on the use of the computer in ethnography:

> I urge all budding fieldworkers to take a course in basic computer applications and collect and record their data with the intention of later punching it on IBM cards and handling it by computer means. I was well advanced in my fieldwork before I learned to appreciate the potentials of the computer, and how it could be used to aid me in the field.

The increasing emphasis on quantification in anthropology represents a step that occurred in some of the other behavioral sciences more than 20 years ago. In a sense, anthropology will be improving the accuracy of its field data in the near future. At the same time, it is hoped that anthropology will not abandon its concern with qualitative thinking. Perhaps the major contribution of the cultural anthropologist will continue to be helping people in Western societies to become more aware that there are world views other than their own, which are equally as valid as their own. According to Magoroh Maruyama (1974:51), in Western culture there is a psychological need to believe in *one* universal truth. This represents a persistence of unidirectional logic derived from the ancient Greek philosophers. Other cultural traditions emphasize other kinds of logic. Perhaps the

Cultural anthropology will continue to show that there are many valid world views.

greatest challenge to anthropologists as myth-makers is to work to include other systems of knowledge as part of the human myth. It is only by comparing our own system of logic with those of other cultures that the strengths and weaknesses of our own system become apparent.

Punching data-processing cards with information from questionnaires used in author's cultural analysis of ethnic relations in Puerto Limon, Costa Rica. (Michael D. Olien)

Anthropology and Outer Space. Anthropological research of the future will not be limited to the planet earth. Anthropologists will be vital to programs of space exploration and colonization. More than any other kind of social scientist, the anthropologist is experienced in dealing with the unusual. Part of the anthropologist's perception is an expectation that behavior, beliefs, and objects will be different from those of his or her own society. Thus the anthropologist will have the type of flexibility needed to cope with the unexpected of outer space. Anthropologist Barbra D. Moskowitz (1975:64) has suggested that if humans encounter new life forms in interplanetary travel, the definition of the word *anthropology* as "the study of humans" will have to be expanded to include the study of all intelligent life forms.

Anthropology may become the study of all intelligent life forms.

Space colonies could provide the basis for a new kind of human diversity. If mating occurred only within the space colony, anthropologists could gain insights into population genetics that are impossible on earth because the gene pools are not closed breeding populations.

Physical anthropologists would also be interested in any types of biological changes that resulted from humans inhabiting environments different from those of earth. Very slight genetic changes could be detected with the help of new kinds of analytical equipment, and this information might be sufficient for long-term projections of biological change. Instead of having to wait tens of thousands of years to see the actual results of slow genetic change, humans could predict patterns of change on the basis of only a few years of study using computer technology. Physical anthropologists, with their knowledge of human evolutionary changes over the past 3 million years, might also conduct research on the anatomy of extraterrestrial beings, if these beings were to allow such research. Extraterrestrial beings, might wish to conduct similar biological studies of earthlings in order to better understand us. If both groups shared their knowledge, each would gain new perspectives about themselves and new ways of thinking about other beings of the universe.

Archaeologists would be useful in space exploration of other planets. The archaeologists' training would give them the best possible insights about the remains of any past intelligent life.

On the basis of analysis of artifacts of a planet being studying, they would be able to make certain deductions about the past inhabitants' way of life.

Linguists would be interested in studying dialect changes as they occurred on space colonies as well as working on new kinds of artificial languages that could be used to contact extraterrestrial beings. If contact with such beings was eventually possible, the linguist would be of great importance in attempting to translate their system of communication into something that earthlings could understand.

Initially the transmission of words between societies of different planets across space would not be very useful. Different beings—if they exist—may have had different evolutionary histories and may exist on planets with entirely different physical environments than earth. The thought patterns and cultural values of inhabitants of another planet might be entirely alien to our own. Thus if we received signals prior to any face-to-face contract, we would be receiving words without their cultural contexts, and it would be difficult to discern their precise meanings. The basic problem in decoding these messages would be our total lack of any prior information or knowledge about the transmitting civilization. We would be faced with the problem of decoding an arbitrary text (Stern 1975:32–33). This situation would be even more difficult than the translation of the Maya writing system, because we possess Mayan cultural remains and there are living descendants of the ancient Mayan writers on earth.

Cultural anthropologists of the future would be important in documenting life on space colonies. The formation of a society has never been viewed by social scientists. If an anthropologist were to accompany a group chosen to being a colony in outer space, in-depth data could be collected about the problems faced by the colonists and the decisions made. Cultural anthropologists could also be among the first to interact with extraterrestrial beings. The anthropologists' awareness of the problems of ethnocentricism would serve to make them fairly neutral observers, even if the culture of these aliens was strange to them. Eventually, earth ethnographers might live among beings of other planets and conduct field research in a manner similar to that employed among non-Western societies today. It must be remembered that extraterrestrial beings may be more advanced or entirely different from any humans or other animal forms that we now know. Therefore certain problems that we cannot anticipate, such as the nature of other beings or their life-style, may limit the possibilities of fieldwork as it is now conducted.

In summary, anthropology promises to be as exciting in the future as it is today.

Future Myth

Anthropology has been depicted as the myth of humankind because it attempts to explain humans in all places and in all times by studying human cultural and biological diversity. We have seen that humans have struggled to provide explanations of their past and their present.

The theories presented in this chapter make it clear that humans also have a need to understand their future. We create "future myths" that explain the kinds of alternatives humans will have to choose between in the future. Such mythmaking is possible because we will not break completely with the human patterns we now know. We project our understanding of the world around us into the future. Our knowledge of humankind's past and present will continue to be of importance in helping to build the human myth of the future.

Humans need to understand the future as well as the past

Anthropology Vocabulary

cloning	future shock	recombinant DNA
cultural selection	futuristics	transience
cyborg	Ik	

Review Questions

1. Why is it more fruitful to think of the future in terms of options and possibilities rather than predictions?
2. Thus far anthropology has played only a minor role in futuristics. Why?
3. How does cultural selection differ from artificial or natural selection?
4. What kinds of political issues may arise in the future over cloning and cyborgization?
5. What kinds of impact might computer technology have on our lives in the next 25 years?

Recommended Reading

Bell, Daniel, ed., 1968, *Toward the Year 2000*. Boston: Houghton Mifflin. A collection of articles based on the work of the Commission on the Year 2000.

Calder, Nigel, ed., 1965, *The World in 1984* (2 vols.). Baltimore: Penguin Books. A collection of articles dealing with a wide range of topics on the future.

Maruyama, Magoroh, and Arthur Harkins, eds., *Cultures Beyond the Earth*. New York: Random House (Vintage Books). A collection of articles dealing with the role of anthropology in outer space. The first articles discuss the scope of problems expected to arise in extraterrestrial communities; the second part is composed of sociocultural fiction.

Toffler, Alvin, 1971, *Future Shock*. New York: Bantam Books. A thought-provoking introduction to the impact of the future on our present way of life.

Turnbull, Colin M., 1972, *The Mountain People*. New York: Touchstone Books. Turnbull's account of the Ik, who he feels provide a sobering view into the possible future of our own society.

Glossary

Abominable Snowman   Humanlike form believed by some to live in the Himalayas. Also called the Yeti.

absolute dating   One of the two major categories of dating; this form of dating provides specific dates. (See **relative dating**.)

acentric society   A type of primate society in which individuals lose their social orientation when under predatory attack and go their separate ways.

Acheulian industry   A hand-ax industry of the Lower Paleolithic associated with *Homo erectus*.

affine   A relative by marriage.

Almas   Semihuman creature believed by some to inhabit Central Asia.

alyha   Socially sanctioned femininelike role among the Mohave that is filled by males.

ambilocal residence   Type of residence pattern in which the husband and wife live with the kin of either, the choice being based on relative need or some other advantage. Found with cognatic descent.

Ameslan   American Sign Language, used by the deaf and now used in the language training of chimpanzees.

amino-acid dating   Based on the rate of change that occurs as the amino-acid molecules realign themselves following the death of the organism.

anthropological linguistics   The study of language by an individual with an anthropological perspective.

anthropology   The study of human beings.

anthropoids   Higher primates; includes monkeys, apes, and humans.

ape   Group of nonhuman primates closest to humans; includes gibbons, orangutans, chimpanzees, and gorillas.

applied anthropology   The use of anthropological knowledge gained from the study of many different societies of the world toward the solution of contemporary social, economic, and technological problems.

arboreal   Adapted for living in trees.

Archaeology   The subfield of anthropology that studies the remains of the past in hopes of reconstructing former ways of life.

area excavation   The excavation of large areas to a depth of at least several meters. Especially useful for determining settlement patterns.

artifacts   Human-made remains left from the past.

artificial selection   Selective breeding of animals and plants by humans that results in desired changes.

Arunta   Aborigine group of central Australia.

aspiration   A slight puff of air released when certain sounds are spoken.

Atlantis   Legendary sunken continent in the Atlantic Ocean.

Australian aborigines   Native peoples of Australia.

Australopithecus   Hominid of Plio-Pleistocene found in Africa.

Australopithecus boisei   Robust *Australopithecus* of East Africa.

avunculocal residence   Form of residence in which husband and wife live with his mother's brother.

Aztecs   Pre-Columbian civilization of Central Mexico.

baka   An evil spirit in the vodun religion.

band   Form of sociopolitical organization found among hunting-and-gathering peoples.

Bigfoot Apelike form believed by some to live in the Northwest of the United States and in Canada. Also called Sasquatch.

bilateral descent Our own system of descent, in which a person relates to close relatives on both father's and mother's side of the family.

bipedalism Type of locomotion used by humans, in which the body is habitually supported on the hindlimbs, which move alternately.

blood brotherhood Form of fictive kinship based on the exchange of blood between individuals.

bound morpheme A morpheme that must be combined with other morphemes in order to have semantic sense, such as a suffix or prefix.

brachiation A hand-over-hand, arm-swinging form of locomotion used by apes, in which the body is suspended by the upper extremities.

brideprice Valuables given by a man when he marries to compensate his wife's kin group for her loss or the loss of children that she might produce.

bride service Labor performed by a male for his wife's kin, either before or after the marriage.

brother-sister marriage A custom that was limited in practice to a few non-Western societies and practiced only by those believed to have been born with divine power.

carbon^{14} dating Absolute-dating technique used to date organic material.

caribou North American reindeer.

carrying capacity The potential of an environment to support human life.

case study perspective Ethnographic approach based on in-depth studies of specific societies.

Çatal Hüyük Early religious city in south central Turkey.

catastrophism The theory of the eighteenth and nineteenth century that fossils were the remnants of previous eras and that they had been destroyed by natural catastrophes.

centripetal society A type of primate society in which individuals band together for mutual protection.

Chan Chan capital of the Chimu empire in Pre-Columbian Peru.

chiefdom Hierarchical tribal society in which some individuals have leadership roles.

chimpanzee African ape; smaller than the gorilla.

Chimu Pre-Incan empire in Peru.

Ch'in Dynasty Early dynasty of China during which centralization of government began.

Chou Dynasty Early dynasty of China (1000–256 BC).

Choukoutien Cave in China where Peking man (*Homo erectus*) was found.

chultun Subterranean chamber found in the Maya area used for storage of water or food.

churinga Flat, oval pieces of wood or stone carved with symbolic designs, used by the Australian aborigines.

circum-Mediterranean The area surrounding the Mediterranean, including southern Europe, the Near East, and North Africa.

circumscription theory An explanation of the origin of the state by the fact that the early stages developed in areas of circumscribed agricultural land.

civilization   A cultural stage usually marked by a state form of organization, urbanism, and writing.

clan   A unilineal group that has stipulated descent, in which kin ties are claimed by the members but in many cases cannot actually be traced.

classic language   A language intimately tied to the first urban civilizations and the invention of writing, and which was spoken by culturally diverse speakers.

classic neanderthal   Neanderthal of western Europe having the most unique features among the forms of Neanderthal.

cloning   The artificial duplicating of organisms.

cognate   A word in one language that resembles a word in another language because they are derived from the same word of an earlier language.

cognatic descent   Descent in which a person is born with a potential claim on a number of kin groups.

comadre   The reciprocal term used by female godparent and female parent in *compadrazgo* relationships.

compadrazgo   A set of complex relationships that develop out of the ritual of Catholic baptism, practiced in southern Europe and Latin America.

compadre   The reciprocal term used by male godparent and male parent in *compadrazgo* relationships.

comparative method   As used in the study of culture during the nineteenth century, it assumed that contemporary primitive peoples reflected early conditions of humankind.

comparative perspective   Synchronic and diachronic comparisons of societies.

comparative philology   An older name for historical linguistics.

competence   A speaker's grasp of the underlying principles of a language.

composite family   Any family form more complex than the nuclear family.

consanguine   A blood relative.

contrastive feature   A variation in sound that makes a difference between two words.

Copper Eskimo   Native American group in northern Canada.

core area   The area of the most intensive exploitation by a nonhuman primate troop within their home range.

cosmology   The study of a society's view of the nature of the universe.

cowboy economy   A reckless, exploitive attitude toward the environment that has led to increasing demands for natural resources.

creationism   Doctrine of divine creation. When capitalized, the term refers to the Biblical version.

Creole   The Hispanic non-Indian people of Venezuela and other parts of Latin America.

Cretaceous period   Last period of the Mesozoic era; the Age of Dinosaurs.

Cro-Magnon   The earliest form of modern human (*Homo sapiens sapiens*) identified in Europe.

cult of the dead   In vodun, veneration of the dead, believed to have supernatural power ranked second only to the Haitian gods.

cultural anthropology   The study of the cultural diversity of contemporary societies, with particular emphasis on beliefs.

cultural evolution The general pattern of cultural development that has occurred in human history.

cultural relativism The belief that every society must be understood in its own terms.

cultural selection The process whereby biological characteristics considered desirable by members of a society increase the chances that individuals possessing those characteristics will mate and produce offspring.

culture A system of knowledge which people use to design their own actions and interpret the behavior of others.

culture area A geographical region within which there is a similarity of culture between societies.

cyborg A part-human, part-machine being.

deductive method Approach that assumes that all data collection takes place in the context of some theoretical framework.

deep structure The underlying structure of a sentence (as opposed to *surface structure*).

démon An evil spirit in the vodun religion.

dendrochronology Tree-ring dating.

devolution A process in which simpler forms of organization develop out of more complex forms.

diachronic studies Comparative study of societies as they change through time in a specified geographical area.

diffusion A process that involves the spread of traits and ideas.

diurnal Active in the daytime.

dominance hierarchy Superordinate-subordinate relationships between adult males of some ground-dwelling Old World monkeys.

dominant characteristic The characteristic which is phenotypically expressed in heterozygous forms.

double unilineal descent Type of unilineal descent in which a person is assigned membership to two distinct kin groups, one on the basis of descent traced through males and one on the basis of descent traced through females.

Dreamtime A belief about the past and about the origins of things held by the Australian aborigines.

Dryopithecus Genus classification of the Miocene fossil apes.

ebene A hallucinogen used by the Yąnomamö.

ecological transition The progressive incorporation of nature into human purposes and action.

egalitarian society A type of social grouping in which there are as many positions of prestige in any given age-sex grade as there are persons capable of filling them.

emic/etic perspective Emic—a set of categories through which the natives view the world; etic—a set of categories used by the Western social scientist to explain social phenomena. Both of these units of analysis are used by the cultural anthropologists in their studies.

environmental determinism A theory that climate causes cultural differences.

Eocene   Second epoch of the Cenozoic era.

ethnocentrism   The belief that one's own way of life is the best or correct way.

ethnographic present   In native societies, the point in time immediately preceding contact with Western civilization.

ethnography   Fieldwork method of cultural anthropology in which a specific group is studied over an extended period of time by an anthropologist actually living with the group and participating in its daily lives.

ethnology   The theoretical method of cultural anthropology; relies on cross-cultural comparison of a number of societies to test hypotheses.

ethnosemantics   The study of the categories that people of different societies use to classify the world around them.

eugenics   The science of improving the human race by careful selection of parents.

evolved Oldowan industry   A tool industry of the Lower Paleolithic associated with *Homo erectus*.

extended family   Generally three generations of kin living together.

family of orientation   The type of nuclear family an individual is born into.

family of procreation   The type of nuclear family that one establishes at marriage.

feral person   A human who has remained isolated from other human beings for a number of years during childhood.

fictive kin   Make-believe but socially important kin.

fluorine dating   A method of chemical dating that measures the fluorine absorbed by an organism after death.

fraternal polyandry   The marriage of a woman to two or more men who are brothers.

free morpheme   Morpheme having semantic meaning by itself.

future shock   The disorientation brought on by drastic, rapid changes in one's own culture.

futuristics   The study of future cultural alternatives, limitations, and choices.

gene pool   The total genes in a breeding population.

genetic drift   The process whereby genes are significantly raised or lowered in small populations.

genotype   The genetic make up of an individual.

geochronology   Relative dating based on climatic changes reflected in the advances and retreats of glaciers or the rising and falling of sea levels.

gibbon   Asian apes, specialized for brachiation.

gorilla   African ape; the largest primate.

gracile *Australopithecus*   Type of *Australopithecus*, also called *Australopithecus Africanus*.

Great Chain of Being   A belief that each living thing on earth was specially created in an unchangeable form, and that each form had a fixed position in a hierarchy of forms.

Great Tradition   The formal literary tradition of a civilization.

group marriage   The quite rare marriage of several women to several men, with no formal pairing off.

hallucinogens   A drug or substance that produces hallucinations.

Han Dynasty   Chinese dynasty, 202 BC to AD 220, that established a centralized government.

hand ax   Typical artifact of the Acheulian industry.

Harappa   A major city of the Indus civilization.

hekura   A Yąnomamö demon.

heterozygous   Containing one dominant and one recessive gene.

historical linguistics   The study of the history, change, and historical relationships of languages.

holistic perspective   The inclusive nature of anthropological research.

home range   A circumscribed area of land within which a primate social group lives.

hominid   Common name for modern humans and their closest evolutionary predecessors.

Homo   Genus name for humans.

Homo erectus   A grade of hominid evolution intermediate between the earlier *Australopithecus* and *Homo* forms and the later *Homo sapiens*.

Homo monstrous   Monstrous races that were thought to exist during ancient and medieval times.

Homo sapiens   A grade in hominid evolution that follows *Homo erectus*. Includes Neanderthals and modern humans.

Homo sapiens neandertalensis   Neanderthal man of Europe and the circum-Mediterranian.

Homo sapiens rhodesiensis   Classification of Neanderthaloids found in sub-Saharan Africa.

Homo sapiens sapiens   Modern humans.

Homo sapiens soloensis   Classification of Neanderthaloids found in Java and China.

homozygous   Refers to a pair of chromosomes with the same genetic material.

huaquero   Person who makes a living at grave robbing.

humor theory   A theory of medicine attributed to Hippocrates, who believed health and temperament to be based on a balance of body fluids.

hungan   a vodun priest. (See *mambo*.)

hwame   Socially sanctioned masculinelike role practiced by Mohave females.

Ik   Native African people of Uganda.

Inca   Largest Pre-Columbian empire of the Andean region.

Indo-European   A language family that includes English and most of the languages of Europe and India.

inductive method   Method that stresses data collection and assumes that synthesis and the generation of inferences can occur only after all data have been collected.

Indus civilization   One of the early civilizations. Located in the Indus River valley of India.

infanticide   The killing of an infant.

intelligence quotient (IQ)   A number representing a score on a test used to measure an individual's intelligence.

International Phonetic Alphabet Sweet's set of symbols to describe the sounds of languages that was adopted by the International Phonetic Association in 1880.

Jericho A site in Jordan; the oldest city thus far discovered.

joint family A form of extended family where two or more sibling families join together, often with brothers heading the household.

kindred An individual's own network of relatives.

!Kung Bushmen Native people of south and southwest Africa who inhabit the Kalahari Desert.

language A system of arbitrary vocal symbols by means of which a social group cooperates.

language family Groupings of languages that are historically linked.

langue French word for "language"; refers to the underlying system.

L'Anse aux Meadows Site in northern Newfoundland thought to represent a transient Norse settlement.

law of independent assortment Mendel's law that hereditary units (chromosomes) are inherited independently of one another.

law of segregation Mendel's law that heredity does not involve a blending of genes but rather that genes act as independent units.

law of superimposition States that the soil layers closest to the surface are the most recent and those farthest from the surface are the oldest, if the layers have not been disturbed.

Lemuriformes Infraorder of prosimians that includes the lemur, indris, sifaka, avahi, and aye-aye.

levirate The marriage of a woman to her deceased husband's brother.

li Code of proper behavior followed by the nobles of the Chou Dynasty in China.

Little Tradition culture of the rural villagers living within a civilization.

Limón Lowland province of eastern Costa Rica.

lineage Unilineal group that has demonstrated descent, in which members of the kin group are able to trace their relationships to the other members of the group.

loa A Haitian vodun god.

local language A language spoken by a local group such as a hunting-and-gathering band or a tribal group. The speakers of such a language share the same culture.

lost tribes of Israel Originally Jews who were deported from the Northern Kingdom of Israel during the reign of the Assyrian kings.

Lower Paleolithic Earliest subdivision of the Old Stone Age. Cultural period of the early Oldowan and the later *Homo erectus* tool industries.

Luapula Native African people of Zambia and Zaïre.

Lugbara Native African people of Uganda and Zaïre.

mambo A vodun priestess. (See *hungan.*)

mana In Polynesia, sacred powers that certain individuals are believed to be born with.

Manataci   The most important supernatural being of the Panare.

marriage section   A type of grouping used to determine marriage partners among some Australian aborigine societies.

massing effect   Principle that progressively higher orders of groupings came into being in times of conflict. Characteristic of tribal peoples.

mastabas   Fairly simple mud-brick tombs constructed by the Egyptians.

matriarchy   A form of family organization in which females dominate. Sometimes also used in the context of political matriarchy, meaning a society ruled by women.

matrifocal family   A form of extended family that is mother-oriented, generally consisting of three successive generations of related females living together.

matrilineal descent   Type of descent traced through a female line, in which children are assigned membership in their mother's kin group.

matrilocal residence   Husband and wife live with her mother.

Maya   Pre-Columbian civilization of southern Mexico, Guatemala, Belize, and Honduras.

Mazatec   A group of Indians of the remote mountain area of southern Mexico.

Mendelian populations   Breeding populations.

Mesoamerica   Term given to one of the Pre-Columbian areas of civilization, which includes most of Mexico and Central America, except Panama and the southeastern half of Costa Rica.

Mesopotamia   A wide plain marked by the Tigris and Euphrates Rivers. Area of earliest civilization, the Sumerian.

Middle Paleolithic   Era of Neanderthals and Neanderthaloids, also called Middle Old Stone Age. Usually associated with Mousterian.

migration   Movement of individuals leaving one breeding population to join another.

Mimbres   Type of Pre-Columbian pottery found in New Mexico.

Miocene   Epoch of the Cenozoic era in which fossil apes became widespread.

Mohave   Native American group of California and adjacent states.

Mohenjo-Daro   A major city of the Indus civilization.

moiety   Large-scale division of society in which everyone is assigned to one of two kin groups on the basis of unilineal descent.

monogamy   Marriage between one man and one woman.

monogenism   The point of view that humans were of a single origin, a single species, and that the variations that appeared were merely varieties of humankind resulting from different climatic conditions.

morpheme   The smallest unit of a language having a definite meaning.

morphemic structure   The structure of the smallest meaningful units in a language.

mother-right   A woman's claim to her children, based on certain knowledge that they are hers, a certainty that the father does not always share.

Mound Builders   A special advanced race of people believed during the nineteenth century to have built the earthen mounds of the eastern United States.

Mousterian   The major stone industry of the Middle Paleolithic period.

Mu   A mythical "lost" continent supposed to have existed in the Pacific Ocean.

mummy bundles   Bodies wrapped in cloth, together with objects of clay, gold, silver, and copper, found at coastal Peruvian Pre-Columbian sites.

mutation   A sudden change in genetic material.

myth   A sacred narrative explaining how the world and people came to be in their present form.

Nacirema   A North American people living in the territory between the Canadian Cree and the Yaqui of northern Mexico.

nadle   The term used for intersex individuals among the Navajo.

nahualli   Aztec vampire witches.

natural selection   Evolutionary process in which the environment exerts pressure that favors reproduction of some individuals over others.

Navajo   Native American group of the Southwest.

Neanderthal   Subspecies of *Homo sapiens* who inhabited Europe, North Africa, and the Middle East from early in the Upper Pleistocene until they disappeared in the middle of the Fourth Glaciation.

Neanderthaloid   Neanderthallike forms of sub-Saharan Africa and the Far East.

new archaeology   Deductive approach; emphasizes hypothesis-testing and experimentation.

New World monkeys   Monkeys of Central and South America. Classified as Ceboidea, or platyrrhine monkey.

nitrogen dating   A chemical dating test that measures the amount of nitrogen still present in a organism that has died.

nocturnal   Active at night.

noncontrastive feature   Sound variation which when substituted for a standard similar sound, does not change a word so that native speakers hear it as a new word.

nonsororal polygyny   A form of polygyny in which a man is married to two or more women at the same time who are not sisters.

nuclear family   Consists of a husband, wife, and their children.

obsidian hydration dating   Measures the absorption of water molecules in obsidian.

occupation levels   Soil strata of a site showing evidence of human occupation.

Oldowan industry   The complex of tools from the early Pleistocene.

Old World monkeys   Monkeys of Asia and Africa. Includes the Colobinae and the Cercopithecinae, also called catarrhine monkeys.

Oligocene   Epoch of the Cenozoic era in which monkeys appear in the fossil record.

orangutan   Largest and heaviest of the Asiatic apes, and the most human-like.

oracle   Medium by which ancestors are consulted.

oyabun-kobun   Form of fictive kinship practiced in Japan.

Palenque   Mayan ceremonial center in southern Mexico.

Panare   A group of Indians living relatively isolated near the Orinoco River in Venezuela.

parole   French word for "speech"; that which is actually spoken.

participant observation   Participation in the day-to-day life of the people being studied by living with them over an extended period of time.

patriarchy   A form of family organization in which males dominate.

patrilineal descent   Type of descent traced through a male line in which children are assigned membership in their father's kin group.

patrilocal residence   The pattern in a society where husband and wife live with his father.

performance   An individual's actual speaking (as opposed to *competence*).

phenotype   Physical appearance of an organism.

phoneme   The smallest sound unit in a language that distinguishes one morpheme from another.

phonemic structure   The structure of the sounds of a language.

phonetics   The study of the sounds of a language.

phratry   A unilineal descent group comprised of several clans or lineages claiming to be related by kinship.

physical anthropology   Subfield of anthropology concerned with human biological diversity.

Pithecanthropus   Java variety of *Homo erectus*.

Pleistocene   Epoch of the Cenozoic era marked by the greatest number of fossil humans and also the Ice Age.

Pliocene   Epoch of the Cenozoic era in which hominids first appear.

pollen analysis   Relative dating technique based on the different percentages of pollen from different species in various soil layers.

polyandry   The marriage of a woman to two or more men.

polygamy   Plural marriage. Includes the various forms of polygyny, polyandry, and group marriage.

polygenism   The belief that there were several species of humans, each specially created.

polygyandry   A form of group marriage where several brothers married to the same wife acquire additional wives who are shared by all of the brothers.

polygyny   The marriage of a male to two or more women.

potassium-argon dating   Determines the age of certain types of rock by measuring the rate of radioactive decay.

power grip   A grip in which all four fingers are wrapped around an object and the thumb is firmly placed against the object to brace it.

precision grip   A grip in which an object is grasped between the fingers alone, usually between the thumb and the first one or two fingers on the thumb side of the hand.

Pre-Columbian   The period of New World history prior to the arrival of Columbus in 1492.

prehensile   Having the ability to grasp.

prehistory   The period prior to writing.

pressure flaking   Tool-making technique in which a piece of bone is used to remove tiny flakes from the cutting edge of the artifact.

primate Any of a taxonomic order of animals (Primate) that includes the prosimians, monkeys, apes, and humans.

profile A cross section of soil layers made visible by excavation.

prognathism A protrusion of the jaw that causes the facial plane to slope outward.

progressive Neanderthal Neanderthals of Eastern Europe and the Near East.

Propliopithecus Oligocene fossil monkey form.

prosimians Lower Primates, including the lemur, loris, and tarsier.

proto-Indo-European Mother language thought to have given rise to languages still being used, such as Hindi, French, German, and English.

punan A Semai word that translates into English roughly as "taboo." It conveys the idea that causing someone unhappiness, especially by frustrating his or her desires, will increase the probability of an accident that will injure him or her physically.

Purgatorius Earliest Prosimian ancestor.

quadrupedalism Locomotion on four feet.

race A subgroup within a single species.

Ramapithecus The most human of any of the Miocene forms. May be the earliest hominid.

rank society A society in which positions of valued status are somehow limited, so that not all those of sufficient talent to occupy such statuses actually achieve them.

recessive characteristic A heritable characteristic that is masked by a dominant gene.

reciprocity The exchange of goods, favors, and labor among a group of people.

recombinant DNA Genetic engineering.

redistribution Major exchange mode of chiefdoms. Payments of goods, money, or services are made to the chief, who in turn redistributes a part of these payments to his subjects.

relative dating Determines whether something is older or more recent than something else.

reinterpretation The process by which old meanings are ascribed to new cultural elements or by which new values change the cultural significance of old forms.

robust *Australopithecus* Type of *Australopithecus*, also called *Australopithecus robustus*.

salvage archaeology Excavation in areas that will be destroyed because of changes imposed on the environment by humans.

Sasquatch Canadian Bigfoot.

satanism Cult worship of the Devil.

segmentary lineage Lineage that fragments after only a few generations, so members are constantly splitting from the lineage and establishing their own lineages.

Semai One of the Senoi groups of the Malay Peninsula.

semantics   The study of word meaning.

semibrachiation   A type of arboreal locomotion used by some monkeys, in which the forelimbs are extended above the head to suspend the body or to propel it through space.

serial monogamy   A form of marriage in which an individual is married to only one spouse at a time but because of divorce may be married two or more times during a lifetime.

sexual dimorphism   Male-female size differences.

shaman   A part-time magicoreligious specialist.

Shang Dynasty   Early dynasty of China (1766–1123 BC).

sibling exchange   System in which a male of one band exchanges his sister with a male of another band in return for that individual's sister.

Sinanthropus pekinensis   The name given to the Chinese *Homo erectus.*

site   The location of an archaeological excavation.

slash-and-burn agriculture   Shifting agriculture in which a plot is cleared and the area is burned and planted. The plot is abandoned after a few years and a new plot cleared.

social Darwinism   The use or misuse of Darwin's biological principles to explain or justify existing forms of human social organization.

social race   A race of humans perceived by members of a society.

society   Large grouping of people who share a common culture.

sociolinguistics   A speciality in linguistics dealing with linguistic variation and social behavior.

sodalities   Groups that cross-cut tribal villages and have some corporate function or purpose, such as clans or warrior societies.

song duel   A means of resolving disputes used by some Eskimo groups in which songs are used to ridicule.

sorcery   Evil obtained through the use of magic.

sororal polygyny   The marriage of a male to two or more women who are sisters.

sororate   The marriage of a man to his deceased wife's sister.

spaceman economy   A nongrowth economy that emphasizes a balance with nature.

speciation   The process whereby populations within a single species become reproductively isolated from one another, leading to the formation of new species.

speech   The spoken aspect of language.

species   A group of organisms that are capable of interbreeding and producing fertile offspring but are reproductively isolated from other such groups.

state   A type of sociopolitical organization in which there are clearly defined social classes, territory, an elite, and a bureaucracy.

stereoscopic vision   Overlapping vision needed for perceiving depth.

stratified society   A society in which members of the same sex and equivalent age status do not have equal access to the basic resources that sustain life.

stratigraphy   The most widely used form of relative dating, which uses the basic principle of superimposition.

Subanun   Tribal people of the Philippines.

Sumerian civilization   Earliest civilization in Mesopotamia.

surface structure   Verbal expression; a level of structure suggested by Chomsky. (See **deep structure.**)

Swanscombe   The earliest of several hominid fossil remains from the second interglacial period and the third glacial period. Intermediate between *Homo erectus* and Neanderthal.

synchronic studies   The comparison of a number of societies at one point in time.

syncretism   A process of merging old and new elements into a functioning unified entity of clear bicultural derivation.

syntactic structure   The structure of a language described by the basic rules of grammar.

synthetic theory   Modern evolutionary theory. Combines Darwin's natural selection and Mendel's genetics.

systems-and-process perspective   The approaches emphasized in modern anthropology that studies human behavior through systems that contribute to the behavior.

tarsier   Small rat-sized prosimian of the Philippines and Indonesia.

Tasaday   Recently discovered native group of the Philippines.

teonanacatl   A hallucinogenic mushroom used by the Aztec.

Teotihuacán   The largest urban center of the Pre-Columbian New World. Located in Central Mexico.

Terra Amata   *Homo erectus* site on the Riviera.

territories   Defended home ranges.

test pit   A pit dug on the periphery of a site to determine the nature of the soil strata.

thermoluminescent dating   A method used for dating inorganic objects that have been heated.

Tiahuanaco   Major Pre-Columbian site in the southern Andes, in Bolivia.

tlacique   An Aztec vampire witch.

totem center   Where the spirits of human ancestral members of the group are thought to reside. A concept of the Australian aborigines.

totemic clan   A kin group in which all members profess a relationship with one another and with a natural species that serves as their symbol.

trade partner   Reciprocal term for two individuals of different tribes who trade with one another and establish a special relationship.

transformational grammar   Chomsky's alternative approach to grammar which emphasizes a generative rather than taxonomic approach.

transience   Nonpermanence.

trench   Excavation of a limited number of adjacent squares stretching across a site.

tribe   A sociopolitical unit based on agriculture or herding, which lacks centralized authority.

tundra   Vast, level, treeless plain of the arctic region.

twin cult   The veneration of twins in vodun because they are thought to have supernatural power.

underproduction   A pattern of very low production, practiced while farming was conducted on a small scale.

uniformitarianism   The doctrine that the processes of nature in action today can account for all past formations of rock and all present features of the landscape.

unilineal descent   Kinship traced exclusively through either the mother's or the father's line.

Upper Paleolithic   The culture produced by the first modern humans, about 40,000 BC, in which they exploited a far larger number of different environmental niches than previous hominids. Characterized by pressure flaking.

Ur   Major city of the Sumerians.

varieties   Differences in appearance between members of a single species once thought to be caused by conditioning factors but now known to be caused by both genetic and conditioning factors.

Vértesszöllös   *Homo erectus* site in Hungary.

vertical excavation   Excavation of limited areas to considerable depths.

vodun   A Haitian folk religion.

voicing   A vibration in the throat that accompanies certain sounds.

wild person   Monstrous human thought to represent the antithesis of civilized humans.

witchcraft   The practices of a witch.

world language   Languages spoken by millions of peoples that have replaced many local and classic languages.

Yąnomamö   Native group who live on the Venezuelen-Brazilian border.

Yeti   Abominable Snowman.

Yir Yoront   Australian aborigine group.

Zande   An African people (also called Azande).

ziggurat   A stepped pyramid of the Sumerians.

zombi   In Haitian vodun beliefs, the victim of an unnatural death whose body has been recovered and is controlled by a sorcerer.

References cited

Abbott, Joan M. W.
1970   Cultural Anthropology and the Man-Environment Relationship: An Historical Discussion. *Kroeber Anthropological Society Papers* 43:10–31.

Aberle, David, et al.
1963   The Incest Taboo and the Mating Patterns of Animals. *American Anthropologist* 65:253–265.

Adams, Frederick U.
1914   *Conquest of the Tropics: The Story of the Creative Enterprises Conducted by the United Fruit Company.* Garden City, N.Y.: Doubleday.

Adams, Robert McC.
1966   *The Evolution of Urban Society: Early Mesopotamia and Prehistoric Mexico.* Chicago: Aldine.

Allegro, John
1970   *The Sacred Mushroom and the Cross.* Garden City, N.Y.: Doubleday.

Anderson, E. N., Jr.
1974   The Life and Culture of Ecotopia. In *Reinventing Anthropology*, Dell Hymes, ed. New York: Random House (Vintage Books), pp. 264–283 [1969].

Anderson, Keith M.
1969   Ethnographic   Analogy   and   Archeological   Interpretation.   *Science* 163(3863):133–138.

Anonymous
1964   It Wasn't Bigfoot After All. *Western Folklore* 23:271–272.
1973   Three Indicted in Connection with Illegally Exported Antiquities. *Archaeology* 26(1):53.

Arambourg, Camille
1955   Sur l'attitude, en station verticale, des Néanderthaliens. *Compfes Rendus de l'Academie des Sciences* (Paris) 240:804–806.

Ardrey, Robert
1961   *African Genesis.* New York: Atheneum.
1966   *The Territorial Imperative.* New York: Atheneum.
1970   *The Social Contract.* New York: Atheneum.

Asimov, Isaac
1971   The Next 100 Years. In *Social Speculations: Visions of Our Time*, Richard Kostelanetz, ed. New York: Morrow, pp. 51–58 [1968].

Ausubel, Nathan
1953   *Pictorial History of the Jewish People.* New York: Crown.

Baade, Fritz
1962   *Race to the Year 2000.* New York: Doubleday.

Barnett, H. G.
1960   *Being a Palauan.* New York: Holt, Rinehart and Winston.

Barzun, Jacques
1965   *Race: A Study in Superstition.* New York: Harper and Row (Harper Torchbooks [1937].

Basso, Ellen B.
1973   *The Kalapalo Indians of Central Brazil.* New York: Holt, Rinehart and Winston.

Bell, Daniel, ed.
1968   *Toward the Year 2000.* Boston: Houghton Mifflin [1967].

Bendysche, Thomas
1863   On the Anthropology of Linnaeus: 1735–1776. *Memoirs of the Anthropological Society of London* 1:421–426.

Bennett, John W.
1976   *The Ecological Transition: Cultural Anthropology and Human Adaptation.* New York: Pergamon Press.

Berndt, Ronald M.
1972   The Walmadjeri and Gugadja. In *Hunters and Gatherers Today*, M. G. Biccheri, ed. New York: Holt, Rinehart and Winston, pp. 177–216.

Berreman, Gerald D.
1975   Himalayan Polyandry and the Domestic Cycle. *American Ethnologist* 2(1):127–138.

Bevan, William
1972   Two Cooks for the Same Kitchen? *Science* 177(4055).

Binford, Lewis R.
1967   Smudge Pits and Hide Smoking: The Use of Analogy in Archaeological Reasoning. *American Antiquity* 32(1):1–12.

Bingham, Harold C.
1932   *Gorillas in a Native Habitat*. Washington, D.C.: Carnegie Institution of Washington, Publication 426, pp. 1–66.

Bleibtreu, Hermann K., and John Meaney
1973   Race and Racism. In *To See Ourselves*, Thomas Weaver, ed. Glenview, Ill.: Scott, Foresman, pp. 184–188.

Bloch, Bernard, and George L. Trager
1942   *Outline of Linguistic Analysis*. Baltimore: Linguistic Society of America.

Boas, Franz
1974   The History of Anthropology. In *Readings in the History of Anthropology*, Regina Darnell, ed. New York: Harper & Row, pp. 260–273 [1904].

Bodley, John
1975   *Victims of Progress*. Menlo Park, Calif.: Cummings Publishing Co.
1976   *Anthropology and Contemporary Human Problems*. Menlo Park, Calif.: Cummings Publishing Co.

Boulding, Kenneth
1966   The Economics of the Coming Spaceship Earth. IN: *Environmental Quality in a Growing Economy*, Henry Jarrett, ed. Baltimore: Johns Hopkins Press.

Bourne, Geoffrey H.
1974   *Primate Odyssey*. New York: Putnam.

Brace, C. Loring
1964a   A Non-Racial Approach Toward the Understanding of Human Diversity. IN: *The Concept of Race*, M. F. Ashley Montagu, ed. New York: Free Press, pp. 103–152.
1964b   On the Race Concept. *Current Anthropology* 5(4):313–320.
1967   *The Stages of Human Evolution: Human and Cultural Origins*. Englewood Cliffs, N.J.: Prentice-Hall.

Brace, C. Loring and M. F. Ashley Montagu
1965   *Man's Evolution: An Introduction to Physical Anthropology*. New York: Macmillan.

Bracewell, Ronald N.
1975   *The Galactic Club: Intelligent Life in Outer Space*. San Francisco: Freeman [1974].

Brumfiel, Elizabeth
1976   Regional Growth in the Eastern Valley of Mexico: A Test of the "Population Pressure" Hypothesis. In *The Early Mesoamerican Village*, Kent V. Flannery, ed. New York: Academic Press, pp. 234–248.

Brunhouse, Robert L.
1973   *In Search of the Maya*. New York: Ballantine Books.

Buffon, de, Comte Georges Louis Leclerc
1749–   *Des epoques de la nature*. In *Histoire naturelle, générale et particuliére*, vol. 5,
1804   7th epoch. Paris: L'Imprimerie Royale.

Burridge, Kenelm
1973   *Encountering Aborigines, a Case Study: Anthropology and the Australian Aboriginal.* New York: Pergamon Press.
Burroughs, Edgar Rice
1917   *A Princess of Mars.* Chicago: A. C. McClurg and Co.
1963   *Tarzan of the Apes.* New York: Ballantine Books [1912].

Calder, Nigel, ed.
1965   *The World in 1984* (2 vols.). Baltimore: Penguin Books.
Calman, W. T.
1949   *Classification of Animals.* New York: Wiley.
Campbell, Bernard G., ed.
1976   *Humankind Emerging.* Boston: Little, Brown.
Carneiro, Robert L.
1973   Classical Evolution. In *Main Currents in Cultural Anthropology,* Raoul and Frada Naroll, eds. New York: Appleton-Century-Crofts, pp. 57–121.
1975   A Theory of the Origin of the State. In *Anthropology: Contemporary Perspectives,* David E. Hunter and Phillip Whitten, eds. Boston: Educational Associates, pp. 144–150 [1970].
Carpenter, C. R.
1934   A Field Study of the Behavior and Social Relations of Howling Monkeys. *Comparative Psychology Monograph* 10(48):1–168.
Carter, G. S.
1951   *Animal Evolution.* New York: Macmillan.
Cartmill, M.
1972   Daubentonia, Woodpeckers and Klinorhynchy. Paper presented at the annual meeting of the American Association of Physical Anthropology, Lawrence, Kansas.
Ceram, C. W.
1951   *Gods, Graves and Scholars: The Story of Archaeology.* New York: Knopf.
Chagnon, Napoleon A.
1968   *Yąnomamö: The Fierce People.* New York: Holt, Rinehart and Winston.
1974   *Studying the Yąnomamö.* New York: Holt, Rinehart and Winston.
1976   Yąnomamö, the True People. *National Geographic* 150(2):211–222.
Chance, M., and C. Jolly
1970   *Social Groups of Monkeys, Apes, and Men.* London: Jonathan Cape.
Chance, Norman A.
1966   *The Eskimo of North Alaska.* New York: Holt, Rinehart and Winston.
Chatterjee, Suhas
1967   Language and Literacy in the North-Eastern Regions. In *A Common Perspective for North-East India, Rathin Mittra and Barun Das Gupta.* Calcutta: Pannalal Das Gupta, pp. 19–23.
Childe, V. Gordon
1952   *Man Makes Himself.* New York: New American Library.
Chomsky, Noam
1965   *Aspects of the Theory of Syntax.* Cambridge, Mass.: M.I.T. Press.
Clark, J. Desmond
1976   African Origins of Man the Toolmaker. In *Human Origins: Louis Leakey and the East African Evidence,* Glynn Isaac and Elizabeth McCown, eds. Menlo Park, Calif: W.A. Benjamin, pp. 1–53.
Clark, W. E. Le Gros
1963   *The Antecedents of Man.* New York: Harper & Row (Harper Torchbooks) [1959].
Cole, Fay-Cooper
1945   *The Peoples of Malaysia.* New York: Van Nostrand.

Constable, George, et al.
1973   *The Neanderthals.* New York: Time-Life Books.
Coon, C. S.; S. M. Garn; and J. B. Birdsell
1950   *Races.* Springfield, Ill.: Thomas.
Conway, Moncure D.
1863   Benjamin Banneker, the Negro Astronomer. *Atlantic Monthly* 11:79–84.
Cotlow, Lewis
1971   *The Twilight of the Primitive.* New York: Ballantine Books.
Cravioto, J.
1970   Complexity of Factors Involved in Protein-Calorie Malnutrition. In *Malnutrition Is a Problem of Ecology,* P. György and O. L. Kline, eds. White Plains, New York: S. Karger, pp. 7–22.
Crick, F. H. C.
1963   Discussion. In *Man and His Future,* Gordon Wolstenholme, ed. Boston: Little, Brown, pp. 274–277.
Culbert, T. Patrick
1974   *The Lost Civilization: The Story of the Classic Maya.* New York: Harper & Row.
Cunnison, Ian
1951   *History on the Luapula.* Manchester, England: Rhodes-Livingstone Paper No. 21.
1954   A Note on the Lunda Concept of Custom. *Rhodes-Livingstone Journal* 14:20–29.
1956a   Perpetual Kinship: A Political Institution of the Luapula Peoples. *Rhodes-Livingstone Journal* 20:28–48.
1956b   Headmanship and the Ritual of Luapula Villages. *Africa* 26:2–16.
1957   History and Genealogies in a Conquest State. *American Anthropologist* 59:20–31.
1959   *The Luapula Peoples of Northern Rhodesia: Custom and History in Tribal Politics.* Manchester, England: Manchester University Press.

Damas, David
1972   The Copper Eskimo. In *Hunters and Gatherers Today,* M. G. Bicchieri, ed. New York: Holt, Rinehart and Winston, pp. 3–50.
Dart, Raymond A., and Dennis Craig
1959   *Adventures with the Missing Link.* New York: Harper & Row.
Darwin, Charles
1958   *The Origin of Species by Means of Natural Selection or the Preservation of Favoured Races in the Struggle for Life.* New York: New American Library (Mentor Books) [1859].
Darwin, Sir Francis, ed.
1961   *Charles Darwin's Autobiography.* New York: Collier Books.
Davis, Shelton H.
1976   Highways and the Future of the Yanomamö. In *Conformity and Conflict,* 3rd ed., James P. Spradley and David W. McCurdy, eds. Boston: Little, Brown, pp. 469–478.
Day, M.
1971   Postcranial Remains of *Homo erectus* from Bed IV, Olduvai Gorge, Tanzania. *Nature* 232:383–387.
de Camp, L. Sprague
1970   *Lost Continents: The Atlantis Theme.* New York: Ballantine Books [1954].
Deniker, Joseph
1900   *The Races of Man: An Outline of Anthropology and Ethnography.* London: Scott.
Dentan, Robert Knox
1968   *The Semai: A Nonviolent People of Malaya.* New York: Holt, Rinehart and Winston.

1970   Living and Working with the Semai. In *Being an Anthropologist: Fieldwork in Eleven Cultures.* New York: Holt, Rinehart and Winston, pp. 85–112.

Devereux, George
1937   Homosexuality Among the Mohave Indians. *Human Biology* 9:498–597.

Diaz, Bernal
1963   *The Conquest of New Spain.* Baltimore: Penguin Books [1568].

Dillon, Lawrence S.
1973   *Evolution: Concepts and Consequences.* Saint Louis: Mosby.

Dobyns, Henry F.
1966   Estimating Aboriginal American Population: An Appraisal of Techniques with a New Hemispheric Estimate. *Current Anthropology* 7(4):395–416, 440–449.

Dobzhansky, Theodosius
1962   *Mankind Evolving: The Evolution of the Human Species.* New Haven: Yale University Press.

Dolhinow, Phyllis
1972   Primate Patterns. In *Primate Patterns,* Phyllis Dolhinow, ed. New York: Holt, Rinehart and Winston.

Dumont, Jean-Paul
1976   *Under the Rainbow: Nature and Supernature Among the Panare Indians.* Austin: University of Texas Press.

Dundes, Alan
1976   In *Encyclopedia of Anthropology,* David E. Hunter and Phillip Whitten, eds. New York: Harper & Row, pp. 279–281.

Durkheim, Emile
1912   *Les formes elementaires de la vie religieuse.* Paris: Bibliothéque de Philosophie Contemporaire.

Editors of *Der Spiegel*
1973   Anatomy of a World Best-Seller: Erich von Däniken's Message from the Unknown. *Encounter* 41(2):8–17.

Editors of Time-Life Books
1972   *Life Before Man.* New York: Time-Life Books.

Edwards, I. E. S.
1947   *The Pyramids of Egypt.* London: Penguin Books.

Ehrlich, Paul R.; Anne H. Ehrlich; and John P. Holdren
1973   *Human Ecology: Problems and Solutions.* San Francisco: Freeman.

Eibl-Eibesfeldt, Irenäus
1975   The Bushmen. In *The Quest for Man,* Vanne Goodall, ed. London: Phaidon Press Ltd., pp. 171–186.

Eichenwald, H. F., and P. C. Fry
1969   Nutrition and Learning. *Science* 163:644–648.

Eimerl, Sarel, and Irven De Vore
1965   *The Primates.* New York: Time-Life Books.

Eiseley, Loren C.
1959   Charles Darwin, Edward Blyth, and the Theory of Natural Selection. *Proceedings of the American Philosophical Society* 103:94–158.

1967   Charles Darwin. In *Human Variation and Origins: An Introduction to Human Biology and Evolution,* W. S. Laughlin and R. H. Osborne, eds. San Francisco: Freeman, pp. 27–35 [1956].

Eliade, Mircea
1964   *Shamanism: Archaic Techniques of Ectasy.* Princeton, N.J.: Princeton University Press.

Elkin, A. P.
1964   *The Australian Aborigines,* 3rd ed. Garden City, N.Y.: Doubleday.

Elliott, J. H.
1970   *The Old World and the New, 1492–1650*. Cambridge, England: Cambridge University Press.

Epstein, A. L.
1954   Divorce Law and the Ability of Marriage Among the Lunda of Kazembe. *Rhodes-Livingstone Journal* 14:1–19.

Erikson, Eric H.
1968   Memorandum on Youth. In *Toward the Year 2000*, Daniel Bell, ed. Boston: Houghton Mifflin, pp. 228–238.

Evans-Pritchard, E. E.
1937   *Witchcraft, Oracles and Magic Among the Azande*. Oxford, England: Oxford University Press.
1965   *Theories of Primitive Religion*. London: Oxford at the Clarendon Press.

Fagan, Brian M.
1972   *In the Beginning: An Introduction to Archaeology*. Boston: Little, Brown.
1973   Belzoni the Plunderer. *Archaeology* 26(1):48–51.

Fleming, Joyce Dudley
1975   Field Report: The State of the Apes. In *Anthropology: Contemporary Perspectives*, David E. Hunter and Phillip Whitten, eds. Boston: Little, Brown, pp. 40–51 [1974].

Foster, George M.
1969   *Applied Anthropology*. Boston: Little, Brown.

Frake, Charles O.
1962   Cultural Ecology and Ethnography. *American Anthropologist* 64(no. 1, pt. 1):53–59.

Frankfort, Henri
1948   *Ancient Egyptian Religion*. New York: Columbia University Press.

Freedman, Maurice
1958   *Lineage Organization in Southeastern China*. London: London School of Economics, Monographs on Social Anthropology, no. 18.

Freud, Sigmund
1950   *Totem and Taboo*. London: Routledge [1913].

Fried, Morton H.
1960   On the Evolution of Social Stratification and the State. In *Culture in History*, S. Diamond, ed. New York: Columbia University Press, pp. 713–731.
1967   *The Evolution of Political Society: An Essay in Political Anthropology*. New York: Random House.
1975a   *The Notion of the Tribe*. Menlo Park, Calif.: Cummings Publishing Co.
1975b   The Myth of the Tribe. *Natural History* Magazine 84 (April):12–13. Copyright © The American Museum of Natural History, 1975. Reprinted by permission.

Friedl, John
1976   *Cultural Anthropology*. New York: Harper's College Press.

Furst, Peter T.
1972   Introduction. In *Flesh of the Gods: The Ritual Use of Hallucinogens*, Peter T. Furst, ed. New York: Praeger, pp. vii–xvi.

Galton, Sir Francis
1891   *Hereditary Genius*. London: Macmillan [1869].

Garbarino, Merwyn S.
1972   *Big Cypress: A Changing Seminole Community*. New York: Holt, Rinehart and Winston.
1976   *Native American Heritage*. Boston: Little, Brown.

Gaster, Theodor H.
1964   *The Dead Sea Scriptures.* Garden City, N.Y.: Doubleday (Anchor Books) [1956].
Geertz, Clifford
1966   Religion as a Cultural System. In *Anthropological Approaches to the Study of Religion*, Michael Banton, ed. London: Travistock, pp. 1–46.
Ginger, Ray
1969   *Six Days or Forever? Tennessee v. John Thomas Scopes.* New York: Quadrangle [1958].
Glacken, Clarence J.
1967   *Traces on the Rhodian Shore: Nature and Culture in Western Thought from Ancient Times to the End of the Eighteenth Century.* Berkeley: University of California Press.
Goodrich, L. Carrington
1951   *A Short History of the Chinese People*, rev. ed. New York: Harper & Row.
Gossett, Thomas F.
1963   *Race: The History of an Idea in America.* Dallas, Texas: Southern Methodist University Press.
Graham, Richard A.
1968   Quoted in the *San Francisco Chronicle and Examiner,* Oct. 27.
Graybill, Donald
1974   Measurement of the Amount and Rate of Site Destruction in Southwestern New Mexico. Paper presented at the annual meeting of the society for American Archaeology, Washington, D.C.
Grayzel, Solomon
1968   *A History of the Jews.* New York: New American Library (Mentor Books) [1947].
Green, John
1973   *The Sasquatch File.* Agassiz, British Columbia: Cheam Publishing Ltd.
Greene, John C.
1961   *The Death of Adam: Evolution and Its Impact on Western Thought.* New York: New American Library (Mentor Books) [1959].

Haldane, J. B. S.
1963   Biological Possibilities for the Human Species in the Next Ten Thousand Years. In *Man and His Future*, Gordon Wolstenholme, ed. Boston: Little, Brown, pp. 337–361.
Hall, Edward
1966   *The Hidden Dimension.* New York: Doubleday.
Haller, John S., Jr.
1970   The Species Problem: Nineteenth-Century Concepts of Racial Inferiority in the Origin of Man Controversy. *American Anthropologist* 72:1319–1329. Reproduced by permission of the American Anthropological Association.
Hamblin, Dora Jane, et al.
1973   *The First Cities.* New York: Time-Life Books.
Harris, George T.
1970   A Conversation with Margaret Mead. *Psychology Today* 4(2):58–64, 74–76.
Harris, Marvin
1970   Referential Ambiguity in the Calculus of Brazilian Racial Identity. In *Afro-American Anthropology: Contemporary Perspectives*, Norman E. Whitten, Jr., and John F. Szwed, eds. New York: Free Press, pp. 75–86.
1975   *Culture, People, Nature: An Introduction to General Anthropology*, 2nd ed. New York: Crowell [1971].
Harrison, Richard J., and William Montagna
1973   *Man*, 2nd ed. Englewood Cliffs, N.J.: Prentice-Hall [1969].

Hawkes, Jacquetta
1968   The Proper Study of Mankind. *Antiquity* 42:255–262.
Hays, H. R.
1964   *From Ape to Angel: An Informal History of Social Anthropology.* New York: Capricorn Books [1958].
Heath, Dwight B.
1973   Economic Aspects of Commercial Archaeology in Costa Rica. *American Antiquity* 38(3):257–265.
Hellmuth, Nicholas
1975   Nakum: A Late Classic Maya Ruin. *Archaeology* 28(4):270–272.
Helms, Mary W.
1969   The Cultural Ecology of a Colonial Tribe. *Ethnology* 8:76–84.
1971   *Asang: Adaptations to Culture Contact in a Miskito Community.* Gainesville: University of Florida Press.
Herndon, James
1972   *How to Survive in Your Native Land.* New York: Bantam Books.
Herskovits, Melville
1945   Problem, Method and Theory in Afroamerican Studies. *Afroamerica* 1:5–24.
1952   Introduction. In *Acculturation in the Americas,* Sol Tax, ed. Chicago: University of Chicago Press, pp. 48–63.
1971   *Life in a Haitian Valley.* New York: Doubleday (Anchor Books) [1937].
Heuvelmans, Bernard
1969   Notice on a Specimen Preserved in Ice of an Unknown Form of Living Hominid: *Homo pongoides. Bulletin of the Royal Institute of Natural Sciences of Belgium.*
Hill, Jane H.
1972   On the Evolutionary Foundations of Language. *American Anthropologist* 74(3):308–317.
Hill, W. C. Osman
1972   *Evolutionary Biology of the Primates.* New York: Academic Press.
Hill, W. W.
1935   The Status of the Hermaphrodite and Transvestite in Navaho Culture. *American Anthropologist* 37:273–279.
Himmelfarb, G.
1959   *Darwin and the Darwinian Revolution.* New York: Norton.
Hocart, A. M.
1914   Mana. *Man* 14:97–101.
Hodgen, Margaret T.
1964   *Early Anthropology in the Sixteenth and Seventeenth Centuries.* Philadelphia: University of Pennsylvania Press.
Hodges, Harold M., Jr.
1974   *Conflict and Consensus: An Introduction to Sociology,* 2nd ed. New York: Harper & Row.
Hoffstetter, Richard
1972   Relationships, Origins, and History of the Ceboid Monkeys and Caviomorph Rodents: A Modern Reinterpretation. In *Evolutionary Biology,* vol. 6, Theodosius Dobzhansky, M. K. Heicht and W. C. Steere, eds. Englewood Cliffs, N.J.: Prentice-Hall, pp. 323–347.
Hooton, Ernest
1947   *Up from the Ape,* rev. ed. New York: Macmillan, p. 15. Copyright 1931, 1946 by Macmillan Publishing Co., Inc., renewed 1959 by Mary C. Hooton and 1974 by Newton W. Hooton. Reprinted by permission.
Hughes, John P.
1962   *The Science of Language: An Introduction to Linguistics.* New York: Random House.

Hunter, David E., and Phillip Whitten
1975   Anthropology as a Point of View. In *Anthropology: Contemporary Perspectives,* David Hunter and Phillip Whitten, eds. Boston: Educational Associates, pp. 1–6.
Hunter, Don and René Dahinden
1973   *Sasquatch.* Toronto: McClelland Stewart Limited.
Hunter, John [Joannes]
1775   *Disputatio Inauguralis quaedam de Hominum Varietatibus* (Inaugural Disputation on the Varieties of Man). Edinburgh: Apud Balfour et Smellie.
Huntington, Ellsworth
1915   *Civilization and Climate.* New Haven: Yale University Press.
Hutton, James
1795   *Theory of the Earth; with Proofs and Illustrations,* vol. 1. London: Printed for Messrs. Caldwell, Junior, and Davies; Edinburgh: William Creech.
Huxley, Aldous
1932   *Brave New World.* London: Chatto and Windus.
Huxley, Thomas Henry
1863   *Evidence as to Man's Place in Nature.* London: Williams and Norgate.

Isaac, Glynn L.
1971   Whither Archaeology? *Antiquity* 45:123–129.
Isaac, Glynn L.; J. W. K. Harris; and D. Crader
1976   Archeological Evidence from the Koobi Fora Formation. In *Earliest Man and Environments in the Lake Rudolf Basin,* Yves Coppens et al., eds. Chicago: University of Chicago Press, pp. 533–551.
Ishino, Iwao
1953   The Oyabun-Kobun: A Japanese Ritual Kinship Institution. *American Anthropologist* 55:695–707.

Janson, H. W.
1952   *Apes and Ape Lore in the Middle Ages and the Renaissance.* London: University of London, Studies of the Warburg Institute, vol. 20.
Jellicoe, Geoffrey A.; Edward D. Mills; and Ove N. Arup
1971   Sea City: A Man-Made Offshore Island for 30,000 Inhabitants. In *Social Speculations: Visions for Our Time,* Richard Kostelanetz, ed. New York: Morrow, pp. 287–293 [1969].
Jolly, Clifford J.
1970   The Seed-Eaters: A New Model of Hominid Differentiation Based on a Baboon Analogy. *Man* 5:5–26.
Jones, Chester Lloyd
1967   *Costa Rica and Civilization in the Caribbean.* New York: Russell and Russell [1935].
Jones, Clarence F., and Paul C. Morrison
1952   Evolution of the Banana Industry of Costa Rica. *Economic Geography* 28:1–19.
Jones, F. Wood
1923   *The Ancestry of Man.* Brisbane: Gillies.

Kahn, Herman, and Anthony Weiner
1967   *The Year 2000.* New York: Macmillan.
Kantner, Claude E., and Robert W. West
1960   *Phonetics: An Introduction to the Principles of Phonetic Science from the Point of View of English Speech.* New York: Harper & Row.
Kardiner, Abram, and Edward Preble
1965   *They Studied Man.* New York: New American Library (Meridian Books) [1961].

Keesing, Roger M.
1975   *Kin Groups and Social Structure.* New York: Holt, Rinehart and Winston.
Kepner, Charles David, Jr.
1936   *Social Aspects of the Banana Industry.* New York: Columbia University Press, Studies in History, Economics and Public Law, no. 414.
Kepner, Charles David, Jr., and Jay Henry Soothill
1935   *The Banana Empire: A Case Study of Economic Imperialism.* New York: Vanguard Press.
King, Thomas F.
1971   A Conflict of Values in American Archaeology. *American Antiquity* 36:255–262.
Kirkpatrick, Dick
1968   The Search for Bigfoot. *National Wildlife* 6(3):42–47.
Kirtley, Bacil F.
1964   Unknown Hominids and New World Legends. *Western Folklore* 23:77–90. Reprinted by permission.
Köhler, Wolfgang
1925   *The Mentality of Apes.* New York: Harcourt Brace Jovanovich.
Kohts, Nadie
1935   Infant Ape and Human Child. *Scientific Memoir, Museum of Darwin,* Moscow, 3:1–596 (published in Russian).
Krantz, Grover S.
1971   Sasquatch Handprints. *Northwest Anthropological Research Notes* 5(2): 145–151.
1972a   Anatomy of the Sasquatch Foot. *Northwest Anthropological Research Notes* 6(1):91–103.
1972b   Additional Notes on Sasquatch Foot Anatomy. *Northwest Anthropological Research Notes* 6(2):230–241.
Kroeber, A. L. and Clyde Kluckhohn
1963   *Culture: A Critical Review of Concepts and Definitions.* New York: Random House (Vintage Books) [1952].
Kummer, Hans
1971   *Primate Societies: Group Techniques of Ecological Adaptation.* Chicago: Aldine.

La Barre, Weston
1972   Hallucinogens and the Shamanic Origins of Religion. In *Flesh of the Gods: The Ritual Use of Hallucinogens,* Peter T. Furst, ed. New York: Praeger, pp. 261–278.
La Fay, Howard
1975   The Maya, Children of Time. *National Geographic* 148(6):729–767. Reprinted by permission.
Lancaster, Jane B.
1975   *Primate Behavior and the Emergence of Human Culture.* New York: Holt, Rinehart and Winston.
Lee, Richard B.
1968   What Hunters Do for a Living, or How to Make Out on Scarce Resources. In *Man the Hunter,* Richard B. Lee and Irven De Vore, eds. Chicago: Aldine, pp. 30–48.
Lee, Richard B., and Irven De Vore
1968   Problems in the Study of Hunters and Gatherers. In *Man the Hunter,* Richard B. Lee and Irven De Vore, eds. Chicago: Aldine, pp. 3–12.
Leyburn, James G.
1966   *The Haitian People,* rev. ed. New Haven, Conn.: Yale University Press [1941].
Lieberman, Leonard
1968   The Debate over Race: A Study in the Sociology of Knowledge. *Phylon* 29:127–141.

Lienhardt, Godfrey
1969   Edward Tylor (1832–1917). In *The Founding Fathers of Social Science*, Timothy
        Raison, ed. Baltimore: Penguin Books, pp. 84–91.
Linden, Eugene
1976   *Apes, Men, and Language.* Baltimore: Penguin Books [1975].
Linton, Ralph
1937   One Hundred Per-Cent American. *The American Mercury* 40:427–429.
Livingstone, Frank B.
1962   On the Non-Existence of Human Races. In *The Concept of Race*, Ashley Mon-
        tagu, ed. New York: Free Press, pp. 46–60.
Lovejoy, Arthur O.
1936   *The Great Chain of Being: A Study of the History of an Idea.* Cambridge, Mass.:
        Harvard University Press.

McCown, Theodore D., and Kenneth A. R. Kennedy
1972   Introduction. In *Climbing Man's Family Tree: A Collection of Major Writings on
        Human Phylogeny, 1699 to 1971*, Theodore D. McCown and Kenneth A. R. Ken-
        nedy, eds. Englewood Cliffs, N.J.: Prentice-Hall, pp. 1–14.
McGimsey, Charles R., III
1972   *Public Archaeology.* New York: Seminar Press.
McKenny, R. E. B.
1910   The Central American Banana Blight. *Science* 31:750–751.
McKern, Thomas
1974   *The Search for Man's Origins.* Reading, Mass.: Addison-Wesley, McCaleb Mod-
        ule in Anthropology, no. 53.
Madsen, William
1957   *Christo-Paganism: A Study of Mexican Religious Syncretism.* New Orleans: Tu-
        lane University, Middle American Research Institute, Publication No. 19, pp.
        105–180.
1960   *The Virgin's Children: Life in an Aztec Village Today.* Austin: University of Texas
        Press.
Malefijt, Annemarie de Waal
1968   Homo monstrosus. *Scientific American* 219:112–118.
1974   *Images of Man: A History of Anthropological Thought.* New York: Knopf.
Malinowski, Bronislaw
1922   *Argonauts of the Western Pacific.* London: Routledge
1967   *A Diary in the Strict Sense of the Term.* London: Routledge & Kegan Paul.
Malson, Lucien
1972   *Wolf Children and the Problem of Human Nature.* New York: Monthly Review
        Press.
Malthus, Thomas R.
1798   *Essay on the Principle of Population.* London: Printed for J. Johnson.
Marler, Peter
1965   Communication in Monkeys and Apes. In *Primate Behavior: Field Studies of
        Monkeys and Apes*, Irven De Vore, ed. New York: Holt, Rinehart and Winston,
        pp. 544–584.
Martin, M. Kay
1969   South American Foragers: A Case Study in Cultural Devolution. *American
        Anthropologist* 71(2):243–260.
Martin, M. Kay, and Barbara Voorhies
1975   *Female of the Species.* New York: Columbia University Press.
Maruyama, Magoroh
1963   The Second Cybernetics: Deviation-Amplifying Mutual Causal Processes.
        American Scientist 51:164–179.

1973   Human Futurists and Urban Planning. *AIP* [American Institute of Planners] *Journal*, Sept.:346–357.
1974   Symbiotization of Cultural Heterogeneity: Scientific Epistemological and Esthetic Bases. *Co-existence* 11:42–56.
1976   Designing a Space Community. *The Futurist*, Oct.:273–281.

Marwick, Max
1970   Introduction. In *Witchcraft and Sorcery*, Max Marwick, ed. Baltimore: Penguin Books, pp. 11–18.

Mason, J. Alden
1957   *The Ancient Civilizations of Peru*. Baltimore: Penguin Books.

May, Stacy, and Galo Plaza
1958   *The United Fruit Company in Latin America*. Washington, D.C.: National Planning Association.

Maybury-Lewis, David
1965   *The Savage and the Innocent*. Cleveland: The World Publishing Co.
1967   *Akwê-Shavante Society*. New York: Oxford University Press.

Mayer, Philip
1970   Witches. In *Witchcraft and Sorcery*, Max Marwick, ed. Baltimore: Penguin Books, pp. 45–64.

Mead, Margaret
1964   Foreword. In *The Australian Aborigines*, by A. P. Elkin. Garden City, N.Y.: Doubleday, pp. vii–ix.

Meadows, Donella H.
1976   A Look at the Future. In *Notes for the Future: An Alternative History of the Past Decade*, Robin Clarke, ed. New York: Universe Books, pp. 56–64.

Mendelssohn, Kurt
1971   A Scientist Looks at the Pyramids. *American Scientist* 59:210–220.

Mercer, Jan, and W. Brown
1973   Racial Differences in IQ: Fact or Artifact. In *The Fallacy of IQ*, C. Senna, ed. New York: Third Press.

Métraux, Alfred
1972   *Voodoo in Haiti*. New York: Schocken Books [1959].

Middleton, John
1954   Some Social Aspects of Lugbara Myth. *Africa* 24:189–199.
1955   The Concept of "Bewitching" in Lugbara. *Africa* 25(3):252–260.
1958   The Political System of the Lugbara of the Nile Congo Divide. In *Tribes Without Rulers*, John Middleton and David Tait, eds. London: Routledge and Kegan Paul, pp. 203–229.
1960   *Lugbara Religion: Ritual and Authority Among an East African People*. London: Oxford University Press.
1965   *The Lugbara of Uganda*. New York: Holt, Rinehart and Winston.

Miller, George A.
1968   Some Psychological Perspectives on the Year 2000. In *Toward the Year 2000*, Daniel Bell, ed. Boston: Houghton Mifflin, pp. 251–264.

Miner, Horace
1956   Body Ritual Among the Nacirema. *American Anthropologist* 58(3):503–507. Reproduced by permission of the American Anthropological Association.

Mintz, Sidney
1972   Introduction to the Second English Edition. In *Voodoo in Haiti*, by Alfred Métraux. New York: Schocken Books, pp. 1–15.

Mitchell, J. Clyde
1965   The Meaning in Misfortune for Urban Africans. In *African Systems of Thought*, M. Fortes and G. Dieterlen, eds. Oxford, England: Oxford University Press.

Montagu, Ashley
1943   Wolf Children. *American Anthropologist* 45:468–472.
1964   *Man's Most Dangerous Myth: The Fallacy of Race*, 4th ed. Cleveland: World.
1965   *The Idea of Race*. Lincoln: The University of Nebraska Press.
1975   Introduction. In *Race and IQ*, Ashley Montagu, ed. London: Oxford University Press, pp. 1–18.
Montesquieu, Baron de la Bréde et de
1899   *The Spirit of the Laws*. New York: Colonial Press [1748].
Moody, Edward J.
1977   Urban Witches. In *Conformity and Conflict: Readings in Cultural Anthropology*, James P. Spradley and David W. McCurdy, eds. Boston: Little, Brown, pp. 427–437.
Moody, Paul Amos
1953   *Introduction to Evolution*. New York: Harper & Row.
Moore, John H.
1974   The Culture Concept as Ideology. *American Ethnologist* 1(3):537–549.
Morris, Desmond
1967   *The Naked Ape*. New York: McGraw-Hill.
1969   Introduction: The Study of Primate Behavior. In *Primate Ethology*, Desmond Morris, ed. Garden City, N.Y.: Doubleday (Anchor Books), pp. 1–8 [1967].
1969   *The Human Zoo*. New York: McGraw-Hill.
Morris, E. H., and R. F. Burgh
1954   *Basketmaker II Sites near Durango, Colorado*. Washington, D.C.: Carnegie Institution of Washington, Publication 604.
Morse, Dan F.
1973   Natives and Anthropologists in Arkansas. In *Anthropology Beyond the University*, Alden Redfield, ed. Athens, Ga.: Southern Anthropological Society Proceedings, no. 7, pp. 26–39.
Morton, Samuel G.
1839   *Crania Americana*. Philadelphia: J. Penington.
Moskowitz, Barbra D.
1975   The Moral Obligations of Anthropology. In *Cultures Beyond the Earth*, Magoroh Maruyama and Arthur Harkins, eds. New York: Random House (Vintage Books), pp. 64–82.
Muller, H. J.
1960   The Guidance of Human Evolution. *Perspective on Biology and Medicine* 3:1–43.
Murdock, George P.
1967   *Ethnographic Atlas*. Pittsburgh: University of Pittsburgh Press.
1968   The Current Status of the World's Hunting and Gathering Peoples. In *Man the Hunter*, Richard B. Lee and Irven De Vore, eds. Chicago: Aldine, pp. 13–20.
Murphy, Earl Finbar
1967   *Governing Nature*. New York: Quadrangle.
Murphy, Yolanda, and Robert F. Murphy
1974   *Women of the Forest*. New York: Columbia University Press.

Napier, John R.
1962   The Evolution of the Hand. *Scientific American* 207(6):62–68.
1972   *Bigfoot: The Yeti and Sasquatch in Myth and Reality*. London: Jonathan Cape.
Napier, John R., and Prue H. Napier
1967   *A Handbook of Living Primates*. London: Academic Press.
Netting, Robert McC.
1971   *The Ecological Approach in Cultural Study*. Reading, Mass.: Addison-Wesley, McCaleb Module in Anthropology.

Nissen, Henry W.
1931   A Field Study of the Chimpanzee. *Comparative Psychology Monograph* 8:11–122.
Nimuendajú, Curt
1946   *The Eastern Timbira.* Berkeley: University of California Press.

Oaksmith, John
1919   *Race and Nationality.* London: Heinemann.
Ogburn, W. F., and N. K. Bose
1959   On the Trail of the Wolf Children. *Genetic Psychology Monographs* 60:117–193.
Olien, Michael D.
1970   *The Negro in Costa Rica: The Role of an Ethnic Minority in a Developing Society.* Winston-Salem, N.C.: Wake Forest University, Overseas Research Center, Developing Nations Monograph Series, no. 3.
1973   *Latin Americans: Contemporary Peoples and Their Cultural Traditions.* New York: Holt, Rinehart and Winston.
1976   United States Colonization Programs for Blacks in Latin America During the 19th Century. In *LAAG Contributions to Afro-American Ethnohistory in Latin America and the Caribbean,* Norman E. Whitten, Jr., comp. Washington, D.C. Contributions of the Latin American Anthropology Group, vol. 1, pp. 7–16.
O'Malley, C. D., and H. W. Magoun
1973   Early Concepts of the Anthropomorpha. In *The Origin and Evolution of Man,* Ashley Montagu, ed. New York: Crowell, pp. 19–34 [1962].
Orwell, George
1949   *1984.* New York: Harcourt, Brace.
Otterbein, Keith F.
1966   *The Andros Islanders: A Study of Family Organization in the Bahamas.* Lawrence: University of Kansas, Social Science Series, no. 14.

Paor, Liam de
1967   *Archaeology: An Illustrated Introduction.* Baltimore: Penguin Books.
Pasternak, Burton
1976   *Introduction to Kinship and Social Organization.* Englewood Cliffs, N.J.: Prentice-Hall.
Patte, Etienne
1955   *Les neanderthaliens: anatomie, physiologie, comparaisons.* Paris: Masson et Cie.
Patterson, Orlando
1967   *The Sociology of Slavery: An Analysis of the Origins, Development and Structure of Negro Slave Society in Jamaica.* London: MacGibbon and Kee.
Pelto, Pertti J.
1970   *Anthropological Research: The Structure of Inquiry.* New York: Harper & Row.
Pilbeam, David
1976   The Naked Ape: An Idea We Could Live Without. In *Anthropology: Contemporary Perspectives,* David E. Hunter and Phillip Whitten, eds. Boston: Educational Associates, pp. 66–75. [1972].
Poirier, Frank E.
1974   *In Search of Ourselves: An Introduction to Physical Anthropology.* Minneapolis: Burgess Publishing Company.
Polo, Marco
1958   *The Travels of Marco Polo.* Baltimore: Penguin Books.
Porschnev, Boris
1958   *Komsomolskaya Pravda,* July 7.
Price, John A.
1973   The Stereotyping of North American Indians in Motion Pictures. *Ethnohistory* 20(2):153–171.

Provencher, Ronald
1975   *Mainland Southeast Asia: An Anthropological Perspective.* Pacific Palisades, Calif.: Goodyear.
Puleston, Dennis E.
1971   An Experimental Approach to the Function of Classic Maya Chultuns. *American Antiquity* 36(3):322–335.

Rasmussen, K.
1932   Intellectual Culture of the Copper Eskimo. Copenhagen: *Report of Fifth Thule Expedition, 1921–1924,* vol. 9.
Redfield, Robert
1956   *Peasant Societies and Culture.* Chicago: University of Chicago Press.
Rentoul, A. C.
1931   Physiological Paternity and the Trobrianders. *Man* 21:152–154.
Reynolds, Philip Keep
1927   *The Banana: Its History, Cultivation and Place Among the Staple Foods.* Boston: Houghton Mifflin.
Richardson, Miles
1975   Anthropologist—the Myth Teller. *American Ethnologist* 2(3):517–533. Reproduced by permission of the American Anthropological Association.
Riley, Carroll L.; J. Charles Kelley; Campbell W. Pennington; and Robert L. Rands
1971   Conclusions. In *Man Across the Sea: Problems of Pre-Columbian Contacts,* Carroll L. Riley et al., eds. Austin, Texas: University of Texas Press, pp. 445–458.
Ripley, William
1899   *The Races of Europe: A Sociological Study.* Englewood Cliffs, N.J.: Prentice-Hall.
Rivers, Caryl
1972   Grave New World. *Saturday Review,* Apr. 8, pp. 23–27.
Robe, Stanley L.
1972   Wild Men and Spain's Brave New World. In *The Wild Man Within,* Edward Dudley and Maximillian Novak, eds. Pittsburgh: University of Pittsburgh Press, pp. 39–53.
Robertson, Merle Greene
1972   Monument Thievery in Mesoamerica. *American Antiquity* 37(2):147–155.
Rosen, S. I.
1974   *Introduction to the Primates Living and Fossil.* Englewood Cliffs, N.J.: Prentice-Hall.
Rowe, John H.
1965   The Renaissance Foundations of Anthropology. *American Anthropologist* 67(1):1–20.

Sadao, Shoji
1971   Buckminster Fuller's Floating City. In *Social Speculations: Visions of Our Time,* Richard Kostelanetz, ed. New York: Morrow, pp. 282–287.
Sahagún, Fray Bernadino de
1963   *The Florentine Codex, Book Eleven: Earthly Things.* Sante Fe, N.M.: The School of American Research [sixteenth century].
Sahlins, Marshall D.
1958   *Social Stratification in Polynesia.* Seattle: University of Washington Press.
1961   The Segmentary Lineage: An Organization of Predatory Expansion. *American Anthropologist* 63(no. 2, pt. 1):322–345.
1968   *Tribesmen.* Englewood Cliffs, N.J.: Prentice-Hall.
1972   *Stone Age Economics.* Chicago: Aldine.
Salinger, J. D.
1961   *Franny and Zooey.* Boston: Little, Brown.

Sanderson, Ivan T.
1967   *Abominable Snowmen: Legend Come to Life.* Philadelphia: Chilton.
1969   Preliminary Description of the External Morphology of What Appeared to Be the Fresh Corpse of a Hitherto Unknown Form of Living Hominid. *Genus* 25:249–278.

Saussure, Ferdinand de
1959   *Course in General Linguistics.* New York: Philosophical Library [1916].

Schaaffhausen, D.
1971   On the Human Skeleton from the Neander Valley. In *Adam, or Ape*, L. S. B. Leakey and Jack and Stephanie Prost, eds. Cambridge, Mass.: Schenkman Publishing Company, pp. 159–164.

Schaller, George B.
1963   *The Mountain Gorilla: Ecology and Behavior.* Chicago: University of Chicago Press.
1964   *The Year of the Gorilla.* Chicago: University of Chicago Press.

Schultz, Adolph H.
1969   *The Life of Primates.* New York: Universe Books.

Sebeok, Thomas A.
1967   Discussion of Communication Processes. In *Social Communication Among Primates*, Stuart A. Altmann, ed. Chicago: University of Chicago Press, pp. 363–369.

Service, Elman R.
1971a   *Profiles in Ethnology*, rev. ed. New York: Harper & Row.
1971b   *Primitive Social Organization: An Evolutionary Perspective*, 2nd ed. New York: Random House [1962].
1975   *Origins of the State and Civilization: The Process of Cultural Evolution.* New York: Norton.

Sharp, Lauriston
1952   Steel Axes for Stone-Age Australians. *Human Organization* 11(2):17–22. Reproduced by permission of the Society for Applied Anthropology.

Shipton, Eric
1961   Forward. In *The Snowman and Company*, by Odette Tchernine. London: Robert Hale Limited, pp. 9–10.

Shouse, Melvin E.
1938   The Lowland Hinterland of Limón, Costa Rica. MA thesis, University of Chicago.

Silverberg, Robert
1970   *The Mound Builders.* New York: Ballantine Books.

Simmonds, N. W.
1959   *Bananas.* London: Longmans, Green and Co., Ltd.

Simons, Elwyn
1963   Some Fallacies in the Study of Hominid Phylogeny. *Science* 141:879–889.
1964   On the Mandible of *Ramapithecus. Proceedings of the National Academy of Science* 51:528.

Simpson, George Eaton
1945   The Belief System of Haitian Vodun. *American Anthropologist* 47(1):35–59.

Singh, J. A. L., and Robert M. Zingg
1942   *Wolf-children and Feral Man.* Denver: Contributions of the University of Denver, vol. 4.

Smith, Bruce D.
1976   "Twitching": A Minor Ailment Affecting Human Paleoecological Research. In *Cultural Change and Continuity*, Charles E. Cleland, ed. New York: Academic Press, pp. 275–292.

Southwick, Charles H.; Mirza Azhar Beg; and M. Rafiq Siddiqi
1965   Rhesus Monkeys in North India. In *Primate Behavior: Field Studies of Monkeys and Apes*, Irven De Vore, ed. New York: Holt, Rinehart and Winston, pp. 111–159.

Spradley, James P., and David W. McCurdy
1975   *Anthropology: The Cultural Perspective.* New York: Wiley.
1977   Culture and the Contemporary World. In *Conformity and Conflict: Readings in Cultural Anthropology*, 3rd ed. James P. Spradley and David W. McCurdy, eds. Boston: Little, Brown, pp. 1–10.

Spuhler, James N., and Gardner Lindzey
1973   Racial Differences in Behavior. In *To See Ourselves*, Thomas Weaver, ed. Glenview, Ill.: Scott, Foresman, pp. 188–192 [1967].

Stack, Carol B.
1974   *All Our Kin: Strategies for Survival in a Black Community.* New York: Harper & Row.
1977   Women and Men. In *Annual Editions, Readings in Anthropology 77/78.* Guilford, Conn.: Dushkin Publishing Group, Inc., pp. 269–273 [1974].

Stanton, William
1960   *The Leopard's Spots: Scientific Attitudes Toward Race in America, 1815–1859.* Chicago: University of Chicago Press.

Stephens, John Lloyd
1841   *Incidents of Travel in Central America, Chiapas and Yucatan* (2 vols.). New York: Harper & Row.

Stephens, William N.
1963   *The Family in Cross-Cultural Perspective.* New York: Holt, Rinehart and Winston.

Stern, Donald K.
1975   First Contact with Nonhuman Cultures: Anthropology in the Space Age. In *Cultures Beyond the Earth*, Magoroh Maruyama and Arthur Harkins, eds. New York: Random House (Vintage Books), pp. 27–63.

Stocking, George W., Jr.
1968   *Race, Culture and Evolution.* New York: Free Press.

Strahler, Arthur N.
1977   *Principles of Physical Geology.* New York: Harper and Row.

Straus, William L., Jr., and A. J. E. Cave
1957   Pathology and Posture of Neanderthal Man. *Quarterly Review of Biology* 32:348–361.

Stross, Brian
1976   *The Origin and Evolution of Language.* Dubuque, Iowa: Brown.

Struhsaker, T. T.
1967   Auditory Communication Among Vervet Monkeys (*Cercopithecus aethiops*). In *Social Communication Among Primates*, S. A. Altmann, ed. Chicago: University of Chicago Press, pp. 281–324.

Stuart, George E.
1975   The Maya Riddle of the Glyphs. *National Geographic* 148(6):768–791. Reprinted by permission.

Stuckert, Robert P.
1959   African Ancestry of the White American Population. *Ohio Journal of Science* 58:155–160.

Swadesh, Morris
1971   *The Origin and Diversification of Language.* Chicago: Aldine.

Tattersall, Ian
1975   *The Evolutionary Significance of Ramapithecus.* Minneapolis: Burgess Publishing Co.

Taylor, Herbert C., Jr.
1971   Vinland and the Way Thither. In *Man Across the Sea*, Carroll L. Riley et al., eds. Austin: University of Texas Press, pp. 242–252.
Tchernine, Odette
1961   *The Snowman and Company*. London: Robert Hale Ltd.
Terman, Lewis M.
1916   *The Measurement of Intelligence*. Boston: Houghton Mifflin.
Thomas, David Hurst
1974   *Predicting the Past*. New York: Holt, Rinehart and Winston.
Tiger, Lionel
1969   *Men in Groups*. New York: Random House.
Tobias, Phillip V.
1976   African Hominids: Dating and Phylogeny. In *Human Origins: Louis Leakey and the East African Evidence*, Glynn L. Isaac and Elizabeth R. McCown, eds. Menlo Park, Calif.: W. A. Benjamin, pp. 377–422.
Toffler, Alvin
1971   *Future Shock*. New York: Bantam Books [1970].
Tonkinson, Robert
1974   *The Jigalong Mob: Aboriginal Victors of the Desert Crusade*. Menlo Park, Calif.: Cummings Publishing Co.
Turnball, Colin M.
1972   *The Mountain People*. New York: Touchstone Books.
1977   The Mountain People. In *Annual Editions, Readings in Anthropology 77/78*. Guilford, Conn.: The Dushkin Publishing Group, Inc., pp. 45– 52 [1973].
Tuttle, R. H.
1969   Knuckle-Walking and the Problem of Human Origins. *Science* 166:935–955.
Tylor, Sir Edward Burnett
1958   *Primitive Culture* (2 vols.). New York: Harper & Row (Harper Torchbooks) [1871].

United States, President's Science Advisory Committee
1967   *The World Food Problem: A Report of the Panel on the World Food Supply* (3 vols.). Washington, D.C.: U.S. Government Printing Office.

Van Hooff, J. A. R. A. M.
1969   The Facial Displays of the Catarrhine Monkeys and Apes. In *Primate Ethology*, Desmond Morris, ed. Garden City, N.Y.: Doubleday (Anchor Books), pp. 9–88.
Verne, Jules
1865   *De la Terre á la Lune (From the Earth to the Moon Direct in 97 Hours 20 Minutes)*. Paris: Collection Hetzel.
1870   *Autour de la Lune (Around the Moon)*. Paris: Collection Hetzel.
1870   *Vingt mille lieues sons les mers (Twenty Thousand Leagues Under the Sea)*. Paris: Rion et Neuville.
Volpe, E. Peter
1967   *Understanding Evolution*. Dubuque, Iowa: Brown.
von Däniken, Erich
1971   *Chariots of the Gods?* New York: Bantam Books [1969].
1974   *The Gold of the Gods*. New York: Bantam Books [1972].

Walker, Alan, and Peter Andrews
1973   Reconstruction of the Dental Arcades of *Ramapithecus wicheri*. *Nature* 244:313–314.
Washburn, S. L.
1960   Tools and Human Evolution. *Scientific American* 203(3):62–75.

Washburn, S. L., and Ruth Moore
1974   *Ape into Man: A Study of Human Evolution.* Boston: Little, Brown.

Wasson, R. Gordon
1972a   What Was the Soma of the Aryans? In *Flesh of the Gods: The Ritual Use of Hal-
        lucinogens,* Peter T. Furst, ed. New York: Praeger, pp. 201–213.
1972b   The Divine Mushroom of Immortality. In *Flesh of the Gods: The Ritual Use of
        Hallucinogens,* Peter T. Furst, ed. New York: Praeger, pp. 185–200.

Watts, Elizabeth S.
1975   *Biology of the Living Primates.* Dubuque, Iowa: Brown.

Weiss, Mark L., and Alan E. Mann
1975   *Human Biology and Behavior: An Anthropological Perspective.* Boston: Little,
        Brown.

Wells, H. G.
1895   *The Time Machine—An Invention.* London: Heinemann.
1898   *The War of the Worlds.* London: Heinemann.

Wells, Rulon S.
1958   De Saussure's System of Linguistics. In *Readings in Linguistics,* Martin Joos,
        ed. New York: American Council of Learned Societies, pp. 1–18.

White, Hayden
1972   The Forms of Wildness: Archaeology of an Idea. In *The Wild Man Within: An
        Image in Western Thought from the Renaissance to Romanticism,* Edward
        Dudley and Maximillian E. Novak, eds. Pittsburgh: University of Pittsburgh
        Press, pp. 3–38.

White, Lynn, Jr.
1969   The Historical Roots of Our Ecologic Crisis. In *The Subversive Science,* Paul
        Sheppard and Daniel McKinley, eds. Boston: Houghton Mifflin, pp. 341–351
        [1967].

Whiting, Beatrice B.
1950   *Paiute Sorcery.* New York: Wenner-Gren Foundation, Viking Fund Publication
        No. 15.

Wilkins, Mira
1974   *The Maturing of Multinational Enterprise: American Business Abroad from 1914
        to 1970.* Cambridge, Mass.: Harvard University Press.

Wilson, Clifford
1975   *The Chariots Still Crash.* New York: New American Library (Signet).

Wilson, E. O., and William Brown, Jr.
1953   The Subspecies Concept and Its Taxonomic Application. *Systematic Zoology*
        2:97–111.

Wittfogel, Karl A.
1957   *Oriental Despotism: A Comparative Study of Total Power.* New Haven, Conn.:
        Yale University Press.
1959   The Theory of Oriental-Society. In *Readings in Anthropology,* vol. 2, Morton H.
        Fried, ed. New York: Thomas Y. Crowell, pp. 94–113 [1938].

Wolf, Eric R., and Sidney W. Mintz
1957   Haciendas and Plantations in Middle America and the Antilles. *Social and Eco-
        nomic Studies* 6:380–412.

Wood, Peter, et al.
1972   *Life Before Man.* New York: Time-Life Books.

Yerkes, Robert M.
1943   *Chimpanzees, A Laboratory Colony.* New Haven, Conn.: Yale University Press.

Zárate, Augustin de
1968   *The Discovery and Conquest of Peru.* Baltimore: Penguin Books [1555].

Zuckerman, Solly
1932   *The Social Life of Monkeys and Apes.* London: Routledge and Kegan Paul Ltd.

Index